The Principles of Computer Hardware

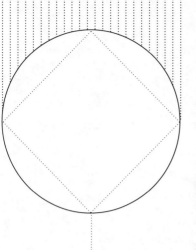

The Principles of
Computer
Hardware

Second Edition

ALAN CLEMENTS

School of Computing and Mathematics, Teesside Polytechnic

OXFORD UNIVERSITY PRESS
1991

Oxford University Press, Walton Street, Oxford OX2 6DP

Oxford New York Toronto
Delhi Bombay Calcutta Madras Karachi
Petaling Jaya Singapore Hong Kong Tokyo
Nairobi Dar es Salaam Cape Town
Melbourne Auckland

and associated companies in
Berlin Ibadan

Oxford is a trade mark of Oxford University Press

British Library Cataloguing in Publication Data

Clements, Alan 1948–
The principles of computer hardware.—2nd ed.
1. Computers
I. Title   621.39
ISBN 0–19–853765–4
ISBN 0–19–853764–6 pbk

Library of Congress Cataloging in Publication Data

Clements, Alan, 1948–
The principles of computer hardware | Alan Clements.—2nd ed.
Includes bibliographical references (p. 632) and index.
1. Electronic digital computers.   I. Title.
TK7888.3.C62   1991   004—dc20   90–7818
ISBN 0–19–853765–4 (hardback)
0–19–853764–6 (paperback)

Typeset by Latimer Trend & Company Ltd, Plymouth

Printed in Malta by Interprint Ltd

For Robert V. Prior

Preface

The principles of computer hardware is intended for students in universities and polytechnics taking a first-level (i.e. introductory) course in electronics, computer science, or information technology.

I have written *The principles of computer hardware* to achieve two goals. The first is to teach students the basic concepts on which the stored-program digital computer is founded. These include the representation and manipulation of information in binary form, the structure of a computer and the flow of information within such a machine, and the exchange of information between its various peripherals. That is, we answer the question: 'How is a computer organized and how does a computer work?' The second is to provide students with a firm foundation for further study later in their course. In particular, the elementary treatment of gates and Boolean algebra provides a basis for a second-level course in digital design, and the introduction to the CPU and assembly-language programming provides a basis for further courses on computer architecture/organization or microprocessor systems design.

At the moment, computer science is not taught in all high schools, and a prior knowledge of computer science is not an entry requirement to many courses in universities and polytechnics. Consequently, the level of this book is aimed at those with no previous knowlege of computer science. The only background information needed by the reader is an appreciation of elementary algebra, which is required in Chapter 2 which deals with Boolean algebra. As all students following a course in computer science or computer technology will also be studying programming in a high-level language (typically Pascal), no attempt is made to teach high-level language programming, and it is assumed that the reader is familiar with many of the basic concepts underlying a high-level language.

While there are some excellent books dealing with the individual subject areas of computer hardware (Boolean algebra, logic circuits, binary arithmetic, computer architecture, memory technology, assembly-language programming, input/output devices, etc.), there are very few really good books that integrate all these themes at a satisfactory level. It is my intention to provide the reader with an insight into all the above topics.

In writing this book, I have set myself three objectives. By adopting an informal style, I hope to increase the enthusiasm of the otherwise faint-hearted programmer who may be put off by the formal approach of other, more traditional, books. I have also tried to give students an insight into computer hardware by explaining why things are as they are, instead of presenting them with information as a piece of dogma to be learned and accepted without question. Moreover, I have included some subjects that would seem out of place in an elementary first-level course. Such topics (e.g. advanced computer arithmetic, timing diagrams, reliability, RISC architectures) have been included to show how the computer hardware of the real world often differs from that of the first-level course in which only the basics are taught. Finally, I have discovered that stating a formula or a theory is not enough—many students like to see an actual application of the formula. Consequently I have, wherever possible, provided examples. Moreover, I have also broadened the range of topics normally found in first-level courses in computer hardware and have provided sections introducing operating systems and local area networks, as these two topics are so intimately related to the hardware of the computer.

Like most introductory books dealing with the architecture of computers, I have chosen a specific microprocessor as a model. The advantage of the microprocessor as a vehicle for teaching the basic principles of computer architecture is its relative simplicity. Most mainframe computers and many minicomputers have sophisticated architectures which confront the students with too much fine detail early in their course. The microprocessor demonstrates almost all the important features of the mainframe computer but has few of its complexities. The microprocessor I have chosen is the 68000 16-bit microprocessor, which has been selected simply because many of the institutions teaching microprocessor systems design use this particular chip. I would emphasize that this book is not designed to provide a practical course in assembly-language programming on the 68000. It is intended only to illustrate the operation of a central processing unit by means of a typical assembly language.

Although aimed at first-year degree students taking a computer science or information technology course or for students of electrical engineering taking a computer technology course, this book should appeal to those on Higher National BTEC courses in computing studies, to those taking Part I of the BCS examination, and to the layperson who just wants to find out how computers work.

Since *The principles of computer hardware* was first published in 1985, I have felt more ambivalent about it than almost anything else I have ever done. On the one hand it has been very successful, has had fairly good reviews, and has been adopted by a much wider range of courses than I had anticipated. Its royalties even gave me the chance to visit friends in Australia.

On the other hand, I have always felt a certain measure of dissatisfaction with my book. Partly because it grew out of lecture notes and therefore lacked the structure that I felt should have been imposed on it, and partly because it represented my opinions and attitudes at the time I wrote it and not those at the time it was published. Whenever I read it, I think: 'Oh dear, did I really write that?' Of course, few people would do something in exactly the same way if they had the opportunity to do it again. I am no exception.

The seond edition has been produced by editing the first edition. As I worked through the original text, I attempted to do three things:

1. To improve the writing and make explanations clearer (I was horrified by the number of sentences that started with 'This . . .').

2. To expand on material that was insufficiently detailed. It is most instructive to re-read something that I wrote a year or more ago. Steps in an argument or a discussion that I once thought followed on logically from each other suddenly appear disjointed and seem to follow no logical pattern. A second edition provides the author with another chance to tidy up some of these confused areas.

3. To update some of the material to reflect changes that have taken place since I started writing the first edition.

In particular, I have rewritten the chapter dealing with the CPU and centred it around the 68000 microprocessor rather than the 6502 microprocessor which now sets a very poor example of microprocessor architecture. Other important changes that have taken place since the early 1980s are the introduction of optical disk technology and the growth of powerful peripherals such as the laser printer. Therefore a description of optical disk systems is provided in the chapter on memory technology.

A few readers of my first edition have commented that there are more references to aircraft and aviation than the law of averages would seem to suggest. While I was writing the first edition, I was also learning to fly light aircraft. Many was the time that I would begin to write a new section immediately following a traumatic flying lesson. After my first spin recovery the instructor said, 'Nice recovery, but there is really no need to scream as we enter the spin.' It's not much fun being in a spinning aeroplane when the ground and sky swap places. Given such experiences, it is hardly surprising that aviation invaded my consciousness.

Reading guide

It has already been stated that this book contains material appropriate to traditional introductory courses in computer hardware and architecture, together with additional material broadening its scope and filling in some of the gaps left in such courses. As students following an introductory course might find it difficult to distinguish between foreground and background material, I am including a guide to their reading.

Chapter 2: The vast majority of Chapter 2 deals with essential topics such as gates, Boolean algebra, and Karnaugh maps. Therefore this chapter is essential reading.

Chapter 3: This chapter introduces bistables (flip-flops) and requires a quantum jump in understanding over earlier sections on gates and similar logic elements. For the purpose of this book, the basic idea of the flip-flop and its application as a memory element in registers is all that is needed. That is, by the end of this course students are expected to be able to design moderately complex circuits built from gates, but are expected only to appreciate the role of sequential circuits. A fuller treatment of sequential circuits belongs to second-level courses in digital design. At the end of

Chapter 3 we introduce some real-world problems in computer design, and these may be omitted on a first reading.

Chapter 4: This chapter deals with the way in which numbers are represented inside a computer, and the way in which they are manipulated in simple arithmetic operations. Apart from some of the coding theory and details of multiplication and division, almost all of this chapter is essential reading. Section 4.8 on floating point arithmetic goes into more detail than some other texts, but this has been necessitated by difficulties that a few students have in understanding how floating point numbers are represented and manipulated. The final part of Chapter 4 introduces multiplication and division and describes how they are actually carried out inside computers. Multiplication and division can be omitted if the student is not interested in how these operations are implemented.

Chapter 5: This is the heart of the book and is concerned with the structure and operation of the computer itself. Section 5.2 deals with the operation of the computer's control unit and may be omitted on a first reading. The control unit is normally encountered in a second- or third-level course, and has been included here for the purposes of completeness, and to give the student an insight into how the computer actually turns a binary-coded instruction into a sequence of events which carry out the instruction. At the end of this chapter we introduce a typical high-performance microprocessor, the 68000, and then briefly look at an alternative to the microprocessors of the mid-1980s. This alternative is the RISC or *reduced instruction set computer architecture* that achieves a high level of performance by overlapping the various stages in the execution of an instruction.

Chapter 6: Having introduced the architecture of a CPU we include an overview of assembly-language programming and the design of simple 68000 assembly-language programs. If the reader is interested only in the structure of the CPU, he or she may omit this chapter.

Chapter 7: This chapter deals with input/output techniques and peripherals such as printers and CRT terminals that enable the computer to communicate with the external world. We also take a brief look at some of the interface chips that facilitate the connection of the computer to its peripherals. Input/ouput techniques, peripherals and their interfaces are essential reading and should not be omitted. However, details of the serial and parallel interfaces may be omitted.

Chapter 8: This chapter examines the way in which information is actually stored within the computer. The student should be aware of the principles governing the operation of both immediate access memory and secondary stores. However, some of the detailed description (thin-film memory, codes for recording) embedded in this section may be omitted on a first reading.

Chapter 9: The techniques whereby networks of computers communicate with each other do not appear in many first-level courses and therefore this chapter may be omitted. However, it is probable that the subject of computer communications will soon worm its way into such courses because of its great importance and impact on computing. In fact, many universities and polytechnics have introduced courses in information technology that include three components: computer hardware and interfacing, programming and software engineering, and communications networks and protocols. For this reason I would expect students to read this chapter even if it does not fall within their syllabus.

Chapter 10: Operating systems and system software as such do not fall within the scope of this book. I have included a brief discussion of operating systems because it leads to the ideas of multiprogramming and memory management—Sections 10.2 and 10.4. These topics are intimately connected with interrupt handling and data storage techniques, and serve as practical examples of the use of the hardware described in Sections 7.2 and 8.4.

The history of this book

Like people, books are born. *The principles of computer hardware* was conceived in December 1980. At the end of every Christmas term the first-year students on the degree course in computer science at Teesside Polytechnic are given tests in each of their subjects in order to monitor their progress. The results of the test in my course on *The principles of computer hardware* were rather poor, so I decided to do something about it. I thought that detailed lecture notes, written in a style accessible to the students, would be the most effective solution.

Unfortunately, I had volunteered to give a short course on computer communications to the staff of the Computer Centre during the Christmas vacation, and did not have enough free time to produce the notes. By accident I found that the week immediately preceding Christmas was the cheapest time of the year for package holidays. So I went to Tenerife for a week, plonked myself down by the pool with folders full of reference material and a bottle of Southern Comfort, and wrote the core of this book—number bases, gates and Boolean algebra, and binary arithmetic. Shortly afterwards I added the section on the structure of the CPU.

These notes appeared to produce the desired improvement in the end-of-year exam result and were well received by the students. In the next academic year the Data Preparation Department of the Computer Centre began to offer an important new facility to lecturers by entering our notes into a Univac 1100. This service enabled me to add new material and clean up the existing text. Now that I could use a word processor to edit my notes, I decided to convert the notes into a book. The conversion process involved adding topics, not covered by our syllabus, to produce a more rounded text. While editing my notes, I discovered what might best be called the *ink-blot* effect. Once text is stored in a computer it tends to expand in all directions because it is very easy to add new material at any point. That is, I can edit and expand a paragraph at any particular point without having to modify the whole text. Modifying the text would have been much more difficult if I had produced a conventional typewritten manuscript, because all changes would involve re-typing or 'cutting and pasting'. The Univac 1100 miniframe computer was replaced by three Prime 750s in 1980 and I am now linked to these by means of a local area network connected to a terminal in my office. Now I can edit and update my notes without leaving my desk.

The rest of the history is described above in my preface to the second edition.

Acknowledgements

Few books are entirely the result of one person's unaided efforts and this is no exception. I would like to thank those who wrote the many books about computers on which my own knowledge, understanding of, and more importantly attitude towards computers are founded. One of the most unpleasant tasks confronting an author is the translation of his or her handwritten manuscript into a typewritten document. This job was tackled by the Data Preparation Department of the Computer Centre at Teesside Polytechnic. Without the help of Marlene Melber and those who work with her, my book may not have appeared. It certainly would not be in its present form.

The greatest help came from my wife, Sue, who proof-read the text, removed my spelling mistakes, modified my punctuation, and blunted my worst assaults on the English language.

As this book has grown out of my lecture notes, I have received many helpful suggestions from my students. Some have checked early drafts, while others have pointed out some of the more incomprehensible sections which have been modified accordingly. I gave a copy of the draft manuscript to a neighbour, Alan Tullo, who is a mathematician but is otherwise unconnected with computer science, and asked him for an overall comment. He not only read it but suggested several modifications to improve the clarity of the text. More importantly, he found some of the blunders I had not noticed.

Finally, I would like to thank all those who reported errors they found in the first edition to me and those who suggested modifications for a second edition. In particular I would like to thank Alan Knowles of Manchester University who read through my draft manuscript and provided me with much valuable feeback.

Teesside A.C.
1990

Contents

Introduction to computer hardware

To begin with I feel I ought to define the terms hardware and software. Of course I could give a deeply philosophical definition, but perhaps an empirical definition is more helpful. If any part of a computer system clatters on the floor when dropped, it is hardware. If it doesn't, it is software.

The *hardware* of a computer includes all the physical components that make up the computer system. These components range from the central processing unit to the memory and input/output devices. The programs that control the operation of the computer are called the *software.* When a program is inside a computer its physical existence lies in the state of electronic switches within the computer, or the magnetization of tiny particles on magnetic tape or disk. That is, we cannot point to a program in a computer any more than we can point to a memory in the brain.

Although hardware and software are very different entities, it is interesting to note that there is often a trade-off between them. Some operations may be carried out either by a special-purpose hardware system or by means of a program stored in memory. In general, the fastest way to perform a given task is to build a circuit dedicated exclusively to the task. This may be a very costly step. Writing a program to perform the same task on an existing computer is considerably cheaper, but the task may take very much longer, as the hardware of the computer may not be optimized to suit the task. Hence the term *trade-off* refers to the exchanging of speed for cost. A similar trade-off exists within human activity. For example, a factory may wish to protect its goods from theft. One possible approach is to seek a hardware solution and position electronic sensors to detect and report any movement. An alternative technique is to program a human being to act as a guard. In this case the software is the *program* that lies in the brain of the general-purpose machine (the human). Computer scientists often refer to the brain as *wetware.*

Why do we teach computer hardware? After all, I can watch a television program without understanding how a cathode ray tube operates, or fly in a Jumbo jet without ever knowing the meaning of thermodynamics. Why then should the lives of computer scientists and programmers be made miserable by forcing them to learn about what goes on inside a computer?

There are several reasons for teaching the principles of computer hardware, the most important of which are:

1. Programming itself involves implicit hardware operations. As an example consider inputting or outputting data. Whenever programmers send data to a computer or receive data from it, they are using hardware devices about which they must have some prior knowledge. Sometimes this involves a knowledge of the format of the data. Suppose data is to be presented on a television-style display (i.e. VDU or CRT terminal). It is clearly sensible to break the data up into segments or pages ending at some logical point and display the data a page at a time. This is better than ending a screen in the middle of a sentence and then expecting the viewer to remember the first half of the sentence.

2. Hardware defines the limitations of the computer. Any computer user must be aware of its restrictions. Clearly, there is no point in buying a computer to, say, allow 80 students simultaneous access to 80 terminals if the computer operating at maximum capacity can service only 40 terminals. Similarly, an on-board navigation computer in an aircraft must have circuits operating at a sufficiently high speed to compute a course correction before the aircraft has strayed too far off track.

3. Programming cannot always be divorced from hardware. While a computer programmer writing packages in COBOL to calculate wages in an office is, largely, far-removed from the finer details of hardware, other programmers are often involved with interfacing a computer to a system. For example, a microprocessor may be used to control the temperature of chemical reaction. Such a system involves converting a temperature into a voltage, transforming the voltage into a digital or numerical value, reading it into the computer, processing this number, outputting another number to a device that converts it into a voltage, and finally using this voltage to control the heater. Such a wide range of activities requires the expertise of the electrical engineer and the programmer. If the job is to be done at all well, they must be able to communicate with each other. Sometimes, they may even be the same person; a programmer well versed in electrical engineering or vice versa.

4. It is aesthetically pleasing to understand hardware. The examples provided at the start of this section are not entirely appropriate. The passenger in an aircraft is not interested in the workings of a jet engine but the pilot is. A detailed knowledge of the engines is not vital to his or her job, but understanding them gives the pilot a measure of satisfaction. Similarly, programmers who understand precisely what happens after their jobs have been submitted to the computer also have more personal satisfaction than their counterparts who regard the internal operation of a computer as a type of black magic.

An overview of the course

It is very difficult to know just what should be included in a course on computer organization and hardware, or what should be excluded from it. Any topic can always be expanded to an arbitrary extent. For example, if we begin with gates and Boolean algebra, do we go on to actual semiconductor devices and then to semiconductor physics? In this course, I have attempted to include those topics relevant to points (1)–(4) above, at an introductory level. However, some of my material may surprise those familiar with more conventional introductory texts. I have included a somewhat wider range of material because the area of influence encompassed by the digital computer has expanded greatly in recent years. I have also gone out of my way to highlight the divergence between theory and practice. For example, while including a conventional introduction to gates and Boolean algebra, I have also made it clear that the designer is concerned with other (economic) considerations as well as logic design. The major subject areas dealt with in this course are:

Computer arithmetic   Our system of arithmetic based on the radix ten has evolved over thousands of years. The computer carries out its internal operations on numbers represented in the radix (or base) two. This anomaly is not due to some magic power inherent in binary arithmetic but simply because it would be uneconomic to design a computer to operate in denary (base ten) arithmetic. At this point I must make a comment. Time and time again, I read in the popular press that the behaviour of digital computers and their characteristics are due to the fact that they operate on bits using binary arithmetic while we humans operate on digits using decimal arithmetic. This idea is nonsense! As there is a simple relationship between binary and decimal numbers, the fact that computers represent information in ***binary*** form is a mere detail of engineering. It is the architecture or organization of a computer that makes it behave in such a different way to the brain.

Basic logic elements and Boolean algebra   It is the type of technology we have today that determines what a computer can do. By starting with the basic logic elements, or gates, from which a computer is made up, we can see how the operation of these gates affects both the way in which the computer carries out arithmetic operations and the way in which the functional parts of a computer interact to execute a program. An introduction to flip-flops and their application to sequential circuits is also included. The flip-flop is a logic element that can store (remember) a single binary digit, and is the basic component of many memory units.

Computer organization   This topic is concerned with how a computer actually operates at the conceptual (i.e. block-diagram) level. That is, we show how the computer goes about reading an instruction from memory, decoding it, and then executing it.

Assembly language   The primitive instructions that directly control the operation of a computer are called machine-code instructions and are composed of sequences of binary values stored in memory. As programming in machine code is exceedingly tedious, an aid to machine-code programming called assembly language has been devised. Assembly language is a form of shorthand permitting the programmer to write machine-code instructions in a simple mnemonic or abbreviated form of plain language. Sometimes high-level languages (Pascal, COBOL, BASIC, FORTRAN etc.) are translated into a series of assembly-language instructions by a compiler as an intermediate step on the way to pure machine code. This intermediate step serves as a debugging tool for programmers who wish to examine the operation of the compiler and the output it produces.

Programmers writing in assembly language require a detailed knowledge of the architecture of the machine they are using, unlike the corresponding programmers operating in high-level languages. At this point I must say that assembly-language programming is introduced to explain the operation of the central processing unit. Apart from certain special exceptions, all programs should be written in a high-level language whenever possible.

Input/output It is no good having a computer unless it can take in new information (programs and data), and output the results of its calculations. In this section we show how information is actually moved into and out of the computer. The operation of three basic input/output devices is described. These are the keyboard, the VDU, and the printer. We also briefly examine the way in which analog signals can be converted into digital form, processed digitally by a computer and then converted back into analog form.

Memory devices A computer needs memory to hold its programs, data and any other information it may require at some time in the future. In this section we look at the *immediate access store* and the *backing store* or the *secondary store.* Basically, an immediate access store provides a computer with any data it requires in approximately the same time it takes the computer to execute one of its assembly-language level operations. The secondary store is very much slower and it takes thousands of times longer to access data in a secondary store than it does in the immediate access store. However, secondary storage is used because it is immensely cheaper than immediate access store. The most popular forms of secondary store are the disk and tape units, which both rely on magnetizing a moving magnetic material to store data. In recent years, optical storage technology has gained prominence because it combines the relatively fast access time of the disk with the large capacity and low cost of the tape deck.

Computer communications Some people thought that the advent of the microprocessor would spell the end of large computer systems. In many ways the reverse has proved true and computer systems have grown even bigger as individual computers are now being linked together to form networks. Networking computers has many advantages, not least of which is the ability of a number of computers in a network to share expensive peripherals such as line-printers. Consequently, a section has been devoted to showing how computers communicate with each other. Three aspects of computer communications are examined. The first is the protocols or rules that govern the way in which information is exchanged between systems in an orderly fashion. The second is the way in which digital information in a computer is encoded in a form suitable for transmission over a serial channel, the characteristics of the physical channel and how data is reconstituted at the receiver. The third provides a brief overview of local area networks. These are networks of computers which are distributed over one site (e.g. an office, or a complex of buildings).

Operating systems   An operating system is a large chunk of software that coordinates all the functional parts of the computer and provides an interface for the user. A major reason for including operating systems in a book on hardware is that two hardware features found on most computers (interrupt handling mechanisms and the stack) facilitate multiprogramming, an important characteristic of many operating systems. Multiprogramming is the ability of a computer to appear to run two or more programs simultaneously. At the end of this section a short introduction to memory management is given. Memory management permits several programs to operate as though each alone occupied the computer's memory and enables a computer with a small, high-speed random access memory, and a large, low-speed serial access memory to appear as if it had a single large high-speed random access memory.

1.1 The digital computer

Before beginning the discussion of computer hardware proper, it is necessary to say what a computer is (and is not), and to define a few terms. If ever an award were to be given to those guilty of mis-information in the field of computer science, it would go to the creators of HAL in *2001*, of R2D2 in *Star Wars* and of K9 in *Doctor Who*. These, and other similar machines, have generated the popular myth that a computer is a reasonably close approximation to a human brain and is a repository for all knowledge so that, somewhere in its memory banks, it contains an infinte accumulation of data. The reality is a little more mundane: a computer is a machine that takes in information from the outside world, processes it according to some pre-determined set of operations and delivers the processed information. Our definition of a computer is remarkably poor, as it attempts to define the word *computer* in terms of the equally complex words *information, operation,* and *process.* Perhaps a better approach is to provide some examples of what a computer can do. We will now look at the role of computers in data processing, numerical computation (popularly called 'number crunching'), workstations, automatic control systems, and electronic systems.

1.1.1 The computer as a data processor

Figure 1.1 represents the more conventional idea of the computer. Here is a system designed to deal with the payroll of a large factory. I am going to call the whole thing a computer, in contrast with those who would say that the CPU (central processing unit) is the computer and all the other devices are peripherals. Somewhere inside the CPU's immediate access memory is a program, a collection of primitive machine-code operations, whose purpose is to calculate an employee's pay based on the number of hours worked, the basic rate of pay, and the overtime rate. Of course, this program would also include many sophistications so that tax, national insurance and any other deductions could be dealt with. The function of the printer in a data-processing system is largely self-explanatory. It is an electromechanical device that prints letters and numbers on a piece of paper and can directly produce the pay-slips. Because the computer's immediate access memory is relatively expensive, only enough is provided to hold the program and the data it is currently processing. The mass of information on the employees is normally held in secondary store as a *disk file*. Whenever the CPU requires information about a particular employee, the appropriate data is taken from the disk (or, more accurately, copied) and placed in the immediate access store. The time taken to perform this operation is a small fraction of a second but is many times slower than reading from the immediate access store. However, the cost of storing information on disk is very low indeed and this compensates for its relative slowness.

The tape transport provides a form of secondary store that is much cheaper than the disk. In many installations the data on the disks is copied onto tape periodically (say every four hours) and the tapes stored in the basement for security reasons. Every so often (more often in some installations than others) the system is said to *crash* and everything grinds to a halt. When this happens the last *tape dump* can be reloaded and the system assumes the state it was in a short time before the crash. Incidentally, *crash* had the original meaning of a failure resulting from a read/write head in a disk drive crashing into the rotating surface of a disk and physically damaging the magnetic coating on its surface. In practice, *crash* has come to mean any system failure.

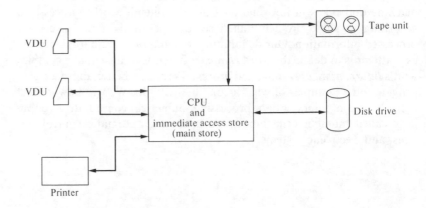

Fig. 1.1 The computer as a data processor.

The visual display units (VDUs) allow operators to enter data directly into the system. This information could be the number of hours an employee has worked in the current week. Conversely, the VDU can be used to ask specific questions, such as 'How much tax did Mr XYZ pay in November?' To be a little more precise, the VDU does not actually ask questions but it allows the programmer to execute a program containing the relevant question. The VDU may even be used to modify the program itself so that new facilities may be added as the system grows. Computers used in data processing are often characterized by their large secondary stores and their extensive use of printers and VDUs.

1.1.2 The computer as a numeric processor

In the above example of a computer as a data processor, the computer devotes much of its time to the manipulation of data in the form of symbols representing information about the employees of a firm. In such applications of the computer, the amount of time spent performing arithmetic (as understood by a mathematician) on numbers is quite small compared with data-processing operations.

Numeric processing or to use the more coloquial term, number crunching, refers to computer applications involving a very large volume of mathematical operations—sometimes billions of operations per job. There are numerous applications of numeric processing, many of which are described as *scientific.* For example, consider the application of computers to the modelling of the processes governing the weather. The atmosphere is a continuous, three-dimensional medium made up of the molecules of a number of different gases. The scientists cannot easily deal with a continuous medium, but can make the problem more tractable by considering the atmosphere to be composed of a very large number of cubes. Each of these cubes is considered to have a uniform temperature, density and pressure. That is, the gas making up the cube shows no variation whatsoever in its physical properties. Variations exist only *between* adjacent cubes. A cube has six faces and the scientist can create a model of how the cube interacts with each of its six immediate neighbours.

The scientist may start by assuming that all cubes are identical (there is no initial interaction between cubes), and then consider what happens when a source of energy, the sun, is applied to the model. The effect of each cube on its neighbour is calculated, and the whole process is repeated cyclically (iteration). In order to get accurate results, the size of the cubes should be small, otherwise the assumption about the cube being uniform will not be valid. Moreover, the number of iterations needed to get the result to converge to a steady-state value is often very large. Consequently, this type of problem often requires very long runs on immensely powerful computers, or supercomputers as they are sometimes called.

Another area in which numeric processing pops up is in certain real-time applications of computers. Here, real-time means that the results of the computations are required within a given time of the start of the computations. For example, consider the application of computers to air-traffic control. A rotating radar antenna measures the bearing and distance (range) of each aircraft (target). At time t, target i at position $P(i,t)$, returns an echo giving its range $r(i,t)$, and bearing $b(i,t)$. Unfortunately, because of the nature of radar signals, a random error is associated with the value of each echo from a target, and this must be taken into account.

The computer obtains the data from the radar receiver for n targets, updated p times every minute. From this raw data, it must compute the position of each aircraft, its track, and warn the controller of any possible conflicts. All this requires considerable high-speed numerical computation.

Computers used in numeric processing applications are frequently characterized by large, powerful and very expensive CPUs, very high-speed memories and relatively modest quantities of input/output devices and secondary storage. Over the last few years special-purpose numeric processors have been designed to augment microprocessors. These are frequently called **numeric coprocessors** and are designed to handle some of the numeric tasks that are not well suited to conventional microprocessors. Numeric coprocessors are now making it possible for microprocessor-based systems to tackle some of the tasks that once required large mainframe computers.

1.1.3 The personal computer and workstation

The 1980s witnessed two significant changes in computing—the introduction of the personal computer and the workstation. Although the personal computer has been around for some time, it is only with the advent of the IBM PC, the Apple Macintosh, the Atari 1024ST and the Amiga that the personal computer has developed from a toy (or curiosity) into a useful tool.

Personal computers bring computing power to people in offices or in their own homes. Commercial software such as word processors, data bases and spreadsheets have revolutionized the office environment, just as computer-aided design (CAD) packages have revolutionized the industrial design environment. For example, today's engineer can design a circuit and simulate its behaviour using one software package and then create a layout for a printed circuit board (PCB) with another package. Indeed, the output from the PCB design package may be suitable for feeding directly into the machine that actually makes the PCBs. We are witnessing the growth of an industry that permits a single individual to design and even produce systems once requiring a whole team of people. Even more impressively, a single engineer can now do in one or two days things that took the design team weeks or even months to do.

Probably the most important application of the personal computer is in word processing. For the first time ordinary people are able to write letters and articles, edit them and then print them. Many personal computers now have quite sophisticated word-processing packages that provide a professional-looking result and even include spelling checkers to remove embarrassing spelling mistakes. When powerful personal computers are coupled to laser printers, it is possible to run desktop publishing packages capable of creating manuscripts that were once the province of the professional publisher.

While everyone who is familiar with the computer also knows about the personal computer, the concept of the workstation is less widely understood. I have looked everywhere for a formal definition of the workstation and have failed to find one. Like almost everything else in the world of computers, people understand what they mean by a piece of jargon, but are often unable to define it formally. So, I am going to provide my own definition of the workstation. **Workstation**: a personal computer that was bought for you by your boss and which you could never afford on your salary in any case. In other words, the workstation is a super personal computer or a personal minicomputer.

Typical workstations are produced by manufacturers such as Apollo, Sun and Xerox. Workstations share many of the characteristics of personal computers and are used by engineers or designers to do the type of things described above. Where they differ from the personal computer is in their performance. Workstations are very powerful indeed and use state-of-the-art microprocessors with 32-bit data buses, very large memories and high-speed clocks. These workstations operate at speeds of ten or more times that of even high-performance personal computers and cost in the region of $20 000–70 000.

Apart from its sheer performance, the most significant feature of the average workstation is its graphics facilities. Personal computers are now generally quite powerful and have large secondary storage facilities, but they lack really sophisticated graphics facilities. The workstation provides the graphics facilities required by the designer using CAD packages. For example, the mechanical engineer needs CAD packages to display objects in three dimensions and to rotate these objects to show how they appear from any particular viewpoint. If objects are to be represented in anything like a reasonable detail, the display system must have a resolution of at least 1000×1000 points (i.e. pixels). Moreover, rotating three-dimensional objects requires a phenomenal amount of computer power.

1.1.4 The computer in automatic control

The vast majority of computers are found neither in data processing roles nor in numeric processing activities. The advent of the microprocessor and low-cost computing has put the computer at the heart of many atuomatic control systems. When used as a control element, the computer is normally embedded in some larger system and is *invisible* to the observer. By invisible I mean that the operator (or the general public) may not be aware of the existence of the computer. Consider the example of a computer installed in a gasoline pump to count and check the cash it receives and then deliver a measured amount of fuel. The user does not care whether the pump is controlled by the latest microprocessor or by a clockwork mechanism, as long as it functions correctly.

A good example of a computer in automatic control is an aircraft's automatic landing system illustrated in Fig. 1.2. In this example, the

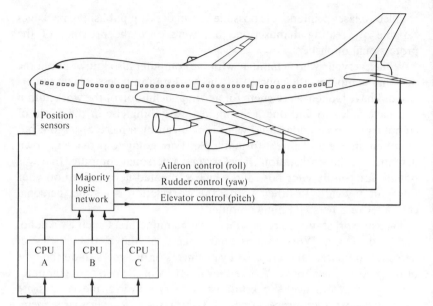

Fig. 1.2 The computer as a control element.

aircraft's position (height, distance from touch down, and distance off the runway centre-line) and speed are determined by various radio techniques in conjunction with a ground-based instrument-landing system. Information about the aircraft's position is fed to the three computers which, individually, determine the error in the aircraft's course. The error is the difference between the aircraft's measured position, and the position it should be in. The resulting outputs from the computer are the signals required to move the aircraft's control surfaces (ailerons, elevator, rudder) and, if necessary, adjust the engine thrust. In this case the computer's program is held in immediate access memory of a variety called read only memory (ROM) which can be read from but not written to. Once the program to land the plane has been developed, it should not need modifying. Note that the automatic-landing system requires three computers, each working on the same problem with the same inputs. The outputs of the computers are fed to a majority logic circuit called a ***voting network***. If all three inputs to the majority logic circuit are the same, its output is identical to its inputs. If one computer fails, the circuit selects its output to be the same as that produced by the two good computers. This arrangement is called ***triple modular redundancy*** and makes the system highly reliable.

Another example of the computer as a complex automatic controller is in the humble automobile. The desire to increase the efficiency and performance of the internal combustion engine, while, at the same time, to reduce the emission of harmful combustion products, has led to the introduction of computerized fuel injection systems (CFIs). Figure 1.3 illustrates the structure of one type of CFI.

1.1.5 The computer as a component

When the microprocessor first appeared, one of its many impacts on

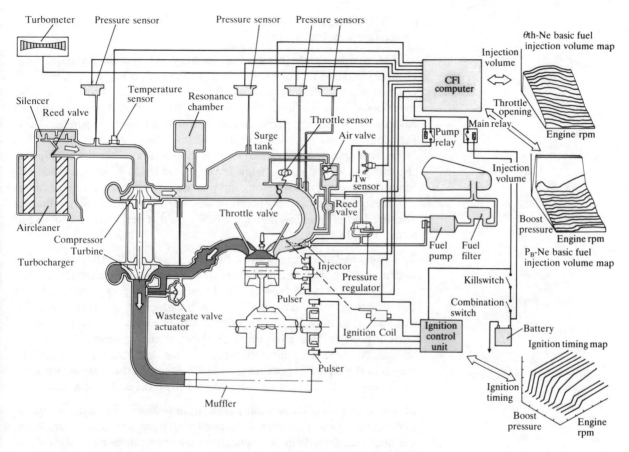

Fig. 1.3 The computerized fuel injection system. This diagram is intended to demonstrate the sophistication of a computerized fuel injection system, rather than to explain how it functions. Reproduced by permission (Honda Ltd).

society was to generate friction between departments of electrical engineering and departments of computer science in universities and polytechnics. Members of both departments thought that the microprocessor belonged to them. A computer scientist sees the microprocessor as little more than a low-cost minicomputer with rather basic facilities. An electronic engineer, on the other hand, sees the microprocessor as just another component, albeit a sophisticated and complex one. In fact, the vast majority of microprocessor applications do indeed fall into the category of the microprocessor as a component. In a sense, the application of a computer as just another electronic component can be thought of as an extension of the computer as an element in control systems.

Consider the application of a microprocessor to a hi-fi cassette deck. At first thought, a microprocessor may seem a little out of place in a system devoted to the processing of analog signals. Microprocessors currently take little part in the processing of the speech and music signals themselves in conventional analog decks, but they do facilitate the control of the cassette deck in four ways.

1. *The control of the mechanical parts of the system*   In older (and cheaper) cassette recorders, the controls (record, play-back, pause, and rewind) were large buttons that directly moved the various cogs and mechanical linkages inside the recorder. Today most high-performance cassette decks employ electronically activated solenoids to perform these functions. By using a microprocessor to read the position of the switches on the front panel, an advanced level of control is possible. For example, if the user presses fast rewind while the deck is in the fast forward mode, the microprocessor can slow, stop, and put the tape in a rewind mode, all in an orderly manner. If this operation were performed manually, without a pause to let the tape slow down, the tape would at best be stretched, and at worst would snap.

2. *The control of a tape counter*   In older cassette decks the tape position indicator is simply a mechanical revolution counter, displaying (typically) from 000 to 999 as the tape moves. By using a microprocessor to perform this function, many new facilities can be added to the tape deck. For example, it is now feasible to ask the cassette deck to rewind from its current position to a given point on the tape and to replay the previous section. As there is a relationship between the tape counter value and the length of the tape, it is possible to indicate either the time elapsed since the beginning of the tape, or the time to go before the end of the tape.

3. *The setting up of the bias and equalization systems*   All audio recording systems have two parameters associated with them, bias and equalization. On nearly all cassette decks a switch selects one of three pairs of values of bias and equalization corresponding to the three basic types of tape (ferro, chrome, and metal). On some of the more advanced decks a microprocessor records a series of tones at the beginning of the tape and then adjusts the values of bias and equalization to the optimum for that particular tape.

4. *Signal processing in a digital tape deck*   Until the mid-1980s conventional microprocessor technology could not be applied to the actual processing of analog signals (i.e. speech and music) economically. Today, we have the compact disc, CD, and digital audio tape, DAT. Sound can be converted to digital form, recorded on tape digitally, played back digitally and then reconverted into analog form ready to feed into an amplifier and loudspeaker system. Special microprocessors that process signals in digital form have been developed to cope with these new recording systems. However, these are very special-purpose devices and are quite unlike conventional microprocessors, even though they are built with the same technology and share common operating principles.

Another example of the computer as a circuit element is provided by the *glass cockpit*. Until the mid-1980s, the flight instrumentation of all large commercial aircraft was almost entirely electromechanical and relied more on the skills of the watchmaker than the electronic engineer. Today these mechanical devices that measure height, speed, engine performance, and attitude of the aircraft are being replaced by electronic displays controlled by microcomputers. Most of the displays are based on the cathode ray tube display—hence the expression glass cockpit. Electronic displays are not only easier to read and more reliable than their mechanical counterparts, but they provide only the information required by the flight crew at any instant. Figure 1.4 illustrates a typical modern aircraft display, which combines a radar image of clouds together with navigational information. In this example the pilot can see that the aircraft is routed from radio beacon WCO to BKP to BED and will miss the area of possible storm activity. Interestingly enough, this type of indicator has been accused of 'deskilling' pilots, since they do not have to create their own mental image of the position of their aircraft with respect to the world from much cruder instruments. Some believe that if they change aircraft type to one without such sophisticated display equipment, they may have lost some of the skills needed to interpret older instruments.

Fig. 1.4 Computer-controlled displays in the glass cockpit. This figure illustrates the primary navigation display (or horizontal situation indicator) that the pilot uses to determine the direction in which the aircraft is travelling (in this case 231 degrees—approximately south west). In addition to the heading, the display indicates the position and density of cloud and the loading of radio beacons. The three arcs indicate range from the aircraft (30, 60, 90 nautical miles). Reproduced by permission. (Smiths Industry.)

1.2 Mainframe, mini, and micro

One of the many ways of categorizing computers is to slot them into three pigeon-holes labelled: *mainframe computer*, *minicomputer*, and *microcomputer*. In the beginning there was only the mainframe computer. The mainframe computer of yesterday was a physically large and fabulously expensive beast complete with a priesthood of programmers, operators and maintenance engineers. Such a colossus was found only in large organizations and often employed as a general-purpose machine for scientific, industrial or data-processing applications. In industry, the mainframe is used to design products and simulate their behaviour as well as to deal with such mundane operations as payroll calculations. Perhaps one of the most notable features of a mainframe is its wide range of peripherals—VDUs, printers, plotters, communications network controllers, and disk and tape drives.

Not only the rich and powerful needed computer power. Scientists in small laboratories wanted to speed up their analysis of scientific data. Engineers wanted to control dams by measuring the flow of water upstream and hence predict the future level of the water. Owners of small companies wanted to keep track of their stock levels, addresses of their clients, their tax returns, invoices and a whole host of data relating to their businesses. In all these cases the mainframe would have proved prohibitively expensive. Computer manufacturers provided a handy solution to such problems in the form of the minicomputer.

The microprocessor is nothing more than a CPU on a single chip of silicon. Its importance is a consequence of its staggeringly low cost and minute size. Alone a microprocessor can do nothing. In conjunction with memory, a power supply, and the necessary peripherals it can be said to form a microcomputer. At the current level of technology most microcomputers have a performance below those of existing minicomputers. A microcomputer costs from $100 to $5000 (although educational 'toys' can be bought for under $100 and simple microprocessor-based controllers may also fall in this price range). It is worth noting that several minicomputer manufacturers have themselves, or in conjunction with others, brought out microprocessors which are functionally equivalent to the CPUs of their own minicomputers. In this way existing minicomputer software can be run on these microcomputers (which run more slowly than their bigger 'mini' brothers).

There is no precise definition of a mainframe, minicomputer, or microcomputer, so we shall list some of the attributes that may be used to characterize them. In one sense we can say that a minicomputer occupies the middle ground of computing, and we can characterize mainframe computers as occupying the high ground and microcomputers as occupying the low ground.

Characteristics of computers

Cost   The minicomputer is much cheaper than the mainframe. Typically, a mini falls in the $10 000–50 000 price range. Equally the microcomputer is cheaper than a minicomputer—although some high-performance microcomputers may fall within the price range of the mini.

Physical size   The mainframe takes up a largish chunk of real estate, often a whole floor of a building. A mini, on the other hand, is frequently quite small, sometimes no larger than the average wardrobe. Although there are some microcomputers almost as large as minis, the average microcomputer sits quite happily on the average office desk. Microcomputers described as *portable* are usually transportable or 'luggable' in the sense that they can be moved from one room to another with relatively little effort. Truly portable computers that can be carried about and used on trains and aeroplanes are now called *laptop portables.*

Peripherals A single mainframe almost certainly has a wide spectrum of users (especially in a university, polytechnic, or research establishment), each with their own particular requirements. Such a diverse range of users demands a wide range of peripherals: disks to store user programs and data, VDUs and printers, telecommunications equipment to link the computer to installations in other towns and even countries, and graphics equipment capable of producing complex diagrams. The mini is frequently dedicated to a single task (say controlling and evaluating an experiment) and often has few peripherals: perhaps a single disk drive, a couple of VDUs and a printer. Having said this, it must be pointed out that some mainframe computers are gradually being replaced by minicomputers or groups of minicomputers in the form of a network.

Performance The performance of a computer is a measure of its computing power. Performance is frequently measured by executing a certain set of instructions a given number of times and then recording the time taken to do this.

Mainframe computers often have very high levels of performance and can execute a hundred million or more instructions a second.

The latest mini has only a fraction of the computational power of the latest mainframe. I say 'latest' because the advance in computer technology is so rapid that today's low-cost mini is often far more powerful than yesterday's mainframe. One of the reasons for the mini's lower computational power is that it frequently uses smaller word lengths than mainframes. The word length of a computer is the number of bits (ones and zeros) in its basic unit of information storage and manipulation. The effects of particular word lengths on computer performance will be dealt with later, but here it is sufficient to state that one result of a short word length is to increase the number of arithmetic operations needed to perform a particular calculation to a given level of precision.

Technology It is reasonably fair to say that today's high-performance mainframe computers are built with the most sophisticated available technology. That is, they use technology that was either in the research laboratory yesterday or was far too expensive to apply to commercial ventures.

Minicomputers often use technology that has been tried and tested in mainframes and has now reached the stage at which it can be miniaturized (with possibly some loss of performance) and produced on a much larger scale. Microcomputers generally use technology that has been developed for very large-scale low-cost production. It is perfectly true that a particular chip may have been developed specifically for microcomputer applications, but the fabrication process used to create the chip will almost certainly be tried and tested.

1.3 The stored-program computer—an overview

Before discussing the stored-program computer, consider first the human being. It is natural to compare today's wonder, the computer, with the human just as the Victorians did with their technology. They coined expressions like, 'He has a screw loose', or 'He has run out of steam', in their endeavour to see their technology in human terms. There have been times when the computer has been compared with the human brain, and periods when the computer has been contrasted with it, and the poor computer called 'a high-speed moron' by those who do not understand the nature of the digital computer.

Figure 1.5 shows how a human may be viewed as a system with *inputs,* a *processing device,* and *outputs.* The inputs are sight (eyes), smell (nose), taste (tongue), touch (skin), sound (ear), and position (muscle tension). Information from these sensors is processed by the brain.

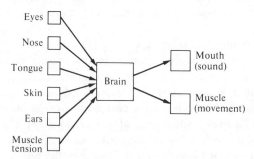

Fig. 1.5 The organization of a human being.

The brain performs two functions. It stores new information and processes the inputs from its sensors. The storage aspect of the brain is important because it modifies the operation of the brain by a process we call learning. Because the brain learns from all new stimuli, it does not always exhibit the same response to a given stimulus. Once a child has been burned by a flame it reacts differently the next time it encounters fire. The ability of a brain to both store and process information is shared by the digital computer. However, most current computers cannot mimic the operation of the brain and therefore simplistic comparisons between the computer and the human brain are often misleading at best and mischievous at worst! A branch of computer science is devoted to the study of computers that do indeed appear to mimic the human brain and share some of the brain's properties. These computers are called neural nets and are in their infancy. We do not cover neural nets in this text.

The output from the brain is used to generate speech or to control the muscles needed to move the body.

Figure 1.6 shows how a computer can be compared with a human. It may have all the inputs a human has, and inputs for a few things we cannot detect. By means of photoelectric devices or radio receivers, a computer can sense ultraviolet light, infra-red, X-rays, or radio waves. The output from the computer is also more versatile than that of humans.

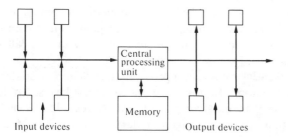

Fig. 1.6 The organization of a computer.

It can produce mechanical movement (by means of motors), or generate light (TV displays), sound (from loudspeakers), or even heat (by passing a current through a resistor).

The computer counterpart of the brain is the central processing unit plus its storage unit (memory). Like the brain, it processes its various inputs and produces an output.

I do not intend to write a treatise on the differences between the brain and the computer, but I feel that it is necessary to make a comment here. Not least because many of my students ask me whether the computer works like the brain and whether computer memory is similar to human memory. It is probable that the processing and memory functions of the brain are closely interrelated, while in the computer they are normally distinct. Many engineers believe that the major breakthrough in computing will come only when computer architecture takes on more of the features of the brain. In particular, the digital computer is *serially* organized and performs a single instruction at a time, while the brain has a highly *parallel* organization and is able to carry out many activities at the same time.

Somewhere in every computer's memory is a block of information that we call a program. The word *program* has the same meaning as it does in the expressions 'programme of studies', or 'programme of music'. A computer program is a collection of actions to be carried out by the computer sequentially. The classic analogy with a computer program is a recipe in a cookery book. The recipe is a sequence of commands that must be obeyed one by one and in the correct order. Our analogy between the computer program and the recipe is particularly appropriate because the cookery instructions involve operations on ingredients, just as the computer carries out operations on data stored in memory.

The central processing unit of a computer reads the instructions making up the program one by one, and executes each instruction as it is brought from memory. The word *execute* means carry out. For example, an instruction 'add A to B' causes the addition of a quantity called A to a quantity called B to be carried out. The actual nature of these instructions does not matter here. What is important is that the most complex actions carried out by a computer can be broken down into a number of more primitive operations. But then again, the most sublime thoughts of Einstein or Beethoven might be reduced to a large number of impulses transmitted across the synapses of the cells in their brains.

The computer performs its operations on information called *data* held within its storage unit. This is also the memory in which the program is located. That is, the program and data used by the computer are located in the same memory but, of course, in different regions of it. A computer that stores instructions and data in the **same** memory unit is called a Von Neumann machine.

Figure 1.7 demonstrates how a program (instructions) and data coexist in the same memory. In this case the memory has seven locations, numbered from 0 to 6. Memory is normally regarded as an array of storage locations (boxes or pigeon-holes). Each of these **boxes** has a unique location or **address** that is said to contain data. For example, in the simple memory of Figure 1.7 address 5 contains the number 7. One great difference between computers and people is that we number m items from 1 to m, while the computer numbers them from 0 to m-1. This is because the computer regards 0 (zero) as a valid identifier. Unfortunately, people often confuse 0 the identifier with 0 meaning 'nothing'.

Information in a computer's memory is accessed by providing the memory with the address (i.e. location) of the desired data. Only one memory location is addressed at a time. If we wish to search through memory for a particular item (because we do not know its address), it is necessary to read the items one at a time until we find the desired item. However, it appears that the human memory works in a very different way. Information is accessed from our memories by applying a **key** to all locations within the memory (brain). This key is some function of the data being accessed and is not related to its location within the brain. Memory locations containing information that **associates** with the key respond to the access. In other words, the brain carries out a parallel search of its memory for the information it requires. Accessing many memory locations in parallel permits more than one location to respond to the access and is therefore very efficient. Suppose someone says 'chip' to you. The word 'chip' is the data that is fed to all parts of your memory for matching. Your brain might produce responses of: chip(silicon), chip (potato), chip(on shoulder), and chip(gambling).

The program in Fig. 1.7 occupies consecutive memory locations 0–3, and the data locations 4–6. The first instruction, 'get [4]', means get (fetch) the contents of memory location number 4 from the memory. We employ square brackets to denote the contents of the address they enclose, so that in this case [4]＝2. The next instruction, at address 1, is 'add it to [5]', and means add the number brought by the previous instruction to the contents of location 5. Thus, the computer adds 2 and 7 to get 9. The third instruction, 'put result in [6]', tells the computer to put the result (i.e. 9) in location 6. This it does, and the 1 that was in location 6 before this instruction was obeyed is replaced by 9. The final instruction in location 3 tells the computer to stop.

We can summarize the operation of a digital computer by means of a little piece of **pseudocode** (pseudocode is a method of writing down an algorithm in a language that is a cross between Pascal and plain English— we shall meet pseudocode again).

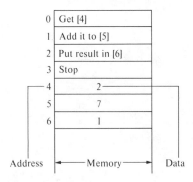

Address	Memory	Data
0	Get [4]	
1	Add it to [5]	
2	Put result in [6]	
3	Stop	
4	2	
5	7	
6	1	

Fig. 1.7 The program and data in memory. *Note*: Throughout this book square brackets denote *the contents of*, so that in the example above, [4] is read as 'the contents of memory location number 4' and is equal to 2.

```
do
   begin
      Read an instruction from memory
      Execute the instruction
   end
repeat forever
```

Summary

In this chapter we have considered how the computer can be looked at as a component or, more traditionally, as part of a large system. Besides acting in the obvious role as a 'computer system', computers are now built into a wide range of everyday items from toys to automobile ignition systems. In particular, we have introduced some of the topics that make up a first-level course in computer architecture or computer organization.

As we progress through this book, we are going to examine how the computer is organized and how it is able to step through instructions in memory and execute them. We will also show how the computer communicates with the world outside the CPU and the memory.

Problems

1. List all the applications of computer you can think of and classify them into the groups we described (e.g. computer as a component).

2. Can a computer ever be capable of feelings, 'free will', and 'original thought'. If not, why not?

3. Some of the current high-performance civil aircraft have *fly-by-wire* control systems. That is, control inputs from the pilot are not fed to the flying control surfaces and engines by wires/mechanical linkages or by hydraulic means. Instead, commands from the pilot are fed to a computer and the computer *interprets* them and carries them out in the fashion it 'thinks' is most appropriate. For example, if the pilot tries to increase the speed to a level at which the airframe might be overstressed, the computer will refuse to obey the command. Some pilots and some members of the public are unhappy about this arrangement. Are their fears rational?

4. The computer has often been referred to as a 'high-speed moron'. Is this statement fair?

5. Computers use binary arithmetic (i.e. all numbers are composed of 1s and 0s) to carry out their operations. Humans normally use decimal arithmetic (0–9) and have symbolic means of representing information (e.g. the Latin alphabet or the Chinese characters). Does this imply a fundamental difference between people and computers?

6. Shortly after the introduction of the computer, someone said that all the computing in the world could be undertaken by two computers. At that time the best computers were no more powerful than today's calculators. The commentator assumed that computers would be used to solve a few scientific problems and little else. As the cost and size of computers has been reduced, the role of computers has increased. Is there a limit to the applications of computers? Do you anticipate any radically new applications of computers?

7. A microprocessor manufacturer, at the release of their new super chip, was asked the question, 'What can your microprocessor do?' He said it was now possible to put it in washing machines so that the user could tell the machine what to do verbally, rather than by adjusting the settings manually. At the same time we live in a world in which many of its inhabitants go short of the very basic necessities of life: water, food, shelter, and elementary health care.

Does the computer make a positive contribution to the future well-being of the world's inhabitants? Is the answer the same if we ask about the computer's short-term effects or its long-term effects?

8. The workstation makes it possible to design and to test (by simulation) everything from other computers to large mechanical structures. Coupled with computer communications networks and computer-aided manufacturing, it could be argued that many people in technologically advanced societies will be able to work entirely from home. Indeed, all their shopping and banking activities can be also be performed from home. Do you think that this step will be advantageous or disadvantageous? What will be the effects on society of a population that can, largely, work from home?

Logic elements and Boolean algebra

We commence our study of the digital computer by investigating the basic elements from which it is constructed. Two distinct classes of component are found in a digital computer—the gate and the flip-flop. These are known as **combinational** or **combinatorial** and **sequential** logic elements, respectively.

Chapter 2 begins by describing the properties of some simple gates and then shows how such gates can be connected together to carry out useful functions in the same way that bricks can be put together to build a house or a school. Following the introduction to gates comes a section on Boolean algebra which provides a formal tool for the analysis of circuits containing gates. Boolean algebra leads on to Karnaugh maps which are nothing more than a graphical technique for the simplification and manipulation of Boolean equations. In the next chapter we look at sequential elements, which are themselves made up of combinational logic elements.

2.1 Analog and digital systems

Before we can appreciate the meaning and implications of **digital** systems, it is necessary to look at the nature of **analog** systems. The word **analog** is derived from the same root as the noun **analogy** and means a quantity that is related to, or resembles, or corresponds to, another quantity. For example, the length of a column of mercury in a thermometer is an analog of the temperature. Analog electronic circuits represent physical quantities in terms of voltages or currents. The most important aspect of an analog system is that analog variables can have any value between their maximum and minimum limits. For example, if a variable X is represented by a voltage in the range $-10\,\mathrm{V}$ to $+10\,\mathrm{V}$, X can have an **infinite** number of values in the range $-10\,\mathrm{V}$ to $+10\,\mathrm{V}$. In other words, we can say that X is **continuous** in value and can change its value by an arbitrarily small amount. If a graph of X is plotted as a function of time, we find that X is also a continuous function of time (see Fig. 2.1).

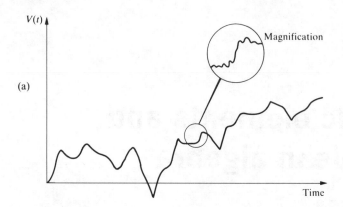

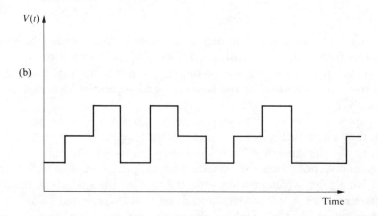

Fig. 2.1 (a) Digital and (b) analog variables.

The design of analog circuits (e.g. most audio amplifiers, cassette tape decks, televisions) is a most demanding process, because analog signals must be processed without changing their *shape*. Any change in the shape of an analog signal results in its degradation or distortion.

Figure 2.1 also shows a digital variable $V(t)$, which is discrete in both *value* and in *time*. That is, $V(t)$ can assume only one of a fixed number of possible values and $V(t)$ changes from one discrete value to another *instantaneously*.

Information inside a computer is represented in digital form. In a digital system all variables and constants must take a value chosen from a set of values called an *alphabet*. In decimal arithmetic we have an alphabet composed of the symbols 0, 1, 2, ..., 9; in Morse code we have an alphabet composed of the four symbols dot, dash, short space, and long space. Other digital systems are Braille, semaphore and the days of the week. An advantage of digital representation of information is that a symbol may be distorted, but as long as the level of distortion is not sufficient for one symbol to be taken for another, the original symbol may always be recognized and reconstituted.

The alphabet selected for digital computers has two symbols, 0 and 1 (sometimes called false and true, or low and high, or off and on). The advantage of such an alphabet is that the symbols can be made as unlike each other as possible to give the maximum discrimination between the two values. Computers once used to store binary information on paper tape—a hole representing one binary value and no hole representing the other. When reading paper tape the computer had only to distinguish between a hole and no hole. Suppose we decided to do away with the binary computer and to replace it with a decimal computer. Imagine that paper tape were to be used by this decimal computer to store the digits 0 to 9. A number on the tape would consist of no hole or a hole in one of nine sizes (ten symbols in all). How do we tell a size six hole from a size five or a size seven? Such a system would require extremely precise electronics.

A single binary digit is known as a *bit* (*bi*nary dig*it*) and is the smallest unit of information possible. That is, a bit cannot be subdivided into smaller units. In current technology, the binary values of information inside a computer are represented by two ranges of voltage. Figure 2.2 illustrates these ranges for a typical logic element found in digital computers.

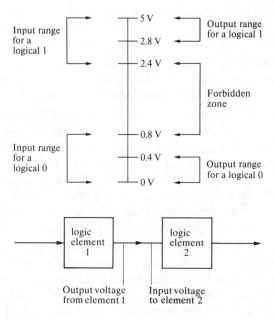

Fig. 2.2 The two states of a typical logic element.

Manufacturers of digital components make a number of promises or guarantees to users. Firstly, for one of the most popular logic families, they guarantee that the output of a gate in a logical zero state shall be in the range 0–0.4 V, and that the output of a gate in a logical one state shall be in the range 2.8–5.0 V. Similarly, they guarantee that the input circuit of a gate shall recognize a voltage in the range 0–0.8 V as a logical zero, and a voltage in the range 2.4–5.0 V as a logical one. By making the input range (for a given logic value) greater than the output range, the designer allows for noise or unwanted signals. For example, a logical zero output of 0.4 V can have a noise spike of 0.2 V added to it to give a total signal level of 0.6 V. This signal, when presented to the input circuit of a gate, is below 0.8 V and is still guaranteed to be recognized as a logical zero. The difference between the input and output ranges for a logic value is known as its *guaranteed noise immunity.* A further discussion of the electrical characteristics of logic elements is given in Chapter 3.

Before we begin to look at gates themselves, we need to clear up a few points concerning binary digital values and the way in which notation is used to describe digital values.

Notes on logical values

1. There are always two discrete states and every logic input or output must assume one of these states. There is no such thing as a valid intermediate state (a state which is neither 1 nor 0).

2. Each logic input or output can exist in only one state at any one time.

3. Each logic state has an inverse or complement which is the opposite of its current state. The complement of a true or one state is a false or zero state, and vice versa.

4. A logic value can be a constant or a variable. If it is a constant it always remains in that state. If it is a variable, it may be switched between the states 0 and 1. A Boolean constant is frequently called a *literal.*

5. A variable is often named by the action it causes to take place. The following logical variables are all self-evident: START, STOP, RESET, COUNT, ADD. It is clearly reasonable to select meaningful names for logical variables just as it is in high-level programming languages.

6. The logical value that causes a signal represented by a variable to carry out the function suggested by its name is arbitrary. If a logical one causes the action, the signal is called active-high. If a logical zero causes the action, the signal is called active-low. Thus, if an active-high signal is labelled START, a logical one (i.e. START = 1) will initiate the action. If it is active-low and labelled $\overline{\text{START}}$, a logical zero will trigger the action. The overbar indicates that START is active-low.

7. Designers and writers frequently wish to avoid saying or writing that a particular signal is set to a logical one or to a logical zero when describing its action in a circuit. Instead, they frequently use the term *asserted* to indicate that a signal is placed in the level that causes its activity to take place. For example, if we say that START is asserted, we mean that it is placed in a high state to cause the action determined by START. Similarly, if we say that $\overline{\text{LOAD}}$ is asserted, we mean that it is placed in a low state to trigger the action.

2.2 Basic gates

We don't use gates to build computers because we like them or because Boolean algebra (i.e. the arithmetic used to describe the properties of gates) is great fun. We use gates because they provide us with a way of mass-producing cheap and reliable digital computers. One of the more remarkable facts about the digital computer is that all its circuits can be considered as nothing more than the interconnection of a few primitive elements called gates. There are three fundamental types of gate: AND,

OR, and NOT (INVERTER), plus two gates that are derived from the other three (i.e. NAND and NOR). Later we shall see that all other gates, and therefore all digital circuits, may be designed from the appropriate interconnection of NAND (or NOR) gates alone. Thus, the most complex digital computer can be reduced to a mass of NAND gates. This fact does not devalue the computer, as the immensely complex human brain is itself just a lot of neurons joined in a particularly complex way.

In this section we are going to define the properties of the five basic gates from which all digital systems are constructed. The word **gate** conveys the idea of a two-state device—open or shut. A gate may be thought of as a black box with one or more input terminals and an output terminal. The digital signals at the input terminals are processed by the gate to produce a digital signal at its output terminal. The nature of the gate determines the actual processing involved. If a gate has two input terminals A and B, and an output terminal C, its output may be written $C = F(A,B)$. This equation is expressed in conventional algebra, where A,B,C are two-valued variables, and F is some logical function.

It is important to stress once again that the output of a gate is a function only of the inputs to the gate. Later, when we introduce **sequential circuits,** we will discover that these circuits have outputs that depend on the **previous** outputs of the circuits as well as their **current** inputs.

To demonstrate that the idea of gates is not only simple and nothing to be afraid of, but also commonplace, consider an example from the analog world. Assume $y = F(x) = 2x^2 + x + 1$. If x is thought of as the input to a black box, and y its output, the circuit of Fig. 2.3 shows how y is generated by a sequence of operations on x. Here the operations performed on the input are those of addition, multiplication, and squaring. The boxes carrying out these operations are entirely analogous to gates in the digital world.

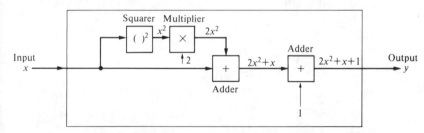

Fig. 2.3 The analog processor.

Before dealing with the gates themselves and their interconnections to form digital (or switching) circuits, it is necessary to define a few elementary conventions. Because we write from left to right, many (but not all) logic circuits are also read from left to right. That is, information flows from left to right with the inputs of gates on the left, and the outputs on the right. As there are often many information paths, and the diagram is drawn on paper in a two-dimensional format, it is frequently necessary for information paths to cross one another. Figure 2.4 shows how this is done. In general, the standard procedure is to regard two lines which simply cross as not being connected. The actual connection of two lines is denoted by a dot at their intersection. The voltage at any point along a line

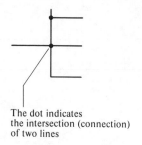

The dot indicates
the intersection (connection)
of two lines

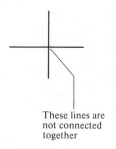

These lines are
not connected
together

Fig. 2.4 Circuit conventions.

(i.e. conductor) is constant, and therefore the logical level is also constant. That is, if one end of a conductor is in a logical state P, then every point along the line is in the same state. If the line is connected to the input of several gates, then the input to each gate is also in a logical state P. A corollary of this is that a line must not be connected to the output of more than one circuit—otherwise the state of the line will be undefined if the outputs differ. In a later part of this book we will introduce 'special' outputs that can be connected together without causing havoc!

The AND gate

The AND gate is a circuit with two or more inputs and a single output. The output of an AND gate is true if and only if each of its inputs is also in a true state. Conversely, if one or more of the inputs to the AND gate is false, the output will also be false. Figure 2.5(a) provides the logical symbol for an AND gate.

The classic way of looking at an AND gate is in terms of an electric circuit or a highway as illustrated in Fig. 2.5(b). Electric current (or traffic) is able to flow along the circuit (road) only if switches (bridges) A and B are closed. The logical symbol for the AND operator is a dot, so that A and B is written A.B. As in normal algebra, the dot is often omitted and A.B can be written AB.

A useful way of describing the relationship between the inputs of gates (and other circuits) and their output(s) is the truth table. In a truth table the value of each output is tabulated for every possible combination of the inputs. As the inputs are two-valued, a circuit with n inputs has 2^n lines in its truth table. The order in which the 2^n possible inputs are taken is not important but by convention the order is:

$$
\left.
\begin{array}{l}
000 \ldots 00 \\
000 \ldots 01 \\
000 \ldots 10 \\
\quad \cdot \\
\quad \cdot \\
\quad \cdot \\
111 \ldots 00 \\
111 \ldots 01 \\
111 \ldots 10 \\
111 \ldots 11
\end{array}
\right\}
\begin{array}{l}
0 \\
\\
\\
\\
2^n \text{ combinations} \\
\\
\\
\\
2^n - 1
\end{array}
\qquad
\begin{array}{l}
\text{e.g. for } n = 3 \\
\end{array}
\qquad
\begin{array}{l}
000 \\
001 \\
010 \\
011 \\
100 \\
101 \\
110 \\
111
\end{array}
$$

Table 2.1 illustrates the truth table for a two-input AND gate, although there is no reason why we cannot have any number of inputs to a gate. Some real gates have three or four inputs, and one gate, the 74133, is a 13-input NAND gate. Later we provide details of some of the types of gate widely available.

When we introduce computer architecture and assembly language programming, we will see how the AND operation can be applied to words. A *word* is a group of bits normally dealt with as a single entity. For example, consider the ANDing of the following two words:

```
11011100 ←——word A
01100101 ←——word B
```
01000100 ←——word C = word (A.B)

Here we have applied the AND operation to each pair of bits so that the ith bit of A is ANDed with the ith bit of B to produce the ith bit of the result C. The AND operation, when applied to words, is called a *logical* operation to distinguish it from an *arithmetic* operation such as addition, subtraction or multiplication. A logical AND is used to mask off certain bits in a word by forcing them to zero. For example, if we wish to clear the leftmost four bits of an eight-bit word to zero, ANDing the word with 00001111 will do the trick.

```
e.g. 11011011 ←——input
     00001111 ←——mask
```
00001011 ←——output

Table 2.1 Truth table for the AND gate

Inputs		Output	
A	B	F=A.B	
0	0	0	False as one or
0	1	0	more inputs are
1	0	0	false
1	1	1	←True as all inputs are true

(a)

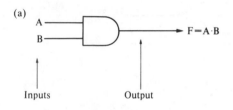

Fig. 2.5 (a) The AND gate, and (b) its representation.

(b)

The OR gate

The logic symbol for an OR gate is given in Fig. 2.6(a). The output of an OR gate is true if either (or both) of its inputs are true. The logical symbol for an OR operation is a plus sign, so that A OR B is written as $A + B$. Table 2.2 provides the truth table for a two-input OR gate.

An OR gate can be represented by the switching circuit of Fig. 2.6(b). A path exists from input to output if either of the two switches are closed.

Note that the use of the term *OR* here is rather different from the English usage of *or*. The *Boolean* OR means (either A or B), or (both A and B), whereas the *English* usage often (but not always) means A or B but not (A and B). For example, consider the use of the word *or* in the two phrases: 'Would you like tea or coffee' and 'Membership is free to students or people under 25'. We shall see that the more common English use of OR corresponds to the Boolean function known as *EXCLUSIVE OR*. The EXCLUSIVE OR is an important function and is frequently abbreviated to written EOR or XOR.

A computer can also perform a logical OR on words as the following example illustrates.

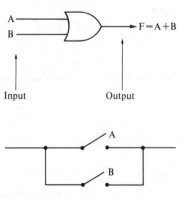

Fig. 2.6 (a) The OR gate, and (b) its representation.

Table 2.2 Truth table for the OR gate

Inputs		Output	
A	B	F=A+B	
0	0	0	←False as both inputs are false
0	1	1	True as one or more inputs are true
1	0	1	
1	1	1	

```
10011100 ←——word A
00100101 ←——word B
10111101 ←——word C = word (A + B)
```

The logical OR operation is used to set one or more bits in a word. *Set* means make a logical one, just as *clear* means reset to a logical zero. For example, the least significant bit of a word is set by ORing it with 00...01. By applying AND and OR operations to a word we can selectively clear or set its bits.

The NOT gate

The NOT gate or *inverter* or *complementer* is a two-terminal device with a single input and a single output. If the input of an invertor is X, its output is NOT X or $\bar{X}$. Figure 2.7(a) illustrates the symbol for an invertor and Table 2.3 provides its truth table. Some teachers vocalize $\bar{X}$ as NOT X (as I do) and others as X NOT.

(a)

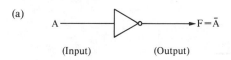

A ————————▷○————→ $F=\bar{A}$

(Input)　　　　　　　(Output)

(b)

Fig. 2.7 (a) The NOT gate or inverter, and (b) its representation.

Input　　　Coil　　　Iron core

Normally closed contacts　　　Output (NOT A)

Table 2.3 Truth table for the inverter

Input A	Output F=$\bar{A}$
0	1
1	0

The operation of the NOT gate may be visualized in terms of the relay illustrated in Fig. 2.7(b). If switch A is open, no current flows through the coil and the iron is unmagnetized. The normally closed contacts are closed so that they form a switch which is on when A is open. If A is now closed, a current flows through the coil, the iron is magnetized and part of the normally closed switch is pulled towards the iron, breaking its circuit and assuming the opposite state to switch A. The relay is used by a computer to control external devices and will be described further when we deal with input and output devices.

The NOT function can also be applied to words:

```
11011100 ←——word A
00100011 ←——word B = word Ā
```

The NAND and NOR gates

The logic symbols for the NAND and NOR gates are given in Fig. 2.8. These two gates are dealt with together because they correspond to an

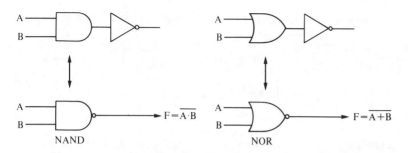

Fig. 2.8 Circuit symbols for the NAND and NOR gates.

AND gate followed by an inverter (Not AND), and an OR gate followed by an inverter (Not OR), respectively. The little circle at the output of a NAND gate represents the symbol for inversion or complementation. It is this circle that converts the AND gate to a NAND gate and an OR gate to a NOR gate. Later, when we introduce the concept of *mixed logic*, we will discover that this circle can be applied to the *inputs* of gates as well as to their outputs.

It should be noted here that $\overline{A.B}$ is not the same as $\overline{A}.\overline{B}$, just as $\overline{A+B}$ is not the same as $\overline{A}+\overline{B}$.

We can get a better feeling for the different effects that the various gates have on two inputs, A and B, by putting all the gates together in a single table (Table 2.6). The EXCLUSIVE OR and its complement, the EXCLUSIVE NOR, are also included in Table 2.6 for reference. The EOR gate is derived from AND, OR, and NOT gates, and appears later in this chapter.

Table 2.4 Truth table for the NAND gate

Inputs A	B	Output $F=\overline{A.B}$
0	0	1
0	1	1
1	0	1
1	1	0

Table 2.5 Truth table for the NOR gate

Inputs A	B	Output $F=\overline{A+B}$
0	0	1
1	0	0
1	0	0
1	1	0

Table 2.6 The truth table of six basic gates

Inputs		Outputs					
		OR	AND	NOR	NAND	EOR	EXNOR
A	B	A+B	A.B	$\overline{A+B}$	$\overline{A.B}$	A⊕B	$\overline{A⊕B}$
0	0	0	0	1	1	0	1
0	1	1	0	0	1	1	0
1	0	1	0	0	1	1	0
1	1	1	1	0	0	0	1

2.2.1 Gates as transmission elements

One of the problems encountered by those teaching digital logic in the early stages of a course is the 'Great, but so what' syndrome. I teach students the properties of gates and they say, 'That's very nice, but what's the point of it all?' A perfectly valid way of looking at gates is to regard them as *transmission* elements that control the flow of information within a computer. Consider each of the AND, OR, and EOR gates with two inputs. One input is a *control* input C that may be set to a logical one or a logical zero state. The other input represents a variable X and we wish to determine the effect the gate has on the transmission of X through it.

Figure 2.9 demonstrates how we can consider each gate to be in one of

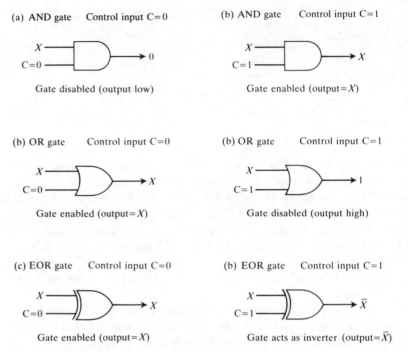

Fig. 2.9 Gates as transmission elements.

two states: one with the control input set at zero and one with the control input set at one. When $C=0$, an AND gate is disabled and its output is forced into a logical zero state. When $C=1$, the AND gate is enabled and its X input is transmitted to the output unchanged. Similarly, an OR gate is enabled by $C=0$ and disabled by $C=1$. However, when the OR gate is disabled, its output is forced into a logical one state. The EOR gate is a more interesting device. When its control input is zero, it transmits its input unchanged. But when $C=1$, it transmits the **complement** of X. The EOR gate can best be regarded as a **programmable inverter**. Later we shall make good use of this property of an EOR gate.

The reason for introducing the concept of a gate as a transmission element is that digital computers can be viewed as a complex network through which information flows and this information is operated on by gates as it flows round the system.

2.2.2 Gates and mixed logic

At this point we are going to introduce the concepts of negative logic and mixed logic. Some students may find that this interrupts their progress toward a better understanding of the gate and may therefore skip ahead to Section 2.3.

We all have our individual crosses to bear. Mine is the way in which a few students regard logical ones and zeroes as if the ones and zeros had some **intrinsic** meaning. If I want to feel really depressed, I ask my class 'What is the state of the inputs to this circuit when the power is first switched on?' A goodly fraction of the class invariably answers, 'zero'. Why do they do this? The question itself was nonsense. They say 'zero' because, somehow, they associate the logical zero state with the human concepts of 'I don't know or care' or 'it is not defined.' Perhaps part of the problem is that we generally use *positive logic* in which high-level signals represent logical one states and these states are called 'true'. As far as digital circuits are concerned, there is no fundamental difference between logical ones and zeros and it is as sensible to choose a logical zero level as the *doing state* as it is to choose a logical one state. Indeed, many of the signals in real digital systems are *active-low,* which means that their activity is carried out by a low-level signal.

Problems arise in students' minds because all the gates we have introduced so far have been described in terms of *positive logic.* This means that, for example, an AND gate requires its inputs to be logical ones for it to produce a logical one output. That is, in *positive logic* high levels (i.e. logical ones) are regarded as true. It is perfectly possible to define a *negative logic* in which low levels (i.e. logical zeros) are regarded as true. In that case, a negative logic AND gate would produce a true output (i.e. zero) whenever all its inputs were true (i.e. zero). But a negative logic AND gate is not the same as a positive logic AND gate, as we are going to demonstrate.

Suppose we regard the logical zero level as true. Applying a 0,0 (true,true) or a 0,1 (true,false) or a 1,0 (false,true) input to the AND gate results in a 0 (i.e. true) output. If we apply 1,1 (false,false) to the AND gate we get a 1 (i.e. false) output. From these results, it should be apparent that an AND gate in positive logic functions as an OR gate in negative logic. If we use a positive logic AND gate in a circuit whose conventions are those of negative logic, the gate functions not as an AND gate but as an OR gate. However, if we go to a distributor selling gates and buy a gate, we ask for an AND gate because by convention gates are invariably described by their positive logic function. For many years engineers have used the symbol for a positive logic AND gate in circuits using active-low signals with the result that the reader is confused and can only understand the circuit by mentally transforming the positive logic gate into its negative logic equivalent.

In *mixed logic* both positive logic and negative logic are used together in the same circuit. The choice of whether to use positive or negative logic is determined only by the desire to improve the clarity of a diagram or explanation. Remember that positive and negative logic are just ways of looking at a logic system. Consider the case in which a system has two inputs A and B and is activated when A = 0 and B = 0. A suitable gate for this is an OR gate, because the output of an OR gate is low only if both its inputs are low. However, although writing down the symbol for an OR gate in this circuit is correct in terms of positive logic, it is misleading to the reader, because it suggests the idea of ORing the signals when we are really ANDing signals (in negative logic terms). Therefore, we often use an AND gate with inverters at its inputs and at its output to suggest that we are ANDing signals. Many designers now use *mixed logic* symbols that

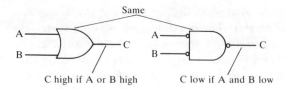

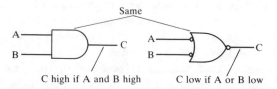

Fig. 2.10 Mixed logic.

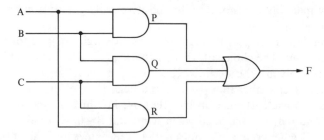

indicate the nature of the operation taking place. Figure 2.10 demonstrates how we do this.

2.3 Some applications of gates

We are now going to look at three simple circuits, each of which is built from a few basic gates. It is my intention to demonstrate that a few gates can be connected together in such a way as to realize a circuit whose function and importance may readily be appreciated by the reader. Following this informal introduction to gates, a more formal section is devoted to the analysis of logic circuits by means of Boolean algebra.

Example 1   Consider the circuit of Fig. 2.11. We can create an 8-line truth table (Table 2.7) for this circuit by writing down all the possible combinations of A, B and C. To obtain the output, F, of the circuit, we include in the truth table the intermediate signals $P=AB$, $Q=BC$ and $R=AC$. P, Q and R are called ***intermediate nodes***.

Fig. 2.11 The use of gates—Example 1.

Figure 2.11 tells us that we can write down the output function, F, as $F=P+Q+R$, where $P=AB$, $Q=BC$, and $R=AC$. Therefore, $F=AB+BC+AC$. By inspecting the truth table for F, we can see that the output is true if two or more of the inputs A, B, and C are true. That is, the arrangement represents a majority logic circuit whose output has the same value as the majority of inputs. We have already seen how such a circuit

Table 2.7 Truth table for the circuit of Fig. 2.11.(Example 1)

Inputs			Intermediate values			Output
A	B	C	P=AB	Q=BC	R=AC	F=P+Q+R
0	0	0	0	0	0	0
0	0	1	0	0	0	0
0	1	0	0	0	0	0
0	1	1	0	1	0	1
1	0	0	0	0	0	0
1	0	1	0	0	1	1
1	1	0	1	0	0	1
1	1	1	1	1	1	1

may be used in an automatic landing system in an aircraft by choosing the output from three independent computers to be the best (i.e. majority) of three inputs.

Example 2 As in the previous example, the circuit of Figure 2.12 has three inputs, one output, and three intermediate values. The truth table for Figure 2.12 is given in Table 2.8.

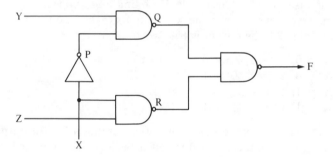

Fig. 2.12 The use of gates—Example 2.

Table 2.8 Truth table for the circuit of Figure 2.12 (Example 2)

Inputs			Intermediate values			Output
X	Y	Z	P=$\overline{X}$	Q=$\overline{YP}$	R=$\overline{XZ}$	F=$\overline{QR}$
0	0	0	1	1	1	0
0	0	1	1	1	1	0
0	1	0	1	0	1	1
0	1	1	1	0	1	1
1	0	0	0	1	1	0
1	0	1	0	1	0	1
1	1	0	0	1	1	0
1	1	1	0	1	0	1

By inspecting the truth table for Fig. 2.12, it can be seen that when the input X is 0, the output, F, is equal to Y. When X is 1, the output is equal to Z. That is, the circuit of Fig. 2.12 is an electronic switch, connecting the output to one of two inputs, Y or Z, depending on the state of a control input X. The circuit of Fig. 2.12 is called a two-input multiplexer and may be represented by the arrangement of Fig. 2.13. Because the word

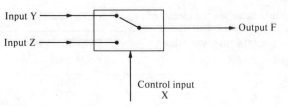

Fig. 2.13 The logical
representation of Fig. 2.12.

multiplexer appears so often in electronics, it is frequently abbreviated to
MUX or MPLX.

From the circuit diagram of Fig. 2.12, an equation for F can readily be
derived by considering the effect of the gates on their inputs.

$$F = \overline{QR}$$
$$Q = \overline{YP}$$
$$P = \overline{X}$$

therefore
$$Q = \overline{Y\overline{X}}$$
$$R = \overline{XZ}$$

therefore
$$F = \overline{\overline{Y\overline{X}}.\overline{XZ}}.$$

When we come to Boolean algebra we will see how this type of
expression can be simplified. Another way of obtaining a Boolean
expression is to use the truth table. Each time a *one* appears in the output
column, we can write down the set of inputs that cause the output to be
true. In Table 2.8 the output is true when

(1) $X = 0, Y = 1, Z = 0$ $(\overline{X}Y\overline{Z})$
(2) $X = 0, Y = 1, Z = 1$ $(\overline{X}YZ)$
(3) $X = 1, Y = 0, Z = 1$ $(X\overline{Y}Z)$
(4) $X = 1, Y = 1, Z = 1$ (XYZ)

There are four possible combinations of inputs that make the output true.
Therefore, the output can be expressed as the logical sum of the four cases
(1)–(4) above:

$$F = \overline{X}Y\overline{Z} + \overline{X}YZ + X\overline{Y}Z + XYZ.$$

That is, the above function is true if any of the above four conditions are
true. A function represented in this way is called a *sum of products* (S of P)
because it is the logical OR of a group of terms each made up of a number
of variables ANDed together. A sum of products expression represents
one of the two standard ways of writing down a Boolean expression.

An alternative form of expression is called a *product of sums* (P of S)
expression and consists of a number of terms ANDed together. The terms
are made up of variables ORed together. A typical 'product of sums'
expression looks like this:

$$F = (A + \overline{B} + C).(\overline{A} + B + C).(\overline{A} + \overline{B} + \overline{C}).$$

Later we shall examine ways of converting sum of products expressions
into product of sums expressions and vice versa.

Each of the terms, (1)–(4) in Example 2 above is called a *minterm*. A
minterm is an AND (product) term that includes each of the variables in

either its true or complemented form. For example, in the case above $\bar{X}Y\bar{Z}$ is a minterm, but if we had had the term $\bar{X}Y$ that would not be a minterm, since $\bar{X}Y$ includes only two of the three variables. When an equation is expressed as a sum of minterms, it is said to be in its *canonical form*. 'Canonical' is just a fancy word that means *standard*.

As the output of the circuit in Fig. 2.12 must be the same whether it is derived from the truth table or from the logic diagram, the two equations we have derived for F must be equivalent, with the result that:

$$\overline{Y\bar{X}.\overline{XZ}} = \bar{X}Y\bar{Z} + \bar{X}YZ + X\bar{Y}Z + XYZ.$$

This equation demonstrates that a given Boolean function can be expressed in more than one way.

The multiplexer of Fig. 2.12 may seem a long way from computers and programming, but I have included it here to demonstrate the relationship between hardware and software. Readers not familiar with the structure of the computer may go directly to Example 3.

The power of a digital computer (or a human brain) lies in its ability to make *decisions*. In the world of computing, *decision taking* corresponds to the conditional branch. For example, in high-level languages we have the following constructs:

IF $(X - 2.0*Z)10,20,30$	FORTRAN
IF X = 5 THEN Z = 27	BASIC
IF t > = 0 THEN I := I + 2;	Pascal

The BASIC and Pascal statements demonstrate two-way branches, and the FORTRAN a three-way branch. In practice, a three-way branch is implemented as two consecutive two-way branches. The conditional branch is implemented by testing for the specified condition (e.g. $X=0$) and then executing the *then* part of the construct if the condition is true, or continuing with the next instruction if it is false. The actual branching is done by loading one of two possible numbers into the *program counter*, which is the part of the CPU that holds the address (i.e. location) of the next instruction to be carried out. By changing this address we can choose between two alternative courses of action. Consider now the arrangement of Fig. 2.14.

Two registers X and Y contain m-bit addresses. The m bits of these registers are fed to m multiplexers whose m outputs supply the m bits of the program counter. The control inputs of the multiplexers are wired together and connected to one bit of the condition code register, CCR. The contents of the condition code register are determined by the results of certain calculations, and its various bits tell us whether the results of the last operation were zero, positive, negative etc. (the representation of negative numbers is dealt with in Chapter 4). In Fig. 2.14 we can see that a particular bit of the CCR can directly feed the contents of registers X or Y to the program counter, and therefore dictate which of two possible sequences of operations are to happen next. We have selected this example to demonstrate how a software operation may be implemented. In practice, the way in which conditional jumps are handled in real com-

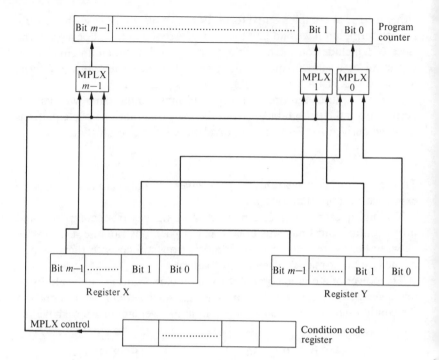

Fig. 2.14 An application of the multiplexer.

puters is somewhat different (but not radically so) to the procedure I have outlined above.

Example 3 Table 2.9 provides us with a truth table for the circuit diagram in Figure 2.15. In this case we have two inputs, two intermediate values and one output.

The circuit of Fig. 2.15 represents one of the most important circuits in digital electronics. Its output is true if one of the inputs is true but not if both inputs are true. We call this the EXCLUSIVE OR (or EOR or XOR) operator, which corresponds to the normal English use of the word *or* (i.e. one or the other but not both). Because the EOR function is so widely used, it has its own symbol:

$$F = A \text{ EOR } B = A \oplus B.$$

Figure 2.16 gives the symbol for an EOR gate. From Table 2.9 we can see that F is true when $A=0$ and $B=1$, or when $A=1$ and $B=0$, so that $F = \bar{A}B + A\bar{B}$. From Fig. 2.15 we have:

Table 2.9 Truth table for the circuit of Figure 2.15 (Example 3)

Inputs		Intermediate values		Output
A	B	$P=A+B$	$Q=\overline{AB}$	$F=PQ$
0	0	0	1	0
0	1	1	1	1
1	0	1	1	1
1	1	1	0	0

Fig. 2.15 The use of gates—Example 3.

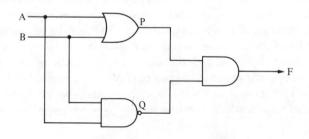

$$F = PQ$$
$$P = A + B$$
$$Q = \overline{AB}.$$
Therefore $F = (A + B).\overline{AB}.$

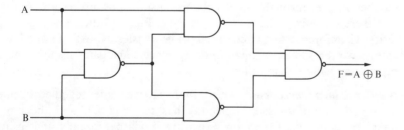

Fig. 2.16 Circuit symbol for an EOR gate.

As these two equations (i.e. $F = \overline{A}B + A\overline{B}$ and $F = (A + B).\overline{AB}$) must be equivalent, we can therefore also build an EOR function in the manner depicted in Fig. 2.17.

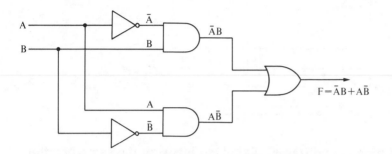

Fig. 2.17 An alternative circuit for an EOR gate.

It is in fact perfectly possible to build an EOR with a single integrated circuit containing four NAND gates (Fig. 2.18). I leave it as an exercise for the reader to verify that Fig. 2.18 does indeed represent an EOR gate.

The EOR is a remarkably versatile logic element which pops up in many places in digital electronics. The output of an EOR is true if its inputs are different, and false if they are the same. Note that the EOR gate, unlike the AND, OR, NAND, and NOR gates, can have only two inputs. The ability of an EOR gate to detect whether its inputs are the same or not allows us to build an equality tester that indicates whether or not two words are identical (Fig. 2.19).

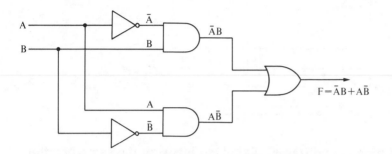

Fig. 2.18 An EOR circuit constructed with NAND gates only.

If the two words in Fig. 2.19 are equal, the outputs of all EORs are zero and therefore the output of the m-input NOR gate is a logical one. Note that in mixed logic we can regard the NOR gate as an AND gate with active-low inputs and an active-high output. Remember that we said that the condition code word is determined by the result of actions within the computer. The output from the NOR gate can be connected to one of the bits of the condition code register so that it can determine which of two courses of action may be taken when a conditional branch is encountered. The condition code register, and its role in the operation of the central processing unit, is discussed in Chapter 5.

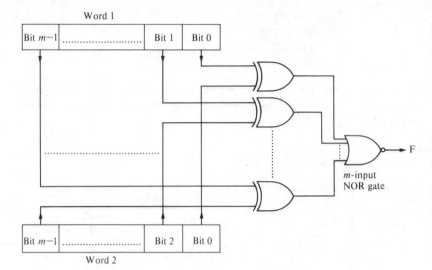

Fig. 2.19 The application of EOR gates in an equality tester.

Comparing different digital circuits with the same function

It should now be apparent that not only can a given function be represented by more than one Boolean expression, but that different combinations of gates may be used to implement the function. This is not the place to go into great depth on the detailed design of logic circuits but it is interesting to see how the designer might of about selecting one particular implementation in preference to another.

Some of the basic criteria by which circuits are judged are listed below. In general, the design of logic circuits is often affected by other factors than those described here.

Speed   The speed of a circuit (i.e. how long it takes the output to respond to a change at an input) is approximately governed by the maximum number of gates through which a change of state must propagate. In Fig. 2.15 there are only 2 gates in series, while in Fig. 2.17 there are 3 gates in series. Therefore the first circuit is 50 per cent faster. Note that not all real gates have the same propagation delay, since some gates respond more rapidly to changes than others.

Number of interconnections   It costs money to wire gates together. Even if a printed circuit is used, somebody has to design it, and the more interconnections used the more expensive it will be. Equally, increasing the number of interconnections in a circuit also increases the probability of failure due to a faulty connection. One parameter of circuit design that takes account of the number of interconnections is the total number of inputs to gates. In Fig. 2.15 there are 6 inputs, while in Fig. 2.17 there are 8 inputs.

Number of packages   Simple gates of the types being discussed here are normally available in 14-pin packages (two pins of which are needed for the power supply). As it costs virtually nothing to add extra gates to the silicon chip, the total number of gates is limited only by the number of pins (i.e. external connections to the chip). Thus, an inverter requires two pins, so 6 inverters are provided on the chip. Similarly, a two-input AND/ NAND/OR/NOR gate needs three pins, so four of these gates are put on the chip. As each of these circuits uses three different types of gate, both circuits require three 14-pin integrated circuits. Even so, the circuit of Fig. 2.15 is better than that of Fig. 2.17 because there are more unused gates left in the ICs, freeing them for use by other parts of the computer system.

Now that we have examined the gate and introduced simple circuits, the next step is to look at Boolean algebra, which provides us with a formal method for analysing circuits containing gates and for synthesizing circuits.

2.4 An introduction to Boolean algebra

George Boole was an English mathematician (1815–1864) who developed a mathematical analysis of logic and published it in his book *An investigation of the laws of thought* in 1854. The algebra of logic of which he laid the foundations would probably have remained a tool of the philosopher, had it not been for the development of electronics in the twentieth century.

In 1938 Claude Shannon published a paper entitled 'A symbolic analysis of relays and switching circuits' which applied Boolean algebra to switching circuits using relays. Such circuits were originally found in telephone exchanges and later in digital computers. Today, Boolean algebra is used to design digital circuits and to analyse their behaviour.

When I was first introduced to conventional algebra as a twelve year old schoolboy, I asked my teacher why we had to learn algebra, as I did not see any point in solving equations. 'Clements,' he said, 'We teach algebra to make the life of schoolboys miserable.' I did not have a happy childhood. A similar question about Boolean algebra often lies at the back of my students' minds. Unlike some of my teachers, I hope to provide more helpful answers to the questions that my students ask me. Digital design is concerned with the conversion of ideas or specifications into actual hardware, and Boolean algebra is a tool that facilitates this process. In particular, Boolean algebra permits an idea to be expressed in a mathematical form, and the resulting expression to be simplified and then translated into the real hardware of gates and other logic elements.

Boolean algebra (or any other algebra) consists of a set of *elements* E, a set of *functions* F that operate on members of E, and a set of basic laws called *axioms* that define the properties of E and F. The set of elements making up a Boolean algebra have two possible values, 0 or 1. These elements may be *variables* or they may be *literals* (i.e. constants) that have fixed values of 0 or 1. A Boolean algebra with n variables has a set of 2^n possible sets of values of these variables.

Only three functions or operations are permitted in Boolean algebra. The first two are the logical OR represented by a plus '+', and the logical AND represented by a dot '.'. The use of these symbols is rather confusing because they are the same as those used for addition and multiplication in everyday life. One reason that these particular symbols have been chosen is that they behave (subject to the postulates of Boolean algebra) rather like conventional addition and multiplication. Some texts use a ∪ (cup) or a ∨ to denote +, and a ∩ (cap) or a ∧ to denote a dot.

The third operation permitted in Boolean algebra is that of negation or complementation and is denoted by a bar over a literal or a variable. The complement of 0 (i.e. $\bar{0}$) is 1, and vice versa. The equation 'X + Y$\bar{Z}$ = A' is read as 'X or Y and not Z equals A'. The priority of an AND operator is higher than that of an OR operator so that the expression means A = X + (Y$\bar{Z}$) and not A = (X + Y)$\bar{Z}$. Note that when this equation is read out its meaning is ambiguous. Some texts use an asterisk to denote negation and some use a stroke '/'. Printers employ these symbols to represent negation because most conventional word processors do not permit overbars. Thus, we can write NOT(X) as $\bar{X}$ or X* or X/.

It should be appreciated that the arithmetic operations of subtraction and division do not exist in Boolean algebra. For example, if we have the Boolean expression X + Y = X + Z, we cannot say that (X + Y) − X = (X + Z) − X and therefore Y = Z. If you don't believe this, then consider the case X = 1, Y = 1, and Z = 0. The left-hand side of the equation yields X + Y = 1 + 1 = 1, and the right-hand side yields X + Z = 1 + 0 = 1. That is, the equation is valid even though Y is not equal to Z.

2.4.1 Basic theorems of Boolean algebra

We approach Boolean algebra by first looking at the action of NOT, OR, and AND operations on constants.

The effect of the three operations +, ., NOT, is best illustrated by means of the truth table given in Table 2.10. These rules may be extended to any number of variables.

Table 2.10 Boolean operations on constants

NOT	AND	OR
$\bar{0}$=1	0.0=0	0+0=0
$\bar{1}$=0	0.1=0	0+1=1
	1.0=0	1+0=1
	1.1=1	1+1=1

Axioms of Boolean algebra

Boolean variables obey similar commutative, distributive, and associative laws as the variables of conventional algebra. That is: If A and B belong to a set of Boolean elements, A.B, A + B, and NOT A and NOT B also belong to the set of Boolean elements. This axiom is called the closure property and implies that Boolean operations on Boolean variables or constants always yield Boolean results.

A + B = B + A
A.B = B.A

The AND and OR operators are **commutative** so that the order of the variables in a sum or product group does not matter.

A.(B + C) = A.B + A.C
A + BC = (A + B)(A + C)

The AND operator behaves like multiplication, and the OR operator like addition in some ways. The **distributive** property states that in an expression containing both AND and OR operators the AND operator takes precedence over the OR.

A.(B.C) = (A.B).C
A + (B + C) = (A + B) + C

The AND and OR operators are **associative** so that the order in which subtotals are calculated does not matter.

The basic axioms of Boolean algebra governing variables, operators and constants are given below.

$$0.X = 0 \qquad 0 + X = X \qquad \overline{\overline{X}} = X$$
$$1.X = X \qquad 1 + X = 1$$
$$X.X = X \qquad X + X = X$$
$$X.\overline{X} = 0 \qquad X + \overline{X} = 1$$

These equations may be proved by substituting all the possible values for X (i.e. 0 or 1). For example, consider $0.X = 0$. If $X = 1$ we have $0.1 = 0$ which is true. Similarly, if $X = 0$ we have $0.0 = 0$ which is also true. Therefore, $0.X = 0$ is true for all possible values of X. A proof in which we test a theorem by examining all possibilities is called *proof by perfect induction*.

Using the above rules, we can readily derive some theorems to help in the simplification of expressions. The following theorems are proved by applying the axioms of Boolean algebra stated above. Although students are expected to be able to prove these theorems from 'first principles', students should learn these theorems because they are very helpful in simplifying more complex expressions.

Theorem 1 $X + XY = X$
Proof: $X + XY = X.1 + X.Y$ (using $1.X = X$ and commutativity)
$$= X(1 + Y) \quad \text{(distributivity)}$$
$$= X(1) \qquad \text{(since } 1 + Y = 1)$$
$$= X$$

Theorem 2 $X + \overline{X}Y = X + Y$
Proof: $X + \overline{X}Y = (X + XY) + \overline{X}Y$ By Theorem 1
$$= X + XY + \overline{X}Y$$
$$= X + Y(X + \overline{X})$$
$$= X + Y(1) = X + Y.$$

Theorem 3 $XY + \overline{X}Z + YZ = XY + \overline{X}Z$
Proof: $XY + \overline{X}Z + YZ = XY + \overline{X}Z + YZ(X + \overline{X})$
$$\text{Remember } (X + \overline{X}) = 1$$
$$= XY + \overline{X}Z + XYZ + \overline{X}YZ$$
$$= XY(1 + Z) + \overline{X}Z(1 + Y)$$
$$= XY(1) + \overline{X}Z(1)$$
$$= XY + \overline{X}Z.$$

We can also prove Theorem 3 by the method of perfect induction. To do this, we set up a truth table, Table 2.11, and demonstrate that the theorem holds for all possible values of X, Y and Z.

As the columns labelled $XY + \overline{X}Z$ and $XY + \overline{X}Z + YZ$ in Table 2.11 are identical, these two expressions must be equivalent.

Theorem 4 $X(X + Y) = X$
Proof: $X(X + Y) = XX + XY$
$$= X + XY$$
$$= X \qquad \text{By Theorem 1}$$

Theorem 5 $X(\overline{X} + Y) = XY$
Proof: $X(\overline{X} + Y) = X\overline{X} + XY$
$$= 0 + XY$$
$$= XY$$

Table 2.11 Proof of Theorem 3 by perfect induction

Inputs			Intermediate values					Output
X	Y	Z	$\overline{X}$	XY	$\overline{X}Z$	YZ	XY+$\overline{X}Z$	XY+$\overline{X}Z$+YZ
0	0	0	1	0	0	0	0	0
0	0	1	1	0	1	0	1	1
0	1	0	1	0	0	0	0	0
0	1	1	1	0	1	1	1	1
1	0	0	0	0	0	0	0	0
1	0	1	0	0	0	0	0	0
1	1	0	0	1	0	0	1	1
1	1	1	0	1	0	1	1	1

Same

Theorem 6 $(X+Y)(X+\overline{Y})=X$

Proof: $(X+Y)(X+\overline{Y})=XX+X\overline{Y}+XY+Y\overline{Y}$

$$=X+X\overline{Y}+XY$$
$$=X(1+\overline{Y}+Y)$$
$$=X$$

Theorem 7 $(X+Y)(\overline{X}+Z)=XZ+\overline{X}Y$

Proof: $(X+Y)(\overline{X}+Z)=X\overline{X}+XZ+\overline{X}Y+YZ$

$$=XZ+\overline{X}Y+YZ$$
$$=XZ+\overline{X}Y \quad \text{By Theorem 3}$$

Theorem 8 $(X+Y)(\overline{X}+Z)(Y+Z)=(X+Y)(\overline{X}+Z)$

Proof: $(X+Y)(\overline{X}+Z)(Y+Z)=(XZ+\overline{X}Y)(Y+Z) \quad \text{By Theorem 7}$

$$=XYZ+XZZ+\overline{X}YY+\overline{X}YZ$$
$$=XZ(Y+1)+\overline{X}Y(1+Z)$$
$$=XZ+\overline{X}Y$$
$$=(X+Y)(\overline{X}+Z) \quad \text{By Theorem 7}$$

An alternative proof for Theorem 8 is provided later.

Theorem 9 $\overline{X.Y.Z}=\overline{X}+\overline{Y}+\overline{Z}$

Proof: To prove that $\overline{XYZ}=\overline{X}+\overline{Y}+\overline{Z}$, we assume that the equation is true and test its consequences.

If $\overline{X}+\overline{Y}+\overline{Z}$ is the complement of XYZ, then from the basic axioms of Boolean algebra, we have:

$$(\overline{X}+\overline{Y}+\overline{Z}).(XYZ)=0$$
$$\text{and } (\overline{X}+\overline{Y}+\overline{Z})+(XYZ)=1$$

Subproof 1. $(\overline{X}+\overline{Y}+\overline{Z}).XYZ = \overline{X}XYZ+\overline{Y}XYZ+\overline{Z}XYZ$

$$=\overline{X}X(YZ)+\overline{Y}Y(YZ)+\overline{Z}Z(XY)$$
$$=0$$

Subproof 2. $(\overline{X}+\overline{Y}+\overline{Z})+XYZ = YZ(X)+\overline{X}+\overline{Y}+\overline{Z}$

$$=YZ+\overline{X}+\overline{Y}+\overline{Z}$$
$$=(\overline{Y}+YZ)+\overline{X}+\overline{Z}$$
$$=\overline{Y}+Z+\overline{Z}+\overline{X}$$
$$=\overline{Y}+1+\overline{X}=1$$

As we have demonstrated that $(\bar{X}+\bar{Y}+\bar{Z}).XYZ=0$ and that $(\bar{X}+\bar{Y}+\bar{Z})+XYZ=1$, then it follows that $\bar{X}+\bar{Y}+\bar{Z}$ is complement of XYZ.

Theorem 10 $\overline{X+Y+Z}=\bar{X}.\bar{Y}.\bar{Z}$

Proof: One possible way of proving Theorem 10 is to use the method we used to prove Theorem 9. For the sake of variety, we will prove Theorem 10 by perfect induction— see Table 2.12.

Table 2.12 Proof of Theorem 10 by perfect induction

X	Y	X	X+Y+Z	$\overline{X+Y+Z}$	$\bar{X}$	$\bar{Y}$	$\bar{Z}$	$\bar{X}.\bar{Y}.\bar{Z}$
0	0	0	0	1	1	1	1	1
0	0	1	1	0	1	1	0	0
0	1	0	1	0	1	0	1	0
0	1	1	1	0	1	0	0	0
1	0	0	1	0	0	1	1	0
1	0	1	1	0	0	1	0	0
1	1	0	1	0	0	0	1	0
1	1	1	1	0	0	0	0	0

↑ _____ ↑
Same

Theorems 9 and 10 are collectively called de Morgan's theorem. In word form, we say that an entire function is complemented by replacing '+' operators by '.' operators, replacing '.' operators by '+' operators, and complementing variables and literals.

Observations

I am concluding with the following observations because they represent .the most frequently encountered misconceptions.

Observation 1 $XY+\bar{X}\bar{Y}$ is not equal to 1
$XY+\bar{X}\bar{Y}$ cannot be simplified

Observation 2 $\bar{X}Y+X\bar{Y}$ is not equal to 1
$\bar{X}Y+X\bar{Y}$ cannot be simplified

Observation 3 $\overline{XY}$ is not equal to $\bar{X}\bar{Y}$

Observation 4 $\overline{X+Y}$ is not equal to $\bar{X}+\bar{Y}$

Observation 5   If a theorem is true for a variable P, it is true for another variable Q. For example, if $P+PZ=P$, then $Q+QZ=Q$. Obvious, isn't it. But students often have trouble dealing with situations in which P is replaced not by Q but by $\bar{P}$. In this case, if we have a theorem $X+XY=X$, then it is also true that $\bar{X}+\bar{X}Y=\bar{X}$. All we have done is to replace X by $\bar{X}$.

Observation 6   If a theorem is true for a variable P, it is true for a compound variable $Q = P$. For example, if $Q = X + YZ$ then by using $P.\overline{P} = 0$, we have $(X + YZ).\overline{X + YZ} = 0$ or $(X + YZ)(\overline{X}.\overline{YZ}) = 0$.

Observation 7 Table 2.13 provides a truth table for all possible functions of two variables A and B. These two variables have $2^2 = 4$ possible different combinations. We can associate a different function with each of these $4^2 = 16$ values to create all possible functions of two variables. N variables have 2^{2^N} functions.

Table 2.13 All possible functions of two variables

Inputs		Functions															
A	B	F_0	F_1	F_2	F_3	F_4	F_5	F_6	F_7	F_8	F_9	F_{10}	F_{11}	F_{12}	F_{13}	F_{14}	F_{15}
0	0	0	1	0	1	0	1	0	1	0	1	0	1	0	1	0	1
0	1	0	0	1	1	0	0	1	1	0	0	1	1	0	0	1	1
1	0	0	0	0	0	1	1	1	1	0	0	0	0	1	1	1	1
1	1	0	0	0	0	0	0	0	0	1	1	1	1	1	1	1	1

Functions:
$F_0 = 0$
$F_1 = $ A NOR B
$F_2 = \overline{A}B$
$F_3 = $ NOT A
$F_4 = A\overline{B}$
$F_5 = $ NOT B
$F_6 = $ A EOR B
$F_7 = $ A NAND B
$F_8 = $ A AND B
$F_9 = $ A ENOR B
$F_{10} = B$
$F_{11} = \overline{A}\overline{B} + \overline{A}B + AB = \overline{A\overline{B}} = \overline{A} + B$
$F_{12} = A$
$F_{13} = \overline{A}\overline{B} + A\overline{B} + AB = \overline{\overline{A}B} = A + \overline{B}$
$F_{14} = $ A OR B
$F_{15} = 1$

Examples of the use of Boolean algebra in simplifying equations

Having presented the basic rules of Boolean algebra, the next step is to show how it is used to simplify Boolean expressions. Such equations are not pulled out of a hat, they are often derived from the description of a particular logic circuit. By simplifying these equations it may be possible to produce a cheaper version of the logic circuit. However, the following equations are generally random functions chosen by me to demonstrate the rules of Boolean algebra.

(a) $X + \overline{Y} + \overline{X}Y + (X + \overline{Y})\overline{X}Y$

(b) $\overline{X}Y\overline{Z} + \overline{X}YZ + X\overline{Y}Z + XYZ$

(c) $\overline{\overline{XY}.\overline{XZ}}$

(d) $(X + \overline{Y})(\overline{X} + Z)(Y + \overline{Z})$

(e) $(W + X + YZ)(\overline{W} + X)(\overline{X} + Y)$

(f) $WX\bar{Z} + \bar{X}YZ + WX\bar{Y} + XYZ + \bar{W}YZ$

(g) $\bar{W}XZ + WZ + XY\bar{Z} + \bar{W}XY$

(h) $(X + Y + Z)(\bar{X} + Y + Z)(\bar{X} + Y + \bar{Z})$.

Solutions

Note: When I simplify Boolean expressions, I try to keep the order of the variables alphabetical, making it easier to pick out logical groupings.

(a) $X + \bar{Y} + \bar{X}Y + (X + \bar{Y})\bar{X}Y = X + \bar{Y} + \bar{X}Y + X\bar{X}Y + \bar{X}\bar{Y}Y$

$\qquad = X + \bar{Y} + \bar{X}Y \qquad$ as $A\bar{A} = 0$

$\qquad = X + \bar{Y} + \bar{X} \qquad$ as $A + \bar{A}B = A + B$

$\qquad = 1 \qquad$ as $A + \bar{A} = 1$.

Note: When a Boolean expression can be reduced to the constant (literal) 1, the expression is always true and is independent of the variables i.e. X,Y.

(b) $\bar{X}Y\bar{Z} + \bar{X}YZ + X\bar{Y}Z + XYZ = \bar{X}Y(\bar{Z} + Z) + XZ(\bar{Y} + Y)$

$\qquad = \bar{X}Y(1) + XZ(1)$

$\qquad = \bar{X}Y + XZ$.

(c) $\overline{\overline{XY}.\overline{XZ}} = \overline{\overline{\overline{XY}}} + \overline{\overline{\overline{XZ}}} \qquad$ by Theorem 9

$\qquad = \bar{X}Y + XZ \qquad$ as $\bar{\bar{F}} = F$.

Note: Both expressions in examples (b) and (c) simplify to $\bar{X}Y + XZ$, demonstrating that these two expressions are equivalent. These equations are those of the multiplexer with (b) derived from the truth table (Table 2.8) and (c) from the circuit diagram of Fig. 2.12.

(d) $(X + \bar{Y})(\bar{X} + Z)(Y + \bar{Z}) = (X\bar{X} + XZ + \bar{X}\bar{Y} + \bar{Y}Z)(Y + \bar{Z})$

$\qquad = (XZ + \bar{X}\bar{Y} + \bar{Y}Z)(Y + \bar{Z}) = (XZ + \bar{X}\bar{Y})(Y + \bar{Z})$

$\qquad\qquad\qquad\qquad\qquad\qquad\qquad$ By Theorem 3

$\qquad = XYZ + XZ\bar{Z} + \bar{X}\bar{Y}Y + \bar{X}\bar{Y}\bar{Z}$

$\qquad = XYZ + \bar{X}\bar{Y}\bar{Z}$.

(e) $(W + X + YZ)(\bar{W} + X)(\bar{X} + Y) = (W\bar{W} + \bar{W}X + \bar{W}YZ + WX + XX$

$\qquad\qquad\qquad\qquad + XYZ)(\bar{X} + Y)$

$\qquad = (\bar{W}X + \bar{W}YZ + WX + X + XYZ)(\bar{X} + Y)$

$\qquad = (X + \bar{W}YZ)(\bar{X} + Y)$

$\qquad = X\bar{X} + XY + \bar{W}\bar{X}YZ + \bar{W}YYZ$

$\qquad = XY + \bar{W}\bar{X}YZ + \bar{W}YZ$

$\qquad = XY + \bar{W}YZ(\bar{X} + 1)$

$\qquad = XY + \bar{W}YZ$.

Note: The above procedure could have been shortened if we had noticed that $(\bar{W} + X)(\bar{X} + Y)$ was of the form $(A + B)(\bar{A} + C) = AC + \bar{A}B$. Continuing along these lines we get:

$(W + X + YZ)(\bar{W} + X)(\bar{X} + Y) = (W + X + YZ)(XY + \bar{W}\bar{X})$

$\qquad = WXY + WW\bar{X} + XXY + \bar{W}\bar{X}X$

$\qquad\qquad + XYYZ + \bar{W}\bar{X}YZ$

$\qquad = WXY + XY + XYZ + \bar{W}\bar{X}YZ$

$$= XY(W+1+Z)+\bar{W}\bar{X}YZ$$
$$= XY+\bar{W}\bar{X}YZ \quad \text{since } (W+1+Z)=1$$
$$= XY+\bar{W}YZ \quad \text{by Theorem 2}$$

(f) $WX\bar{Z}+\bar{X}YZ+WX\bar{Y}+XYZ+\bar{W}YZ = WX\bar{Z}+YZ(\bar{X}+X+\bar{W})+WX\bar{Y}$
$$= WX\bar{Z}+YZ+WX\bar{Y}$$
$$= WX(\bar{Y}+\bar{Z})+YZ$$

Note that $YZ=\overline{\bar{Y}+\bar{Z}}$ so that we can invoke $A+\bar{A}B = A+B$
$$= WX+YZ.$$

(g) $\bar{W}XZ+WZ+XY\bar{Z}+\bar{W}XY = Z(\bar{W}X+W)+XY\bar{Z}+\bar{W}XY$
$$= Z(X+W)+XY\bar{Z}+\bar{W}XY$$
$$= XZ+WZ+XY\bar{Z}+\bar{W}XY$$
$$= X(Z+Y\bar{Z})+WZ+\bar{W}XY$$
$$= X(Z+Y)+WZ+\bar{W}XY$$
$$= XZ+XY+WZ+\bar{W}XY$$
$$= XZ+XY(1+\bar{W})+WZ$$
$$= XZ+XY+WZ.$$

(h) $(X+Y+Z)(\bar{X}+Y+Z)(\bar{X}+Y+\bar{Z}) = (Y+Z)(\bar{X}+Y+\bar{Z})$
$$\text{as } (A+B)(A+\bar{B})=A$$
$$= Z(\bar{X}+Y)+Y\bar{Z}$$
$$\text{as } (A+B)(\bar{A}+C)=AC+\bar{A}B$$
$$= \bar{X}Z+YZ+Y\bar{Z}$$
$$= \bar{X}Z+Y(Z+\bar{Z})$$
$$= \bar{X}Z+Y.$$

The design of a two-bit multiplier

So far all the applications of Boolean algebra have been textbook examples, without any real significance other than to provide a test bed for the rules of Boolean algebra. The following example illustrates how Boolean algebra is applied to a practical problem.

Suppose a designer wishes to produce a two-bit by two-bit binary multiplier. The two two-bit inputs are X_1,X_0 and Y_1,Y_0 and the four-bit product at the output terminals is Z_3,Z_2,Z_1,Z_0. We have not yet introduced binary arithmetic (Chapter 4), but nothing difficult is involved here. We begin by considering the block diagram of the system (Fig. 2.20a) and constructing its truth table.

The multiplier has four inputs, X_1,X_0,Y_1,Y_0 indicating a 16-line truth table) and four outputs. Table 2.14 provides a truth table for the binary multiplier. Each 4-bit input represents the product of two two-bit numbers

(a)

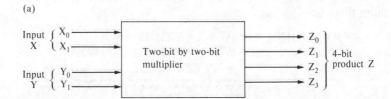

Fig. 2.20 (a) A 2-bit multiplier.

Table 2.14 Truth table for a 2-bit by 2-bit multiplier

| | Inputs | | | | Outputs | | | |
| | X | | Y | | Z | | | |
$X \times Y = Z$	X_1	X_0	Y_1	Y_0	Z_3	Z_2	Z_1	Z_0
$0 \times 0 = 0$	0	0	0	0	0	0	0	0
$0 \times 1 = 0$	0	0	0	1	0	0	0	0
$0 \times 2 = 0$	0	0	1	0	0	0	0	0
$0 \times 3 = 0$	0	0	1	1	0	0	0	0
$1 \times 0 = 0$	0	1	0	0	0	0	0	0
$1 \times 1 = 1$	0	1	0	1	0	0	0	1
$1 \times 2 = 2$	0	1	1	0	0	0	1	0
$1 \times 3 = 3$	0	1	1	1	0	0	1	1
$2 \times 0 = 0$	1	0	0	0	0	0	0	0
$2 \times 1 = 2$	1	0	0	1	0	0	1	0
$2 \times 2 = 4$	1	0	1	0	0	1	0	0
$2 \times 3 = 6$	1	0	1	1	0	1	1	0
$3 \times 0 = 0$	1	1	0	0	0	0	0	0
$3 \times 1 = 3$	1	1	0	1	0	0	1	1
$3 \times 2 = 6$	1	1	1	0	0	1	1	0
$3 \times 3 = 9$	1	1	1	1	1	0	0	1

(b)

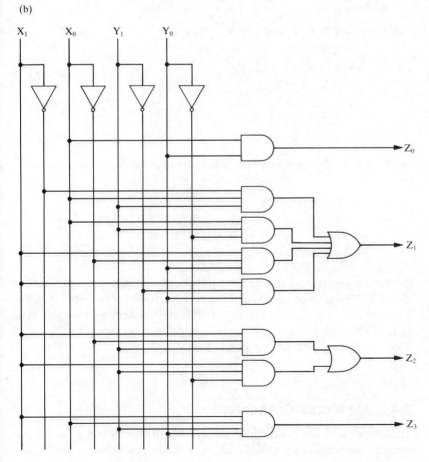

Fig. 2.20 (b) a possible circuit for the 2-bit multiplier.

so that, for example, an input of $X_1, X_0, Y_1, Y_0 = 1110$ represents the product 11×10 or 3×2. The corresponding output is a 4-bit product, which, in this case, is 6 or 0110 in binary form.

From Table 2.14, we can derive expressions for the four outputs, Z_0 to Z_3. Note that whenever a truth table has m output columns, a set of m Boolean equations must be derived. One equation is associated with each of the m columns. To derive an expression for Z_0, the four minterms in the Z_0 column are ORed logically.

$$\begin{aligned} Z_0 &= \bar{X}_1 X_0 \bar{Y}_1 Y_0 + \bar{X}_1 X_0 Y_1 Y_0 + X_1 X_0 \bar{Y}_1 Y_0 + X_1 X_0 Y_1 Y_0 \\ &= \bar{X}_1 X_0 Y_0 (\bar{Y}_1 + Y_1) + X_1 X_0 Y_0 (\bar{Y}_1 + Y_1) \\ &= \bar{X}_1 X_0 Y_0 + X_1 X_0 Y_0 \\ &= X_0 Y_0 (\bar{X}_1 + X_1) \\ &= X_0 Y_0 \end{aligned}$$

$$\begin{aligned} Z_1 &= \bar{X}_1 X_0 Y_1 \bar{Y}_0 + \bar{X}_1 X_0 Y_1 Y_0 + X_1 \bar{X}_0 \bar{Y}_1 Y_0 + X_1 \bar{X}_0 Y_1 Y_0 \\ &\quad + X_1 X_0 \bar{Y}_1 Y_0 + X_1 X_0 Y_1 \bar{Y}_0 \\ &= \bar{X}_1 X_0 Y_1 (\bar{Y}_0 + Y_0) + X_1 \bar{X}_0 Y_0 (\bar{Y}_1 + Y_1) + X_1 X_0 \bar{Y}_1 Y_0 + X_1 X_0 Y_1 \bar{Y}_0 \\ &= \bar{X}_1 X_0 Y_1 + X_1 \bar{X}_0 Y_0 + X_1 X_0 \bar{Y}_1 Y_0 + X_1 X_0 Y_1 \bar{Y}_0 \\ &= X_0 Y_1 (\bar{X}_1 + X_1 \bar{Y}_0) + X_1 Y_0 (\bar{X}_0 + X_0 \bar{Y}_1) \\ &= X_0 Y_1 (\bar{X}_1 + \bar{Y}_0) + X_1 Y_0 (\bar{X}_0 + \bar{Y}_1) \\ &= \bar{X}_1 X_0 Y_1 + X_0 Y_1 \bar{Y}_0 + X_1 \bar{X}_0 Y_0 + X_1 \bar{Y}_1 Y_0 \end{aligned}$$

$$\begin{aligned} Z_2 &= X_1 \bar{X}_0 Y_1 \bar{Y}_0 + X_1 \bar{X}_0 Y_1 Y_0 + X_1 X_0 Y_1 \bar{Y}_0 \\ &= X_1 \bar{X}_0 Y_1 (\bar{Y}_0 + Y_0) + X_1 X_0 Y_1 \bar{Y}_0 \\ &= X_1 \bar{X}_0 Y_1 + X_1 X_0 Y_1 \bar{Y}_0 \\ &= X_1 Y_1 (\bar{X}_0 + X_0 \bar{Y}_0) \\ &= X_1 Y_1 (\bar{X}_0 + \bar{Y}_0) \\ &= X_1 \bar{X}_0 Y_1 + X_1 Y_1 \bar{Y}_0 \end{aligned}$$

$$Z_3 = X_1 X_0 Y_1 Y_0$$

We have now obtained four simplified *sum of products* expressions for Z_0 to Z_3.

i.e. $\begin{aligned} Z_0 &= X_0 Y_0 \\ Z_1 &= \bar{X}_1 X_0 Y_1 + X_0 Y_1 \bar{Y}_0 + X_1 \bar{X}_0 Y_0 + X_1 \bar{Y}_1 Y_0 \\ Z_2 &= X_1 \bar{X}_0 Y_1 + X_1 Y_1 \bar{Y}_0 \\ Z_3 &= X_1 X_0 Y_1 Y_0 \end{aligned}$

It is interesting to note that each of the above expressions is symmetric in X and Y. This is to be expected: if the problem itself is symmetric in X and Y (i.e. $3 \times 1 = 1 \times 3$), then the result should also demonstrate this symmetry. There are many ways of realizing the expressions for Z_0 to Z_3. Figure 2.20(b) illustrates one possible way.

2.4.2 De Morgan's theorem

Theorems 9 and 10 provide the designer with an exceedingly powerful tool because they enable an AND function to be implemented by an OR gate and inverter, or they enable an OR gate to be implemented by an AND gate and inverter. When an entire function is complemented, de Morgan's theorem states that the ANDs are changed into ORs, and vice versa. Variables (and any literals) are complemented. It should be noted that here *variables* means also groups of variables. De Morgan's theorem is of great importance when the implementation of logic functions in terms of NAND and NOR gates only is considered.

The reader may wonder why we should wish to implement circuits in NAND (or NOR) logic only. There are several reasons for this, but in general NAND gates operate at a higher speed than AND gates and NAND gates can be built with fewer components (at the chip level). Later we shall examine in more detail how a circuit can be designed entirely with NAND gates only. The following examples illustrate the application of de Morgan's theorem.

1. $F = \overline{XY + XZ}$
$ = \overline{XY}.\overline{XZ}$
$ = (\bar{X} + \bar{Y})(\bar{X} + \bar{Z})$

The + becomes ., and the two groups of variables are complemented.

The processs is continued by applying de Morgan to the two complemented groups.

2. $F = \overline{AB + CD + AD}$
$ = \overline{AB}.\overline{CD}.\overline{AD}$
$ = (\bar{A} + \bar{B})(\bar{C} + \bar{D})(\bar{A} + \bar{D})$.

3. $F = \overline{AB(C + BD)}$
$ = \bar{A} + \bar{B} + \overline{C + BD}$
$ = \bar{A} + \bar{B} + \bar{C}.\overline{BD}$
$ = \bar{A} + \bar{B} + \bar{C}(\bar{B} + \bar{D})$

4. A proof of Theorem 8 by de Morgan's theorem

$(X + Y)(\bar{X} + Z)(Y + Z) = \overline{\overline{(X + Y)(\bar{X} + Z)(Y + Z)}}$
$\phantom{(X + Y)(\bar{X} + Z)(Y + Z)} = \overline{\overline{X + Y} + \overline{\bar{X} + Z} + \overline{Y + Z}}$
$\phantom{(X + Y)(\bar{X} + Z)(Y + Z)} = \overline{\bar{X}\bar{Y} + X\bar{Z} + \bar{Y}\bar{Z}}$
$\phantom{(X + Y)(\bar{X} + Z)(Y + Z)} = \overline{\bar{X}\bar{Y} + X\bar{Z}} \qquad \text{By Theorem 3}$
$\phantom{(X + Y)(\bar{X} + Z)(Y + Z)} = \overline{\bar{X}\bar{Y}}.\overline{X\bar{Z}} = (X + Y)(\bar{X} + Z)$

2.4.3 Implementing logic functions in NAND or NOR logic only

We have already stated that some gates are intrinsically better than others (i.e. they are faster or cheaper). For example, the NAND gate is both faster and cheaper than the corresponding AND gate. The same is true for the NOR gate and the OR gate. Consequently, it is frequently necessary to realize a circuit using one type of gate only. Engineers sometimes adopt one particular type of gate with which to implement a digital circuit because there is not a uniform range of gates available. That is, for obvious economic reasons manufacturers do not sell a uniform range of gates (e.g. 2-input AND, 3-input AND, ..., 10-input AND, 2-input OR, ... etc.). For example, there are many types of NAND gate, from the quad two-input NAND to the thirteen-input NAND, but there are few types of AND gates.

NAND logic

We first look at the way in which circuits can be constructed from nothing but NAND gates and then demonstrate that we can fabricate circuits with NOR gates only. To construct a circuit solely in terms of NAND gates, de Morgan's theorem must be invoked to get rid of all '+' operators in the expression. For example, suppose we wish to generate the expression $F = A + B + C$ using NAND gates only. We begin by applying a double negation to the expression, as this does not alter the expression's value but it does give us the opportunity to apply de Morgan's theorem.

$$F = A + B + C \qquad \text{Double negation has no effect}$$
$$F = \overline{\overline{F}} = \overline{\overline{A + B + C}} \qquad \text{on the value of a function}$$
$$F = \overline{\overline{A}.\overline{B}.\overline{C}} \qquad \text{Apply de Morgan's theorem}$$

We have now converted the OR function into a NAND function. The three NOT functions can be implemented in terms of NOT gates, or by means of two-input NAND gates with their inputs connected together. Figure 2.21 shows how the function $F = A + B + C$ can be implemented in NAND logic only. If the inputs of a NAND gate are A and B, and the output is C, then $C = \overline{AB}$. But if $A = B$ then $C = \overline{AA}$ or $C = \overline{A}$. The reader can better understand this if he or she refers to the truth table for the NAND gate, and imagines the effect of removing the lines $A,B = 0,1$ and $A,B = 1,0$. It is important to note that we are not applying de Morgan's theorem here to simplify Boolean expressions. We wish only to convert the expression into a form suitable for realization in terms of NAND (or NOR) gates. Indeed, the final expression may be much more complex than its original form.

Applying the above techniques to our multiplier we get:

$$Z_0 = X_0 Y_0 = \overline{\overline{X_0 Y_0}} \quad \text{(i.e. NAND gate followed by NOT gate} = \text{AND gate)}$$

$$Z_1 = \overline{X_1} X_0 Y_1 + X_0 Y_1 \overline{Y_0} + X_1 \overline{X_0} Y_0 + X_1 \overline{Y_1} Y_0$$
$$= \overline{\overline{\overline{X_1} X_0 Y_1 + X_0 Y_1 \overline{Y_0} + X_1 \overline{X_0} Y_0 + X_1 \overline{Y_1} Y_0}}$$
$$= \overline{\overline{\overline{X_1} X_0 Y_1} . \overline{X_0 Y_1 \overline{Y_0}} . \overline{X_1 \overline{X_0} Y_0} . \overline{X_1 \overline{Y_1} Y_0}}$$

Fig. 2.21 Implementing F=A+B+C in NAND logic only.

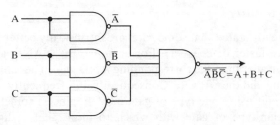

$$Z_2 = X_1\bar{X}_0Y_1 + X_1Y_1\bar{Y}_0 = \overline{\overline{X_1\bar{X}_0Y_1 + X_1Y_1\bar{Y}_0}} = \overline{\overline{X_1\bar{X}_0Y_1} \cdot \overline{X_1Y_1\bar{Y}_0}}$$

$$Z_3 = X_1X_0Y_1Y_0 = \overline{\overline{X_1X_0Y_1Y_0}}$$

Figure 2.22 shows the implementation of the multiplier in terms of NAND logic only. Note that it performs exactly the same function as the circuit of Fig. 2.20(b).

NOR logic

The procedures described above may equally be applied to the implementation of circuits using NOR gates only. By way of illustration, the value of Z_3 above is converted to NOR logic form.

$$Z_3 = X_1X_0Y_1Y_0$$

$$= \overline{\overline{X_1X_0Y_1Y_0}}$$

$$= \overline{\bar{X}_1 + \bar{X}_0 + \bar{Y}_1 + \bar{Y}_0}$$

Note that $\bar{X}$ may be implemented by an inverter or by a NOR gate with its inputs connected together.

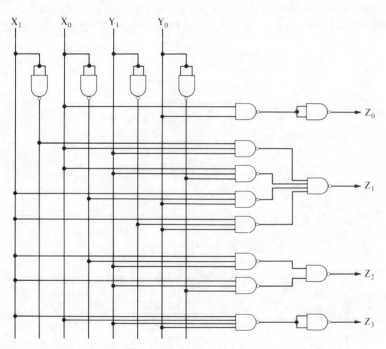

Fig. 2.22 Implementing the multiplier circuit in NAND logic only.

2.4.4 Karnaugh maps

The Karnaugh map, or more simply the K map, is a graphical technique for the representation and simplification of a Boolean expression. Although the Karnaugh map can simplify equations with five or six variables, we will use it to solve problems with only three or four variables. Other techniques such as the Quine–McCluskey method may be applied to the simplification of Boolean expessions in more than six variables. However, these techniques are beyond the scope of this book.

I find that students appreciate Karnaugh maps because they show unambiguously when a Boolean expression has been reduced to its most simple form. Students who use algebraic techniques to simplify an expression often reach a point at which they cannot proceed, as they are unable to find further simplifications. However, they are not certain whether the equation is indeed in its most simple form or whether they just cannot see the next step.

The Karnaugh map is a two-dimensional form of the (one-dimensional) truth table, drawn in such a way that the simpification of a Boolean expression can immediately be seen from the location of ones on the map. The key to the Karnaugh map is that adjacent squares (horizontally and vertically adjacent, but not diagonally adjacent) differ by only one variable. A system with n variables has 2^n lines in its truth table and 2^n squares on its Karnaugh map. Each square on the Karnaugh map is associated with a line in the truth table.

Figure 2.23 shows Karnaugh maps for one to four variables. As one- and two-variable maps represent trivial cases, they are not considered further. Consider now the three-variable map. Figure 2.24 shows the truth table for a three-variable function and the corresponding Karnaugh map.

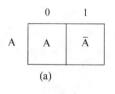

(a)

	0	1
A	A	$\bar{A}$

$$\begin{array}{c|c|c} B \backslash A & 0 & 1 \\ \hline 0 & \bar{A}\bar{B} & A\bar{B} \\ \hline 1 & \bar{A}B & AB \end{array}$$

(b)

(c)

C \ AB	00	01	11	10
0	$\bar{A}\bar{B}\bar{C}$	$\bar{A}B\bar{C}$	$AB\bar{C}$	$A\bar{B}\bar{C}$
1	$\bar{A}\bar{B}C$	$\bar{A}BC$	ABC	$A\bar{B}C$

(d)

CD \ AB	00	01	11	10
00	$\bar{A}\bar{B}\bar{C}\bar{D}$	$\bar{A}B\bar{C}\bar{D}$	$AB\bar{C}\bar{D}$	$A\bar{B}\bar{C}\bar{D}$
01	$\bar{A}\bar{B}\bar{C}D$	$\bar{A}B\bar{C}D$	$AB\bar{C}D$	$A\bar{B}\bar{C}D$
11	$\bar{A}\bar{B}CD$	$\bar{A}BCD$	$ABCD$	$A\bar{B}CD$
10	$\bar{A}\bar{B}C\bar{D}$	$\bar{A}BC\bar{D}$	$ABC\bar{D}$	$A\bar{B}C\bar{D}$

Fig. 2.23 The Karnaugh map:
(a) one-variable; (b) two-variable; (c) three-variable; (d) four-variable.

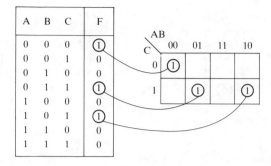

Fig. 2.24 The relationship between the truth table and the Karnaugh map for $F = \overline{A}\overline{B}\overline{C} + \overline{A}BC + A\overline{B}C$.

Each of the three ones in the truth table is mapped on to its appropriate square on the Karnaugh map.

A three-variable Karnaugh map has four vertical columns, one for each of the four possible values of two out of the three variables. For example, if the three variables are A, B, and C, the four columns represent all the possible combinations of A and B. Thus, the first (leftmost) column is labelled 00 and represents the case A = 0, B = 0. The next column is labelled 01, and represents the case A = 0, B = 1. The next column is labelled 11 (not 10), and represents the case A = 1, B = 1. Remember that adjacent columns differ by only one variable at a time. The fourth column, 10, represents the case A = 1, B = 0. In fact, a Karnaugh map is made up of all possible 2^n *minterms* for a system with n variables.

A three-variable Karnaugh map has two horizontal rows, the upper row corresponding to C = 0, and the lower to C = 1. Any square on the Karnaugh map represents a unique combination of the three variables, from ABC to $\overline{A}\overline{B}\overline{C}$. Figure 2.24 demonstrates how a function of three variables, $F = \overline{A}\overline{B}\overline{C} + \overline{A}BC + A\overline{B}C$, is plotted on a Karnaugh map.

It should be clear from Figure 2.24 how the entries in the table are plotted on the Karnaugh map. At this point it is worth noting that no two ones plotted on the Karnaugh map of Fig. 2.24 are adjacent to each other, and that the function $F = \overline{A}\overline{B}\overline{C} + \overline{A}BC + A\overline{B}C$ cannot be simplified. To keep the Karnaugh maps as clear and uncluttered as possible, squares that do not contain a one are left unmarked even though they must, of course, contain a zero. A square containing a logical one is said to be covered by a one.

Now consider the two functions $F_1 = AB\overline{C} + ABC$, and $F_2 = AB$ (Fig. 2.25). The Karnaugh map for F_1 has two separate adjacent squares covered, corresponding to $AB\overline{C}$ and ABC. The Karnaugh map for F_2 has a *group of two squares* covered, corresponding to the column A = 1, B = 1. As the function for F_2 does not involve the variable C, a one is entered in the squares for which A = B = 1 and C = 0, and A = B = 1 and C = 1.

It is immediately obvious that these two Karnaugh maps are identical, so that $F_1 = F_2$ and $AB\overline{C} + ABC = AB$. From the rules of Boolean algebra $AB\overline{C} + ABC = AB(C + \overline{C}) = AB(1) = AB$. It should be apparent that two adjacent squares in a Karnaugh map can be grouped together to form a single simpler term. It is this property that the Karnaugh map exploits to simplify expressions.

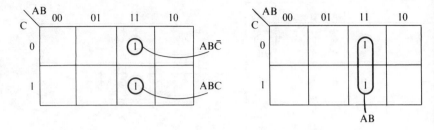

Fig. 2.25 Plotting two functions on the Karnaugh maps.

$$F_1 = AB\bar{C} + ABC \qquad\qquad F_2 = AB$$

Simplifying sum of products expression with a Karnaugh map

The first step in simplifying a Boolean expression by means of a Karnaugh map is to plot all the ones in the function's truth table on the Karnaugh map. The next step is to combine adjacent ones into groups of one, two, four, eight, or sixteen. The groups of minterms should be as large as possible—a single group of four minterms yields a simpler expression than two groups of two minterms. The final stage in simplifying an expression is reached when each of the groups of minterms (i.e. the product terms) are ORed together to form the simplified sum of products expression. This process is best demonstrated by means of examples. In what follows, a four-variable map is chosen to illustrate the examples.

Before we actually use the Karnaugh map to simplify Boolean expressions, we have to demonstrate how product terms are plotted on the map. Fig. 2.26 presents six functions plotted on Karnaugh maps. In these diagrams various sum of products expressions have been plotted directly from the equations themselves, rather than from the minterms of the truth table. The following notes should help in understanding these diagrams.

1. For a four-variable map:
   1-variable product term covers 8 squares
   2-variable product terms cover 4 squares
   3-variable product terms cover 2 squares
   4-variable product terms cover 1 squares

2. A square covered by a one may belong to more than one term in the sum of products expression. For example, in Fig. 2.26(b) the minterm $\bar{A}\bar{B}CD$ belongs to two groups, $\bar{A}\bar{B}$ and CD. If a 'one' on the Karnaugh map appears in two groups, it is equivalent to adding the corresponding minterm to the overall expression for the function plotted on the map twice. Repeating a term in a Boolean expression does not alter the value of the expression, because one of the axioms of Boolean algebra is $X + X = X$.

3. The Karnaugh map is not a square or a rectangle as it appears in these diagrams. A Karnaugh map is a *torus* or *doughnut* shape. That is, the top edge is adjacent to the bottom edge and, the left-hand edge is adjacent to the right-hand edge. For example, in Fig. 2.26(d) the term $\bar{A}D$ covers the two minterms $\bar{A}\bar{B}\bar{C}D$ and $\bar{A}B\bar{C}D$ at the top, and the two minterms $\bar{A}\bar{B}CD$ and $\bar{A}BCD$ at the bottom of the map. Similarly, in Fig. 2.26(e) the term $\bar{B}\bar{D}$ covers all four corners of the map.

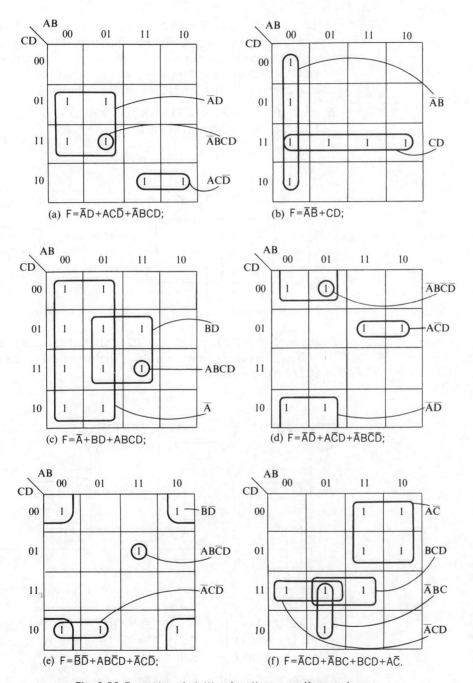

Fig. 2.26 Examples of plotting functions on a Karnaugh map.

4. In order either to read a product term from the map, or to plot a product term on the map, it is necessary to ask the question, what minterms (squares) are covered by this term?

Having shown how terms are plotted on the Karnaugh map, the next step is to apply the map to the simplification of the expressions. Once more, we demonstrate this process by means of examples. In each case, the original unsimplified function is plotted on the left-hand side of the page, and the regrouped ones are plotted on the right-hand side.

Example 1 $F = AB + \bar{A}B\bar{C}D + \bar{A}BCD + A\bar{B}C\bar{D}$ (Fig. 2.27). The simplified function is $F = AB + BD + A\bar{C}\bar{D}$.

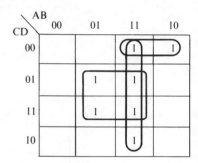

Fig. 2.27 Karnaugh map for Example 1.

Example 2 $F = A\bar{C}\bar{D} + \bar{A}\bar{B}C + \bar{A}CD + A\bar{B}D$ (Fig. 2.28). In this case there is only one regrouping possible. The simplified function is $F = \bar{B}D + A\bar{C}\bar{D} + \bar{A}CD + \bar{A}\bar{B}C$.

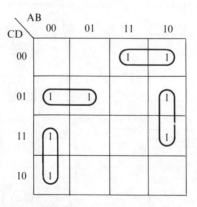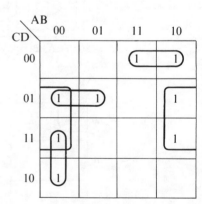

Fig. 2.28 Karnaugh map for Example 2.

Example 3 $F = \bar{A}\bar{B}\bar{C}\bar{D} + A\bar{B}\bar{C}\bar{D} + \bar{A}B\bar{C}D + AB\bar{C}D + \bar{A}BCD + ABCD + \bar{A}\bar{B}CD + A\bar{B}CD$ (Fig. 2.29). The function can be simplified to two product terms with the result that $F = \bar{B}\bar{D} + BD$.

Example 4 $F = \bar{A}\bar{B}\bar{C} + \bar{A}B\bar{C} + \bar{A}BC + AB\bar{C} + ABC$ (Fig. 2.30). In this case we can see that it is possible to group the minterms together in two ways, both of which are equally valid. That is, there are two equally correct simplifications of the expression.

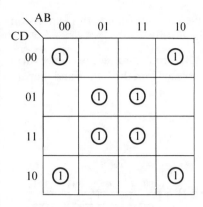

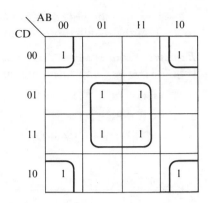

Fig. 2.29 Karnaugh map for Example 3.

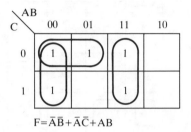

$$F = \bar{A}\bar{B} + \bar{A}\bar{C} + AB$$

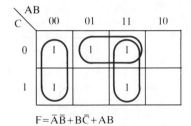

$$F = \bar{A}\bar{B} + B\bar{C} + AB$$

Fig. 2.30 Example 4—expressing a simplification in two ways $F = \bar{A}\bar{B}\bar{C} + \bar{A}B\bar{C} + \bar{A}B\bar{C} + AB\bar{C} + ABC$.

Applications of Karnaugh maps

Apart from the use of Karnaugh maps in the simplification of Boolean expressions, they can be applied to the conversion of sum-of-products form to the corresponding product-of-sums form. The first step in this process involves the generation of the complement of the expression.

The example given in Fig. 2.31 demonstrates how the complement of $F = \bar{C}\bar{D} + \bar{A}\bar{B} + A\bar{B} + C\bar{D}$ may be determined. If the squares on a Karnaugh map covered by ones represent F, then the remaining squares covered by zeros represent the complement of F, $\bar{F}$. From the right-hand diagram $\bar{F} = BD$.

In order to convert from the sum-of-products form to the product-of-sums form, it is first necessary to calculate $\bar{F}$ in a sum-of-products form (in

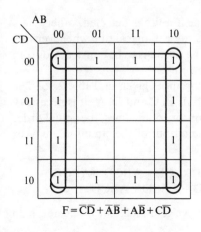

$$F = \bar{C}\bar{D} + \bar{A}\bar{B} + A\bar{B} + C\bar{D}$$

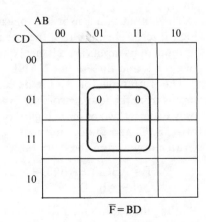

$$\bar{F} = BD$$

Fig. 2.31 Using a Karnaugh map to calculate a complement.

the way we have described above) and then to complement this expression to get F in the required product-of-sums form.

Example Convert $F = ABC + \bar{C}D + \bar{A}BD$ into product-of-sums form (Fig. 2.32). The complement of F may be read from the right-hand map as

$$\bar{F} = \bar{C}\bar{D} + \bar{B}C + \bar{A}\bar{D}$$
$$\text{So } F = \overline{\bar{C}\bar{D} + \bar{B}C + \bar{A}\bar{D}}$$
$$= (C + D)(B + \bar{C})(A + D)$$

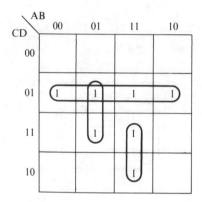
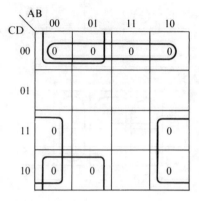

Karnaugh map of F   Karnaugh map of $\bar{F}$

Fig. 2.32 Converting from S of P to P of S form.

Using the Karnaugh map to design a circuit with NAND logic

Now that we have demonstrated how Karnaugh maps can be used to simplify Boolean expressions, we are going to apply the Karnaugh map to the design of a simple logic circuit using NAND logic only. Consider a fire detection circuit that protects a room against fire by means of four sensors. These are a flame detector, a smoke detector, and two high-temperature detectors located at the opposite ends of the room. As such detectors are prone to error or false alarms, the fire alarm is triggered only when two or more of the sensors simultaneously indicate the presence of a fire.

The output of a sensor is a logical one if a fire is detected, otherwise a logical zero. The output of the circuit is to be a logical one whenever two or more of its inputs are a logical one. The circuit is to be constructed from two-input and three-input NAND gates only.

The truth table for the fire detector circuit is given in Table 2.15. The inputs from the four sensors are labelled A, B, C and D. As it is necessary only to detect two or more logical ones on any of the lines, the actual order of A, B, C, and D does not matter. The output of the circuit, F, may be written down from the truth table:

$$F = \bar{A}\bar{B}CD + \bar{A}B\bar{C}D + \bar{A}BC\bar{D} + \bar{A}BCD + A\bar{B}\bar{C}D + A\bar{B}C\bar{D}$$
$$+ A\bar{B}CD + AB\bar{C}\bar{D} + AB\bar{C}D + ABC\bar{D} + ABCD.$$

Plotting these terms on a Karnaugh map we get Fig. 2.33(a). The next step is to group these terms together into six groups of four (Fig. 2.33(b)). Therefore, the simplified sum of products form of F is given by

$$F = AB + AC + AD + BC + BD + CD.$$

In order to convert the expression into NAND logic only form, it is necessary to eliminate the five logical OR operators:

$$F = \overline{\overline{F}} = \overline{\overline{AB + AC + AD + BC + BD + CD}}$$
$$= \overline{\overline{AB} \cdot \overline{AC} \cdot \overline{AD} \cdot \overline{BC} \cdot \overline{BD} \cdot \overline{CD}}$$

Although we have realized the expression in NAND logic as required, it calls for a six-input NAND gate. If the expression for F is examined, it can be seen that six terms are NANDed together, which is the same as ANDing them and then inverting the result. Because of the associative property of Boolean variables, we can write X(YZ) = (XY)Z, and hence extending this to our equations we get

$$F = \overline{\overline{\overline{AB} \cdot \overline{AC}} \cdot \overline{\overline{AD} \cdot \overline{BC}} \cdot \overline{\overline{BD} \cdot \overline{CD}}}$$

Figure 2.34 shows how this expression may be implemented in terms of two- and three-input NAND gates.

Table 2.15 Truth table for a fire detector

Inputs				Output
A	B	C	D	F
0	0	0	0	0
0	0	0	1	0
0	0	1	0	0
0	0	1	1	1
0	1	0	0	0
0	1	0	1	1
0	1	1	0	1
0	1	1	1	1
1	0	0	0	0
1	0	0	1	1
1	0	1	0	1
1	0	1	1	1
1	1	0	0	1
1	1	0	1	1
1	1	1	0	1
1	1	1	1	1

F is true if two or more inputs are true

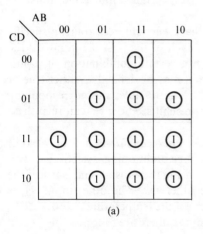

(a)

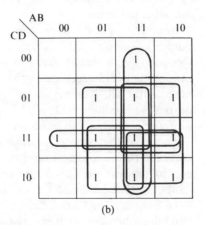

(b)

Fig. 2.33 (a) Karnaugh map for Table 2.15; (b) grouping the minterms of (a).

We could have attacked this problem in a slightly different way. If the Karnaugh map is examined it is apparent that because most squares are covered by ones, the remaining squares, covered by zeros, give $\overline{F}$ in a moderately simple form (Fig. 2.35).

$$\overline{F} = \overline{A}\overline{B}\overline{D} + \overline{A}\overline{B}\overline{C} + \overline{A}C\overline{D} + \overline{B}C\overline{D}$$

and
$$F = \overline{\overline{A}\overline{B}\overline{D} + \overline{A}\overline{B}\overline{C} + \overline{A}C\overline{D} + \overline{B}C\overline{D}}$$
$$= \overline{\overline{A}\overline{B}\overline{D} \cdot \overline{A}\overline{B}\overline{C} \cdot \overline{A}C\overline{D} \cdot \overline{B}C\overline{D}}.$$

I leave it as an exercise to the reader to work out whether this expression can be realized with as few gates as the one above.

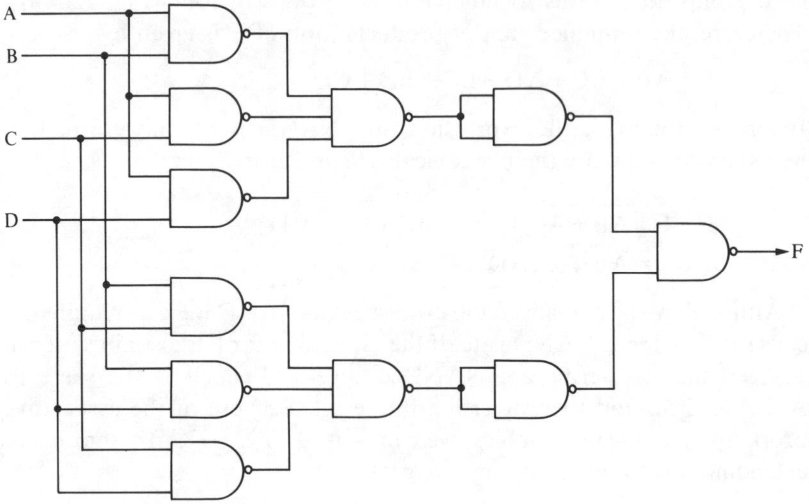

60 · Logic elements and Boolean algebra

Fig. 2.34 Implementing the fire detection circuit.

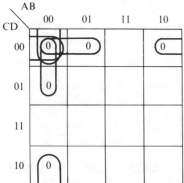

Fig. 2.35 Karnaugh map for F̄.

Table 2.16 Truth table for a pair of thermostats

Inputs		Meaning
C	H	
0	0	Temperature OK
0	1	Too hot
1	0	Too cold
1	1	?

Karnaugh maps and don't care conditions

We are now going to demonstrate how Karnaugh maps can be applied to a class of problems in which the truth table corresponding to a given system is not fully specified. That is, for certain input conditions the output is undefined.

In all the logic design problems we have encountered so far, a specific output value has been associated with each of the possible input values. Occasionally, a system exists in which a certain combination of inputs cannot happen. In such cases, the output may be defined as either true or false. After all, if a particular input is impossible, the corresponding output is meaningless. Or is it? Later we shall see how we can turn these meaningless outputs to good use.

To make the concept of ***impossible input conditions*** a little clearer, consider the following example. An air-conditioning system has two control inputs. One, C, is from a cold-sensing thermostat, and is true if the temperature is below 15°C, and false otherwise. The other input, H, is from a hot-sensing thermostat and is true if the temperature is above 22°C, and false otherwise. As there are two inputs, there are four possible logical conditions as illustrated in Table 2.16.

The input condition $C = 1, H = 1$ has no real meaning, as it is impossible to be too hot and too cold simultaneously. Such an input condition could arise only if one of the thermostats had become faulty. Consider now the following example of an air-conditioning unit with four inputs and four outputs. Table 2.17 defines the meaning of the inputs to the controller.

The controller has four outputs P, Q, R, and S. When $P = 1$ a heater is switched on, and when $Q = 1$ a cooler is switched on. Similarly, a humidifier is switched on by $R = 1$, and a dehumidifier by $S = 1$. In each case a logical zero switches off the appropriate device. The relationship between the inputs and outputs is as follows.

If the temperature and humidity are both within limits, switch off the heater and the chiller. The humidifier and dehumidifier are both switched off unless stated otherwise. If the humidity is within limits, switch on the

Table 2.17 Truth table for a climate controller

Input	Name	Meaning when input=0	Meaning when input=1
H	Hot	temperature < upper limit	temperature > upper limit
C	Cold	temperature > lower limit	temperature < lower limit
W	Wet	humidity < upper limit	humidity > upper limit
D	Dry	humidity > lower limit	humidity < lower limit

heater if the temperature is too low, and switch on the cooler if the temperature is too high.

If the temperature is within limits, switch on the heater if the humidity is too low, and the cooler if the humidity is too high. If the humidity is high, and the temperature low, switch on the heater. If the humidity is low, and the temperature high, switch on the cooler.

If both the temperature and humidity are high, switch on the cooler and dehumidifier. If both the temperature and humidity are too low, switch on the heater and humidifier.

The relationship between the inputs and outputs can now be expressed in terms of a truth table (Table 2.18). We can draw Karnaugh maps for P to S, plotting a 0, 1, or X as necessary. Remember that an X corresponds to a don't care condition. Consider P first (Fig. 2.36).

The don't care conditions are so called because the corresponding input conditions cannot occur. Of course, any real combinatorial digital circuit must have a particular logical output for each of the 2^n inputs. In other words, if an input which is classified as ***don't care*** is applied to the circuit, it ***must*** produce either a logical one or a zero at the output. We choose the output to be a one or a zero to simplify the design of the circuit. That is, if an X can be used to turn a group of ones into a larger group of ones on a Karnaugh map, it is taken as a logical one. Otherwise it is made a zero.

Fig. 2.36 Karnaugh map for P.

Table 2.18 Truth table for a climate controller

H	C	W	D	Condition	P	Q	R	S
0	0	0	0	OK	0	0	0	0
0	0	0	1	Dry	1	0	0	0
0	0	1	0	Wet	0	1	0	0
0	0	1	1	Impossible	X	X	X	X
0	1	0	0	Cold	1	0	0	0
0	1	0	1	Cold and dry	1	0	1	0
0	1	1	0	Cold and wet	1	0	0	0
0	1	1	1	Impossible	X	X	X	X
1	0	0	0	Hot	0	1	0	0
1	0	0	1	Hot and dry	0	1	0	0
1	0	1	0	Hot and wet	0	1	0	1
1	0	1	1	Impossible	X	X	X	X
1	1	0	0	Impossible	X	X	X	X
1	1	0	1	Impossible	X	X	X	X
1	1	1	0	Impossible	X	X	X	X
1	1	1	1	Impossible	X	X	X	X

The table has column group headers: **Inputs** (H, C, W, D, Condition) and **Outputs** (P, Q, R, S).

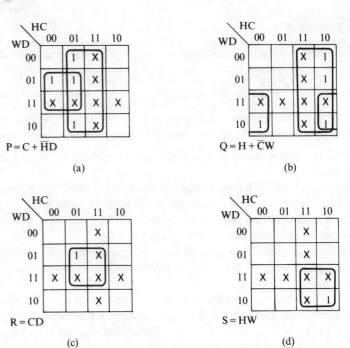

Fig. 2.37 Simplified Karnaugh maps for (a) P; (b) Q; (c) R; (d) S.

The Karnaugh map of Fig. 2.37(a) corresponds to output P. Six of the don't care conditions are included within the groupings to get $P = C + \bar{H}D$. Figures 2.37(b)–(d) provide Karnaugh maps for Q. R. and S, respectively.

2.5 Special-purpose logic elements

So far, we have dealt with the primitive logic elements from which all digital systems can be constructed. As technology has progressed, larger and larger numbers of components have been fabricated on single chips of silicon to produce more complex circuits. It is now possible to obtain chips with several gates connected together in order to perform a particular logic function. Such circuits are called medium scale integration (MSI), in contrast with the gates themselves which fall in the category of small scale integration (SSI).

By the 1970s entire systems began to appear on a single chip, of which the microprocessor is the most spectacular example. The technology used to make such complex systems is called large scale integration (LSI). The late 1980s was said to be the era of very large scale integration (VLSI). Interestingly enough, VLSI is not being used primarily to create very powerful computers on a chip, but is applied to the production of exceedingly large memory arrays capable of holding up to 4M bits of data (i.e. $2^{22} = 4\,194\,304$ bits). The late 1980s has seen the rise of ultra high-speed *gallium arsenide* technology with subnanosecond propagation delays per gate. It is possible that gallium arsenide technology might replace some of the applications now exclusively met by silicon technology.

2.5.1 SSI

Figure 2.38 illustrates one of the popular SSI gates available in 14-pin DIL (dual-in-line) packages. Dual-in-line simply means that there are two parallel rows of pins. The rows are 0.3 inches apart and the pins are spaced by 0.1 inch. Two pins are needed for the power supply ($V_{cc} = +5.0$ V, and ground $= 0$ V). In each example in Fig. 2.38 as many gates of a given type as possible are put in the package. For all practical purposes, the number of gates in a DIL SSI circuit is limited only by the number of pins to the DIL package. Fig. 2.39 illustrates the construction of this type of integrated circuit together with some larger packages. The physical size of the package does not necessarily correspond to the complexity of the device, but rather to the number of external connections (pins).

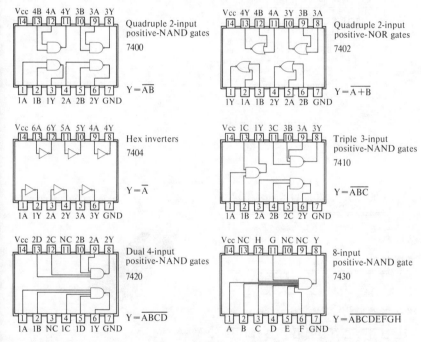

Fig. 2.38 Some basic SSI gates in 14-pin DIL packages. $V_{cc}=+5$ V power supply, GND=ground.

Figure 2.40 illustrates one of the elementary special purpose logic functions built from basic gates. These are called AND–OR–INVERT gates. These are still SSI circuits and implement some frequently appearing logic functions. For example, the 7454 generates the function $F = \overline{AB + CD + EF + GH}$, the inverse of a sum-of-products expression. If an equation can be expressed in the form above, it can be generated by a single chip rather than the two or more chips needed if basic gates were used. When more than about 10–20 gates are put on a single chip to achieve a logical function such as a multiplexer, the circuit is called an MSI chip.

2.5.2 The multiplexer

A particularly common functioning arising regularly in digital design is the *multiplexer*. We have already encountered a simple two-input multi-

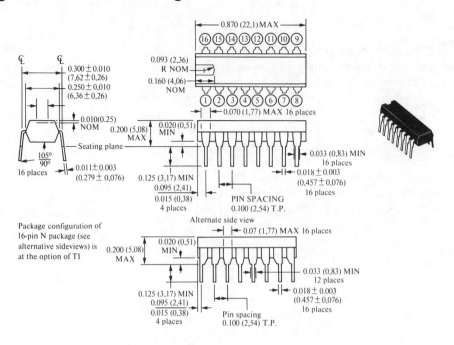

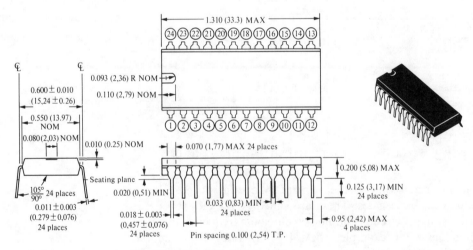

Fig. 2.39 The DIL package.

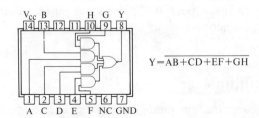

Fig. 2.40 The 7454
AND–OR–INVERT gate.

$$Y = \overline{AB + CD + EF + GH}$$

plexer in Example 2 on page 33. Figure 2.41 shows the 74157, a quadruple two-input multiplexer, which is available in a 16-pin MSI circuit. Each of the four Y outputs is connected to the corresponding A input pin when SELECT = 0, and to the B input when SELECT = 1. The $\overline{\text{STROBE}}$ input forces all Y outputs into logical zero states whenever $\overline{\text{STROBE}}$ = 1. The use of a multiplexer to switch between two alternative sources of data has already been discussed earlier in the example of the implementation of the conditional branch.

Figure 2.42 illustrates a 1-of-8 data multiplexer, the 74151, which has 8 data inputs, $D_0, D_1, D_2, \ldots, D_7$, an output Y (plus its complement $W = \overline{Y}$), and three data select inputs, A,B,C. When A,B,C = 0,0,0, the output is $Y = D_0$, and when ABC = 1,0,0, $Y = D_1$, etc. That is, if the binary value at the data select input is i, the output is given by $Y = D_i$. A typical application of the 74LS151 is in the selection of one out of eight logical conditions within a digital system. Figure 2.43 demonstrates how the 74LS151 might be used in conjunction with a computer's condition code register, CCR, to select one of eight logical conditions. Eight inputs from the CCR are connected to eight points in the central processing unit of a computer. By applying a suitable code to ABC, one of those eight points can be tested by examining the output at Y.

2.5.3 The demultiplexer

The inverse function of the multiplexer is the **demultiplexer**. Figure 2.44(a) illustrates the 74138, a three-line to eight-line demultiplexer. The truth table for this device is given in Table 2.19.

The eight outputs, $\overline{Y}_0$ to $\overline{Y}_7$, are active-low and remain in a logical one state unless the corresponding input is selected. The device has three

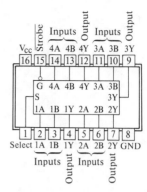

Fig. 2.41 The 74157 quadruple two-input multiplexer.

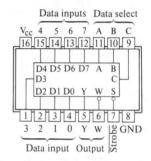

Fig. 2.42 The 74151 one-of-eight multiplexer.

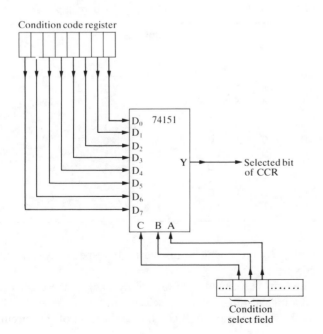

Fig. 2.43 Using the 74LS151.

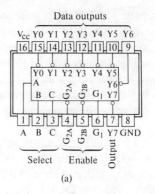

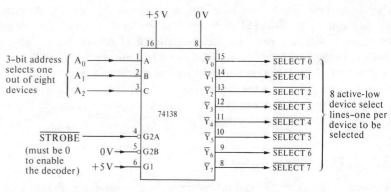

Fig. 2.44 (a) The 74138 three-line to eight-line demultiplexer; (b) applying the 74138 as a device selector.

Note: Only one of the 8 devices enabled by $\overline{\text{SELECT 0}}$ to $\overline{\text{SELECT 7}}$ can be active at any instant

(b)

Table 2.19 Truth table for 74LS138 3-line to 8-line demultiplexer

Inputs						Outputs							
Enable			Select										
G_1	$\bar{G}_2$	$\bar{G}_3$	C	B	A	$\bar{Y}_0$	$\bar{Y}_1$	$\bar{Y}_2$	$\bar{Y}_3$	$\bar{Y}_4$	$\bar{Y}_5$	$\bar{Y}_6$	$\bar{Y}_7$
X	1	1	X	X	X	1	1	1	1	1	1	1	1
0	X	X	X	X	X	1	1	1	1	1	1	1	1
1	0	0	0	0	0	0	1	1	1	1	1	1	1
1	0	0	0	0	1	1	0	1	1	1	1	1	1
1	0	0	0	1	0	1	1	0	1	1	1	1	1
1	0	0	0	1	1	1	1	1	0	1	1	1	1
1	0	0	1	0	0	1	1	1	1	0	1	1	1
1	0	0	1	0	1	1	1	1	1	1	0	1	1
1	0	0	1	1	0	1	1	1	1	1	1	0	1
1	0	0	1	1	1	1	1	1	1	1	1	1	0

enable inputs, $G_1, \bar{G}_2, \bar{G}_3$, which must be 1,0,0, respectively, for the chip to be selected.

When the chip is selected, one (and only one) of the eight outputs is forced into a logical zero state. The selected output depends on the three-bit code at the select inputs, A,B,C. One application of this circuit is as a device selector. Suppose there are eight devices and only one can be active (in use) at a time. If each device is enabled by a logical zero at its input, then the binary code applied to CBA will determine which device is selected. Figure 2.44(b) demonstrates how the 74138 is applied in this way.

The demultiplexer generates the 2^n **minterms** of an n-bit function. By ORing together the appropriate minterms we can generate an arbitrary sum-of-products expression in n variables. For example, Fig. 2.45 demonstrates how a three-line to eight-line decoder can be used to implement a full-adder (see Chapter 4 for details of this). Note that the outputs of the 74LS138 are active-low and therefore it is necessary to employ a NAND gate to generate the sum-of-products expression.

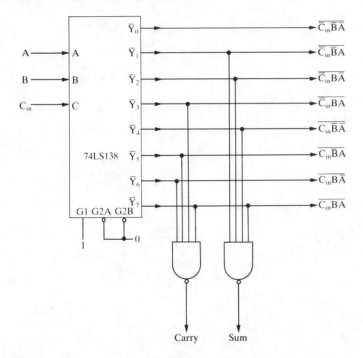

Fig. 2.45 Generating logic functions with a demultiplexer.

Another application of the demultiplexer might be in decoding a binary string. Consider the ISO/ASCII character code (to be described in Chapter 4). This code represents the alphanumeric characters (A to Z, 0 to 9, and symbols such as !,@,£,$,%, ...) together with certain non-printing symbols such as back-space and carriage return. The codes of some of these non-printing control codes are as follows:

Mnemonic	Name	Value
BS	Back space	00001000
LF	Line feed	00001010
CR	Carriage return	00001101
HT	Horizontal tabulate	00001001
VT	Vertical tabulate	00001011

Suppose we have a system that receives an ASCII/ISO code from a keyboard and we wish to decode its function in hardware. By examining the control codes above, it can be seen that all the codes of interest start with 00001. We can use the most significant four bits to enable a decoder and a 74LS138 three-line to eight-line decoder to distinguish between these codes. Figure 2.46 demonstrates how this is achieved. Each output from the decoder can be fed to a circuit to perform the appropriate action (e.g. carriage return).

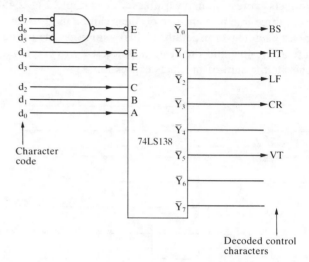

Fig. 2.46 Detecting control codes.

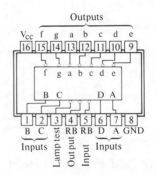

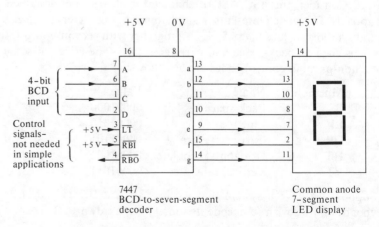

Fig. 2.47 The 7447 BCD-to-seven-segment decoder.

2.5.4 Code-converters

Among the many other special purpose logic elements is the *code-converter* that transforms one binary code into another. For example, Fig. 2.47 shows how a 7447 BCD-to-seven-segment decoder is used to display a single decimal digit. The ten digits 0 to 9 can be made up of two to seven straight-line segments, as can be seen from any digital watch. The 7447 is designed to convert a 4-bit BCD code (see Chapter 4) into the combination of segments needed to form the corresponding decimal digit.

There are several other MSI building blocks including a number of arithmetic elements, ranging from the full-adder, which calculates the sum of three bits, to a complete 8-bit arithmetic unit. Chapter 4 deals with the full adder.

2.6 Tri-state logic

The logic elements introduced at the beginning of this chapter are used to create functional units in which one or more logical outputs are generated from a number of inputs. A computer is made up of the interconnection of such functional units together with the storage elements to be described in Chapter 3. Here we are going to examine a special type of gate (a gate with a tri-state output) that enables the various functional units of a computer to be interconnected.

Buses

Figure 2.48 shows a system composed of five functional units, A, B, C, D, and E. These units are linked together by means of two data highways (or buses), P and Q, permitting data to be moved from one unit to another. Buses are not strictly necessary; it would be possible to provide direct connections between those parts of a digital system which exchange information. Equally, public highways are not necessary; each home could have a private path to all other homes, factories shops and services with which it needs to communicate. In both these cases the sheer number of interconnections would be uneconomic unless there are very few functional units (or homes).

A bus is normally represented diagrammatically by a single line (or double line) as in Fig. 2.48. The actual bus is made up of a number of lines (i.e. electrical connections) and Fig. 2.49 shows how they are arranged. Processes A and B are able to transmit data to the bus or receive data from it. We are not concerned with the nature of the processes A and B here, but simply wish to show how they communicate with each other. For clarity, the connections to only one line of the bus are shown. Similar arrangements exist for d_1 to d_{m-1}.

Suppose A wishes to send data to B. It puts data on the bus via gate A_{out}, and B receives the data via gate B_{in}. Such an arrangement is, in fact, unworkable, and a glance at Fig. 2.50 will show why. Each line of the bus has a number of outputs connected to it (from A, B, . . .) and Fig. 2.50

Fig. 2.48 Functional units and buses.

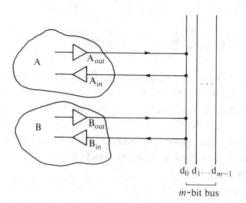

Fig. 2.49 Connecting circuits to buses.

$d_0 \, d_1 \ldots d_{m-1}$

m-bit bus

demonstrates the consequence of connecting together two outputs in differing logical states.

In Fig. 2.50 output A is in a logical one state and is pulled up towards + 5 V by a switch inside the gate. Similarly, output B is a logical zero state and is pulled down towards 0 V by another switch. These switches are transistors which are either conducting or non-conducting. Because the two outputs are of differing states and are wired together, two problems exist. The first is philosophical. As the logical level along a conductor is constant, because the voltage at all points along the conductor is constant, and yet its ends are connected to different voltages, the logical level on the conductor is undefined and breaks one of the rules of Boolean algebra. That is, there is no such thing as a valid indeterminate state lying between

Fig. 2.50 The outputs of two gates connected together.

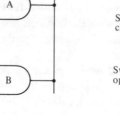
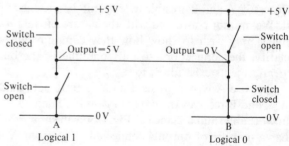

a logical one and a logical zero. Secondly, and more practically, a direct physical path exists between the $+5\,V$ power supply and ground $(0\,V)$. This is a short-circuit and the current flowing through the two output circuits will destroy them.

The difficulty of connecting outputs together is resolved by the tri-state gate. Tri-state logic is not, as its name suggests, an extension of Boolean algebra into ternary or three-valued logic. It is a method of resolving the conflict of Fig. 2.50 by disconnecting from the bus all those gates not actively engaged in transmitting data.

Figure 2.51 illustrates a gate with a tri-state output. The gate shown here is an inverter (complementer) for the sake of simplicity. In fact, any type of gate can have a tri-state output. All tri-state gates have a special input labelled ENABLE. When ENABLE $= 1$, the gate behaves normally, and its output is either a logical 1 or a logical 0 depending on its input. When ENABLE $= 0$, both switches in the output circuit of the gate are open, and the output is physically disonnected from the gate's internal circuitry. If I were to ask what state the output is in when ENABLE $= 0$, the answer should be that the question is meaningless. In fact, because the output of an un-enabled tri-state gate is normally connected to a bus, the logic level at the output terminal is the same as that on the bus to which it is connected. For this reason, the output of a tri-state gate in its **_third state_** is said to be **_floating_**. It floats up and down with the bus traffic. Most practical tri-state gates do, in fact, have active-low enable inputs.

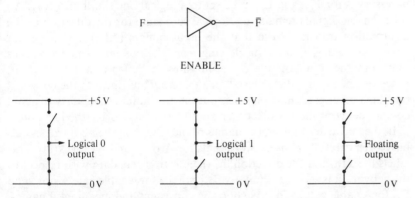

Fig. 2.51 The tri-state output.

The truth table of an inverter with a tri-state output is given in Table 2.20. Figure 2.52 shows how tri-state gates are actually used to implement a bused structure. The gates shown are called buffers because, when enabled, their outputs are equal to their inputs. They simply serve to connect or disconnect the networks to the bus. The outputs of networks A, B, and C are placed on the bus by three tri-state buffers AO, BO, and CO, which are enabled by signals E_{AO}, E_{BO}, and E_{CO}, respectively. If any network wishes to put data on to the bus it must set its enable signal (e.g. E_{BO}) to a logical one. Note that it is vital that no more than one of E_{AO}, E_{BO}, and E_{CO} be true at any instant.

Each of the networks receives data from the bus via their own input buffers (AI, BI, and CI). If a network wishes to receive data, it enables its input buffer by asserting one of E_{AI}, E_{BI}, or E_{CI}, as appropriate. For

Table 2.20 Truth table for tri-state gate

ENABLE	A	Output	
0	0	X	Here X
0	1	X	represents
1	0	1	'floating'
1	1	0	

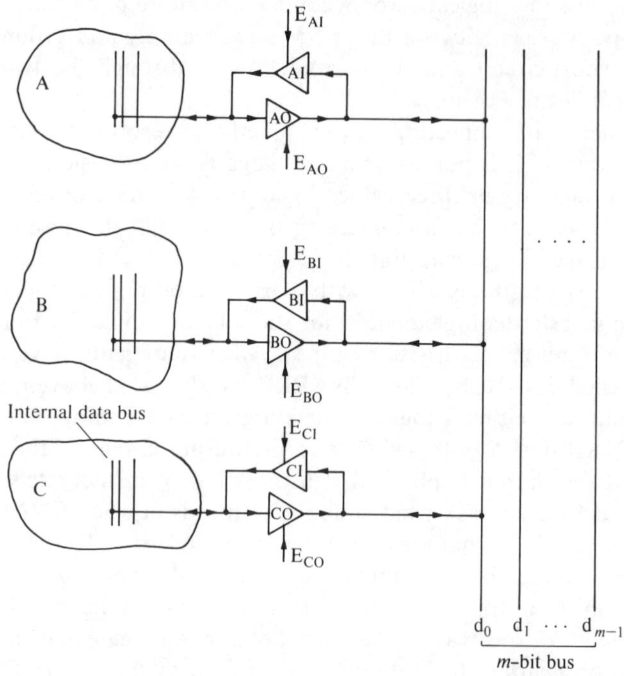

Fig. 2.52 The tri-state gate and the bus.

example, if network C wishes to transmit data to network A, all that is necessary is for E_{CO} and E_{AI} to be set to a logical one simultaneously. All other enable signals remain in a logical zero state for the duration of the information transfer. Note that the input buffers (AI, BI, CI) are not always necessary. If the data flowing from the bus into a network goes only into the input of one or more gates, a buffer is not needed. If, however, the input data is placed on an *internal* bus (local to the network) on which other gates may put their output, the buffer is necessary to avoid conflict between the various other outputs that may drive the local bus.

In the above description the names of the gates and their control signals have been carefully chosen. AO stands for A(out), and AI for A(in). This labels the gate and the direction in which it transfers data with respect to the network it is serving. Similarly, E_{AO} stands for 'enable gate A out', and E_{AI} for 'enable gate A in'. By choosing consistent and meaningful names, the reading of circuit diagrams and their associated text is made easier.

Further details of a bused system will be elaborated on in Chapter 3, and Chapter 5 on the structure of the CPU will make extensive use of buses in its description of how the CPU actually carries out basic computer operations.

Summary

In this chapter we have looked at the basic set of elements used to create any digital system—the AND, OR, and NOT gates. We have demonstrated how simple functions can be generated from gates by first converting a problem in words into a truth table and then using either graphical or algebraic methods to convert the truth table into a logical expression and finally into a circuit made up of gates.

In the next chapter we look at sequential circuits built from flip-flops. As the term *sequential* suggests, these circuits involve the time factor, because the logical state of a sequential device is determined by its current inputs and its past history (or behaviour). Sequential circuits form the basis of counters and data storage devices. Once we have covered sequential circuits, we will have covered all the basic building blocks necessary to design a digital system of any complexity (e.g. the digital computer).

Worked examples

Question 1

A circuit has four inputs, A, B, C, D, representing the sixteen natural binary integers from 0000 (0) to 1111 (15). A is the most significant bit and D the least significant bit. The output of the circuit, F, is true if the input is divisible by a multiple of 4,5,6, or 7, with the exception of 15, in which case the output is false. Zero is not divisible by 4, 5, 6, or 7.

(a) Draw a truth table to represent the algorithm.

(b) From the truth table obtain a simplified sum of products expression for F by means of Boolean algebraic techniques.

(c) Draw a Karnaugh map and hence obtain a simplified sum-of-products expression for F.

(d) Express F in product-of-sums form.

(e) Design a logic circuit to implement F using NAND gates only.

Solution 1

(a) The truth table is shown in Table 2.21.

(b) From the truth table a sum of products for F can be obtained by writing down the sum of the minterms:

$$F = \bar{A}B\bar{C}\bar{D} + \bar{A}B\bar{C}D + \bar{A}BC\bar{D} + \bar{A}BCD + A\bar{B}\bar{C}\bar{D} + A\bar{B}C\bar{D} + AB\bar{C}\bar{D} + AB\bar{C}\bar{D}.$$

By means of Boolean algebra the expressions can be simplified to

$$F = \bar{A}B\bar{C}(\bar{D} + D) + \bar{A}BC(\bar{D} + D) + A\bar{B}\bar{D}(\bar{C} + C) + AB\bar{D}(\bar{C} + C)$$

$$= \bar{A}B\bar{C} + \bar{A}BC + A\bar{B}\bar{D} + AB\bar{D}$$

$$= \bar{A}B(\bar{C} + C) + A\bar{D}(\bar{B} + B)$$

$$= \bar{A}B + A\bar{D}.$$

Table 2.21

Inputs				Number value	F	Comment
A	B	C	D			
0	0	0	0	0	0	
0	0	0	1	1	0	
0	0	1	0	2	0	
0	0	1	1	3	0	
0	1	0	0	4	1	divisible by 4
0	1	0	1	5	1	divisible by 5
0	1	1	0	6	1	divisible by 6
0	1	1	1	7	1	divisible by 7
1	0	0	0	8	1	divisible by 4
1	0	0	1	9	0	
1	0	1	0	10	1	divisible by 5
1	0	1	1	11	0	
1	1	0	0	12	1	divisible by 6
1	1	0	1	13	0	
1	1	1	0	14	1	divisible by 7
1	1	1	1	15	0	false by definition

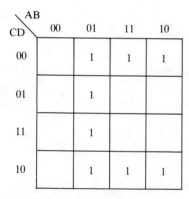

Fig. 2.53

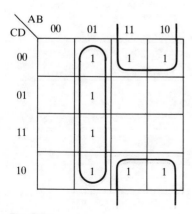

Fig. 2.54

(c) The Karnaugh map for F is given in Fig. 2.53. The squares covered by ones can be formed into two groups of four, as indicated in Fig. 2.54.

This gives $F = \bar{A}B + A\bar{D}$ which is (reassuringly) the same as the result obtained in part (b) above.

(d) To obtain a product-of-sums expression, it is necessary to generate the complement of F in a sum-of-products form, and then complement it.

$$F = \bar{A}B + A\bar{D}$$

$$\bar{F} = \overline{\bar{A}B + A\bar{D}}$$

$$= (A + \bar{B})(\bar{A} + D) \qquad \text{complement in product-of-sums form}$$

$$= A\bar{A} + AD + \bar{A}\bar{B} + \bar{B}D$$

$$= AD + \bar{A}\bar{B} + \bar{B}D$$

$$= AD + \bar{A}\bar{B} \qquad \text{complement in sum-of-products form}$$

$$F = \overline{AD + \bar{A}\bar{B}}$$

$$= (\bar{A} + \bar{D})(A + B) \qquad \text{function in required product-of-sums form}$$

Note that the complement of F in sum of products form could have been obtained directly from the Karnaugh map of F by considering the squares covered by zeros.

(e) To convert the expression $F = \bar{A}B + A\bar{D}$ into NAND logic form, the '+' must be eliminated.

$$F = \bar{\bar{F}} = \overline{\overline{\bar{A}B + A\bar{D}}} = \overline{\overline{\bar{A}B} \cdot \overline{A\bar{D}}}.$$

The inverse functions A and B can be generated by two-input NAND gates with their inputs connected together. Figure 2.55 implements F in NAND logic only.

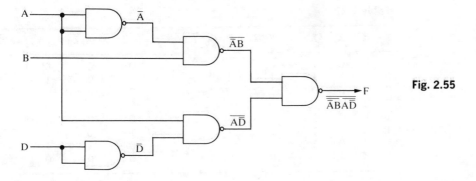

Fig. 2.55

Question 2

(a) Using AND, OR, and NOT gates only, design circuit diagrams to generate P and Q from inputs X, Y, and Z, where $P = (X + \bar{Y})(Y \oplus Z)$ and $Q = \bar{Y}Z + XY\bar{Z}$. Do not simplify, or otherwise modify, these expressions.

(b) By means of a truth table establish a relationship between P and Q.

(c) Compare the circuit diagrams of P and Q in terms of speed (propagation delay) and cost of implementation.

Solution 2

(a) The circuit diagram for $P = (X + \bar{Y})(Y \oplus Z) = (X + \bar{Y})(Y\bar{Z} + \bar{Y}Z)$ is shown in Fig. 2.56, and that for $Q = \bar{Y}Z + XY\bar{Z}$ in Fig. 2.57.

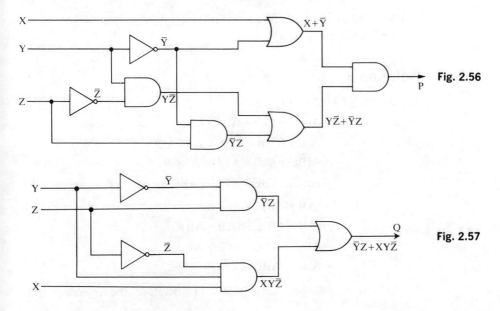

Fig. 2.56

Fig. 2.57

(b) The truth table for P and Q is shown in Table 2.22.

From this table it can be seen that $P = Q$.

Table 2.22

X	Y	Z	$X+\bar{Y}$	$Y\oplus Z$	$P=(X+\bar{Y})(Y\oplus Z)$	$\bar{Y}Z$	$XY\bar{Z}$	$P=\bar{Y}Z+XY\bar{Z}$
0	0	0	1	0	0	0	0	0
0	0	1	1	1	1	1	0	1
0	1	0	0	1	0	0	0	0
0	1	1	0	0	0	0	0	0
1	0	0	1	0	0	0	0	0
1	0	1	1	1	1	1	0	1
1	1	0	1	1	1	0	1	1
1	1	1	1	0	0	0	0	0

(c) *Propagation delay*. The maximum delay in the circuit for P is 4 gates in series in the Y path (i.e. NOT gate, AND gate, OR gate, AND gate). Maximum delay in circuit for Q is 3 gates in series in both Y and Z paths (i.e. NOT gate, AND gate, OR gate). Therefore the circuit for Q is 33% faster than that for P.

Cost. Total number of gates needed to implement P = 7. Total number of gates needed to implement Q = 5. Total inputs in the circuit for P = 12. Total inputs in the circuit for Q = 9.

Clearly, the circuit for Q is better than that for P both in terms of the number of gates and the number of inputs to the gates.

Question 3

(a) Show that the EXCLUSIVE OR, EOR, operator is associative, so that $A\oplus(B\oplus C)=(A\oplus B)\oplus C$.

(b) Show that any logic function can be implemented in terms of EOR and AND gates only.

Solution 3

(a)
$$A\oplus(B\oplus C)=A\oplus(B\bar{C}+\bar{B}C)$$
$$=A\overline{(B\bar{C}+\bar{B}C)}+\bar{A}(B\bar{C}+\bar{B}C)$$
$$=A(\bar{B}+C)(\bar{B}+C)+\bar{A}B\bar{C}+\bar{A}\bar{B}C$$
$$=A(\bar{B}\bar{C}+BC)+\bar{A}B\bar{C}+\bar{A}\bar{B}C$$
$$=A\bar{B}\bar{C}+ABC+\bar{A}B\bar{C}+\bar{A}\bar{B}C$$

$$(A\oplus B)\oplus C=(A\bar{B}+\bar{A}B)\oplus C$$
$$=(A\bar{B}+\bar{A}B)\bar{C}+\overline{(A\bar{B}+\bar{A}B)}C$$
$$=A\bar{B}\bar{C}+\bar{A}B\bar{C}+(\bar{A}\bar{B}+AB)C$$
$$=A\bar{B}\bar{C}+\bar{A}B\bar{C}+\bar{A}\bar{B}C+ABC.$$

Both these expressions are equal and therefore the operator $\oplus$ is associative.

(b) Consider $F=A\oplus B$.

$$F=A\bar{B}+\bar{A}B$$

If $A = 0$ $F = B$

If $A = 1$ $F = \bar{B}$.

In other words, if one input to an EOR gate is connected to a logical one, the other input appears at the output in a complemented form. Therefore, the EOR gate can act as an inverter.

If an EOR gate connected as an inverter is applied to the output of an AND gate, the AND gate is transformed into a NAND gate. As all logic functions can be generated by NAND gates only, then all logic functions can be generated by AND gates and EOR gates acting as inverter.

Question 4

Design a BCD-to-seven-segment decoder. The decoder has a 4-bit natural binary BCD input represented by DCBA, where A is the least significant bit. Assume that the BCD input can never be greater than 9. A seven-segment decoder is illustrated in Fig. 2.58, and when one of its seven outputs (a to g) is true, the corresponding segment of the display is illuminated.

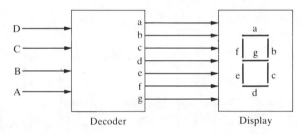

Fig. 2.58

Solution 4

The truth table for this problem is given in Table 2.23.

We can now solve the equation for segments a to g. By using Karnaugh maps the don't care conditions can be catered for. Figure 2.59 shows Karnaugh maps for segment a. From the map $a = CA + BA + D + \bar{C}B$.

An alternative approach is to obtain a by considering the zeros on the map (Fig. 2.60). From the Karnaugh map $\bar{a} = \bar{D}\bar{C}\bar{B}A + C\bar{A}$. Therefore

$$a = \overline{\bar{D}\bar{C}\bar{B}A + C\bar{A}} = (D + C + B + \bar{A})(\bar{C} + A)$$
$$= D\bar{C} + DA + C\bar{C} + CA + \bar{C}B + BA + \bar{C}\bar{A} + \bar{A}A$$
$$= D\bar{C} + DA + CA + \bar{C}B + BA + \bar{C}\bar{A}$$
$$= D\bar{C} + CA + BA + \bar{C}\bar{A}.$$

This expression offers no improvement over the first realization of a.

Figure 2.61 shows Karnaugh maps for segment b, giving $b = \bar{C} + \bar{B}\bar{A} + BA$.

Plotting zeros on the Karnaugh map for b we get Fig. 2.62, giving $\bar{b} = C\bar{B}A + CB\bar{A}$. Therefore,

$$b = \overline{C\bar{B}A + CB\bar{A}} = (\bar{C} + B + \bar{A})(\bar{C} + \bar{B} + A)$$
$$= \bar{C} + BA + \bar{B}\bar{A}.$$

Table 2.23

Inputs				Character	Outputs						
D	C	B	A		a	b	c	d	e	f	g
0	0	0	0	0	1	1	1	1	1	1	0
0	0	0	1	1	0	1	1	0	0	0	0
0	0	1	0	2	1	1	0	1	1	0	1
0	0	1	1	3	1	1	1	1	0	0	1
0	1	0	0	4	0	1	1	0	0	1	1
0	1	0	1	5	1	0	1	1	0	1	1
0	1	1	0	6	0	0	1	1	1	1	1
0	1	1	1	7	1	1	1	0	0	0	0
1	0	0	0	8	1	1	1	1	1	1	1
1	0	0	1	9	1	1	1	0	0	1	1
1	0	1	0		X	X	X	X	X	X	X
1	1	0	0		X	X	X	X	X	X	X
1	1	0	0		X	X	X	X	X	X	X
1	1	0	1		X	X	X	X	X	X	X
1	1	1	0		X	X	X	X	X	X	X
1	1	1	1		X	X	X	X	X	X	X

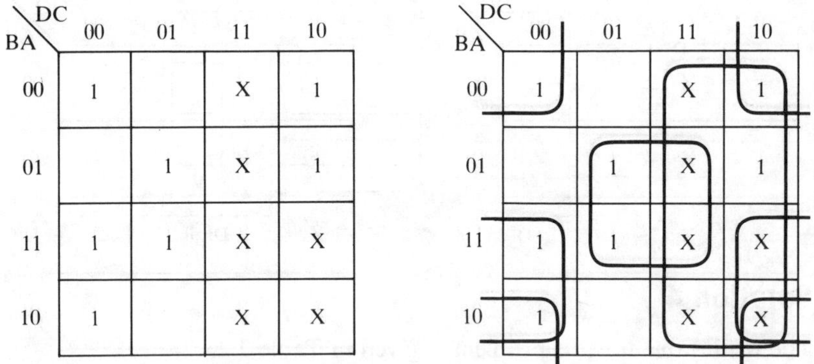

forbidden (don't care outputs)

Fig. 2.59

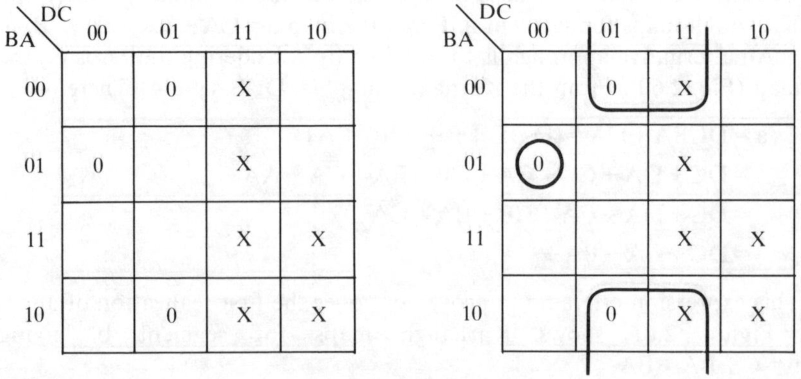

BA\DC	00	01	11	10
00	1		X	1
01		1	X	1
11	1	1	X	X
10	1		X	X

BA\DC	00	01	11	10
00	1		X	1
01		1	X	1
11	1	1	X	X
10	1		X	X

Fig. 2.60

BA\DC	00	01	11	10
00		0	X	
01	0		X	
11			X	X
10		0	X	X

BA\DC	00	01	11	10
00		0	X	
01	0		X	
11			X	X
10		0	X	X

This expression yields the same result as that obtained directly by considering the ones on the Karnaugh map.

The equations for the remaining five segments can be considered in a similar way.

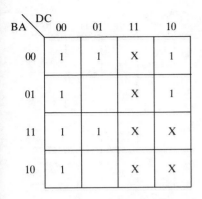
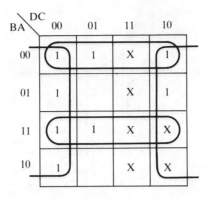

Fig. 2.61

DC BA	00	01	11	10
00			X	
01		0	X	
11			X	X
10		0	X	X

DC BA	00	01	11	10
00			X	
01		0	X	
11			X	X
10		0	X	X

Fig. 2.62

Question 5

A logic circuit has two 2-bit natural binary inputs A and B. A is given by A_1, A_0 where A_1 is the most significant bit. Similarly for B. The circuit has three outputs, X, Y and Z. The relationship between A and B, and X, Y, Z is as follows.

	X Y Z
$A > B$	1 0 0
$A < B$	0 1 0
$A = B$	0 0 1

Design a circuit to implement this function.

Solution 5

The truth table for this problem is given in Table 2.24.

We can use Karnaugh maps to derive expressions for X, Y, Z as shown in Fig. 2.63. I have chosen this example because of its symmetry. Notice how the result for X is almost identical to that for Y (the variables have simply been complemented). You would expect this symmetry from the very nature of the problem.

Table 2.24

A A_1 A_0	B B_1 B_0	A>B X	A<B Y	A=B Z
0 0	0 0	0	0	1
0 0	0 1	0	1	0
0 0	1 0	0	1	0
0 0	1 1	0	1	0
0 1	0 0	1	0	0
0 1	0 1	0	0	1
0 1	1 0	0	1	0
0 1	1 1	0	1	0
1 0	0 0	1	0	0
1 0	0 1	1	0	0
1 0	1 0	0	0	1
1 0	1 1	0	1	0
1 1	0 0	1	0	0
1 1	0 1	1	0	0
1 1	1 0	1	0	0
1 1	1 1	0	0	1

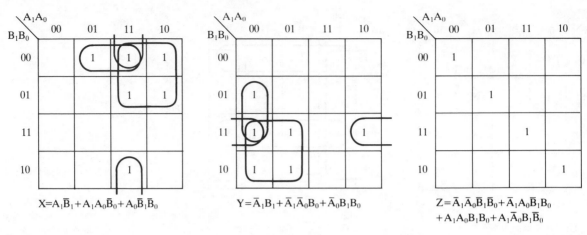

$$X = A_1\bar{B}_1 + A_1 A_0 \bar{B}_0 + A_0 \bar{B}_1 \bar{B}_0$$

$$Y = \bar{A}_1 B_1 + \bar{A}_1 \bar{A}_0 B_0 + \bar{A}_0 B_1 B_0$$

$$Z = \bar{A}_1 \bar{A}_0 \bar{B}_1 \bar{B}_0 + \bar{A}_1 A_0 \bar{B}_1 B_0$$
$$+ A_1 A_0 B_1 B_0 + A_1 \bar{A}_0 B_1 \bar{B}_0$$

Fig. 2.63

Problems

1. Tabulate the values of the variables, P, Q, R, S, T, U in Fig. 2.64 for all possible input variables A, B, C, D.

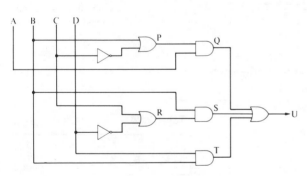

Fig. 2.64

Note: The truth table for this question should be in the form of Table 2.25.

2. For Fig. 2.64 obtain a Boolean expression for the output, U, in terms of the inputs A, B, C, D. This expression need not be simplified.

3. Use a truth table to obtain the relationship between outputs X and Y, and the input variables A, B, C for the circuit shown in Fig. 2.65. From the truth table write down Boolean expressions for X and Y. Derive expressions for X and Y by considering the Boolean equations of the gates.

Demonstrate that the two results (i.e. those derived from the truth table and those derived from the Boolean equations) are equivalent by substituting literals (000, 001, etc.) for A, B, C in the Boolean equations.

Table 2.25

Inputs				Intermediate values					Output
A	B	C	D	$P = B + \bar{C}$	$Q = P.A$	$R = C + \bar{D}$	$S = B.R$	$T = B.D$	$U = Q + S + T$
0	0	0	0	1	0	1	0	0	0
0	0	0	1	.	.	.	.	.	.
0	0	1	0	.	.	.	.	.	.
0	0	1	1	.	.	.	.	.	.
0	1	0	0	.	.	.	.	.	.
		.		.	.	.	.	.	.
		.							
1	1	1	1	1	1	1	1	1	1

Fig. 2.65

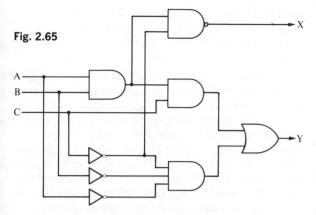

4. Draw logic diagrams using AND, OR, NOT gates only, to implement the following Boolean expressions:

(a) $F = A\bar{B} + \bar{A}B$ 　　　(b) $F = (A + B + C)(AB + AC)$

(c) $F = (A + \bar{C})(A + B\bar{D})$. 　(d) $F = \overline{\bar{A} + \bar{C}}.\overline{A + B\bar{D}}$

(e) $F = (A\bar{B} + \bar{A}B + A\bar{C})(\overline{\bar{A}B + A\bar{B} + A\bar{C}})$.

Do not simplify the expressions.

5. Plot the following functions on a Karnaugh map.

(a) $F = ABC + ABC$

(b) $F = ABC + ABC + ABC$

(c) $F = A + AB + AC + ABC$

(d) $F = (A + B)(AC + D)$

(e) $F = ABCD + ABCD + BD$.

6. Simplify the following expressions by means of Boolean algebra. That is, do not use Karnaugh maps.

(a) $A\bar{B}\bar{C} + \bar{A}\bar{B}C + \bar{A}B\bar{C} + \bar{A}\bar{B}C$

(b) $ABC + \bar{A}BC + A\bar{B}C + AB\bar{C} + \bar{A}\bar{B}C + \bar{A}B\bar{C}$

(c) $ABC + A\bar{B}\bar{C} + \bar{A}\bar{B}C + \bar{A}B\bar{C} + A\bar{B}\bar{C} + AB\bar{C} + \bar{A}\bar{B}\bar{C} + \bar{A}BC$

(d) $(A + B + C)(A + \bar{B} + \bar{C})(A + B + \bar{C})(A + \bar{B} + C)$

(e) $(A\bar{B} + \bar{A}B + A\bar{C})(\overline{\bar{A}B + A\bar{B} + A\bar{C}})$

(f) $A + \bar{B} + (A + CD)(A + \bar{B}\bar{C})$

(g) $\bar{A}\bar{B} + \bar{B}\bar{C} + A\bar{B}C + AB\bar{C}D$

(h) $(\bar{A} + B)(A + \bar{B} + C)(A + B + \bar{C})(\bar{A} + B + \bar{C})(\bar{A} + \bar{B} + C)$

7. Use de Morgan's theorem to complement the following expressions. Do not simplify the expressions either before or after you complement them.

(a) $\bar{X}\bar{Y} + XY$ 　　(b) $XYZ + \bar{X}\bar{Y}$

(c) $X(Y + Z) + \bar{X}\bar{Y}$ 　(d) $WX(\bar{Y}Z + YZ)$

(e) $WX(W\bar{Z} + \bar{Y}Z)$ 　(f) $XY + \bar{X}\bar{Y}(WZ + \bar{W}Z)$

8. Convert the following expressions to sum-of-products form.

(a) $(A + B)(\bar{B} + C)(\bar{A} + C)$

(b) $(C + D)(A\bar{B} + AC)(A\bar{C} + B)$

(c) $(A + B + C)(A + CD)(D + F)$

9. Convert the following expressions to product-of-sums form.

(a) $AB + \bar{A}\bar{B} + BC$ 　　　(b) $AB + \bar{A}C + BC$

(c) $\bar{A}\bar{B}(\bar{C}\bar{D} + A(B + \bar{C} + D))$ 　(d) $AB\bar{C} + \bar{A}B\bar{C} + \bar{A}B\bar{C}$
　　　　　　　　　　　　　　　　　$+ \bar{A}\bar{B}C$

10. A circuit has four inputs, P, Q, R, S, representing the natural binary numbers $0000 = 0$, to $1111 = 15$. P is the most significant bit. The circuit has one output, X, which is true if the number represented by the input is divisible by three. (Regard zero as being indivisible by three.)

Design a truth table for this circuit, and hence obtain and expression for X in terms of P,Q,R, and S. Give the circuit diagram of an arrangement of AND, OR, and NOT gates to implement this circuit.

Design a second circuit to implement this function using NAND gates only.

11. A device accepts natural binary numbers in the range 0000 to 1111, which represent 0 to 15. The output of the circuit is true if the input to the circuit represents a prime number and is false otherwise. Design a circuit using AND, OR, and NOT gates to carry out this function. Note that zero (0000) and one (0001) are not considered as prime numbers.

12. A logic circuit accepts a natural binary number DCBA in the range 0 to 15. The output is the square of the input (e.g. if $DCBA = 0101_2 = 5_{10}$ the output is $00010101_2 = 25_{10}$). Design a circuit to implement this function.

13. A logic circuit has three inputs A, B, C, where A is the least significant bit. The circuit has eight outputs, Y_0 to Y_7. For any binary code applied to the input terminals (A, B, C), one and one only of the outputs goes true—the others remain false.

Thus, if $C = 1$, $B = 0$, $A = 0$ the output Y_4 is true. Design a logic network to implement this circuit. Such a circuit is called a demultiplexer, which we have already met.

14. A 4-bit binary number is applied to a circuit on four lines A, B, C, D. The circuit has a single output, F, which is true if the number is in the range three to twelve, inclusive.

Draw a truth table for this problem, and obtain a simplified expression for F in terms of the inputs.

Implement the circuit (a) in terms of NAND gates only; (b) in terms of NOR gates only.

15. A circuit has four inputs D, C, B, A encoded in 8421 natural binary form. The inputs in the range $0000 = 0$ to $1011 = 11$ represent the months of the year from January (0) to December (11). Inputs in the range 1100–1111 (i.e.

12–15) cannot occur. The output of the circuit is a logical one if the month represented by the input has 31 days. Otherwise the output is false. The output for inputs in the range 1100 to 1111 is undefined.

(a) Draw a truth table to represent the problem and use it to construct a Karnaugh map.

(b) Use the Karnaugh map to obtain a simplified expression for the function

(c) Construct a circuit to implement the function using AND, OR, and NOT gates.

(d) Construct a circuit to implement the function using NAND gates only.

(e) Construct a circuit to implement the function using NOR gates only.

16. A multiplexer has eight inputs Y_0–Y_7 and a single output Z. A further three inputs A, B, C (A = lsb) determine which output the single input X is connected to. For example, if A, B, C = 110, the output Y_6 = X and all other outputs are low. Design a circuit to implement this function.

17. A *priority encoder* is a circuit with m inputs and $\log_2 m$ outputs. A typical priority encoder may have eight inputs and three outputs. If one of the m inputs is asserted, the binary code corresponding to the *location* of the asserted input appears at the output. For example, if input Y_3 is asserted the output code is 011. However, if more than one input is asserted the output code reflects the position of the *highest* input. That is, if input 3 is asserted the output code is 011 but if input 5 is also (i.e. concurrently) asserted, the output goes to 101 to reflect the higher priority. The priority encoder is used to determine which of a group of competing devices can gain access to a system. Design an 8-input, 3-output priority encoder.

Sequential logic

Each logic circuit we have encountered up to this point has been a *combinational* circuit whose output is a function of its inputs only. That is, given a knowledge of a combinational circuit's inputs together with its Boolean function, we can always calculate the state of its outputs. Circuits whose outputs depend not only on their current inputs, but also on their *past* inputs, are called *sequential circuits*. Even if we know the structure of a sequential circuit (i.e. its Boolean transfer function) and its current inputs, we cannot determine its output state *without* a knowledge of its past history (i.e. its previous internal states). In this chapter we are going to look at some simple sequential circuits. The basic building block of sequential circuits is the *flip-flop* or *bistable,* just as the basic building block of the combinational circuit is the gate.

It is not my intention to deal with sequential circuits at anything other than an introductory level, as their full treatment forms an entire branch of digital engineering. Sequential circuits cannot, however, be omitted from elementary texts on computer hardware because they are needed to implement registers, counters and shifters, all of which are fundamental to the operation of the central processing unit.

A bistable is so called because, for a given input, its output can remain in one of two stable states indefinitely. That is, for a particular set of inputs, the output may assume either a logical zero or a logical one, the actual value depending on the previous inputs. Such a circuit has the ability to remember what has happened to it in the past and is therefore a form of memory element. A more detailed discussion of memory elements is given in Chapter 8. A bistable is the smallest possible memory cell and can store only a single bit of information. The term flip-flop, which is synonymous with bistable, is onomatopoeic and gives the impression of the circuit going *flip* into one state and then *flop* into its complement. Once upon a time bistables were constructed from electromagnetic relays and really did make a 'flip-flop' sound as they clocked from one state into another.

There are two approaches to the description of flip-flops. One is to demonstrate what they do by defining their characteristics, as an *abstract* model and then to point out how they may be designed. That is, we say this is a flip-flop and this is how it behaves—now let's see what it can do. The other way of approaching flip-flops is to demonstrate how a flip-flop can be implemented with just two gates and then show how its special properties are put to work. I intend to follow the latter path. Readers who do not like this approach may skip ahead to the summary of flip-flops at the end of this section and then return when they have a global picture of the flip-flop.

3.1 The RS flip-flop

We begin our discussion of the flip-flop with the simplest member of the family, the RS flip-flop. Figure 3.1 illustrates one of the most complex circuits in this book. Although it involves no more than two simple two-input NOR gates, its operation is not immediately apparent. The circuit has two inputs, A and B, and two outputs, X and Y. A truth table for the NOR gate is provided alongside Fig. 3.1 for reference. From the equations governing the gates we can readily write down expressions for outputs X and Y in terms of inputs A and B.

Fig. 3.1 Two cross-coupled NOR gates.

A B	$\overline{A+B}$
0 0	1
0 1	0
1 0	0
1 1	0

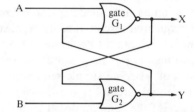

1. $X = \overline{A + Y}$

2. $Y = \overline{B + X}$

If we substitute the value for Y from equation (2) in equation (1), we get:

3. $X = \overline{A + \overline{B + X}} = \overline{A} . \overline{\overline{B + X}}$

$$= \overline{A} . (B + X)$$

$$= \overline{A}B + \overline{A}X$$

As Boolean algebra does not define the operations of division or subtraction, we are left with a rather nasty-looking equation in which the *output* is a function of the *output*. Equation (3) is correct but its meaning is not immediately apparent. We have to look for another way of analysing the behaviour of cross-coupled gates. Perhaps a better approach to understanding this circuit is to assume a value for output X and for the inputs and then see where it leads us.

Analysing a sequential circuit by assuming initial conditions

Figure 3.2 shows the NOR gate circuit with the initial condition $X = 1$ and $A = B = 0$. As the inputs to gate G_2 are $X = 1$, $B = 0$, its output, $\overline{X + B}$, must be 0. The inputs to gate G_1 are $Y = 0$ and $A = 0$, so that its output, X, is $\overline{Y + A}$, which is 1. Now note that this situation is self-consistent. The output of gate G_1 is 1, which is fed back to the input of gate G_1 to keep X

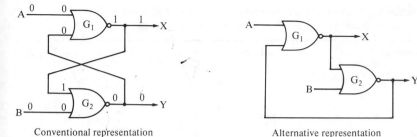

Conventional representation   Alternative representation

Fig. 3.2 The operation of Fig. 3.1.

in a logical 1 state. That is, the output actually maintains itself. Such a circuit is called **cross-coupled** because the output is fed back to the input. It should now be a little more clear why the above equation for X (i.e. equation 3) has X on both sides of the equal sign (i.e. $X = \overline{AB} + \overline{A}X$).

If we had assumed the initial state of X to be 0 and inputs $A = B = 0$, we could have proceeded as follows:

The inputs to G_2 are $X = 0$, $B = 0$ and therefore its output is $Y = \overline{X + B} = \overline{0 + 0} = 1$. The inputs to G_1 are $Y = 1$ and $A = 0$, and its output is $X = \overline{Y + A} = \overline{1 + 0} = 0$. Once more we can see that the circuit is self-consistent. Note that for the inputs $A = B = 0$, the output can remain indefinitely in either a zero or a one state.

The next step in the analysis of the circuit's behaviour is to consider what happens if we modify the inputs A and B. We will assume that the X output is initially a logical one state.

If input B to gate G_2 goes high while input A remains low, the output of gate G_2 (i.e. Y) is unaffected, because the output of a NOR gate is low if either of its inputs are high. As X is already high, the state of B has no effect on the state of Y.

If now input A goes high while B remains low, the output, X, of gate G_1 must fall to a logical zero state. The inputs to a gate G_2 are now both in logical zero states, and its output Y rises to a logical one. However, as Y is fed back to the input of gate G_1, the output X is maintained at a logical zero if A goes to a zero. Thus, the effect of setting A to a one causes output X to flip over from a one to a zero, and to remain in that state when A returns to a zero. Table 3.1 provides a truth table for the circuit of Fig. 3.1. Two tables are presented—one appropriate to the circuit we have described and one with its inputs and outputs relabelled.

Table 3.1(a) corresponds exactly to the two NOR gates of Fig. 3.1, and Table 3.1(b) to the **idealized** form of this circuit which is called an RS flip-flop. There are two differences between Tables 3.1(a) and 3.1(b). Table 3.1(b) uses the **conventional** labelling of an RS flip-flop, with inputs R and S, and an output Q. The other difference is in the entry for the case in which $A = B = 1$, and $R = S = 1$. The effect of these differences will be dealt with later.

We have already stated that the circuit of Fig. 3.1 defines its output in terms of itself (i.e. $X = \overline{AB} + \overline{A}X$). The truth table approach gets around this problem by creating a **new** variable, X^+ (or Q^+), where X^+ is the new output corresponding to the **old** output X, and the current inputs A and B. Similarly, the equation can be re-written as $X^+ = \overline{AB} + \overline{A}X$. The input and

Table 3.1 Truth table corresponding to the circuit of Fig. 3.1
(a) Truth table for Fig. 3.1   (b) Relabelled truth table

| Inputs | | | Output | Inputs | | | Output |
A	B	X	X^+	R	S	Q	Q^+
0	0	0	0	0	0	0	0
0	0	1	1	0	0	1	1
0	1	0	1	0	1	0	1
0	1	1	1	0	1	1	1
1	0	0	0	1	0	0	0
1	0	1	0	1	0	1	0
1	1	0	0	1	1	0	?
1	1	1	0	1	1	1	?
↑			↑	↑			↑
Old X			New X	Old Q			New Q

The truth table is interpreted as follows. The output of the circuit is currently X (or Q), and the new inputs to be applied to the input terminals are A,B (or R,S). When these new inputs are applied to the circuit, its output is given by X^+ (or Q^+). For example, if the current output X is 1, and the new values of A and B are A=1, B=0, then the new output, X^+, will be 0. This value of X^+ then becomes the next value of X when new inputs A and B are applied to the circuit.

output columns of the truth table are now not only separated in space (e.g. input wires on the left and output wires on the right) but also in time. The current output X is combined with inputs A and B to generate a new output X^+. The value of X that produced X^+ no longer exists and belongs only to the past.

The labels R and S in Table 3.1(b) correspond to *reset* and *set*, respectively. The word 'reset' means 'make zero' (clear has the same meaning) and 'set' means 'make one'. The output of all flip-flops is called Q by a historical convention. Examining the truth table reveals that whenever R = 1, the output Q is *reset* to zero. Similarly, when S = 1 the output is *set* to one. When R and S are both zero, the output does not change. That is, $Q^+ = Q$.

If both R and S are simultaneously high, the output is conceptually undefined (hence the question marks in the truth table), as the output cannot be set and reset at the same time. In the case of the RS flip-flop implemented by two NOR gates, the output X does, in fact, go low when A = B = 1. In practice, the user of an RS flip-flop must avoid the condition R = S = 1. This statement is, perhaps, a little too harsh. It is possible to assert both the R and S inputs to an RS flip-flop simultaneously—if you know exactly how the flip-flop will behave under these circumstances.

The two-NOR-gate flip-flop of Fig. 3.2 has two outputs X and Y. An examination of the circuit for all inputs except A = B = 1 reveals that X and Y are complements. Because of the symmetric nature of flip-flops, almost all flip-flops have two outputs, Q and its complement $\overline{Q}$. However, the complement of Q may not always be available to the user of the flip-flop since many commercial devices leave $\overline{Q}$ buried on the chip and not brought out to a pin. Fig. 3.3 gives the circuit representation of an RS flip-flop.

There are two general ways of presenting the truth table of the RS, or any other, flip-flops. The truth tables presented so far are exhaustive in the sense that for each set of possible inputs two lines are needed, one for Q=0 and one for Q=1. An alternative approach is to employ the *algebraic* value of Q and is illustrated by Table 3.2.

When R=S=0 the new output, Q+, is simply the old output Q. In other words, the output does not change state and remains in its previous state as long as R and S are both 0. The inputs R=S=1 result in the output $Q^+ = X$. The special symbol X is used in truth tables to indicate an *indeterminate* (undefined) condition or, as we have already seen, a *don't care* condition. An *indeterminate* condition is one whose outcome cannot be calculated, while a *don't care* condition is one whose outcome does not matter to the designer.

3.1.1 Building an RS flip-flop from NAND gates

We can construct an RS flip-flop from two cross-coupled NAND gates just as easily as from two NOR gates. Figure 3.4 illustrates a two-NAND-gate flip-flop whose truth table is given in Table 3.3. The only significant difference between the NOR gate flip-flop of Fig. 3.1 and the NAND gate flip-flop of Fig. 3.4 is that the inputs to the NAND gate flip-flop are *active-low*. If we were to place inverters at the $\overline{R}$ and $\overline{S}$ inputs to the NAND gate flip-flop, it would then be logically equivalent to a NOR gate flip-flop.

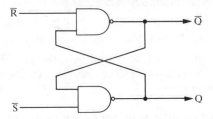

The *no-change* input to the NAND gate flip-flop is $\overline{R},\overline{S} = 1,1$; the output is cleared by forcing $\overline{R} = 0$ and set by forcing $\overline{S} = 0$; the *forbidden* input state is $\overline{R},\overline{S} = 0,0$. Suppose, however, that we did force the inputs of a NAND-gate RS flip-flop into the state 0,0 and then released the inputs to 1,1 to enter the no-change state. What would happen? The answer is that we cannot predict the final outcome. Initially, when both inputs are zero, the outputs of the RS flip-flop must *both* be logical ones (because the output of a NAND gate is a one if either of its inputs is a zero). The real problem arises when the inputs change state from 0,0 to 1,1. Due to tiny imperfections, either one or the other input would go high before its neighbour and cause the flip-flop to be set or reset.

Real applications of RS flip-flops may employ either two NAND or two NOR gates depending only on which gates provide the simpler solution. In practice, the majority of RS flip-flops are constructed from NAND gates because most circuits use active-low signals. We began our discussion of RS flip-flops with the NOR gate circuit (unlike other texts that introduce first the more common NAND gate flip-flop) because I have discovered that many students find it hard to come to terms with negative logic (i.e. logic in which the low state is the active state).

Fig. 3.3 The RS flip-flop.

Table 3.2 Alternative truth table for RS flip-flop

Inputs		Output	Description
R	S	Q^+	
0	0	Q	No change
0	1	1	Output set
1	0	0	Output clear
1	1	X	Forbidden

Fig. 3.4 RS flip-flop constructed from two NAND gates.

Table 3.3 Truth table of RS flip-flop constructed from two NAND gates

Inputs		Output	Comment
R	S	Q^+	
$\overline{0}$	$\overline{0}$	X	Forbidden
0	1	0	Clear
1	0	1	Set
1	1	Q	No change

Not that if $\overline{R}=\overline{S}=0$, the output is forced to 1.

3.1.2 Applications of the RS flip-flop

An important application of RS flip-flops is in the recording of short-lived events. If the Q output of a flip-flop is in a zero state, a logical one pulse at its S input (assuming the R input is zero) will cause Q to be set to a one, and to remain at a one, until the R input resets Q. A pulse and its effect on an RS flip-flop is illustrated in Fig. 3.5.

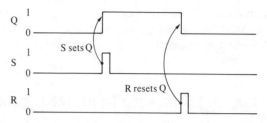

Fig. 3.5 The effect of a pulse on an RS flip-flop.

Consider the following application of RS flip-flops to an indicator circuit. If an aircraft is flown outside its *performance envelope* no immediate damage may be done, but its structure might be permanently weakened. To keep things simple, we will consider three possible events which are considered harmful and might endanger the aircraft:

1. Exceeding the maximum permissible speed V_{ne}.
2. Extending the flaps at speeds above the flap-limiting speed V_{fl}. That is, the flaps must not be lowered if the aircraft is going faster than V_{fl}.
3. Exceeding the maximum acceleration (g-force) G_{max}. If any of the above parameters are exceeded (even for only an instant), a lasting record of the event must be made.

Figure 3.6 shows the arrangement of warning lights to indicate that one of the above conditions has been violated. The acceleration and speed of the aircraft are measured by transducers that convert acceleration or velocity into a voltage. The voltages from the transducers are compared with the three thresholds (V_{ne}, V_{fl}, G_{max}) in comparators, whose outputs are true if the threshold is exceeded, otherwise false. In order to detect the extension of flaps above the flap-limiting speed, the output of the comparator is ANDed with a signal from the flap actuator circuits which is true when the flaps are down.

The signals from the comparators are fed, via OR gates, to the S inputs of three RS flip-flops. Initially, on switching on the system, the flip-flops are automatically reset by applying a logical one pulse to all R inputs simultaneously. If at any time one of the S inputs becomes true, the output of that flip-flop is set to a logical one and triggers an alarm. All outputs are ORed together to illuminate a master warning light. A master alarm signal removes the necessity of the pilot having to scan all the warning lights periodically. An additional feature of the circuit is a test facility. When the warning test button is pushed, all warning lights should be illuminated and remain so until the reset button is pressed. A test facility verifies the correct operation of the flip-flops and the warning lights.

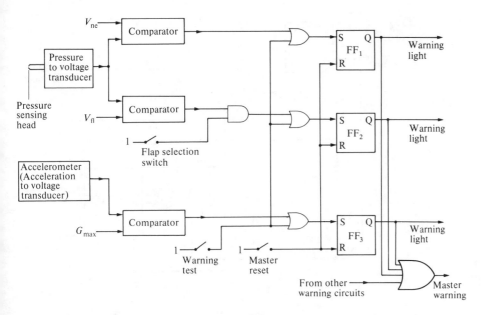

Fig. 3.6 The application of an RS flip-flop to a warning system.

A pulse-train generator

Another simple application of the RS flip-flop is illustrated by the pulse-train generator of Fig. 3.7, which generates a sequence of N pulses each time it is triggered. The value of N is user-supplied and is fed to the circuit by switches. Assume that initially the R and S inputs to the flip-flop are $R = 0$ and $S = 0$ and that its output Q is a logical zero.

When a logical one pulse is applied to the flip-flop's S (i.e. START) input, its Q output rises to a logical one and enables AND gate G_1. A train of clock pulses at the second input of G_1 now appears at the output of the AND gate. The gated pulse train is applied to the input of a *counter* (to be described later) which counts pulses and generates a three-bit output on Q_a, Q_b, Q_c, corresponding to the number of pulses counted in the range 0 to 7. The outputs of the counter are fed to an equality detector composed of three EOR gates G_2–G_4. A second input to the equality detector is C_a, C_b, C_c, and is user-supplied.

Initially the counter is in a reset state ($Q_a = Q_b = Q_c = 0$). As the counter counts upward from zero, the equality detector compares its output with the user-supplied inputs C_a, C_b, C_c. When the output of the counter is equal to the user-supplied input, the output of gate G_5 goes high and resets the RS flip-flop. Resetting the RS flip-flop has the effect of forcing the counter to zero and disabling the AND gate G_1. Therefore, no further clock pulses appear at the output of G_1. In this application of the RS flip-flop, its S input is triggered to start an action and its R input is triggered to terminate the action.

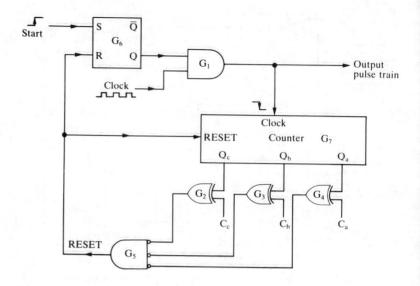

Fig. 3.7 The pulse-train generator.

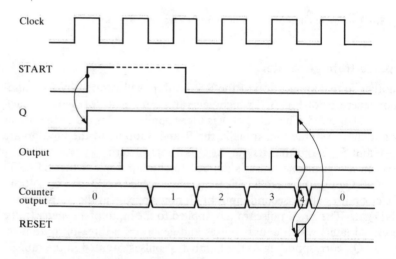

3.1.3 The clocked RS flip-flop

The RS flip-flop of Fig. 3.1 responds immediately to signals applied to its inputs according to its truth table. There are, however, situations when we want the RS flip-flop to ignore its inputs until a suitable time. The circuit of Fig. 3.8 demonstrates how this is accomplished.

In the inner box lies a normal, unmodified, RS flip-flop. Its inputs, R' and S', are derived from the external inputs R and S by ANDing them with a clock input C. As long as $C=0$, the inputs to the RS flip-flop, R' and S', are forced to remain at zero, no matter what is happening to R and S. While these R' and S' inputs are zero, the output of the RS flip-flop remains constant. Whenever $C=1$, the external R and S inputs to the circuit are transferred to the flip-flop so that $R'=R$ and $S'=S$, and the flip-flop responds accordingly. The clock input may be thought of as an inhibitor, restraining the flip-flop from acting until the right time. Figure

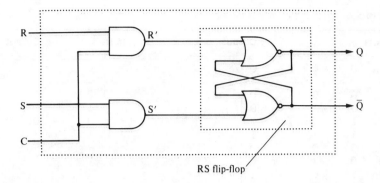

Fig. 3.8 The clocked RS flip-flop.

3.9 demonstrates how we can conveniently build a clocked RS flip-flop from NAND gates. The subject of clocked flip-flops is dealt with in more detail later in this section.

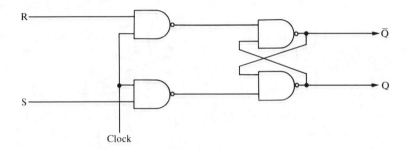

Fig. 3.9 Designing a clocked RS flip-flop with NAND gates.

3.2 The D flip-flop

Like the RS flip-flop, the D flip-flop has two control inputs, one called D and the other C. The D input is often referred to as the data input and C as the clock input. The D flip-flop is, by its nature, a clocked flip-flop and we will use the term '***clocking*** the D flip-flop' to refer to the act of pulsing the C input high and then low.

Whenever a D flip-flop is clocked, the value at its D input is transferred to its Q output and the output then remains constant until the next time it is clocked. Some people call the D flip-flop a ***staticizer*** because it records the state of the D input and holds it constant until it is once more clocked. Others call it a ***delay element*** because, if the D input changes state at time T but the flip-flop is clocked t seconds later, the output Q does not change state until t seconds after the input. I think of it as a census taker. When it is clocked it takes a census of the input and remembers it until the next census is taken. The truth table for a D flip-flop is given in Table 3.4.

The possible circuit of a D flip-flop is provided in Fig. 3.10 and consists of an RS flip-flop plus a few gates. The effect of the two AND gates is to turn the RS flip-flop into a clocked RS flip-flop. As long as the C input to the AND gates is low, the R and S inputs are clamped at zero and Q cannot change.

When C goes high, the S input is connected to D and the R input to $\overline{D}$.

Table 3.4 Truth table for a D flip-flop

Inputs			Output		Inputs		Output
C	D	Q	Q^+		C	D	Q^+
0	0	0	0		0	0	Q
0	0	1	0	No change	1	1	Q
0	1	0	1		0	0	0
0	1	1	1		1	1	1
1	0	0	0				
1	0	1	0	$Q^+ \leftarrow D$			
1	1	0	1				
1	1	1	1				

(alternative form)

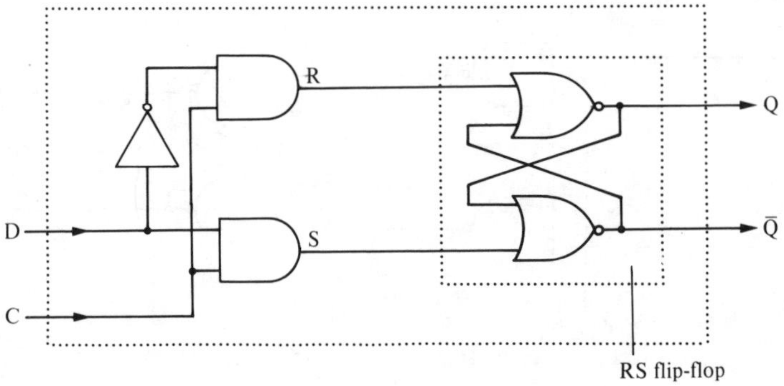

Fig. 3.10 The circuit of a D flip-flop.

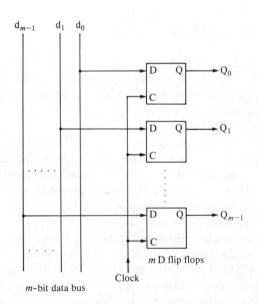

Fig. 3.11 An application of D flip-flops.

Therefore, (R,S) must be either (0,1) if D=1, or (1,0) if D=0. Consequently, D=1 sets the RS flip-flop, and D=0 clears it.

A typical example of the application of D flip-flops is provided by Fig. 3.11 in which an *m*-bit wide data bus transfers data from one part of a digital system to another. Data on the bus is constantly changing as different devices use it to transmit their data from one register to another.

The D inputs of a group of *m* D flip-flops are connected to the *m* lines of the bus. The clock inputs of all flip-flops are connected together, allowing them to be clocked simultaneously. As long as C = 0, the flip-flops ignore data on the bus and their Q outputs remain unchanged. Suppose some device wishes to transfer its data to the flip-flops. It first puts its data on the bus and then the flip-flops are clocked, latching the data into them. When the clock has returned to zero, the data remains frozen in the flip-flops. In Chapter 5 we shall discover that a computer is composed of little more than combinational logic elements, buses and groups of flip-flops called *registers* which transmit data to and receive data from buses.

3.3 Clocked flip-flops

We now take a break from describing flip-flops and look more closely at the idea of *clocking* sequential circuits. We have already briefly encountered the clocked D flip-flop and the clocked RS flip-flop. A flip-flop is described in two ways, firstly by its type (RS, D, JK), and secondly by the way in which it is clocked. A digital device, when clocked, responds to the signal at its inputs. The whole idea behind clocked circuits is to allow logic elements to respond to their inputs only when the inputs are valid.

Figure 3.12 demonstrates the effect of circuit delays on a system. Two inputs A and B are acted upon by *processes* A and B to produce signals that are fed to process C. The nature of the processes is not important since we are interested only in the way in which they delay signals passing through them. Imagine that at time *t* = 0, the inputs to processes A and B become valid (i.e. they are the correct inputs to be operated on by the

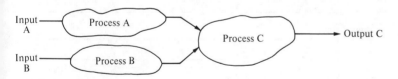

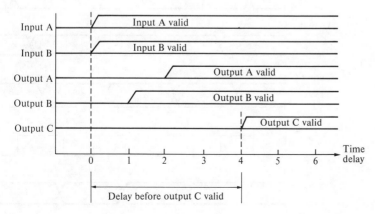

Fig. 3.12 Clocked systems.

processes). Assume that process A in Fig. 3.12 introduces a two-unit delay and process B a one-unit delay.

The outputs of processes A and B are fed to process C which has a two-unit delay. Clearly, the desired output from C due to inputs A and B is not valid until at least four time units after $t = 0$. The output at C changes at least once before it settles down to the intended value. This poses a problem. How does an observer at the output of process C know when to act upon the data from C?

If a D flip-flop is placed at the output of process C, and is clocked, say, four units of time after $t = 0$, the desired data will be latched into the flip-flop and held constant until the next clock pulse. Clocked systems hold digital information constant in flip-flops while the information is operated on by groups of logic elements, analogous to the processes of Fig. 3.12. Between clock pulses, the outputs of the flip-flops are processed by the logic elements and the new data values are presented to the inputs of flip-flops.

After a suitable time delay (longer than the time taken for the slowest process to be completed), the flip-flops are clocked. The outputs of the processes are held constant until the next time the flip-flops are clocked. A

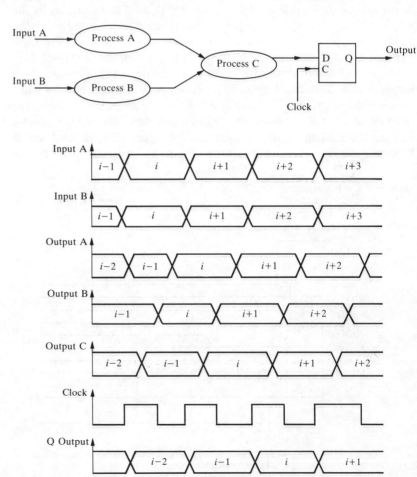

Fig. 3.13 The effect of latching the output of process C.

clocked system is often called *synchronous,* as all processes are started simultaneously on each new clock pulse. An *asynchronous* system is one in which the end of one process signals (i.e. triggers) the start of the next. Obviously, an asynchronous system must be faster than the corresponding synchronous system. Asynchronous systems are, however, more complex and difficult to design than synchronous systems and 'popular wisdom' says that they are best avoided because they are inherently less reliable than synchronous circuits.

The effect of adding a single D flip-flop at the output of process C is illustrated by the timing diagram of Fig. 3.13. Now consider the effect of placing D flip-flops at the outputs of processes A and B, and at the output of process C. Each of these flip-flops is clocked simultaneously every two units of time. Figure 3.14 gives the timing diagram for this version of our circuit with processes A, B, and C. In this case, we can see that a new input can be accepted every two units of time, rather than every four units of time as Fig. 3.13 would suggest. The secret of our increase in throughput is called *pipelining* because we are operating on different data at different

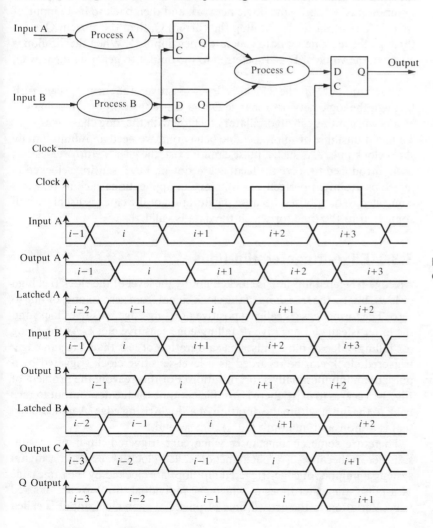

Fig. 3.14 Latching the input and output of all processes.

stages in the pipeline. For example, when process A and process B are operating on data i, process C is operating on data $i-1$ and the latched output from process C corresponds to data $i-2$.

Ways of clocking flip-flops

There are three types of clocked flip-flop:

1. level-sensitive
2. edge-sensitive
3. master–slave.

A *level-sensitive* clock triggers a flip-flop whenever the clock is in a particular logical state (some flip-flops are clocked by a logical one and some by a logical zero). The clocked RS flip-flop of Fig. 3.8 is level-sensitive because the RS flip-flop responds to its R and S inputs whenever the clock input is high. Unfortunately, a level-sensitive clock is unsuitable for certain applications. Consider the circuit of Fig. 3.15. The output of a D flip-flop is fed through a logic network and then back to its D input. If we call the output of the flip-flop the current Q, then the current Q is fed through the logic network to generate a new input D. When the flip-flop is clocked, the value of D is transferred to the output to generate the new Q, Q^+.

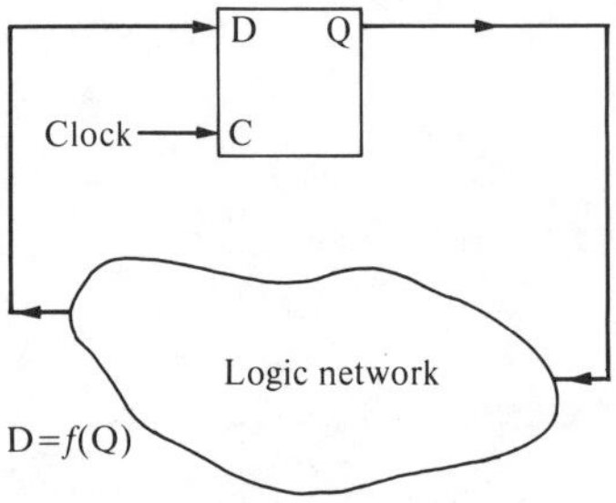

Unfortunately, if the clock is level-sensitive, the new Q can rush through the logic network, change D and hence the output. This chain of events will continue in an oscillatory fashion with the 'dog chasing its tail'. To avoid unstable or unpredictable behaviour, we need an infinitesimally short clock pulse. As such a pulse cannot exist, the *edge-sensitive* clock has been introduced to solve the feedback problem. Level-sensitive clocked D flip-flops are often perfectly satisfactory in applications such as registers connected to data buses, because the duration of the clock is usually small compared to the time for which the data is valid.

Fig. 3.15 Feedback and the level-sensitive clock.

3.3.1 Edge-triggered flip-flops

An edge-triggered flip-flop is clocked not by the level of the clock (i.e. high or low), but by the *transition* of the clock signal from zero to one, or one to zero. The former case is called a positive or rising-edge sensitive clock, and the latter is called a negative or falling-edge sensitive clock. As the rising (or falling) edge of most pulses has a duration of less than 5 ns, an edge-triggered clock can be regarded as a level-sensitive clock triggered by a pulse of an infinitesimally short duration. For this reason, the problem of Fig. 3.15 ceases to exist; there is insufficient time for the new output to race back to the input within the duration of a single rising edge. A nanosecond (ns) is a thousand millionth (10^{-9}) of a second.

There are some circumstances when edge-triggered flip-flops are unsatisfactory because of a phenomenon called clock *skew.* If, in a digital system, a number of edge-triggered flip-flops are clocked by the same edge of a pulse, the exact times at which the individual flip-flops are clocked vary. Variation in the arrival time of pulses at each clock input is called *clock skew* and is caused by the different paths by which clock pulses reach each flip-flop. Electrical impulses move through circuits at somewhat less than the speed of light, which is 30 cm per nanosecond. Unless each flip-flop is located at the same distance from the source of the clock pulse and unless any additional delays in each path due to other logic elements are identical, the clock pulse will arrive at the flip-flops at different instants. Suppose that the output of flip-flop A is connected to the input of flip-flop B, and they are nominally clocked together. Ideally, at the moment of clocking, the old output of A is clocked into B. If, by bad design or bad luck, flip-flop A is triggered a few nanoseconds *before* flip-flop B, B sees the *new* output from A, not the *old* (i.e. previous) output—it is as if A were clocked by a separate and earlier clock. A solution to this problem is provided by the *master–slave* clocked flip-flop.

3.3.2 The master–slave flip-flop

The master–slave (MS) flip-flop has the external appearance of a single flip-flop, but internally is arranged as two flip-flops operating in series. One of these flip-flops is called the *master* and the other the *slave.* On the rising edge of the clock pulse, the input data is copied into the master flip-flop (see Fig. 3.16). At this point, the output terminals of the MS flip-flop are not affected and do not change state (since they are derived from the slave flip-flop which is in a hold state since its clock is low). As the master flip-flop of Fig. 3.16 uses a level-sensitive RS flip-flop, the master responds to data at its RS inputs as long as $C=1$. The data at the RS inputs is latched by the master at the instant C goes low.

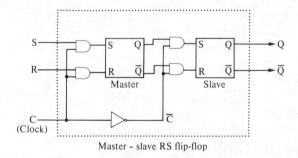

Master – slave RS flip-flop

Fig. 3.16 The master–slave RS flip-flop.

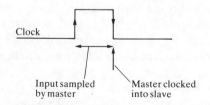

On the falling edge of the clock, data at the master's output terminals is copied into the slave flip-flop. Only now may the output terminals change state. Master–slave flip-flops totally isolate their input terminals from their output terminals, simply because the output of the slave flip-flop does not change until after the input conditions have been sampled and latched internally in the master. Conceptually, the master–slave flip-flop behaves like an air-lock in a submarine or space craft. An air-lock exists to transfer people between regions of different pressure (air-to-vacuum or air-to-water) without ever permitting a direct path between the two pressure regions. A flip-flop is analogous to an air-lock because its output must not be fed directly back to its input. To operate an air-lock in a submarine, divers in the water open the air-lock, enter and close the door behind them. The divers are now isolated from both the water outside and the air inside. When the divers open the door into the submarine, they step inside and close the air-lock door behind them.

In order to understand how the three different types of clocked flip-flop behave, consider Fig. 3.17, where for a given input waveform, the output waveforms for three different types of clocked D flip-flop are presented.

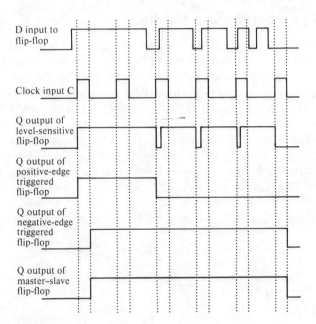

Fig. 3.17 A comparison of flip-flop clocking modes.

3.4 The JK flip-flop

The JK flip-flop is possibly the most useful of the flip-flops described here because it can be configured, or programmed, to operate in one of two modes. All JK flip-flops are clocked, and the majority of them operate on the master–slave principle. The truth table for a JK flip-flop is given in Table 3.5.

For all values of J and K, except J = K = 1, the JK flip-flop behaves exactly like an RS flip-flop with *J* acting as the *set* input, and *K* acting as the *reset* input. When J and K are both true, the output of the JK flip-flop *toggles,* or changes state, each time the flip-flop is clocked. That is, if Q was a zero it becomes a one, and vice versa. It is this property that puts the JK flip-flop at the heart of many counter circuits, the operation of which is

Table 3.5 Truth table for JK flip-flop

(a) Truth table for JK flip-flop					(b) Alternative form of truth table		
Inputs			**Output**		**Inputs**		**Output**
J	K	Q	Q^+		J	K	Q^+
0	0	0	0	No change	0	0	Q
0	0	1	1		0	1	0
0	1	0	0	Reset Q	1	0	1
0	1	1	0		1	1	$\bar{Q}$
1	0	0	1	Set Q			
1	0	1	1				
1	1	0	1	Toggle Q			
1	1	1	0				

(algebraic form)

dealt with in the next section. The logic symbol for a JK flip-flop is given in Fig. 3.18. Note that a **bubble** at the clock input to a flip-flop indicates that the flip-flop changes state on the falling edge of a clock pulse. Figure 3.19 demonstrates how a JK flip-flop can be constructed from NAND gates.

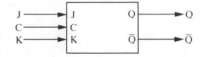

Fig. 3.18 The representation of the JK flip-flop.

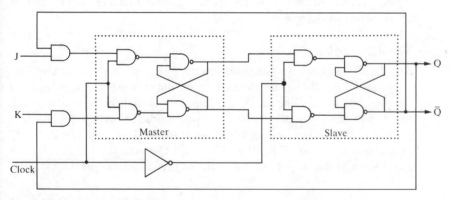

Fig. 3.19 Circuit of a JK flip-flop.

3.5 Summary of flip-flop types

Over the years I have been teaching students about the operation of flip-flops, I have discovered that some confuse the different types of flip-flop. Therefore, we are providing a summary of flip-flop behaviour here. To understand flip-flops, it is necessary to appreciate that, unlike combinational circuits, flip-flops have *internal states* as well as external inputs. That is, the output of a flip-flop depends on its internal state, which, in turn, depends on the previous inputs of the flip-flop. Flip-flops are therefore *memory elements.* The most common forms of flip-flop are the D flip-flop, the RS flip-flop and the JK flip-flop. Each flip-flop has two outputs, Q and its complement $\overline{Q}$, although the complementary output is not always connected to a pin in an integrated circuit. The majority of flip-flops are clocked and have a clock input which is used to trigger the flip-flop.

The D flip-flop

The D flip-flop is the easiest flip-flop to understand. D flip-flops have two inputs, a D (data) input and a C (clock) input. The output of a D flip-flop is constant (i.e. it remains in its previous state) until its C input is clocked. When its C input is clocked, its Q output becomes equal to D *until the next time it is clocked.*

The RS flip-flop

An RS flip-flop has two inputs, R (reset) and S (set), plus a third input, C (clock), if it is a clocked flip-flop. As long as both R and S are zero, the Q output of the RS flip-flop is constant and remains in its previous state. When R = 1 and S = 0, the Q output is forced to zero (and remains at zero when R returns to zero). When S = 1 and R = 0, the Q output is forced to one (and remains at one when S returns to zero). The input conditions R = S = 1 produce an indeterminate state and should be avoided by the user of the RS flip-flop. Clocked RS flip-flops behave as we have described, except that their R and S inputs are treated as zero until the flip-flop is clocked. When the RS flip-flop is clocked, its Q output behaves as we have just described.

The JK flip-flop

The JK flip-flop always has three inputs, J, K, and a clock input C. As long as a JK flip-flop is not clocked, its output is constant (i.e. remains in the previous state). When a JK flip-flop is clocked, it behaves like an RS flip-flop (when J = R, K = S) for all input conditions except J = K = 1. If J = K = 0, the output does not change state. If J = 1 and K = 0, the Q output is reset to zero. If K = 1 and J = 0, the Q output is set to one. If both J and K are 1, the output changes state (or toggles) each time it is clocked.

3.6 Applications of sequential elements

Just as the logic gate is combined with other gates to form combinational circuits such as adders and multiplexers, flip-flops can be combined together to create a class of circuits called sequential circuits. Here, we are concerned with two particular types of sequential circuit: the *shift register* and the *counter*.

3.6.1 Shift registers

We have already seen that a collection of *m* D-type flip-flops is able to store an *m*-bit word. By slightly modifying the circuit of the register we can build a *right-shift register*, a register whereby all the bits can be moved one place right every time the register is clocked. For example, the binary pattern.

01110101
becomes 00111010 after the register is clocked once
and   00011101 after it is clocked twice.

Note that a *zero* has been shifted in from the left-hand end, and the *one* at the right-hand end has been lost. I used the expression *binary pattern* above because, as we shall see later, the byte 01110101 can represent many things. However, when a pattern represents a fixed-point binary number, shifting it one place right has the effect of dividing the number by two (just as shifting a decimal number one place right divides it by ten).

Figure 3.20 demonstrates how a shift register can be constructed from D flip-flops. The Q output of each flip-flop is connected to the D input of the flip-flop on its right. All clock inputs are connected together so that each flip-flop is clocked simultaneously. When the ith stage is clocked, its output, Q_i, takes on the value from the stage on its left, that is, $Q_i \leftarrow Q_{i+1}$. Data presented at an external input, D_{in}, is shifted into the $(m-1)$th stage at each clock pulse.

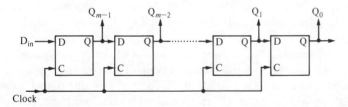

Fig. 3.20 A shift register.

An example of the operation of a 5-bit shift register is given in Fig. 3.21. In this case D_{in} is connected to a logical zero so that zeros are shifted into the left-hand stage, Q_4. It should be obvious that the flip-flops must either be edge-triggered or master–slave flip-flops, otherwise if a level-sensitive flip-flop were used, the value at the input to the left-hand stage would ripple through all stages as soon as the clock were high.

The output of the right-hand stage, Q_0, in Fig. 3.21 consists of a series of five sequential pulses, corresponding to the five bits of the word in the shift register (i.e. 11010). A shift register is often used to convert a parallel word of m bits into a serial word of m consecutive bits. Such a circuit is called a parallel-to-serial convertor. If the output of an m-bit parallel-to-serial convertor is connected to the D_{in} input of an m-bit shift register, after m clock pulses the information in the parallel-to-serial convertor has been

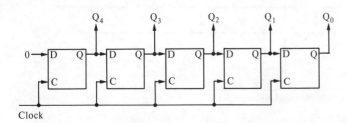

Fig. 3.21 An example of a shift register.

transferred to the second (right-hand) shift register. This shift register is called a serial-to-parallel convertor and is depicted in Fig. 3.22. Note that there is almost no difference between a parallel-to-serial convertor and a serial-to-parallel convertor. Many data-transmission systems (see Chapter 10) operate on this principle.

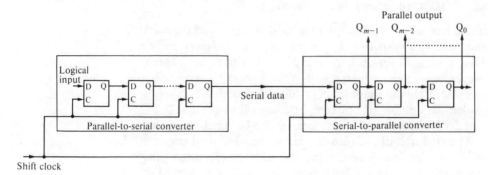

Fig. 3.22 The serial-to-parallel converter.

The only flaw in our shift register (when operating as a parallel-to-serial convertor) is the lack of any facilities for loading it with m bits of data at one go, rather than by shifting in m bits through D_{in}. A right-shift register with a parallel load capacity is shown in Fig. 3.23. A two-input multiplexer, composed of two AND gates, an OR gate and an inverter, switches the D input of a flip-flop between the output of the previous stage (shift mode), and the load input (load mode). The control inputs of all multiplexers are connected together, to form the mode control, labelled load/$\overline{\text{shift}}$. When we label a variable name1/$\overline{\text{name2}}$, we mean that when the variable is high it carries out action name1 and when it is low it carries out action name2. In the case above, if load/$\overline{\text{shift}}=0$ the operation performed is a shift and if load/$\overline{\text{shift}} = 1$ the operation performed is a load.

We can construct a shift register from JK flip-flops just as easily as from RS flip-flops as Fig. 3.24 demonstrates. I leave it as an exercise to the reader to work out how this arrangement operates. In a later section on computer instructions, it will be seen that there are a number of different

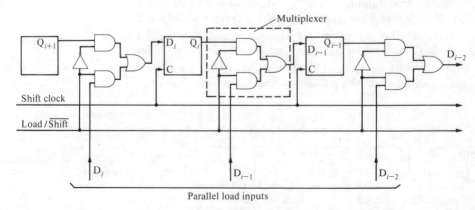

Fig. 3.23 A shift register with a parallel load capability.

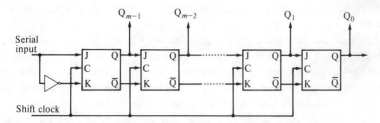

Fig. 3.24 A shift register composed of JK flip-flops.

types of shift (circular, arithmetic, logical). In practice, these other types of shift are all derived from the basic shift register described above. Although we have considered the right-shift register, a left-shift register is equally easy to design. The input of the ith stage, D_i, is connected to the output of the $(i-1)$th stage so that, at each clock pulse, $Q_i \leftarrow D_{i-1}$. In terms of the previous example:

$$01110101$$
$$\text{becomes } 11101010.$$

The structure of a left-shift register composed of JK flip-flops is described in Fig. 3.25.

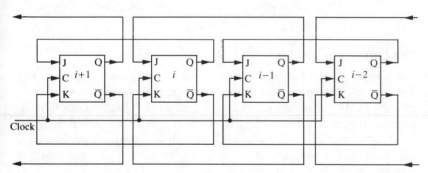

Fig. 3.25 The left-shift register.

3.6.2 Asynchronous counters

A counter is a special type of sequential circuit with a single clock input and a number of outputs. Each time the counter is clocked, one or more of the outputs change state. These outputs form a sequence with N unique values. After the Nth value has been observed at the counter's output terminals, the next clock pulse causes the counter to assume the same output as it had at the start of the sequence. That is, the sequence is cyclic. For example, a counter may display the sequence 01234501234501 ..., or the sequence 9731097310973 ... A counter composed of m flip-flops can generate an arbitrary sequence with a length of not greater than 2^m cycles before the sequence begins to repeat itself.

One of the tools frequently employed to illustrate the operation of sequential circuits is the ***state diagram.*** Any system with internal memory (e.g. the flip-flop) and external inputs can be said to be in a state which is a function of its internal and external inputs. A state diagram shows some (or all) of the possible states of a given system. Each of the states is normally represented by a labelled circle and the states are linked by unidirectional lines showing the paths by which one state becomes another state.

The state diagram of a JK flip-flop has only two states, S_1 and S_2 as we can see from Fig. 3.26. S_1 represents the state $Q=0$, and S_2 represents the state $Q=1$. Transitions between states are determined by the values of the JK inputs at the time the flip-flop is clocked. Table 3.6 defines the four possible input conditions, C_1, C_2, C_3, and C_4, in terms of J and K.

From Figure 3.26 it can be seen that conditions C_3 or C_4 cause a transition from state S_1 to state S_2. Similarly, conditions C_2 or C_4 cause a transition from state S_2 to state S_1. Note that condition C_4 causes a change of state from S_1 to S_2 and also from S_2 to S_1. This is, of course, the condition $J=K=1$ which causes the JK flip-flop to toggle its output. Note also, that some conditions cause a state to change to *itself*, that is, there is no overall change. Thus, conditions C_1 or C_2, when applied to the system in state S_1, have the effect of leaving the system in state S_1.

Table 3.6 Relationship between J,K and conditions C_1–C_4

J	K	Condition
0	0	C_1
0	1	C_2
1	0	C_3
1	1	C_4

Fig. 3.26 The state diagram of a JK flip-flop.

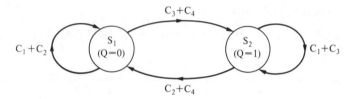

The binary up-counter

The state diagram of a simple three-bit binary up-counter is given in Fig. 3.27. In this example, there is only a single path from one state to its neighbour. As the system is clocked, it cycles through the states S_0 to S_7, which represent the natural binary numbers 0 to 7. The actual design of counters in general can be quite involved, although the basic principle is to ask 'what input conditions are required by the flip-flops to cause them to change from state S_i to state S_{i+1}?'

The design of an *asynchronous* natural binary up-counter is rather more simple than the general case (i.e. of a counter for an arbitrary sequence). A three-bit binary counter composed of JK flip-flops is given in Fig. 3.28, together with its timing diagram. The JK inputs to each flip-flop are connected to constant logical one levels. Consequently, whenever a flip-flop is clocked, its output changes state. The flip-flops are arranged so that the Q output of one device triggers the clock input of the next device (i.e. the output Q_i of stage i triggers the input of stage $i+1$). The flip-flops in Fig. 3.28 are master–slave clocked and their outputs change on the negative edge of the clock pulse.

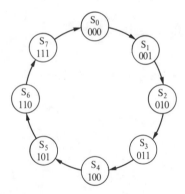

Fig. 3.27 The state diagram of a 3-bit counter.

The asynchronous binary up-counter of Fig. 3.28 is also called a ripple-counter because the output of the first stage triggers the input of the second stage and the output of the second stage triggers the input of the third stage, and so on. Consequently, a change of state at the output of the first stage *ripples through* the counter until it clocks the final stage.

The binary down-counter

Figure 3.29 demonstrates the effect of connecting the $\overline{Q}$ output of each

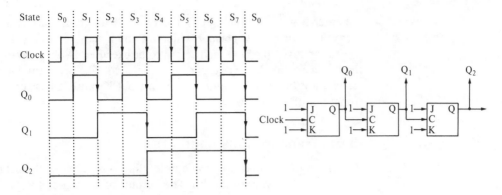

Fig. 3.28 The asynchronous binary counter.

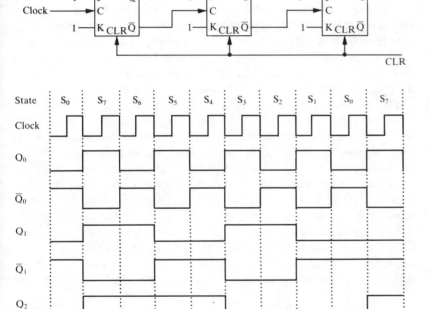

Fig. 3.29 The asynchronous binary down-counter.

stage in a ripple-counter to the clock input of the next stage. If we examine the timing diagram of this counter, we discover that it is a binary *down-counter* that counts backwards from 7 to 0.

Many flip-flops are rather more sophisticated than those described above (we shall see some examples of practical flip-flops later) and have additional inputs that force the output of the flip-flop into a known state. The JK flip-flops in the down-counter of Fig. 3.29 all have a CLR (i.e. clear) input that forces the Q output to zero whenever CLR is asserted. By connecting all CLR inputs together, we can reset the counter to zero by asserting CLR.

Counters find many applications in digital computers. Anticipating

Chapter 5 we will find that at the heart of all computers is a *program counter* or *instruction counter* which, at any instant, contains the number (i.e. address) of the next instruction to be executed. After each instruction has been executed, the counter is incremented. The program counter is so called, not because it counts programs, but because it has the circuit, or function, of a counter.

3.6.3 Synchronous counters

Synchronous counters are made up of flip-flops that are all clocked at the same time (i.e. synchronously). The outputs of all stages of a synchronous counter become valid at the same time (to a reasonable approximation) and the ripple-through effect associated with asynchronous counters is entirely absent. Synchronous counters can be easily designed to count through any arbitrary sequence just as well as the natural sequence $0,1,2,3,\ldots$.

We design a synchronous counter by means of a *state diagram* and the *excitation table* for the appropriate flip-flop (either RS or JK). An excitation table is nothing more than a version of a flip-flop's truth table arranged to display the input states required to force a given output transition. Table 3.7 illustrates the excitation table of a JK flip-flop. Suppose we wish to force the Q output of a JK flip-flop to make the transition from 0 to 1 the next time it is clocked. Table 3.7 tells us that the J,K input should be 1,d (where d = don't care). If we set J = 1 and K = 0, the flip-flop is *set* when it is clocked and Q becomes 1. If, however, we set J = 1 and K = 1, the flip-flop is toggled when it is clocked and the output Q = 0 is toggled to Q = 1. Clearly, the state of the K input does not matter when we wish to set Q^+ to 1 given that Q = 0 and J = 1. It should now be clear why all the transitions in the JK's excitation table have a don't care input. A given state can be reached from more than one starting point.

The next step in designing a synchronous counter is to construct a truth table for the system to determine the JK inputs required to force a transition to the required next state for each of the possible states in the table. It is much easier to explain this step by example rather than by algorithm.

Suppose we wish to design a synchronous counter to count through the natural sequence $0,1,2,3,4,5,6,7,8,9,0,\ldots$ (such a counter is called a binary coded decimal or modulo-10 counter). As there are ten states, we require four JK flip-flops because $2^3 < 10 < 2^4$. Table 3.8 provides a truth table for this counter.

To understand Table 3.8 it is necessary to look along a line and to say, 'Given this state and the next state, what must the inputs of the flip-flops be to force the transition to the next state?' For example, in the first line the current state is 0,0,0,0 and the next state is 0,0,0,1. The values for the four pairs of J,K inputs are obtained from the excitation table in Table 3.7. Three of these outputs cause the transition $0 \rightarrow 0$ and one causes the transition $0 \rightarrow 1$. Therefore, three pairs of J,K inputs required are 0,d (for the 0 to 0 transitions) and the other J,K input is 1,d for the 0 to 1 transition.

Table 3.7 Excitation table of a JK flip-flop

Inputs		Transition		
J	K	Q	$\rightarrow$	Q^+
0	d	0	$\rightarrow$	0
1	d	0	$\rightarrow$	1
d	1	1	$\rightarrow$	0
d	0	1	$\rightarrow$	1

Note that d denotes a *don't care* condition and indicates that the variable marked by a d may be a zero or a one state. For example, J=0, K=1 forces Q=1 into the state Q^+=0. Similarly, J=1, K=1 forces Q=1 into the state Q^+=0. Therefore we can say that the input conditions necessary to force the state Q=1 into Q^+=0 is J,K=d,1.

Table 3.8 Truth table for a synchronous counter

| | Outputs | | | | Next state | | | | Inputs | | | | | | | |
Count	Q_d	Q_c	Q_b	Q_a	Q^+_d	Q^+_c	Q^+_b	Q^+_a	J_d	K_d	J_c	K_c	J_b	K_b	J_a	K_a
0	0	0	0	0	0	0	0	1	0	d	0	d	0	d	1	d
1	0	0	0	1	0	0	1	0	0	d	0	d	1	d	d	1
2	0	0	1	0	0	0	1	1	0	d	0	d	d	0	1	d
3	0	0	1	1	0	1	0	0	0	d	1	d	d	1	d	1
4	0	1	0	0	0	1	0	1	0	d	d	0	0	d	1	d
5	0	1	0	1	0	1	1	0	0	d	d	0	1	d	d	1
6	0	1	1	0	0	1	1	1	0	d	d	0	d	0	1	d
7	0	1	1	1	1	0	0	0	1	d	d	1	d	1	d	1
8	1	0	0	0	1	0	0	1	d	0	0	d	0	d	1	d
9	1	0	0	1	0	0	0	0	d	1	0	d	0	d	d	1
10	1	0	1	0	X	X	X	X	X	X	X	X	X	X	X	X
11	1	0	1	1	X	X	X	X	X	X	X	X	X	X	X	X
12	1	1	0	0	X	X	X	X	X	X	X	X	X	X	X	X
13	1	1	0	1	X	X	X	X	X	X	X	X	X	X	X	X
14	1	1	1	0	X	X	X	X	X	X	X	X	X	X	X	X
15	1	1	1	1	X	X	X	X	X	X	X	X	X	X	X	X

Note that the ds in the table correspond to don't care conditions due to the excitation table of the JK flip-flop. The Xs correspond to don't care conditions due to unused states (the counter never enters states 1010 to 1111). There is, of course, no fundamental difference between X and d. I have chosen different symbols in order to distinguish between the *origins* of the don't care states.

From the truth table of the synchronous counter we can write down eight Karnaugh maps for the Js and Ks. Figure 3.30 gives the Karnaugh maps for this counter. These maps can be simplified to give:

$$J_d = Q_c Q_b Q_a \qquad K_d = Q_a$$
$$J_c = Q_b Q_a \qquad K_c = Q_b Q_a$$
$$J_b = \overline{Q_d} Q_a \qquad K_b = Q_a$$
$$J_a = 1 \qquad K_a = 1$$

We can now write down the circuit diagram of the synchronous counter (Fig. 3.31). The same technique can be employed to construct a vounter that will step through any arbitrary sequence. We will revisit this technique when we look at state machines.

3.7 Practical sequential logic elements

Just as some of the semiconductor manufacturers have provided a range of combinational logic elements in single packages, they have done the same with sequential logic elements. Indeed, there are far more special-purpose sequential logic elements than combinational logic elements. Figure 3.32 gives an indication of just two of the many flip-flops available in a single DIL package (a pair of edge-triggered D flip-flops and a pair of JK flip-flops). Practical flip-flops are more complex than those presented hitherto in this chapter. Real circuits have to cater for real-world problems. We have already said that the output of a flip-flop is a function of its current inputs and its previous output. What happens when a flip-

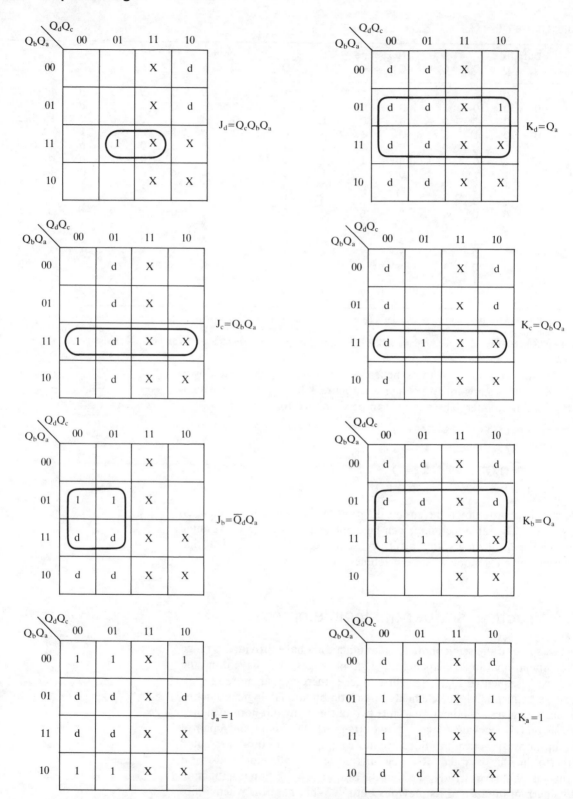

Fig. 3.30 Karnaugh maps for a synchronous counter.

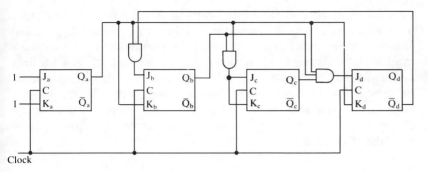

Fig. 3.31 Circuit diagram of a synchronous counter.

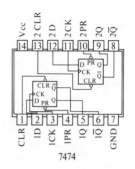

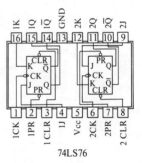

74LS74 function table

Inputs				Outputs	
$\overline{PR}$	$\overline{CLR}$	Clock	D	Q	$\overline{Q}$
0	1	X	X	1	0
1	0	X	X	0	1
0	0	X	X	1	1
1	1	↑	1	1	0
1	1	↑	0	0	1
1	1	0	X	Q_0	$\overline{Q}_0$

74LS76 function table

Inputs					Outputs	
$\overline{PR}$	$\overline{CLR}$	Clock	J	K	Q	$\overline{Q}$
0	1	X	X	X	1	0
1	0	X	X	X	0	1
0	0	X	X	X	1	1
1	1	↓	0	0	Q_0	$\overline{Q}_0$
1	1	↓	1	0	1	0
1	1	↓	0	1	0	1
1	1	↓	1	1	Toggle	Toggle
1	1	1	X	X	Q_0	$\overline{Q}_0$

Note: The entries ↑ or ↓ in the 'clock' column correspond to a rising
or falling edge respectively

Fig. 3.32 Some flip-flops available in DIL packages.

flop is first switched on? The answer is quite simple. The Q output takes on a random state, assuming no input is being applied that will force Q into a 0 or 1 state.

Random states may be fine at the gaming tables in Monte Carlo; they are less helpful when the control systems of a nuclear reactor are first energized. For this reason, many flip-flops are provided with special control inputs that are used to place them in a known state. The 74LS74, a dual positive-edge triggered D flip-flop illustrated in Fig. 3.32, has two active-low control inputs called preset and clear (abbreviated $\overline{PR}$ and $\overline{CLR}$). In normal operation both $\overline{PR}$ and $\overline{CLR}$ remain in logical one states. If $\overline{PR} = 0$ the Q output is set to a logical one, and if $\overline{CLR} = 0$ the Q output is cleared to a logical zero. As in the case of the RS flip-flop, the condition $\overline{PR} = \overline{CLR} = 0$ should not be allowed to occur.

These preset and clear inputs are unconditional in the sense that they override all activity at the other inputs of this flip-flop. For example, asserting $\overline{PR}$ will set Q to 1 irrespective of the state of the flip-flop's C and D inputs. When a digital system is made up from many flip-flops, which must be set or cleared at the application of power, their $\overline{PR}$ or $\overline{CLR}$ lines are connected to a common $\overline{RESET}$ line and this line is momentarily brought to a logical zero level by a single pulse shortly after the power is switched on. Note that the active-low $\overline{PR}$ and $\overline{CLR}$ inputs of the 74LS76 JK flip-flop behave in exactly the same way as the corresponding inputs in the 74LS74 D flip-flop.

The register

It is possible to obtain single DIL packages containing several flip-flops connected together to implement a register. Figure 3.33 illustrates the 74LS373, an octal D flip-flop, which is available in a 20-pin DIL package with eight inputs, eight outputs, two power-supply pins and two control inputs. The clock input, G, is a level-sensitive clock, which, when high, causes the value at D_i to be transferred to Q_i. All eight clocks are connected together internally so that the G input clocks each flip-flop simultaneously.

The 74LS373's other control input is called $\overline{OUTPUT\ ENABLE}$, which we will abbreviate to $\overline{OE}$. When $\overline{OE} = 0$, the flip-flop behaves exactly as we would expect. When $\overline{OE} = 1$, the eight Q outputs are internally disconnected from the output pins of the device. That is, the 74LS373 has tri-state outputs and $\overline{OE}$ is used to turn off the chip's output circuits when it is not driving a bus.

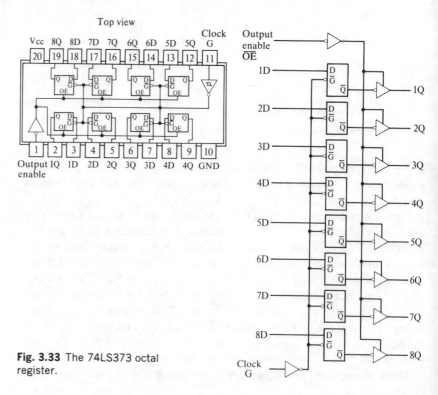

Fig. 3.33 The 74LS373 octal register.

Figure 3.34 demonstrates how the 74LS373 octal register might be used in a computer or some similar digital system: Four 74LS373 octal registers are connected to a common data bus. Each register is arranged so that both its outputs and its inputs are connected to the same bus. Consequently, each register can transmit data onto the bus or receive data from the bus. Four control lines are connected to the register's $\overline{OE}$ inputs so that the output circuits of the registers can be enabled individually. Each of these four lines is connected to one of the outputs of a 74LS139 2-line to 4-line decoder. Note that the 74LS139 contains *two* complete 2-line to 4-line decoders in a single 16-pin package. Thus, for each of the four possible 2-bit codes at the inputs to the 74LS139 one (and only one) of the 74LS139's outputs is asserted active low and therefore only one of the registers has its outputs enabled.

The two-bit binary *source* code at the input of IC5a causes one of its output lines to go low and hence forces the corresponding octal register to

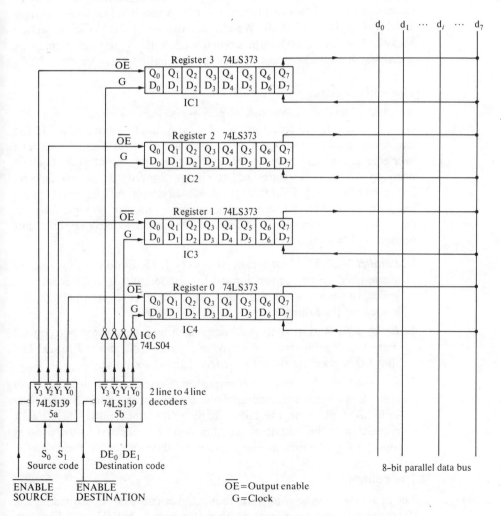

Fig. 3.34 A register array using 74LS373 octal D flip-flops.

put its output onto the data bus. For example, if the source code at the input to IC5a is 01, register 1 has its output enabled and the contents of register 1 are placed on the bus. The outputs of all other registers remain internally disconnected from the bus.

A second 2-line to 4-line decoder, IC5b, in conjunction with four inverters, converts a 2-bit *destination* code into one of four active-high lines. For each of the four possible codes at the input to IC5b, one of the four lines connected to the G inputs of the registers goes high, clocking that register.

Whenever the two decoders are enabled, the source code selects the register putting data onto the bus and the destination code selects the register receiving the data. If the contents of register 1 are to be copied into register 3, the source code is set to 01 and the destination code to 11. The two decoders are enabled and the data transfer is made. We can easily relate the example of Fig. 3.34 to the digital computer. One of the most fundamental operations in computing is the *assignment* which can be represented in a high-level language as B: = A and in a low-level language as MOVE A,B or LDA B. We can see from Fig. 3.34 that the action MOVE A,B (i.e. transfer the contents of A to B) is implemented by specifying *A* as the source and *B* as the destination.

The shift register

Another widely available special-purpose sequential circuit is the shift register. The internal structure, pin-out, and function table of a 74LS95 parallel-access bidirectional shift register are given in Figure 3.35. The user accesses the shift register through its pins and cannot make connections to the internal parts of its circuit. Indeed, its actual *internal* implementation may differ from the *published* circuit. As long as it behaves like its published circuit, the precise implementation of its logic function does not matter to the end user. The 74LS95 is a particularly versatile shift register and has the following functions.

1. *Parallel load.* The four bits of data to be loaded into the shift register are applied to its parallel inputs, the mode control input is set to a logical one and a clock pulse applied to the clock 2 input. The data is loaded on the falling edge of the clock 2 pulse.

2. *Right-shift.* A shift right is accomplished by setting the mode control input to a logical zero and applying a pulse to the clock 1 input. The shift takes place on the falling edge of the clock pulse.

3. *Left-shift.* A shift left is accomplished by setting the mode control input to a logical one, and applying a pulse to the clock 2 input. The shift takes place on the falling edge of the clock pulse. A left-shift requires that the output of each flip-flop be connected to the parallel input of the previous flip-flop, and serial data entered at the D input.

The counter

The final type of special-purpose sequential circuit to be described here is the counter. There are a large number of counters available and Fig. 3.36

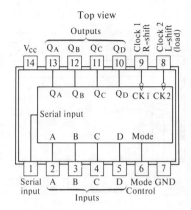

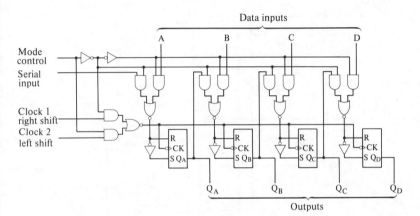

Fig. 3.35 The 74LS95 shift register.

illustrates a typical counter, the 74177 4-bit presettable binary counter. When we call a counter (or any other digital circuit) *presettable,* we mean that it can be loaded or initialized with predetermined data. In other words, we can preset its internal state by loading it from an external source. The pin-out of the 74177 is given in Fig. 3.36 together with its internal arrangement. Note that in Fig. 3.36 there is a T flip-flop. The T stands for *toggle,* because its output changes state every time it is clocked. The T flip-flop is functionally equivalent to a JK flip-flop with $J = K = 1$.

The counter is arranged as a divide by 2 stage followed by a divide by 8 stage. To divide by 16 (i.e. count from 0000 to 1111) it is necessary to connect the output of the first stage (Q_a) to the clock of the succeeding stages (clock 2). We do this by connecting pin 5 to pin 6 externally. The count input is applied to clock 1 and on each falling edge of the clock pulse the contents of the counter are incremented by one. The $\overline{\text{CLR}}$ input sets the value of each Q output to zero when $\overline{\text{CLR}} = 0$. The COUNT/$\overline{\text{LOAD}}$ input permits normal counting when high, and allows four bits to be loaded into the counter when low. This facility is used to preset the counter so that it counts up from I (rather than 0), where I is the value loaded into it.

We have now dealt with all the circuits needed to design a general-

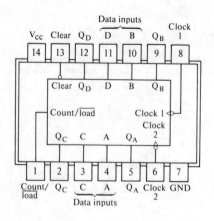

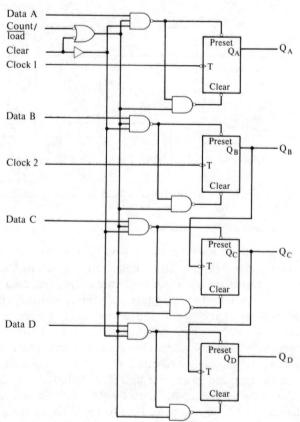

Fig. 3.36 The 74177 4-bit binary counter.

purpose digital computer. However, before we move on to a rather different topic, we should take a brief look at a topic that lays the foundation for a further course in sequential systems.

3.8 An introduction to state machines

No discussion of sequential circuits would be complete without at least a mention of ***state machines***. The state machine offers the designer a formal way of specifying, designing, testing and analysing sequential systems. Since the study of state machines is very much a second-level course in digital design, we shall simply introduce some of the basic concepts here.

It would be nearly impossible to find a text on state machines without encountering the general state machines called **Mealy** machines and **Moore** machines (after G. H. Mealy and E. Moore). Figure 3.37 illustrates the structure of a Mealy estate machine and Figure 3.38 the structure of a Moore state machine. Both machines have a combinational network that operates on the machine's inputs and on its **internal states** to produce a new internal state. The output of the Mealy machine is a function of the current inputs and the internal state of the machine, while the output of a Moore machine is a function of the internal state of the machine only.

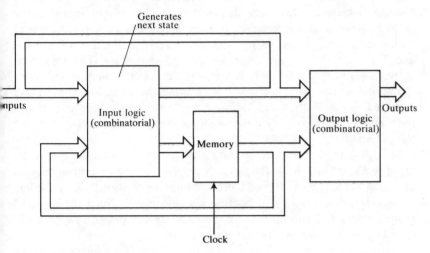

Fig. 3.37 The Mealy machine.

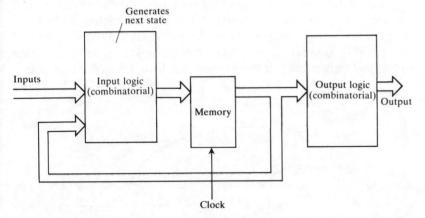

Fig. 3.38 The Moore machine.

Simple example of a state machine

As we have said above, the state-machine approach to the design of sequential circuits is by no means trivial. Here, we will design a simple state machine by means of an example.

Suppose we require a **sequence detector** that has an input X and an output Y. If a certain sequence of bits appears at the input of the detector, the output goes true. Sequence detectors are widely used in digital systems to split a stream of bits into units or *frames* by providing special bit patterns between adjacent frames and then using a sequence detector to identify the start of a frame.

In the following example we design a sequence detector that produces a true output Y whenever it detects the sequence 010 at its X input.

For example, if the input sequence is

000110011010110001011,

the output sequence will be

000000000001000000100.

We solve the problem by constructing a state diagram as illustrated in Figure 3.39. Each *circle* represents a particular state of the system and *transitions* between states are determined by the current input to the system at the next clock pulse. A state is marked name/value, where 'name' is the label we use to describe the state (e.g. A,B,C,D, in Fig. 3.39) and 'value' is the output corresponding to that state. The transition between states is labelled a/b, where a is the input condition and b the output value after the next clock. For example, the transition from state B to state C is labelled 1/0 and indicates that if the system is in state B and the input is 1, the next clock pulse will force the system into state C and set the output to 0.

State A is the initial starting state in Fig. 3.39. Suppose we record an input while in state A. If the input is a zero we may be on our way to detecting the sequence 010 and therefore we move to state B along the line marked 0/0 (the output is 0 because we have not detected the required sequence yet). If the input is 1, we return to state A because we have not even begun to detect the start of the sequence.

From state B there are two possible transitions. If we detect a zero we remain in state B because we are still at the start of the desired sequence. If we detect a one, we move on to state C (we have now detected 01). From state C a further one input takes us right back to state A (because we have received 011). However, if we detect a zero we move to state D and set the output to 1 to indicate that the sequence has been detected. From state D

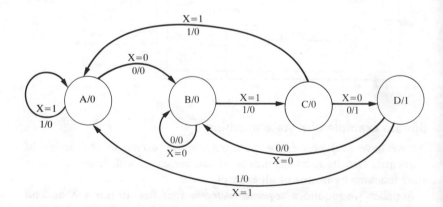

Fig. 3.39 State diagram for a 010 sequence detector.

we move back to state A if the next input is a one, and back to state B if it is a zero.

From the state diagram we can construct a state table that defines the output and the next state corresponding to each current state and input. Table 3.9 provides a state table for Fig. 3.39 and Table 3.10 expands Table 3.9 to provide numeric states 0,0 to 1,1 (i.e. Q_1, Q_2 where Q_1 and Q_2 are the outputs of flip-flops that hold the internal state). Finally, we can construct Table 3.11 to determine the JK input of each JK flip-flop that will force the appropriate state transition, given the next input X. Table 3.11 is derived by using the excitation table of the JK flip-flop (see Table 3.7). The final step is to create a circuit diagram from Table 3.11 (i.e. Fig. 3.40).

Now that we have introduced the idea of sequential systems, the next step in our introduction to logic systems is to consider some of the more *practical* considerations that interest the systems designer.

Table 3.9 State table for a 010 sequence detector

Current state	Output	Next state	
		X=0	X=1
A	0	B	A
B	0	B	C
C	0	D	A
D	1	B	A

Table 3.10 Modified state table for a sequence detector

State	Q_1	Q_2	Output	Next state	
				X=0	X=1
A	0	0	0	0,1	0,0
B	0	1	0	0,1	1,0
C	1	0	0	1,1	0,0
D	1	1	1	0,1	0,0

Table 3.11 Determining the JK inputs of the sequence detector

Current state			Next state		Inputs			
Q_1	Q_2	X	Q_1	Q_2	J_1	K_1	J_2	K_2
0	0	0	0	1	0	d	1	d
0	0	1	0	0	0	d	0	d
0	1	0	0	1	0	d	d	0
0	1	1	1	0	1	d	d	1
1	0	0	1	1	d	0	1	d
1	0	1	0	0	d	1	0	d
1	1	0	0	1	d	1	d	0
1	1	1	0	0	d	1	d	1

$J_1 = Q_1 + Q_2 X$ $K_1 = Q_2 + X$
$J_2 = \overline{X}$ $K_2 = X$

3.9 Practical considerations in logic design

Any student undertaking an introductory course in logic design or reading an elementary text on Boolean algebra may be left with the impression that designing a digital system involves little more than simplifying a few Boolean equations, turning the results into a circuit diagram and then putting it together. In practice this is not so.

In the real world the designer is subject to a number of constraints. The

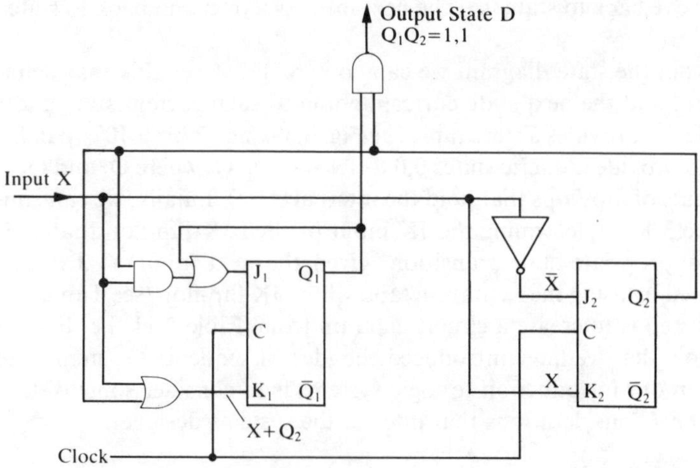

Fig. 3.40 Circuit of a 010 sequence detector.

logic elements available to designers are not only characterized in terms of Boolean algebra, they have other important properties that cannot be neglected. Moreover, the designer's employer is not interested in just any solution, he or she is interested in a cheap solution. The blind application of conventional Boolean algebra does not always lead to the most cost-effective solution to a problem. An astronaut was once asked how it felt to be strapped into his space capsule. He is reported to have replied, 'How would you feel sitting on top of a million critical components, each supplied by the company that put in the lowest bid?' Here we are going to take a brief look at some of the characteristics of logic elements that are of greatest interest to the design engineer. This is not intended to be a rigorous approach covering all the practical aspects of digital design, but is intended as an informal guide to some of the areas of digital design of interest to the engineer.

3.9.1 Electrical characteristics of gates

A glance at a manufacturer's data sheet for even the simplest of logic elements will reveal one or more pages of information. This data sheet is really a set of *promises* from the manufacturer to the user. The basic parameters of a typical logic element are given in Table 3.12.

Logic elements are produced by a number of different manufacturing processes. One of the basic types of logic element is called TTL (transistor–transistor logic), and a particular widely used variant of TTL is called low-power Schottky TTL (LS TTL). The actual details of the manufacture and the properties of various logic families are well beyond the scope of this book so we will just look at one representative member of this typical family. Microprocessors and memory elements are largely manufactured with NMOS or CMOS technologies. NMOS and CMOS chips can be connected to TTL logic elements (i.e. they employ similar signal levels).

The *operating temperature range* tells designers how cold or how hot they can let their equipment become without the characteristics of the logic element drifting outside their stated ranges.

Table 3.12 Sample data for a logic element (low-power Schottky TTL)

Temperature range (commercial)		0°C to +70°C			
Temperature range (military)		−55°C to +125°C			
Operating voltage		5 V±5 per cent			
Maximum ratings					
Storage temperature		−65°C to +150°C			
Supply voltage		−0.5 V to +7 V			
D.c. input current		−30 mA to +5.0 mA			
D.c. characteristics		Min	Typical	Max	
V_{OH}	output high voltage	2.7	3.4		V
V_{OL}	output low voltage			0.4	V
V_{IH}	input high voltage	2.0			V
V_{IL}	input low voltage			0.8	V
I_{IL}	input low current			−0.36	mA
I_{IH}	input high current			40	µA
I_{OH}	output high current			−400	µA
I_{OL}	output low current			+8	mA
Switching characteristics					
t_{LH}	low to high delay	10 ns (max)			
t_{HL}	high to low delay	12 ns (max)			

Considerations of temperature are frequently of little importance to the designers of domestic equipment where the environment is often maintained from approximately 10°C to 25°C. However, automobile manufacturers may find the thermal behaviour of logic elements one of their most important parameters. The manufacturers have to sell their cars in markets as far apart as Alaska and the Sahara.

The voltage characteristics of a logic element define the worst-case input and output conditions. Ideally, we would like logic elements to have logical zero outputs of 0 V and logical one outputs of +5 V (i.e. the power-supply level) to provide the greatest discrimination between digital signals. The LS TTL logic element of Table 3.12 does not display maximum discrimination between its logical zero and logical one states. For example, V_{OL} is the maximum output voltage when the output is in a low-level state. If V_{OL} is quoted as 0.4 V, it implies that the output for a logical zero may lie anywhere in the range 0 V to 0.4 V. The low-level output will never be greater than 0.4 V unless, of course, the device is faulty.

Similarly, V_{IL} defines the maximum input voltage that an element will reliably recognize as a logical zero. A V_{IL} of 0.8 V means that an input in the range 0–0.8 V is guaranteed to be interpreted as a logical zero. Note that V_{IL} is quoted as 0.8 V and V_{OL} as 0.4 V. The difference between these two figures is called the *noise margin* of the device. If we know that an output in a low state will be 0.4 V or less, and that an input will see a voltage of up to 0.8 V as a low state, then up to 0.4 V may be added to the output without any error occurring. The *additional* 0.4 V allows for noise in the system. Noise is the general term given to all unwanted signals.

Another important set of electrical parameters consists of those concerning the flow of current between gates. In an ideal world no current would flow between gates. Unfortunately, for the input of a gate to maintain a given logic level it must absorb some current from the gate driving it. That is, from the output to which it is connected. For example, from Table 3.12 it can be seen that the maximum input current into a gate in a high state, I_{IH}, is 40 μA (40×10^{-6} A).

The maximum current into an output in a logic one state, I_{IH}, is given as -400 μA. The minus sign indicates that current flows *out of* the gate. This is because, by convention, current flowing into a gate is defined as positive. Current flows into an output in a logical zero state, and out of an output in a logical one state. However, we frequently forget the sign of the current into or out of a gate, since we are usually more concerned with the magnitude of a current rather than its sign (i.e. direction).

A fundamental difference exists between I_{IH} and I_{OH}. While I_{IH} represents the current taken by the input of a gate, I_{OH} represents the maximum current which may be supplied by the output circuit of a gate. The actual output current of a gate will always be a value between 0 and I_{OH} or I_{OL}. When the output of a gate is connected to the input of another gate the output current of one gate must be exactly equal to the input current of the gate to which it is connected. A basic law of electronics states that the current flowing along a given path must be the same at all points along the path. Figure 3.41 illustrates the electrical conditions of a gate with a logical zero output driving two inputs, and the conditions of a gate with a logical one output driving four inputs.

When several inputs are connected to one output, the total current drawn by the inputs must not exceed the maximum current which the output can supply. If there are *n* inputs, it follows that I_{OH} must be greater

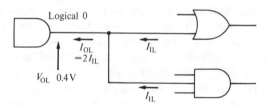

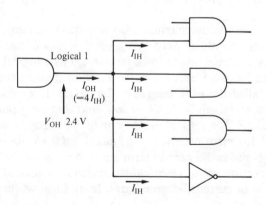

Fig. 3.41 The electrical characteristics of gates in the logical zero and the logical one states.

than, or equal to, nI_{IH} for reliable operation. For the example above, in the high-level state one output can supply enough current to drive $400/40 = 10$ inputs. The four basic equations which govern the electrical operation of gates are:

$$V_{OL} < V_{IL}$$
$$V_{OH} > V_{IH}$$
$$I_{OL} > nI_{IL} \text{ for } n \text{ inputs connected to one output}$$
$$I_{OH} > nI_{IH} \text{ for } n \text{ inputs connected to one output}$$

Effect of finite progapation delays on logic elements

Another important set of properties of all logic elements is their timing characteristics. Up to now it has been generally assumed that if a number of Boolean values are applied to the input terminals of an arrangement of gates, then the correct output (i.e. that determined by the Boolean equations of the gates) will appear instantaneously at the output of the circuit. This is not so. In general, a simple gate has a propagation delay of approximately 10 ns. One nanosecond is an unbelievably short period of time in human terms—but not in electronic terms. The propagation delay introduced by logic elements is one of the greatest problems designers have to contend with. We have already seen some of the effects of delays in Section 3.3 when we introduced clocked flip-flops.

Figure 3.42 illustrates the effects of propagation delay on a single inverter. A pulse with sharp (i.e. vertical) rising and falling edges is applied to the input of an inverter. An inverted pulse is produced at its output which is delayed with respect to the input pulse. Moreover, the edges of the output pulse are no longer vertical. The time t_{HL} is the time delay between the rising edge of the input pulse and the point at which the output of the gate has reached V_{OL}. Similarly, t_{LH} represents the time between the falling edge of the input and the time at which the output reaches V_{OH}.

It might be thought that the effect of time delays on the passage of signals through gates simply reduces the speed at which a digital system may operate. Unfortunately, propagation delays have more sinister effects, as shown by Fig. 3.43. By the rules of Boolean algebra the output of the AND gate should be permanently zero.

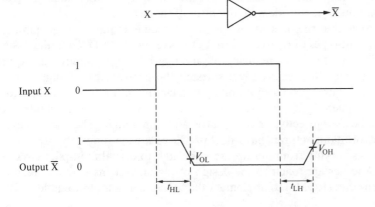

Fig. 3.42 The propagation delay of an inverter.

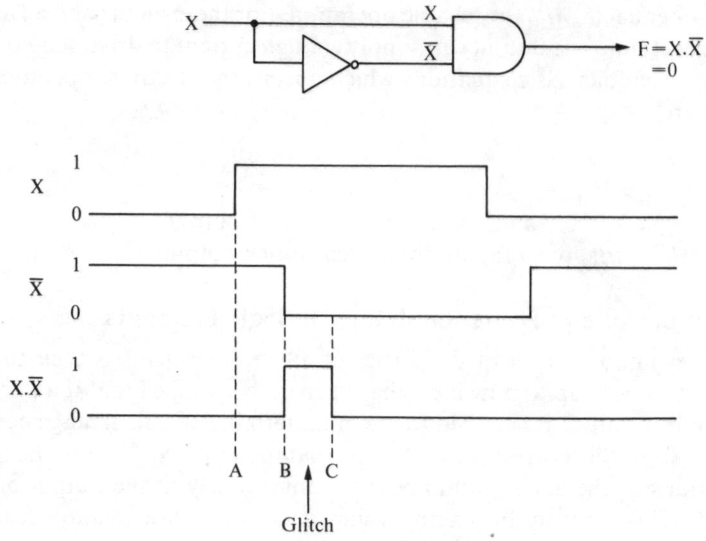

Fig. 3.43 The side-effect of propagation delay in a gate.

Now examine its timing diagram. At point A the input, X, rises from zero to one. However, the $\overline{X}$ input to the AND gate does not fall to zero until a time has elapsed equal to the propagation delay of the inverter. Consequently, for a short time the inputs of the AND gate are both true, and its output rises to a logical one from points B to C (after its own internal delay). The short pulse at the output of the AND gate is called a glitch, and can be very troublesome in digital systems. There are two solutions to this problem. One is to apply special design techniques to the Boolean logic to remove the glitch. The other is to connect the output to a flip-flop, and to clock the flip-flop after any glitches have died away.

3.9.2 Economic considerations of digital design

Economic considerations in designing digital systems vary widely with the application. For example, an engineer designing an on-board computer in a satellite is concerned largely with optimizing three parameters: weight, reliability, and power consumption. The designer of washing machine controllers may be concerned almost entirely with minimizing the cost of the circuit because a small saving multiplied by a large number of units amounts to a considerable quantity of money.

As all but the most trivial of digital circuits require a large number of different types of gate (two-input OR, five-input AND, etc.), the designer will look at ways of reducing the number of integrated circuits required. Sometimes the designer will sidestep the problem by asking, 'Has any manufacturer produced an integrated circuit with a function close to my requirements?' If the answer is yes, then a commercially available circuit can be used directly, or with a little additional logic. The major semiconductor manufacturers have now produced a wide range of basic building blocks varying from multiplexers through to digital multiplier circuits.

Another approach to the design of digital systems is to use read-only memories (ROMs) to implement the function as a look-up table. A ROM is a device with n-address input lines specifying 2^n unique locations within it. Each location, when accessed, produces an m-bit value on its m-output lines. It is called **read-only** because the output corresponding to a given input cannot be modified (i.e. written into) by the user.

Figure 3.44 shows how a 16×4 ROM implements the multiplier circuit of Fig. 2.20(b). The four address inputs X_1, X_0, Y_1, Y_0 select one of the sixteen possible locations, each containing a 4-bit word corresponding to the desired result. The manufacturer or user of the ROM writes the appropriate output into each of the sixteen locations. For example, the location 1011, corresponding to 10×11 ($=2 \times 3$), has 0110 ($=6$) written into it. The ROM directly implements not the circuit but the truth table. For each input the corresponding output is stored. The ROM look-up table does not even require Boolean algebra to simplify the sum-of-products expression derived from the truth table. Not only does a ROM look-up table save a large number of SSI and MSI logic elements, but the ROMs themselves can be readily replaced to permit the logic functions to be modified (to correct errors or to add improved facilities). Unfortunately, ROM look-up tables are limited to about seventeen inputs and eight outputs. (i.e. $8 \times 2^{17} = 1M$ bits).

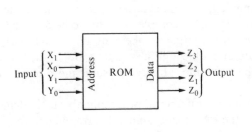

Input	Outputs
$X_1 X_0 Y_1 Y_0$	$Z_3 Z_2 Z_1 Z_0$
0000	0000
0001	0000
0010	0000
0011	0000
0100	0000
0101	0001
0110	0010
0111	0011
1000	0000
1001	0010
1010	0100
1011	0110
1100	0000
1101	0011
1110	0110
1111	1001

Fig. 3.44 Using a ROM to replace logic elements.

Yet another technique open to the designer involves **programmable logic**. General-purpose logic arrays (collections of different types of gate on a single chip) are now widely available. The chip contains a regular structure of basic gates that are interconnected to generate a certain class of logical expressions. By breaking links between the various gates, the chip can be configured to carry out a specific function. Links between gates are broken by passing a large current through them that destroys a fusible link. The digital designer selects the appropriate device from a manufacturer's catalogue and adapts the Boolean equations to fit the type of gates on the chip. The engineer then plugs the chip into a special programming machine which interconnects the gates in the desired way. Actually, the interconnections are there already, the programmer does not make new connections, but destroys unwanted connections.

Figure 3.45 illustrates how programmable logic devices operate. At the cross-points between the vertical and horizontal lines are tiny fuses. If the fuse is left intact an electrical connection exists, linking the vertical and

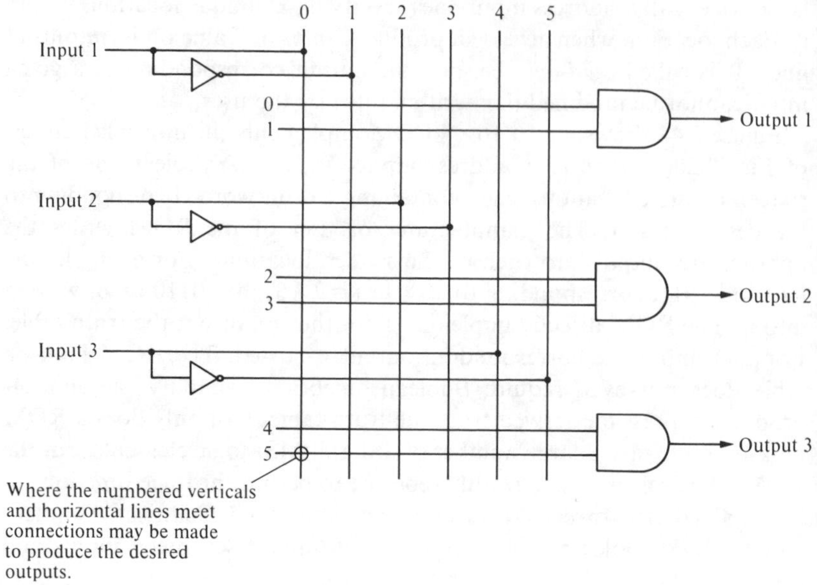

Fig. 3.45 A simplified example of programmable array logic.

Where the numbered verticals and horizontal lines meet connections may be made to produce the desired outputs.

horizontal lines. If a large pulse of current is passed through the fuse during the chip's programming, the link is broken because the fuse melts. Programmable logic elements enable complex systems to be designed and implemented without requiring large numbers of chips. Without the present generation of programmable logic elements, many of the low-cost microcomputers would be much more bulky, consume more power, and cost considerably more.

Today's designers have a large number of programmable logic elements at their disposal. There is the PAL (programmable array logic), the PLA (programmable logic array) and the PROM (programmable read-only memory). Figure 3.46 illustrates these logic elements, each of which contains an AND gate array and an OR gate array. The difference between the various types of programmable logic element depends on whether one or both of the AND or OR arrays are programmable. A programmable logic array is the most versatile device and contains both programmable AND and OR arrays. Many applications do not require such a versatile logic element and the programmable logic element with its fixed AND array and programmable OR array, or the programmable array logic with its fixed OR array and programmable AND array, are more suitable. Programmable logic elements are generally available in 20- or 24-pin packages, have 16 or more inputs/outputs and contain tens of gates.

Device manufacturers have now developed logic languages that can be run on small computers (e.g. PCs) which make it possible to program these programmable logic elements. That is, the operator can express the required functions in Boolean form and the software will generate the data necessary to program the device.

A recent innovation in programmable logic is the electrically programmable and erasable logic element. These can be programmed in a

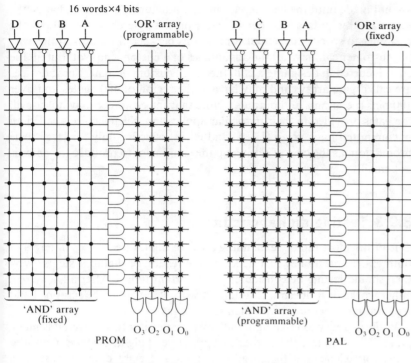

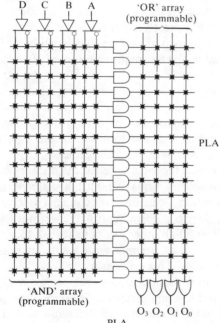

Fig. 3.46 Programmable logic element.

special machine and then erased and reprogrammed (if necessary). Reprogrammable logic elements represent a considerable saving at the design stage.

Programmable logic can be taken one step further. A large number of gates are fabricated on a chip, but the interconnections between the gates are not made until the last step in the manufacturing process. That is, the manufacturer puts a number of gates on a single chip and allows the customer to specify the actual connections between the gates. In this way the customer can have all the advantages of a custom chip without all the costs incurred in designing a chip (i.e. a full custom design). These devices are called gate arrays and may have in the region of 4000 gates and over 100 pins (i.e. inputs and outputs). Note that the customer may not use all the gates provided in their particular application. Such a chip is called an uncommitted logic array (ULA) and is cost-effective only for large-scale production, as the cost of setting up the equipment to produce the chips is not small.

3.9.3 Testing digital circuits

One of the most rapidly expanding areas of digital electronics in terms of both effort and money invested is in the testing of digital systems. Why then should testing be considered so important today? After all, a system either works or it doesn't. If it doesn't work it can easily be scrapped and replaced more economically than repairing it.

While it is easy to test a light bulb by plugging it into a socket, it is much more difficult to test all but the most primitive of digital systems. Consider a memory element with ten address lines and eight data outposts (i.e. 1K bytes). How many tests do we need to perform to verify that the memory is working correctly? Obviously the memory can be tested by writing a pattern into each of its $2^{10} = 1024$ locations and then reading the pattern back. That is, the test requires a total of 1024 read and 1024 write cycles.

But wait a moment. How do we know that the memory will store *every* possible data pattern at each possible word location? The test can be extended to include each location by writing all possible data values into a location before testing the next location. In this case there are $2^8 = 256$ tests/location, or $2^8 \times 2^{10} = 2^{18}$ tests altogether.

At last we have now thoroughly tested the memory component. No we have not! Some memories display a fault called *pattern sensitivity* in which writing data to location X can affect the contents of location Y. In order to eliminate errors due to pattern sensitivity, we must write a pattern to location X and then fill all other locations with Y to see if X is disturbed. So for each of our 2^{18} tests, we must write a different pattern in each of the other $2^{10} - 1$ word cells. This gives us a total of $2^{18} \times 2^{10}$ or 2^{28} tests.

The above example demonstrates that to test a digital system with external inputs and internal states is *effectively* impossible. Even if tests could be carried out at a rate of over 10 million/second, most reasonably complex digital systems (e.g. a microprocessor chip) would take longer to test than the anticipated life of the entire universe.

A way out of this dilemma is to seek tests that provide a reasonable level of confidence in their ability to detect a large fraction of possible faults without requiring an excessive amount of time. The first step in devising such tests is to distinguish between the idea of a *defect* and a *fault*. A real system fails because of a defect in its manufacture. For example, a digital system may fail because of a defect at the component level (a crystal defect in a silicon chip), or at the system level (a solder splash joining together two adjacent tracks on a printed circuit board). The observed failure is termed a *fault*.

Although there are an infinite number of possible defects that might cause a system to fail, their *effects* are relatively few. In simpler terms, an automobile may suffer from many defects, but many of these defects result in a single observable fault—the car does not move. That is, a *fault* is the observable effect due to a defect. Digital systems can be described in terms of *fault models* (i.e. the list of observable effects of defects). Typical faults are:

1. **Stuck-at-one.** The input or output of a circuit remains in a logical one state independently of all other circuit conditions. This is usually written s_a_1.

2. *Stuck-at-zero.* In this case the input or output is permanently stuck in a zero state (i.e. s_a_0).

3. **Bridging faults.** Two inputs or outputs of a circuit are effectively connected together and cannot assume independent logic levels. That is, they must both be zeros or ones.

It is possible to devise a longer list of fault models, but the stuck-at fault model is able to detect a surprisingly large number of defects. In other words, if we test a system by considering all possible stuck-at-1 and stuck-at-0 faults, we are likely to detect almost all of the probable defects.

The sensitive path test

A *sensitive path* between an input and an output is constructed to make the output a function of the input being tested (i.e. the output is sensitive to a change in the input). Figure 3.47(a) illustrates a path to be tested between input A and output K. Figure 3.47(b) demonstrates how we have chosen the sensitive path by ensuring that a change in input A is propagated through the circuit.

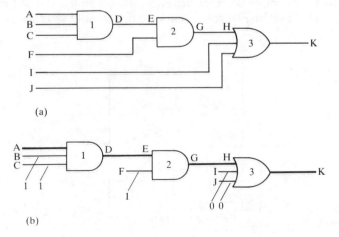

(a)

(b)

Fig. 3.47 (a) Testing a digital circuit; (b) establishing a sensitive path.

By setting inputs B and C to AND gate 1 high, input A is propagated through the gate to AND gate 2. Output D of AND gate 1 is connected to input E of the two-input AND gate 2. The second input of AND gate 2, F, must be set to 1 to propagate E through gate 2. Output G of AND gate 2 is connected to input H of the three-input OR gate 3. In this case, inputs I and J must be set to a logical zero to propagate input H (i.e. A) through the OR gate.

By setting inputs B,C,F,H,J to 1,1,1,0,0, the output K = A and therefore by setting A to 0 and then to 1, we can test the sensitive path between A and K and determine whether the A-stuck-at fault exists.

A *fault-list* can be prepared for the circuit which, in this case, might consist of A s_a_0, A s_a_1, B s_a_0, B s_a_1, ... A convenient notation for the fault list is: A/0, A/1, B/0, B/1, ... etc. The '/' is read as 'stuck at'.

To test for A s_a_0 (i.e. A/0), the other inputs are set to the values necessary to create a sensitive path and A is switched from 0 to 1. If the output changes state, A is not stuck at zero. The same test also detects A/1.

Fault tests are designed by engineers (possibly using CAD techniques) and can be implemented either manually or by means of computer-controlled automatic test equipment (ATE). This sets up the appropriate input signals and tests the output against the expected value. We can specify the sensitive path for A in the circuit of Fig. 3.47(b) as A.B.C.F.$\bar{I}$.$\bar{J}$.

It is not always possible to test digital circuits by the above means because of the *topological* properties of some digital circuits. For example, a digital signal may take more than one route through a circuit and certain faults may lead to a situation in which an error is cancelled at a particular node. Similarly, it is possible to have logic circuits that have an *undetectable* fault. Figure 3.48 provides an example of such a circuit. Note that this type of undetectable fault is due to redundancy in the circuit and can be eliminated by redesigning the circuit. Alternatively, a circuit can be made more easy to test by connecting some of its internal nodes to pins so that they can be directly examined.

Sequential circuits are particularly difficult to test, partially because flip-flops exhibit more complex behaviour than simple gates but mainly because they have *internal* states that cannot normally be observed from

Fig. 3.48 A circuit with an undetectable fault. In order to establish a sensitive path for internal node D, it is necessary to set inputs G and F to OR gate 5 to zero. G is set to zero by setting inputs A and B to 0,1. F is set to zero by setting imputs A and C to 1,1. Unfortunately, setting G and H to zero requires that input A be both 0 and 1 *simultaneously*. This is a contradiction and therefore node D cannot be tested for a stuck-at-zero fault.

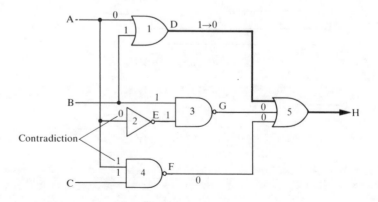

outside the circuit. One possible solution to the testing of sequential circuits is to design them with in-built test facilities. What this means is that the sequential circuit has a means of pre-loading its internal registers with known values and a means of observing the outputs of the flip-flops. In practice, four control signals might be used: a run/test input to force the normal mode or the test mode, a clock input that shifts data into or out of the circuit, and a serial input that can be used to pre-load the internal flip-flops and an output that can be used to observe the outputs of the internal flip-flops. Figure 3.49 illustrates a serial circuit with built-in test facilities.

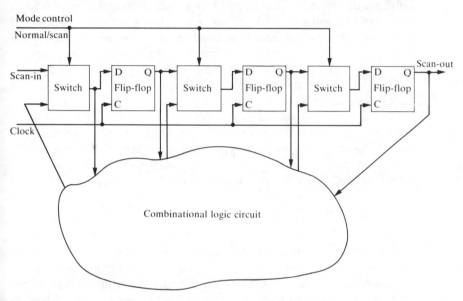

Fig. 3.49 Testing sequential circuits.

3.10 Computers and reliability

Reliability is one of the major factors in both the selection of components for incorporation in a computer, and in its actual design. The domestic consumer is often not directly conscious of the importance of *reliability*. When I go into camera shop, the salesperson says 'Nice job this, F1.4, self-focusing, automatic exposure, motor drive . . .'. I buy it. It breaks down a week later.

If I buy computer equipment for my employer, I don't ask the salesperson about irrelevant or frivolous features. Instead, I am concerned about its mean time between failure (MTBF) and its mean time to repair (MTTR), since professional equipment often has to operate continuously for long periods of time. Sometimes, the failure of such equipment is both expensive and embarrassing. At other times the failure is disastrous. For example, the failure of a computer in a time-sharing bureau leads to a direct loss of income and an additional loss in the form of goodwill, whereas the total failure of a computer operating control rods in an nuclear reactor is too frightening to contemplate. Before we deal with reliability formally, note the word *total* in the last sentence—later we shall see how systems can be made more reliable by choosing designs which tolerate a partial failure of the system.

There are two widely held personal theories of reliability: one is that demons live in all manufactured devices and that their aim is to cause a breakdown at the worst possible time. The other is that a device is programmed by its manufacturers to fail at the precise moment its guarantee ends. Neither of these theories is entirely true, as a device may fail from one of many causes, and it is almost impossible to say when a given device is going to fail. However, when dealing with large numbers of nominally identical devices, it is possible to say something about the *average* device. The reliability of a device is defined as $1 - p$, where p is the probability of its failure in a given time. For example, if there is a one in ten chance of a particular component failing within a year (i.e. $p = 0.1$), it may be said to be 90 per cent reliable.

Consider a very large number of components of which, after a time t, N are still working (the rest have failed). The change of N as a function of time is represented by dN/dt, and is negative because N is decreasing. The ratio of the rate of decrease of N to the population of working devices is called the failure rate, L, and is denoted by

$$L = \frac{-dN}{dt}/N.$$

The failure rate is often expressed in units of failures per cent per 1000 hours, although the period of time varies from application to application. For example, if a component is said to exhibit a failure rate of 0.003% per 1000 hours, a batch of 1 000 000 components can be expected to show 30 failures after 1000 hours of use.

From the above expression $dN/N = -L\,dt$. Assuming (for the moment) that the failure rate is constant, the expression can be integrated to give

$$\log N = -Lt + C, \text{ where } C \text{ is a constant of integration,}$$

or

$$N = e^{-Lt+C} = e^{-Lt} \times e^C = Ke^{-Lt}, \qquad \text{where } K = e^C.$$

K represents the initial number of components at $t = 0$, and is normally written N_0. We now have

$$N = N_0 e^{-Lt}.$$

Incidentally, this equation is also the same as the equation governing the decay of radioactive material. If we define the reliability, $r(t)$, of a batch of N_0 components as N/N_0 (that is the current survivors divided by the original population) then we can write

$$r(t) = \frac{N(t)}{N_0} = e^{-Lt}.$$

A more useful concept than failure rate is mean time between failure,

MTBF, because it gives an idea of the *expected* lifetime of a component. MTBF is defined as:

$$\frac{\sum_{i=1}^{N_0} \text{life of component } i}{N_0} = \int_0^\infty r(t)\,\mathrm{d}t.$$

Integrating this expression yields $\text{MTBF} = m = 1/L$.

Thus, $r(t) = e^{t/m}$. It should be noted that the mean time between failure, m is obtained by *measurement*. That is, the failure rate of a batch of components must be measured by observing their behaviour. Of course, the component you buy may not be a student of statistics, and may therefore fail at the earliest inconvenient moment.

While it is desirable to have components with a large MTBF, it is just as desirable to have components or systems that can be rapidly repaired when they do fail. Another useful parameter is the MTTR (mean time to repair), also called MTRF (mean time to repair a fault). These two parameters can be combined to give the availability or up-time ratio of a system. That is,

$$\text{availability} = \frac{\text{MTBF}}{\text{MTBF} + \text{MTTR}}.$$

We have assumed that the failure rate, L, and therefore m, is a constant. In practice, this is not entirely true. Figure 3.50 shows the classic *bath-tub* curve of the failure rate of a component as a function of time. The left-hand part of the curve is the *infant mortality* of the component and corresponds to the initial high failure rate in a batch of components due to manufacturing errors. The flat portion of the curve corresponds to a constant failure rate, and represents the useful life of the batch of components. The rise in failure rate at the end of the batch's lifetime corresponds to old age and is due to the wearing out of components.

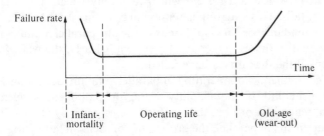

Fig. 3.50 The reliability curve.

It is now common for some manufacturers to *burn in* their components, before selling them. That is, the components are run, often at a high temperature to accelerate their ageing, to get them over the infant mortality region. Components failing during the burn-in period are discarded, and the buyer gets a more reliable component. Of course, components that have been burnt in are appreciably more expensive than components straight off the production line.

The failure of components is a function of *temperature* and it has been observed that an increase in the temperature of components reduces their reliability. Since the effect of temperature on reliability is remarkably predictable (this has been demonstrated by experiments and is in line with the thermal behaviour of molecules), it is possible to carry out *accelerated ageing* tests on components simply by raising their temperature.

3.10.1 Failure of systems of components

All the above would be useless to computer engineers if it could not be applied to groups of components to enable the designer to determine the overall failure rate of a system made up of many components with known failure rates.

Suppose a system is composed of two components R_1 and R_2. If we know that the reliability of these components is r_1 and r_2, respectively, we can calculate the reliability of the system. For this calculation we will assume that the system, as a whole, fails if either R_1 or R_2 fails.

The reliability of a system made up of components operating in series (i.e. one out, all out) is the product of their individual reliabilities. Thus, the reliability of our two-component system is $r = r_1 \times r_2$. For example, if R_1 is 99 per cent reliable and R_2 is 95 per cent reliable, then the overall reliability is $0.99 \times 0.95 = 0.94$, or 94 per cent. Note that this formula is reassuringly in line with common sense. The overall reliability is dependent on the lowest reliability in the expression—that is, the system is as good as its weakest link. The reliability of a system made up of links or components operating in series is given in Fig. 3.51.

Fig. 3.51 The reliability of components in series is the product of individual reliabilities. That is, $r = r_1 r_2 \ldots r_n$.

3.10.2 Increasing reliability through redundancy

It is possible to design a system which fails only when more than one component fails. This situation is represented by Fig. 3.52. Such a system involves redundancy or *back-up.* For example, the parallel modules in Fig. 3.52 may be disk drives in a computer system. Clearly, the whole system fails when all the disk drives have failed.

When components are operating in parallel, a failure occurs only when all components fail. If the reliability of the ith component is given by r_i, then its unreliability, or probability of failure, is given by $(1 - r_i)$. If there are n components in parallel, the probability of them all failing together is $(1 - r_1)(1 - r_2) \cdots (1 - r_n)$. Therefore, the reliability of the system is given by

$$1 - \text{system unreliability} = 1 - (1 - r_1)(1 - r_2) \cdots (1 - r_n).$$

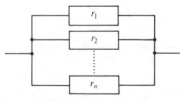

Fig. 3.52 Reliability of components in parallel = 1 − unreliability and is given by $1 - (1 - r_1)(1 - r_2) \ldots (1 - r_n)$.

Consider now the two components R_1 and R_2 with reliabilities 99 per cent and 98 per cent operating in parallel. The overall system reliability is

$$1 - (1 - 0.99)(1 - 0.98) = 1 - (0.01)(0.02) = 1 - 0.0002$$
$$= 0.9998 \text{ or } 99.98 \text{ per cent}$$

Notice how parallel components can have a dramatic effect on overall reliability. In practice there are slight penalties to be paid for using parallel systems, as the components, or pathways, linking the parallel modules may themselves fail.

In a real system the reliability can be calculated, and redundancy added, where necessary, to strengthen weak links in the chain. For example, consider the system illustrated in Fig. 3.53, which has an ALU, memory module, three VDUs, three disk controllers, and three disk drives. Table 3.13 provides the reliabilities of the individual components.

Table 3.13 Component reliability

Component	Reliability
VDU	0.98
CPU	0.999
Memory	0.8
Disk controller	0.995
Disk drive	0.8

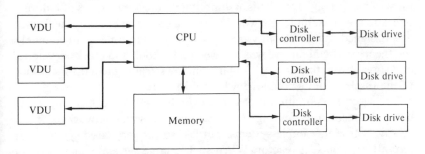

Fig. 3.53 A small computer system.

If it is assumed that the system will still give a reduced, but acceptable, level of service with just a CPU, memory module, and a single disk controller and associated drive, then Fig. 3.54 shows the system from a reliability point of view. The overall reliability is determined by four groups in series: the VDUs, the CPU, the memory, the disk controllers and disk drives. Note that the VDUs are in parallel as a failure occurs only when all three VDUs fail. Similarly, each disk controller or its associated disk drive must fail before the system fails.

The reliability of each of these four links is:

VDUs $\quad 1-(1-0.98)(1-0.98)(1-0.98)=1-0.000008=0.999992$
CPU $\quad 0.999$
Memory $\quad 0.8$
Disk drive and controller $\quad 1-(1-0.995 \times 0.8)(1-0.995 \times 0.8)$
$$(1-0.995 \times 0.8)$$
$$=1-(1-0.796)(1-0.796)(1-0.796)$$
$$=1-0.008495=0.9915.$$

The overall system reliability is given by the product of the individual reliabilities of the four links operating in series:

$$0.999992 \times 0.999 \times 0.8 \times 0.9915 = 0.7924 \quad \text{or} \quad 79 \text{ per cent.}$$

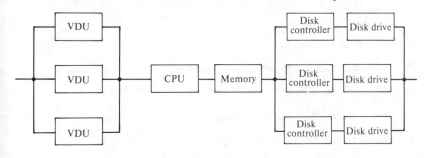

Fig. 3.54 The reliability of the computer in Fig. 3.53.

It should be appreciated that the above result is almost entirely dominated by the low reliability of the memory module. Suppose the manufacturer puts two memory modules in parallel. The reliability of the memory system would now be $1-(1-0.8)(1-0.8)$, or 0.96, and the reliability of the system 0.9509 or 95 per cent.

From what I have said above, reliability may look like a science. It is not. It is a black art. The computer designer or any other engineer should not grow too complacent. Reliability calculations are based on two assumptions. The first is that the reliability of a component is constant for most of its life (Fig. 3.50). This assumption ignores new modes of failure in operation. For example, the world's first passenger jet aircraft, the Comet, was designed using reliability theory known at that time. Unfortunately, the theory of metal fatigue was not well understood and cracks developed and spread from the aircraft's square windows, leading to a disintegration of the fuselage and a consequent loss of the aircraft.

The second assumption is that the overall reliability can be calculated using the techniques for Fig. 3.50 (parallel and serial networks). This is relatively true for simple systems, but less so for very large systems—an aircraft or a nuclear reactor. When such a large system is analysed, the analysis itself is made by an engineer operating under certain assumptions. Some of these may involve human behaviour. For example, the reliability of a system may depend strongly on its maintenance. If, because of economic pressures, the maintenance is not carried out according to the manufacturer's specifications, the reliability of the system will not match its reliability on paper.

Summary

In this chapter we have looked at the flip-flop that provides data storage facilities in a computer and which can be used to create counters and shift registers as well as more general forms of state machine.

We have also examined some of the topics that are of interest to the designer as well as the more mundane logical properties of a circuit. In particular, we have introduced the electrical properties of logic elements, their reliability and some of the problems of testing digital circuits.

Worked examples

Question 1

Design an 8-bit shift register to perform the following operations:

(a) load each stage from an 8-bit data bus (parallel load)

(b) logical shift left (0 in, MSB lost)

(c) logical shift right (0 in, LSB lost)

(d) arithmetic shift left (same as logical shift left)

(e) arithmetic shift right (MSB replicated, LSB lost)

(f) circular shift left (MSB moves to LSB position)

(g) circular shift right (LSB moves to MSB position).

The circuit is composed of eight master–slave JK flip-flops and has a clock input which causes operations (a)–(g) above to be carried out on its falling edge. There are five control inputs:—

R   When R = 1 shift right, when R = 0 shift left.
S   When S = 1 perform a shift operation, when S = 0 a parallel load.
L   When L = 1 perform a logical shift (if S = 1).
A   When A = 1 perform an arithmetic shift (if S = 1).
C   When C = 1 perform a circular shift (if S = 1).

Note that illegal combinations of L, A, and C cannot occur, and therefore more than one of L, A, and C, will never be true simultaneously.

For all eight stages of the shift register obtain algebraic expressions for J and K in terms of R, S, L, A, C, and the outputs of the flip-flops.

Solution 1

Figure 3.55 illustrates five stages of the shift register. These are the end stages Q_7 and Q_0, the most significant and least significant-bit stages, respectively. A non-end stage, Q_i, together with its left-hand neighbour (Q_{i+1}) and its right-hand neighbour (Q_{i-1}) must also be considered.

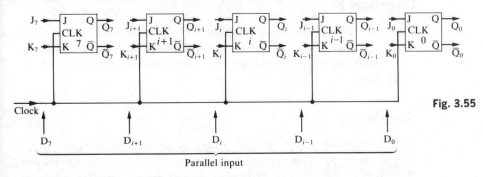

Fig. 3.55

All stages except 0 and 7 perform the same functions: parallel load, shift right and shift left. As the JK flip-flops always load data from one source or another, only the inputs J = 1, K = 0, or J = 0, K = 1 have to be considered. Consequently, $J = \overline{K}$, and we need only derive an expression for J, as the corresponding value for K can be obtained from an inverter.

Stage i

Parallel load $J_i = D_i$ $S = 0$
Shift right $J_i = Q_{i+1}$ $S = 1$, $R = 1$
Shift left $J_i = Q_{i-1}$ $S = 1$, $R = 0$

Therefore, $J_i = \overline{S}D_i + S(RQ_{i+1} + \overline{R}Q_{i-1})$

Stage 0 (LSB)

Parallel load		$J_0 = D_0$	$S = 0$
Shift right	logical	$J_0 = Q_1$	$S = 1$, $R = 1$, $L = 1$
	arithmetic	$J_0 = Q_1$	$S = 1$, $R = 1$, $A = 1$
	circular	$J_0 = Q_1$	$S = 1$, $R = 1$, $C = 1$
Shift left	logical	$J_0 = 0$	$S = 1$, $R = 0$, $L = 1$
	arithmetic	$J_0 = 0$	$S = 1$, $R = 0$, $A = 1$
	circular	$J_0 = Q_7$	$S = 1$, $R = 0$, $C = 1$

$$\text{Therefore, } J_0 = \overline{S}D_0 + S(RLQ_1 + RAQ_1 + RCQ_1 + \overline{R}L0 + \overline{R}A0 + \overline{R}CQ_7)$$
$$= \overline{S}D_0 + S(RQ_1 + \overline{R}CQ_7).$$

This expression simplifies because $L + A + C$ must be true as one type of shift, or another, must be taking place if $S = 1$.

Stage 7 (MSB)

Parallel load		$J_7 = D_7$	$S = 0$
Shift right	logical	$J_7 = 0$	$S = 1$, $R = 1$, $L = 1$
	arithmetic	$J_7 = Q_7$	$S = 1$, $R = 1$, $A = 1$
	circular	$J_7 = Q_0$	$S = 1$, $R = 1$, $C = 1$
Shift left	logical	$J_7 = Q_6$	$S = 1$, $R = 0$, $L = 1$
	arithmetic	$J_7 = Q_6$	$S = 1$, $R = 0$, $A = 1$
	circular	$J_7 = Q_6$	$S = 1$, $R = 0$, $C = 1$

$$\text{Therefore, } J_7 = \overline{S}D_7 + S(RL0 + RAQ_7 + RCQ_0 + \overline{R}LQ_6 + \overline{R}AQ_6 + \overline{R}CQ_6)$$
$$= \overline{S}D_7 + S(R(AQ_7 + CQ_0) + \overline{R}Q_6)$$

Question 2

Design a 4-bit asynchronous ripple-through decade-counter to count from 0 to 9 cyclically. Use JK master–slave flip-flops with an unconditional active-low clear input. Provide a timing diagram to illustrate the operation of the circuit.

Solution 2

A decade counter can be derived from a binary counter by resetting it to zero at the appropriate point. A four-stage binary counter counts from 0000 to 1111 (i.e. 0 to 15). To create a decade counter the state ten (1010) must be detected and used to reset the flip-flops.

Fig. 3.56

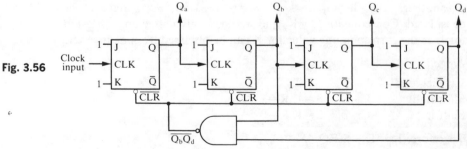

The binary counter counts normally from 0 to 9. On the tenth count $Q_d = 1$, and $Q_b = 1$. This is detected by the NAND gate whose output goes low, resetting the flip-flops. The count of ten exists momentarily.

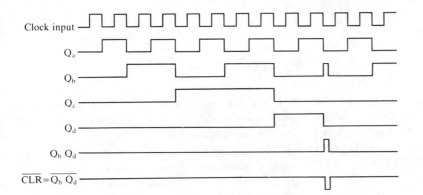

Fig. 3.57

Note that the reset pulse must be long enough to reset all flip-flops to zero. If the reset pulse were too short and, say, O_b was reset before Q_d, the output might be reset to 1000. The counting sequence would now be: 0,1,2,3,4,5,6,7,8,9,(10),8,9,8,9, ... However, such a problem is unlikely to occur in this case, since the reset pulse is not removed until at least the output of one flip-flop and the NAND gate has changed state. The combined duration of flip-flop reset time plus a gate delay, will provide sufficient time to ensure that all flip-flops are reset. It is possible to imagine situations in which the circuit would not function correctly. Suppose the minimum reset pulse required to guarantee the reset of a flip-flop were 50 ns. Suppose also that the minimum time between the application of a reset pulse and the transition $Q \leftarrow 0$ were 10 ns, and that the propagation delay of a NAND gate were 10 ns. It would indeed be possible for the above error to occur. This example demonstrates the dangers of designing asynchronous circuits!

Problems

1. Explain why it is necessary to employ clocked flip-flops in sequential circuits (as opposed to unclocked flip-flops)? What are the three basic clocking modes and why is it necessary to cater for so many clocking modes?

2. Why have not D and RS flip-flops been replaced by the JK flip-flop, since the JK flip-flop can, apparently, do everything a D flip-flop or an RS flip-flop can do?

3. For the input and clock signals shown in Fig. 3.58, provide a timing diagram for the Q output of a D flip-flop. Assume that the flip-flop is

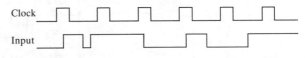

Fig. 3.58

(a) level sensitive;

(b) positive edge triggered;

(c) negative edge triggered;

(d) a master–slave flip-flop.

4. Assuming that the initial state of the circuit shown in Fig. 3.59 is given by C = 1, D = 1, P = 1, and Q = 0, complete the table. This question should be attempted by calculating the effect of the new C and D on the inputs to both cross-coupled pairs of NOR gates, and therefore on the outputs P and Q. As P and Q are also inputs to the NOR gates, the change in P and Q should be taken into account when calculating the effect of the next inputs C and D. Remember that the output of a NOR is 1 if both its inputs are 0, and is 0 otherwise.

Modify the circuit to provide a new input S which, when 1, will at any time set P to 1 and Q to 0. Provide another input R which will similarly set P to 0 and Q to 1. Note that R and S cannot both be a 1 at the same time, and therefore the condition R = S = 1 need not be considered.

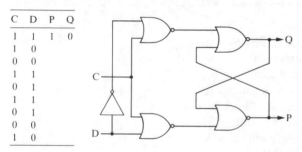

C	D	P	Q
1	1	1	0
1	0		
0	0		
1	1		
0	1		
1	1		
0	1		
0	0		
1	0		

Fig. 3.59

5. What additional logic is required to convert a JK flip-flop into a D flip-flop?

6. Demonstrate that the flip-flops shown in Fig. 3.60 are equivalent.

7. A T flip-flop has a single clock input and outputs Q and $\overline{Q}$. Its Q output toggles (changes state) each time it is clocked. The T flip-flop behaves exactly like a JK flip-flop with its J and K inputs connected permanently to a logical one. Design a T flip-flop using a D flip-flop.

8. Investigate the behaviour of the circuit shown in Fig. 3.61.

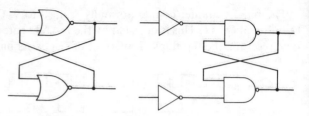

Fig. 3.60

9. Explain the meaning of the terms *asynchronous* and *synchronous* in the context of sequential logic systems. What is the significance of these terms?

10. Design a synchronous binary duodecimal (i.e. base 12) counter that counts through the natural binary sequence from 0 (0000) to 11 (1011) and then returns to zero on the next count. The counter is to be built from four JK flip-flops.

11. Design a modulo 13 counter using:

(a) JK flip-flops;

(b) RS flip-flops (with a master–slave clock).

12. Design a *programmable* modulo 10/modulo 12 synchronous counter using JK flip-flops. The counter has a control input, TEN/$\overline{\text{TWELVE}}$, which when high causes the counter to count modulo ten. When low, TEN/$\overline{\text{TWELVE}}$ causes the counter to count modulo 12.

13. How would you determine the maximum rate at which a synchronous counter could be clocked?

14. Design a simple digital time-of-day clock that can display the time from 00:00:00 to 23:59:59. Assume that you have a clock pulse input derived from the public electricity supply of 50 Hz (Europe) or 60 Hz (USA).

15. The circuit in Fig. 3.62 represents a *Johnson* counter. This is also called a *twisted* ring counter because feedback from the last (rightmost) stage is fed back to the first stage by crossing over the Q and $\overline{Q}$ connections. Investigate its operation.

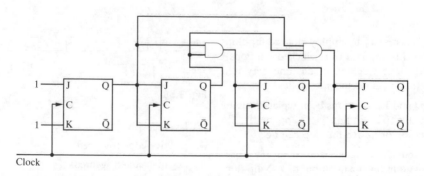

Clock

Fig. 3.61

Fig. 3.62

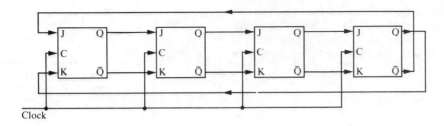

Fig. 3.63

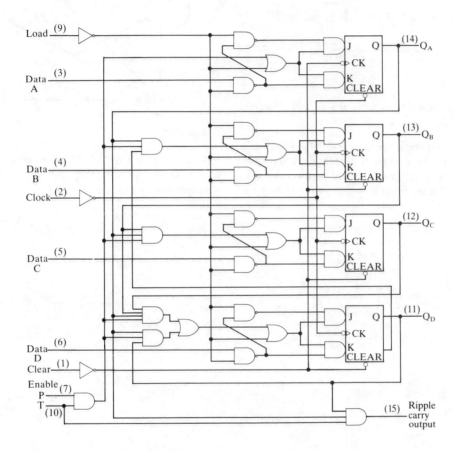

16. Figure 3.63 shows a 74162 synchronous decade (i.e. modulo 10) counter. Investigate its operation. Explain the function of the various control inputs. Note that the flip-flops are master–slave JKs with asynchronous (i.e. unconditional) clear inputs.

17. What are the most important constraints on the designer who is working on:

(a) a washing machine controller;

(b) the on-board navigation computer of a space probe;

(c) a controller in a pacemaker for surgical implantation.

18. Design a counter using JK flip-flops to count through the following sequence.

Q_2	Q_1	Q_0	
0	0	1	
0	1	0	
0	1	1	
1	1	0	
1	1	1	
0	0	1	sequence repeats

19. Investigate the action of the circuit shown in Fig. 3.64 when it is presented with the input sequence 111000001011111. The first bit is the right-most bit. Assume that all flip-flops are reset to Q=0 before the first bit is received.

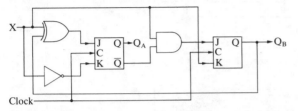

Clock

Fig. 3.64

20. Design a state machine to implement the state diagram shown in Fig. 3.65.

21. A highly reliable computer has five CPU modules each with a probability of failure of 0.01 per cent per 1000 hours. If the system gives an acceptable level of performance with at least three CPUs operational, what is the reliability of the system?

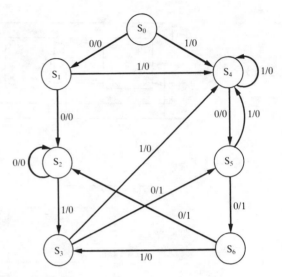

Fig. 3.65

A computer has an MTBF of 5000 hours. If a given system uses one of these computers, what is the probability of failure due to a failure of the CPU over a period of 100 hours?

Computer arithmetic

4

Because of the ease with which binary logic elements can be manufactured and because of their remarkably low price, it was inevitable that the binary number system was chosen to represent numerical data within a digital computer. In this chapter we are going to examine how numbers are represented in digital computers, how they are converted from one base to another, and how they are manipulated within the computer. We begin with an examination of binary codes in general and show how patterns of ones and zeros can represent a wide range of different quantities.

The main theme of this chapter is the class of binary codes used to represent numbers in digital computers. We look at how numbers are converted from the familiar decimal form to binary form and vice versa. In the middle of the chapter we take a break from numeric data and examine briefly codes that enable the computer to determine whether data has been corrupted (i.e. inadvertently modified). Other topics included here are ways in which we represent and handle negative as well as positive numbers and how we perform simple arithmetic operations in assembly language. We also look at the way in which the computer deals with very large and very small numbers by means of a system called *floating point*. Finally, we introduce the operations of multiplication and division and demonstrate how they may be carried out.

4.1 Characters, words, and bytes

The smallest quantity of information that can be stored and manipulated inside a computer is the *bit*. Digital computers store information in their memories in the form of groups of bits called words. The number of bits per word varies from computer to computer. Typical computer word lengths are:

Cray-1 supercomputer	64 bits
ICL 1900 series mainframe	24 bits
UNIVAC 1100 mainframe	36 bits
PDP-11 minicomputer	16 bits
VAX minicomputer	32 bits

8085, Z80, 6502, 6809 microprocessors	8 bits
68000, 8086 microprocessors	16 bits
68020, 80386 microprocessors	32 bits
Typical microcontrollers	4 bits

A group of 8 bits has come to be known as a **byte**. Often a word is spoken of as being 2 or 4 bytes long, because its bits can be formed into 2 or 4 groups of eight, respectively. Microprocessors and minicomputers are normally byte-oriented with word lengths and addresses of 8, 16 or 32 bits. But beware—some early computers grouped bits into sixes and called them bytes. One of the greatest irritations of computer science is its flexible jargon. Some computer manufacturers have hijacked the term **word** and redefined it to mean a 16-bit value (as opposed to a byte which is an 8-bit value and a long word which they use to indicate a 32-bit value). Throughout this text we will use **word** to mean the basic unit of information operated on by a computer except when we are describing the 68000 microprocessor in the next chapter.

An n-bit word can be arranged into 2^n unique bit patterns and may represent many things, because there is no intrinsic meaning associated with a pattern of ones and zeros. The meaning of a particular pattern of bits is the meaning given to it by the programmer. As Humpty Dumpty said to Alice 'A word means exactly what I choose it to mean, nothing more and nothing less.' The computer itself cannot tell the meaning of the word, but simply treats it in the way the programmer dictates. For example, a programmer could read the name of a person into the computer and then perform an arithmetic operation on the pattern of bits representing the name (say multiply it by two). The computer would happily carry out the operation although the result would be meaningless. If this is not clear, consider the following example. In a Chinese restaurant, 46 represents **bamboo shoots** and 27 represents **egg fried rice**. If I were to ask for a portion of 73, I would be most unlikely to get egg fried rice with bamboo shoots!

The following are some entities a word may represent.

1. An **instruction.** An instruction or operation to be performed by the CPU is normally represented by a single word. The relationship between the bit pattern of the instruction and what it does is arbitrary and is determined by the designer of the computer. A particular sequence of bits that means **add A to B** to one computer might have an entirely different meaning to another computer. Some computers require two or more consecutive words to make up an instruction.

2. A **numeric quantity.** A word, either alone or as part of a sequence of words, may represent a numerical quantity. Numbers can be represented in one of many formats: BCD integer, unsigned binary integer, signed binary integer, BCD floating point, binary floating point, complex integer, complex floating point, double-precision integer etc. The meaning of some of these terms and the way in which the computer carries out its operations in the number system represented by the term will be examined later.

3. A *character*. There are many applications of computers in which text is input, processed, and the results printed. The most obvious and spectacular example is the word processor. Programs themselves are frequently in text form when they are first submitted to the computer. The alphanumeric characters (A–Z, a–z, 0–9) and the symbols *,−,+,!,?, etc. are assigned binary patterns so that they can be stored and manipulated within the computer. Fortunately, one particular code is now in widespread use throughout the computer industry called the ISO 7-bit character code. This is also known as the ASCII code (American Standard Code for Information Interchange), and represents a character by 7 bits, allowing a maximum of $2^7 = 128$ different characters. Of these 128 characters, 96 are the normal printing characters (including both upper and lower case). The remaining 32 characters are *non-printing*. These include carriage return, back-space, line feed etc. Table 4.1 defines the relationship between the bits of the ISO/ASCII code and the character it represents.

Table 4.1 The ISO character code

$b_3b_2b_1b_0$	$b_6b_5b_4$	0 000	1 001	2 010	3 011	4 100	5 101	6 110	7 111
0	0000	NUL	DLC	SP	0	@	P		p
1	0001	SOH	DC1	!	1	A	Q	a	q
2	0010	STX	DC2	''	2	B	R	b	r
3	0011	ETX	DC3	#	3	C	S	c	s
4	0100	EOT	DC4	$	4	D	T	d	t
5	0101	ENQ	NAK	%	5	E	U	e	u
6	0110	ACK	SYN	&	6	F	V	f	v
7	0111	BEL	ETB	'	7	G	W	g	w
8	1000	BS	CAN	(	8	H	X	h	x
9	1001	HT	EM	)	9	I	Y	i	y
A	1010	LF	SUB	*	:	J	Z	j	z
B	1011	VT	ESC	+	;	K	[	k	{
C	1100	FF	FS	,	<	L	\	l		
D	1101	CR	GS	−	=	M	]	m	}
E	1110	SO	RS	.	>	N	^	n	~
F	1111	SI	VS	/	?	O	−	o	DEL

Control characters ← → ← Printing characters →

We obtain the 7-bit ISO (ASCII) binary code for a character by reading the most significant three bits in the column in which it appears and the least significant four bits in the row in which it appears. Thus, the character W is in the 101 column and the 0111 row, so that its ISO code is 1010111 (or 57 in hexadecimal form). Similarly, the code for a carriage return (CR) is 0001101.

4. A *picture element.* One of the many entities that has to be digitally encoded is the picture or graphical display. Pictures vary widely in their complexity and there are a correspondingly large number of ways of representing pictorial information. For example, pictures can be *parameterized* and stored as a set of parameters. When the picture is to be displayed or printed, it is recreated from its parameters. There parameters are the ingredients of a picture and correspond to lines, arcs and polygons and their positions within the picture.

Another way of storing pictorial information is to employ symbols that can be put together to make a picture. Such an approach is

Teletext character codes

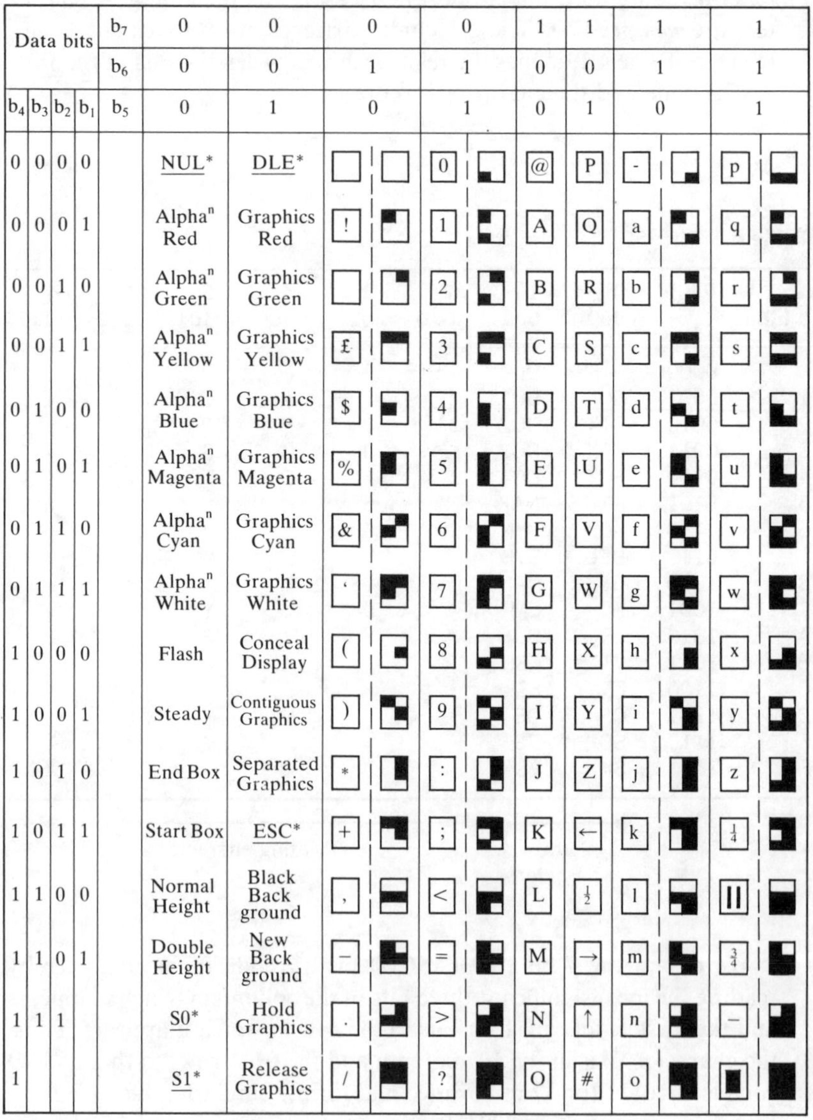

Data bits				$b_7=0$ / $b_6=0$ / $b_5=0$	$b_7=0$ / $b_6=0$ / $b_5=1$	$b_7=0$ / $b_6=1$ / $b_5=0$	$b_7=0$ / $b_6=1$ / $b_5=1$	$b_7=1$ / $b_6=0$ / $b_5=0$	$b_7=1$ / $b_6=0$ / $b_5=1$	$b_7=1$ / $b_6=1$ / $b_5=0$	$b_7=1$ / $b_6=1$ / $b_5=1$
b_4	b_3	b_2	b_1								
0	0	0	0	NUL*	DLE*		0	@	P		p
0	0	0	1	Alphaⁿ Red	Graphics Red	!	1	A	Q	a	q
0	0	1	0	Alphaⁿ Green	Graphics Green		2	B	R	b	r
0	0	1	1	Alphaⁿ Yellow	Graphics Yellow	£	3	C	S	c	s
0	1	0	0	Alphaⁿ Blue	Graphics Blue	$	4	D	T	d	t
0	1	0	1	Alphaⁿ Magenta	Graphics Magenta	%	5	E	U	e	u
0	1	1	0	Alphaⁿ Cyan	Graphics Cyan	&	6	F	V	f	v
0	1	1	1	Alphaⁿ White	Graphics White	'	7	G	W	g	w
1	0	0	0	Flash	Conceal Display	(	8	H	X	h	x
1	0	0	1	Steady	Contiguous Graphics	)	9	I	Y	i	y
1	0	1	0	End Box	Separated Graphics	*	:	J	Z	j	z
1	0	1	1	Start Box	ESC*	+	;	K	←	k	¼
1	1	0	0	Normal Height	Black Background	,	<	L	½	l	‖
1	1	0	1	Double Height	New Background	−	=	M	→	m	¾
1	1	1		S0*	Hold Graphics	.	>	N	↑	n	—
1				S1*	Release Graphics	/	?	O	#	o	■

Black represents display colour, and white represents background.
* These control characters are reserved for compatibility with other data codes.

Fig. 4.1 Encoding graphics symbols.

popular with small microprocessor systems and generally employs an 8-bit code to represent the symbols from which the picture is to be constructed. Teletext, Ceefax and Oracle pictures are all drawn in this way. Figure 4.1 illustrates a typical set of graphics symbols.

More complex and detailed pictures cannot readily be parameterized or reduced to a few fairly crude symbols. Often, the only way such a picture can be stored is as a bit-map. Any picture can be transformed into a rectangular array of *pixels* or picture elements. By analogy with the bit, a pixel is the smallest unit of information of which a picture is composed. Unlike a bit, the pixel can have *attributes* such as colour. Consider an A4 size picture (approximately 210 mm by 296 mm). If we wish to store a reasonably high definition A4 picture, we must use approximately 12 pixels/mm in both the horizontal and vertical axes. That is, 1 square millimetre is made up of $12 \times 12 = 144$ pixels and therefore the entire picture is composed of $210 \times 296 \times 144 = 8\,951\,040$ pixels. This represents over 1M bytes of storage. If the picture were *coloured* and each pixel could have one of 256 different colours, the total storage requirement would be over 8M bytes. From these parameters it should now be clear why high-quality computer graphics requires such expensive equipment. Typical high-quality colour video displays have a resolution of 1024 by 1024 (i.e. 2^{20} pixels) per frame. There are, however, rather complex techniques for *compressing* the amount of storage required by a picture. Such techniques operate by locating areas of a constant colour and intensity and storing the shape and location of the area and its colour. Encoding pictures in this way is similar to the ideas behind parameterizing that we discussed earlier.

4.2 Number bases

We represent numbers in the decimal system by means of positional notation. By *positional* we mean that the value or *weight* of a digit depends on its location within a number. As each digit moves one place left, it is multiplied by ten (the base or radix) and as it moves one place right it is divided by ten. Thus, the 9 in 95 is worth ten times the 9 in 59. If this seems obvious and not worthy of mention consider the Romans. They conquered most of the known world, invented Latin grammar, kept the lions well-fed, found time for the odd orgy or two, and yet their mathematics was terribly cumbersome. Because they did not use a positional system, each new large number had to have its own special symbol. Their number system was one of give and take so that if $X = 10$ and $I = 1$, then $XI = 11$ (i.e. $10 + 1$) and $IX = 9$ (i.e. $10 - 1$).

A number N when expressed in positional notation in the base b is written $a_n a_{n-1} a_{n-2} \cdots a_1 a_0 . a_{-1} a_{-2} \cdots a_{-m}$ and is defined as

$$a_n b^n + a_{n-1} b^{n-1} + \cdots + a_1 b^1 + a_0 b^0 + a_{-1} b^{-1} + a_{-2} b^{-2} + \cdots + a_{-m} b^{-m}$$

$$= \sum_{i=-m}^{n} a_i b^i.$$

The *a*s in the above equation are called *digits* and may have one of *b* possible values. Positional notation employs the *radix point* to separate the integer and fractional parts of the number. In decimal arithmetic we speak of the *decimal* point and in binary arithmetic we speak of the *binary* point.

Now let's look at some examples of how the above formula works. The decimal number 1982 is equal to

$$1 \times 10^3 + 9 \times 10^2 + 8 \times 10^1 + 2 \times 10^0.$$

Similarly, 12.34 is equal to

$$1 \times 10^1 + 2 \times 10^0 + 3 \times 10^{-1} + 4 \times 10^{-2}.$$

The value of the binary number 10110.11 is given by

$$1 \times 2^4 + 0 \times 2^3 + 1 \times 2^2 + 1 \times 2^1 + 0 \times 2^0 + 1 \times 2^{-1} + 1 \times 2^{-2},$$

or, in decimal,

$$16 + 4 + 2 + 0.5 + 0.25 = 22.75.$$

If we decided to adopt base seven, the number 123 would be equal to the decimal number

$$1 \times 7^2 + 2 \times 7^1 + 3 \times 7^0 = 49 + 14 + 3 = 66.$$

To be more precise in the use of our terminology, we should make it clear that we are talking about *natural* positional numbers here. The natural numbers have positional weights of 1,10,100,1000, . . . (decimal) or 1,2,4,8,16,32, . . . (binary). It is, in fact, perfectly possible to have weightings that are not successive powers of an integer. For example, we can choose a binary weighting of 2,4,4,2, which means that the number 1010 is interpreted as $1 \times 2 + 0 \times 4 + 1 \times 4 + 0 \times 2 = 6$.

Currently, those involved with computers are interested in four bases: decimal, binary, octal and hexadecimal.

Decimal	$b = 10$	$a = \{0,1,2,3,4,5,6,7,8,9\}$
Binary	$b = 2$	$a = \{0,1\}$
Octal	$b = 8$	$a = \{0,1,2,3,4,5,6,7\}$
Hexadecimal	$b = 16$	$a = \{0,1,2,3,4,5,6,7,8,9,A,B,C,D,E,F,\}$

When it is necessary to indicate the base of a number, we use a subscript. For example 123_{10} means 123 in base ten, while 123_8 means 123 octal.

People normally work in decimal and computers in binary. We shall see later that the purpose of the octal and hexadecimal systems is as an aid to human memory. It is almost impossible to remember long strings of binary digits. By converting them to the octal or hexadecimal bases (a very easy task) the shorter octal or hexadecimal numbers can be more readily committed to memory. Furthermore, as octal and hexadecimal numbers are more compact than binary numbers (1 octal digit = 3 binary digits and 1 hex digit = 4 binary digits), they are used in computer texts and *core-dumps*. The latter term refers to a print-out of part of the computer's memory, an operation normally performed as a diagnostic aid when all else has failed. For example, the eight-bit binary number 10001001 is equivalent to the hexadecimal number 89. Clearly, 89 is easier to remember than 10001001.

There are occasions when binary numbers offer people advantages over other forms of representation. Suppose a computer-controlled chemical plant has three heaters, three valves, and two pumps, which are designated $H_1, H_2, H_3, V_1, V_2, V_3, P_1, P_2$, respectively. An 8-bit word from the computer is fed to an interface unit, which converts the binary ones and zeros into electrical signals that switch on (logical one), or switch off (logical zero), the corresponding device. For example, the binary word 01010011 has the effect described in Table 4.2 when presented to the control unit.

By inspecting the binary value of the control word, the status of all devices is immediately apparent. If the output had been represented in decimal (83), hexadecimal (53), or octal (123), the relationship between the number and its intended action would not be so obvious.

How many decimal digits does it require to represent a binary number? If we are going to represent decimal numbers in binary form, we need to know how many binary digits are required to express, say, an n-digit decimal number. Suppose we require m bits to represent the largest n-digit decimal number, which is, of course, $99\ldots999$ or $10^n - 1$.

We require the largest binary number in m bits (i.e. $11\ldots111$) to be equal to or greater than the largest decimal number in n bits (i.e. $99\ldots999$). That is,

$$10^n - 1 \leqslant 2^m - 1, \text{ i.e. } 10^n \leqslant 2^m.$$

Taking logarithms to base ten we get:

$$\log_{10}10^n \leqslant \log_{10}2^m$$

$$n\log_{10}10 \leqslant m\log_{10}2$$

$$n \leqslant m\log_{10}2 = 0.30103m$$

$$m \geqslant 3.322n.$$

In other words, it takes approximately $3.3n$ bits to represent an n-bit decimal number. For example, if we wish to represent decimal numbers up to 1 000 000 in binary, we must use at least 6×3.3 bits which indicates a 20-bit word length.

If there is one point that I would like to emphasize here, it is that the rules of arithmetic are the same in base x as they are in base y. In other words, all the rules we learned for base ten arithmetic can be applied to base 2, base 16, or even base 5 arithmetic. For example, the base five numbers 123_5 and 221_5 represent, in decimal, $1 \times 5^2 + 2 \times 5^1 + 3 \times 5^0 = 38_{10}$, and $2 \times 5^2 + 2 \times 5^1 + 1 \times 5^0 = 61_{10}$, respectively. If we add 123_5 to 221_5 we get 344_5, which is equal to the decimal number $3 \times 5^2 + 4 \times 5^1 + 4 \times 5^0 = 99_{10}$. Adding the decimal numbers 38_{10} and 61_{10} also gives us 99_{10}.

Now that we have looked at the structure of binary and decimal numbers, the next step is to consider how we convert a number in one base into its equivalent value in another base.

Table 4.2 Decoding the binary sequence 01010011

Bit	Value	Component	Action
7	0	Heater 1	off
6	1	Heater 2	on
5	0	Heater 3	off
4	1	Valve 1	on
3	0	Valve 2	off
2	0	Valve 3	off
1	1	Pump 1	on
0	1	Pump 2	on

4.3 Number-base conversion

It is sometimes necessary to convert numbers from one base to another by means of a pencil-and-paper method. This is particularly true when working with microprocessors at the assembly language or machine-code level. In general, computer users need not concern themselves with conversion between number bases, as the computer will have software to convert a decimal input into the computer's own internal binary representation of the input. Once the computer has done its job, it converts the binary results into decimal form before printing them.

A knowledge of the *effect* of number bases on arithmetic operations is sometimes quite vital, as, for example, even some of the simplest of decimal fractions (say $1/10 = 0.1$) have no exact binary equivalent. Suppose the computer were asked to add 0.1 to itself and stop when the result reached 1. The computer might never stop because 0.1 is not exactly represented by a binary number, with the result that the sum of ten binary representations of 0.1 is never exactly 1. It may be 1.0000000000001 or 0.99999999999, which is almost as good as 1, but it is not the same as 1, and a test for equality with 1 will always fail.

4.3.1 Conversion of integers

In this section we are going to demonstrate how integers are converted from one base to another.

Decimal to binary

To convert a decimal integer to binary, divide the number successively by 2, and after each division record the remainder which is either 1 or 0. The process is terminated only when the result of the division is 0 remainder 1. Note that in all the following conversions R is the remainder after a division.

For example, 123_{10} becomes

$$
\begin{aligned}
123 \div 2 &= 61 \quad R = 1 \\
61 \div 2 &= 30 \quad R = 1 \\
30 \div 2 &= 15 \quad R = 0 \\
15 \div 2 &= 7 \quad R = 1 \\
7 \div 2 &= 3 \quad R = 1 \\
3 \div 2 &= 1 \quad R = 1 \\
1 \div 2 &= 0 \quad R = 1
\end{aligned}
$$

The result is read from the most significant bit (the last remainder) upwards to give:

$$123_{10} = 1111011_2.$$

Decimal to octal

The process is as above except that division by 8 is used. In this case, the remainder is a number in the range 0 to 7. As before, the process of conversion ends when the final result is 0 remainder R (where $0 \leqslant R < 8$).

For example, 4629_{10} becomes

$$
\begin{array}{llll}
4629 \div 8 = 578 & R = 5 \\
578 \div 8 = & 72 & R = 2 \\
72 \div 8 = & 9 & R = 0 \\
9 \div 8 = & 1 & R = 1 \\
1 \div 8 = & 0 & R = 1 \\
\end{array}
$$

Therefore, $4629_{10} = 11025_8$.

Decimal to hexadecimal

Decimal numbers are converted from decimal into hexadecimal form in exactly the same way that decimal numbers are converted into binary form. However, in this case the remainder lies in the decimal range 0 to 15, corresponding to the hexadecimal range 0 to F.

For example, 53241_{10} becomes

$$
\begin{array}{llll}
53241 \div 16 = 3327 & R = 9 \\
3327 \div 16 = & 207 & R = 15_{10} = F \\
207 \div 16 = & 12 & R = 15_{10} = F \\
12 \div 16 = & 0 & R = 12_{10} = C \\
\end{array}
$$

Therefore, $53241_{10} = CFF9_{16}$

Binary to decimal

It is possible to convert a binary number to decimal by adding together the requisite powers of two. This technique is suitable for relatively small binary numbers up to about seven or eight bits.

For example, 1010111_2 is represented by:

$$
\begin{array}{ccccccccc}
64 & 32 & 16 & 8 & 4 & 2 & 1 & & 64 \\
1 & 0 & 1 & 0 & 1 & 1 & 1 & = & 16 \\
& & & & & & & & 4 \\
& & & & & & & & 2 \\
& & & & & & & & +1 \\
\hline
& & & & & & & & 87 \\
\end{array}
$$

A more methodical technique is based on a recursive algorithm as follows. Take the left-most non-zero bit, double it and add it to the bit on its right. Now take this result, double it and add it to the next bit on the right. Continue in this way until the least significant bit has been added in. The recursive procedure may be expressed mathematically as:

$$(a_0 + 2(a_1 + 2(a_2 + \cdots))),$$

where the least significant bit of the binary number is a_0.

For example, 1010111_2 becomes $\quad 1 \quad 0 \quad 1 \quad 0 \quad 1 \quad 1 \quad 1$

$$\frac{2}{2}$$

$$\frac{4}{5}$$

$$\frac{10}{10}$$

$$\frac{20}{21}$$

$$\frac{42}{43}$$

$$\frac{86}{87}$$

Therefore, $1010111_2 = 87_{10}$.

Octal to decimal

Remember that we said that any rule that applies to base X also applies to base Y. If we convert binary numbers to decimal by continually adding $2a_i$ to a_{i-1}, then we convert from octal to decimal by continually adding $8a_i$ to a_{i-1}. An octal number is expressed in decimal form as:

$$(a_0 + 8(a_1 + 8(a_2 + \cdots))).$$

We take the left-most digit, multiply it by eight and add it to the digit on its right. We then multiply this subtotal by eight and add it to the next digit on its right. The process ends when the left-most digit has been added to the subtotal.

For example, 6437_8 becomes $\quad 6 \quad 4 \quad 3 \quad 7$

$$\frac{48}{52}$$

$$\frac{416}{419}$$

$$\frac{3352}{3359}$$

Therefore, $6437_8 = 3359_{10}$.

Hexadecimal to decimal

The method is identical to the procedures for binary and octal except that 16 is used as a multiplier.

For example, $1AC_{16}$ becomes $\quad 1 \quad A \quad C$

$$\frac{16}{26}$$

$$\frac{416}{428}$$

Therefore, $1AC_{16} = 428_{10}$

Conversions between binary, octal, and hexadecimal

In much of this book, binary numbers will be represented in hexadecimal form. Although some texts favour the octal format, I find octal numbers ill-fitted to the representation of 8 or 16-bit binary values. We shall use hexadecimal representations of binary numbers simply because of the ease with which conversions may be made between binary and hexadecimal numbers.

Binary to octal

Form the bits into groups of *three* starting at the binary point and moving leftwards. Replace each group of three bits with the corresponding octal digit (0 to 7).

For example, 11001011101_2 becomes   11   001   011   101
                3   1   3   5

Therefore, $11001011101_2 = 3135_8$.

Note how the binary number has been *condensed* to a more manageable size.

Binary to hexadecimal

The binary number is formed into groups of *four* bits starting at the decimal point. Each group is replaced by a hexadecimal digit from 0 to 9, A, B, C, D, E, F.

For example, 11001011101_2 becomes   110   0101   1101
               6   5   D

Therefore, $11001011101_2 = 65D_{16}$.

Octal to binary

Converting an octal number into its binary equivalent requires the reverse procedure of converting from binary to octal. Each octal digit is simply replaced by its 3-bit binary equivalent. It is important to remember that a (say) 3 must be replaced by 011 and not 11.

For example, 41357_8 becomes   4   1   3   5   7
           100   001   011   101   111

Therefore, $41357_8 = 100001011101111_2$.

Hexadecimal to binary

Each hexadecimal digit is replaced by its 4-bit binary equivalent.

For example, $AB4C_{16}$ becomes   A   B   4   C
          1010   1011   0100   1100

Therefore, $AB4C_{16} = 1010101101001100_2$.

Conversion between hexadecimal and octal values is best performed via binary. For example, to convert the hexadecimal number 12BC to octal form we perform the following actions:

$12BC_{16} = 1\ 0010\ 1011\ 1100_2$ (form groups of four bits from the right)

$1001010111100_2 = 1\ 001\ 010\ 111\ 100_2$ (after regrouping)

$1\ 001\ 010\ 111\ 100_2 = 11274_8$ (convert 3-bit groups to octal digits)

4.3.2 Conversion of fractions

The conversion of fractions from one base to another is carried out in a similar way to the conversion of integers, although it is rather more tedious to manipulate fractions manually. Fortunately, it is rare to have to perform actual pencil and paper conversion of fractions outside the class room. One way of effectively abolishing fractions is to treat all fractions as integers scaled by an appropriate factor. For example, the binary fraction 0.10101 is equal to the integer 10101 divided by 2^5 (i.e. 32), so that, for example, 0.10101 is the same as $10101/2^5 = 21/32 = 0.65625$.

Converting binary fractions to decimal fractions

The algorithm for converting binary fractions to their decimal equivalent is based on the fact that a bit in one column is worth half the value of a bit in the column on its left. Starting at the rightmost non-zero bit, take that bit and halve it. Now add the result to the next bit on its left. Halve this result and add it to the next bit on the left. Continute until the binary point is reached.

For example, consider the conversion of 0.01101_2 into decimal form.

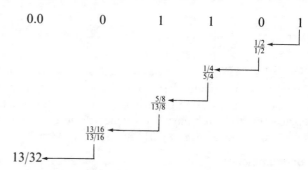

Therefore, $0.01101_2 = 13/32$.

Converting decimal fractions to binary fractions

The decimal fraction is multiplied by two and the integer part noted. The integer, which will be either 1 or 0, is then stripped from the number to leave a fractional part. The new fraction is multiplied by two and the integer part noted. We continue in this way until the process ends or a sufficient degree of precision has been achieved. The binary fraction is formed by reading the integer parts from the top to the bottom as illustrated below.

For example, 0.6875_{10} becomes

$0.6875 \times 2 \rightarrow \mathbf{1}.3750$
$0.3750 \times 2 \rightarrow \mathbf{0}.7500$
$0.7500 \times 2 \rightarrow \mathbf{1}.5000$
$0.5000 \times 2 \rightarrow \mathbf{1}.0000$
0.0000×2 ends the process

Therefore, $0.6875_{10} = 0.1011_2$.

Now consider 0.1_{10}
$$0.1000 \times 2 \rightarrow \mathbf{0}.2000$$
$$0.2000 \times 2 \rightarrow \mathbf{0}.4000$$
$$0.4000 \times 2 \rightarrow \mathbf{0}.8000$$
$$0.8000 \times 2 \rightarrow \mathbf{1}.6000$$
$$0.6000 \times 2 \rightarrow \mathbf{1}.2000$$
$$0.2000 \times 2 \rightarrow \mathbf{0}.4000$$
$$0.4000 \times 2 \rightarrow \mathbf{0}.8000$$
$$0.8000 \times 2 \rightarrow \mathbf{1}.6000$$
$$0.6000 \times 2 \rightarrow \mathbf{1}.2000$$
$$0.2000 \times 2 \rightarrow \mathbf{0}.4000$$
$$0.4000 \times 2 \rightarrow \mathbf{0}.8000$$
$$\text{etc.}$$

Therefore, $0.1_{10} = 0.00011001100_2$, etc.

As I pointed out before 0.1 cannot be expressed exactly in terms of binary fractions.

Converting between octal/hexadecimal fractions and decimal fractions

We can convert between octal or hexadecimal fractions and decimal fractions using the same algorithms we used for binary conversions. All we have to change is the base (i.e. 2 to 8 or 2 to 16). Consider the following example.

Convert 0.12_{10} into its octal equivalent.

$$0.12 \times 8 \rightarrow \mathbf{0}.96$$
$$0.96 \times 8 \rightarrow \mathbf{7}.68$$
$$0.68 \times 8 \rightarrow \mathbf{5}.44$$
$$0.44 \times 8 \rightarrow \mathbf{3}.52$$
$$0.52 \times 8 \rightarrow \mathbf{4}.16$$
$$0.16 \times 8 \rightarrow \mathbf{1}.28$$
$$\text{etc.}$$

Therefore, $0.12_{10} = 0.075341_8$.

Similarly consider the conversion of 0.123_{16} into a decimal fraction:

$$
\begin{array}{cccc}
0 & 1 & 2 & 3 \\
\frac{291}{4096} \leftarrow & \frac{35/256}{291/256} \leftarrow & \frac{3/16}{35/16} & \leftarrow
\end{array}
$$

Binary to octal/hexadecimal fraction conversion and vice versa

The conversion of binary fractions to octal (hexadecimal) bases, is as easy as the corresponding integer conversions. The only point worth mentioning is that when binary digits are split into groups of three (four), we start grouping bits at the binary point and move to the right. Any group of digits remaining on the right containing fewer than three (four) bits must be made up to three (four) bits by the addition of zeros to the right of the least significant bit. The following examples illustrate this point.

Binary to octal $0.10101100_2 \rightarrow 0.101\ 011\ 0(00)_2 \rightarrow 0.530_8$
Binary to octal $0.10101111_2 \rightarrow 0.101\ 011\ 11(0)_2 \rightarrow 0.536_8$
Binary to hexadecimal $0.10101100_2 \rightarrow 0.1010\ 1100_2 \rightarrow 0.AC_{16}$
Binary to hexadecimal $0.101011001_2 \rightarrow 0.1010\ 1100\ 1(000)_2 \rightarrow 0.AC8_{16}$
Octal to binary $0.456_8 \rightarrow 0.100\ 101\ 110_2 \rightarrow 0.100101110_2$
Hexadecimal to binary $0.ABC_{16} \rightarrow 0.1010\ 1011\ 1100_2 \rightarrow 0.101010111100_2$

Numbers containing an integer part and a fraction part (e.g. 110101.11010 in base two or 123.125 in decimal) are converted from one base to another in two stages. The integer part is converted and then the fractional part (using any appropriate conversion technique).

4.4 Special-purpose codes

Throughout this book a group of binary digits will generally represent one of three things: a numerical quantity, an instruction, or an ISO character. However, in the world of computing and digital systems there are many different codes, each one best suited to the particular job for which it was designed.

4.4.1 BCD codes

A particularly widespread code is called BCD or binary-coded decimal. In theory BCD is a case of having your cake and eating it. It has already been stated that computer designers are forced to rely on two-state logic elements on purely economic grounds. This, in turn, leads to the world of binary arithmetic and the consequent problems of converting between binary and decimal representations of numeric quantities. Binary-coded decimal numbers accept the inevitability of two-state logic by coding the individual decimal digits into groups of four bits. Table 4.3 shows how the ten digits, 0 to 9, are represented in BCD, and how a decimal number is converted to a BCD form.

BCD arithmetic is identical to decimal arithmetic and differs only in the way the ten digits are represented. The following example shows how a BCD addition is carried out.

$$
\begin{array}{ll}
1942 \rightarrow & 0001\ 1001\ 0100\ 0010 \\
+\,2379 \rightarrow & +\,0010\ 0011\ 0111\ 1001 \\
\hline
4321 & 0100\ 0011\ 0010\ 0001
\end{array}
$$

Although BCD seems a good idea because it makes decimal to binary conversion easy, it suffers from two disadvantages. The first is that BCD arithmetic is more complex than binary arithmetic simply because the binary tables (i.e. addition, subtraction, multiplication and division) are exceedingly small and may be implemented in hardware by a few gates. On the other hand, the decimal tables involve all combinations of the digits 0–9. Today's digital technology makes these disadvantages less evident than in the early days of computer technology, where each gate was a large and

Table 4.3 The BCD code

Decimal	BCD
0	0000
1	0001
2	0010
3	0011
4	0100
5	0101
6	0110
7	0111
8	1000
9	1001

To convert a decimal number into its BCD equivalent, we simply encode each digit into the appropriate 4-bit BCD code. For example, the decimal number 1942 is encoded as 0001 1001 0100 0010, which, after compaction, becomes 0001100101000010.

expensive item. However, once a trend has started it tends to gain momentum and to continue long after its original driving force has vanished. This is particularly true in the world of computing where, in the early days, one of the main criteria of circuit design was the minimization of the total number of valves or transistors in a circuit. Today, the number of transistors in a circuit is one of the designer's smallest problems.

The major disadvantage of BCD lies in its inefficient use of storage. As computer owners have to pay for memory modules, it is reasonable to use the smallest quantity of memory for a given job. A BCD digit requires four bits of storage but only ten symbols are mapped onto ten of the sixteen possible binary codes. Consequently, the binary codes 1010–1111 (10 to 15) are redundant and represent wasted storage. As we demonstrated earlier in this chapter, natural binary numbers require an average of approximately 3.322 bits per decimal digit.

In spite of the disadvantage of BCD, it is frequently found in applications requiring little storage, such as pocket calculators or digital watches. Microprocessors often have special instructions to aid BCD operations, and many interpreters for the language BASIC perform all numeric operations on BCD numbers. There are in fact a number of different ways of representing BCD numbers in addition to the basic BCD code presented above. Each of these codes has desirable properties making it suitable for a particular application. Other BCD codes are not relevant to this text.

4.4.2 Unweighted codes

The binary code described in Section 4.2 is often called pure binary, natural binary, or 8421 weighted binary. The 8, 4, 2, and 1 represent the *weightings* of each of the columns in the positional code. There are many other positional codes that do not have a natural binary weighting. Some codes are called *unweighted* because the value of a bit does not depend on its *position* in a number. Each of these codes does, however, have special properties that make it suitable for a specific application. One such unweighted code is called a *unit distance code*.

Before we can define a unit distance code, we have to introduce the idea of the *distance* between two binary values. The *Hamming* distance between two words is the number of places (i.e. positions) in which they differ. The examples in Table 4.4 should make this clear.

In a unit distance code, the distance between consecutive code words is constant and equal to one. That is, no two consecutive code words differ in more than one bit position. Natural binary number are most certainly not

Table 4.4 The Hamming distance

Word 1	00101101	00101101	00101101	00101101
Word 2	00101100	11101100	11101101	00100101
Places different	√	√ √	√ √	√
Hamming distance	1	3	2	1

The Hamming distance is simply the number of positions in which two binary sequences differ.

Table 4.5 The 4-bit Gray code (an unweighted unit distance code)

Decimal value	Natural binary value	Gray code
0	0000	0000
1	0001	0001
2	0010	0011
3	0011	0010
4	0100	0110
5	0101	0111
6	0110	0101
7	0111	0100
8	1000	1100
9	1001	1101
10	1010	1111
11	1011	1110
12	1100	1010
13	1101	1011
14	1110	1001
15	1111	1000

members of the domain of unit distance codes. For example, the sequential natural binary numbers $0111 = 7$ and $1000 = 8$ differ by a Hamming distance of four. The most widely encountered unit distance code is the *Gray code*, the first 16 values of which are given in Table 4.5.

The Gray code is often associated with optical encoders, a mechanism for converting the angle of a shaft into a binary value. Figure 4.2(a) shows an optical encoder using a natural binary code and Fig. 4.2(b) shows the same arrangement but with a Gray encoder disk. An optical encoder allows the angular position of a shaft to be determined electronically without any physical connection between the shaft and the measuring equipment. On the end of the shaft is a glass or plastic disk with a number of concentric tracks, one for each of the bits in the code representing the position of the shaft. A four-bit code may be suitable for a wind direction indicator connected to a weather vane, while a ten-bit code may be required to indicate the position of a shaft in a machine.

Each of the tracks is divided into a number of sectors which are either opaque or transparent. On one side of the disk are a number of light sources (LEDs or incandescent light bulbs), one per track. On the other side of the disk are an equal number of photoelectric sensors. Each sensor is situated directly opposite its light source. Thus, for any position of the disk, a particular combination of the photo-electric cells detects a light beam, depending on whether or not there is a transparent sector between the light source and detector.

The natural binary code can, under certain circumstances, create

Sector	Angle	Binary code
0	0–45	0 0 0
1	45–90	0 0 1
2	90–135	0 1 0
3	135–180	0 1 1
4	180–225	1 0 0
5	225–270	1 0 1
6	270–315	1 1 0
7	315–360	1 1 1

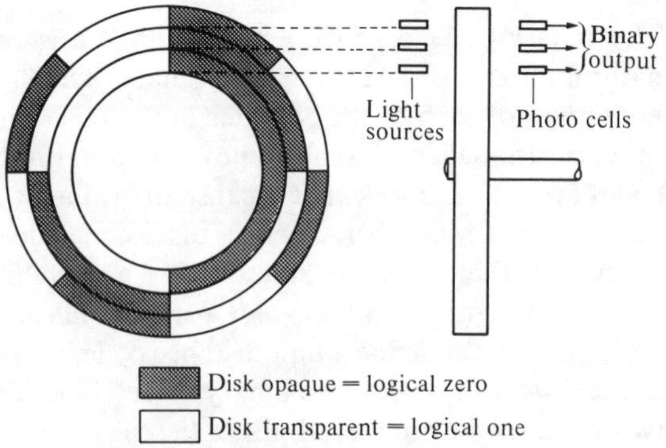

Disk opaque = logical zero

Disk transparent = logical one

(a)

Sector	Angle	Gray code
0	0–45	0 0 0
1	45–90	0 0 1
2	90–135	0 1 1
3	135–180	0 1 0
4	180–225	1 1 0
5	225–270	1 1 1
6	270–315	1 0 1
7	315–360	1 0 0

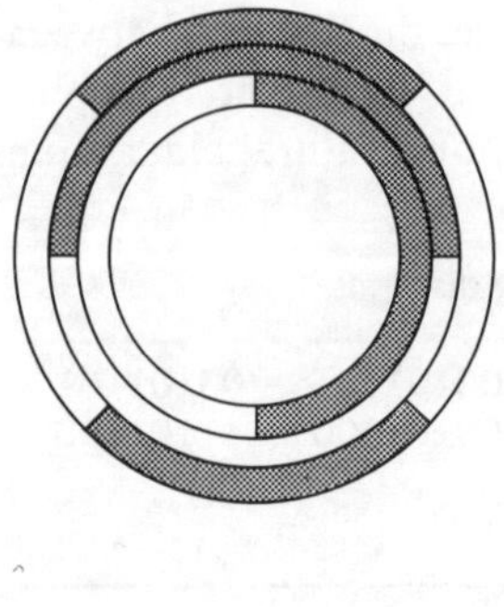

(b)

Fig. 4.2 (a) A natural binary-encoded optical encoder; (b) a Gray-encoded optical encoder.

problems, because more than one bit of the output code changes when the shaft rotates from one code to the next code. Unfortunately, as the photoelectric cells cannot be perfectly aligned, the light source is not a point source, and the edges of the sectors are not perfect straight edges, when two bits change state one bit may change before the other. For example, the change from, say, 001 to 010 may be seen as the sequence 001, 000, 010. Because the least significant bit changes before the middle bit, the spurious code 000 is generated momentarily. In some applications this can be very troublesome. From Fig. 4.2(b) it can be seen that a Gray encoded disk has the property that only one bit at a time changes, solving the problems inherent in the natural binary system. Once the Gray code has been read into a digital system it may be converted into a natural binary code for processing in the normal way.

Gray codes can be converted into natural binary codes and vice versa by the EOR gate logic of Fig. 4.3.

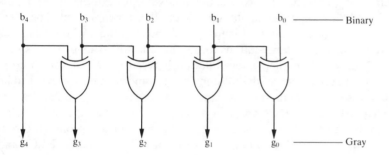

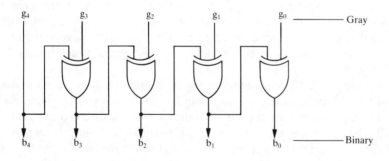

Fig. 4.3 Converting binary codes to Gray codes and vice versa.

4.4.3 Error-detecting codes

The subject of error-detecting codes is large enough to fill a number of text books. Here we shall look only at two classes of error-detecting codes: codes with a single parity bit and Hamming codes. Error detecting codes or EDCs have the ability to detect that a word has been corrupted. The Hamming code to be described later is not only an EDC, it is also an error-correcting code, ECC, because it can be used to correct a corrupted word. Of course, the ECC is also an EDC while the EDC is not necessarily an ECC. When in the realm of EDCs and ECCs we use two special terms:

source code and code word. A source code is an unencoded piece of information and a code word is a source word that has been encoded.

Before we introduce EDCs and ECCs, we must ask ourselves why they are needed. In any electronic system there are unwanted random signals, collectively called noise, that may interfere with the correct operation of the system. These random signals arise from a variety of causes, ranging from the thermal motion of electrons in a digital system, to electromagnetic radiation from nearby lightning strikes and power-line transients caused by the switching of inductive loads (e.g. starting motors in vacuum cleaners or elevators). The magnitude of these unwanted signals is generally tiny compared with digital signals inside the computer. The two electrical levels representing the zero and one binary states are so well separated that one level is almost never spontaneously converted into the other level inside a digital computer under normal operating conditions.

Whenever digital signals are transmitted over a long distance by cables, their magnitude is diminished, making it possible for external noise signals to exceed the level of the digital signals and thus corrupt them. The effect of electrical noise is familiar to most people because those who tune radios or televisions to distant stations know that the sound or picture is of a lower quality than when a local station is received. Whenever an error occurs in the reception of digital signals, it is important for the event to be detected so that a request for retransmission of the corrupted data can be made. ECCs and EDCs are also required by data storage technology. Many of the techniques used to store digital data are prone to errors (albeit with a very low probability of error). Consequently, ECCs and EDCs are frequently used to determine whether data has been corrupted during the process of storage and retrieval.

A popular method of error detection is implemented by transmitting the desired digital information (i.e. the source word) plus one or more *check bits* whose value is a function of the information bits. Note that some codes that are not included here create code words that are very complex functions of the source word and do not simply append check bits to the source word.

Because check bits convey no new information, they are called *redundant* bits. At the receiving end of a data link the information bits are used to calculate (locally) the check bits. If the received check bits are the same as the locally generated check bits, error-free transmission is assumed, otherwise the receiver must send a message back to the transmitter asking it to repeat the lost data. If an error is detected in a stored word, it cannot be corrected by asking the computer what it was, because there is no other copy of the word. Consequently the operating system must be informed of the error and then left to take appropriate action (usually by aborting the current task). Fortunately, some memories use error-correcting codes and are able to repair the damage done by an error before the word is passed to the computer.

As an example of the application of check bits consider a simple two-digit decimal code with a single decimal check digit. The check digit is calculated by adding up the two source digits modulo ten (modulo ten simply means that we ignore any carry when we add the digits—the modulo ten value of $6+7$ is 3). If the two source digits are 4 and 9, the code word is 493 (the check digit is 3). Suppose that during transmission or storage the code word is corrupted and becomes 463. If we re-evaluate the check digit we get $4+6=10=0$ (modulo ten). As the recorded check digit is 3, we know that an error must have occurred.

How error-detecting codes work

The idea behind EDCs is that an m-bit source code can convey 2^m unique messages. If r check bits are added to the m message digits to create an n-bit code word, then there are $2^n=2^{m+r}$ possible code words. Of these code words only 2^m are valid. Should a code word be received which is not one of these 2^m values, an error may be assumed.

Figure 4.4(a) demonstrates how EDCs operate. Imagine an n-dimensional space in which each point is represented by the value of an n-component vector. If we assume that the vectors are made up of binary components, an n-dimensional space will contain 2^n possible elements. Each of these elements corresponds to a particular code word. For

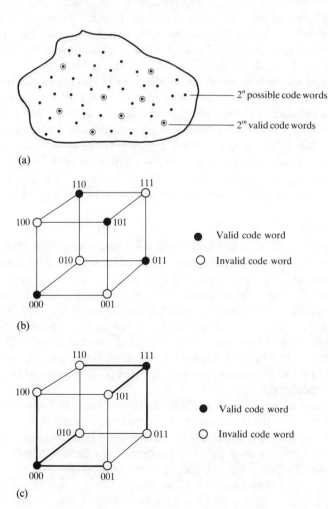

(a)

(b)

(c)

● Valid code word
○ Invalid code word

Fig. 4.4 (a) The principle of the EDC; (b) all possible code words in three-dimensional space; (c) an error-correcting code in three-dimensional space.

example, an eight-dimensional space has 256 possible elements. Suppose that only m of the n bits of each vector are used to generate a unique code word and the other $n - m = r$ bits are generated from some function of the m-bit source word. The n-dimensional space will contain 2^m **valid** code words, 2^n **possible** code words and $2^n - 2^m$ **error states.**

If we read a word from memory or from some communication system, we can check its location within the n-dimensional space. If the word is located at one of the 2^m valid points we assume that it is error free. If it falls in one of the $2^n - 2^m$ error states, we can reject it.

Figure 4.4(b) demonstrates an error-detecting code for $n = 3$. Each of the $2^3 = 8$ possible code words are represented by a corner of the three-dimensional cube. Of the eight possible code words, four have been marked as valid by heavy shading (i.e. 000, 011, 101, 110). If we choose a code word from this space, we can see at once whether it represents a valid code or not (it is valid if there is an even number of ones in the code word).

In Fig. 4.4(c) we have drawn another three-dimensional cube, but in this case only one message bit is used ($m = 1$ and $r = 2$). Here there are only two valid code words, 000 and 111. Note that each valid code word is separated from another valid code word by a Hamming distance of three. If an invalid code word is detected we can attempt to correct the error by choosing the valid code word **nearest** to the code word in error. Thus, if the invalid code word we receive is 001, we assume that the correct code was 000 (because 001 is closer to 000 than to 111). All error-correcting codes operate on the principle that valid code words are separated by a Hamming distance of at least **three.** Consequently, we can select an error-correcting strategy that says, 'if we detect an invalid code word, we will try to correct the error by selecting the nearest valid code to the code word in error.' Since valid codes are separated by a minimum of three units from each other, a single error moves a code word one unit from its correct value, but it remains two units from any other valid code word.

Parity EDCs

The simplest error-detecting code involves a single **parity** bit. There are two types of parity, even parity and odd parity. We will deal with even parity codes first. An error-detecting code with a single even parity check bit chooses the parity bit to make the total number of ones in the word even. Here, the total number of bits includes the parity bit itself. Thus, if the message (i.e. source word) is 0101101, the parity bit is chosen to be 0 as there are four **ones** in the word. The code word now becomes 00101101 — the parity bit has been appended to the most significant bit position, although in principle there is no reason why the parity bit should be placed at any particular point.

Suppose that the above code word is transmitted, and is received as 00101100 because the least significant bit has been changed from 1 to 0. The parity of the word calculated at the receiver is odd (there are 3 ones), and an error is assumed to have occurred. We cannot tell from the received word which bit is in error, so we cannot correct the error. Note that if there had been two errors, no parity violation would have been detected, and the errors would not have been flagged. Single parity check bits are helpful only when errors are relatively infrequent and tend to occur singly.

In a system with odd parity, the parity bit is chosen to make the total number of ones odd. Table 4.6 gives the eight valid code words for a 3-bit source word, for both even and odd parities. In each case the parity bit is the most significant bit. Note that the even parity code of Table 4.6 corresponds to the example we introduced in Fig. 4.4(b).

The simple single parity bit error-detecting code can be extended to create *block* EDCs which are also called *matrix* EDCs. A block EDC uses two types of parity check bit: a *vertical* parity bit and a *horizontal* (or *longitudinal*) parity bit. Imagine a block of data composed of a sequence or source words. Each source word can be written vertically to form a column and the sequence of source words can be written one after another to create a block. Figure 4.5(a) demonstrates a simple block of six 3-bit source words.

Table 4.6 Odd and even parity codes

Message	Code word (even parity)	Code word (odd parity)
000	0000	1000
001	1001	0001
010	1010	0010
011	0011	1011
100	1100	0100
101	0101	1101
110	0110	1110
111	1111	0111
	↑ Even parity bit	↑ Odd parity bit

(a)

Bit	word1	word2	word3	word4	word5	word6
D_0	0	1	1	0	1	0
D_1	1	0	0	1	0	1
D_2	1	1	0	1	1	0

The source words are 110, 101, 001, 110, 101, and 010 and have been written down as a block or matrix.

(b)

Bit	word1	word2	word3	word4	word5	word6	word7
D_0	0	1	1	0	1	0	1
D_1	1	0	0	1	0	1	1
D_2	1	1	0	1	1	0	0
D_3	0	0	1	0	0	1	0 ←Vertical parity bits

↑ Horizontal parity word

A vertical even parity bit has been appended to each column to create a new row labelled D_3. Similarly, a horizontal parity bit has been appended to each row to create a new column labelled word7.

Fig. 4.5 (a) The block code error-detecting code; (b) detecting errors with horizontal and vertical parity bits; (c) using vertical and horizontal parity to correct an error.

(c)

Bit	word1	word2	word3	word4	word5	word6	word7	
D_0	0	1	1	0	1	0	1	✓
D_1	1	0	1	1	0	1	1	X
D_2	1	1	0	1	1	0	0	✓
D_3	0	0	1	0	0	1	0	✓
	✓	✓	X	✓	✓	✓	✓	

By detecting a parity error in a row, we can detect the position of the bit in error (i.e. in this case bit D_1). By detecting a parity error in a column, we can detect the word in error (i.e. in this case word3). Now we can locate the actual error which is bit D_1 of word3.

We can generate a parity bit for each source word (i.e. column) and append it to the bottom of each column to create a new row. Each of these parity bits is called a vertical parity bit. Since a block of source words is made up of a number of columns, a parity word can be formed by calculating the parity across the bits. Each code word (i.e. column) in Fig. 4.5(b) is composed of four bits: D_0, D_1, D_2, D_3 (where D_3 is the vertical parity bit). We can now derive a horizontal parity bit by calculating the parity across the columns. That is, we create a parity bit across all the D_0s. Horizontal parity bits for D_1, D_2, and the vertical parity bits, D_3, can be generated in a similar way. Figure 4.5(b) shows how the source words of Fig. 4.5(a) are transformed into a block error-detecting code.

If a single error occurs in a particular word, we can detect which word is in error from the vertical parity bit. However, the horizontal parity bit will tell us which bit in the block is in error (i.e. an error in D_0 or D_1, etc.). Now we know the column and the row in which the error occurs, we can locate the exact position of the error. As we know which bit has been corrupted we can reverse it and *correct* the error. The block error-detecting code is also an error-correcting code.

Figure 4.5(c) demonstrates the action of a block error-detecting code. A tick marks each row or column where the parity is correct, and a cross where it is not. In this example, the bit in error is detected by the intersection of the row and column in which it creates a parity violation. Thus, although the word 1001 is received incorrectly as 1101 it can be corrected. While the block parity code can detect and correct single errors, it can detect (but not correct) certain combinations of multiple error. Block EDCs/ECCs are sometimes found in data transmission systems and in the storage of serial data on magnetic tape.

4.4.4 Hamming codes

Hamming codes are possibly the simplest class of error-detecting and -correcting codes that can be applied to a single code word (in contrast with a block error-correcting code that is applied to a group of words). A Hamming code takes an m-bit source word and generates r parity check bits to create an n-bit code word. The r parity check bits are selected so that a single error in the code word can be detected, located and therefore corrected.

Hamming codes are designated $H_{n,m}$ where, for example, $H_{7,4}$ represents a Hamming code with a code word of seven bits and a source word of four bits. The following sequence of bits represents a $H_{7,4}$ code word:

7	6	5	4	3	2	1	←bit position
I_4	I_3	I_2	C_3	I_1	C_2	C_1	

I = information (i.e. message bit)
C = code bit

The information (i.e. source word) bits are numbered I_1, I_2, I_3, and I_4, while the check bits are numbered C_1, C_2, and C_3. Similarly the bit positions in the code word are numbered from one to seven. Note that the check bits are located in **binary** positions in the code word (i.e. positions 1, 2, and 4).

The code bits are generated from the source word according to the following equations:

$$C_3 = I_2 \oplus I_3 \oplus I_4$$
$$C_2 = I_1 \oplus I_3 \oplus I_4$$
$$C_1 = I_1 \oplus I_2 \oplus I_4.$$

Suppose we have a source word equal to $I_4, I_3, I_2, I_1 = 1,1,0,1$. The check bits are calculated as

$$C_3 = 0 \oplus 1 \oplus 1 = 0$$
$$C_2 = 1 \oplus 1 \oplus 1 = 1$$
$$C_1 = 1 \oplus 0 \oplus 1 = 0.$$

The code word is therefore

$$I_4, I_3, I_2, C_3, I_1, C_2, C_1, = 1,1,0,0,1,1,0.$$

Suppose now that the code word is corrupted during storage (or transmission). Assume that I_3 is switched from 1 to 0. The resulting code word is now 1000110. Using the new code word we can recalculate the check bits to give

$$C_3 = 0 \oplus 0 \oplus 1 = 1$$
$$C_2 = 1 \oplus 0 \oplus 1 = 0$$
$$C_1 = 1 \oplus 0 \oplus 1 = 0.$$

The new check bits are 1,0,0 and the stored check bits are 0,1,0. If we take the EOR of the old and new check bits we get $1 \oplus 0$, $0 \oplus 1$, $0 \oplus 0 = 1,1,0$. Note that $1,1,0 = 6$ and points to bit position 6 in the code word. It is this bit that is in error. How does a Hamming code perform this apparent magic trick? The answer can be found in the equations for the parity check bits. The check bits are calculated in such a way that any single bit error will change the particular combination of check bits that points to its location.

The Hamming code described above can detect and correct a single error. By adding a further check bit we can create a Hamming code that can detect two errors and correct one error.

4.4.5 Huffman codes

This short introduction to Huffman codes has been included to show that there is more than one way of 'skinning the cat'. Huffman codes differ from all other encoding techniques described in this book, because they employ a variable-length code word. The idea of a Huffman code is not new. When Samual Morse devised his famous code he sent his assistant round to the printer's to count the number of letters (i.e. A to Z) in each pigeon hole in which they were stored. As, for example, the letter *E* appears so frequently in English language text there were many Es. Equally, there were relatively few Qs. So, Samual Morse created a code whereby frequently used letters had short codes, while infrequently used letters had long codes. For example, the letter E has a morse symbol '.', and the letter Q has the symbol '__.__'.

A similar arrangement can be extended to binary codes. It must be stated that Huffman codes are applied only to information in which some letters or groups of letters appear more frequently than others. Plain text (e.g. written English) is such a case. To keep things simple, consider the following example. A grocer sells only four items (I did say we were keeping things simple), potatoes, onions, beans, and avocado pears. Being a thoroughly modern trader (and a computer scientist) the grocer has a computerized business. Every time an item is bought, it is encoded in binary form and stored on disk. Because business is brisk and disk space limited, the grocer wishes to code transactions in such a way as to use the least possible storage. Initially the grocer tried the 2-bit binary code described in Table 4.7.

If there are *n* transactions, the total storage required to record them is 2*n* bits. At first sight it would seem that there is no way the grocer can get away with less than two bits to encode each transaction. However, after a little thought, the grocer realizes that most customers buy potatoes and therefore devises the encoding scheme of Table 4.8.

Now there are four codes of different lengths. One code has a one-bit length, one has a two-bit length, and two have three-bit lengths. After a week's trading, the total storage space occupied will be the number of transactions for each item multiplied by the length of its code. The average code length will be:

$$1 \times \tfrac{3}{4} + 2 \times \tfrac{1}{8} + 3 \times \tfrac{1}{16} + 3 \times \tfrac{1}{16} = 1\tfrac{3}{8} = 1.375.$$

By adopting this code, a Huffman code, the average storage has been reduced from two bits per transaction to 1.375 bits per transaction, a saving of 31.25 per cent. A Huffman code is often represented in the form of a binary tree, the tree in Fig. 4.6 corresponding to the grocer's example.

The diagram in Fig. 4.6 is sometimes called a *trellis* and is read from left to right. From the left, each of the four terminal nodes (labelled node 0, node 10 etc.) can be reached by following the marked paths. These paths are marked by a 1 or a 0 depending on the bit to be decoded. The example below should clarify things.

The grocer's disk contains the following string of bits, 001100101110. What codes does this string correspond to?

The first (left-most) bit of the string is 0. From the trellis it can be seen that a first bit 0 leads immediately to a terminal node. Thus, the first code is 0. Similarly, the second code is also zero. The third code begins with a 1 and we must examine another bit to continue. This is also a one, and another bit must be read. The third bit is a zero leading to a terminal node 110. This process can be continued until the string is broken down into the sequence

Table 4.7 Coding four items with a 2-bit code

Item	Code
Potatoes	00
Onions	01
Beans	10
Avocado pears	11

Table 4.8 A Huffman code for four items

Item	Percentage of transactions	Code
Potatoes	75	0
Onions	12.5	10
Beans	6.25	110
Avocado pears	6.25	111

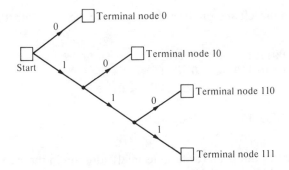

Fig. 4.6 A Huffman code.

0 0 110 0 10 111 0 = potatoes, potatoes, beans, potatoes, onions, avocados, potatoes.

Now that we have looked at some general binary codes, we are going to return to numeric codes and examine how a computer performs simple arithmetic operations. The following section ties together binary arithmetic and the digital logic we learned in Chapter 2.

4.5 Binary arithmetic

Now that we have introduced binary numbers and demonstrated how it is possible to convert between binary and decimal formats, the next step is to look at how binary numbers are manipulated. Binary arithmetic follows exactly the same rules as decimal arithmetic and all that we have to do to work with binary numbers is to learn the binary tables. These are somewhat more easy than their decimal equivalents as Table 4.9 demonstrates by providing the binary tables for addition, subtraction, and multiplication.

A remarkable fact about binary arithmetic is that if we did not worry about the *carry* in addition and the *borrow* in subtraction, then the operations of addition and subtraction would be identical. Such an arithmetic in which addition and subtraction are equivalent does exist and has some important applications; this is called modulo-2 arithmetic.

The addition of n-bit numbers is entirely straightforward, except that when adding the two bits in each column, a carry bit from the previous stage must also added in. Each carry bit results from a carry-out from the column on its right. In the following example, we present the numbers to

Table 4.9 The binary tables

Addition	Subtraction	Multiplication
0+0=0	0−0=0	0×0=0
0+1=1	0−1=1 borrow 1	0×1=0
1+0=1	1−0=1	1×0=0
1+1=0 carry 1	1−1=0	1×1=1

be added on the left and on the right we include the carry bits that must be added in.

$$
\begin{array}{ll}
00110111 \rightarrow & 00110111 \\
+\,01010110 \rightarrow & 01010110 \\
& 111\ \ 11 \quad \leftarrow\text{carries} \\[4pt]
\hline \\[-8pt]
10001101 \rightarrow & 10001101
\end{array}
$$

We can carry out octal (or hexadecimal) addition in the same way that we carry out binary addition. All we have to remember is that if we add together two digits whose sum is greater than eight (or 16), we must convert the result into a carry digit whose value is eight (or 16) plus the remainder which is the sum less eight (or 16). For example, if we add 5 and 7 in octal, we get 14 which is 4 carry 1 (i.e. 4 plus 8).

Consider the octal addition $12345 + 67013$.

$$
\begin{array}{ll}
12345 \rightarrow & 12345 \\
67013 \rightarrow & 67013 \\
& 11\ \ \ 1 \ \leftarrow\text{carries} \\[4pt]
\hline \\[-8pt]
101360 \rightarrow & 101360
\end{array}
$$

Subtraction can also be carried out in a conventional fashion, although we shall see later that a computer does not subtract numbers in the way we do because negative numbers are not usually represented in a *sign plus magnitude* form but by means of their *complements:*

$$
\begin{array}{ll}
\quad 01010110 & \quad\ 86 \\
-\ 00101010 & -42 \\
\quad\ 1\ 1 \quad \leftarrow\text{borrows} & \quad\ \underline{} \\
\quad\ \underline{} & \quad\ 44 \\
\quad 00101100
\end{array}
$$

The multiplication of binary numbers can be done by the *pencil and paper* method of shifting and adding, although in practice the computer uses a somewhat modified technique.

$$
\begin{array}{rr}
01101 & 13 \\
\times\,01010 & \times\,10 \\
\hline
00000 & 130 \\
01101 & \\
00000 & \\
01101 & \\
00000 & \\
\hline
0010000010 &
\end{array}
$$

4.5.1 The half-adder

Having looked at gates, Boolean algebra and binary arithmetic, we can now consider the design of a circuit to add binary numbers. The most primitive circuit used in binary addition is called the *half-adder* or HA, and adds together two bits to give a sum, S, and a carry, C as described in Table 4.10. The sum, S, is given by $S = A\overline{B} + \overline{A}B$ and the carry by $C = AB$.

From the earlier section on gates we know that this circuit may be realized in at least three different ways—see Fig. 4.7. This circuit, whatever its implementation, is often represented in many texts by the symbol in Fig. 4.8.

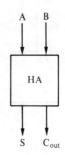

Fig. 4.8 The circuit representation of a half-adder.

Table 4.10 Truth table for half-adder

A	B	S	C	
0	0	0	0	From this truth table it can be seen that the sum of two bits is their EXCLUSIVE OR so that $S = \overline{A}B + A\overline{B} = A \otimes B$. The carry is given by $C = AB$.
0	1	1	0	
1	0	1	0	
1	1	0	1	
		↑	↑	
		Sum	Carry	

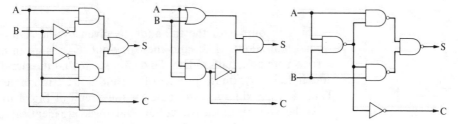

Fig. 4.7 Three ways of implementing a half-adder.

4.5.2 The full-adder

Unfortunately, the half-adder is of little use as it stands. When two *n*-bit numbers are added together we have to take account of any carry bits. Adding bits a_i of A and b_i of B together must include provision for adding in the carry bit c_{i-1} from the results of the addition in the column to the right of a_i and b_i. This is represented diagrammatically as:

$$\begin{array}{l} a_{n-1}\ldots a_2\ a_1\ a_0 \\ +\,b_{n-1}\ldots b_2\ b_1\ b_0 \\ \hline \end{array} \rightarrow \begin{array}{l} a_{n-1}\ldots a_2\ a_1\ a_0 \\ b_{n-1}\ldots b_2\ b_1\ b_0 \\ +\,c_{n-2}\ldots c_1\ c_0 \\ \hline \end{array}$$

When people perform an addition they deal with the carry automatically, without thinking about it. More specifically they say, 'If a carry is generated we add it to the next column, if it is not we do nothing'. In human terms *doing nothing* and *adding zero* are equivalent. As far as the

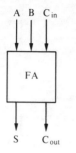

Fig. 4.9 The circuit representation of a full-adder.

logic necessary to carry out the addition is concerned, we always add in the carry from the previous stage, where the carry bit has the value 0 or 1.

The full-adder, represented by the symbol of Fig. 4.9, adds together two bits, plus a carry-in from the previous stage, to generate a sum and a carry-out. Table 4.11 provides the truth table for a full adder.

The conventional way of realizing the circuit for a full-adder is to connect two half-adders in tandem. Conceptually, a full-adder requires that the two bits of A and B be added together and then the carry-in should be added to the result. Figure 4.10 shows a possible representation of the full-adder in terms of two half-adders.

Table 4.11 Truth table for full adder

C_{in}	A	B	S	C_{out}	
0	0	0	0	0	
0	0	1	1	0	
0	1	0	1	0	same as for half-adder
0	1	1	0	1	
1	0	0	1	0	
1	0	1	0	1	
1	1	0	0	1	
1	1	1	1	1	
↑			↑	↑	
Carry-in			Sum	Carry-out	

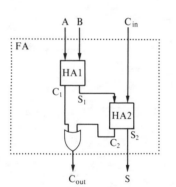

Fig. 4.10 Implementing a full-adder by two half-adders.

The sum output of the full-adder is given by the sum output of the second half-adder, HA2, and the carry-out, C_{out}, is given by ORing the carries from both half-adders. To demonstrate that the circuit of Fig. 4.10 does indeed perform the process of full addition a truth table may be used. Table 4.12 provides a truth table for the circuit of Fig. 4.10.

As the contents of the two columns arrowed are identical to those of the corresponding columns of the truth table for the full-adder, we must conclude that our circuit is that of a full-adder. In practice the full-adder is not often implemented in this way as the propagation path through the two half-adders involves six units of delay. An alternative full-adder

Table 4.12 Truth table for a full-adder implemented by two half-adders

C_{in}	A	B	S_1	C_1	S_2	C_2	C_{out}
0	0	0	0	0	0	0	0
0	0	1	1	0	1	0	0
0	1	0	1	0	1	0	0
0	1	1	0	1	0	0	1
1	0	0	0	0	1	0	0
1	0	1	1	0	0	1	1
1	1	0	1	0	0	1	1
1	1	1	0	1	1	0	1
					↑		↑
					Sum		Carry-out

circuit may be derived directly from the equations for the sum and the carry from the truth table. Let the sum be S, the carry-out C_o and the carry-in C.

$$S = \bar{C}\bar{A}B + \bar{C}A\bar{B} + C\bar{A}\bar{B} + CAB$$

$$\begin{aligned}
\text{and } C_o &= \bar{C}AB + C\bar{A}B + CA\bar{B} + CAB \\
&= \bar{C}AB + C\bar{A}B + CA(\bar{B} + B) \\
&= \bar{C}AB + C\bar{A}B + CA \\
&= \bar{C}AB + C(\bar{A}B + A) = \bar{C}AB + C(A + B) \\
&= \bar{C}AB + CB + CA \\
&= A(\bar{C}B + C) + CB = A(B + C) + CB \\
&= CA + CB + AB
\end{aligned}$$

Note that the carry-out represents a ***majority logic function*** which is true if two or more of the inputs are true. The circuit diagram of the full-adder corresponding to the above equations is given in Fig. 4.11. This circuit contains more gates than the equivalent realization in terms of half-adders (12 against 9) but it is faster. The maximum propagation delay is three gates in series.

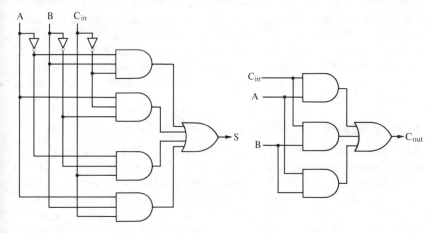

Fig. 4.11 A possible circuit for the full-adder.

4.5.3 The addition of words

Even a full adder on its own is not a great deal of help, as we frequently wish to add two n-bit numbers together. We will now look at ways in which two n-bit numbers can be added together using full-adders. We begin with the ***serial full-adder*** and then describe the ***parallel full-adder***.

It is perfectly possible to add two n-bit numbers, A and B, together, serially, a bit at a time by means of the scheme given in Fig. 4.12. The contents of the shift registers containing the n-bit words A and B are shifted into the full-adder a bit at a time. The result of each addition is shifted into a result or sum register. A single flip-flop holds the carry bit so that the old carry-out becomes the next carry-in.

After n clock pulses, the sum register, S, contains the sum of A and B. Serial adders are frequently included in some (often older) text books with the comment that 'as the serial adder uses only one full-adder, it is cheaper

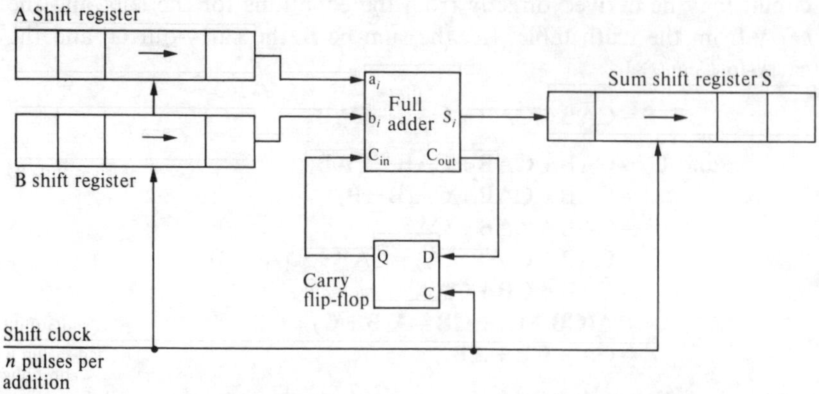

Fig. 4.12 The serial adder.

than a parallel adder using *n* full-adders. However, because the serial adder adds one bit of its two inputs together at a time, it is slower than the corresponding parallel adder.' Such a statement may have been true in the past but it is not now. With the present ability to put 500 000 or more transistors on a chip, a circuit can be designed to optimize its performance rather than reduce the number of gates. I have included the serial adder here to show the contrast between serial operations (bit by bit) and parallel operations involving all the bits of a word at once. In Chapter 10, we will discover that computers communicate with each other (over long distances) serially, a bit at a time, rather than by parallel transmission, a word at a time.

Parallel adders

The more practical form of adder is the ***parallel*** adder of Fig. 4.13 which employs *n* full-adders to add together two *n*-bit numbers. The carry-out of each full-adder becomes the carry-in of the stage on its left. A parallel adder adds the *n* bits of word A to the *n* bits of word B in one simultaneous operation. The term ***parallel*** implies that all *n* additions take place at the same time. It is tempting to think that the parallel adder is *n* times faster than the corresponding serial adder. In practice a real parallel adder is slowed down by the effect of the carry-bit propagation through the stages of the full-adder. We shall shortly return to this topic.

There are several points worth noting about Fig. 4.13. Firstly, it might be thought that the first stage could be replaced by a half-adder since it does not have a carry-in (there is no stage to its right). However, by using a full-adder for this stage, the carry-in may be set to zero for normal addition, or it may be set to 1 to generate A + B + 1 (the '+' here

Fig. 4.13 The parallel adder.

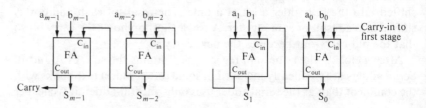

signifying addition and not logical OR). If B were set to zero, $A + 1$ would be generated and the circuit functions as an incrementer. A facility to add in *one* to the sum of A plus B will prove very useful when we come to complementary arithmetic.

Another feature of this circuit concerns the carry-out from the last (most significant bit) stage. If two n-bit words are added and the result is greater than $111\ldots 1$, then a carry-out is generated. As the computer cannot store words longer than n bits, the sum cannot be stored in the memory as a single entity. The carry-out of the most-significant stage may be latched into a flip-flop (normally forming part of the computer's condition code register). When addition is performed by software as part of a program, it is usual for the programmer to test the carry bit to check if the result has gone out of range.

A final point about the parallel adder concerns the meaning of the term *parallel*. It must be apparent that while the first stage can add a_0 to b_0 to get s_0 as soon as A and B are presented to the input terminals of the full-adder, the second stage must wait for the first stage's carry-out to be added in to a_1 plus b_1 before it can be sure that its own output is valid. In the worst case of $111\ldots 1 + 1$, the carry must ripple through all the stages. The full-adder we have described here is parallel in the sense that all the bits of A are added to all the bits of B in a single operation *without* the need for a number of separate clock cycles. Once the values of A and B have been presented to the inputs of the full adders, the system must wait until the circuit has had time to settle down and for all carries to propagate, before the next operation is started.

In many digital systems the clock period is determined by the worst-case settling time required by the slowest circuit in the system. More sophisticated digital systems have a variable clock pulse, with the duration of each pulse tailored to the worst-case delay possible for the current operation being carried out. It is possible to reduce partially the effect of the *ripple through carry* in a parallel adder. Arrangements called *carry look-ahead circuits* can be used to anticipate a carry over a group of say four full-adders. That is, the carry-out to stage $i + 5$ is calculated by examining the inputs to stages $i + 4$, $i + 3$, $i + 2$, $i + 1$, and the carry-in to stage $i + 1$, by means of a special high-speed circuit. This anticipated carry can be fed to the fifth stage to avoid the delay that would be incurred if a ripple-through carry were used. The exact nature of these circuits is beyond the scope of this book.

The full-subtractor

Using the techniques we have applied to the full-adder it is possible to design a full-subtractor in the same way. As the full-subtractor is not used widely I leave its design as an exercise to the reader.

4.6 Signed numbers

Any real computer must be able to deal with negative numbers as well as positive numbers. Before we examine how the computer handles negative numbers we should consider how we deal with them. I believe that people do not, in fact, actually use negative numbers. They use positive numbers (the '5' in -5 is the same as in $+5$), and place a negative sign in front of the number to remind them that it must be treated in a special way when it takes part in arithmetic operations. In other words we treat all numbers as positive and use a sign (i.e. $+$ or $-$) to determine what we have to do with the numbers. For example, consider the following two operations:

$$
\begin{array}{rr}
8 & 8 \\
+5 \quad \text{and} \quad & -5 \\
\hline
13 & 3 \\
\hline
\end{array}
$$

In each of the above examples the numbers are the *same*, but the *operations* we performed on them were *different*; in the first case we added them together and in the second case we subtracted them. This technique can be extended to computer arithmetic to give the *sign* and *magnitude* representation of a negative number.

4.6.1 Sign and magnitude representation

An n-bit word can have 2^n possible different values from 0 to 2^{n-1}. For example, an 8-bit word can represent the numbers 0, 1, ..., 254, 255. One way of representing a negative number is to take the most significant bit and reserve it to indicate the sign of the number. The usual convention is to choose the sign bit to be 0 to represent positive numbers and to choose it to be 1 to represent negative numbers. We can express the value of a sign and magnitude number in the form $(-1)^S \times M$, where S is the sign bit of the number and M is its magnitude. If $S=0$, $(-1)^0 = +1$ and the number is positive and if $S=1$, $(-1)^1 = -1$ and the number is negative.

For example, in eight bits we can interpret the two numbers 00001101 and 10001101 as

$$
\underset{\substack{\downarrow \\ \text{Sign} \\ \text{bit}}}{0} \quad \underset{\substack{\text{Number} \\ \text{magnitude}}}{\underline{0001101}} \quad = +13_{10} \quad \text{and} \quad \underset{\substack{\downarrow \\ \text{Sign} \\ \text{bit}}}{1} \quad \underset{\substack{\text{Number} \\ \text{magnitude}}}{\underline{0001101}} \quad = -13_{10}.
$$

Using a sign and magnitude representation is a perfectly valid way to represent signed numbers, although it is not widely used in integer arithmetic. The range of a sign and magnitude number in n bits is given by

$$
-(2^{n-1}-1) \quad \text{to} \quad +(2^{n-1}-1) \quad \text{or} \quad -2^{n-1}+1 \quad \text{to} \quad 2^{n-1}-1.
$$

All we have done is to take an n-bit number, use one bit to represent the sign and let the remaining $n-1$ bits represent the number. Thus, an 8-bit number can represent from -127 (11111111) to $+127$ (01111111). One of the objections to this system is that it has two values for zero:

$00000000 = +0$ and $10000000 = -0$

Personally, I do not see this as a particular problem, given the current ability to produce complex digital devices economically. Possibly the sign and magnitude notation was abandoned in the earlier days of computers when each and every gate was a precious item. The most widespread reason for rejecting this system is simply that it requires separate adders and subtractors. We shall soon see that other ways of representing negative numbers remove the need for separate adders and subtractors. However, I would emphasize that today the additional cost of a subtractor in a CPU is negligible.

Examples of addition and subtraction in sign and magnitude arithmetic are given below. It must be remembered that the most significant bit is a *sign bit* and does not take part in the calculation itself. This is in contrast with twos complement arithmetic (see later) in which the sign bit forms an integral part of the number when it is used in calculations. In each of the four examples below, we perform the calculation by first converting the sign bit to a $+$ve or to a $-$ve sign. Then we perform the calculation and convert the sign of the result into a sign bit.

Sign and magnitude value	Number with sign bit converted into a sign	Result with sign converted into sign bit
1. 001011 $+001110$ →	$+01011$ $+01110$	
	$+11001$	→ 011001
2. 001011 $+100110$ →	$+01011$ -00110	
	$+00101$	→ 000101
3. 001011 $+110110$ →	$+01011$ -10110	
	-01011	→ 101011
4. 001011 -001001 →	$+01011$ -01001	
	00010	→ 000010

4.6.2 Complementary arithmetic

In complementary arithmetic the *negativeness* of a number is contained within the number itself. Because of this, the concept of signs ('$+$' and '$-$') may, effectively, be dispensed with. If we add X to Y the operation is that of addition if X is positive and Y is positive, but if Y is negative the end result is that of subtraction (assuming that Y is represented by its negative form). It is important to point out here that complementary arithmetic is used to represent and to manipulate **both** positive and negative numbers. To demonstrate that there is nothing magical about complementary arithmetic it is worthwhile first examining decimal complements.

Tens complement arithmetic

The 10s complement of an n-digit decimal number, N, is defined as $10^n - N$. The 10s complement may also be calculated by subtracting each of the digits of N from 9 and adding 1 to the result. Consider the 4-digit decimal number 1234. Its 10s complement is

(a) $10^4 - 1234 = 8766$ or (b)   9999
                                    $-$ 1234
                                    _____

                                    $8765 + 1 = 8766$

Suppose we add this complement to another number (say) 8576. We get

$$\begin{array}{r} 8576 \\ +8766 \\ \hline 17342 \end{array}$$

Now let us examine the effect of subtracting 1234 from 8576 by conventional means.

$$\begin{array}{r} 8576 \\ -1234 \\ \hline 7342 \end{array}$$

Notice that the results of the two operations are similar in the least significant four digits, but differ in the fifth digit by 10^4. The reason for this is not hard to find. Consider the subtraction of Y from X. We wish to calculate $Z = X - Y$, which we do by adding the 10s complement of Y to X. The 10s complement of Y is $10^4 - Y$. Therefore we get

$$Z = X + (10^4 - Y) = 10^4 + (X - Y).$$

In other words, we get the desired result, $X - Y$, together with an **unwanted** digit in the left-most position. This digit may be discarded. Note that complementing a number **twice** results in the original number. For example, $-1234 \rightarrow 10^4 - 1234 = 8876$. Complementing twice, we get $-(-1234) \rightarrow -(8876) = 10^4 - 8876 = 1234$. Note that I have used the arrow '$\rightarrow$' to replace 'is represented by'.

4.6.3 Twos complement representation

The equivalent of 10s complement in binary arithmetic is twos complement. To form the twos complement of an n-bit binary number, N, we evaluate $2^n - N$. For example, in 5 bits, if $N = 5 = 00101$, then the twos complement of N is given by $2^5 - 00101 = 100000 - 00101 = 11011$. It is important to note here that 11011 represents -00101 (-5) or $+27$ depending only on whether we interpret the bit pattern ***11011*** as a twos complement integer or as an unsigned integer.

If we add the twos complement of N (i.e. 11011) to another binary number, we should execute the operation of subtraction. In the following demonstrations we add 11011 to 01100 (i.e. 12).

$$
\begin{array}{ll}
\quad 01100 & \quad 12 \\
+\,11011 & +\,(-5) \\
\hline
100111 & \quad 7 \\
\end{array}
$$

As in the case of the decimal example in 10s complement arithmetic, we get the correct answer, together with the $2^n = 2^5$ term, which is discarded. Before continuing further, it is worthwhile examining the effect of adding all the combinations of positive and negative values for a pair of numbers. It is important to note that the result of each of these four examples must be interpreted as a twos complement value.

Let $X = 9 = 01001$ and $Y = 6 = 00110$:

$$-X \rightarrow 100000 - 01001 = 10111$$
$$-Y \rightarrow 100000 - 00110 = 11010$$

$$
\begin{array}{lll}
1. & +X & \quad 01001 \\
   & +Y & +00110 \\
   &   & \hline \\
   &   & \quad 01111 = +15 \\
\end{array}
\qquad
\begin{array}{lll}
2. & +X & \quad 01001 \\
   & -Y & +11010 \\
   &   & \hline \\
   &   & 100011 = +3 \\
\end{array}
$$

$$
\begin{array}{lll}
3. & -X & \quad 10111 \\
   & +Y & +00110 \\
   &   & \hline \\
   &   & \quad 11101 = -3 \\
\end{array}
\qquad
\begin{array}{lll}
4. & -X & \quad 10111 \\
   & -Y & +11010 \\
   &   & \hline \\
   &   & 110001 = -15. \\
\end{array}
$$

All four examples give us the result we would expect when the result is interpreted as a twos complement number. However, as Examples 3 and 4 give negative results, they may require a little further explanation. The result in Example 3 is -3. The two complement representation of -3 is $100000 - 00011 = 11101$. Similarly, in Example 4 the twos complement representation of -15 is $100000 - 01111 = 10001$.

Example 4 evaluates $-X + -Y$ to get a result of -15 but with the addition of a 2^n term. In Example 4, where both numbers are negative, we have $(2^n - X) + (2^n - Y) = 2^n + (2^n - X - Y)$. The first part of our expression is the redundant 2^n and the second part is the twos complement representation of $-X - Y$. We can now see that the twos complement system works for all possible combinations of positive and negative numbers.

Calculating twos complement values

The twos complement system would not be so attractive if it were not for the ease with which twos complements can be formed. Consider the twos complement of N, which is defined as: $-N \rightarrow 2^n - N$.

Suppose we rearranged the equation by subtracting 1 from the 2^n and adding it to the result:

$$-N \to \quad (2^n - 1) \quad -N + 1$$
$$\to \underbrace{111 \ldots 1}_{} -N + 1.$$

n places

For example, in 8 bits ($n = 8$) we have:

$$-N \to 2^8 - N$$
$$\to 100000000 - N$$
$$\to 100000000 - 1 - N + 1 \quad \text{(after rearranging)}$$
$$\to \ 11111111 - N + 1.$$

The evaluation of the twos complement of N becomes particularly easy because, if a bit of N is 0, subtracting it from 1 gives 1, and if the bit is 1, subtracting it from 1 gives 0. In other words, $1 - N_i = \bar{N_i}$. That is, to form the twos complement of a number we simply invert the bits and add 1. For example, in five bits we have

$$7 = 00111$$
$$-7 = \overline{00111} + 1 = 11000 + 1 = 11001.$$

Evaluating twos complement numbers in the above fashion is attractive because it is easy to perform with hardware. To implement an adder/subtractor the logic of Fig. 4.14 is used. This diagram shows how, with the addition of a little extra logic, a parallel binary adder may readily be converted into an adder/subtractor for twos complement numbers.

Each of the EOR gates has two inputs b_i (where $i = 0$ to $n - 1$), and C, a control signal. The output of the EOR is $b_i\bar{C} + \bar{b_i}C$. If C is 0 then $\bar{C} = 1$ and the output is b_i. If C is 1 then $\bar{C} = 0$ and the output is $\bar{b_i}$. The n EORs form a chain of programmable invertors, inverting the input if $C = 1$ and passing the input unchanged if $C = 0$. Note also that the carry-in input to the first full-adder is C. When addition is being performed $C = 0$ and the carry-in is zero. However, when we perform subtraction $C = 1$, so that one is added to the result of the addition. This ***one*** is needed to form the twos complement of B; we have already inverted B's bits so that adding the one forms the twos complement of B, enabling the subtraction of B from A to take place.

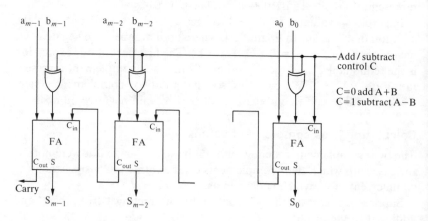

Fig. 4.14 The binary adder/subtractor.

Properties of twos complement numbers

1. The twos complement system is a true complement system in that $+X+(-X)=0$. For example, in five bits $+13=01101$ and $-13=10011$. The sum of $+13$ and -13 is:

$$\begin{array}{r} 01101 \\ +\,10011 \\ \hline 100000=0 \end{array}$$

2. There is a unique zero $00\ldots0$.

3. If the number is positive the most significant bit is 0, and if it is negative the MSB is 1. Thus, the MSB is a sign bit.

4. The range of twos complement numbers in n bits is from -2^{n-1} to $+2^{n-1}-1$. For $n=5$, this range is from -16 to $+15$. Note that the total number of different numbers is 32 (16 negative, zero, and 15 positive). What this demonstrates is that a 5-bit number can uniquely describe 32 items, and it is up to us whether we choose to call these items the natural binary integers 0 to 31, or the signed twos complement numbers -16 to $+15$.

5. The complement of the complement of X is X (i.e. $-(-X)=X$). In five bits $+12=01100$ and $-12\rightarrow10011+1=10100$. If we form the twos complement of -12 (i.e. 10100) in the usual fashion by inverting the bits and adding 1, we get $\overline{10100}+1=01011+1=01100$, which is the same as the number we started with. Please note that a negative number is represented by its complement. It is not equal to its complement.

Let us now see what happens if we violate the range of twos complement numbers. That is, we will carry out an operation whose result falls outside the range of values that can be represented by twos complement numbers. If we choose a five-bit representation, we know that the range of valid signed numbers is -16 to $+15$. Suppose we first add 5 and 6 and then try 12 and 13.

Case 1		Case 2	
$5=$	00101	$12=$	01100
$+6=$	00110	$+13=$	01101
$\overline{}$	$\overline{}$	$\overline{}$	$\overline{}$
11	$01011=11_{10}$	25	$11001=-7_{10}$ (as a twos complement number)

In Case 1 we get the expected answer of $+11$, but in Case 2 we get a negative result because the sign bit is '1'. If the answer were regarded as an unsigned binary number it would be $+25$ which is, of course, the correct answer. Once the twos complement system has been chosen to represent signed numbers, all answers must be interpreted in this light.

Similarly, if we add together two negative numbers whose total is less than -16, we also go out of range. For example, if we add $-9=10111$ and $-12=10100$, we get:

$$
\begin{array}{ll}
-9 & \quad 10111 \\
-12 & +10100 \\
\hline
-21 & \quad 101011 \quad \text{gives a positive result } 01011 = +11_{10}
\end{array}
$$

Both of these cases represent a condition called **arithmetic overflow**. Arithmetic overflow occurs during a twos complement addition if the result of adding two positive numbers yields a negative result, or if the result of adding two negative numbers yields a positive result. Overflow represents an out-of-range condition and can result from operations other than addition (e.g. multiplication). We can express arithmetic overflow during an addition algebraically. If we let a_{n-1} be the sign bit of A, b_{n-1} be the sign bit of B, and s_{n-1} be the sign bit of the sum of A and B, then

$$
V = a_{n-1}\,\overline{b_{n-1}}\,\overline{s_{n-1}} + \overline{a_{n-1}}\,b_{n-1}\,s_{n-1}.
$$

That is, if the sign bits of A and B are the same but the sign bit of the result is different, arithmetic overflow has occurred. It is important to note that arithmetic overflow is a consequence of twos complement arithmetic, and should not be confused with carry-out, which is the carry bit generated by the addition of the two most significant bits of the numbers.

An alternative view of twos complement numbers

We have seen that a binary integer, N, lying in the range $0 \leqslant N < 2^{n-1}$, is represented in a negative form by the expression $2^n - N$. We have also seen that this expression can be readily evaluated by inverting the bits of N and adding 1 to the result.

Another way of looking at a twos complement number is to regard it as a conventional binary number represented in the positional notation but with the sign of the most significant bit negative. That is,

$$
-N = -d_{n-1}2^{n-1} + d_{n-2}2^{n-2} + \cdots + d_0 2^0,
$$

where d_{n-1}, d_{n-2}, ..., d_0 are the bits of the twos complement number D. Consider the representation of 14, and the twos complement form of -14, in five bits:

$$
\begin{array}{ll}
& +14 = 01110 \\
& -14 \rightarrow 2^n - N = 2^5 - 14 = 32 - 14 = 18 = 10010_2 \\
\text{or} \quad & -14 \rightarrow \overline{01110} + 1 = 10001 + 1 = 10010_2.
\end{array}
$$

From what we have said earlier, we can regard the twos complement representation of -14 (i.e. 10010) as

$$
\begin{aligned}
& -1 \times 2^4 + 0 \times 2^3 + 0 \times 2^2 + 1 \times 2^1 + 0 \times 2^0 \\
= & -16 + (0 + 0 + 2 + 0) \\
= & -16 + 2 = -14
\end{aligned}
$$

It is possible to demonstrate that a twos complement number is indeed represented in this way. In what follows N represents a positive integer, and D the twos complement form of $-N$. We wish to prove that $-N = D$.

That is, $-N = -2^{n-1} + \sum_{i=0}^{n-2} d_i 2^i.$ (1)

In terms of the bits of N and D we have

$$-(N_{n-1}N_{n-2}\ldots N_1 N_0) = d_{n-1}d_{n-2}\ldots d_1 d_0 = D.$$ (2)

The bits of D are formed from the bits of N by inverting and adding 1.

$$\overline{N}_{n-1}\overline{N}_{n-2}\cdots\overline{N}_0 + 1 = d_{n-1}d_{n-2}\cdots d_0.$$ (3)

Substituting (3) in (1) to eliminate D we get

$$-N = -2^{n-1} + \sum_{i=0}^{n-2} \overline{N}_i 2^i + 1.$$

But $\overline{N}_i = 1 - N_i$, so that

$$-\overline{N} = -2^{n-1} + \sum_{i=0}^{n-2} (1 - N_i)2^i + 1$$

$$= -2^{n-1} + \sum_{i=0}^{n-2} 2^i - \sum_{i=0}^{n-2} N_i 2^i + 1$$

$$= -2^{n-1} + (2^{n-1} - 1) - \sum_{i=0}^{n-2} N_i 2^i + 1$$

$$= -2^{n-1} + (2^{n-1} - 1) + 1 - N \quad \text{(because } \sum_{i=0}^{n-2} N_i 2^i = N \text{ as the most}$$

significant bit of N is zero for N to be within its stated range)

$$= -2^{n-1} + 2^{n-1} - N = -N.$$

Representing twos complement numbers graphically

We can visualize numbers in the twos complement system by imagining numbers arranged around a circle. Figure 4.15 demonstrates such an arrangement for 4-bit numbers in which a circle has been divided up by 16 radials and these radials numbered from 0000 to 1111. Suppose we also decide to number the radials according to their twos complement values,

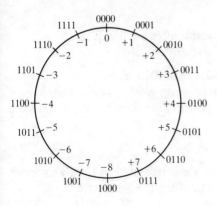

Fig. 4.15 Visualizing twos complement numbers.

so that 0000 to 0111 are numbered 0 to 7, while 1000 to 1111 are numbered -8 to -1. Notice how stepping one place *clockwise* increases a number and stepping one place *anticlockwise* decreases a number. We can now see how adding numbers to a negative value causes the result to move in the direction of zero. For example, if we add 0011 ($+3$) to 1100 (-4) we get 1111 which is -1. If we had added 0101 ($+5$) to 1100, we would have got (1)0001 which is $+1$ and lies to the right of zero.

4.6.4 Ones complement representation

An alternative to twos complement arithmetic is *ones complement* arithmetic in which the representation of a negative number, N, in n bits is given by $2^n - N - 1$. The ones complement representation of a number is one less than the corresponding twos complement representation and is formed more simply by inverting the bits of N. For example, for $n=5$ consider the subtraction of 4 from 9. The binary value of four is 00100 and its ones complement is 11011:

$$
\begin{array}{rl}
+9 = +01001 \rightarrow & 01001 \\
-4 = -\overline{00100} \rightarrow & +11011 \\
\hline
& 100100 \quad \leftarrow \text{result after addition} \\
+ & \llcorner\!\!\longrightarrow 1 \\
\hline
& 00101 \quad \leftarrow \text{result after adding in the} \\
& \qquad\qquad \text{end-around-carry}
\end{array}
$$

After the addition has been completed, the left-most bit of the result is added to the least significant bit of the result in an arrangement called end-around-carry. This provides us with the final and correct result. Note that if the result of the initial addition yields a carry-out of zero, the result is negative and adding in the carry-out (i.e. zero) also gives the correct answer. Consider the following example:

$$
\begin{array}{rl}
-9 = -01001 \rightarrow & 10110 \\
+4 = -\overline{00100} \rightarrow & +00100 \\
\hline
& 011010 \quad \leftarrow \text{result after addition} \\
+ & \llcorner\!\!\longrightarrow 0 \\
\hline
& 11010 \quad \leftarrow \text{result after adding in the} \\
& \qquad\qquad \text{end-around-carry}
\end{array}
$$

Note that in ones complement 11010 is -00101 (i.e. -5).

We can demonstrate that end-around-carry works in ones complement arithmetic as follows. Suppose we wish to compute $X - Y$. We add the ones complement of Y to X to get

$$ X + (2^n - Y - 1) = 2^n + (X - Y) - 1. $$

By transferring the carry-out, 2^n, to the least significant bit, we correct the result $(X - Y) - 1$ to $(X - Y)$ by cancelling the '-1' term.

If we add together two ones complement negative numbers we get

$$-X + -Y = (2^n - X - 1) + (2^n - Y - 1)$$
$$= 2^n - 1 + 2^n - 1 - (X + Y).$$

If we apply end-around-carry to this result, the *first* 2^n term cancels the *first* -1 term to leave $2^n - 1 - (X + Y)$. This is, of course, the correct result in ones complement form.

The ones complement system is not a true complement as $X + (-X)$ is not zero. Furthermore, there are two representations for zero: $00\ldots0$ and $11\ldots1$. The ones complement system is not as widely used as the twos complement system for representing signed numbers, but it is found in some computers.

It is instructive to compare the various ways of representing numbers we have encountered so far. Table 4.13 shows how the sequence of 5-bit

Table 4.13 The representation of negative numbers

Binary code	Pure binary	Sign and magnitude	Ones complement	Twos complement
00000	0	0	0	0
00001	1	1	1	1
00010	2	2	2	2
00011	3	3	3	3
00100	4	4	4	4
00101	5	5	5	5
00110	6	6	6	6
00111	7	7	7	7
01000	8	8	8	8
01001	9	9	9	9
01010	10	10	10	10
01011	11	11	11	11
01100	12	12	12	12
01101	13	13	13	13
01110	14	14	14	14
01111	15	15	15	15
10000	16	−0	−15	−16
10001	17	−1	−14	−15
10010	18	−2	−13	−14
10011	19	−3	−12	−13
10100	20	−4	−11	−12
10101	21	−5	−10	−11
10110	22	−6	−9	−10
10111	23	−7	−8	−9
11000	24	−8	−7	−8
11001	25	−9	−6	−7
11010	26	−10	−5	−6
11011	27	−11	−4	−5
11100	28	−12	−3	−4
11101	29	−13	−2	−3
11110	30	−14	−1	−2
11111	31	−15	−0	−1

binary numbers for $n = 5$ for pure binary numbers, sign and magnitude, ones complement, and twos complement representations.

4.7 Computer arithmetic and assembly-language programming

Having dealt with the addition and subtraction of binary numbers at the hardware level in terms of full adders, it is time to see how these operations are carried out at the software level in terms of assembly language. I do not wish to pre-empt later sections on assembly language, but the following notes should help.

Assembly language is the most primitive language (excepting machine code which is the binary form of an assembly language) in which programs can be written and is the *host* or *native* language of the computer. An assembly language uses *mnemonics* to represent the various operations that may be performed by the computer. For example, ADD = add, SUB = subtract, BRA = branch etc. Mnemonics vary from computer to computer, although the meanings of many mnemonics are self-evident.

Following the mnemonic is often a *symbolic* name that refers to a variable. If we write ADD.B NUM_1,D0 we mean add the 8-bit number we have called (or 'labelled') NUM_1 to the contents of a data register numbered *D0*. The '.B' following an instruction (i.e. mnemonic) indicates that we are working with 8-bit numbers. A data register is a special purpose data storage element that is located within the CPU rather than in the main memory. NUM_1 refers not to the number but to its location in memory. As many computers allow us to specify only one memory resident operand, it is necessary to have special registers in the computer to hold intermediate results (i.e. data registers—in the case of the 68000 there are eight, called D0–D7). Throughout this book most assembly language examples will refer to the 68000 microprocessor. The reasons for this are as follows:

1. It can use an 8-bit data word which is of manageable size for student examples. A short data word does not necessarily restrict the things we can do.

2. The architecture and the assembly language of the 68000 are both easy to use and understand. Furthermore, its architecture is not untypical of the mainstream computer. Some computers are less typical of computers in general and are therefore less well suited to teaching purposes.

3. The 68000 can operate on byte (8-bit), word (16-bit) or long word (32-bit) values. Note that byte, word and long word are used here to refer to particular word lengths—this is Motorola's terminology.

When carrying out operations with a '.B' suffix (e.g. ADD.B, SUB.B, MOVE.B), the 68000 uses an 8-bit data word and can therefore represent unsigned binary numbers in the range 0 to 255 (i.e. 0 to $2^8 - 1$), and signed twos complement numbers in the range -128 to $+127$.

Suppose we wish to perform the operation $R := P + Q$ by adding together the numbers P and Q, and calling the result R. P, Q, and R are names referring to physical locations within the 68000's memory. We use symbolic names because we do not want to be bothered with trying to remember addresses. A program that will evaluate $R := P + Q$ is

```
MOVE.B P,D0
ADD.B  Q,D0
MOVE.B D0,R
```

The first instruction causes the contents of the memory location we have called P to be moved to data register D0. The mnemonic, 'MOVE.B' means **move** a byte from its **source** to its **destination**. Note that 68000 assembly language instructions are written in the form

```
operation <source>,<destination>
```

with the result that MOVE.B X,Y moves the byte X into the byte Y. Not all computers follow the same convention—the 8086 microprocessor uses the convention `operation <destination>,<source>`

In a real program it would normally be necessary for the programmer to 'tell' the assembler where the locations P, Q, and R are located in the memory. The MOVE.B operation does not affect the number in P. It is a most important rule that unless the contents of a memory location or register are modified by writing a new number into it, they do not change. Perhaps it would have been better to call the 'MOVE' instruction 'COPY' as this expresses the action of MOVE more exactly.

The second instruction, ADD.B Q,D0, means add the contents of memory location called Q to the contents of D0. Figure 4.16 shows the location of the program and its data in memory. A memory map is a diagrammatic representation of the layout of data or instructions in memory.

The final instruction, MOVE.B D0,R, stores the contents of data register D0 to a memory location, which in our case is called R. There is nothing difficult about this example. However, the reader may ask 'But are we operating with unsigned binary numbers or with twos complement numbers?' The answer is that it does not matter. The same addition operation will serve both cases: it is how the programmer **deals** with the result that matters.

At the end of an arithmetic (and some other types of) operation the CPU updates its condition code register, CCR. The format of the 68000's CCR is defined in Fig. 4.17.

Here we are concerned only with bits 0 and 1, which represent carry and overflow, respectively. The computer does not know what the programmer is up to. So, at the end of an arithmetic operation it says:

1. Was a carry generated (a 1 propagated out of bit 7 of the result)?
2. If I assume the number was in twos complement form, was there an overflow?

It is up to the **programmer** to use the information in the condition code register according to the application. Consider now the two programs:

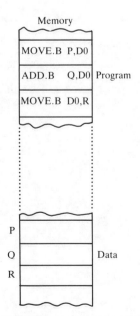

Fig. 4.16 Memory map of a simple program.

Fig. 4.17 Format of the 68000's
condition code register.

X=extend bit (1 if a carry was generated by an arithmetic operation)
N=negative flag (1 if msb=1)
Z=zero flag (1 if all bits of operand=0)
V=overflow flag (1 if last operation generated arithmetic overflow)
C=carry bit (1 if last operation generated a carry out of msb)

```
Case 1                     Case 2
MOVE.B P,D0                MOVE.B P,D0
ADD.B  Q,D0                ADD.B  Q,D0
BCS    ERROR               BVS    ERROR
MOVE.B D0,R               MOVE.B D0,R
  .                          .
  .                          .
  .                          .
ERROR                      ERROR
```

In Case 1 we have assumed that the arithmetic is unsigned binary. If, after the ADD.B Q,D0 operation, the sum of the two numbers is greater than 255, a one is propagated from the most significant bit position into the carry. The following instruction, BCS, means branch if carry set. Thus, if a carry has been generated, the next instruction, MOVE.B D0,R, is not executed. Instead a branch or jump is made to the part of the program called 'ERROR'. This part of the program (not shown here) must be designed to deal with the problem. If a branch is not made, the next instruction immediately following the conditional branch is executed.

In Case 2 the arithmetic has been assumed to be in twos complement form. The program is identical to Case 1 except that after the addition we test to see if the overflow bit has been set. The V bit in the 68000 is set after arithmetic operations *on the assumption that* twos complement representation of signed numbers is being used.

Dealing with large integers

The principal limitation of these examples is that they handle only 8-bit numbers. While I have nothing against small numbers personally, there are times when numbers greater than 255 impinge on my life. In these circumstances I can use the 68000's ability to deal with 16-bit or 32-bit numbers. For example, if we wish to perform 16-bit addition we write ADD.W Q,D0, and if we wish to add 32-bit numbers we write ADD.L Q,D0. The 68000 is able to perform 32-bit arithmetic because its registers are really 32 bits wide. When we perform a byte operation such as ADD.B D0,Q, we are using only the least significant eight bits of a 32-bit register. Similarly, 16-bit operations such as ADD.W D0,D2 involve only the least significant 16 bits of registers D0 and D2.

Sometimes it is necessary to perform arithmetic on even longer words. In such cases we can regard a large word as being made up of units of 32 bits (or even 16 or 8 bits). Unless speed is of the utmost importance, creating large numbers by chaining together smaller units of data is more cost-effective than buying a computer with the required word length.

Imagine that I need to deal with unsigned numbers up to 2^{64} (i.e. 1.8447×10^{19}). To create a 64-bit word all I need do is to take two 32-bit words in memory and regard them as a 64-bit entity. Using the previous example with P, Q, and R we can draw the memory map of Fig. 4.18.

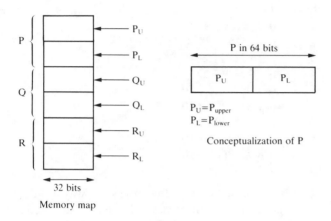

$P_U = P_{upper}$
$P_L = P_{lower}$

Conceptualization of P

Memory map

Fig. 4.18 Memory map of a system for double-precision arithmetic.

Our 64-bit word is now composed of two halves. P is represented by P_U (the 32 most significant bits), and P_L (the 32 least significant bits). I have drawn the memory map with P_L and P_U adjacent to each other, although there is no reason why this must be done in practice. To add P and Q to get R we must perform the following operations:

$$\begin{array}{r} P_U \ P_L \\ + Q_U \ Q_L \\ \hline R_U \ R_L \end{array}$$

That is, we add P_L to Q_L to get R_L, and then P_U to Q_U to get R_U. The only point to note is that when P_L is added to Q_L any carry generated must be added to the $(P_U + Q_U)$ column. In terms of assembly language the program to add P and Q is:

```
MOVE.L PL,D0
ADD.L  QL,D0
MOVE.L D0,RL
MOVE.L PU,D0
ADDX.L QU,D0
MOVE.L D0,RU
```

The first three lines of the above fragment of code calculate the least significant 32 bits of the result in exactly the same way we calculated 8-bit answers. When we come to add P_U to Q_U to create the most significant 32 bits of the result we use a special addition instruction, ADDX.L, that automatically adds in any carry bit when P_U is added to Q_U. The instruction ADDX.L QU,D0 adds the 32 bits in the memory location specified by the symbolic name Q_U to the 32-bit value already in D0, together with the current value of the X bit in the 68000s CCR. The 68000's X bit, or extend bit, is effectively equal to its carry bit. There are some differences between the C and X bits in the CCR, but, as far as we are concerned, the X bit is a copy of the C bit. We can extend this example to deal with numbers made up of an arbitrary number of units. The range of unsigned integers for a given number of bytes is:

Bytes	Range
1	0–255
2	0–65 535
3	0–16 777 215
4	0–4 294 967 296
5	$0–1.0995116 \times 10^{12}$
6	$0–2.8147498 \times 10^{14}$
7	$0–7.2057594 \times 10^{16}$
8	$0–1.8446744 \times 10^{19}$
9	$0–4.7223665 \times 10^{21}$
10	$0–1.2089258 \times 10^{24}$

Subtraction is performed in very much the same way as addition (that is, from the programmer's point of view). The 68000 subtraction instruction has the mnemonic SUB and SUB.B X,Y subtracts byte operand X from byte operand Y and deposits the result in Y. To subtract Q from P to get R, the following program is used:

```
MOVE.B P,D0    Put P into data register D0
SUB.B  Q,D0    Subtract Q
MOVE.B D0,R    Store the result in R
```

Note that in the above fragment of code we have added comments to the right of our mnemonic instructions. A program written in a high-level language like Pascal is often self-documenting because the act of reading it tells the reader what is happening in a clear and unambiguous fashion. Unfortunately, in an assembly language program the morass of detail entirely obscures the point of the program. Consequently, without a copious quantity of comment, the program soon becomes incomprehensible—even to its author.

In the next section we look at how the CPU deals with really large and microscopically small numbers without demanding excessive amounts of storage to represent them.

4.8 Floating point numbers

Before I go any further I have to admit that floating point arithmetic is not one of the great fun-subjects of computer science. While the basic ideas of floating point arithmetic are perfectly simple, the details of their implementation get rather involved.

Before we introduce floating point numbers themselves, we are going to show how *fixed point* numbers are handled by a computer. We have already demonstrated that to deal with large numbers on a machine having a small word length, we just chain words together, but have not yet looked at how the computer deals with binary fractions. Fortunately, a binary (or decimal) fraction presents no problems. Consider the following two calculations in decimal arithmetic.

Case 1 Integer arithmetic   Case 2 Fixed point arithmetic

$$
\begin{array}{r}
7632135 \\
+\ 1794821 \\
\hline
9426956
\end{array}
\qquad
\begin{array}{r}
763.2135 \\
+\ 179.4821 \\
\hline
942.6956
\end{array}
$$

Although Case 1 uses *integer* arithmetic and Case 2 uses *fractional* arithmetic, the calculations are entirely identical. We can extend this principle to computer arithmetic. All the computer programmer has to do is to remember where the binary point is assumed to lie. All input to the computer is scaled to match this convention and all output is similarly scaled. The internal operations themselves are carried out as if the numbers were in integer form. This arrangement is called fixed-point arithmetic, because the binary point is assumed to remain in the same position. That is, there are always the same number of digits before and after the binary point. The advantage of the fixed-point representation of numbers is that no specially complex software or hardware is needed to implement it.

A simple example should make the idea of fixed-point arithmetic clearer. Consider an eight-bit fixed-point number with the four most significant bits representing the integer part and the four least significant bits representing the fractional part.

Let us see what happens if we wish to add the two numbers 3.625 and 6.5, and print the result. An input program first converts these numbers to binary form:

$$3.625_{10} \rightarrow 11.101_2 \rightarrow 0011.1010_2 \text{ (in 8 bits)}$$

$$6.5_{10} \rightarrow 110.1_2 \rightarrow 0110.1000_2 \text{ (in 8 bits)}$$

The computer now regards these numbers as 00111010 and 01101000, respectively. Remember, that the binary point is only imaginary. These numbers are added in the normal way to give

$$
\begin{array}{r}
00111010 \\
+\ 01101000 \\
\hline
10100010
\end{array}
= 162 \text{ (if interpreted as unsigned binary).}
$$

The output program now takes the result and splits it into an integer part 1010, and a fractional part .0010, and prints the correct answer 10.125. Note that a fixed-point number may be spread over several words to achieve a greater range of values than allowed by a single word.

The fixed point representation of fractional numbers is very useful in some circumstances, particularly for financial calculations. In these the smallest fractional part may be (say) 0.1 of a penny or 0.001 pound. The largest integer part may be (say) 1 000 000 pounds. To represent such a quantity in (say) BCD a total of $6 \times 4 + 3 \times 4 = 36$ bits are required. In a byte-oriented computer five bytes would be needed for each number.

Fixed point numbers have their limitations. What about the astrophysicist who is examining the behaviour of the sun? An astrophysicist is confronted with quantities such as the mass of the sun (1 990 000 000 000 000 000 000 000 000 000 000 g) and the mass of an electron (0.000 000 000 000 000 000 000 000 000 910 956 g).

If astrophysicists were to resort to fixed-point arithmetic, they would need to take an extravagantly large number of bytes to represent a wide range of numbers. A single byte represents numbers in the range 0–255, or approximately 0 to 1/4 thousand. If our physicist wanted to work with astronomically large and microscopically small numbers, roughly 14 bytes would be required for the integer part of the number and 12 bytes for the fractional part—a 26-byte (208–bit) number! A clue to a way out of our dilemma is to note that both numbers contain a large number of zeros but few significant digits.

4.8.1 The representation of floating point numbers

Digital computers often represent and store numbers in a *floating point* format. Just as we represent the decimal number 1234.56 by 0.123456×10^4, the computer handles binary numbers in a similar way. For example, 1101101.1101101 may be represented internally as $0.11011011101101 \times 2^7$ (the 7 is, of course, also stored in a binary format). Floating point notation is sometimes called scientific notation. Before looking at floating point numbers in more detail it is necessary to consider the ideas of range, precision and accuracy which are closely related to the way numbers are represented in floating point format.

Range The range of a number tells us how big or how small it can be. In the example of the astrophysicist we were dealing with numbers as large as 2×10^{33} to those as small as 9×10^{-28}, representing a range of approximately 10^{61}, or 61 decades. The range of numbers represented in a digital computer must be sufficient for the vast majority of calculations that are likely to be performed. If the computer is to be employed in a dedicated application where the range of data to be handled is known to be quite small, then the range of valid numbers may be restricted, simplifying the hardware/software requirements.

Precision The precision of a number is a measure of its *exactness* and corresponds to the number of significant figures used to represent it. For example, the constant π may be written as 3.142 or 3.141592. The latter case is more precise than the former because it represents π to one part in 10^7 while the former represents π to one part in 10^4.

Accuracy Accuracy has been included here largely to contrast it with precision, a term often incorrectly thought to mean the same as accuracy. Accuracy is the measure of *correctness* of a quantity. For example, we can say $\pi = 3.141$ or $\pi = 3.241592$. We can now see that in the former case we have a low precision number which is more accurate than its higher precision neighbour. In an ideal world accuracy and precision would go hand-in-hand. It is up to the computer programmer to design numerical algorithms that preserve the accuracy that the available precision allows. One of the potential hazards of computation is calculations of the form:

$$\frac{A+B}{A-B} \quad \text{e.g.} \quad \frac{1234.5687+1234.5678}{1234.5687-1234.5678} = \frac{2469.1365}{0.0009}$$

When the denominator of the expression is evaluated we are left with 0.0009, a number with only one decimal place of precision. Although the calculation shows eight figures of precision, it may be very inaccurate indeed.

A floating point number is represented in the form:

$$a \times r^e,$$

where a is the **mantissa** (also called an argument), r is the **radix** or base, and e is the **exponent** or characteristic. The way in which a computer stores floating point numbers is by dividing the binary sequence representing the number into the two fields illustrated in Fig. 4.19.

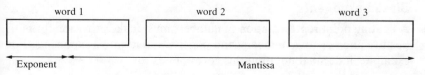

Fig. 4.19 Storing a binary floating point number as exponent and mantissa.

The radix r is understood and need not be stored explicitly by the computer. Throughout the remainder of this section the value of the radix in all floating point numbers is assumed to be two. In some computers the radix of the exponent is octal or hexadecimal, so that the mantissa is multiplied by 8^e or 16^e, respectively. For example, if a floating point number has a mantissa 0.101011 and an **octal** exponent of 4 (i.e. 0100 in 4 bits), the number is equal to 0.101011×8^4 or 0.101011×2^{12} which is 101011000000.

It is not necessary for a floating point number to occupy a single storage location. Indeed with an 8-bit word, such a representation would be useless. Often a number of words are grouped to form the floating point number as described in Fig. 4.20. It is worthwhile noting that the division between exponent and mantissa need not fall at a word boundary. That is, a mantissa might, typically, occupy three bytes and the exponent one byte of a two 16-bit word floating point number.

Fig. 4.20 Using several words to represent a single FP number.

4.8.2 The normalization of floating point numbers

By convention the floating point mantissa is always **_normalized_** (unless it is equal to zero) so that it is expressed in the form $0.1 \ldots \times 2^e$. For the moment we are considering positive manitssas only. If the result of a calculation were to yield $0.01 \ldots \times 2^e$, the result would be normalized to give $0.1 \ldots \times 2^{e-1}$. Similarly, the result $1.01 \ldots \times 2^e$ would be normalized to $0.101 \ldots \times 2^{e+1}$).

By normalizing a mantissa, the greatest possible advantage is taken of the available precision. For example, the unnormalized 8-bit mantissa 0.00001010 has only four significant bits, while the normalized 8-bit mantissa 0.10100011 has eight significant bits. It is worth noting here that there is a slight difference between normalized decimal numbers as used by engineers and scientists, and normalized binary numbers. A decimal floating point number is normalized so that its mantissa lies in the range $1.00 \ldots 0$ to $9.99 \ldots 9$. A positive floating point normalized binary mantissa x is of the form

$$x = 0.100 \ldots 0 \text{ to } 0.11 \ldots 11.$$

That is, $\frac{1}{2} \leqslant x < 1$. A special exception has to be made in the case of zero, as this number cannot, of course, be normalized. A negative, twos complement, floating point mantissa is stored in the form

$$x = 1.01 \ldots . 1 \text{ to } 1.00 \ldots . 0.$$

In this case the negative mantissa, x, is constrained so that $-\frac{1}{2} > x \geqslant -1$. The floating point number is therefore limited to one of the three ranges described by Fig. 4.21.

Fig. 4.21 Range of valid normalized twos complement mantissas.

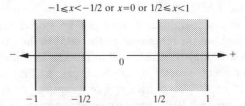

A far more common representation of floating point mantissas uses a sign and magnitude representation so that normalized mantissas lie in the range $0.1000 \ldots 00$ to $0.1111 \ldots 11$ for positive numbers and $1.1000 \ldots 00$ to $1.1111 \ldots 11$ for negative numbers. As we shall soon see, the IEEE format for floating point numbers uses a sign and magnitude format for the mantissa with a leading 1 in front of the binary point (i.e. mantissas fall in the range $-1.111 \ldots 11$ to $-1.000 \ldots 00$ or $+1.000 \ldots 00$ to $+1.111 \ldots 11$). That is, a mantissa x is constrained to lie in the ranges: $-2 < x \leqslant -1$ or $x = 0$ or $1 \leqslant x < 2$.

Biased exponents

A floating point representation of numbers must make provision for both positive and negative numbers, and positive and negative exponents. For example, in decimal notation this corresponds to:

$$+0.123 \times 10^{12}, \qquad -0.756 \times 10^{9}$$
$$+0.176 \times 10^{-3}, \qquad -0.459 \times 10^{-7}.$$

The mantissa of a floating point number is often represented as a twos complement number. The exponent, however, is sometimes represented in a **biased** form. If we take an m-bit exponent, there are 2^m possible unsigned integer values of the exponent from $00\ldots0$ to $11\ldots1$. Suppose now we re-label these numbers not from 0 to 2^m-1, but from -2^{m-1} to $+2^{m-1}-1$ by subtracting a constant value (or bias) of 2^{m-1} from each of the numbers.

What we have is a continuous natural binary series from 0 to N that represents a series of numbers from $-B$ to $N-B$. For example, if the series (in decimal) were 0,1,2,3,4,5,6,7, we could subtract, say, $B=4$ from each number of the series to generate a new series $-4,-3,-2,-1,0,1,2,3$. We have really invented a new method of representing negative numbers by adding a constant to the most negative number to make the result equal to zero. In the example above, we have added 4 to each number so that -4 is represented by 0 and -3 by $+1$, etc.

We create a biased exponent by adding a constant to the true exponent so that the biased exponent is given by $b'=b+B$, where b' is the biased exponent, b the true exponent and B a weighting. The weighting B is frequently either 2^{m-1} or $2^{m-1}-1$. Consider what happens for the case where $m=4$ and $B=2^3=8$ (see Table 4.14).

The true exponent ranges from -8 to $+7$, allowing us to represent powers of two from 2^{-8} to 2^{+7}, while the biased exponent ranges from 0 to $+15$. The advantage of the biased representation of exponents is that the most negative exponent is represented by zero. Conveniently, the floating point value of zero is represented by

$$0.0\ldots0 \times 2^0$$

which is zero times the most negative exponent (see Fig. 4.22). By choosing the biased exponent system we arrange that zero is represented by a zero mantissa and a zero exponent as Fig. 4.22 demonstrates.

Note that the biased exponent representation of exponents is also called **excess n**, where n is typically 2^{m-1}. For example, a 6-bit exponent may be called **excess 32** because the stored exponent exceeds the true exponent by 32. In this case, the smallest true exponent that can be represented is -32 and is stored as an excess 32 value of 0. The maximum true exponent that can be represented is 31 and this is stored as 63.

A second advantage of the biased exponent representation is that the stored (i.e. biased) exponents form a natural binary sequence. This sequence is monotonic so that increasing the exponent by 1 involves adding one to the binary exponent, and decreasing the exponent by 1 involves subtracting one from the binary exponent. In both cases the binary biased exponent can be considered as behaving like an unsigned binary number.

Table 4.14 Relationship between *true* and *biased* exponents

Binary representation of exponent	True exponent	Biased form
0000	-8	0
0001	-7	1
0010	-6	2
0011	-5	3
0100	-4	4
0101	-3	5
0110	-2	6
0111	-1	7
1000	0	8
1001	1	9
1010	2	10
1011	3	11
1100	4	12
1101	5	13
1110	6	14
1111	7	15

For example, if $n=1010.1111$, we normalize it to 0.10101111×2^4. The true exponent is $+4$ which is stored as a biased exponent of $4+8$ which is 12, or 1100 in binary form.

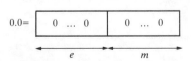

Fig. 4.22 Representing zero with a biased exponent.

4.8.3 Possible floating point systems

In order to choose a floating point representation for a given computer, the programmer must select the following items:

1. the number of words used (i.e. total number of bits);
2. the representation of the mantissa (2s complement etc.);
3. the representation of the exponent (biased etc.);
4. the number of bits devoted to the mantissa and exponent;
5. the location of the mantissa (exponent first or mantissa first).

Point (4) is worthy of elaboration. Once the programmer has decided on the total number of bits in the floating point representation (an integral number of word lengths) the programmer must partition this representation into mantissa and exponent. If the programmer dedicates a large number of bits to the exponent, the result is a floating point number with a very big range. These (exponent) bits have been obtained at the expense of the mantissa which reduces the precision of the floating point number. Conversely, increasing the bits available for the mantissa improves the precision at the expense of the range.

Because of the five points above, the numbers of ways in which a floating point number may be represented is legion, with (almost) no two machines using the same format. Things are now getting better with the introduction of microprocessors; as we shall see later the IEEE has introduced specifications for floating point numbers (Fig. 4.24). The examples of Fig. 4.23 illustrate the representations adopted by a few computer users.

UNIVAC 1100

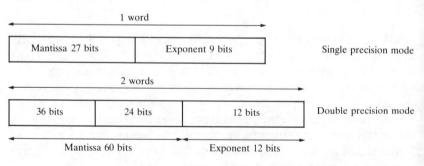

Fig. 4.23 Some floating point formats.

CDC 3600

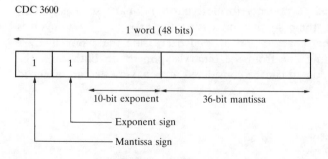

The Univac single precision mode provides a range of approximately 10^{-76} to 10^{+76} with a precision of 8 decimal places. In the double precision mode the range is increased to 10^{614} to 10^{-614}, and the precision is equivalent to 18 decimal places. Double precision mode is used in numerical arithmetic where great precision is sometimes necessary. In general, the use of double precision slows the running of a program considerably unless the computer has a special high-speed floating point unit.

The IEEE floating point format

The Institute of Electrical and Electronics Engineers (IEEE) has produced a standard floating point format for arithmetic operations in mini- and microcomputers (i.e. ANSI/IEEE standard 754-1985). To cater for a number of different applications, the IEEE has specified three basic formats, called *single, double,* and *quad.* Table 4.15 defines the principal features of these three floating point formats.

IEEE floating point numbers are normalized so that their mantissas lie in the range $1 \leqslant F < 2$. This range corresponds to a mantissa with an integer part equal to 1. An IEEE format floating point number X is formally defined as:

$$X = -1^S \times 2^{E-B} \times 1.F,$$

where

S = sign bit, 0 = positive mantissa, 1 = negative mantissa
E = exponent biased by B
F = fractional mantissa
(note that the mantissa is 1.F and has an implicit leading one).

Table 4.15 Basic IEEE floating point formats

Type	Single	Double	Quadruple
Field width in bits			
S=sign	1	1	1
E=exponent	8	11	15
L=leading bit	1	1	1
F=fraction	23	52	111
Total width	32	64	128
Sign bit	0=+, 1=−	0=+, 1=−	0=+, 1=−
Exponent			
Maximum E	255	2047	32767
Minimum E	0	0	0
Bias	127	1023	16383

Normalized numbers: (all formats)
  Range of exponents (min. E+1) to (max. E−1)

  Represented number $-1^S \times 2^{E-bias} \times$ L.F.
A signed zero is represented by the minimum exponent, L=0, and F=0, for all three formats.
  The maximum exponent has a special function and is used to represent signed infinity for all three formats.

For example, a single format 32-bit floating point number has a bias of 127 and a 23-bit fractional mantissa. There are two particular points of interest. The first is that a sign and magnitude representation has been adopted for the mantissa. If $S = 1$ the mantissa is negative and if $S = 0$ it is positive.

The second point is that the mantissa is always normalized and lies in the range $1.000\ldots00$ to $1.111\ldots11$. Note that an IEEE floating point number is normalized differently to the floating point numbers we have encountered earlier. If the mantissa is always normalized, it follows that the leading 1, the integer part, is redundant when the IEEE format floating point number is stored in memory. If we know that a 1 must be located to the left of the fractional mantissa, there is no need to store it. In this way a bit of storage is saved, permitting the precision of the mantissa to be extended by one bit. The format of the number when stored in memory is given in Fig. 4.24.

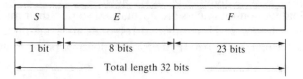

Fig. 4.24 Format of the IEEE 32-bit floating point format.

As an example of the use of the IEEE 32-bit format, consider the representation of the decimal number -2345.125 on a machine having a 16-bit wordlength:

$$-2345.125_{10} = -100100101001.001_2 \text{ (as an equivalent binary number)}$$
$$= -1.00100101001001 \times 2^{11} \text{ (as a normalized binary number).}$$

The mantissa is negative so the sign bit S is 1.

The biased exponent is given by $+11 + 127 = 138 = 10001010_2$.

The fractional part of the mantissa is $.00100101001001000000000$ (in 23 bits)

Therefore, the IEEE single format representation of -2345.125 is

$$11000101000100101001001000000000.$$

This number is stored as two consecutive 16-bit words:

$$1100010100010010 \quad 1001001000000000.$$

In order to minimize storage space in a 16-bit memory, floating point numbers are *packed* so that the sign bit, exponent and mantissa share part of two or more machine words. When floating point operations are carried out, the numbers are first unpacked and the mantissa separated from the exponent. For example, the basic single precision format specifies a 23-bit fractional mantissa, giving a 24-bit mantissa when unpacked and the leading 1 reinserted. If the processor on which the floating point numbers are being processed has a 16-bit word length, the unpacked mantissa will occupy 24 bits out of the 32 bits taken up by two words.

If, when a number is unpacked, the number of bits in its exponent and mantissa is allowed to increase to fill the available space, the format is said to be *extended*. By extending the format in this way, the range and precision of the floating point number are considerably increased. For example, a single format number is stored as a 32-bit quantity. When it is unpacked the 23-bit fractional mantissa is increased to 24 bits by including the leading 1 and then the mantissa is extended to 32 bit (either as a single 32-bit word or as two 16-bit words). All calculations are then performed using the 32-bit extended precision mantissa. This is particularly helpful when transcendental functions (e.g. $\sin x$, $\cos x$) are evaluated. After a sequence of floating operations have been carried out in the extended format, the floating point number is re-packed and stored in memory in its basic form.

Note that in 32-bit single IEEE format, the maximum exponent E_{max} is $+127$ and the minimum exponent E_{min} is -126 and not $+128$ to -127 as we might expect. The special value $E_{min} - 1$ (i.e. -127) is used to encode zero and $E_{max} + 1$ is used to encode plus or minus infinity or a 'NaN'. A NaN is a special entity catered for in the IEEE format and is 'Not a Number'. The use of NaNs is covered by the IEEE standard and they permit the manipulation of formats outside the IEEE standard.

4.8.4 Floating point arithmetic

Unlike integer and fixed-point number representations, floating point numbers cannot be added in one simple operation. A moment's thought should demonstrate why this is so. Consider an example in decimal arithmetic. Let $A = 12345$ and $B = 567.89$. In floating point form these numbers can be represented by:

$$A = 0.12345 \times 10^5 \text{ and } B = 0.56789 \times 10^3$$

If these numbers were to be added by hand, no problems would arise.

```
    12345
+    567.89
  _____
  12912.89
```

However, as these numbers are held in a normalized floating point format we have the problem below.

$$0.12345 \times 10^5$$
$$+ 0.56789 \times 10^3$$

Addition cannot take place as long as the exponents are *different*. To perform a floating point addition (or subtraction) the following steps must be carried out:

1. Identify the number with the smaller exponent.
2. Make the smaller exponent equal to the larger exponent by dividing the mantissa of the smaller number by the same factor by which its exponent was increased.

3. Add (or subtract) the mantissas.

4. If necessary, normalize the result (post-normalization).

In the above example we have $A = 0.12345 \times 10^5$ and $B = 0.56789 \times 10^3$. The exponent of B is smaller than that of A, which results in an increase of 2 in B's exponent and a corresponding division of B's mantissa by 10^2 to give 0.0056789×10^5. We can now add A to the denormalized B.

$$
\begin{array}{r}
A = 0.1234500 \times 10^5 \\
+\, B = 0.0056789 \times 10^5 \\
\hline
0.1291289 \times 10^5
\end{array}
$$

This result is already in a normalized form and does not need post-normalizing. Note that the answer is expressed to a precision of seven significant figures while A and B are each expressed to a precision of five significant figures. If the result were stored in a computer, its mantissa would have to be reduced to five figures after the decimal point (because we were working with five-digit mantissas).

When people do arithmetic they often resort to what may best be called *floating precision*. If they want greater precision they simply use more digits. Computers use a fixed representation for floating point numbers so that the precision may not increase as a result of calculation. Consider the following binary example of floating point addition.

$$
\begin{array}{l}
A = 0.11001 \times 2^4 \\
B = 0.10001 \times 2^3.
\end{array}
$$

The exponent of B must be increased by 1 and the mantissa of B divided by 2 (i.e. shifted one place right) to make both exponents equal to 4:

$$
\begin{array}{r}
A = 0.11001 \quad\, \times 2^4 \\
B = 0.010001 \times 2^4 \\
\hline
1.000011 \times 2^4
\end{array}
$$

In this case the result has overflowed and must be post-normalized by dividing the mantissa by two and incrementing the exponent.

$$
A + B = 1.000011 \times 2^4 \rightarrow 0.1000011 \times 2^5.
$$

We have also gained two extra places of precision, forcing us to take some form of action. For example, we can simply truncate the number to get:

$$
A + B = 0.10000 \times 2^5.
$$

A more formal procedure for the addition of floating point numbers is given in Fig. 4.25 as a flow chart.

A few points to note about this flow chart are:

1. Because (in many implementations) the exponent shares part of a word with the mantissa, it is necessary to separate them before the process of addition can begin. As we pointed out before, this is called *unpacking*.

2. If the two exponents differ by more than $p + 1$, where p is the number of

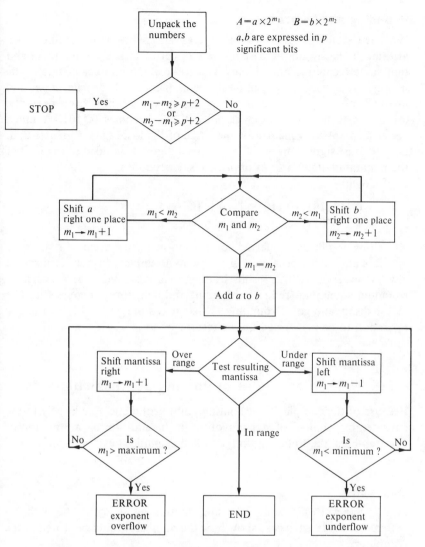

$A = a \times 2^{m_1}$ $B = b \times 2^{m_2}$

a, b are expressed in p significant bits

Fig. 4.25 Flow chart for floating point addition/subtraction.

significant bits in the mantissa, then the smaller number is too small to affect the larger and hence the result is effectively equal to the larger number, and no further action takes place. For example, there is no point in adding 0.1234×10^{20} to 0.4567×10^{2}, because adding 0.4567×10^{2} to 0.1234×10^{20} has no effect on a 4-digit mantissa.

3. During post-normalization the exponent is checked to see if it is less than its minimum possible value, and greater than its maximum possible value. This corresponds to testing for *exponent underflow* and *overflow*, respectively. Each of these cases represent conditions in which the number is outside the range of numbers which the computer can handle. Exponent underflow would generally lead to the number being made equal to zero, while exponent overflow would result in an error condition and may require the intervention of the operating system.

Rounding and truncation

We have seen that some of the operations involved in floating point arithmetic lead to an increase in the number of bits in the mantissa and that some technique must be invoked to keep the number of bits in the mantissa constant. The simplest technique is called *truncation* and involves nothing more than dropping unwanted bits. For example, 0.1101101 truncated to four significant bits becomes 0.1101. A much better technique is *rounding.* If the value of the lost digits is greater than half the least significant bit of the retained digits, 1 is added to the LSB of the remaining digits. For example, consider rounding to 4 significant bits the following numbers:

$$0.1101101 \rightarrow 0.1101 + 1 = 0.1110$$
$$0.1101011 \rightarrow 0.1101$$

Rounding is always preferred to truncation partly because it is more accurate and partly because it gives rise to an unbiased error. Truncation always undervalues the result, leading to a systematic error, whereas rounding sometimes reduces the result and sometimes increases it. The major disadvantage of rounding is that it requires a further arithmetic operation to be performed on the result.

4.8.5 Worked examples of floating point calculations

Because of the complexity of floating point arithmetic, due largely to the considerable number of steps involved in the addition or subtraction of two numbers, the following fully worked examples have been included.

Question 1

Add together 10.125 and 32.1 using floating point arithmetic with the format below. In each case show how the numbers would be stored in the computer.

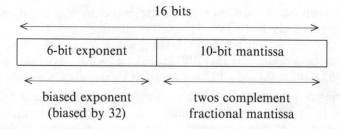

Solution 1

$10.125 \rightarrow 1010.001_2$
$\qquad \rightarrow 0.101000100_2 \times 2^4$

The exponent is 4 or, in biased form, $4 + 32 = 36 = 100100$.

The floating point representation of 10.125 is

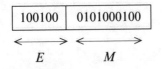

$$\xleftarrow{\hspace{1.5cm}}\xrightarrow{\hspace{1.5cm}}$$
$$E \qquad\qquad M$$

$32.1 \rightarrow 100000.00011001100\ldots$
$\rightarrow 0.100000000110011 \times 2^6$
$\rightarrow 0.100000001_2 \times 2^6$ after rounding.

The exponent is 6 or, in biased form, $6 + 32 = 38$
The floating point representation of 32.1 is

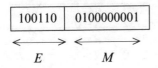

$$\xleftarrow{\hspace{1.5cm}}\xrightarrow{\hspace{1.5cm}}$$
$$E \qquad\qquad M$$

As these numbers have different exponents, the smaller mantissa must be scaled.

$$100100 \quad 0.101000100 \;\rightarrow\; 100110 \quad 0.00101000100$$
$$E \qquad M \qquad\qquad E \qquad\quad M$$

We can now add the mantissas:

$$
\begin{array}{r}
0.00101000100 \\
+\,0.100000001 \\
\hline
0.10101001000
\end{array}
$$

This result may now be rounded to 10 bits (0.101010010) and our final answer is

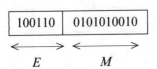

$$\xleftarrow{\hspace{1.5cm}}\xrightarrow{\hspace{1.5cm}}$$
$$E \qquad\qquad M$$

The decimal equivalent of this binary number represents $0.101010010 \times 2^6 = 101010.010 = 42.25$. Note that the correct answer is 42.225. The error has been introduced because the mantissa is restricted to 10 bits.

Question 2

Assuming a 6-bit biased exponent (i.e. excess 32) and a 10-bit twos complement mantissa, perform the following operations. In each case compare the calculated result with the true result. During the calculation of the 10-bit mantissa rounding may be employed. During successive floating point operations (e.g. scaling the mantissa) truncation must be used.

(a)	157.3	(b)	157.3	(c)	157.3	(d)	157.3
	+ 257.1		− 12.6		− 142.7		+ 158.3

Solution 2a

$$
\begin{array}{r}
157.3 \\
+\,257.1 \\
\hline
414.4 \\
\end{array}
$$

Step 1   Convert 157 to binary

$$
\begin{array}{lll}
157 \div 2 = 78 & R = 1 \\
78 \div 2 = 39 & R = 0 \\
39 \div 2 = 19 & R = 1 \\
19 \div 2 = 9 & R = 1 \\
9 \div 2 = 4 & R = 1 \\
4 \div 2 = 2 & R = 0 \\
2 \div 2 = 1 & R = 0 \\
1 \div 2 = 0 & R = 1 \\
\end{array}
$$

Therefore, $157_{10} = 10011101_2$.

Step 2   Convert 0.3 to binary

$$
\begin{array}{l}
0.3 \times 2 = 0.6 \\
0.6 \times 2 = 1.2 \\
0.2 \times 2 = 0.4 \\
0.4 \times 2 = 0.8 \\
0.8 \times 2 = 1.6 \\
\end{array}
$$

Therefore, $0.3_{10} = 0.01001\ldots{}_2$.

Step 3   Normalize the fixed-point binary number

$$
157.3 = 10011101.01001\ldots
$$
$$
= 0.1001110101001 \times 2^8.
$$

Step 4   Round the mantissa to ten bits

0.100111010|1001

greater than 1/2 lsb of 10 remaining bits

0.100111011 rounded mantissa.

Thus, the floating point representation of 157.3 is 0.100111011×2^8. The exponent is $+8$ (true). In biased form we must add 2^5 ($=32$) to this to get 40. This number would actually be stored as 1010000100111011.

Step 5   Convert 257.1 to a normalized floating point number, rounded to 10 bits

$$
257.1_{10} = 0.100000001_2 \times 2^9.
$$

Step 6   Compare exponents

$$
0.100111011 \times 2^8
$$
$$
0.100000001 \times 2^9.
$$

Step 7 Make the smaller exponent equal to the larger exponent, and shift its mantissa right for each increment of the exponent.

$$0.0100111011 \times 2^9$$
$$0.100000001 \ \times 2^9.$$

Step 8 Add mantissas

0.010011101×2^9 Note the smaller mantissa has been
$\underline{0.100000001 \times 2^9}$ truncated to 10 bits
$\overline{0.110011110 \times 2^9.}$

The result is already normalized and needs no further processing. This corresponds to $0.110011110 \times 2^9 = 110011110_2 = 414_{10}$, and differs from the exact answer (414.4) by 0.4.

Solution 2b

$$\begin{array}{r} 157.3 \\ - \ \ 12.6 \\ \hline 144.7 \end{array}$$

Step 1 Convert 157.3 to binary

$157.3_{10} = 0.100111011_2 \times 2^8$ (normalized and rounded).

Step 2 Convert 12.6 to binary

$$12.6_{10} = 1100.10011001100_2$$
$$= 0.110010011011 \times 2^4$$
$$= 0.110010011 \times 2^4 \text{ (floating-point rounded binary).}$$

Step 3 Form twos complement of mantissa

$$0.110010011 \rightarrow 1.001101100 \text{ (invert bits)}$$
$$\rightarrow 1.001101101 \text{ (add 1).}$$

Step 4 Equalize exponents

$$1.001101101 \times 2^4 \rightarrow 1.111100110(1101) \times 2^8$$
$$\rightarrow 1.111100110 \times 2^8$$

Note 1 When shifting negative numbers right the sign bit is propagated.
Note 2 The bits shifted out have been dropped.

Step 5 Perform addition $0.100111011 \ \times 2^8$
$\underline{ \ \ 1.111100110 \ \times 2^8}$
$ \ \ 10.100100001 \ \times 2^8$

Note The leftmost 1 in the carry-bit position is the result of twos complement arithmetic and is neglected.

$\text{Result} = 0.1001000001 \times 2^8 = 10010000.1_2 = 144.5_{10}$

The exact answer is 144.7.

Solution 2c

$$
\begin{array}{r}
157.3 \\
-142.7 \\
\hline
14.6
\end{array}
$$

Step 1 Convert 157.3 to binary

$157.3_{10} = 0.100111011_2 \times 2^8$ (normalized and rounded)

Step 2 Convert 142.7 to binary

$142.7_{10} = 10001110.1011001_2$
$= 0.100011101 \times 2^8$ (normalized and rounded).

Step 3 Form twos complement of the mantissa

$0.100011101 \rightarrow 1.011100010$ (invert bits)
$\rightarrow 1.011100011$ (add 1).

Step 4 Perform addition

$$
\begin{array}{r}
0.100111011 \times 2^8 \\
1.011100011 \times 2^8 \\
\hline
10.000011110 \times 2^8
\end{array}
$$

The answer is 0.000011110×2^8.

Step 5 Normalize the result

$0.000011110 \times 2^8 \rightarrow 0.1111000000 \times 2^4$
$\rightarrow 15_{10}.$

The exact answer is 14.6.

Solution 2d

$$
\begin{array}{r}
157.3 \\
-158.3 \\
\hline
-001.0
\end{array}
$$

Step 1 $157.3 = 0.100111011 \times 2^8$ (normalized and rounded).

Step 2 $158.3 = 10011110.01001$ (fixed-point binary)
$= 0.1001111001001 \times 2^8$ (floating-point binary)
$= 0.100111101 \times 2^8$ (floating-point, rounded binary).

Step 3   Form twos complement of mantissa

$$0.100111101 \rightarrow 1.011000010 \text{ (invert bits)}$$
$$\rightarrow 1.011000011 \text{ (add 1)}.$$

Step 4   Perform addition (exponents are the same here)

$$
\begin{array}{l}
0.100111011 \times 2^8 \\
\underline{1.011000011 \times 2^8} \\
1.111111110 \times 2^8
\end{array}
$$

The answer is negative (sign bit = 1), but is not normalized.

Step 5   Normalize the result

$$1.111111110 \times 2^8 = 1.000000000 \times 2^0$$
$$= -1_{10}.$$

Note the operation of the arithmetic shift left

$$1.111111110 \times 2^8 \rightarrow 1.111111100 \times 2^7$$
$$\rightarrow 1.111111000 \times 2^6$$
$$\rightarrow 1.11111000 \times 2^5$$
$$\text{etc.}$$

4.9 Multiplication and division

In this final part of our excursion into digital arithmetic, we are going to look at what might best be called *advanced* computer arithmetic. Advanced computer arithmetic is concerned with those numerical operations involving multiplication and division. Such operations and their derivatives (reciprocals, square roots, exponentiation, trigonometric functions) are very important in many areas of computation, especially numerical computation. At least one good reason for studying multiplication and division is that there seems to be an infinite number of ways of performing these operations and hence there is a correspondingly large number of Ph.D.s (or expenses-paid visits to conferences in the USA) to be won by inventing new forms of multiplier.

The newcomer to computing is often surprised to find that most of the popular 8-bit microprocessors cannot perform multiplication directly. Any programmer who wishes to multiply two numbers with a typical 8-bit chip must resort to an algorithm involving shifting and adding. Equally, the newcomer might think that the omission of multiplication from the CPUs instructions set is a horrendous oversight entirely devaluing the microprocessor. This is not so. It is remarkable how little multiplication or any similar higher order arithmetic operations appear in many programs. For example, the principal operation carried out by editors, assemblers, compilers, or text processors is the searching of data areas for a match with a given string. In fact the most frequent application of multiplication is not in arithmetic, but in calculating the addresses of array elements. For example, the location of the element $x(i, j)$ in the m-row by n-column matrix, X, is given by $(A + mi + j)$, where A is the address of the first element.

Here we consider only multiplication and division, since other mathematical functions are normally derived from multiplication. Indeed, division itself will later be defined as an iterative process involving multiplication.

4.9.1 Multiplication

Binary multiplication is, in principle, no more complex than decimal multiplication. In many ways it is easier, as the whole binary multiplication table can be reduced to

$$0 \times 0 = 0$$
$$0 \times 1 = 0$$
$$1 \times 0 = 0$$
$$1 \times 1 = 1$$

Note that the multiplication of two bits is identical to their logical AND. When we consider the multiplication of strings of bits, things become more complex and the way in which multiplication is carried out, or mechanized, varies widely from machine to machine. Basically the faster (and more expensive) the computer, the more complex the hardware used to implement multiplication. The simpler machines form the product of two numbers by *shifting and adding*, very much as people do. High-speed computers perform multiplication in a single operation by means of a very large logic array involving hundreds of gates.

Unsigned multiplication

The so-called *pencil and paper* algorithm used by people to calculate the product of two multi-digit numbers, involves the multiplication of an n-digit number by a *single* digit followed by shifting and adding. We can apply the same approach to unsigned binary numbers in the following way. The multiplier bits are examined, one at a time, starting with the least significant bit. If the current multiplier bit is *one* the multiplicand is written down; if it is *zero* then n zeros are written down instead. Then the next bit of the multiplier is examined, but this time we write the multiplicand (or zero) one place to the left of the last digits we wrote down. Each of these groups of n digits is called a *partial product*. When all partial products have been formed, they are added up to give the result of the multiplication. An example should make this clear:

10×13 Multiplier $= 1101_2$

                   Multiplicand $= 1010_2$

1010	
1101	
1010	Step 1
0000	Step 2
1010	Step 3
1010	Step 4
10000010	Step 5

Step 1 First multiplier bit $= 1$, write down multiplicand
Step 2 Second multiplier bit $= 0$, write down zeros shifted left
Step 3 Third multiplier bit $= 1$, write down multiplicand shifted left
Step 4 Fourth multiplier bit $= 1$, write down multiplicand shifted left
Step 5 Add together four partial products.

The result, $10000010_2 = 130$, is eight bits long. It should be appreciated from the above algorithm that the multiplication of two n-bit numbers yields a $2n$-bit product.

Digital computers do not implement the pencil and paper algorithm in the above way, as this would require the storing of n partial products, followed by the simultaneous addition of n words. A better technique is to add up the partial products as they are formed. A possible algorithm for the multiplication of two n-bit unsigned binary numbers is given in Table 4.16. We will consider the previous example of 1101×1010 using the algorithm of Table 4.16. The mechanization of the product of 1101×1010 is presented in Table 4.17.

Multiplication without a multiplication instruction

The algorithm described in Table 4.16 can readily be applied to a typical microprocessor. We shall assume that the microprocessor does not have its own multiplication instruction (a statement which is true of most 8-bit microprocessors).

The flow chart in Fig. 4.26 illustrates a multiplication algorithm for the 68000 microprocessor. Note that the reader who is unfamiliar with the

Table 4.16 An algorithm for multiplication

(a)	Set a counter to n.
(b)	Clear the $2n$-bit partial product register.
(c)	Examine the right-most bit of the multiplier (initially the least significant bit). If it is *one* add the multiplicand to the n most significant bits of the partial product.
(d)	Shift the partial product one place to the right.
(e)	Shift the multiplier one place to the right (the right-most bit is, of course, lost).
(f)	Decrement the counter. If the result is not zero repeat from step (c). If the result is zero read the product from the partial product register.

Table 4.17 Mechanizing unsigned multiplication
Multiplier = 1101.   Multiplicand = 1010

Step	Counter	Multiplier	Partial product	Cycle
(a) and (b)	4	1101	00000000	
(c)	4	1101	10100000	1
(d) and (e)	4	0110	01010000	1
(f)	3	0110	01010000	1
(c)	3	0110	01010000	2
(d) and (e)	3	0011	00101000	2
(f)	2	0011	00101000	2
(c)	2	0011	11001000	3
(d) and (e)	2	0001	01100100	3
(f)	1	0001	01100100	3
(c)	1	0001	100000100	4
(d) and (e)	1	0000	10000010	4
(f)	0	0000	10000010	4

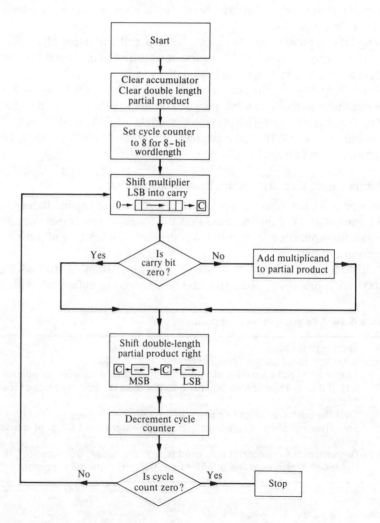

Fig. 4.26 Flow chart for unsigned multiplication.

Table 4.18 A 68000 program for multiplication

```
        ORG     $1000   data origin
P       DS.B    1       multiplier location (byte)
Q       DS.B    1       multiplicand location (byte)
R       DS.W    1       destination of result (word)
        ORG     $2000   origin of program
        CLR.W   D0      clear partial product
        CLR.W   D2      clear register used to hold Q
        MOVE.B  Q,D2    get multiplicand in D2
        LSL.W   #8,D2   shift D2 left by one byte
        MOVE.B  #8,D1   set counter to 8
LOOP    LSR.B   P       shift multiplier bit into carry
        BCC     SHIFT   if clear shift partial product right
        ADD.W   D2,D0   add multiplicand to ms byte
SHIFT   ROR.W   #1,D0   rotate partial product ms byte
        SUB.B   #1,D1   decrement counter
        BNE     LOOP    loop until all bits done
        MOVE.W  D0,R    store product ms byte
```

68000 microprocessor and its assembly language may skip this section until he or she has read Chapters 5 and 6. We are using the 68000's add and shift instructions to perform multiplication, although the 68000 does, in fact, have its own multiply and divide instructions. Table 4.18 provides a suitable 68000 program for 8-bit multiplication.

Signed multiplication

The multiplication algorithm we have just discussed is valid only for unsigned integers or unsigned fixed point numbers. As many computers represent signed numbers by means of twos complement notation, it is necessary to find some way of forming the product of twos complement numbers. It is, of course, possible to convert negative numbers into a modulus-only form, calculate the product and then convert it into a twos complement form if it is negative. This approach wastes time.

Before introducing a suitable algorithm, it is worthwhile demonstrating that the twos complement representation of negative numbers cannot be used with the basic shifting and adding algorithm described above. That is, twos complement arithmetic 'works' for addition and subtraction, but not for multiplication or division (without using special algorithms). For example, consider the product of X and $-Y$.

Twos complement form of $-Y = 2^n - Y$.

The product $X(Y) = X(2^n - Y) = 2^n X - XY$.

The *expected* result, $-XY$, should be represented in twos complement form by $2^{2n} - XY$. Note that the most significant bit is 2^{2n} (not 2^n) because multiplication automatically yields a double-length product. In order to get the correct twos complement result it is necessary to add a correction factor of

$$2^{2n} - 2^n X = 2^n(2^n - X).$$

This correction is the twos complement of X scaled by 2^n. As an illustration consider the product of $X = 15$ and $Y = -13$ in five bits.

$$X = \quad 15 = 01111_2$$
$$Y = -13 = 10011_2$$

2^9	2^8	2^7	2^6	2^5	2^4	2^3	2^2	2^1	2^0	
				0	1	1	1	1		X
				1	0	0	1	1		Y (2s complement form)
				0	1	1	1	1		
			0	1	1	1	1			
		0	0	0	0	0				
	0	0	0	0	0					
0	1	1	1	1						
0	1	0	0	0	1	1	1	0	1	uncorrected result
1	0	0	0	1						correction factor
1	1	0	0	1	1	1	1	0	1	corrected result

The final result in ten bits, $1100111101_2 = -195_{10}$, is correct. Similarly, when X is negative and Y positive, a correction factor of $2^n(2^n - Y)$ must be added to the result.

When both multiplier and multiplicand are negative the following situation exists:

$$(2^n - X)(2^n - Y) = 2^{2n} - 2^n X - 2^n Y + XY.$$

In this case correction factors of $2^n X$ and $2^n Y$ must be added to the result. The 2^{2n} is a carry-out bit from the msb position and can be neglected.

Booth's algorithm

The classic approach to the multiplication of signed numbers in twos complement form is provided by Booth's algorithm. This algorithm works for two positive numbers, one negative and one positive, or both negative. Booth's algorithm is broadly similar to conventional unsigned multiplication but with the following differences. In Booth's algorithm *two* bits of the multiplier are examined together, to determine which of three courses of action is to take place next. The algorithm is defined below.

1. If the current multiplier bit is 1 and the next lower-order multiplier bit is 0, subtract the multiplicand from the partial product.

2. If the current multiplier bit is 0 and the next lower-order multiplier bit is 1, add the multiplicand to the partial product.

3. If the current multiplier bit is the same as the next lower-order multiplier bit, do nothing.

   Note 1. When adding the multiplicand to the partial product, discard any carry bit generated by the addition.

Note 2. When the partial product is shifted, an arithmetic shift is used and the sign bit propagated.

Note 3. Initially, when the current bit of the multiplier is its least significant bit, the next lower-order bit of the multiplier is assumed to be zero.

The flow chart for Booth's algorithm is given in Fig. 4.27. In order to illustrate the operation of Booth's algorithm, consider the three products: 13×15, -13×15, and $-13 \times (-15)$. Table 4.19 demonstrates how Booth's algorithm mechanizes these three multiplications.

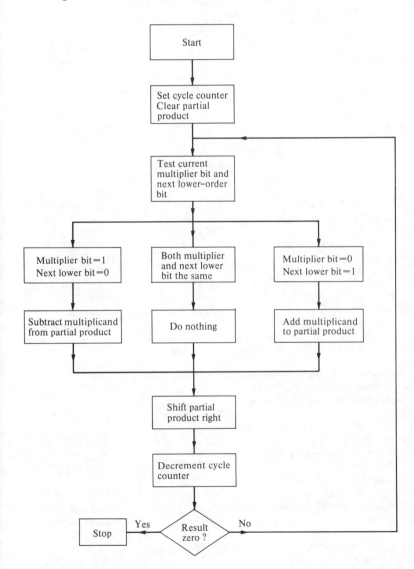

Fig. 4.27 Flow chart for Booth's algorithm.

High-speed multiplication

I do not intend to delve deeply into the subject of high-speed multiplication as large portions of advanced textbooks are devoted to this topic

Table 4.19 Mechanizing Booth's algorithm—three examples

1. Multiplicand=01111=+15
   Multiplier =01101=+13

Step	Multiplier bit	Partial product
		0000000000
Subtract multiplicand	011010	1000100000
Shift partial product right		1100010000
Add multiplicand	01101	10011110000
Shift partial product right		0001111000
Subtract multiplicand	01101	1010011000
Shift partial product right		1101001100
Do nothing	01101	1101001100
Shift partial product right		1110100110
Add multiplicand	01101	10110000110
Shift partial product right		0011000011

The final result is 0011000011_2 which is equal to +195. Note that the underlined numbers represent the bits to be examined at each stage.

2. Multiplicand=01111=+15
   Multiplier =10011=−13

Step	Multiplier bit	Partial product
		0000000000
Subtract multiplicand	100110	1001000000
Shift partial product right		1100010000
Do nothing	10011	1100010000
Shift partial product right		1110001000
Add multiplicand	10011	10101101000
Shift partial product right		0010110100
Do nothing	10011	0010110100
Shift partial product right		0001011010
Subtract multiplicand	10011	1001111010
Shift partial product right		1100111101

The result is 1100111101_2 which corresponds to −195.

3. Multiplicand=10001=−15
   Multiplier =10011=−13

Step	Multiplier bit	Partial product
Subtract multiplicand	100110	0111100000
Shift partial product right		0011110000
Do nothing	10011	0011110000
Shift partial product right		0001111000
Add multiplicand	10011	1010011000
Shift partial product right		1101001100
Do nothing	10011	1101001100
Shift partial product right		1110100110
Subtract multiplicand	10011	10110000110
Shift partial product right		0011000011

The result is 0011000011_2 which corresponds to +195.

alone. Here some alternative ways of forming products to the method of shifting and adding are explained.

We have seen in an earlier example in Chapter 2 that it is possible to construct a 2-bit by 2-bit multiplier by means of logic gates. This process can be extended to larger numbers of bits. Currently, 16-bit by 16-bit single-chip multipliers can be bought which will generate the 32-bit product in less than 50 ns. Figure 4.28 illustrates the type of logic array used to directly multiply two numbers.

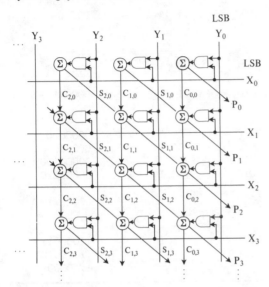

Fig. 4.28 The multiplier array.

An alternative approach is to use a look-up table in which all the possible results of the product of two numbers are stored in ROM. Table 4.20 shows how two 4-bit numbers may be multiplied by storing all $2^8 = 256$ possible results in a ROM. Table 4.20 is a larger version of Table 2.14.

The 4-bit multiplier and 4-bit multiplicand together form an 8-bit address which selects one of 256 locations within the ROM. In each of these locations the product of the multiplier (most significant 4 address bits) and the multiplicand (least significant 4 address bits) are stored. For example, the product of 2 and 3 is given by the contents of location 00100011, which is 00000110.

The disadvantage of this technique is the rapid increase in the size of the ROM as the number of bits in the multiplier and multiplicand increases. Table 4.21 provides the relationship between the size of a multiplier and the number of bits a PROM requires to hold the appropriate multiplication table.

The multiplication of two 8-bit numbers requires a memory capacity of 1 048 576 bits. Forming the product of even larger numbers directly by look-up table becomes impracticable. Fortunately, it is possible to calculate the product of two $2n$-bit numbers by using an n-bit multiplier.

Before showing how we proceed with binary numbers, let's take a look at the product of two 2-digit decimal numbers, and then extend the technique to binary arithmetic.

Table 4.20 Multiplication by means of a look-up table

Address		Data
Multiplier	Multiplicand	Result
0000	0000	00000000
0000	0001	00000000
:	:	:
0000	1111	00000000
:	:	
0001	0000	00000000
0001	0001	00000001
	:	
0001	1111	00001111
:	:	:
0010	0000	00000000
0010	0001	00000010
0010	0010	00000100
0010	0011	00000110
:	:	:
0010	1111	00011110
:	:	:
1111	1101	11000011
1111	1110	11010010
1111	1111	11100001

Table 4.21 Relationship between multiplier size and array size

Multiplier bits n	Address bits $2n$	Lines in table 2^{2n}	Total of bits in ROM $2n \times 2^{2n}$
2	4	16	64
3	6	64	384
4	8	256	1 024
5	10	1 024	10 240
6	12	4 096	49 152
7	14	16 384	229 376
8	16	65 536	1 048 576

$$
\begin{aligned}
34 \times 27 &= (3 \times 10 + 4)(2 \times 10 + 7) \\
&= 3 \times 2 \times 10^2 + 3 \times 7 \times 10 + 4 \times 2 \times 10 + 4 \times 7 \\
&= 6 \times 10^2 + 21 \times 10 + 8 \times 10 + 28 \\
&= 6 \times 10^2 + 29 \times 10 + 28 \\
&= 600 + 290 + 28 \\
&= 918
\end{aligned}
$$

Now consider the generation of the product of two 8-bit numbers by means of 4-bit multipliers.

Let the two 8-bit numbers A and B be represented by

$$A = \boxed{\begin{array}{c|c} A_u & A_1 \end{array}} \qquad B = \boxed{\begin{array}{c|c} B_u & B_1 \end{array}}$$
$$\leftarrow 4 \rightarrow \leftarrow 4 \rightarrow \qquad \leftarrow 4 \rightarrow \leftarrow 4 \rightarrow$$

A_u represents the four most significant bits of A, and A_1 the four least significant bits. We have already encountered the idea of splitting up numbers when we performed 64-bit addition on a 32-bit microprocessor in Section 4.7.

A and B can be represented algebraically as follows:

$$A = A_u \times 16 + A_1 \text{ and } B = B_u \times 16 + B_1$$

Consequently, $AB = (A_u \times 16 + A_1)(B_u \times 16 + B_1)$
$$= 256 A_u B_u + 16 A_u B_1 + 16 A_1 B_u + A_1 B_1$$

This expression requires the evaluation of four 4-bit products ($A_u B_u$, $A_u B_1$, $A_1 B_u$, $A_1 B_1$), the shifting of the products by 8 or 4 positions (i.e. multiplication by 256 or 16), and the addition of four partial products. Figure 4.29 shows how this may be achieved.

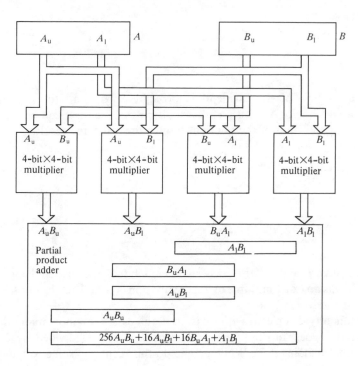

Fig. 4.29 High-speed multiplication.

4.9.2 Division

Division is the inverse of multiplication and is performed by repeatedly subtracting the **divisor** from the **dividend** until the result is either zero or less than the divisor. The number of times the divisor is subtracted is called the *quotient*, and the number left after the final subtraction is the *remainder*. That is,

$$\frac{dividend}{divisor} = quotient + \frac{remainder}{divisor}$$

Alternatively, we can write

$$dividend = quotient \times divisor + remainder.$$

Before we consider binary division let's examine decimal division using the traditional pencil and paper technique. The following example illustrates the division of 575 by 25.

$$\overset{quotient}{divisor\,)\overline{dividend}} \qquad 25\overline{)575}$$

The first step is to compare the two digits of the divisor with the most significant two digits of the dividend and ask how many times the divisor goes into these two digits. The answer is 2 (i.e. $2 \times 25 = 50$), and 2×25 is subtracted from 57. The number 2 is entered as the most significant digit of the quotient to produce the situation below.

$$\begin{array}{r} 2 \\ 25\overline{)575} \\ 50 \\ \hline 7 \end{array}$$

The next digit of the dividend is brought down, and the divisor is compared with 75. As 75 is an exact multiple of 25, a three can be entered in the next position of the quotient to give the following result.

$$\begin{array}{r} 23 \\ 25\overline{)575} \\ 50 \\ \hline 75 \\ 75 \\ \hline 00 \end{array}$$

As we have examined the least significant bit of the dividend and the divisor was an exact multiple of 75, the division is complete, the quotient is 23 with a zero remainder.

A difficulty associated with division lies in estimating how many times the divisor goes into the partial dividend (i.e. 57 was divided by 25 to produce 2 remainder 7). While people do this mentally, some way has to be found to mechanize it for application to computers. Luckily this process is easier in binary arithmetic. Consider the above example using unsigned binary arithmetic:

$$25 = 11001_2 \qquad 575 = 1000111111_2$$

$$\begin{array}{r} 11001\overline{)1000111111} \\ 11001 \end{array}$$

The five bits of the divisor do not go into the first five bits of the dividend, so a zero is entered into the quotient and the divisor is compared with the first six bits of the dividend:

```
              01
       11001)1000111111
              11001
             ──────
             001010
```

The divisor goes into the first six bits of the dividend once, to leave a partial dividend 001010(1111). The next bit of the dividend is brought down to give

```
              010
       11001)1000111111
              11001
             ──────
             010101
              11001
```

The partial dividend is less than the divisor, and a zero is entered into the next bit of the quotient. The process continues as follows.

```
                010111
         11001)1000111111
                11001
               ──────────
               00101011
                 11001
               ──────────
               000100101
                  11001
               ──────────
               000011001
                  11001
               ──────────
               0000000000
```

In this case the partial quotient is zero, so that the final result is 10111, remainder 0.

Restoring division

The classic pencil and paper algorithm we have just discussed can be implemented in digital form with little modification. The only real change is to the way in which the divisor is compared with the partial dividend. People do the comparison mentally; computers must perform a subtraction and test the sign of the result. If the subtraction yields a positive result, a one is entered into the quotient, but if the result is negative a zero is entered in the quotient and the divisor added back to the partial dividend to restore it to its previous value.

A suitable algorithm for restoring division is as follows:

1. Align the divisor with the most significant bit of the dividend.
2. Subtract the divisor from the partial dividend.

3. If the resulting partial dividend is negative, place a zero in the quotient, and add back the divisor to restore the partial dividend.

4. If the resulting partial dividend is positive, place a one in the quotient.

5. Perform a test to determine end of division. If the divisor is aligned so that its least significant bit corresponds to the least significant bit of the partial dividend, stop. The final partial product is the remainder. Otherwise, continue with Step 6.

6. Shift the divisor one place right. Repeat from Step 2.

The flow chart corresponding to this algorithm is given in Fig. 4.30. As an example of this algorithm consider the division of 01100111_2 by 1001_2,

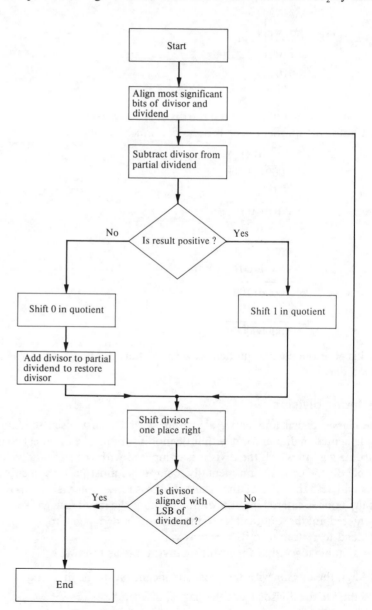

Fig. 4.30 The flow chart for restoring division.

which corresponds to 103 divided by 9 and should yield a quotient 11 and a remainder 4. Figure 4.31 illustrates the division process, step by step.

Non-restoring division

It is possible to modify the restoring division algorithm of Fig. 4.30 to achieve a reduction in the time taken to execute the division process. Basically, the non-restoring division algorithm is almost identical to the restoring algorithm. The only difference is that the so-called restoring operation is eliminated. From the flow chart for restoring division (Fig. 4.30), it can be seen that after a partial dividend has been restored by adding back the divisor, one half the divisor is subtracted in the next cycle. This is because each cycle includes a shift-divisor-right operation which is equivalent to dividing the divisor by two. Thus, the restore divisor operation in the current cycle followed by the subtract half the divisor in the following cycle is equivalent to a single operation of add half the divisor to the partial dividend. That is, $D - D/2 = + D/2$, where D is the divisor. Figure 4.32 gives the flow chart for non-restoring division. After the divisor has been subtracted from the partial dividend, the new partial dividend is tested. If it is negative, zero is shifted into the least significant position of the quotient and half the divisor is added back to the partial dividend. If it is positive, one is shifted into the least significant position of the quotient and half the divisor is subtracted from the partial dividend. Fig. 4.33 repeats the example of Fig. 4.31 using non-restoring division.

Step	Description	Partial dividend	Divisor	Quotient
		01100111	00001001	00000000
1	Align	01100111	01001000	00000000
2	Subtract divisor from partial dividend	00011111	01001000	00000000
4	Result positive shift in 1 in quotient	00011111	01001000	00000001
5	Test			
6	Shift divisor one place right	00011111	00100100	00000001
2	Subtract divisor from partial dividend	−00000101	00100100	00000001
3	Restore divisor, shift in 0 in quotient	00011111	00100100	00000010
5	Test			
6	Shift divisor one place right	00011111	00010010	00000010
2	Subtract divisor from partial dividend	00001101	00010010	00000010
4	Result positive shift in 1 in quotient	00001101	00010010	00000101
5	Test			
6	Shift divisor one place right	00001101	00001001	00000101
2	Subtract divisor from partial dividend	00000100	00001001	00000101
4	Result positive shift in 1 in quotient	00000100	00001001	00001011
5	Test			

Quotient=1011, remainder=100

Figure 4.31 Restoring division for 1001)͞01͞10͞01͞11

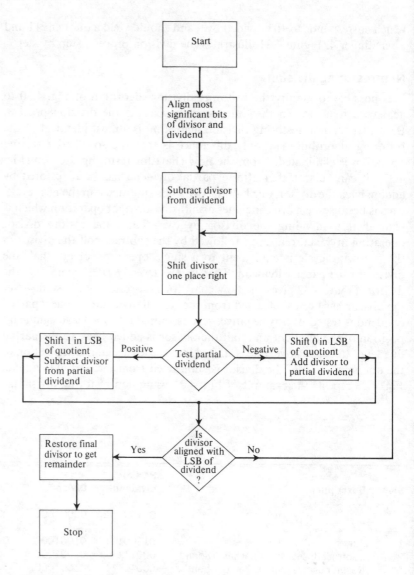

Fig. 4.32 The flow chart for non-restoring division.

Division by multiplication

Because both computers and microprocessors perform division far less frequently than multiplication, there is less special-purpose hardware for division. It is, however, possible to perform division by means of multiplication, addition and shifting. As high-speed multipliers are readily available, they can be applied to division.

Suppose we wish to divide a dividend N by a divisor D to obtain a quotient Q, so that $Q = N/D$. The first step is to scale D so that it lies in the range:

$$\tfrac{1}{2} \leqslant D < 1.$$

The above operation is carried out by shifting D left or right and recording the number of shifts. This is entirely analogous to normalization in

Step	Description	Partial dividend	Divisor	Quotient
		01100111	00001001	00000000
1	Align divisor	01100111	01001000	00000000
2	Subtract divisor from partial dividend	00011111	01001000	00000000
3	Shift divisor right	00011111	00100100	00000000
4	Test partial dividend enter 1 in quotient and subtract divisor from partial dividend	−00011111	00100100	00000001
6	Test for end of process	−00000101	00100100	00000001
3	Shift divisor right	−00000101	00010010	00000001
5	Test partial dividend enter 0 in quotient and subtract divisor from partial dividend	00001101	00010010	00000010
6	Test for end of process	00001101	00010010	00000010
3	Shift divisor right	00001101	00001001	00000010
4	Test partial dividend enter partial 1 in quotient and subtract divisor from partial dividend	00000100	00001001	00000101
6	Test for end of process	00000100	00001001	00000101
3	Shift divisor right	00000100	0000100.1	00000101
4	Test partial dividend enter 1 in quotient and subtract divisor from partial dividend	−00000000.1	0000100.1	00001011
6	Test for end of process	−00000000.1	0000100.1	00001011
7	Restore last partial dividend	00000100	0000100.1	00001011

Figure 4.33 An example of non-restoring division for $1001\overline{)01100111}$

floating point arithmetic. A new number, Z, is defined in terms of D as $Z = 1 - D$. As D lies between $\frac{1}{2}$ and unity, it follows that Z lies between zero and $\frac{1}{2}$.

An elementary rule of arithmetic states that if the top and bottom of a fraction are multiplied by the same number, the value of the fraction remains unaltered.

Thus, $Q = N/D = KN/KD$.

Suppose $K = 1 + Z$; then

$$Q = \frac{N}{D} = \frac{N(1+Z)}{D(1+Z)} = \frac{N(1+Z)}{(1-Z)(1+Z)} = \frac{N(1+Z)}{1-Z^2}.$$

If we now repeat the process with $K = (1 + Z^2)$, Q becomes

$$\frac{N(1+Z)}{1-Z^2} \cdot \frac{1+Z^2}{1+Z^2} = \frac{N(1+Z)(1+Z^2)}{1-Z^4}.$$

This process may be repeated n times with the result that:

$$Q = \frac{N}{D} = \frac{N(1+Z)(1+Z^2)(1+Z^4)\cdots(1+Z^{2^{n-1}})}{1-Z^{2^n}}.$$

Since Z is less than unity, the value of Z^{2^n} rapidly approaches zero as n is increased. Consequently, the approximate value of Q is given by:

$$Q = N(1 + Z^1)(1 + Z^2)(1 + Z^4) \cdots (1 + Z^{2^{n-1}})$$

For 8-bit precision n need be only 3, and if $n = 5$ the quotient yields a precision of 32 bits. As the divisor was scaled to lie between $\frac{1}{2}$ and unity, the corresponding quotient, Q, calculated from the above formula must be scaled by the same factor to produce the desired result.

Summary

In this chapter we have looked at how numerical information is represented inside a digital computer. We have concentrated on the binary representation of numbers, since digital computers handle binary-encoded information efficiently. Both positive and negative numbers must be stored and manipulated by a computer. We have looked at how digital computers represent negative numbers. Once more, it must be emphasized that negative numbers are stored in a form that represents them. For example, the twos complement representation of the number -5 behaves like -5 when it takes part in addition and subtraction. This representation is not the same as -5 and cannot be directly used in, say, multiplication operations.

Since digital computers sometimes have to work with very large and very small numbers, we have covered some of the ways in which the so-called 'scientific notation' is used to encode both large and small numbers. These numbers are stored in the form of a mantissa and a magnitude (i.e. the exponent or the numbers of zeros before/after the binary point), and are called floating point numbers. Until recently, almost every computer used its own representation of floating point numbers. Today, the IEEE standard for the format of floating point numbers is rapidly replacing all *ad hoc* floating point formats.

At the end of this chapter we have briefly introduced the operations of multiplication and division and have demonstrated how they can be mechanized in digital computers.

Worked examples

Question 1

When two n-bit twos complement integers, A and B, are added together to form a sum S, the possibility of arithmetic overflow exists. The definition of arithmetic overflow is:

$$V = \overline{s_{n-1}} a_{n-1} b_{n-1} + s_{n-1} \overline{a_{n-1}} \, \overline{b_{n-1}}$$

where s_{n-1}, a_{n-1}, and b_{n-1} are the most significant bits of the sum, A, and B, respectively.

This equation is not generally used in real computers to detect overflow because it requires the storage of a_{n-1} and b_{n-1}, one of which is normally destroyed by the addition.

The actual method of detecting overflow is to compare the carry-in to the most significant stage of the parallel adder with the carry-out from the same stage. If they are different overflow is said to occur. That is:

$$V = c_n \overline{c_{n-1}} + \overline{c_n} c_{n-1}.$$

Prove that the above method of detecting overflow by examining the carry bits of the parallel adder is valid.

Solution 1

The most significant stage of a parallel adder can be represented by the diagram in Fig. 4.34.

The msb stage adds together a_{n-1}, b_{n-1}, and c_{n-1} to generate a sum bit, s_{n-1}, and a carry-out, c_n. There are four possible combinations of A and B which can be added together:

$$(+A)+(+B), \quad (+A)+(-B), \quad (-A)+(+B), \quad (-A)+(-B).$$

As adding two numbers of differing sign cannot result in arithmetic overflow, we need consider only the cases where A and B are both positive, or both negative.

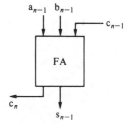

Fig. 4.34

Case 1 A and B positive $a_{n-1}=0$, $b_{n-1}=0$

The final stage adds $a_{n-1}+b_{n-1}+c_{n-1}$ to get c_{n-1}, as a_{n-1} and b_{n-1} are both zero. That is, the carry-out, c_n, is zero; and $s_{n-1}=c_{n-1}$. We know overflow occurs if $s_{n-1}=1$, therefore overflow occurs if the sum is negative and $\overline{c_n} c_{n-1}=1$.

Case 2 A and B negative $a_{n-1}=1$, $b_{n-1}=1$.

The final stage adds $a_{n-1}+b_{n-1}+c_{n-1}=1+1+c_{n-1}$, to get a sum, $s_{n-1}=c_{n-1}$, and a carry-out $c_{n=1}$. Overflow occurs if the sum is positive and $s_{n-1}=0$. That is, if $c_n \overline{c_{n-1}}=1$.

Considering both cases, overflow occurs if $\overline{c_n} c_{n-1} + c_n \overline{c_{n-1}} = 1$.

Question 2

A 32-bit IEEE floating-point number has the following format:

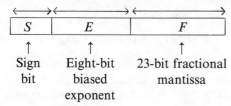

A number N is represented by $N = (-1^S) \times 2^{E-127} \times 1.F$

Carry out the operation $42.6875 - 0.09375$.

Solution 2

$N = (-1)^S \times 2^{E-127} \times 1.F$ where $S =$ sign bit, $E =$ exponent biased by 127, $F = $ *fractional* mantissa.

S	E (i.e. actual exponent + 127)	F (i.e. fractional part of mantissa)
←→	←——————————→	←——————————————→
1 bit	7 bits	23 bits

$42.6875_{10} = 101010.1011_2$
$= 1.010101011 \times 2^5$ (note that $F = .010101011$)

$S = 0$ (positive), $E = 5 + 127$ (i.e. actual exponent + bias) $= 132 = 10000100_2$
$F = 01010101100000000000000$ (in 23 bits).

Therefore, 42.6875_{10} is represented by

0	10000100	01010101100000000000000
S	E	F

Similarly,

$$-0.09375_{10} = -0.00011_2 = -1.1_2 \times 2^{-4},$$

$S = 1$ (negative), $E = -4 + 127 = 123 = 01111011_2$ (in 8 bits),
$F = 10000000000000000000000$ (fractional part in 23 bits).

Therefore, -0.09375_{10} is represented by

1	01111011	10000000000000000000000
S	E	F

To add these floating point numbers, the exponent must be the same. Do this by making the smaller exponent equal to the larger exponent and scaling the mantissa accordingly.

Note that when floating point operations are performed, the leading one in the mantissa must be restored (i.e. $M = 1.F$).

Mantissa of larger number $= 1.01010101100000000000000$

Mantissa of smaller number $= -1.10000000000000000000000$.

Shift mantissa of smaller number right by nine places (i.e. the difference between the exponents)

$$-0.00000000110000000000000.$$

Subtract mantissas to get $+1.01010100110000000000000$.

The new floating point number is represented by

0	10000100	01010100110000000000000.
S	E + 127	F

The new value is given by

$$(0)^{-1} \times 2^{10000100_2 - 127} \times 1.0101010011_2$$
$$= +2^5 \times 1.0101010011$$
$$= +101010.10011_2 = 42.59375_{10}.$$

Problems

1. Convert the following decimal integers to their natural binary equivalents:

(a) 15   (b) 42
(c) 235   (d) 4090
(e) 40 900   (f) 65 530.

2. Convert the following natural binary numbers to their decimal equivalents.

(a) 110   (b) 1110110
(c) 11011   (d) 11111110111

3. Complete Table 4.22

Table 4.22

Decimal	Binary	Octal	Hexadecimal
37			
73			
	10101010		
	11011011101		
		42	
		772	
			256
			ABC

4. Convert the following base five numbers into their base nine equivalents (for example, $23_5 = 14_9$):

(a) 24   (b) 144
(c) 444   (d) 1234

5. Convert the following decimal numbers to their binary equivalents. Calculate the answer to five binary places and round the result up or down as necessary.

(a) 1.5   (b) 1.1
(c) 1/3   (d) 1024.0625
(e) 3.141592   (f) 1/SQRT(2)

6. Convert the following binary numbers to their decimal equivalents.

(a) 1.1   (b) 0.001
(c) 101.101   (d) 11011.101010
(e) 111.111111   (f) 10.1111101

7. Complete Table 4.23. Calculate all values to four places after the radix point.

Table 4.23

Decimal	Binary	Octal	Hexadecimal
0.37			
0.73			
	11011.011101		
	111.1011		
		0.70	
		1.101	
			2.56
			AB.C

8. Calculate the error (both absolute and as a percentage) if the following decimal fractions are converted to binary fractions, correct to 5 binary places.

Note Convert the decimal number to six binary digits and then round up the 5th bit if the 6th bit is a 1.

(a) 0.675   (b) 0.42
(c) 0.1975   (d) 0.1
(e) 0.01   (f) 0.001

9. An electronics engineer has invented a new logic device which has three states: $-1, 0, +1$. These states are represented by $\bar{1}, 0,$ and 1, respectively. This arrangement may be used to form a **balanced ternary** system with a radix 3, but where the 'trits' represent $-1, 0, +1$ instead of $0, 1, 2$. The examples in Table 4.24 illustrate how this system works.

Write down the first 15 decimal numbers in the balanced ternary base.

Table 4.24

Ternary	Balanced ternary	Decimal
11	$1\,1$	4
12	$1\bar{1}\bar{1}$	5
22	$10\bar{1}$	8
1012	$11\bar{1}\bar{1}$	32

10. The results of an experiment fall in the range -4 to $+9$. A scientist wishes to read the results into a computer and then process them. The scientist decides to use a 4-bit binary code to represent each of the possible inputs. Devise a 4-bit code capable of representing numbers in the range −4 to +9.

11. Design a natural binary to Gray code converter. The circuit has four inputs and four outputs. For example, the input 1000 results in the output 1100.

12. Decode the Huffman code below, assuming that the valid codes are P=0, Q=10, R=110, and S=111. How many bits would be required if P, Q, R, and S had been encoded as 00, 01, 10, 11, respectively?

00000111011100000010111111110101001111100010

13. The hexadecimal dump from part of a microcomputer's memory is as follows:

0000 4265 6769 6EFA 47FE BB87 2686 3253 7A29
0010 C98F E000 6CCD.

The dump is made up of a series of strings of characters, each string being composed of nine groups of four hexadecimal characters. The first four characters in each string provide the starting address of the following 16 bytes. For example, the first byte in the second string (i.e. C9) is at address $0010 and the second byte (i.e. $8F) is at address $0011.

The 22 bytes of data in the two strings represent the following sequence of items:

(a) five consecutive ISO/ASCII encoded characters

(b) one unsigned 16-bit integer

(c) one twos complement 16-bit integer

(d) one unsigned 16-bit fraction

(e) one 6-digit natural BCD integer

(f) one 4-byte floating point number with a sign bit and true fraction plus an exponent biased by 64

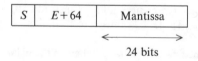

24 bits

(g) one 16-bit unsigned fixed point number with a 12-bit integer part and a 4-bit fraction.

Decode the hexadecimal data, assuming that it is interpreted as above.

14. A message can be coded to protect it from unauthorized readers by EORing it with a binary sequence of the same length to product an encoded message. The encoded message is decoded by EORing it with the *same* sequence that was used to decode it. If the ISO/ASCII-encoded message used to generate the code is ALANCLEMENTS, what does the following encoded message (expressed in hexadecimal form) mean?

09 09 0D 02 0C 6C 12 02 17 02 10 73

15. A single-bit error-detecting code appends a bit, called a parity bit, to a source word to produce a code word. An even parity bit is chosen to make the total number of ones in the code word even (this includes the parity bit itself). For example, the source words 0110111 and 1100110 are coded as 01101111 and 11001100, respectively. In these cases the parity bit has been located in the LSB position.

Indicate which of the following hexadecimal numbers have parity errors.

$00, $07, $FF, $A5, $5A, $70, $FE.

16. A single parity bit error detecting code will detect all single-bit errors in a code word. What other classes of error does this type of error-detecting code detect. What classes of error will not be detected?

17. A checksum digit is the least-significant digit formed when a sequence of numbers are added together. For example, the **decimal** checksum of the sequence 98731 is 8 because $9+8+7+3+1=28$ and 8 is the least significant digit. Similarly, the checksum of the hexadecimal sequence A3, 02, 49, FF is ED because $A3+02+49+FF=1ED$.

The purpose of a checksum is to detect errors in a sequence of digits after they have been transmitted or stored in memory or on tape. The following hexadecimal sequences are terminated by a checksum. Which, if any, are in error?

(a)   0001020304050F

(b)   11223344556675

(c)   FFA32415751464

The position of the checksum in the above three strings is the right-most byte. Does it matter where the checksum is located? What happens if there is an error in the checksum itself?

18. Almost all computer hardware courses include a section on number bases and the conversion of numbers between bases. Does the base in which a computer represents numbers really matter to the computer user or even to the student of computer science?

19. Perform the following binary additions:

(a) 10110
    + 101

(b)   100111
      111001
    + 101101

(c)   11011011
      10111011
      00101011
    + 01111111

20. Perform the following octal additions:

(a)   42
    + 53

(b)   3357
    + 2741

(c)   777
      543
    + 420

(d)   437
      426
      772
    + 747

21. Perform the following hexadecimal additions:

(a)
$$\begin{array}{r} 42 \\ +\,53 \\ \hline \end{array}$$

(b)
$$\begin{array}{r} 3357 \\ +\,2741 \\ \hline \end{array}$$

(c)
$$\begin{array}{r} 777 \\ 543 \\ +\,420 \\ \hline \end{array}$$

(d)
$$\begin{array}{r} ABCD \\ FE10 \\ +\,123A \\ \hline \end{array}$$

22. Using 8-bit arithmetic throughout, express the following decimal numbers in twos complement binary form:

(a) -4 (b) -5 (c) 0 (d) -25
(e) -42 (f) -128 (g) -127 (h) -111.

23. Perform the following decimal subtractions in 8-bit twos complement arithmetic. Note that some of the answers will result in arithmetic overflow. Indicate where overflow has occurred:

(a)
$$\begin{array}{r} 20 \\ -\,5 \\ \hline \end{array}$$

(b)
$$\begin{array}{r} 127 \\ -\,126 \\ \hline \end{array}$$

(c)
$$\begin{array}{r} 127 \\ -\,128 \\ \hline \end{array}$$

(d)
$$\begin{array}{r} 5 \\ -\,20 \\ \hline \end{array}$$

(e)
$$\begin{array}{r} 69 \\ -\,42 \\ \hline \end{array}$$

(f)
$$\begin{array}{r} -20 \\ -\,111 \\ \hline \end{array}$$

(g)
$$\begin{array}{r} -127 \\ -\,2 \\ \hline \end{array}$$

(h)
$$\begin{array}{r} -42 \\ +\,69 \\ +\,120 \\ \hline \end{array}$$

24. Using twos complement binary arithmetic with a 12-bit word, write down the range of numbers capable of being represented (both in decimal and binary formats) by giving the smallest and largest numbers. What happens when the smallest and largest numbers are

(a) incremented?   (b) decremented?

25. Distinguish between *overflow* and *carry* when these terms are applied to twos complement arithmetic on n-bit words.

26. Write down an algebraic expression giving the value of the n-bit integer $N = a_{n-1}, a_{n-2}, \ldots, a_1, a_0$ for the case where N represents a twos complement number.

Hence prove that (in twos complement notation) the representation of a signed binary number in $n+1$ bits may be derived from its representation in n bits by repeating the leftmost bit. For example, if $n = -12 = 10100$ in *five* bits, $n = -12 = 110100$ in *six* bits.

27. Perform the additions below on 4-bit binary numbers:

(a)
$$\begin{array}{r} 0011 \\ +\,1100 \\ \hline \end{array}$$

(b)
$$\begin{array}{r} 1111 \\ +\,0001 \\ \hline \end{array}$$

(c)
$$\begin{array}{r} 0110 \\ +\,0111 \\ \hline \end{array}$$

(d)
$$\begin{array}{r} 1100 \\ +\,1010 \\ \hline \end{array}$$

In each case, regard the numbers as being (i) unsigned integer, (ii) twos complement integer, and (iii) sign and magnitude integer. Calculate the answer and comment on it where necessary.

28.

(a) Write down the largest base 5 positive integer in n digits.

(b) Write down the largest base 7 number in m digits.

(c) It is necessary to represent n-digit base 5 numbers in base 7. What is the minimum number (m) of digits needed to represent all possible n-digit base 5 numbers? (*Hint*: The largest m-digit base 7 number should be greater than or equal to the largest n-digit base 5 number.)

29. A 4-bit binary adder adds together two 4-bit numbers, A and B, to produce a 4-bit sum, S, and a single-bit carry-out C. What is the range of outputs (i.e. largest and smallest values) that the adder is capable of producing? Give your answer in both binary and decimal forms.

An adder is designed to add together two binary-coded decimal (BCD) digits to produce a single-digit sum and a one-bit carry-out. What is the range of valid outputs that this circuit may produce?

The designer of the BCD adder decides to use a pure binary adder to add together two BCD digits as if they were pure 4-bit binary numbers. Under what circumstances does the binary adder give the correct BCD result? Under what circumstances is the result incorrect (i.e. the 4-bit binary result differs from the required BCD result)?

What algorithm must the designer apply to the 4-bit output of the binary adder to convert it to a BCD adder?

30. Design a full subtractor circuit which will subtract bit X together with a borrow-in bit B_i from bit Y to produce a difference bit $D = Y - X - B_i$, and a borrow-out B_0.

31. In the negabinary system an i-bit binary integer, N, is expressed using positional rotation as:

$$N = a_0 \times (-1)^0 \times 2^0 + a_1 \times (-1)^1 \times 2^1 + \cdots + a_{i-1} \times (-1)^{i-1} \times 2^{i-1}$$

This is the same as conventional natural 8421 binary weighted numbers, except that alternate positions have the additional weighting $+1$ and -1.
For example,

$$1101 = (-1 \times 1 \times 8) + (+1 \times 1 \times 4) + (-1 \times 0 \times 2)$$
$$+ (+1 \times 1 \times 1)$$
$$= -8 + 4 + 1 = -3$$

(a) The following 4-bit numbers are represented in negabinary form. Express them as signed decimal values:

(i) 0000   (ii) 0101   (iv) 1010   (v) 1111.

(b) Perform the following additions on 4-bit negadecimal numbers. The result is a 6-bit negadecimal value. You must work out your own algorithm:

(i)
$$\begin{array}{r} 0000 \\ +\,0001 \\ \hline \end{array}$$

(ii)
$$\begin{array}{r} 1010 \\ +\,0101 \\ \hline \end{array}$$

(iii)
$$\begin{array}{r} 1101 \\ +\,1011 \\ \hline \end{array}$$

(iv)
$$\begin{array}{r} 1111 \\ +\,1111. \\ \hline \end{array}$$

(c) Convert the following signed decimal into their 6-bit negabinary counterparts:

(i) 4   (ii) -4 (iii) -7 (iv) $+7$ (v) 10.

(d) What is the range of values that can be expressed as an n-bit negabinary value? That is, what is the largest positive decimal number and what is the largest negative decimal number that can be converted into an *n*-bit negabinary form?

32. The following floating point format has been designed to give you an 'easy' introduction to the manipulation of floating point numbers. Questions 2 and 3 provide more realistic (and more tedious) examples.

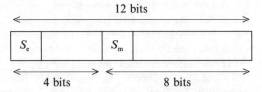

12 bits

4 bits   8 bits

The exponent consists of a 3-bit absolute value plus a sign bit, S_e. The mantissa consists of a 7-bit absolute value plus a sign bit, S_m. For example, the binary pattern 1101011010000 represents $+0.11010000 \times 2^{-5}$. Note that both mantissa and exponent are represented in sign and magnitude form.

For the above format write down the range of numbers capable of being represented. Using this format perform the following operations:

(a) 25
   $+16$

(b) 25
   -16

(c) 12.25
   $+1.125$

(d) 1.125
   -0.625.

33. A computer has a 24-bit word length which, for the purpose of floating-point operations, is divided into an 8-bit biased exponent, and a 16-bit twos complement mantissa. Write down the range of numbers capable of being represented in this format and their precision.

34. For the floating-point format of the previous question, perform the following operations:

(a) 276.123
   -159.014

(b) 276.123
   $+276.123$

(c) -276.123
   $+275.123$

(d) 1563.123
   -0.042

(e) 276.123
   $+76.123$

(f) 276.123
   -76.123

Use the following assumptions:

(i) The numbers are stored as 24-bit words.

(ii) Floating point operations are carried out on an 18-bit mantissa (two extra bits in the ALU). That is, the 16-bit mantissa from the memory becomes an 18-bit mantissa while floating point calculations are being carried out.

(iii) During the floating point operations all mantissa bits generated in the 19th position are dropped (i.e. truncation, not rounding).

(iv) The final value has its 18-bit mantissa rounded to 16 bits, and is then packed with the exponent into a 24-bit word, and stored in memory.

In each case, convert the final 24-bit floating point result into a decimal value and compare it with the expected result.

35. The twos complement fractional part of a normalized floating-point number X is constrained to lie within one of the three ranges:

$$-1 \leqslant X < -\tfrac{1}{2}, \quad X = 0, \quad \tfrac{1}{2} \leqslant X < 1.$$

Explain why this is so and illustrate your answer with a five-bit mantissa.

The central processing unit

The central processing unit (CPU) lies at the heart of a computer and is responsible for stepping through the instructions of a program in an orderly fashion, reading them from memory, executing them, and controlling the operation of the computer's memory and input/output devices. That is, the CPU includes all the components required to fetch instructions from memory, decode them, execute them and transfer any data to and from memory or peripherals. The CPU excludes instruction and program memory and all input/output devices. In this chapter we are going to look at the structure or *organization* of a CPU. We begin by describing a very simple CPU based on the 68000 microprocessor. In the middle part of this chapter we examine the control unit of a CPU that is responsible for taking an instruction and causing the appropriate actions to take place. At the end of the chapter we introduce the 'reduced instruction set computer' (i.e. RISC) that provides an alternative way of implementing a CPU to the complex instruction set 68000 described throughout this text.

By the way, you should be aware that my definition of the CPU excludes the memory that holds the programs and data, because a few other writers include memory as part of the CPU. I have chosen to regard the CPU as excluding memory, since my definition of the CPU closely matches the structure of many of the microprocessors that are now so widely used. However, my diagrams of the CPU will include the memory system because CPU operations cannot be explained without reference to the memory that holds programs and data. In a later chapter we will look at the memory system in some detail.

Before we look at the way in which a CPU works, it is important to understand the relationship between the CPU, the memory and the program. Let's take a simple program to calculate the area of a circle and see how the computer deals with it. In what follows the computer is a hypothetical machine devoid of all the nasty complications associated with reality.

We know that the area of a circle, A, can be calculated from the formula $\pi \times r^2$. When people evaluate the area of a circle, they perform many of the necessary steps automatically at a **subconscious** level. However, when they come to write programs, they must tell the computer exactly what it must do, step by step. To illustrate this point, take a look at the expression $\pi \times r \times r$. We write $r \times r$, but we mean a number, which we have given the symbol r, multiplied by itself. We never confuse the symbol r with the value that we give to r when we evaluate the expression. This may seem an obvious point, but students often have great difficulty when they come to the concepts of an **address** and **data** in assembly language. Although people never confuse the symbol for the radius (i.e. r) and its value, say 4 cm, you must remember that an address (i.e. the place where the value of r is stored) and data (i.e. the value of r) are both binary quantities inside the computer.

Figure 5.1 illustrates the relationship between the program, memory and processor. The memory has been divided into five parts: program, constants, variables, input, and output. The program is composed of the sequence of operations to be carried out, or executed. The constants (in this case there is only one—π) are numbers used by the program but which do not change during its execution. The variables represent numbers created and modified by the program. Thus, when the program 'squares r' it reads the value of the number in the memory location it has called r, squares it, and puts the result back in the same location. Thus the original value of r is lost. Note that a programmer may sometimes wish to retain

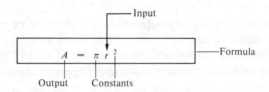

Fig. 5.1 The relationship between the memory, processor, and program.

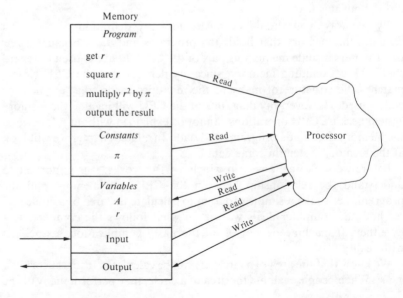

the original value of r, rather than by overwriting it with r^2. In such a case, r^2 would be stored in another memory location.

Although the variables (i.e. the values held in memory locations) are often numerical quantities, there is no reason why this must always be so. For example, the variables used by a word processor are the letters (and other symbols) of the text being manipulated. Indeed, it is perfectly possible for the variable to be another program. That is, one program can operate on, or modify, another program.

Any program must be able to communicate with the outside world, otherwise all its efforts are to no effect. I have labelled two memory locations in Fig. 5.1 *input* and *output,* so that reading from the *input* location causes information to be taken from an input device (say a keyboard) and writing to the *output* location causes information to be moved from the computer to an output device (say a VDU). Regarding input and output as memory locations is not entirely fictional: as we shall later discover, some computers really do perform all input/output transactions via the memory.

The processor may either read data from a memory location or write data to a memory location. Of the five regions of memory described above, three are read-only, one is write-only, and one can be read from or written to.

5.1 The structure of the CPU

We are now going to look at the structure of a CPU. In order to keep things simple, we will build up a CPU step by step. Figure 5.2 provides the

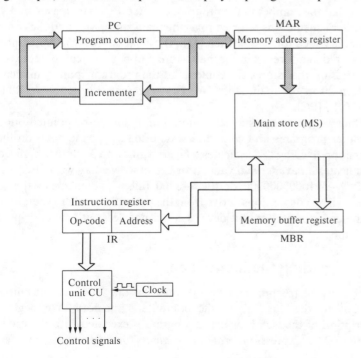

Fig. 5.2 The address paths of the CPU.

block diagram of part of a CPU. In this diagram only the *address paths* and the paths needed to read an instruction from memory are shown for clarity. That is, I have omitted the data paths required to actually execute instructions. The address paths represent highways along which addresses flow from one part of the CPU to another. An address is a number representing the location of an item of data within the memory. In terms of the example in which we evaluated the area of a circle, r is the symbolic address of the radius. There are two types of information flow in a computer: address and data (the latter is usually taken to mean instructions, constants and variables).

Register transfer language

We are going to adopt a shorthand called register-transfer language (RTL) in order to help us to explain how the CPU in Fig. 5.2 works. One or more letters, or letters followed by numerals, denote registers or storage locations. Square brackets denote the contents of the registers they enclose, and a left arrow ($\leftarrow$) indicates the transfer of the contents of a register. The left-hand side of an equation denotes the *result* of the action defined on the right-hand side of the equation. For example, the expression

$$[MAR] \leftarrow [PC]$$

means that the contents of the program counter, PC, are transferred (i.e. copied) into the memory address register, MAR. Note that the contents of the PC are not modified by this operation. Similarly, the expression

$$[PC] \leftarrow [PC] + 1$$

means that the number in the program counter, PC, is increased by 1. The computer's memory is referred to as the main store, MS, and the contents of memory location x is written [MS(x)]. That is, [MS(x)] represents the data stored at address x in the main store. Suppose the computer executes an operation that stores the contents of the program counter in memory location 20 in the main store. We can represent this action in RTL as [MS(20)]←[PC].

While we are on the subject of notation, it should be pointed out that computer programs and computer texts often adopt the notation that a number prefixed by '%' indicates a *binary* value and a number prefixed by '$' indicates a *hexadecimal* value. For example, we may write [PC]←1024 or [PC]←%10000000000 or [PC]←$400 (all of which mean the same thing). These conventions derive from the past when earlier generations of computer input and output devices could not deal with superscripts and subscripts.

5.1.1 Reading the instruction

Before any instruction can be executed by the CPU, it must first be brought to the CPU from the computer's memory. We begin our description of the way in which a program is executed with the program counter. The expression *program counter* (or instruction counter or location counter) is rather a misnomer. It does not count programs, or anything else, but contains the address of the next instruction in memory to be executed. It can be said to **point** to the next instruction to be executed. If, for example, [PC] = 5 (i.e. the PC contains the number 5), the next instruction to be executed is to be found in memory location 5.

The execution of an instruction begins with the contents of the program counter being moved to the memory address register (i.e. [MAR]←[PC]). Once the contents of the program counter have been transferred to the memory address register, the contents of program counter are incremented (increased by 1) and moved back to the program counter (i.e. [PC]←[PC]+1]). That is, the program counter is pointing to the next instruction while the current instruction is being executed.

The memory address register, MAR, holds the address of the location in the main store, MS, into which data is being written in a write cycle, or from which data is being read in a read cycle. Now, the MAR contains a copy of the contents of the PC, so that when a read cycle is performed, the instruction to be executed is read from the memory and transferred to the memory buffer register, MBR. We can represent this operation in RTL terms as:

[MBR]←[MS([MAR])]

We interpret the expression [MS([MAR])] as 'the contents of the main store whose address is given by the contents of the MAR'. The MBR is a temporary holding place for data received from memory in a read cycle, or for data to be transferred to memory in a write cycle. Some texts refer to the MBR as the memory data register, MDR. At this point, the MBR contains the **bit pattern** of the instruction to be executed.

The instruction is next moved from the MBR to the instruction register, IR, where it is divided into two **fields**. A field is a part of a word in which the bits are grouped together into a logical entity. For example, a person's name is divided into two fields: given name and family name. One field in the IR contains the operation code (op-code), that tells the CPU what operation is to be carried out. The other field, called the **operand field**, contains the address of the data to be used by the instruction. Sometimes the operand field is redundant, as not all op-codes refer to a location in memory. We shall soon see that the operand field can provide a **constant** to be employed by the operation code, rather than the address of the data required by the op-code.

Here it is necessary to make two points. First, the type of instructions we are describing belongs to a class of instructions called **one-address instructions.** That is, the instructions consist of only two fields: the op-code and the operand. There are other classes of instruction (e.g. two-address or three-address instructions) that have two or more operands. The second point worth noting is that the CPU we are describing is highly simplified. Many real machines have such long instruction formats that it is necessary to break up an instruction and store it in consecutive memory locations. All this means in practice is that the CPU must perform two or more read cycles to fetch an instruction.

The control unit, CU, takes the op-code from the IR, together with a stream of clock pulses, and generates signals that control all parts of the CPU. In many computers the time between individual clock pulses is in the range 0.01–$1\,\mu s$ (i.e. 10^{-8} to $10^{-6}\,s$). It is the control unit that is responsible for moving the contents of the program counter into the MAR, executing a read cycle, and moving the contents of the MBR to the IR. Later we look at the control unit, which is the most complex part of the CPU, in more detail and demonstrate how it goes about interpreting an op-code.

The above sequence of operations in which the next instruction is moved from memory to the instruction register is known as a *fetch* phase. All instructions in a conventional computer are executed in a two-phase operation called a fetch–execute cycle. During the fetch phase, the instruction is read from memory and decoded by the control unit. The fetch phase is followed by an *execute* phase in which the control unit generates all the signals necessary to execute the instruction. Table 5.1 puts together the sequence of operations taking place in a fetch phase. Note that in Table 5.1 *FETCH* is a label that serves to indicate a particular line in the sequence of operations. The notation *IR(op-code)* means the operation-code field of the instruction register.

Table 5.1 The FETCH phase expressed in register transfer language

FETCH	[MAR] ←[PC]	copy PC to MAR
	[PC] ←[PC]+1	increment PC
	[MBR] ←[MS([MAR])]	read instruction
	[IR] ←[MBR]	move it to IR
	CU ←[IR(op-code)]	

5.1.2 The CPU's data paths

Now that we've sorted out the fetch phase, let's see what else we need to actually execute instructions. In Fig. 5.3 new data paths have been added to the simplified CPU of Fig. 5.2, together with an address path from the address field of the IR to the PC.

Other modifications to Fig. 5.2 included in Fig. 5.3 are the addition of a data register, D0, and an arithmetic and logical unit, ALU. The data register holds temporary or intermediate results during a calculation. A data register is necessary in a one-address machine, because diadic operations (e.g. $+$, $-$, $*$, $/$ etc.) take place on one operand specified by the instruction and the contents of the data register. The result of the operation is deposited in the data register, destroying one of the original operands. Later we shall see that a real microprocessor like the 68000 has more than one data register (the 68000 has eight from D0–D7). Some of yesterday's computers and many of the first-generation 8-bit microprocessors had only one general-purpose data register which was called the *accumulator*.

For example, if we add the contents of memory location 1234 to the data register, the data that was in the data register is replaced by the

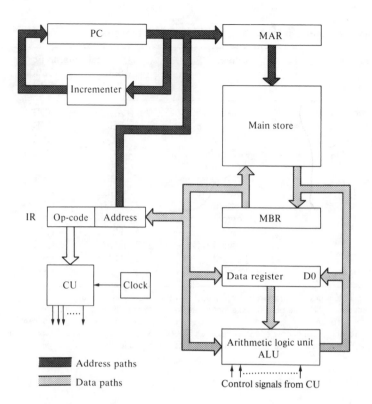

Fig. 5.3 The address and data paths of the CPU. *Note:* I have called the data register D0 to make it compatible with the 68000 microprocessor which has eight data registers D0 to D7. Many microprocessors with a single data register call the data register an accumulator.

previous contents of the data register plus the contents of location 1234 specified by the instruction.

The ALU is the *workhorse* of the CPU because it carries out all the calculations. Arithmetic and logical operations are applied either to the contents of the data register alone or to the contents of the data register and the contents of the MBR. The output of the ALU is fed back to the data register or to the MBR.

Two types of operation are carried out by the ALU; arithmetic and logical. The fundamental difference between an arithmetic and a logical operation is that in logical operations a carry is not generated when bit A_i of word A and bit B_i of B are operated upon. Table 5.2 provides examples of typical arithmetic and logical operations.

Having developed our computer a little further, we can now execute an elementary program. Consider the operation $P = Q + R$. Here the '+' symbol means arithmetic addition. The program required to carry out this operation is given below and is the same as the program we introduced in Chapter 4 when dealing with addition. Remember that P, Q, and R are *symbolic* names that refer to the *locations* of the variables in memory. The extension '.B' in the following mnemonics defines a byte (i.e. 8-bit) operand.

```
MOVE.B Q,D0  Load data register D0 with the contents of Q.
ADD.B  R,D0  Add to data register D0 the contents of R.
MOVE.B D0,P  Store the contents of data register D0 in P.
```

Table 5.2 Some typical arithmetic and logical operations

Operation	Class	Typical mnemonic 6502 CPU	68000 CPU
Addition	Arithmetic	ADC	ADD
Subtraction	Arithmetic	SBC	SUB
Negation	Arithmetic	NEG	NEG
Multiplication	Arithmetic	—	MULU
Division	Arithmetic	—	DIVU
Divide by 2	Arithmetic	ASR	ASR
Multiply by 2	Arithmetic	ASL	ASL
OR	Logical	ORA	OR
AND	Logical	AND	AND
NOT	Logical	NOT	NOT
EOR	Logical	EOR	EOR
Shift left	Logical	LSL	LSL
Shift right	Logical	LSR	LSR

The 6502 is a first-generation microprocessor with a single general-purpose data register (i.e. accumulator). The 68000 is a second-generation microprocessor with eight general-purpose data registers. Note that 6502 instructions require a single operand (e.g. ADC Q) since there is only one data register. 68000 instructions may take two operands (e.g. ADD Q,D3) since one of eight data registers can be specified.

Note that the one address machine requires a rather cumbersome sequence of operations just to carry out a simple action—adding two numbers.

If we had a three address format, we could have written:

ADD.B Q,R,P Add contents of Q to R and put the result in P.

Three-address machines are faster than one-address machines, as they can do in one instruction things that take other machines three cycles. However, the power of three-address machines can be achieved only by means of a complex and expensive CPU and memory system.

The way in which the CPU operates can best be seen by examining the execution of the instruction ADD.B R,D0 in terms of register-transfer language. Table 5.3 gives the sequence of operations carried out during the fetch and execute phases of an ADD.B R,D0 instruction. These operations tell us what is actually going on inside the computer.

Two operations sharing the same line are executed simultaneously. Incidentally, operations of the form [PC]←[MAR] or [D0]←[D0]+[MAR] are often referred to as *microinstructions*. Each assembly level instruction (e.g. MOVE.B, ADD.B) is executed as a series of microinstructions. In general, microinstructions and microprogramming are the province of the computer designer, although some machines are microprogrammable by the user. Section 5.2.1 on the operation of the control unit takes a further look at microinstructions.

Table 5.3 A FETCH/EXECUTE cycle expressed in RTL

FETCH	[MAR] ← [PC]	move contents of PC to MAR
	[PC] ← [PC]+1	increment contents of the PC
	[MBR] ← [MS([MAR])]	read from the main store
	[IR] ← [MBR]	move contents of MBR to IR
	CU ← [IR(op-code)]	move op-code from IR to CU
ADD	[MAR] ← [IR(address)]	move address of operand to MAR
	[MBR] ← [MS([MAR])]	read data
	ALU ← [MBR], ALU ← [DO]	perform addition
	[DO] ← ALU	move output of ALU to data register

Note that during the fetch phase the op-code is fed to the control unit by the operation CU←[IR(op-code)] and the CU uses it to generate all the internal signals required to place the ALU in its addition mode. When the ALU is programmed for addition it adds together the data at its two input terminals to produce a sum at its output terminals.

5.1.3 Executing conditional instructions

So far, we have considered the architecture of a CPU capable of executing simple programs in a purely sequential mode—no mechanism yet exists for making choices or repeating a group of instructions. To do this, the CPU must be able to execute either absolute branches (GOTOs) or conditional branches. A *branch* is an instruction that forces the CPU to execute an instruction out of the normal sequence. The word *branch* generally implies switching between two courses of action, while *jump* implies a non-sequential flow of control. Both terms are used in computer science, often quite interchangeably. A *conditional branch* allows high-level constructs such as IF THEN ELSE to be implemented. The block diagram of Fig. 5.4 shows the new address and data paths required by the CPU to execute conditional branches.

Three items have been added to our computer of Fig. 5.3: a carry flip-flop, a condition code register, CCR, and a path between the address field of the instruction register and the program counter. Note that the terms *condition code register* and *processor status register*, PSR, are interchangeable. Some texts use PSR and some CCR. We describe these three elements first and then demonstrate how they can be used together to implement conditional branches.

The action of the *carry flip-flop* is quite straightforward. Whenever, for example, an addition or subtraction is performed, the result goes to the data register and the carry, or borrow, bit is retained in the carry flip-flop. For example, the addition 00000100 + 00000001 provides a sum 00000101 and a carry bit C = 0, while the sum 10000110 + 10001110 provides a sum 00010100 and a carry bit C = 1. Similarly, if the contents of the data register are moved (shifted) left or right by one bit, the bit that would 'fall off the edge' is transferred to the carry flip-flop. For these reasons, the carry bit may be thought of as a one-bit extension of the data register.

After the CPU carries out an arithmetic or a logical operation, it updates the bits of its *condition code register* to reflect the nature of the result. The bits of the CCR of interest here are:

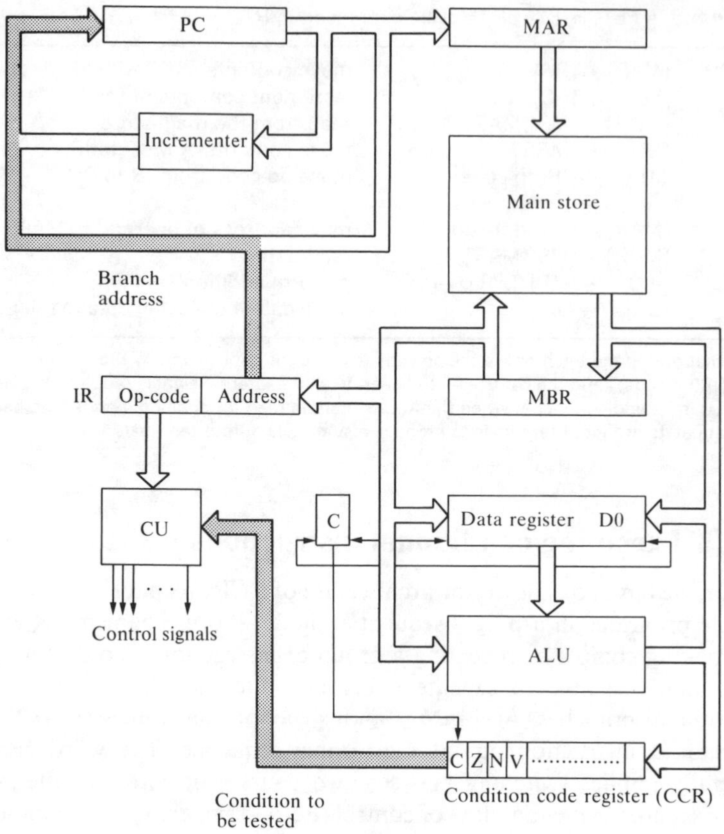

Fig. 5.4 Information paths in the CPU and conditional instructions. Note that the carry bit, C, is shown twice for clarity—once as part of the CCR and once as an extension of the data register.

C = Carry	Set if a carry was generated in the last operation. The C bit is, of course, the same as the carry bit in the carry flip-flop.
Z = Zero	Set if the last operation generated a zero result.
N = Negative	Set if the last result generated a negative result, in twos complement terms (i.e., its MSB = 1).
V = Overflow	Set if the last operation resulted in an arithmetic overflow. That is, an operation on one or two signed twos complement values gave a result that was outside its allowable range. (An arithmetic overflow occurs during addition if the sign bit of the result is different to the sign bit of both operands.)

The examples in 8-bit arithmetic shown in Table 5.4 should demonstrate the effect of binary addition on the contents of the CCR. In each of the examples the C, Z, N, and V bits of the CCR are presented to show how they relate to the addition.

Note that the CPU does not **assume** anything about the nature of the operation it is carrying out. For example, if the programmer adds the ASCII code for the letter 'A' (i.e. $41) to the ASCII code for the letter 'B' (i.e. $42), the result will be $83 or %10000011. This result causes the N bit

Table 5.4 How the CCR is affected by addition

Operand 1 + Operand 2 = Result	CCR status bits
00000011 + 00000100 = 00000111	C=0, Z=0, N=0, V=0
11111111 + 00000001 = 00000000	C=1, Z=1, N=0, V=0
01100110 + 00110010 = 10011000	C=0, Z=0, N=1, V=1
11001001 + 10100000 = 01101001	C=1, Z=0, N=0, V=1

of the CCR to be set to one, even though the concept of negativeness is, in this case, quite meaningless.

The CCR is connected to the control unit, enabling certain types of instruction to interrogate the CCR. For example, instructions exist that test whether the last operation performed by the central processor yielded a positive result, or whether the carry bit was set, or whether arithmetic overflow occurred. There is, of course, no point in carrying out an interrogation unless the results are acted upon. We need a mechanism that does one thing if the result of the test is true and does another thing if the result of the test is false. The final modification included in Fig. 5.4 to the CPU of Fig. 5.3 is the addition of a path between the address field of the instruction register and the program counter. It is this feature that enables the computer to respond to the result of its interrogation of the CCR.

An instruction can test one or more bits of the CCR and, if the bit is clear, the next instruction is obtained from memory in the normal way. But if the bit is set, the next instruction is obtained from the location whose address is in the instruction register. This type of instruction is known as a **conditional branch** or conditional jump. In the above description we said that a branch is made if a certain bit of the CCR is set; equally a branch can be made if the bit is clear. The way in which conditional branches are actually implemented inside the computer is discussed in Section 5.2 on the control unit. Table 5.5 illustrates some of the conditional branch instructions implemented by a typical microprocessor.

Branch operations can be written in register-transfer language in an 'IF condition THEN action' format. Below are two examples of conditional branches expressed in terms of RTL. The mnemonic BCC is read as

Table 5.5 Typical conditional branch instructions

BCC	Branch on carry clear	branch if C=0
BCS	Branch on carry set	branch if C=1
BEQ	Branch on zero result	branch if Z=1
BNE	Branch on non-zero result	branch if Z=0
BMI	Branch on minus result (2s comp)	branch if N=1
BPL	Branch on positive result (2s comp)	branch if N=0
BVC	Branch on overflow clear (2s comp)	branch if V=0
BVS	Branch on overflow set (2s comp)	branch if V=1
BGE	Branch on greater than or equal to	branch if $N\bar{V}+\bar{N}V=1$
BGT	Branch on greater than	branch if $NV\bar{Z}+\bar{N}\bar{V}\bar{Z}=1$
BHI	Branch if higher than	branch if $\bar{C}.\bar{Z}=1$
BLE	Branch if less than	branch if $Z+\bar{N}V+N\bar{V}=1$
BLS	Branch if lower than or the same	branch if $C+Z=1$

'branch on carry clear' and BEQ as 'branch on zero' *or* 'branch on equal'. The notation [C] is read as 'the carry bit' and could equally be represented by [CCR(C)].

```
BCC address: IF [C]=0 THEN [PC]←[IR(address)]
BEQ address: IF [Z]=1 THEN [PC]←[IR(address)]
```

5.1.4 Dealing with literal operands

We have considered all operands to be addresses and assumed all instructions (e.g. MOVE.B, ADD.B, and BCC etc.) refer to an address somewhere within the CPU's memory. Sometimes we wish to use operands that represent the *actual* value of the data being referred to by the op-code part of the instruction. For example, we may wish to add the number 12 to the contents of data register D0. It is perfectly possible to store the value 12 in memory at location, say, 100 and then execute the instruction, ADD.B 100,D0. A much better solution is to execute the operation ADD.B #12,D0, in which the operand is the *actual* (i.e. literal) number used by the op-code 'ADD.B'. Although the symbol '#' appears as part of the operand when this instruction is written in mnemonic form, the assembler uses a different code for

```
ADD.B #⟨literal⟩,⟨destination⟩
```

than it does for

```
ADD.B ⟨address⟩,⟨destination⟩.
```

The notation '⟨address⟩' means that the contents of the angle brackets should be replaced by the appropriate address whenever the instruction is actually used by a programmer. Similarly, ⟨destination⟩ means that the programmer should write the appropriate destination for the operand (i.e. in our examples the destination is D0).

The instruction ADD.B #12,D0 is defined in RTL as: [D0]←[D0]+12. Figure 5.5 shows that an additional data path between the operand field of the IR and the ALU is required to deal with literal operands.

5.1.5 An example of a simple assembly-language program

In order to fit together the things we have learned in this section, a programming example on our hypothetical computer should help. A suitable basic one-address instruction set for this computer is described in Table 5.6, where M and N are the symbolic names of operands used by instructions and the suffix '.B' indicates that the operand size is a byte. The instructions in Table 5.6 are typical of those of the 68000 microprocessor, except for the IN and OUT instructions. Note that in Table 5.6 each instruction has a 2-digit hexadecimal op-code and a 2-digit operand. For example, the instruction to store the contents of the data register in memory location 5, MOVE.B D0,5, is represented by the code 0105. I

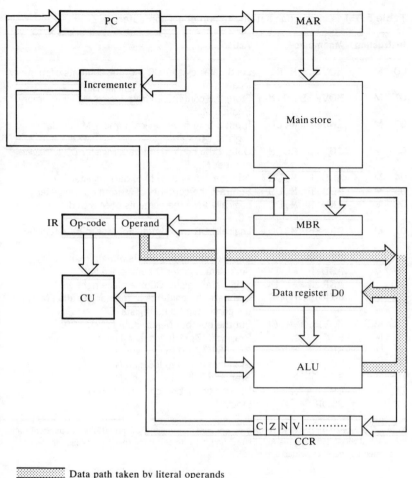

Fig. 5.5 Dealing with literal operands.

Data path taken by literal operands
e.g. MOVE #123,D0 [D0]←[IR(Operand)]
    ADD   #123,D0 [D0]←[D0]+[IR(Operand)]

have not used actual 68000 operation codes, as the relationship between a 68000 op-code and its mnemonic is rather complex.

Two operations in Table 5.6 that cannot be carried out by our present computer are the input and output instructions, IN.B M,D0 and OUT.B D0,M, respectively. To implement these instructions, we would need data paths from the data register to and from our peripherals.

For the purpose of our example we will assume that the input/output device is a VDU and has device number 0. To read data from the VDU's keyboard we execute the instruction IN.B 0,D0, and to display a number on its screen we execute OUT.B D0,0. Please note that there is a 'simple fiction' here. For the sake of simplicity, I have assumed that the keyboard and VDU send and receive numbers. This is not true, as keyboards and VDUs invariably regard data as being ISO/ASCII encoded.

To make our example more realistic we would have had to transform

Table 5.6 The instruction set of a hypothetical computer

Instruction		Mnemonic	Action
00	M	MOVE.B M,D0	Load data register D0 with the contents of memory location M.
01	M	MOVE.B D0,M	Store the contents of data register D0 in memory location M.
02	M	IN.B M,D0	Input a byte from device number M into data register D0.
03	M	OUT.B D0,M	Output the contents of data register D0 to device number M.
04	M	ADD.B M.D0	Add the contents of M to data register D0.
05	M	SUB.B M,D0	Subtract the contents of M from data register D0.
06	M	AND.B M,D0	Logically AND the contents of M with data register D0.
07	M	OR.B M,D0	Logically OR the contents of M with data register D0.
08		NEG.B D0	Complement the contents of data register D0.
09		ASL.B #1,D0	Shift data register D0 one place left.
0A		ASR.B #1,D0	Shift data register D0 one place right.
0B	M	CMP.B M,D0	Compare the contents of memory location M with the contents of data register D0.
0C	M	MOVE.B #M,D0	Put the number M into data register D0.
0D	N	BEQ N	Branch if [Z]=1 to location N.
0E	N	BNE N	Branch if [Z]=0 to location N.
0F	N	BCC N	Branch if [C]=0 to location N.
10	N	BCS N	Branch if [C]=1 to location N.
11	N	BRA N	Unconditional branch to location N.
12		STOP	Stop.

Note   The **branch on zero** and **branch on not zero** instructions (0D and 0E) are dependent on the state of the Z flag from the ALU. The Z flag is set to one if the result of the last operation performed by the ALU yielded a zero value.

data from the keyboard from its ISO/ASCII code into its binary equivalent and to convert a number into an ISO/ASCII string before sending it to the VDU.

The problem we wish to solve is: read a series of numbers from the keyboard that are terminated by a zero, add them together, multiply the result by 10 and print the answer on the VDU. In a high-level language, this program may be written in the BASIC or Pascal forms in Table 5.7.

Some people who write programs in assembly language first draw a flow chart for their algorithm and then convert it into assembly language; others write the program in a high-level language (often Pascal) and then code each of the statements into a number of assembly language operations. Yet others write assembly language directly from the problem. These latter people seldom get their programs right and often they fail their exams. Since preparing the second edition of *The Principles of Computer Hardware*, the size of my classes has become so large that I have stopped trying to mark students' work on the basis of their programs. I take their scripts to the top of a flight of stairs and then hurl them into space. Then I award marks according to where each script lands. This takes most of the effort out of marking, but it is not particularly fair.

Table 5.7 A program to add a sequence numbers terminated by zero expressed in both BASIC and Pascal

BASIC	Pascal
10 T=0	**Program** *sum* (*input, output*);
20 INPUT N	**Var** *N, T*: *integer*;
30 T=T+N	**begin**
40 IF N<>0 THEN GOTO 20	$T:=0$;
50 T=T * 10	**repeat**
60 PRINT T	*read* (*N*);
70 STOP	$T:=T+N$
	until *N=0*;
	$T:=T*10$;
	write (*T*)
	end.

However, why should I give my students a false impression about life by trying to be fair to them?

A flow chart for the algorithm to add a sequence of numbers terminated by zero is given in Fig. 5.6. Flow charts were once a popular method of representing algorithms in a graphical form before they were coded into either high-level language or assembly language. In general, the use of flow charts is strongly discouraged today. Although the flow chart is able to illustrate a simple algorithm quite elegantly, it is unsuited to complex algorithms, because it tends to confuse the structure of an algorithm with the implementation of the algorithm. Moreover, a flow chart can be very

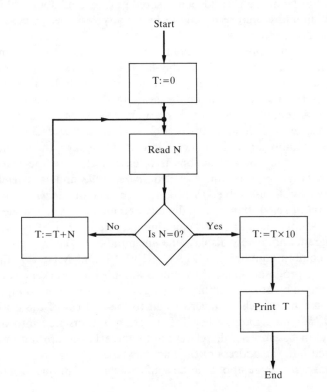

Fig. 5.6 A flow chart to execute the algorithm of Table 5.7.

Table 5.8 Expressing the algorithm of Table 5.7 in pseudocode

```
Module Sum_times_ten
  Clear Total
  REPEAT
    Get Number
    Total:=total+number
  UNTIL Number=0
  Total:=Total * 10
  Print Total
End Sum_times_ten
```

difficult to modify if the algorithm is ever changed at a later date. A much better approach to program design is the use of *pseudocode.* A pseudocode version of the algorithm is given in Table 5.8. We will introduce pseudocode briefly here to demonstrate how we can express algorithms. Later we look at pseudocode in more detail.

Pseudocode is difficult to define precisely and, perhaps, the best way of describing it is to call it 'Home-made Pascal without all the fiddly rules'. Pseudocode allows a programmer to write an algorithm in almost plain English using some of the constructs of structured programming (e.g. IF THEN ELSE or WHILE … DO, etc.). In the example in Table 5.8, control actions are presented in capitals, variables in lower case and plain English actions in bold text. These actions (e.g. **Clear, Get** Number, **Print**) all express quite adequately the action to be carried out. The actions can, themselves, be represented by other sequences of pseudocode operations. When an algorithm has been expressed in pseudocode, the programmer can then translate each of the pseudocode actions or control constructs in an almost semi-automatic fashion.

Notice that the algorithm of Fig. 5.6 requires a number to be multiplied by 10. As our instruction set lacks any facilities for direct multiplication, we must resort either to repeated addition or write a program to do multiplication. An alternative solution is to note that $10x = (2 \times 2x + x) \times 2$.

Before we begin to construct the program, we have to decide where to put it in the computer's memory. For convenience we may assume that the program starts at location 0. We do not know yet how long the program will be, but from the pseudocode it should not exceed about 20 instructions. It should therefore be safe to locate any variables at hexadecimal location 20 onwards.

Table 5.9 presents the program in assembly-language form. It is important to note that an assembly-language program is not executed directly by a computer; it is in a form that can readily be understood by people. Here I must comment on the meaning of 'understood' in the above sentence. Assembly language is easy to understand in the sense that the meaning of each individual instruction is clear to the reader. However, because assembly language is such a low-level language, the meaning (i.e. effect) of a group of instructions is often not clear to the reader. An assembly-language program is called *source code* and is *assembled* or translated by an assembler to produce a binary or *machine code* form (called *object code*), that can be directly executed by the computer.

The first column in Table 5.9 containing the numbers 1–19 is not part of the program and merely displays the line number for later reference. The second column containing TOTAL, REPEAT and MULT is the label field of the program. These three words are labels or markers which may be referred to by other assembly-language instructions. For example, BEQ MULT means branch on a zero result to the address of the instruction labelled 'MULT'. Later, when the program is translated into machine code by an assembler, all references to these labels are automatically translated into the address of the line they label.

At first sight, there appear to be some mnemonics in this program not

Table 5.9 The algorithm of Table 5.7/5.8 expressed in assembly language

```
1.              NAM      EXAMPLE
2.              ORG      $20          Data origin $20 (i.e. 32 decimal)
3.    TOTAL     DS.B     1            Reserve a byte of storage for 'TOTAL'
4.              ORG      0            Origin of the program
5.              MOVE.B   #0,D0        [D0]←0
6.              MOVE.B   D0,TOTAL     [TOTAL]←[D0]
7.    REPEAT    IN.B     0,D0         [D0]←Input
8.              BEQ      MULT         IF [Z]=1 THEN [PC]←MULT
9.              ADD.B    TOTAL,D0     [D0]←[D0]+[TOTAL]
10.             MOVE.B   D0,TOTAL     [TOTAL]←[D0]
11.             BRA      REPEAT       [PC]←REPEAT
12.   MULT      MOVE.B   TOTAL,D0     [D0]←[TOTAL]
13.             ASL.B    #1,D0        [D0]←[D0] * 2
14.             ASL.B    #1,D0        [D0]←[D0] * 2
15.             ADD.B    TOTAL,D0     [D0]←[D0]+[TOTAL]
16.             ASL.B    #1,D0        [D0]←[D0] * 2
17.             OUT.B    D0,0         Output←[D0]
18.             STOP
19.             END
```

$\longleftarrow\underline{\hspace{3cm}}\longrightarrow$ $\longleftarrow\underline{\hspace{5cm}}\longrightarrow$

The program   The comments

Notes
1. The line number is not part of the program. It is included here to help us to refer to specific lines in the program. In this example, the comments have been provided in RTL form to remind the reader what the instruction does. The instruction field of a real program would attempt to inform the reader what the algorithm was doing.
2. The actual start of each line (i.e. column one) is reserved for labels (e.g. TOTAL, REPEAT and MULT).
3. The comment field to the right of instructions and assembler directives is ignored by the assembler. I have provided comments in RTL form to define the action of each instruction. Real programs use comments in plain English to help the reader understand the meaning of the program.

appearing in the instruction set (lines 1, 2, 3, 4, 19). These are not assembly-language operations but are called *assembler directives* or *pseudo operations.* Assembler directives are not translated into executable instructions. They simply tell the assembler things it needs to know about the program.

The first assembler directive, NAM, names the program (in this case EXAMPLE). The second assembler directive, ORG, sets the origin or *beginning* to $20. That is, any program or data following this directive is to be located at address $20 and successive locations. It is perhaps best to imagine an assembler as having a 'location counter' that keeps track of where the final machine code is to go in memory. As each new mnemonic is assembled, the location counter is incremented. The effect of an ORG N directive is to reset the value of the location counter to N.

The assembler directive DS.B, *define storage,* reserves one or more byte-size memory locations for the named value. Thus, 'TOTAL DS.B 1' reserves a single byte for the item called 'TOTAL'. The second ORG 0 resets the origin to 0 so that the program will be loaded into memory starting at address 0. The final assembler directive, END, tells the assembler that the end of the program has been reached.

One operation included in the program of Table 5.6 and not yet described is the arithmetic shift left instruction, ASL, that shifts the bit pattern of the operand left. ASL.B #1,D0 shifts the 8 least significant bits in data register D0 one place left and introduces a zero into the now vacated least significant bit position (i.e. the contents of D0 are multiplied by two). The '#1' indicates that there is to be a single left shift. Fig. 5.7 describes the operation of the ASL instruction.

Fig. 5.7 The operation of a shift instruction (ASL). Note that the 68000 form of this instruction is ASL #1, D0. The #1 indicates a shift one place.

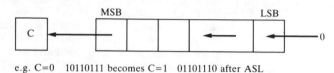

e.g. C=0   10110111 becomes C=1   01101110 after ASL

For the sake of simplicity, it is assumed that the sum of the numbers will not produce an out-of-range result when multiplied by ten. That is, we do not have to worry about a carry-out being generated from the most significant bit (MSB) position when an ASL is executed.

Once the program has been assembled and placed in the main store of the computer, it can be executed. The layout or *memory map* of the program is given in Fig. 5.8. A memory map is a snapshot of the contents of a computer's memory and shows the locations of data and programs within the memory.

Each memory location in our hypothetical computer holds four digits. The first two (i.e. most significant) digits of an instruction define the operation code and the second two point to the memory location accessed by the op-code. Exceptions to this are the IN and OUT operations, in which a peripheral is accessed, and the MOVE.B #⟨literal⟩,D0 operation in which the two digits specified by 'literal' are loaded into data register D0. Some op-codes do not require an operand field and their operand fields are indicated by XX in Fig. 5.8.

Fig. 5.8 Memory map of a machine-code program.

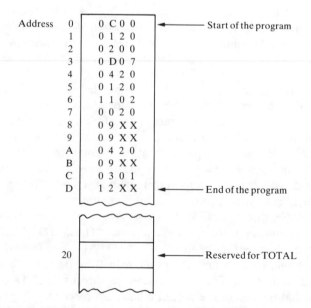

Note: XX represents two don't care hexadecimal digits.

Now that we have taken a brief look at the CPU of a hypothetical simple computer, we will look at the structure of a more complex CPU.

5.1.6 The architecture of a typical high-performance CPU

It is reasonably true to say that in recent years computer architecture has been driven by advances in technology rather than advances in computer science or programming. That is, the programmer or the end user of a computer gets what the engineer is able to produce economically. If we

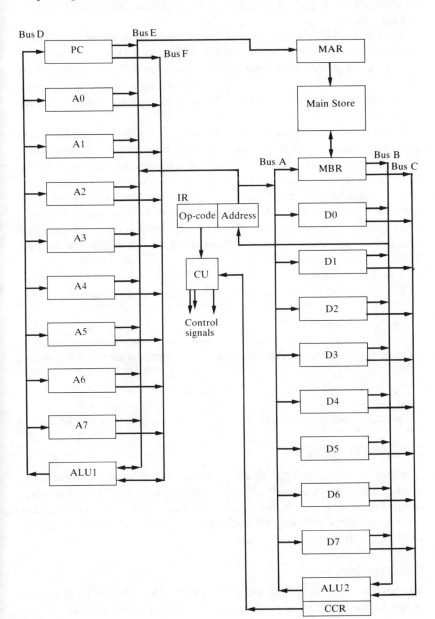

Fig. 5.9 The architecture of a high-performance CPU.

forget, for a moment, the mainframe and the minicomputer, the 1970s saw the introduction of the 8-bit microprocessor with very few internal registers. Because of advances in semiconductor technology, many microprocessors introduced in the 1980s operate on 16- or 32-bit words and have more on-chip registers.

We are going to take a brief look at the architecture of a CPU that is more representative of today's powerful microprocessors. Figure 5.9 illustrates the structure of a CPU with multiple buses and register arrays (rather than the single data register structure of Figs. 5.3–5.5). Although Fig. 5.9 is intended only as an example of a CPU, it is very similar to the structure of the 68000 microprocessor that we describe in more detail in the next chapter.

The CPU in Fig. 5.9 has the same control registers as the more primitive CPUs described earlier (i.e. PC, MAR, MBR, IR). However, the major change is the provision of eight data registers, D0–D7, and eight address registers, A0–A7. The provision of 16 user-accessible registers requires a rather different instruction format to the one-address format described earlier.

In order to access the data and address registers easily, we need to resort to a two-address instruction format. That is, the instruction requires three fields: an op-code, an operand address and a register address. As only one address is a memory address, it is, perhaps, more proper to call this a 'one and a half address format' than a two-address format, because many computers have no more than sixteen registers and the register address need occupy no more than four bits. The 68000 uses both a one and a half and a true two-address format as illustrated by the instruction formats below.

Op-code	Source operand address	Destination operand address

e.g. MOVE 1234,2000

Op-code	Source operand address	Destination operand register

e.g. MOVE 1234,D0

Op-code	Source operand register	Destination operand address

e.g. MOVE D0,1234

Although we are going to deal with the 68000 16-bit microprocessor in more detail later, we provide an indication of some of the instructions that can be executed by the 68000 in Table 5.10. Each instruction is provided in mnemonic form and briefly described in RTL. These definitions are meant to be illustrative rather than definitive.

Data registers

The 68000's eight data registers D0–D7 make this microprocessor more powerful than some of its predecessors that had only one general-purpose

Table 5.10 Some typical 68000 instructions

ADD	address,D*i*	[D*i*]←[D*i*]+[MS(address)]
ASL	#number,address	Shift [MS(address)] left by <number> bits
ASR	#number,address	Shift [MS(address)] right by <number> bits
DIVU	address,D*i*	[D*i*]←[D*i*]/[MS(address)]
MULU	address,D*i*	[D*i*]←[D*i*]*[MS(address)]
NEG	address	[MS(address)]←[$\overline{\text{MS(address)}}$]
AND	address,D*i*	[D*i*]←[D*i*] . [MS(address)]
OR	address,D*i*	[D*i*]←[D*i*]+[MS(address)]
EOR	address,D*i*	[D*i*]←[D*i*]⊕[MS(address)]
NOT	address	[MS(address)]←[$\overline{\text{MS(address)}}$]
SUB	address,D*i*	[D*i*]←[D*i*]−[MS(address)]
TST	address	[MS(address)]−0
CMP	address,D*i*	[D*i*]−[MS(address)]
EXG	R*i*,R*j*	[R*i*]←[R*j*], [R*j*]←[R*i*]
MOVE	address,D*i*	[D*i*]←[MS(address)]
MOVE	D*i*,address	[MS(address)]←[D*i*]
MOVE	#data,D*i*	[D*i*]←data
MOVE	#data,address	[MS(address)]←data
LEA	address,A*i*	[A*i*]←address
BRA	address	[PC]←address
BCC	address	IFC=0 THEN [PC]←address

data register (accumulator). Modern technology allows us to put several data registers on a chip, where once only one or two such registers could be accommodated economically. The only difference between these registers and locations in memory is that the registers are on-chip and can be accessed more rapidly than locations within the main store.

We do not really **need** more than one accumulator or data register in a one-address machine. However, by providing several data registers, the programmer is able to store frequently used data values on-chip rather than in the computer's main store. By doing this we can speed up the execution of programs, because data in registers does not have to be fetched from the main store. For example, ADD.B D0,D1 adds the contents of D0 to D1 and deposits the result in D1 and requires no references to memory (i.e. read or write cycles). The only difficulty associated with the use of multiple registers is the burden it sometimes places on the programmer. That is, the programmer has to decide what register is going to hold what variable. Fortunately, most programmers write in high-level languages and the job of deciding what register holds what data is left to the compiler, sparing programmers the tricky problem of register allocation.

Address registers

One of the greatest differences between the architecture of the CPU of Fig. 5.9 and that of the simple CPUs described earlier is the addition of eight address registers, A0–A7. Address registers are so called because they are used to hold the address of operands to be accessed in memory. I do not intend to go into details about the function of address registers here, because they are described in much more detail later. However, it is worthwhile hinting at how they are actually used.

Many real microprocessors store instructions in more than one memory word so that the op-code in one word is followed by the address of the operand in the next. While this arrangement permits efficient memory usage, it is relatively slow because more than one memory access is required per fetch cycle. The operation of the CPU can be speeded up by first loading the address of the operand into an **address register** and then using instructions that specify the location of an operand in terms of an address register. That is, once we have loaded the address of an operand into an address register, we do not have to refer to the operand again explicitly. We can access the operand via the address register (which means that we can invariably use a single-word instruction to access the operand as opposed to a two-word instruction). For example, the instruction ADD.B (A1),D0 means add the contents of the memory location pointed at by address register A1 to the contents of data register D0. In RTL form, this is represented by:

$$[D0] \leftarrow [D0] + [MS([A1])]$$

Note that we write ADD.B (A1),D0 in the assembly-language instruction, rather than ADD.B A1,D0, because we mean that the operand is not the contents of A1, but the contents of the memory location whose address is in A1. That is, ADD.B A1,D0 means $[D0] \leftarrow [D0] + [A1]$, while ADD.B (A1),D0 means $[D0] \leftarrow [D0] + [MS([A1])]$. Of course, we have to set up the contents of A1 initially and that may require a multiple-word instruction. However, once the appropriate operand address is in A1, we can access the operand simply by specifying the pointer to it in A1.

Another application of address registers is in the **dynamic** computation of addresses by the computer. Because we can apply arithmetic operations to the contents of an address register, we can work with variable addresses. The calculation of addresses at **run-time** enables us to operate on tables and other data structures as we shall soon see.

Before we look at how assembly-language programs are written for the 68000 microprocessor (in Chapter 6), we are going to examine the control unit of a CPU. Readers not interested in how an instruction is decoded and executed may skip ahead to Chapter 6. I have also provided an introduction to RISC architectures in this text because they represent a trend away from traditional complex architectures such as the 68000. Since it is difficult to discuss RISC architectures without an understanding of microprogramming, I have placed the section on RISC architectures after microprogramming.

5.2 The control unit

The precise way in which a digital computer interprets machine-code instructions is rather complex and, consequently, the discussion of its control unit, CU, is often relegated to more advanced courses on computer architecture. Here we are going to provide an overview of the control unit's operation and demonstrate how it enables the CPU to carry out the instruction currently in the instruction register. That is, we are going to show how a pattern of bits in the instruction register is used to generate the sequence of actions taking place during the execution of an instruction. The model of the CPU we are going to use to illustrate the operation of the control unit is presented in Fig. 5.10 (as before we have included a program and data memory in this figure, even though memory is not part of the CPU). We have provided a rather simple CPU in order to reduce the level of complexity and have stripped the CPU of any unnecessary detail to make its internal operation easier to understand.

There are two radically different approaches to the design of the control unit. The first, dealt with in Section 5.2.1, is to make the control unit itself a 'computer within a computer', and turn each machine instruction into a sequence of even more primitive instructions called *microinstructions*. The

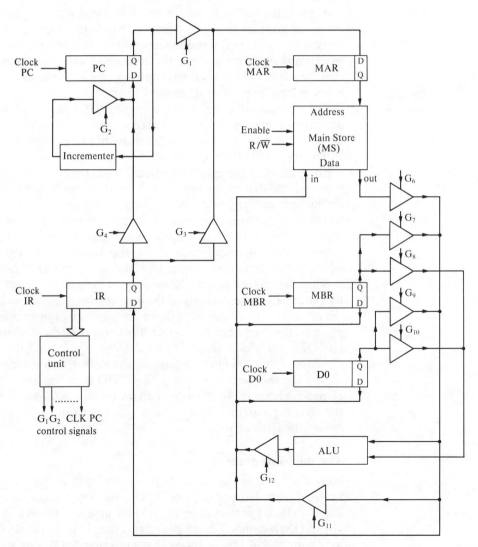

Fig. 5.10 Controlling the flow of data within the CPU.

alternative approach (see Section 5.2.2) is to ask what sequence of logical and arithmetic operations are needed to carry out an instruction, and then to design the appropriate logic circuit to bring this about.

5.2.1 Microprogrammed control unit

Before describing the control unit, we need to define three terms: macro-level instruction, micro-level instruction and interpretation. The natural or *native language* of a computer is its machine code, whose mnemonic representation is called assembly language. Assembly language instructions are also called *macroinstructions*. Each *macroinstruction* is *interpreted* by means of a number of very primitive actions called *microinstructions*. In other words, there is a language even more primitive than machine code.

A microinstruction is the smallest event that can take place within a computer and may consist of clocking a flip-flop or moving data from one register to another. The process whereby a macroinstruction is executed by carrying out a series of microinstructions is called *interpretation*. Note that the use of the term macroinstruction here has nothing to do with the noun 'macro' used by programmers.

The internal structure of the primitive CPU illustrated in Fig. 5.10 differs from those of Figs. 5.2–5.5 used to describe the fetch–execute cycle, because Fig. 5.10 includes the *mechanism* by which information is moved within the CPU. Each of the registers (program counter, MAR, data register, etc.) is made up of D flip-flops. When the clock input to a register is pulsed, the data at the register's D input terminals is transferred to its output terminals and held constant until the register is clocked again. The connections between the registers are by means of m-bit wide data highways. In Fig. 5.10 such highways are drawn in a single line.

Suppose we wish our computer to perform a fetch/execute cycle in which the op-code corresponds to addition (i.e. ADD.B ⟨address⟩,D0) and has the effect of adding the contents of the memory location specified by ⟨address⟩ to the contents of the data register (i.e. D0) and depositing the result in D0. We can write down the sequence of operations that take place during the execution of ADD.B not only in terms of register-transfer language, but also in terms of the enabling of gates and the clocking of flip-flops. Table 5.11 illustrates the sequence of microinstructions executed during the fetch–execute cycle of an ADD.B instruction. It should be emphasized that the fetch phase of all instructions is *identical* and it is only the execute phase that varies according to the nature of the op-code read during the fetch phase.

The microprogram

Now imagine that the output of the control unit in Fig. 5.10 consists of twelve signals that enable gates G_1–G_{12}, two signals that control the MS, and five clock signals that pulse the clock inputs of the PC, MAR, MBR, IR, and D0 registers. Table 5.12 presents the 19 outputs of the control unit as a sequence of binary values that are generated during the fetch and execute phases of an ADD.B instruction.

Table 5.11 Interpreting a fetch–execute cycle in terms of RTL

Step	Register-transfer language	Operations required
1	[MAR] ←[PC]	enable G_1, clock MAR
1a	INC ←[PC]	
2	[PC] ←INC	enable G_2, clock PC
3	[MBR] ←[MS([MAR])]	enable MS, R/$\overline{W}$=1, enable G_6 enable G_{11}, clock MBR
4	[IR] ←[MBR]	enable G_7, clock IR
4a	CU ←[IR(op-code)]	
5	[MAR] ←[IR(address)]	enable G_3, clock MAR
6	[MBR] ←[MS([MAR])]	enable MS, R/$\overline{W}$=1, enable G_6, enable G_{11}, clock MBR
7	ALU ←[MBR]	enable G_7
7a	ALU ←[D0]	enable G_{10}
8	[D0] ←ALU	enable G_{12}, clock data register

Notes
1. Where there is no entry in the column labelled 'Operations required', that operation happens automatically. For example, the output of the program counter is always connected to the input of the incrementer, and therefore no explicit operation is needed to move the contents of the PC to the incrementer.
2. Any three-state gate not explicitly mentioned is not enabled.
3. Steps 1, 1a are carried out simultaneously, as are 4, 4a and 7, 7a.

Table 5.12 Control signals generated during the fetch and execute phases of an ADD instruction

Step	Gate control signals												MS control		Register clocks				
	G_1	G_2	G_3	G_4	G_5	G_6	G_7	G_8	G_9	G_{10}	G_{11}	G_{12}	ENABLE	R/$\overline{W}$	PC	MAR	MBR	DO	IR
1	1	0	0	0	0	0	0	0	0	0	0	0	0	X	0	1	0	0	0
2	0	1	0	0	0	0	0	0	0	0	0	0	0	X	1	0	0	0	0
3	0	0	0	0	0	1	0	0	0	0	1	0	1	1	0	0	1	0	0
4	0	0	0	0	0	0	1	0	0	0	0	0	0	X	0	0	0	0	1
5	0	0	1	0	0	0	0	0	0	0	0	0	0	X	0	1	0	0	0
6	0	0	0	0	0	1	0	0	0	0	1	0	1	1	0	0	1	0	0
7	0	0	0	0	0	0	1	0	0	1	0	0	0	X	0	0	0	0	0
8	0	0	0	0	0	0	0	0	0	0	0	1	0	X	0	0	0	1	0

When the main store, MS, is accessed by ENABLE=1, a memory read or write cycle may take place. The R/$\overline{W}$ (i.e. read/write) signal determines the nature of the memory access when ENABLE=1. When R/$\overline{W}$=0 the cycle is a write cycle, and when R/$\overline{W}$=1 the cycle is a read cycle. The R/$\overline{W}$ signal is undefined whenever ENABLE=0.

If, for each of the eight steps in Table 5.12, the nineteen signals are fed to the various parts of the CPU in Fig. 5.10, then the fetch–execute cycle will be carried out. In a real computer very many more than 19 control signals are generated by the CU. A typical value would be in the range 64 to 200. One of the most significant differences between a microinstruction and a macroinstruction is that the former contains many fields and may provide several operands, while the macroinstruction frequently specifies only an op-code and one or two operands.

The eight steps in Table 5.11 represent a *microprogram* that interprets a fetch phase followed by an ADD.B instruction.

We have demonstrated that a macroinstruction is interpreted by a sequence of microinstructions and that there is a microprogram for each of a CPU's op-codes. We now have to look at the microprogram itself and consider the hardware required to execute it. The microprogram is executed by a mechanism similar to that which executes the macroprogram (i.e. machine code) itself (wheels within wheels?). For example, the microprogrammed control unit has a microprogram counter instead of a program counter.

The basic structure of a microprogrammed control unit is given in Fig. 5.11. The microprogrammed control unit has a microprogram counter, a microprogram memory and a microinstruction register. The microinstruction address from the microprogram counter is applied to the address input of the microprogram memory and the data output of the memory fed to the microinstruction register. Information in the microinstruction register is divided into four fields: next microinstruction address field, microprogram counter load-control field, condition select field and CPU control field. Most of the bits in the microinstruction register belong to the CPU control field and control the flow of information within the CPU by enabling tristate gates and clocking registers as described above.

Microinstruction sequence control

If the microprogram counter were to step through the microprogram

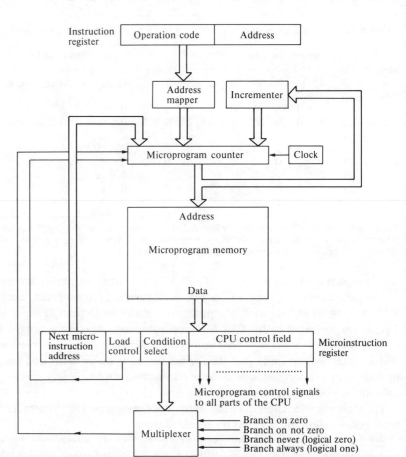

Fig. 5.11 The microprogrammed control unit.

memory in the natural sequence, 0, 1, 2, 3,..., etc., a stream of consecutive microinstructions would appear in the microinstruction register, causing the CPU to behave in the way described by Table 5.11. The CPU control bits of each microinstruction would determine the flow of information within the CPU. However, just as in the case of the macroprogram control unit, it is often necessary to modify the sequence in which microinstructions are executed. For example, we may wish to repeat a group of microinstructions n times, or we may wish to jump from a fetch phase to an execute phase, or we may wish to call a procedure.

Microinstruction sequence control is determined by three fields of the microinstruction register, enabling the microprogram counter to implement both conditional and unconditional branches to locations within the microprogram memory. We shall soon see that this activity is necessary to execute macroinstructions such as BRA, BCC, BCS, BEQ, etc.

In normal operation, the microprogram counter steps through microinstructions sequentially and the next microprogram address is the current address plus one. By loading the contents of the **next microinstruction address** field of the current microinstruction field into the microprogram counter, a branch can be made to any point in the microprogram memory. In other words each microinstruction determines whether the next microinstruction is taken in sequence or whether it is taken from the next address field of the current microinstruction. The obvious question to ask is, 'What determines whether the microprogram counter continues in sequence or is loaded from the **next microinstruction address field** of the current microinstruction?'

The **microprogram counter load control** field of the microinstruction register tells the microprogram counter whether to take its next address from the incrementer and continue in sequence, or whether to get its next microinstruction address from the address mapper (see below), or whether to use the address in the next address field of the microinstruction register.

The **condition select** field of the miscroinstruction register implements conditional branches at the macroinstruction level by executing a conditional branch at the microinstruction level. In the simplified arrangement of Fig. 5.11, one of four conditions may be selected. These conditions are obtained from the ALU and are usually the flag bits of the condition code register (e.g. Z, N, C, V). The condition select field determines which of the CCR bits are to be fed to the output of the condition select multiplexer. If the output of the multiplexer is true, a jump is made to the address specified by the contents of the next microinstruction address field, otherwise the microprogram continues sequentially. In Fig. 5.11 two of the conditions are obtained from the CCR and two bits are permanently true and false. A false condition implies 'branch never' (i.e. continue) and a true condition implies 'branch always' (i.e. goto).

A conditional branch at the macroinstruction level (e.g. BEQ) is interpreted by microinstructions in the following way. The condition select field of the microinstruction selects the appropriate status bit of the CCR to be tested. For example, if the macroinstruction is BEQ, the Z bit is selected. The microprogram counter load control field contains the operation 'branch to the address in the microinstruction register on selected condition true'. Thus, if the selected condition is true (i.e. $Z = 1$), a jump is made to a point in the microprogram that implements the corresponding jump in the macroprogram. If the selected condition is false (i.e. $Z = 0$), the current sequence of microinstructions is terminated by the start of a new fetch–execute cycle.

Implementing the fetch–execute cycle

The first part of each microprogram executed by the control unit corresponds to a macroinstruction fetch phase and ends with the macroinstruction op-code being deposited in the instruction register. The op-code is fed to the *address mapper*, which is a look-up table containing the starting address of the microprogram for each of the possible op-codes. That is, the address mapper translates the arbitrary bit pattern of the op-code into the location of the corresponding microprogram that will execute the op-code. After this microprogram has been executed, an unconditional jump is made to the start of the microprogram that interprets the macroinstruction fetch phase, and the process continues.

The above description of the microprogrammed control unit is, of course, grossly simplified. In practice the microprogram normally includes facilities for dealing with interrupts, the main memory (MS), and input/output. One of the great advantages of a microprogrammed control unit is that it is possible to alter the content of the microprogram memory (sometimes called the control store) and hence design your own machine-level instructions.

In fact it is perfectly possible to choose a set of microprograms that will execute the machine code of an entirely different computer. In this case the computer is said to *emulate* another computer. Such a facility is useful if you are changing your old computer to a new one whose own machine code is incompatible with your old programs. Emulation applies to programs that exist in binary (object) form on tape or disk. By writing microprograms (on the new machine) to interpret the machine code of the old machine, it is possible to use the old software and still get the advantages of the new machine. In the next section we briefly describe components that can be used to create a microprogrammed control unit. Readers not interested in this level of detail may skip to Section 5.2.3.

5.2.2 An introduction to bit-slice components

While most readers of this text will already be familiar with the microprocessor, few will have encountered the term *bit-slice*. A microprocessor can best be described as a *CPU on a chip* and is satisfactory in many applications requiring low-cost computer power. Alternatives to the microprocessor are the minicomputer or the mainframe. The bit-slice component provides a middle path between microcomputer and mainframe that enables the engineer to design moderately powerful or special-purpose digital computers. Bit-slice components, as their name suggests, are really subsections of a microprocessor that can be put together to create a custom CPU. For example, a 32-bit computer is made by putting together eight 4-bit bit-slice chips.

Bit-slice components are divided into two types corresponding to the functional division within the microprocessor (i.e. microprogram control and ALU). Typical bit-slice components are the Am2910 sequencer (a control unit) and the Am2901 ALU that forms a 4-bit slice of an arithmetic logic unit. By using an Am2910, several Am2901s, some additional logic and a microprogram in ROM, a CPU with a user-defined instruction set and word length may be created. Of course, the designer does not have to construct a new CPU out of bit-slice components. Instead he or she can emulate an existing microprocessor and operate it at a higher speed, or even add machine-level instructions to enhance it.

The bit-slice ALU

The arrangement of an Am2901 bit-slice ALU element is given in Fig. 5.12. At its heart lies an arithmetic logic unit that can generate one of eight functions of two inputs R and S. These functions vary from R plus S to the exclusive NOR of R and S. The values of R and S may be selected from a register file of 16 general-purpose data registers, an external input, a Q register, or zero. An additional feature of the Am2901 is its ability to shift the contents of the Q register (and also its ALU output) right or left to facilitate multiplication or division where a double-length result is required.

The 2901 is controlled (programmed) by means of a 9-bit wide control input that selects the source of the data taking part in an arithmetic or logical operation, determines the particular operation to be executed and controls the destination (together with any shifting) of the result. Typical operations which may be carried out by the Am2901 are:

1. $[R(7)] \leftarrow [R(7)] + [R(1)]$
2. $[R(6)] \leftarrow ([R(6)] + [R(5)])/2$
3. $[R(9)] \leftarrow$ NOT $[R(9)]$
4. $[R(12)] \leftarrow [R(12)] + 1$

where $[R(i)]$ is one of the AM2901's 16 data registers.

An arithmetic unit of any length (as long as it is a multiple of 4) is constructed by connecting together a number of Am2901s. Figure 5.13 illustrates how four Am2901s are put together to create a 16-bit ALU. The Am2901s' inputs are divided into four groups: the nine ALU functions, source and destination operand control bits, the A and B register select inputs (each four bits) and a direct data input (16 bits) that allows the ALU to receive data from the main store. The output of the ALU is a 16-bit word that may be gated onto the system address or data bus. In addition to the 4-bit slices themselves, additional logic is required to deal with the various types of shift operators (logical, arithmetic and circular) and a carry flip-flop is needed to hold the carry bit.

When Figs. 5.13 and, say, 5.5 are compared, it may appear that the ALU formed by four bit-slice units represents only a fraction of the central processor unit, since there is no program counter, incrementer, or

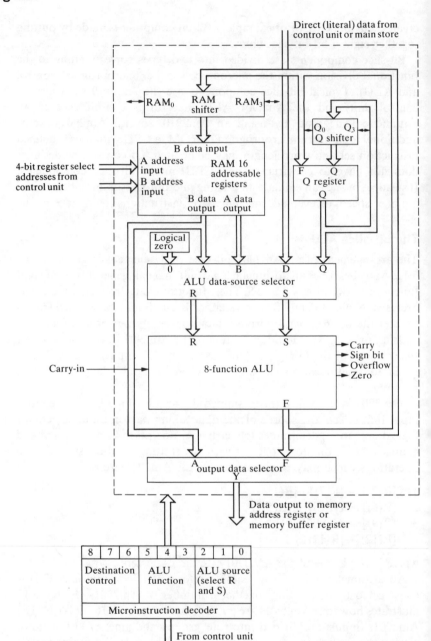

Fig. 5.12 The Am2901 bit-slice ALU.

data register. As the 2901 has 16 registers, one of the registers may be assigned to serve as the program counter. A special incrementer for the program counter is not necessary, because the ALU may be used to increment the contents of the program counter. Designers may use these registers in any way they desire. For example, they may choose to implement eight addressable data registers, two stack pointers (described later), two index registers, a program counter and three scratchpad registers. Flexibility is the most powerful feature of bit-slice microprocessors.

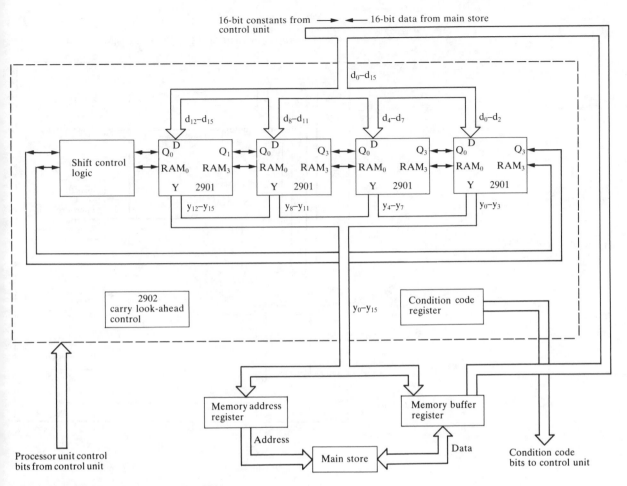

Fig. 5.13 A 16-bit ALU using four Am2901s.

Bit-slice control

The control section of a bit-slice microprocessor is considerably more complex than its arithmetic and logical section, both in the way it operates and the amount of circuitry required to implement it. We are now going to describe the microprogram control unit that steps through the microprogram.

A complex control unit is normally constructed from several bit-slice sequencers, but a modest control unit may be made from, say, a single Am2910 microprogram controller, containing a 12-bit microprogram counter capable of stepping through up to 4096 words of a microprogram. The internal arrangement of an Am2910 is illustrated in Fig. 5.14. The output of the Am2910 is a 12-bit address that points to the current microinstruction in the microprogram memory.

The address of the next microinstruction may be obtained from any one of four sources by means of a multiplexer within the Am2910. The first source is the microprogram counter which may be incremented after each

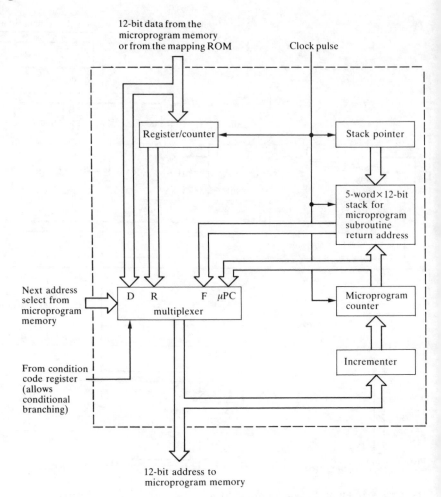

Fig. 5.14 The Am2910 microprogram sequencer.

12-bit data from the microprogram memory or from the mapping ROM

Clock pulse

Register/counter

Stack pointer

5-word×12-bit stack for microprogram subroutine return address

Next address select from microprogram memory

D   R   F   μPC

multiplexer

Microprogram counter

From condition code register (allows conditional branching)

Incrementer

12-bit address to microprogram memory

microinstruction access, so that it steps through the microinstructions sequentially.

A second source of microinstruction address comes from an external input (e.g. the next microinstruction address field of the current microinstruction) which allows a branch in the microcode. The third input to the multiplexer is from a microaddress stack, holding return addresses so that microinstruction subroutines may be terminated with an operation that pops the return address off the stack (we deal with the stack and subroutines in the next chapter). The fourth source of the microinstruction address comes from a register/counter that may be preloaded with a number N and then used as a loop termination counter to permit a sequence of microinstructions to be repeated $(N+1)$ times.

The source of the next microinstruction address is determined by a multiplexer controlled by a 4-bit input to the Am2910. In order to understand how the control unit determines the execution of a macroinstruction, it is necessary to refer to Fig. 5.15 (which is essentially the same as Fig. 5.11). If we assume that an op-code is in the CPU's instruction register, the following sequence of events takes place:

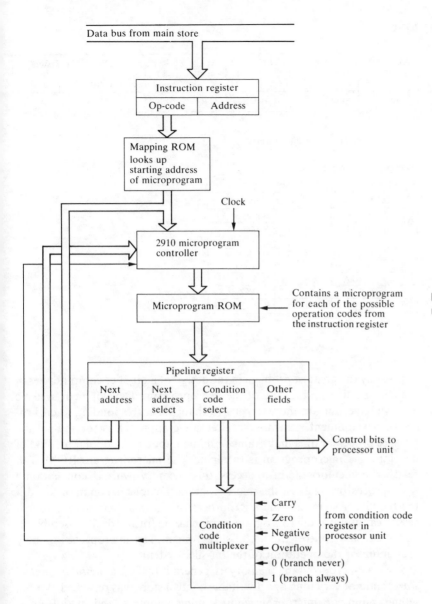

Fig. 5.15 The structure of a microprogrammed control unit.

1. The op-code is fed to the input of a mapping ROM which looks up the starting address of the relevant microprogram in a table of addresses. The first address of the microprogram to interpret the macroinstruction is clocked into the Am2910's microprogram counter and also appears at the output of the Am2910, where it selects the first microinstruction from the microprogram memory.

2. The microinstruction is held in a pipeline register, so-called because it holds the current microinstruction while the control unit is busy fetching the *next* microinstruction.

3. The microinstruction is used to control the operation of the CPU. Microinstructions are typically 64–128 bits wide and are divided into a number of fields with each field directly controlling part of the computer. Figure 5.16 illustrates a hypothetical microinstruction.

Branch address	Next microinstruction select	Condition code select	ALU shift control	ALU source select	ALU destination control	ALU function	Register A and B addresses	Direct data constant	System bus control
16 bits	4 bits	4 bits	3 bits	3 bits	3 bits	3 bits	8 bits	16 bits	4 bits

64-bit microinstruction format

Examples of microprogram fields

Source select

Code	R	S
0	A	Q
1	A	B
2	0	Q
3	0	B
4	0	A
5	D	A
6	D	Q
7	D	0

ALU function

Code	Function
0	R plus S
1	S minus R
2	R minus S
3	R OR S
4	R AND S
5	R AND S
6	R EX OR S
7	R EXNOR S

Fig. 5.16 The structure of a typical microinstruction.

Possibly the greatest problem in the design of a bit-slice computer lies in the construction and testing of the microprogram. Development systems are available but are more expensive than the corresponding microprocessor development systems. An alternative approach is to emulate the bit-slice processor on a mainframe or minicomputer. A popular method of developing a microprogram is to replace the microprogram ROM with read/write memory and to access this memory with a conventional microprocessor. That is, the microprogram memory is common to both the bit-slice system and the microprocessor. In this way, the microprocessor can input a microprogram in mnemonic form, edit it, assemble it, and then pass control to the bit-slice system. The microprocessor may even monitor the operation of the bit-slice system.

Such a microprogram memory is generally called a *writable control store,* and not very long ago a writable control store was regarded as a big selling point of microprogrammed minicomputers and mainframes. Unfortunately, few designers or salespeople realized that a microprogrammable control store was of very little practical use in most applications of their computers. Even if a computer user has the expertise to design new microprogrammed macroinstructions, it is unlikely that the system software and compilers will be able to make use of these new instructions.

Bit-slice systems are more costly than microprocessor systems and their development presents a formidable design task. Equally, their application to many problems provides the most cost effective solution. One application of bit-slice components is in the production of minicomputers or even mainframes. Another common application of bit-slice computers is in the emulation of large mainframe computers. Clearly, by choosing the macrocode of the bit-slice computer to be that of a given mainframe it is possible to run software written for the mainframe on the relatively low cost bit-slice machine.

5.2.3 The random logic control unit

The type of control unit featured in Section 5.2.1 performs the interpretation of a machine-code instruction by means of a microprogram stored in a read-only memory. The complexity of a microprogrammed control unit is not directly related to the complexity of the machine-code instructions it interprets, just as the complexity of a computer at the machine-code level is not related to the complexity of the high-level language programs being run on it. The above statement is correct to a first approximation but it must be admitted that designers sometimes attempt to provide machine-level instructions that are close to some of the more complex facilities offered by high-level languages. In such cases, there is indeed a relationship between the complexity of the high-level language and the complexity of the control unit.

When engineers design a random logic control unit, RALU, they ask 'What sequence of microinstructions is needed to execute each machine-code instruction and what logic elements do we need to implement them?' In other words, designers resort to the Boolean techniques we have already come across in Chapter 2. The word 'random' in the expression *random logic element* implies that the arrangement of gates from which the control unit is constructed varies widely from computer to computer. Perhaps a better term than *random* logic would be *ad hoc* logic. The same microprogrammed control unit can readily be adapted to suit many different computers with relatively little modification, but the random logic control unit is dedicated to a specific CPU and cannot easily be modified.

Before designing a random logic control unit, let's consider an ultra-simple CPU. It is possible to use the CPU structures described earlier in this section. However, by adopting another design I hope to show the reader that the structure of the CPU is chosen by an engineer and is not rigidly fixed. When designing any computer, the engineer has to weigh up the trade-offs between computational power, speed, and cost. The *architecture* of the computer we are going to consider is essentially the same as that of the CPU described earlier. However, the *implementation* is rather different because the internal bus structure has been much simplified. Note that we use the term *architecture* to describe the functional capabilities of a computer. A computer's architecture is independent of the way in which the computer is physically implemented.

Figure 5.17 presents the structure of a primitive CPU. It is primitive because the number of buses and functional units have been reduced to the bare minimum, making the CPU cheap to produce but reducing its speed. As there is only one internal bus, several microinstructions cannot be carried out simultaneously in order to execute operations in parallel. For example, there is no separate incrementer for the program counter, forcing the ALU to be used to increment the contents of the PC. Consequently, the ALU and associated data paths are not available for other operations while the program counter is being incremented.

In Fig. 5.17 a single bus is connected to all registers, the main store and the ALU, permitting the transfer of only one data word at a time from a source to a destination. The main store receives the address of a memory

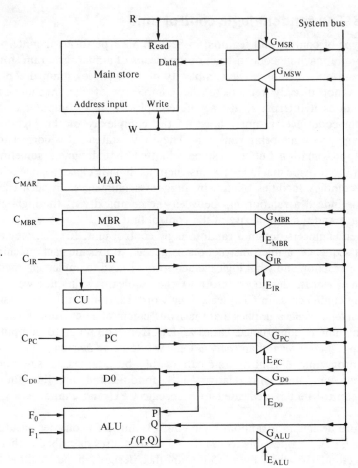

Fig. 5.17 The structure of a primitive CPU.

location to be accessed directly from the MAR, whose output is permanently connected to the address input of the MS. A fixed or **dedicated** connection between the MAR and MS is possible, because the main store never receives an address input from any source other than the memory address register. A permanent connection is a good thing because it removes the need for bus control circuits.

The bidirectional data bus from the main store is connected to the system bus by tri-state gates G_{MSR} and G_{MSW}. During a memory write cycle (W true), data is transferred from the system bus to the memory via gate G_{MSW}. In a read cycle (R true), data is transferred from the memory to the system bus via gate G_{MSR}.

The MBR, data register, program counter, and instruction register are each arranged in exactly the same way with respect to the internal bus. When one of these registers wishes to place data on the bus, its tri-state gate is enabled. Conversely, data is copied into a register from the bus by clocking the register. Note that the instruction register, IR, is arranged so that it can receive data from the main store directly, without the data having to pass through the MBR as indicated earlier in this chapter.

The ALU receives data from two sources, the internal bus and the data register, and places its own output on the system bus. This arrangement begs the question, 'If the ALU gets data from the system bus how can it put data on the same bus at the same time?'. There are two possible solutions to this dilemma. The first is to put a register in the ALU to hold input data constant while the system bus is connected to the output of the ALU. That is, the ALU is provided with its own personal 'MBR'.

Another solution relies on an effect hitherto considered harmful—the propagation delay experienced by digital signals passing through a logic network. When data is presented to the ALU's inputs, it ripples through the gates of the ALU to appear at the ALU's output terminals after a delay of the order of 50 ns. Suppose that the contents of the MBR are fed to the ALU by enabling gate G_{MBR}, and that sufficient time has elapsed for the output of the ALU to settle. If now gate G_{MBR} is disabled, the input to the ALU is no longer valid. However, the output of the ALU cannot change instantly because of internal delays. Consequently, if gate G_{ALU} is enabled and the data register clocked, the system bus may be used for the data transfer before the output of the ALU changes. This is a sort of digital juggling trick.

The ALU is controlled by a 2-bit code, F_0, F_1, that determines its functions as defined in Table 5.13. These are representative of real instructions, although a practical ALU would implement, typically, sixteen different functions.

In order to keep the design of a random logic control unit as simple as possible, we will construct a 3-bit op-code giving a total of eight instructions. The repertoire of instructions in Table 5.14 presents a very primitive instruction set indeed, but it does include many of the types of instruction found in real processors.

Table 5.13 Decoding the ALU control code, F_0, F_1

F_1	F_0	Function
0	0	add P to Q
0	1	subtract Q from P
1	0	increment Q
1	1	decrement Q

Table 5.14 A primitive instruction set for the CPU of Fig. 5.17

Op-code	Mnemonic		Operation
000	LOAD	M	$[D0] \leftarrow [MS(M)]$
001	STORE	M	$[MS(M)] \leftarrow [D0]$
010	ADD	M	$[D0] \leftarrow [D0] + [MS(M)]$
011	SUB	M	$[D0] \leftarrow [D0] - [MS(M)]$
100	INC	M	$[MS(M)] \leftarrow [MS(M)] + 1$
101	DEC	M	$[MS(M)] \leftarrow [MS(M)] - 1$
110	BRA	M	$[PC] \leftarrow M$
111	BEQ	M	IF Z=1 THEN $[PC] \leftarrow M$

Note that M defines the memory location used by the instruction.

Having constructed an instruction set, the next step is to define each of the instructions in terms of RTL, and determine the sequence of operations necessary to carry them out on the computer in Fig. 5.17. Table 5.15 lists all clock signals, denoted by $C_{register}$, and all tri-state bus controller signals, denoted by $E_{source\ of\ data}$, required to execute each of the CPU's instructions. The symbol Z is the *zero-flag* bit from the CCR which is assumed to be part of the ALU.

Table 5.15 Interpreting the instruction set of Table 5.14 in RTL and microinstructions

Instruction	Op-code	Operations (RTL)	Control actions	
Fetch	—	$[MAR]\leftarrow[PC]$ $[IR]\leftarrow[MS([MAR])]$ $ALU\leftarrow[PC]$ $[PC]\leftarrow ALU$	$E_{PC}=1,$ $R=1,$ $E_{PC}=1,$ $E_{ALU}=1,$	C_{MAR} C_{IR} $F_1,F_0=1,0$ C_{PC}
LOAD	000	$[MAR]\leftarrow[IR]$ $[D0]\leftarrow[MS([MAR])]$	$E_{IR}=1,$ $R=1,$	C_{MAR} C_{D0}
STORE	001	$[MAR]\leftarrow[IR]$ $[MS([MAR])]\leftarrow[D0]$	$E_{IR}=1,$ $E_{D0}=1,$	C_{MAR} $W=1$
ADD	010	$[MAR]\leftarrow[IR]$ $[MBR]\leftarrow[MS([MAR])]$ $ALU\leftarrow[MBR]$ $[D0]\leftarrow ALU$	$E_{IR}=1,$ $R=1,$ $E_{MBR}=1,$ $E_{ALU}=1,$	C_{MAR} C_{MBR} $F_1,F_0=0,0$ C_{D0}
SUB	011	$[MAR]\leftarrow[IR]$ $[MBR]\leftarrow[MS([MAR])]$ $ALU\leftarrow[MBR]$ $[D0]\leftarrow ALU$	$E_{IR}=1,$ $R=1,$ $E_{MBR}=1,$ $E_{ALU}=1,$	C_{MAR} C_{MBR} $F_1,F_0=0,1$ C_{D0}
INC	100	$[MAR]\leftarrow[IR]$ $[MBR]\leftarrow[MS([MAR])]$ $[ALU]\leftarrow[MBR]$ $[MBR]\leftarrow ALU$ $[MS([MAR])]\leftarrow[MBR]$	$E_{IR}=1,$ $R=1,$ $E_{MBR}=1,$ $E_{ALU}=1,$ $E_{MBR}=1,$	C_{MAR} C_{MBR} $F_1,F_0=1,0$ C_{MBR} $W=1$
DEC	101	$[MAR]\leftarrow[IR]$ $[MBR]\leftarrow[MS([MAR])]$ $ALU\leftarrow[MBR]$ $[MBR]\leftarrow ALU$ $[MS([MAR])]\leftarrow[MBR]$	$E_{IR}=1,$ $R=1,$ $E_{MBR}=1,$ $E_{ALU}=1,$ $E_{MBR}=1,$	C_{MAR} C_{MBR} $F_1,F_0=1,1$ C_{MBR} $W=1$
BRA	110	$[PC]\leftarrow[IR]$	$E_{IR}=1,$	C_{PC}
BEQ	111	IF $Z=1$ THEN $[PC]\leftarrow[IR]$	IF $Z=1$ THEN $E_{IR}=1, C_{PC}$	

From op-code to operation

In order to execute an instruction we have to do two things: convert the 3-bit op-code into one of eight possible sequences of action and then cause these actions to take place.

Figure 5.18 shows how the instructions are decoded and is similar in operation to the three-line to eight-line decoder described in Chapter 2. For each of the eight possible 3-bit op-codes, one and only one of the eight outputs is placed in an active-high condition. For example, if the op-code corresponding to ADD (i.e. 010), is loaded into the IR during a fetch phase, Output 2 from the AND gate array, **ADD,** is asserted high while all other AND gate outputs remain low.

It is no good simply detecting and decoding a particular instruction. The control unit has to carry out the sequence of microinstructions that

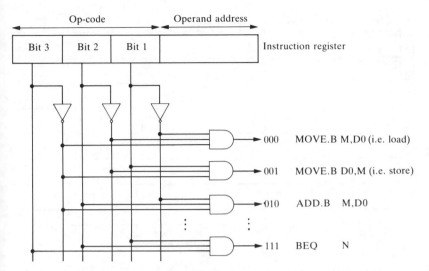

Fig. 5.18 The instruction decoder.

will execute the instruction. To do this we require a source of signals to trigger each of the microinstructions. A circuit that produces a stream of trigger signals is called a *sequencer* and Fig. 5.19 provides the logic diagram of a suitable eight-step sequencer. The outputs of three JK flip-flops arranged as a 3-bit binary up-counter are connected to eight three-input AND gates to generate timing signals T_0–T_7. Figure 5.20 illustrates the timing pulses created by this circuit. Note that the timing decoder is similar to the instruction decoder of Fig. 5.17. As not all macroinstruc-

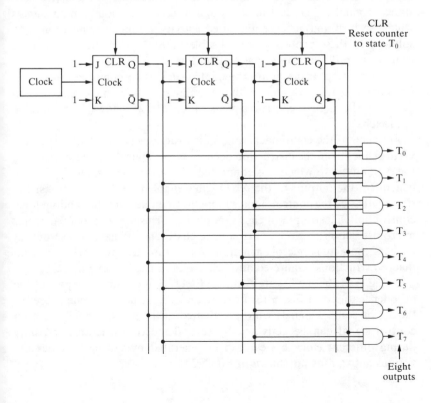

Fig. 5.19 The timing-pulse generator.

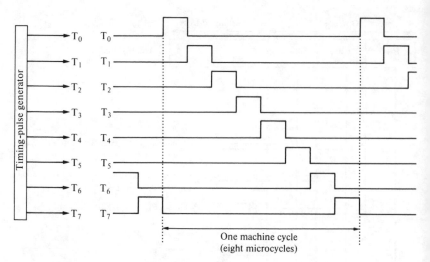

Fig. 5.20 The outputs of the timing-pulse generator.

tions require the same number of microinstructions to interpret them, the sequencer of Fig. 5.19 has a reset input that can be used to reset the sequencer by returning it to state T_0.

The sequencer of Fig. 5.18 is illustrative rather than practical, as spurious pulses may be generated at the timing pulse outputs due to the use of an asynchronous counter. All outputs of an asynchronous counter do not change state at the same instant and therefore the bit pattern at its output may pass through several states (for only a few nanoseconds) before it settles down to its final value. Unfortunately, these transient states or glitches may last long enough to create spurious timing signals which, in turn, may trigger undesired activity within the control unit. A solution to these problems is to disable the output of the timing pulse generator until the counter has settled down.

The next step in designing the control unit is to combine the signals from the instruction decoder with the timing signals from the sequencer to generate the actual control signals. Figure 5.21 shows one possible approach.

For each of the eight machine-level instructions (plus fetch) one of the vertical lines from the instruction decoder is in a logical one state, enabling the AND gates to which it is connected. As the timing signals, T_0–T_7, are generated, the outputs of the AND gates enabled by the current instruction synthesize the control signals required to implement the random logic control unit. The output of each AND gate corresponding to a particular microinstruction (e.g. C_{MAR}) is connected to an OR gate whose output triggers the actual microinstruction. As we pointed out earlier, not all macroinstructions require eight clock cycles to execute them.

In Fig. 5.21 the AND gates with EXECUTE as an input are part of the decoder featured in Fig. 5.18. For each microinstruction, some subset of the set of control signals will be activated at a defined time. Thus each control signal can be activated by several macroinstructions (possibly during different clock cycles) and is generated by ORing together the various activations (as shown in Fig. 5.23).

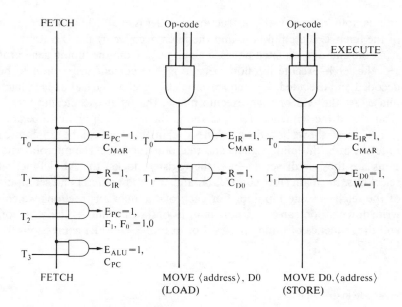

Fig. 5.21 The random logic control unit.

The fetch–execute flip-flop

So far we have devised a mechanism to interpret each macroinstruction but have not tackled the problem of the two-phase fetch–execute cycle. As the control unit is always in one of two states (fetch or execute), an RS flip-flop provides a convenient way of switching from one state to another. When $Q = 0$ the current operation is a fetch phase, and when $Q = 1$ an execute phase is being performed. Figure 5.22 is an extension of Fig. 5.21

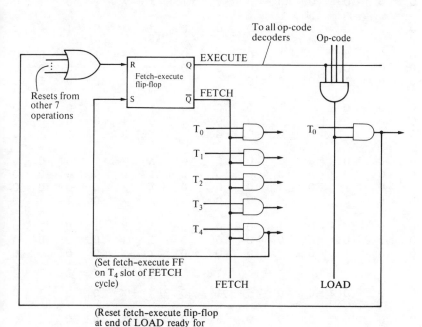

Fig. 5.22 The fetch–execute flip-flop.

and demonstrates how the instruction decoder is enabled by the Q output of the fetch–execute flip-flop, and the fetch decoder by the $\overline{Q}$ output.

At the end of each fetch phase, a clock pulse from the timing generator sets the fetch–execute flip-flop, permitting the current instruction to be decoded and executed. The sequencer is also reset at the end of each fetch phase. At the end of each execute phase, the fetch–execute flip-flop is cleared and the sequencer reset, enabling the next fetch phase to begin.

Table 5.16 shows how the machine-level instructions can be represented in terms of both timing signals and microinstructions. The microinstructions are the bus driver enables, the register clocks, the ALU function select bits, the main store controls (R and W), and the reset and set inputs of the fetch–execute flip-flop. For each of the microinstructions we can write down a Boolean expression in terms of the machine-level instruction and the sequence of timing pulses. For example, consider expressions for E_{MBR}, E_{IR}, C_{MAR}.

Table 5.16 The interpretation of machine-code instructions

Instruction	Time	Enables MBR	IR	PC	DO	ALU	Clocks MAR	MBR	IR	PC	DO	ALU F_1	F_0	MS R	W	FF R	S
Fetch	T_0	0	0	1	0	0	1	0	0	0	0	X	X	0	0	0	0
	T_1	0	0	0	0	0	0	0	1	0	0	X	X	1	0	0	0
	T_2	0	0	1	0	0	0	0	0	0	0	1	0	0	0	0	0
	T_3	0	0	0	0	1	0	0	0	1	0	X	X	0	0	0	0
	T_4	0	1	0	0	0	1	0	0	0	0	X	X	0	0	0	1
LOAD	T_0	0	0	0	0	0	0	0	0	0	1	X	X	1	0	1	0
STORE	T_0	0	0	0	1	0	0	0	0	0	0	X	X	0	1	1	0
ADD	T_0	0	0	0	0	0	0	1	0	0	0	X	X	1	0	0	0
	T_1	1	0	0	0	0	0	0	0	0	0	0	0	0	0	0	0
	T_2	0	0	0	0	1	0	0	0	0	1	X	X	0	0	1	0
SUB	T_0	0	0	0	0	0	0	1	0	0	0	X	X	1	0	0	0
	T_1	1	0	0	0	0	0	0	0	0	0	0	1	0	0	0	0
	T_2	0	0	0	0	1	0	0	0	0	1	X	X	0	0	1	0
INC	T_0	0	0	0	0	0	0	1	0	0	0	X	X	1	0	0	0
	T_1	1	0	0	0	0	0	0	0	0	0	1	0	0	0	0	0
	T_2	0	0	0	0	1	0	1	0	0	0	X	X	0	0	0	0
	T_3	1	0	0	0	0	0	0	0	0	0	X	X	0	1	1	0
DEC	T_0	0	0	0	0	0	0	1	0	0	0	X	X	1	0	0	0
	T_1	1	0	0	0	0	0	0	0	0	0	1	1	0	0	0	0
	T_2	0	0	0	0	1	0	1	0	0	0	X	X	0	0	0	0
	T_3	1	0	0	0	0	0	0	0	0	0	X	X	0	1	1	0
BRA	T_0	0	1	0	0	0	0	0	0	1	0	X	X	0	0	1	0
BEQ	T_0	0	1	0	0	0	0	0	0	Z	0	X	X	0	0	1	0

Note: Z=zero flag from condition code register.

$$E_{MBR} = ADD.T_1 + SUB.T_1 + INC.T_1 + INC.T_3 + DEC.T_1 + DEC.T_3$$
$$E_{IR} = Fetch.T_4 + BRA.T_0 + BEQ.T_0$$
$$C_{MAR} = Fetch.T_0 + Fetch.T_4$$

A more detailed diagram of a control unit built from random logic that will interpret the instruction set of Table 5.14 is given in Fig. 5.23 and puts together the sub-units of Figs. 5.18–5.22. We should note, of course, that this CPU is very highly simplified and illustrates the nature of the random logic CU rather than its exact design.

Table 5.15 could also be used to implement a microprogrammed control unit, in which case the lines of the table represent consecutive words in the control store.

Random logic versus microprogramming

The two approaches to the design of a control unit we have covered are radically different, and any designer has to choose between them. We cannot go into the details of control unit design here, and will therefore point out the most significant features of microprogrammed and random logic control units.

1. Random logic control units are faster than their microprogrammed counterparts. This must always be so because the random logic control unit is optimized for its particular application. Moreover, a microprogrammed control unit is slowed by the need to read a microinstruction from the microprogram memory. Memory accesses are generally slower than basic Boolean operations.

2. Microprogramming offers a flexible design. As the microprogram lives in (read only) memory, it can easily be modified at either the design or the production stage. A random logic control unit is strictly one-off and cannot readily be modified to incorporate new features in the processor (e.g. additional machine-level instructions), and sometimes it is difficult to remove design errors without considerable modification of the hardware.

3. Microprogramming had its high point in the early 1970s when main store was relatively slow (1–2 μs), while the access time of the control store used to hold microprograms was much smaller (e.g. 50–100 ns). It was then sensible to design complex machine-level instructions that were executed very rapidly as microcode. Today, things have changed and main store with access times of below 100 ns is the norm rather than the exception. Faster main stores make microprogramming less attractive because hard-wired random logic control units can be designed to execute instructions much more rapidly than microcoded control units. Many of today's most powerful microprocessors are internally microprogrammed but the microprogram cannot be modified by the user. The new generation of RISC (reduced instruction set computers) architectures are not microprogrammed.

Now that we have covered microprogramming, we can introduce the RISC architecture. Since RISC architectures represent a break from the

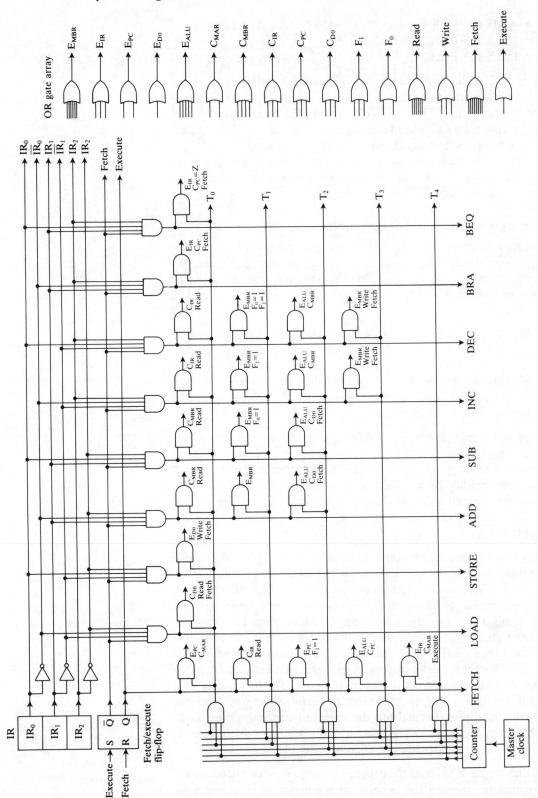

Fig. 5.23 Details of a random logic unit.

tradition of the 68000 and similar microprocessors, the reader might like to leave this section until he or she has covered some of the material in later chapters. Furthermore, the discussion of RISC architectures involves topics not yet introduced. In some ways it would have been better to leave the section on RISC to much later in the text. However, I did not wish to break the sequence of topics by returning to computer architectures.

5.3 An introduction to RISC processors

Since the introduction of the microprocessor in the mid 1970s there seems to have been an almost unbroken trend towards more and more complex (you might even say Baroque) architectures. These architectures have developed rather like a snowball by adding more and more layers to a central core as they roll downhill. A reaction against this trend began at IBM with their 801 architecture and continued at Berkeley where Patterson and Ditzel coined the term 'RISC', or reduced instruction set computer, to describe a new class of architectures that have reversed previous trends in microcomputer design. Since then, several major manufacturers have launched their own processors based on the principles established at Berkeley.

According to popular wisdom RISC architectures are streamlined versions of traditional complex instruction set computers (which have become known as CISCs to delinate them from RISCs). This notion is both misleading and dangerous, as it implies that RISC processors are in some way cruder versions of existing architectures. In brief, RISC architectures redeploy to better effect some of the silicon real estate used to implement complex instructions and elaborate addressing modes in conventional microprocessors of the 68000 and 8086 generation. The term RISC should really stand for regular instruction set computer.

If the RISC philosophy is so appealing, why was it not developed much earlier? The short answer to this question is that RISC architectures make sense only in a 32-bit world because they rely on large instruction formats to limit the effect of the processor–memory bottleneck. In other words it is the move from 8-bit and 16-bit architectures to 32-bit architectures that has made the development of RISC architectures almost inevitable.

If we consider the historical progression of microcomputer architectures as they moved from 8-bit to 16-bit to RISC machines, one of the trends that stands out most clearly is the way in which each new architecture has been designed. It is (to a certain extent) true to say that those who designed 8-bit architectures were striving to put a computer on a chip, rather than to design an optimum computing engine. Designers of 16-bit machines attempted to rationalize 8-bit processors by adding features to improve their performance (e.g. including new addressing modes and more general-purpose registers). The designers of RISC architectures have taken the design process back to fundamentals by studying what many computers actually do and by starting from a blank sheet (as opposed to modifying an existing chip *à la* Intel).

Two of the most significant factors in computer architecture that have influenced the design of today's microprocessors are microprogramming and the desire to help the compiler writers by providing ever more complex instruction sets. By complex instructions we mean instruction of the 68000 form, for example, MOVE 12(A3,D0),D2, or ADD (A6)−,D3. Such instructions permit quite complex sequences of actions to be carried out by a single machine-level instruction. In the first example the contents of A3 is added to the contents of D0 together with the literal 12. The resulting sum is used as an effective address, the contents of which are loaded into register D2.

Microprogramming achieved its high point in the 1970s when ferrite core memory was relatively slow (access times of greater than 1 µs) and semiconductor high-speed random access memory was very expensive. Quite naturally, computer designers used the slow main store to hold the complex instructions that made up the machine-level program. Machine-level instructions are interpreted by microcode in the much faster micro-program control store. Today, it is possible to obtain semicondutor memory suitable for use in main stores with an access time of 80 ns or less, and therefore the previous advantages of microprogramming either disappear or even prove a hindrance. A significant feature of all architectures claiming to belong to the RISC group is their lack of microprogramming and their ability to execute an op-code in a single machine cycle. A converse of this is that complex multi-action instructions cannot be directly executed by RISC architectures.

5.3.1 Instruction usage

Extensive research has been carried out by a number of independent computer scientists over a decade or more into the way in which computers execute programs. Their studies demonstrate that the relative frequency with which different classes of instructions are executed is not uniform and that some types of instruction are executed far more frequently than others. Instruction usage statistics are legion. The following have been compiled by Fairclough, who divided the instructions into eight groups according to type. The figures provide the average number of instructions, expressed as a percentage, for each instruction group. The mean value below represents the results averaged over both program types and computer architecture.

Group	1	2	3	4	5	6	7	8
Mean value	45.28	28.73	10.75	5.92	3.91	2.93	2.05	0.44

The eight instruction groups are as follows:

1. data movement
2. program modification (i.e. branch, call, return)
3. arithmetic
4. compare
5. logical
6. shift
7. bit manipulation

8. input/output and miscellaneous.

The above data convincingly demonstrate that the most common instruction type is the assignment or data movement primitive of the form P: = Q in a high-level language or MOVE P,Q or LDA P in a low-level language. Similarly, the program modification group that includes conditional and unconditional branches together with subroutine calls and returns, forms the second most common group of instructions. Taken together, the data movement and program modification groups account for 74 per cent of all instructions. A corollary of this statement is that we can expect a large program to contain only 26 per cent of instructions that are not data movement or program modification primitives.

An inescapable inference from such results is that processor designers would be better employed devoting their time to optimizing the way in which their machines handle instructions in groups one and two, than in seeking new 'powerful' instructions. In the early days of the microprocessor, chip manufacturers went out of their way to provide special instructions that were unique to their products. These instructions were then heavily promoted by the company's sales force. Today, we can see that their efforts should have been directed towards the goal of optimizing the most frequently used instructions. RISC architectures have been designed to exploit the programming environment in which most instructions are data movement or program control instructions. As an example of the way in which the designers of RISC architectures approach computer designs consider how a literal operand might be encoded.

An obvious question to ask is, 'What is the range of the majority of operands?' It has been reported by Tanenbaum that 56 per cent of all constant values lie in the range −15 to +15 and that 98 per cent of all constant values lie in the range −511 to +511. Consequently, the inclusion of a 5-bit constant field in an instruction would cover just over half the occurrences of a literal. RISC architectures have sufficiently long instruction lengths to include a literal field that caters for the majority of all literals.

Measurements made by Tanenbaum and by Halbert and Kessler have indicated that for over 95 per cent of dynamically called procedures twelve words of storage are sufficient for all their arguments and local values. That is, if an architecture has twelve or so words of on-chip register storage, it should be able to handle all the operands required by most procedures without accessing main store. This both reduces the processor–memory bus traffic and permits small address fields within the instruction format. Moreover, a really efficient architecture should make provision for each procedure to have associated with it about twelve on-chip registers. The transfer of data between registers should be very fast. We shall later see that RISC architectures can actually remove the need to transfer data between procedures.

Having described some of the ingredients that go into an efficient architecture, the next step is to look at the characteristics of first-generation RISCs. After that we describe the characteristics of RISC processors in more detail.

5.3.2 Characteristics of RISC architectures

The above discussion can be summarized to provide a list of the desired characteristics of an efficient RISC architecture.

1. RISC processors should have sufficient on-chip memory (i.e. registers) to help overcome the worst effects of the processor–memory bottleneck. Internal memory can be accessed more rapidly than off-chip main store. We have seen that procedures require, on average, in the region of twelve words for local storage and parameter passing. This fact indicates that it is indeed feasible to adopt on-chip storage.

2. Since instructions in the program modification group, which includes procedure call and return instructions, are so frequently executed, an effective architecture should make provisions for the efficient passing of parameters between procedures.

3. RISC processors should not attempt to implement infrequently used instructions. Complex instructions both waste silicon real estate and conflict with the requirements of point 4 below. Moreover, the inclusion of complex instructions increases the time taken to design, fabricate and test a processor.

4. If a RISC processor is to be fast, it should execute on average approximately one instruction per clock cycle. This restriction also imposes a limit on the maximum complexity of instructions.

5. A corollary of point 4 is that an efficient architecture should not be microprogrammed, as microprogramming interprets an instruction by executing microinstructions. In the limit, a RISC processor is close to a microprogrammed architecture in which the distinction between machine cycle and microcycle has vanished.

6. An efficient processor should have a single instruction format (or at least very few formats). By providing a single instruction format, the decoding of an instruction into its component fields can be performed by a minimum level of decoding logic.

7. In order to reduce the time taken to execute an instruction, the multilength instructions associated with first- and second-generation microprocessors should be abandoned. As it would be unreasonable to perform multiple accesses to the program store to read each instruction, it follows that the word length of a RISC processor should be sufficient to accommodate the operation code field and one or more operand fields. A corollary of this statement is that a high-speed RISC processor may not necessarily be as efficient as a conventional microprocessor in its utilization of program memory space.

We now look at the three fundamental aspects of the RISC architecture: its use of a large number of on-chip registers, its use of multiple overlapping register windows to considerably reduce the need to transfer parameters between procedures, and its pipelining mechanism that permits the overlapping of instruction execution.

The Berkeley RISC architecture adopts a three-register instruction format of the form specified below. Each operand field permits one of 32 internal registers to be accessed.

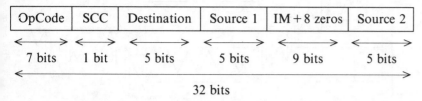

For our current purposes we are not interested in the two fields labelled 'SCC' and 'IM + 8 zero' above, as these are concerned with updating the condition code register and with providing a literal, respectively.

The RISC format permits instructions of the form ADD X,Y,Z, where X, Y, and Z are internal registers. Since five bits are allocated to each operand field, it follows that the RISC has $2^5 = 32$ internal registers. This last statement is emphatically not true, since the RISC has 138 user-accessible general-purpose internal registers. The reason for the discrepancy between the number of registers directly addressable and the actual number of registers is due to a mechanism called windowing that gives the programmer a view of only a subset of all registers at any instant.

5.3.3 Register windows

An important design feature of the Berkeley RISC architecture is the way in which it can allocate register space to every new procedure. Although only twelve or so registers are required by each invocation of a procedure, the successive nesting of procedures rapidly increases the number of on-chip registers assigned to procedures (if each procedure is to have its own local variables). It might be thought that any attempt to dedicate a set of registers to each new procedure is impractical, since the repeated calling of nested procedures will require an unlimited amount of storage.

Fortunately, although procedures can be nested to an arbitrary depth, the average behaviour of programs does not demonstrate pathological behaviour with respect to procedure nesting. Much RISC literature refers to research by Halbert and Kessler, and by Tamir and Sequin, demonstrating that most procedures are not nested to any great depth. These results indicate that it might be feasible to adopt a modest number of local register sets for a sequence of nested procedures.

Figure 5.24 provides a graphical representation of the execution of a program in terms of the depth of nesting of procedures. What this figure demonstrates is that even though procedures may be nested to depths greater than 12, there are long runs of procedure invocations that do not require, for example, a nesting level of greater than five from some arbitrary point.

A mechanism for implementing local variable work space for procedures adopted by the designers of the Berkeley RISC is to handle up to eight nested procedures by providing on-chip work space for each

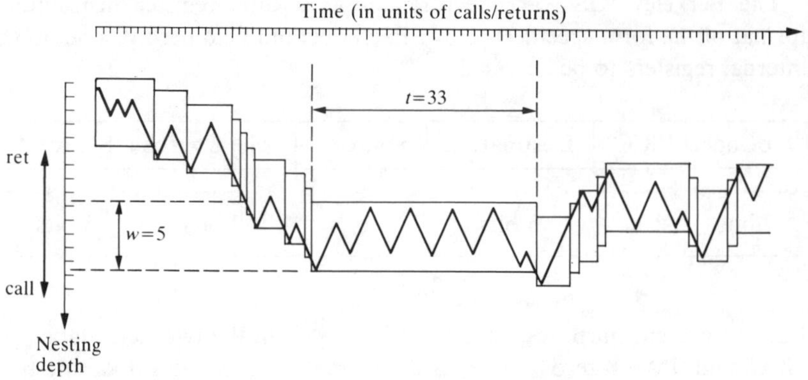

Time (in units of calls/returns)

$t=33$

ret

Fig. 5.24 Nested procedures as a function of time.

$w=5$

call

Nesting
depth

procedure. Any further nesting will force the CPU to resort to external memory space for local variable storage, as we shall soon see.

Memory space used by procedures can, to a reasonable approximation, be divided into four types:

Global space. Global space is a region of logical address space that is directly accessible by all procedures. It is used to hold constants and data that may be required from any point within the program. Most conventional microprocessors have only internal global registers.

Local space. Local space is a region of logical address space that is private to the procedure. That is, no other procedure can access the current procedure's local address space from outside the procedure. Local space is employed as working space by the current procedure.

Imported parameter space. Imported parameter space holds the parameters imported by the current procedure from its parent. In RISC terminology these are called the 'high' registers.

Exported parameter space. Exported parameter space holds the parameters exported by the current procedure to its child. In RISC terminology these are called the 'low' registers.

Windows and parameter passing

One of the reasons for the relatively high frequency of data movement operations is the need to pass parameters to procedures and to receive them from procedures. Any system that removes (or at least reduces) this two-way transfer of data is likely to considerably speed up program execution. The Berkeley RISC architecture solves the problem of parameter passing by means of multiple overlapped windows. A window is the set of registers visible to the current procedure. Figure 5.25 illustrates the structure of the RISC's overlapping windows.

Suppose that the processor is currently using the ith window set. A special-purpose register, called the window pointer (WP), indicates the current active window. In this case the WP contains the value i. As described above, each window is divided into four parts: registers R0–R9 are the global register set, registers R10–R15 are used by the procedure to receive parameters from its parent (and to pass parameters back to its parent), registers R16–R25 are ten local registers that cannot be accessed

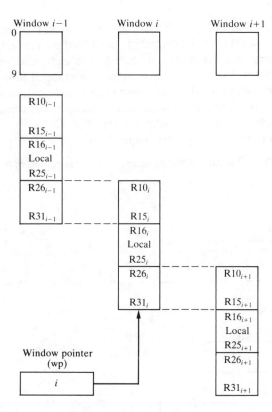

Fig. 5.25 Structure of the RISC's overlapping windows.

directly by any other procedure, and registers R26–R31 are used by the procedure to pass parameters to and from its own child (i.e. a procedure called by itself).

All windows consist of 32 registers, R0–R31, and each of these registers can be addressed by a RISC instruction which contains five address bits per operand field. In this section we will use the mnemonics of the Berkeley RISC wherever possible when describing the operation of a RISC architecture. An instruction of the form ADD R3,R12,R25 implements [R25]←[R3]+[R12], where R3 is within the window's global address space, R12 is within its import from (or export to) parent procedure space, and R25 is within its local address space. Note that RISC arithmetic and logical instructions always involve 32-bit values (there are no 8-bit or 16-bit operations).

Whenever a procedure is invoked by an instruction of the form CALLR Rd,⟨address⟩, the contents of the window pointer are incremented by 1 and the current value of the program counter saved in register Rd of the new window. Note that the Berkeley RISC does not employ a conventional stack in external main memory to save subroutine return addresses.

Once a new window has been invoked (in Fig. 5.25 this is window i), the new procedure sees a different set of registers to the previous window. Global registers R0–R9 are an exception since they are common to all windows. Window R10 of the child procedure corresponds to (i.e. is the same as) window R26 of the calling (i.e. parent) procedure.

The complete structure of RISC's window system is given in Fig. 5.26. On the left-hand side of the diagram is the actual register array that holds all the on-chip general-purpose registers. The eight columns associated with windows 0–7 show how each window is mapped onto the physical memory array and how the overlapping regions are organized. Note that the windows are organized in a circular fashion so that window 0 follows window 7 and window 7 precedes window 0.

The total number of registers required are:

10 global + 8 × 10 local + 8 × 6 parameter transfer registers = 138 registers.

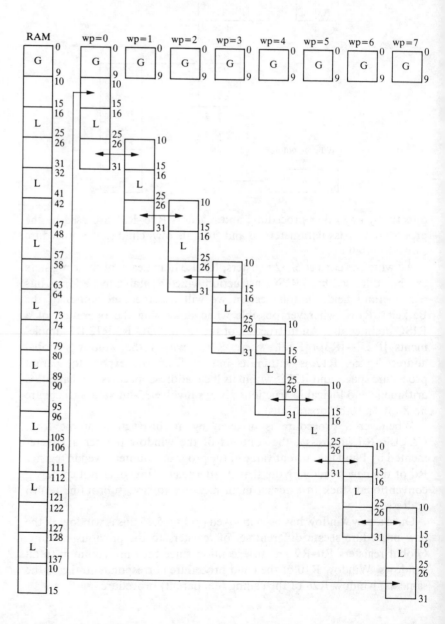

Fig. 5.26 Detailed structure of RISC's windows.

Window overflow

Unfortunately, the on-chip resources of any processor are finite and, in the case of the Berkeley RISCs, the registers are limited to eight windows. If procedures are nested to a depth greater than or equal to eight, window overflow is said to occur, as there is no longer a new window for the next procedure invocation. When an overflow takes place, the only thing left to do is to employ external memory to hold the overflow data. In practice the oldest window is saved rather than the new window created by the procedure just called.

If the number of procedure returns minus the number of procedure calls exceeds eight, window underflow takes place. Window underflow is the converse of window overflow and the youngest window saved in main store must be returned to a window.

5.3.4 RISC architecture and pipelining

Once again it is worth remarking that conventional complex instruction set microprocessors have traded complexity for efficiency. That is, they have implemented an ability to interpret very complex instructions but have done so at the expense of the efficient use of the chip's facilities. As elsewhere in this text, efficiency can be taken as a measure of the processor's throughput. In this section we show how the regular structure of the RISC permits it to carry out a number of internal operations in parallel.

Figure 5.27 illustrates the machine cycle of a hypothetical simple microprocessor that executes an instruction of the form ADD P (i.e. $[A] \leftarrow [A] + [M(P)]$, where A is some on-chip general-purpose register/ accumulator and P is a general memory location). The instruction is executed in the following five phases.

Instruction fetch. Read the instruction from the system memory and increment the program counter.

Instruction decode. Decode the instruction read from memory during the previous phase. The nature of the instruction decode phase is very dependent on the complexity of the instruction encoding. A regularly encoded instruction might be decoded in a few nanoseconds with two levels of gating while a complex instruction format might require ROM-based look-up tables to implement the decoding.

Operand fetch. The operand specified by the instruction is read from the system memory or an on-chip register and loaded into the CPU.

Execute. The operation specified by the instruction is carried out.

Operand store. The result of the execution phase is written into the operand destination. This may be an on-chip register or a location in external memory.

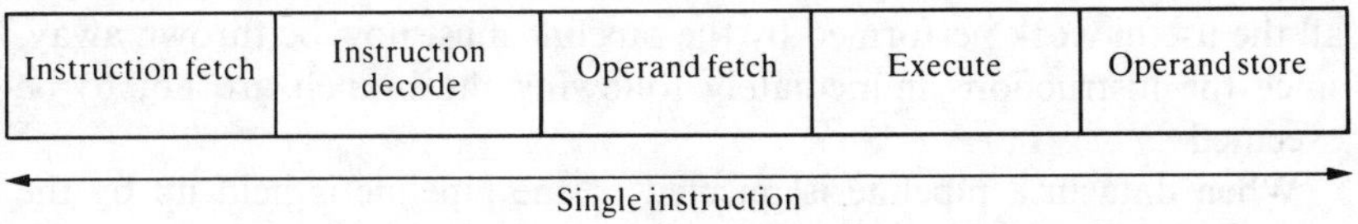

Instruction fetch	Instruction decode	Operand fetch	Execute	Operand store

← Single instruction →

Fig. 5.27 Structure of a machine cycle.

Each of the above five phases may take a specific time (although the time taken would normally be an integer multiple of the system's master clock period). Some instructions may require less than five phases. For example an instruction like CMP R1,R2 compares R1 and R2 by subtracting R1 from R2 to set the condition codes and does not, therefore, need an operand store phase.

The inefficiency resulting from the arrangement of Fig. 5.27 is immediately apparent. Consider the execution phase of instruction interpretation. This phase might take one fifth of an instruction cycle, leaving the instruction execution unit idle for the remaining 80% of the time. The same rule applies to the other functional units of the processor, which also lie idle for 80 per cent of the time. A technique called pipelining can be employed to increase the effective speed of the processor by overlapping in time the various stages in the execution of an instruction. In the simplest of terms, a pipelined processor can execute instruction i while fetching instruction $i+1$ at the same time.

The way in which a RISC processor may implement pipelining is described in Fig. 5.28. The RISC processor overlaps the instruction fetch from external memory phase with three internal phases: operand fetch, execute and operand store. Note that the three internal phases take approximately the same time as the instruction fetch, because these operations take place within the CPU itself and operands are fetched from and stored in the CPU's own register file. Moreover, since the RISC has a very simple and regular instruction format, the instruction decoding phase is not necessary.

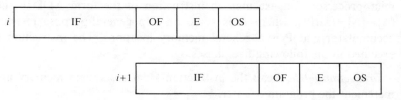

Fig. 5.28 Instruction pipelining.

IF=instruction fetch   OF=operand fetch   E=execute   OS=operand store

Pipelining is, unfortunately, not without quite considerable disadvantages. Here we provide an overview of the two fundamental problems encountered by the designer of pipelined systems: pipeline bubbles created by branch instructions and data dependency.

A pipeline is an ordered structure that thrives on regularity. At any stage in the execution of a program, a pipeline contains components of two or more instructions at varying stages in their execution. Consider now Fig. 5.29 in which a sequence of instructions is being executed in a pipeline processor. When the processor encounters a branch instruction, it is forced to reload its program counter with a new value. This means that all the useful work performed by the pipeline must now be thrown away, since the instructions immediately following the branch are not to be executed.

When data in a pipeline is rejected or the pipeline is held up by the

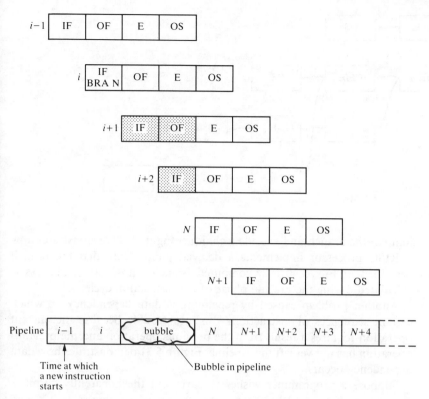

Fig. 5.29 The effect of a branch instruction in pipelining.

introduction of idle states, we say that a bubble has been introduced. Of course, the longer the pipeline the more instructions that must be rejected once the branch is encountered.

As we have already demonstrated that program control instructions are so frequent, any realistic processor using pipelining must do something to overcome the problem of bubbles caused by this class of instructions. The Berkeley RISC machines reduce the effect of bubbles by refusing to throw away the instruction immediately following a branch. That is, the instruction following a branch is always executed. Consider the effect of the following sequence of instructions:

```
ADD    R1,R2,R3      [R3]←[R1]+[R2]
JMPX   N             [PC]←[N] i.e. goto address N
ADD    R3,R4,R5      [R5]←[R3]+[R4]
ADD    R7,R8,R9      Not executed because of branch taken
```

The processor calculates R5: = R1 + R2 + R4 before executing the branch. This sequence of instructions is most strange to the eyes of a conventional assembly-language programmer, who is not accustomed to seeing an instruction executed after a branch has been taken.

Unfortunately, it is not always possible to arrange a program in such a way as to include a 'useful' instruction immediately after a branch. Whenever this happens, the compiler must introduce a no operation (NOP) instruction after the branch and accept the inevitability of a bubble. RISC literature generally refers to this mechanism as the delayed

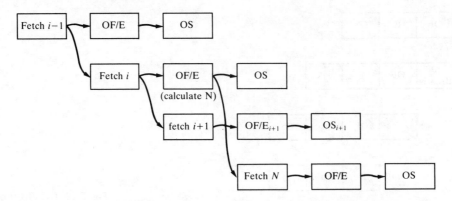

Fig. 5.30 The delayed jump.

jump or the branch-and-execute technique. Figure 5.30 demonstrates how a RISC processor implements a delayed jump. Note that the branch described in Fig. 5.30 is a computed branch whose target address is calculated during the execute phase of the instruction cycle.

Another problem caused by pipelining is data dependency, in which certain sequences of instructions run into trouble because the current operation requires a result from the previous operation and the previous operation has not yet left the pipeline. Figure 5.31 demonstrates how data dependency occurs.

Suppose a programmer wishes to carry out the apparently harmless calculation $X := (A+B)AND(A+B-C)$. Assuming that A,B,C,X and two temporary values, Temp1 and Temp2, are in registers in the current window, we can write

```
ADD    A,B,Temp1        [Temp1]←[A]+[B]
SUB    Temp1,C,Temp2    [Temp2]←[Temp1]−[C]
AND    Temp1,Temp2,X    [X]←[Temp1].[Temp2]
```

Instruction $i+1$ in Fig. 5.31 begins execution during the operand fetch phase of the previous instruction. However, instruction $i+1$ cannot continue on to its next phase, operand fetch, because the very operand it requires does not get written back to the register file for another two clock

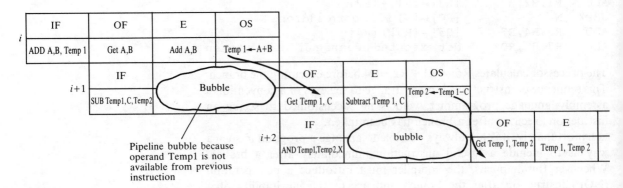

Fig. 5.31 The effect of data dependency.

cycles. Consequently a bubble must be introduced in the pipeline while instruction $i+1$ waits for its data. In a similar fashion, the logical AND operation also introduces a bubble as it too requires the result of a previous operation which is in the pipeline.

Figure 5.32 demonstrates a technique called internal forwarding designed to overcome the effects of data dependency. The example provided corresponds to a three-stage pipeline like the RISC. The following sequence of operations is to be executed:

```
1. ADD R1,R2,R3       [R3]←[R1]+[R2]
2. ADD R4,R5,R6       [R6]←[R4]+[R5]
3. ADD R3,R4,R7       [R7]←[R3]+[R4]
4. ADD R7,R1,R8       [R8]←[R1]+[R7]
```

In this example, instruction 3 uses an operand generated by instruction 1 (i.e. the contents of register R3). However, because of the intervening instruction 2, the destination operand generated by instruction 1 has time to be written into the register file before it is read as a source operand by instruction 3.

Instruction 3 generates a destination operand R7 which is required as a source operand by the next instruction. If the processor were to read the source operand requested by instruction 4 from the register file, it would see the old value of R7. By means of internal forwarding, the processor transfers R7 from instruction 3's execution unit directly to the execution unit of instruction 4 (see Fig. 5.32).

5.3.5 Accessing external memory

In their ruthless pursuit of efficiency, the designers of the Berkeley RISC architecture have severely restricted the way in which it accesses external memory. Conventional CISC processors frequently have a wealth of addressing modes that can be used in conjunction with many memory reference instructions. For example, a CISC like the 68020 implements

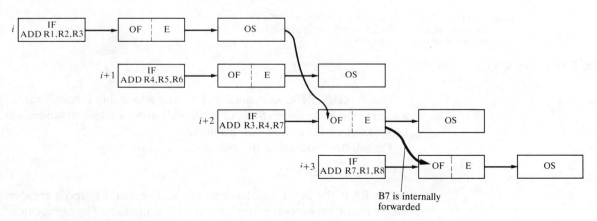

Fig. 5.32 Internal forwarding.

ADD D0, − (A5) which adds the contents of D0 to the top of the stack pointed at by A5 and then pushes the result on to this stack.

The Berkeley RISC permits only two types of reference to external memory: a load and a store. Consequently, all arithmetic and logical operations carried out by the RISC apply only to source and destination operands in registers. Similarly, the Berkeley RISC provides a limited number of addressing modes with which to access an operand in the main store. The reason for these severe restrictions on external memory accesses is not hard to find. Before we look at the Berkeley RISC in detail, we are going to discuss some of the general principles of load and store instructions in a RISC environment.

The load register operation of the form LOAD (Rx)S2,Rd has the effect $[Rd] \leftarrow [M([Rx] + S2)]$. Figure 5.33 demonstrates the sequence of actions required by this instruction. During the source fetch phase, register Rx, which is used to calculate the effective address, is read from the register file and used to calculate the effective address of the operand in the execute phase. However, now that we have performed the 'execute phase' we cannot move to the store operand phase, since the operand has not been read from the main store. Therefore the main store must be accessed to read the operand and a store operand phase executed to load the operand into destination register Rd.

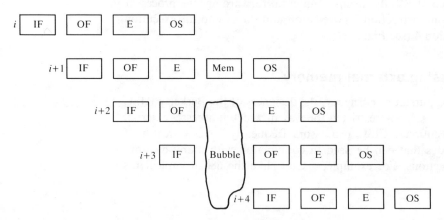

Instruction $i+1$ is LOAD Rx (S2), Rd (i.e. $[Rd] \longleftarrow [M([Rx]+S2)]$).
A bubble in the pipeline is caused by the additional memory reference in the instruction interpretation.

Fig. 5.33 Executing a LOAD instruction.

The Berkeley RISC implements two basic addressing modes: indexed and program counter relative. All other addressing modes can (and must) be synthesized from these two primitives.

The effective address in the indexed mode is given by

$$EA = [Rx] + S2$$

where Rx is the index register (one of the 32 general purpose registers accessible by the current procedure) and S2 is an offset. The offset can be either a general purpose register or a 13-bit constant (see Fig. 5.34).

The effective address in the program counter relative mode is given by

EA= [PC] +S2

where PC represents the contents of the program counter and S2 is an offset as above.

These addressing modes include quite a powerful 'toolbox': zero, one or two pointers and a constant offset. If you wonder how we can use an addressing mode without an index (i.e. pointer) register, note that R0 in the global register set permanently contains the constant zero. Note that there is a difference between addressing modes permitted by load and store operations. A load instruction permits the second source, S2, to be either an immediate value or a second register, while a store instruction permits S2 to be a 13-bit immediate value only.

The RISC has just two basic instruction formats as defined in Fig. 5.34, although there are slight variations on these two formats. The short immediate format provides a 5-bit destination, a 5-bit source_1 operand and a 14-bit short source_2 operand. The short immediate format has two variations: one that specifies a 13-bit literal for source_2 and one that specifies a 5-bit source_2 register address. Bit 13 is used to specify whether the source_2 operand is a 13-bit literal or a 5-bit register pointer.

The long immediate format provides a 19-bit source operand by concatenating the two source operand fields. Immediate fields with 13 and 19 bits may sound a little strange at first sight. However, since 13 + 19 = 32, RISC permits a full 32-bit value to be loaded into a window register in two operations. A typical microprocessor might take the same number of instruction bits to perform the same action (i.e. a 32-bit operation code field followed by a 32-bit literal). In plain English, the RISC processor can load 32-bit constants just as efficiently as many microprocessors (even if the idea of a 13-bit load followed by a 19-bit load seems a little bizarre).

Conditional instructions do not require a destination address and therefore the five bits, 19–23, normally used to specify a destination

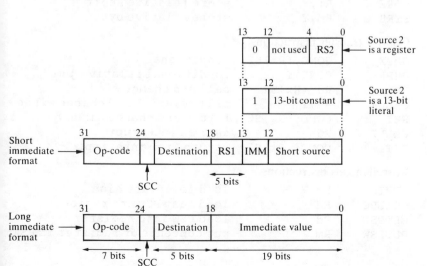

Fig. 5.34 The RISC instruction format. Note: SCC determines whether the condition codes are updated by the current instruction.

register are used to specify the condition (one of 16 since bit 23 is not used by conditional instructions).

The RISC instruction set is described below:

Register to register

SLL	Rs,S2,Rd	shift left logical
SRA	Rs,S2,Rd	shift right arithmetic
SRL	Rs,S2,Rd	shift right logical
AND	Rs,S2,Rd	logical AND
OR	Rs,S2,Rd	logical OR
XOR	Rs,S2,Rd	exclusive OR
ADD	Rs,S2,Rd	add
ADDC	Rs,S2,Rd	add with carry
SUB	Rs,S2,Rd	subtract
SUBC	Rs,S2,Rd	subtract with borrow
SUBI	Rs,S2,Rd	subtract reverse
SUBCI	Rs,S2,Rd	subtract reverse with borrow

Load instructions

LDXW	(Rx)S2,Rd	load long
LDXHU	(Rx)S2,Rd	load short unsigned
LDXHS	(Rx)S2,Rd	load short signed
LDXBU	(Rx)S2,Rd	load byte unsigned
LDXBS	(Rx)S2,Rd	load byte signed
LDRW	Y,Rd	load relative long
LDRHU	Y,Rd	load relative short unsigned
LDRHS	Y,Rd	load relative short signed
LDRBU	Y,Rd	load relative byte unsigned
LDRBS	Y,Rd	load relative byte signed

Store instructions

STXW	Rm,(Rx)S2	store long
STXH	Rm,(Rx)S2	store short
STXB	Rm,(Rx)S2	store byte
STRW	Rm,Y	store relative long
STRH	Rm,Y	store relative short
STRB	Rm,Y	store relative byte

Control transfer instructions

JMPX	COND,(Rx)S2	conditional jump
JMPR	COND,Y	conditional relative jump
CALLX	Rd,(Rx)S2	call and change window
CALLR	Rd,Y	call relative and change window
RET	COND,(Rx)S2	return and change window
CALLI	Rd	call an interrupt
RETI	COND,(Rx)S2	return from interrupt

Miscellaneous instructions

LDHI	Rd,Y	load immediate high
GETLPC	Rd	load last PC into register
GETPSW	Rd	load PSW into register
PUTPSW	Rm	put contents of register in PSW

Summary

The central processing unit lies at the heart of any computer system and is responsible for reading instructions from memory, decoding them and then interpreting (i.e. executing) them. In this chapter we have looked at the principal parts of a CPU and have described how they cooperate to execute a program. We began our discussion of the CPU with a simple model that could do no more than read sequential instructions. Then we gradually added the components and data paths required to execute instructions, to deal with literal operands and to implement conditional branches. The hypothetical architecture we have introduced provides us with a starting point for the description of a real microprocessor, the 68000, in the next chapter.

The most complex part of a CPU is its control unit, which is responsible for interpreting the pattern of bits making up an instruction. We have looked at the two fundamental ways of carrying out this interpretation: one by means of random logic and the other by means of a microprogram. The random logic control unit uses a pulse generator and an instruction decoder together with an array of AND and OR gates to synthesize all the signals necessary to control the flow of data in the CPU. The microprogrammed control unit uses the instruction to look up a sequence of microinstructions in read-only memory. The bits of these microinstructions are used to directly control the rest of the CPU.

Although much of this text is based on a modern complex instruction-set computer, the 68000, we have introduced some of the principles governing the reduced instruction-set computers that have done so much to increase the performance of microprocessors in the late 1980s and early 1990s. RISC architectures have taken a step backwards and returned to the fundamental principles governing the von Neumann computer. By using large register sets with a simple instruction set that is suited to pipelining, RISC processors have dramatically increased the processing power that could be put on a single chip.

Problems

1. What is the largest program that can be addressed by processors with the following number of address bits? The largest program is the same as the processor's address space and is measured in bytes.

(a) 12 bits

(b) 16 bits

(c) 24 bits

(d) 32 bits

(e) 48 bits

2. A 68000-based system is to be used for word processing. Assume that all its memory space is to be populated by read/write memory and that 1 Mbyte is allocated to the operating system, word processor and text buffer space. The remaining memory space can hold a text file. If the average English word contains five ISO/ASCII-encoded characters and one page of text is composed of approximately 35 lines of 12 words, how many pages of text can be held in the 68000's memory space at any instant?

3. Suppose a 68000 is to be used to process digital images (e.g. in a laser printer). An image is made up of an array of n by n pixels. Each pixel may have one of 16 grey levels (from all white to all black). If a picture measures 20×20 cm, what is the maximum resolution that can be supported by a 68000 (in terms of pixels per cm^2)?

4. The Von Neumann stored program computer locates program and data in the same memory. What are the advantages and disadvantages of a system that has separate program and data memories?

5. What is the meaning (in plain English) of the following operations expressed in RTL?

(a) [D3]←4

(b) [D3]←[MS(4)]

(c) [MS(4)]←[MS(2)]

(d) [MS(5)]←[MS([MS(2)])]

(e) [D4]←[MS([D2])]

(f) [D1]←[MS[4+[D2]])]

6. Explain the function of the following registers in a CPU:

(a) PC

(b) MAR

(c) MBR

(d) IR

7. Explain the meaning of a 'fetch cycle' and describe its action in RTL.

8. Some microprocessors have one accumulator, some have two. The 68000 has eight data registers (accumulators). How do you think that you might go about determining the 'ideal' number of general purpose data register a computer should have?

9. What is a microinstruction?

10. What is an assembler directive and why do you think that it is sometimes called a 'pseudo operation'?

11. Define the following (68000) instructions in RTL:

(a) `MOVE #1234,1234`

(b) `MOVE 1234,D3`

(c) `MOVE (A1),1234`

(d) `MOVE (A1),A1`

(e) `MOVE #1234,(A1)`

12. What are the characteristics of a RISC architecture that distinguish it from a CISC architecture like the 68000?

13. Pipelining permits the computer designer to increase the effective speed of a processor by overlapping operations. What are the problems caused by pipelining?

Assembly-language programming and the 68000 microprocessor

6

Following our examination of the CPU and its control unit, the next step is to look at a real CPU in greater detail. Although we could have chosen to illustrate the central processor unit of a mainframe or a minicomputer, we are going to describe a microprocessor. It is reasonable to choose a microprocessor because they are so widely available and are less complex than mainframes.

We have decided to use the 68000 microprocessor as a vehicle for teaching microprocessor architecture and for introducing assembly-language programming. The 68000 has been selected for a number of reasons. First, it represents a reasonably state-of-the-art architecture and is found in a wide variety of powerful microcomputers. Second, it has a moderately sophisticated architecture incorporating many facilities once found only on more powerful minicomputers and mainframe computers. By the way, there are other members of the 68000 family as well as the 68000 itself. Fortunately the 68000 we describe here is compatible with the 68008, 68010, 68020, 68030, and the 68040 in the sense that assembly-language programs written for the 68000 will run on the 68020, etc. However, programs written in 68020 or 68030 assembly language will not necessarily run on the 68000, because the newer and more powerful devices have enhanced 68000 instruction sets.

Before continuing, we must clear up two points of potential confusion. The 68000 has 32-bit wide internal data registers and can therefore properly be called a 32-bit microprocessor. However, the 68000 has only a 16-bit external data bus, so that 32-bit operands must be moved to and from memory as two consecutive 16-bit words. Consequently, the 68000 can equally be called a 16-bit microprocessor. It would be reasonably true to say that the 68000 is a 32-bit computer from the standpoint of the programmer using it, and a 16-bit computer from the standpoint of the engineer designing systems around it. A few writers refer to the 68000 as a 16/32-bit microprocessor.

A second point about the 68000 to note is that although the 68000 is a

16-bit *word*-oriented machine, it is *byte addressable.* That is, successive bytes in memory are stored at consecutive byte addresses 0,1,2,3 . . . and any particular byte in memory can be individually read from or written to. Since a word is composed of *two* bytes, successive words are stored at consecutive *even* addresses 0,2,4,6, ... The 68000 stores the *most-significant* byte of a word (i.e. bits D_{08}–D_{15}) at the *even* address and the *least-significant* byte of a word (i.e. bits D_{00}–D_{07}) at the *odd* address. For example, if we execute the operation MOVE.W D0,1234, bits D_{00}–D_{07} of D0 are stored at byte address 1235 and bits D_{08}–D_{15} of D0 are stored at byte address 1234. Figure 6.1 illustrate how the 68000's memory space is organized.

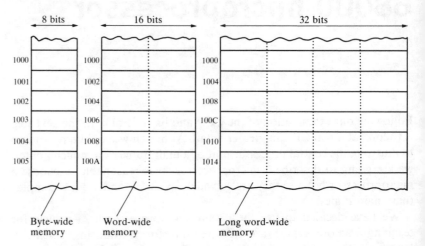

Fig. 6.1 The 68000's memory space.

The least-significant bit of the 68000's PC is bit zero, while the least-significant bit of the address bus is A_{01}. Since the 68000 always addresses a word on an even address boundary (i.e. 0, 2, 4, 6, . . .), the state of address bit A_{00} does not determine the word selected by the 68000. Two active-low pins from the 68000 $\overline{\text{UDS}}$, upper data strobe, and $\overline{\text{LDS}}$, lower data strobe, are used to select either the upper byte of a word, the lower byte of a word or the entire word. Figure 6.2 demonstrates how $\overline{\text{LDS}}$ and $\overline{\text{UDS}}$ are employed by the 68000.

One of the most important differences between microprocessors and other computers is that the designers of the microprocessor are subject to two special restrictions: the number of gates that can be put on a single chip is determined by the available technology and the number of external connections to the chip is limited to about 64, although chips are now appearing with many more pins (i.e. over 100) by using special packages called *pin grid arrays.*

In order to keep the number of external connections to the 68000 to a reasonable number (i.e. to permit it to be fitted in a 64-pin package), only 23 of the 68000's 32 address lines are connected to pins. (Remember that there is no A_{00}—since the smallest unit of data that the address bus can specify is a 16-bit word.) Although the 68000 has a 32-bit program counter and eight 32-bit address registers, it can access only 2^{24} bytes of memory. Address bits A_{24}–A_{31} are 'trapped on the chip' and cannot be used to

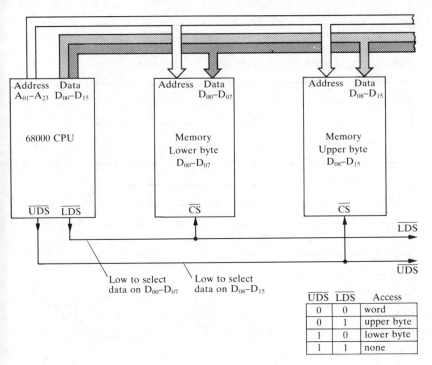

Fig. 6.2 Addressing bytes and words.

UDS	LDS	Access
0	0	word
0	1	upper byte
1	0	lower byte
1	1	none

access memory. Fortunately, the 68000's 2^{24} bytes (i.e. 16M bytes) of addressable memory is more than enough for most applications of the 68000. The newer 68020 is housed in pin grid array and supports a full 32-bit address bus.

Because of their limitations, microprocessors are inherently less complex than mainframe computers (even though *today's* microcomputer is more powerful than yesterday's mainframe). While we could have gone to the other extreme from the mainframe and have selected an 8-bit microprocessor with its very simple internal architecture to illustrate most of the important concepts of microprocessor architecture, it is much more rewarding to teach the architecture of a more sophisticated CPU—even if it does slightly complicate matters. In any case, many of the older 8-bit microprocessors lack features that are now regarded as an essential part in any course on computer technology.

The simplified programmer's model of the 68000 is given in Fig. 6.3. A microprocessor, or any other computer, can be viewed in three different ways. Designers see its internal structure and organization; they have created the device and must have an intimate knowledge of all its aspects, particularly the control unit. Engineers who interface the microprocessor to all the other components of a system are interested in its electrical properties and wish to know about the voltages and currents at each of the pins, the timing requirements and protocols observed by the various signals entering or leaving the chip. Programmers are not interested in such fine detail and require little more than a programming model of the machine. That is, programmers need to know its instruction set and the

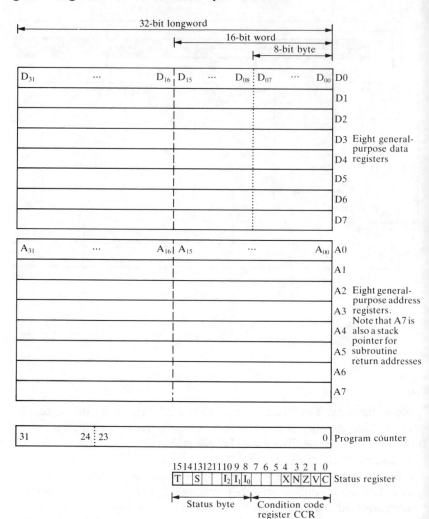

Fig. 6.3 The programmer's model of the 68000 microprocessor.

arrangement of its internal registers; they are interested in what it does and not in how it does it.

Microprocessor word lengths

In our previous discussion of the CPU, we did not look closely at the length of the units of data manipulated by the CPU. A real computer has a particular data word length, which is, for 8-bit and 16-bit microprocessors, normally the same size as the words stored in the memory locations of the main store. Thirty-two bit microprocessors have either 32-bit wide memories or else they store 32-bit quantities in two consecutive locations of 16-bit memory.

The actual word length associated with any computer is a compromise between many factors and represents the designer's attempt to satisfy a sector of the computer market. As time passes, the maximum economic word length increases with technological progress. In less than a decade, microprocessor word lengths have increased from 4 to 32 bits. At first sight, it might be thought that the minimum word size of a computer must be equal to the number of bits in the op-code field plus the number of bits in the address field of an instruction register. That is,

$$\text{minimum wordlength} = \log_2 (\text{number of instructions}) + \log_2 (\text{number of memory locations}).$$

For example, if there are 256 instructions and the largest program to be run is 65 536 locations, then the minimum word length would be

$$\log_2(256) + \log_2(65536) = 8 + 16 = 24.$$

Fortunately, at least for the designers of microprocessors, the minimum word length suggested by the above equation is not necessary. There are several ways of reducing the minimum word length required by a particular computer. For example, the number of address bits may be reduced by **segmentation.** Segmentation divides the available memory space into a number of units called pages or segments, so that, for example, a 16M byte (2^{24} byte) memory space may be divided into 256 segments of 65 536 (i.e. 2^{16}) locations. Whenever the computer specifies an address, it employs 16 bits to select a location within a segment and eight bits to select a particular segment as illustrated in Fig. 6.4. In other words, the 24-bit effective address of an operand is derived from the 16-bit operand address plus the eight most-significant bits from a segment register.

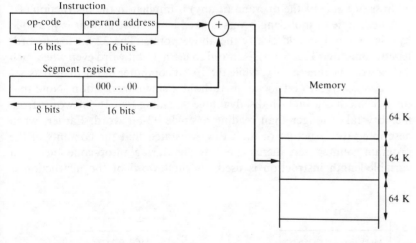

Fig. 6.4 Accessing a large memory by segmentation.

As long as locations within a given segment are selected, the CPU is effectively dealing with 16-bit addresses. It should be obvious that this arrangement becomes both complex and time wasting whenever it is necessary to hop from one segment to another many times during the execution of a program. Segmentation is used by the Intel 8086 16-bit microprocessor.

Another way of reducing the minimum word length is to store the op-code and operand fields of an instruction in separate memory locations, an approach adopted by virtually all microprocessors. A 16-bit word length allows up to 65 536 different instructions, but no microprocessor or even mainframe really has 65 536 *different* instructions. The majority of CPUs have relatively few basic instructions (20–100 or so). The total of 65 536 unique op-codes is made up of a large number of variations on individual instructions. For example, the 68000 instruction MOVE Di,Dj, where i and j each selects one of eight data registers, has a total of $2^{3+3} = 64$ variations.

During the fetch cycle, the op-code is read from the memory and examined. If an operand is required by the instruction, one or more extra read operations are carried out and an operand formed from a string of consecutive 16-bit words from memory. Consequently, we have, say, a 32-bit instruction stored as two consecutive 16-bit words. Some of the 68000's instructions are 80 bits long and these are stored as five consecutive 16-bit words.

Multilength instructions have two advantages. By using a 16-bit word length, the cost of the system can be greatly reduced, because a 16-bit data highway costs much less than a 32-bit data highway. Moreover, not all instructions need be a full 32 bits long, so that a 16-bit instruction does not waste memory space by occupying a 32-bit word. One of the figures of merit of a computer is the number of bytes it requires to store a particular program. A compact program is clearly better than a long program since it uses less memory. Some instructions, such as MOVE or ADD, require the address of an operand, while other instructions, such as STOP (i.e. stop executing) or NOP (no operation) do not need an operand field. The latter instructions are said to have an *inherent addressing mode*, as the address or value of the operand (if any) is implicit in the instruction.

An example of multilength versus fixed length instructions is provided by Fig. 6.5 and should clarify the above points. The 32-bit fixed-word-length computer, Fig. 6.5(a), is forced to use a 32-bit word even when such a long word is unnecessary, while the 16-bit computer in Fig. 6.5(b) uses 1 or 2 consecutive 16-bit locations to hold a single instruction. Note that this scheme has a built-in disadvantage—reading two 16-bit words from memory takes longer than reading a single 32-bit word. Earlier, when describing the structure of the CPU, we stated that the contents of the program counter were incremented by one during an op-code fetch. If a variable-length instruction is used, the first word of the instruction is

Fig. 6.5 Comparison of (a) 32-bit and (b) 16-bit word length.

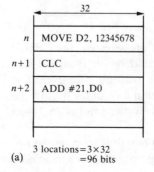

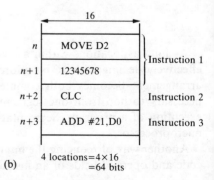

examined during the instruction fetch phase and the program counter incremented by 1, 2, or 3 words, accordingly.

Assembler directives

The lines making up an assembly-language program can be classified into two types: executable statements and assembler directives. An executable statement is an instruction, written in mnemonic form, that the assembler will translate into the machine code of the target microprocessor. An *assembler directive* is a statement that tells the assembler something it needs to know about the program it is assembling. For example, an assembler directive *TTL* means 'title' and the statement TTL Clements informs the assembler that the current program is called 'Clements'. Similarly, the assembler directive *END* indicates to the assembler that the end of the program has been reached and there are no more lines to read. 68000 assemblers reserve the first (i.e. leftmost) column for labels so that any string of characters starting in the first column is interpreted as a symbolic name. One exception is the asterisk. An asterisk in the first column indicates that the remainder of the line is a comment and should be ignored.

Throughout this chapter we will be introducing various executable statements. Here we are going to mention a few of the most important assembly directives used by the 68000 programmer.

EQU The equate directive permits the programmer to equate a symbolic name to a numeric value. If we write Tuesday EQU 3, we can use the symbolic name Tuesday instead of its actual value, 3.

DC The define constant directive permits a constant to be set up and loaded into memory. DC is qualified by .B, .W, .L for 8-bit, 16-bit and 32-bit constants, respectively. The assembler directive DC.B 12,255 would place the values 12 and 255 (i.e. 00001100 and 11111111) in successive memory locations.

DS The define storage directive tells the assembler to reserve memory locations and also takes a .B, .W, or a .L qualifier. For example, LIST DS.L 4 tells the assembler to reserve four consecutive long words in memory and to equate the name of the first word with 'LIST'.

ORG The origin directive tell the assembler to set the program counter to a particular value and is used to define where a program or data is to be located in memory.

The following fragment of a meaningless assembly-language program illustrates the use of some of these assembler directives. Note that we can specify ISO/ASCII characters by enclosing them in quotes. For example, 'Alan' is equivalent to the string of bytes: $41, $6C, $61, $6E.

```
        ORG    $001000        Data starts at location 1000
Buffer  DS.W   24             Save 24 words of storage
POINTER DS.L   1              Save a 32-bit longword
```

```
Date    DC.B    '25 May 1988'       Store the ISO/ASCII string
*                                   32,35,20,4D,41,79,20,31,39,38,38,
*                                   in successive memory locations
*
Test    DC.B    0,12                Store 0 and 12 in successive locations
*
        ORG     $000200             Start of actual program
        LEA     Buffer,A0           ....first executable instruction
        .
        .
        END                         End of program
```

6.1 The 68000's registers

The 68000 is well endowed with registers, at least by comparison with earlier microprocessors. It has eight 32-bit general-purpose data registers, eight 32-bit address registers, an 8-bit condition code register, an 8-bit status byte and a 32-bit program counter. The status byte is not discussed further in this section as it is accessed only by the operating system and is not used during the execution of 'user programs'.

6.1.1 Data registers of the 68000

The programmer's model of the 68000 illustrated in Fig. 6.3 is, effectively, the same as the architecture of the more advanced CPU that we introduced in the previous chapter. The 68000 has eight general-purpose data registers, numbered D0–D7. Any operation that can be applied to Di can also be applied to Dj. In other words, there are no special-purpose data registers reserved for certain types of instruction. Some microprocessors do not permit all instructions to be applied to each of their registers. In these cases, learning assembly language becomes rather like learning to conjugate irregular foreign verbs.

Why has the 68000 got eight data registers? I have heard it said that a CPU should have either one data register (i.e. accumulator) or an infinite number of data registers and nothing in between. The advantage of multiple data registers is that frequently used data can be kept on-chip rather than in the system's main store, in order to speed up the processing. Unfortunately, the provision of multiple registers puts considerable pressure on the assembly-language programmer to remember what data is in what register.

Times have changed and a trend arose in the mid 1980s towards machines with many registers. The RISC I (reduced instruction-set computer) microprocessor designed at Berkeley has over 100 internal registers. Fortunately, the pressure on programmers to allocate data to particular registers has been removed by modern high-level languages that automatically assign data to registers. Although some engineers might program the 68000 in assembly language, very few would ever contemplate programming today's RISC machines in anything other than a high-level language.

The 68000 is limited to eight data registers, mainly because of the number of bits devoted to coding its instructions (i.e. it takes three bits to point to one of eight data registers). As the number of bits allocated to the 68000's instructions is an integer multiple of 16-bit words and most instructions contain the op-code and operand register in a single 16-bit word, any increase in the number of data registers would require a reduction in the number of bits dedicated to the op-code. In other words, there is a trade-off between the number of *different* instructions and the number of registers that can be specified by a given op-code length.

There is little difference between on-chip registers and memory locations as far as the programmer is concerned; both can hold data. However, because registers are on-chip they can be accessed more rapidly than locations inside the main store. Since registers have short addresses (i.e. 0–7) while memory locations may require 32-bit addresses, it is possible to design short instructions to access on-chip registers. For these reasons, it is good practice to keep frequently-used data in registers rather than in memory.

Programmers writing in high-level languages do not have to worry about how data is allocated to registers or to memory, because a compiler performs data allocation automatically (if not optimally). When writing in assembly language, the programmer must decide what data goes in memory and what should be stored in the registers. Any register can be used to hold any variable and what goes where is left entirely up to the programmer. I usually allocate variables in the order D0, D1, etc. Whenever I have a *global* variable (i.e. one that applies to the main program and subroutines called by it), I usually allocate registers starting at D7 and work backwards. For example, I often use D7 as a global error register. This is my personal style and I find it helps me to read my own assembly-language programs. Some assemblers permit data registers to be renamed to reflect the variables they hold. For example, D0 might be renamed 'Monday' and the operation MOVE.B 12,D0 written in the form MOVE.B 12, Monday.

A particularly interesting feature of the 68000 is its ability to perform operations on multi-length operands. As we pointed out in the previous chapter, many of the 68000's operations can be applied to an 8-bit, a 16-bit, or a 32-bit operand and the terms *byte,* *word* and *long word* will be used to refer to 8-bit, 16-bit and 32-bit values, respectively, whenever we refer to the 68000. Up to now, we have used the term *word* to imply a more general unit of data.

The 68000's data registers are written D0–D7 If we wish to refer to an individual *bit,* we write D_{00} to D_{31}. Should we wish to refer to a *bit of a register,* we write, say, D3(12), which is read as bit 12 of D3. More usually, we refer to a range of bits and indicate, for example, bits 8–31, inclusive, of D4 by D4(8:31).

The 68000 assembly language indicates byte, word or longword operations by appending .B, .W or .L, respectively, to a mnemonic. When a byte operation is applied to the contents of a data register, only bits D_{00}–D_{07} of the register are affected. Similarly, a word operation affects bits D_{00}–D_{15} of the register. Note that only the lower-order byte or word of a register is affected by a byte or a word operation. For example, applying a byte operation to data register D1 affects only bits 0–7 and leaves bits 8–31 unchanged. CLR.B D1 has the effect of forcing the contents of D1 to $XXXXXXXXXXXXXXXXXXXXXXXX$00000000, where the Xs represent the old bits of D1 before the CLR.B D1 was executed. If [D1] = \$12345678 *before* the CLR.B D1, [D1] = \$12345600 *after* it.

Some further examples should make the action of byte, word, and long word operations clearer.

```
ADD.L    D0,D1        [D1(0:31)]←[D1(0:31)]+[D0(0:31)]
ADD.W    D0,D1        [D1(0:15)]←[D1(0:15)]+[D0(0:15)]
ADD.B    D0,D1        [D1(0:7)]←[D1(0:7)]+[D0(0:7)]
```

Throughout this text, if the slice of a register is not specified by $(0:m)$, we generally mean the bits of the register appropriate to the operand size (i.e. .B, .W, .L). For example, D3 and D3(0:31) are equivalent when referring to a long word operand. However, the slice notation is not always employed unless I specifically wish to emphasize that we are operating on a slice of a register.

If we assume that the initial contents of D0 and D1 are \$12345678 and \$ABCDEF98, respectively, the ADD operation has the following effects on the contents of D1 and the carry bit, C.

```
ADD.L    D0,D1        results in [D1]=BE024610 and [C]=0
ADD.W    D0,D1        results in [D1]=ABCD4610 and [C]=1
ADD.B    D0,D1        results in [D1]=ABCDEF10 and [C]=1
```

The carry and other bits of the CCR are determined only by the result of operations on bits 0–7 for a byte operation, by the result of operations on bits 0–15 for a word operation, and by the result of operations on bits 0–31 for a long word operation. For example, when adding two byte operands by means of ADD.B D0,D1, the carry out is generated by the addition of D0(7) + D1(7) + Carry_in_to_bit_7.

6.1.2 Address registers of the 68000

We have already seen that the 68000 has eight 32-bit address registers, called A0–A7, that are used as *pointer registers* in the calculation of operand addresses. In fact, it would not be inaccurate to call them *index* or *modifier* registers (although these more general terms are not used by the makers of the 68000). Here we should state that A0–A6 are identical in that whatever we can do to Ai we can also do to Aj. Address register A7 has an *additional* function to those of A0–A6 because A7 is used by the 68000 as a system stack pointer for the storage of subroutine return addresses.

In some ways, the address registers can be used in almost exactly the same fashion as the 68000's data registers. For example, we can move data to or from them and we can add data to them. However, there are a number of important differences between the 68000's address and data registers. First, operations on the address registers do not affect the status of the 68000's condition code register. The 68000's manufacturers have argued that programmers should be allowed to carry out address calculations without modifying the value of the CCR, because the CCR should reflect the status of the CPU due to operations on data. For example, if you are in the process of adding up a series of numbers, you should not have to worry about modifying the CCR every time you have to calculate the address of the next number in the series.

A second feature of the 68000's address registers is that they are available only for word and long word operations. No instruction may operate only on the low-order byte of an address register.

A third and most important feature of the 68000's address registers is that the contents of an address register are considered to be a *single entity* and byte and word divisions are meaningless. It is not difficult to appreciate the logical basis for the decision to treat the contents of an address register as a single entity. If an address register is used to point to the location of an item in memory, the concept of separate and independent fields within the address register is quite meaningless. Moreover, the manufacturers of the 68000 regard all addresses as signed, twos complement values. Consequently, if we perform an operation on the lower-order word of an address register, the sign bit is extended from A_{15} to bits A_{16}–A_{31}. For example, the operation 'load A3 with the 16-bit value $8022' (i.e. MOVEA.W #$8022,A3) has the effect:

[A3]←$FFFF8022.

Similarly, the operation 'load A3 with the 16-bit constant $7022' has the effect:

[A3]←$00007022.

You may find the concept of twos complement and therefore *negative* addresses rather strange (I once did). However, if you think of a positive address as meaning *forward* and a negative address as meaning *backward*, all will soon be clear. Suppose address register A1 contains the value 1280. If address register A2 contains the value −40 (stored as the appropriate twos complement value), adding A1 + A2 to create a composite address results in the value 1240, which is 40 locations *back* from the address pointed at by A1.

Remember that only bits A_{01}–A_{23} of the address registers or the PC can be connected to the address bus. Consequently, bits A_{24}–A_{31} of addresses (but not data!) represent don't care conditions, because they play no role in accessing data in physical memory. Addresses stored in memory are held as two 16-bit consecutive words. It is only when addresses are used to access physical memory that bits A_{24}–A_{31} are disregarded. For example, the operations MOVE D3,$12345678 and MOVE D3,$44345678 have the same effect as far as the hardware of the system is concerned, since the eight most-significant bits of both addresses are not used to select a memory location.

Human ingenuity being what it is, I know of at least one programmer who has turned this disadvantage into an advantage. The programmer argued that address bits A_{24}–A_{31} take no part in accessing data and can therefore be treated as tag bits identifying the type of data being addressed. That is, the eight most-significant bits of an address are coded to reflect the nature of the item being accessed (i.e. its data type such as integer, floating point, ISO/ASCII string, etc.) These eight bits do not appear on the address bus when the corresponding item is accessed from memory and therefore they do not affect the way in which memory is accessed. However, they are used by the software to determine the type of operation that can take place on the associated data. The 68000 does have a true 32-bit address bus and all its address bits take part in the selection of data in memory.

Although many of the operations that can be applied to the contents of data registers can also be applied to the contents of address registers, the designers of assemblers for the 68000 have included some *special* mnemonics for operations on address registers. The following examples illustrate some of these mnemonics. In each case, the destination operand is an *address register.*

```
ADDA.L    D1,A3    ADDA  = add to address register
MOVEA.L   D1,A2    MOVEA = move to an address register
SUBA.W    D1,A3    SUBA  = subtract from an address register
```

Life is often difficult for the assembly-language programmer because some assemblers for the 68000 permit only the use of the ADD mnemonic for both ADD.W A1,D1 and for ADD.W D1,A1. Equally, other assemblers *demand* that the programmer write ADDA.W D1,A1 and will reject ADD.W D1,A1. The purpose of forcing programmers to write MOVEA, ADDA and SUBA instead of MOVE, ADD and SUB when specifying address registers as destinations is to remind them that they are dealing with *addresses* and that these addresses are treated differently to data values (e.g. because of sign-extension). Practical applications of the 68000's address registers are provided when we discuss addressing modes.

6.2 An introduction to the 68000's instruction set

We are now going to describe some of the 68000's assembly-language instructions. In the following section my intention is to demonstrate a few of the things a microprocessor can do, rather than to provide an assembly-language primer. A more detailed definition of the 68000 instruction set is given in Appendix A1.

The 68000's instruction set is more primitive than the average student might imagine, although, in fact, the 68000 represents a great leap forward over eight-bit microprocessors of the 8080, Z80, 6800 and 6502 era. When we say that the 68000 has a relatively simple instruction set, we mean that it is not able to carry out floating point operations directly and that it cannot perform the, say, string matching operations found in editors and text processors. Of course, any complex operation can be implemented in terms of a sequence of primitive machine-code operations, just as a sophisticated computer can be made up of a large number of primitive gates.

6.2.1 Data movement instructions

There are five classes of machine-code instructions: data movement, arithmetic, logical, branch, and control. Data movement involves nothing more complex than copying an item of data from one place to another. It has been reported that 70 per cent of all assembly-language instructions in a typical program perform data (or address) movement. We are going to define some of the 68000's data movement instructions as soon as we have cleared up a few matters of terminology. In order to avoid unnecessary complexity, I have dropped the operand size qualifiers .B, .W and .L from instructions, as we are more interested in what these instructions do rather than in whether the instruction is applied to a byte, word or long word. Assemblers for the 68000 usually permit the programmer to omit the qualifier after an instruction by assuming a default value of .W (i.e. ADD D1, D2 is the same as ADD.W D1,D2). Similarly, I have dropped the notation $Di(0:15)$ whenever it is clear that Di can clearly be interpreted as meaning the 'lower order word' of Di.

All 68000 dual-operand instructions are written in the form **operation source, destination,** where **source** refers to the location of the source operand and **destination** refers to the location of the destination operand. For example, MOVE D3,D4 means put the contents of D3 (i.e. the source operand) in D4 (i.e. the destination operand). The reader should appreciate that some microprocessor assemblers (e.g. the 8086) accept instructions in the form **operation destination, source**!

Typical 68000 data/address movement instructions

```
MOVE   Di,Dj      [Dj]←[Di]
MOVE   M,Di       [Di]←[MS(M)]
MOVE   Di,M       [MS(M)]←[Di]
EXG    Di,Dj      [Dj]←[Di], D[i]←[Dj]
SWAP   Di         [Di(0:15)]←[Di(16:31)],
                  [Di(16:31)]←[Di(0:15)]
LEA    M, Ai      [Ai]←M
```

The operation EXG exchanges the contents of two registers (it is intrinsically a long-word operation). EXG is used to transfer the contents of an address register into a data register and vice versa. SWAP exchanges the upper and lower order words of a given register. LEA (load effective address) loads an address into an address register. That is, LEA M,A2 loads the *address* of M into A2 and not the *contents* of M.

6.2.2 Arithmetic and logical operations

Arithmetic operations are those that act on data as if it were a **numeric** quantity. We have already seen that ADD M,Di adds the contents of memory location M to the contents data register Di and stores the result in Di. Other arithmetic operations implemented by the 68000 are SUB (subtract), DIVU and DIVS (unsigned and signed divide), MULU and MULS (unsigned and signed divide), and NEG (negate). Logic operations are those involving Boolean operations on the bits of a word (e.g. AND, OR, EOR, NOT). The following instructions illustrate some of the arithmetic and logical instructions found on the 68000. Note that [X] represents the contents of the X bit in the CCR and is, for most practical purposes, a copy of the carry bit.

```
ADD  Di,Dj      [Dj]←[Di]+[Dj]
ADDX Di,Dj      [Di]←[Di]+[Dj]+[X]
SUB  Di,Dj      [Dj]←[Dj]-[Di]
SUBX Di,Dj      [Dj]←[Dj]-[Di]-[X]
MULU Di,Dj      [Dj(0:31)]←[Di(0:15)]×[Dj(0:15)]
DIVU Di,Dj      [Dj(0:15)]←[Dj(0:31)]/[Di(0:15)]
                [Dj(16:31)]←remainder
AND  Di,Dj      [Dj]←[Di].[Dj]
OR   Di,Dj      [Dj]←[Di]+[Dj]
EOR  Di,Dj      [Dj]←[Di]⊕[Dj]
NOT  Di         [Di]←[Di]
```

The 68000 has a full complement of both arithmetic and logical shifts operations, which are briefly defined in Fig. 6.6. All a shift operation does

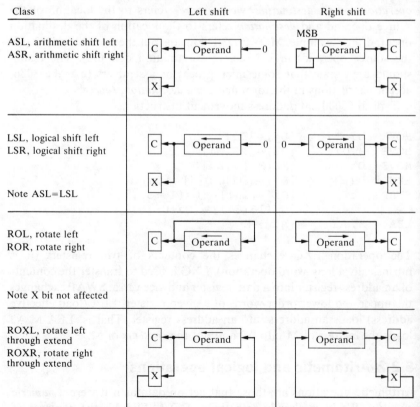

Fig. 6.6 The 68000's shift instructions.

is to move a group of bits one or more places left or right. Logical shifts introduce a zero into the bit position vacated by the shift. Arithmetic shifts treat the data shifted as a signed twos complement value which means that the sign bit is propagated in an arithmetic shift right. Circular shifts treat the data being shifted as a *ring* with the most-significant bit adjacent to the least-significant bit. Circular shifts result in the most-significant bit being shifted into the least-significant bit position (left shift), or vice versa for a right shift.

6.2.3 Branch instructions

The 68000 has fourteen branch instructions of the form B_{cc}, where *cc* is one of 14 possible combinations (e.g. BCC, BCS, BVC, BVS, etc.). Branch instructions are dealt with later and all we need say here is that a branch causes the program to continue execution at a point other than the next instruction in sequence following the current instruction. Without branch instructions we would not be able to implement high-level language constructs such as IF . . . THEN . . . ELSE or DO . . . WHILE.

Two very important program control instructions from the programmer's point of view are BSR, branch to subroutine, and JSR, jump to subroutine. Both these permit a program to call a procedure as we shall see in a later section when we deal with subroutines.

6.2.4 System control instructions

System control instructions cannot be described in any detail here, as they relate to topics not yet introduced. Broadly speaking, control instructions are used by the operating system rather than the applications programmer.

Typical system control instructions set the priorities of interrupt request handlers or they determine the operating status of the processor.

6.3 Applications of some of the 68000's instructions

In order to illustrate the effect of some of the 68000's instructions on actual data, sequences of instructions together with sample data are given in Table 6.1. For simplicity's sake, all operands are byte values. Three data locations, whose symbolic names are NUM1, NUM2, and NUM3, provide two sources and a destination for data taking part in the operations. Some operations are *diadic*, operating on NUM1 and NUM2 to produce NUM3, while others are *monadic*, operating on NUM1 to produce NUM2. Although the actions of all the instructions in Table 6.1 are self-evident, Appendix A1 provides the full definition of all the 68000's instructions. However, we should note that ASL.B #1,D0 means 'shift the lower-order byte in D0 one place left'—the #1 specifies the number 1 (as opposed to address 1). When the contents of a register or memory location are shifted left, a zero enters the least-significant bit position and the most-significant bit is shifted out into the carry bit of the CCR.

Table 6.1 Illustrating the effect of some 68000 instructions

1 Addition	2 Subtraction	3 Logical AND	4 Logical OR
MOVE.B NUM1,D0 ADD.B NUM2,D0 MOVE.B D0,NUM3	MOVE.B NUM1,D0 SUB.B NUM2,D0 MOVE.B D0,NUM3	MOVE.B NUM1,D0 AND.B NUM2,D0 MOVE.B D0,NUM3	MOVE.B NUM1,D0 OR.B NUM2,D1 MOVE.B D0,NUM3

	NUM1	01010101		NUM1	01010101		NUM1	01010101		NUM1	01010101
	NUM2	00010111		NUM2	00010111		NUM2	00010111		NUM2	00010111
	NUM3	01101100		NUM3	00111110		NUM3	00010101		NUM3	01010111

5 Logical EOR	6 Shift left	7 Shift right	8 Rotate left
MOVE.B NUM1,D0 EOR.B NUM2,D0 MOVE.B D0,NUM3	MOVE.B NUM1,D0 ASL.B #1,D0 MOVE.B D0,NUM2	MOVE.B NUM1,D0 LSR.B #1,D0 MOVE.B D0,NUM2	MOVE.B NUM1,D0 ROL.B #1,D0 MOVE.B D0,NUM2

	NUM1	01010101		NUM1	01010101		NUM1	01010101		NUM1	01010101
	NUM2	00010111		NUM2	10101010		NUM2	00101010		NUM2	10101010
	NUM3	01000010									

In each of the eight examples, the sequence of instructions is provided above a memory map of the data acted on by them. Note that the memory maps are those existing after the instructions have been executed.

The 68000, like many other processors, permits certain operations to act on either the contents of a data register, or on the contents of a memory location. In Examples 6–8 in Table 6.1, the shifting operations act on a data register so that the reader can see the *before* and *after* effect, with NUM1 holding the data before the operations, and NUM2 the data after them. In practical programs, operations would be applied directly to memory locations.

Applying logical operations

It is immediately obvious how arithmetic operations are applied to real applications, as everyone is familiar with numerical calculations in everyday life. The application of logical operations is less obvious.

In Chapter 4 we saw how a group of bits can represent the status of devices connected to the computer. The examples provided were pumps, heaters, and valves that were turned on or off by the value of a particular bit in a control word. It is in the manipulation of individual bits within a word that logical operations are needed.

Consider the control of a system with eight single-bit inputs (P,Q,R,S,T,U,V,W), and eight single-bit outputs, (A,B,C,D,E,F,G,H). We are not interested in the details of input/output techniques here and assume that the reading of a memory location whose address is 'INPUT' loads the values of P–W into a data register. Similarly, writing the contents of a data register to memory location 'OUTPUT' has the effect of setting up the eight output bits A–H. The format of the input and output control words is defined in Fig. 6.7.

Suppose that the following control operations must be performed.

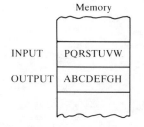

Fig. 6.7 The memory maps of the two input/output ports.

```
IF ((P=1) AND (Q=0)) OR ((P=0) AND (S=1))
  THEN
    BEGIN
      C:=1; E:=0
    END
  ELSE
    BEGIN
      C:=0; E:=1
    END
ENDIF
```

The above action involves the testing of three bits of INPUT (P, Q, and S), and then setting or clearing two bits of OUTPUT (C and E). An important consideration is that the bits of OUTPUT not involved in the algorithm must not be affected in any way by operations on bits C and E. The sequence of instructions shown in Table 6.2 will execute the desired action.

Table 6.2 An example of the application of logical operations

see page 237. for typical branch instruction

	MOVE.B	INPUT,D0	Get input status
	AND.B	#%11000000,D0	Mask out all bits but P and Q
	CMP.B	#%10000000,D0	Test for P=1, Q=0
	BEQ	TRUE	Goto action on test true
	MOVE.B	INPUT,D0	Get input status again
	AND.B	#%10010000,D0	Mask out all bits but P and S
	CMP.B	#%00010000,D0	Test for P=0, S=1
	BEQ	TRUE	Goto action on test true
FALSE	MOVE.B	D0,OUTPUT	Get output control word
	AND.B	#%11011111,D0	Clear bit C
	OR.B	#%00001000,D0	Set bit E
	MOVE.B	D0,OUTPUT	Set up new output control word
	BRA	EXIT	Branch past actions on test true
TRUE	MOVE.B	OUTPUT,D0	Get output control word
	AND.B	#%11110111,D0	Clear bit E
	OR.B	#%00100000,D0	Set bit C
	MOVE.B	D0,OUTPUT	Set up new output control word
EXIT			Continue

The assembly-language symbol '%' means that the following number is to be interpreted by the assembler as a binary value and the symbol '$' means that the following number is interpreted as a hexadecimal value. Once more the advantage of programming in binary (in certain circumstances) is self-evident, as AND.B #%11000000,D0 tells the reader much more than the hexadecimal and decimal forms of the operand: AND.B #$C0,D0 and AND.B #192,D0, respectively.

Remember that the assembly-language symbol '#' (pronounced 'hash') informs the assembler that the following value is not the address of a memory location containing the operand, but the actual operand itself. Thus, AND.B #%11000000,D0 means form the logical AND between the binary value 11000000 and the contents of D0. If we had made a mistake in the program and had written AND.B %11000000,D0 (rather than AND.B #%11000000,D0), the instruction would have the effect of ANDing D0 with the *contents* of memory location %11000000 (i.e. 192). The use of the '#' symbol is called immediate addressing and is dealt with in more detail later in this chapter.

In Table 6.2 the operation 'CMP' causes a comparison to be made between the two operands specified by the instruction and sets the bits of the CCR accordingly. The effect of CMP.B #%00010000,D0 is to compare the contents of D0 with the binary value 00010000, which is done by subtraction (i.e. [D0] − 00010000). The result of the subtraction is discarded, leaving the contents of D0 unaffected by the CMP operation. Only the bits of the CCR are modified. If D0 contains 00010000, the subtraction yields zero, setting the Z (zero) flag of the CCR. The following operation, 'BEQ TRUE', results in a branch to the instruction whose address is labelled 'TRUE'. All 68000 comparison instructions are of the form *CMP source, destination* which results in the comparison of destination with source. Note that the difference between CMP Di,Dj and SUB Di,Dj is that the former simply evaluates Dj–Di and throws away the result, while the latter evaluates Dj–Di and puts the result in Dj.

The label 'FALSE' is a dummy label and is not in any way used by the assembly program. It merely serves as a reminder to the programmer of the action to be taken as a result of the test being false. At the end of this sequence is an instruction 'BRA EXIT'. A BRA (branch) is equivalent to a 'GOTO' in a high-level language and causes a branch round the action taken if the result of the test is true.

6.4 Addressing modes

The subject of addressing modes is concerned with how the address of an operand is calculated by the CPU. Up to this point we have dealt largely with the *absolute addressing* mode in which the actual address in memory of an operand is specified by the instruction, or with *register direct* addressing in which the address of an operand is a register. We are going to introduce other ways of specifying the location of an operand. We now need to introduce a new term, *effective address*, which is a general expression for the address of an operand. The term *effective address* is necessary because the address of an operand can be obtained or *calculated* in several different ways and we require a way of referring to an address that is independent of the way in which we calculate it.

6.4.1 Absolute addressing

In absolute addressing the operand field of the instruction provides the address of the operand in memory. For example, the instruction MOVE 1234,D0 copies the contents of memory location 1234 into data register D0. A few examples of instructions with absolute addresses are given below.

```
MOVE  1234,D0          [D0]←[1234]
MOVE  D0,1234          [1234]←[D0]
MOVE  1234,1224        [1224]←[1234]
ADD   1234,D0          [D0]←[D0]+[1234]
SUB   TEMP,D2          [D2]←[D2]-[TEMP]
```

Note that [1234] means the contents of memory location 1234 and is a short-hand form of [MS(1234)]. Sometimes I shall write [M] and sometimes I shall write [MS(M)] to indicate the contents of memory location M.

In practice, assembly-language programmers seldom use numeric addresses (e.g. 1234) and invariably use symbolic addresses (e.g. DAY_OF_WEEK). For example, in the simple algebraic expression, $x := y + z$, the letters x, y, and z are all symbolic values (as opposed to the actual locations of these variables in memory). We frequently use numeric values as addresses in this chapter, because we are trying to demonstrate what happens when machine-code instructions are executed.

Absolute addressing is used whenever the address of a variable is constant. A constant address implies that the same location in memory will always hold the same variable (e.g. 1234 might always be used to hold a variable TEMP_X). I know that this sounds like a statement of the obvious, but there are occasions when variables are moved about in memory. If you write a program and send it to colleagues to run on their computer, it is possible that they may wish to put the program in a different region of memory. In that case, all absolute addresses referring to the locations of data will have to be changed.

6.4.2 Immediate addressing

Immediate addressing, sometimes called literal addressing, is provided by all computers and microprocessors and allows the programmer to specify a *constant*. The value following the op-code in an instruction is not a reference to the address of an operand but is the actual operand itself. In many assembly languages, the symbol '#' precedes the operand to indicate immediate addressing. Assemblers differ in their conventions—some use '@' to indicate immediate operands. The four instructions below show how absolute and immediate addressing modes are represented in 68000 assembly language and in RTL, respectively.

```
Assembly language form    RTL form              Name
MOVE 1234,D0              [D0]←[1234]           Absolute addressing
MOVE #1234,D0            [D0]←1234             Immediate addressing
ADD  1234,D0             [D0]←[D0]+[1234]      Absolute addressing
ADD  #1234,D0           [D0]←[D0]+1234        Immediate addressing
```

The symbol '#' is not part of the instruction. It is a message to the assembler telling it to select that code for 'move data' that uses the immediate addressing mode. Do not confuse the symbol # with the symbols $ or %. The $ indicates only that the following number is hexadecimal and the % indicates that the following number is binary.

The symbols '$' and '%' are necessary, because most computers cannot deal with subscripts and, therefore, the conventional way of indicating the base by a subscript is impossible. For example, MOVE #25,D0, MOVE #$19,D0 and MOVE #%00011001,D0 have identical effects.

Examples of the application of immediate addressing

Immediate addressing is used whenever the value of the operand taking part in an instruction is known at the time the program is written. That is, it is used to handle constants as opposed to variables. Immediate addressing has the advantage that it is faster than absolute addressing, because only one memory reference is required to read the instruction during the fetch phase. When the operation MOVE #5,D0 is read from memory in a fetch cycle, the operand, 5, is available immediately without a further memory access to location 5 to read the actual operand. Some of the applications of immediate addressing are given below.

1. *As an arithmetic constant*

```
MOVE  NUM,D0        [D0]←[MS(NUM)]
ADD   #22,D0        [D0]←[D0]+22
MOVE  D0,NUM        [MS(NUM)]←[D0]
```

The above sequence results in the data in memory location NUM being increased by 22. That is, [NUM]←[NUM]+22. Actually, the 68000 can add an immediate operand to a memory location directly without using a data register by means of the ADDI (add immediate) instruction. The instruction, ADDI #22,NUM adds the constant value 22 to the contents of the location NUM.

2. *In a comparison with a constant.* Consider the test on a variable, NUM, to determine whether it lies in the range $7 < \text{NUM} < 25$.

```
        MOVE    NUM,D0     Get NUM in D0
        CMP     #8,D0      Compare it with 8
        BMI     FALSE      IF negative NUM≤7
        CMP     #25,D0     Compare it with 25
        BPL     FALSE      IF positive NUM>24
TRUE    ...
          .
          .
          .
FALSE   ...
```

3. *As a method of terminating loop structures.* A typical loop structure is illustrated in both BASIC and Pascal below.

```
BASIC                    Pascal
10 FOR I=1 TO N          FOR I:=1 TO N DO
 .                       BEGIN
 .
 .                         .
50 NEXT I                  .
                           .
                         END;
```

The above construct may readily be translated into 68000 assembly language. The loop counter is stored in data register D0.

```
           MOVE     #1,D0          Load D0 with initial value of I (=loop counter)
NEXT       ...                     Start of loop
           .                       Body of loop
           .                       .
           .                       .
           ADD      #1,D0          Increment loop counter
           CMP      #N+1,D0        End of loop test
           BNE      NEXT           IF not end THEN repeat loop.
```

At the end of the loop, the counter is incremented by the instruction ADD #1,D0. The counter, D0, is then compared with its terminal value by CMP #N+1,D0. Note that the comparison is with $N+1$, because the counter is incremented before it is tested. On the last time round the loop, I becomes $N+1$ after incrementing and the branch to NEXT is not taken, allowing the loop to be exited. The same loop construct can be written in a much more elegant fashion. At this point in the text we are interested only in the application of immediate addressing as a means of setting up counters.

6.4.3 Self-modifying code

Up to now we have dealt with fixed addresses that do not change during the execution of a program. In the next section we look at address register indirect addressing that allows the programmer to specify addresses not known at the time the program is written (e.g. the nth location in a table or a list). Before we deal with register indirect addressing, it is worthwhile demonstrating that without it a programmer's life would be very difficult. That is, I intend to show that it is difficult to access data structures such as tables or lists unless the computer is provided with some way of changing addresses *during* the execution of a program. We know how to add together several numbers. Now imagine adding together one hundred numbers stored in consecutive locations. The following fragment of program demonstrates a possible, but highly impractical, approach.

```
MOVE    NUM1,D0      Put first number in D0
ADD     NUM2,D0      Add second number to D0
ADD     NUM3,D0      Add third number to running total
  .
  .
  .
ADD     NUM99,D0     Add in 99th number
ADD     NUM100,D0    Add in last number
```

Clearly, there has to be a better solution to this problem. What we want is an instruction that will add in number 1 when we execute it the first time, number 2 when we execute it the second time, and number i when we execute it the ith time.

One way out of this tedious approach is to resort to a self-modifying program. I must point out that the use of self-modifying programs is extremely bad practice and is something that no programmer should ever resort to. It is even worse than using the wrong knife at a banquet. I introduce the idea of self-modifying code here only to demonstrate a primitive form of address modification. Readers who do not wish to learn about how variable addresses can be created by modifying instructions in memory can jump ahead to Section 6.4.4.

The following is an example of self-modifying code.

```
          TTL     SELFMOD
NUM1      EQU     $002000
NUM2      EQU     $002002
          ORG     $001000
          MOVE    #99,D0          [D0]←99
          MOVE    NUM1,D1         [D1]←[NUM1]
*
LOOP      ADD     NUM2,D1         [D1]←[D1]+[NUM2]
          ADD     #2,LOOP+2       [LOOP+2]←[LOOP+2]+2
          SUB     #1,D0           [D0]←[D0]-1
          BNE     LOOP            IF Z≠0 THEN [PC]←LOOP
                                  (i.e. branch on non-zero to LOOP)
```

The key to this program is the two instructions 'ADD NUM2,D1' and 'ADD #2,LOOP + 2'. The first instruction adds the contents of memory location NUM2 to the contents of D1 (which initially contains NUM1). The following instruction increments the contents of memory location 'LOOP + 2', which is two bytes on from the location marked by the label 'LOOP'. Here we are operating on the *instruction* 'ADD NUM2,D1' (hence the expression 'self-modifying code'). Adding 2 to the memory location specified by LOOP + 2 adds 2 to the operand field of the instruction ADD NUM2,D1. That is, the *address* of the operand is modified from NUM2 to NUM2 + 2, which is, of course, NUM3. In this way, 'NUM2' gets added to NUM1 99 times, but on each occasion we have a different 'NUM2', because it has been altered by the operation ADD #2,LOOP + 2. Remember that we add *two* to the operand field of ADD NUM2,D1, because the 100 16-bit numbers are stored in consecutive even addresses ($002000, $002002, $002004, . . .). Figure 6.8 illustrates the memory map of a system, written in 68000 machine code, that will implement the above program.

The program resides at memory locations $001000 to $001014, and the 100 numbers are stored in the range $002000 to $0020C7. It should now be clear that the instruction ADD #2,LOOP + 2 (06780002100A) causes the pointer to NUM2 (initially $002002) to be incremented, so that the next number to be added is in location $002004. Note also that the instruction BNE LOOP has a branch address 'F2'. The twos complement value $F2 represents − 14 and tells the computer to branch back 14 bytes from the current value of the PC. We shall discuss this further when we come to relative addressing.

There are several arguments against self-modifying code. Self-modify-

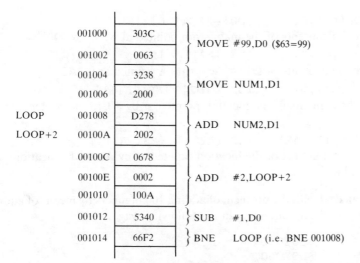

001000	303C
001002	0063

MOVE #99,D0 ($63=99)

001004	3238
001006	2000

MOVE NUM1,D1

LOOP 001008 | D278

LOOP+2 00100A | 2002

ADD NUM2,D1

00100C	0678
00100E	0002
001010	100A

ADD #2,LOOP+2

001012 | 5340 } SUB #1,D0

001014 | 66F2 } BNE LOOP (i.e. BNE 001008)

Fig. 6.8 The memory map of a self-modifying program.

ing code cannot (for obvious reasons) be placed in permanent read-only memory (ROM). More importantly, a bug in a self-modifying program is likely to prove disastrous. If an op-code is accidentally modified (instead of an operand) the program will almost certainly crash (i.e. run wild). Yet another argument against the use of self-modifying code is its almost total incomprehensibility to the reader. A program relying on self-modifying code is exceedingly difficult for anyone other than its author to follow, and even the author can have difficulties.

6.4.4 Address register indirect addressing

Address register indirect addressing provides a neat solution to the above problem in which we wanted to add together a large series of numbers. Address register indirect addressing is so called because it uses an address register to point at the location of the operand in memory. We should note here that some other texts call this addressing mode 'indexed addressing' or 'modifier based addressing'. However, the manufacturers of the 68000 reserve the term 'indexed addressing' to indicate a particular variant of address register indirect addressing in which the effective address of an operand is calculated by adding the contents of *two* modifier registers, as we shall see later.

In address register indirect addressing, the operand field of an instruction holds the address of the address register (i.e. A0–A7) to be used in calculating the true address of the operand. The *actual* address of the operand is given by the contents of the address register specified in the instruction. For example if the instruction is CLR (A0), and [A0] = 10, the contents of memory location 10 are cleared. That is, in address register indirect addressing the effective address of an operand is provided by the contents of the address register specified by the instruction.

Address register indirect addressing is indicated to the 68000 assembler by enclosing the address register in parentheses. The following instructions illustrate this addressing mode and provide RTL definitions for the action to be carried out, together with a plain language description.

```
MOVE (A0),D0        [D0]←[MS([A0])]
```
Move the contents of the main store pointed at by A0 to D0
```
MOVE D1,(A2)        [MS([A2])]←[D1]
```
Move the contents of D1 to the location pointed at by A2
```
ADD  (A1),D2        [D2]←[D2]+[MS([A1])]
```
Add the contents of the location pointed at by A1 to the contents of D2
```
MOVE (A1),(A2)      [MS([A2])]←[MS([A1])]
```
Move the contents of the location pointed at by A1 to the location pointed at by A2

We can deal with the problem of adding 100 numbers by means of address register indirect addressing in the following way.

```
          ORG     $001000
NUM1      EQU     $002000
          CLR     D0          D0 is the number counter
          MOVEA   #NUM1,A0    A0 points to the first number
          CLR     D1          Clear the total in D1
LOOP      ADD     (A0),D1     Add in the number pointed at by A0
          ADDA    #2,A0       Point to the next number in the list
          ADD     #1,D0       Increment the number counter
          CMP     #100,D0     Have we added the 100 numbers?
          BNE     LOOP        If not then repeat
```

A more general form of the 68000's address register indirect addressing mode is its **_address register indirect addressing mode with displacement._** In this case, the effective address of an operand is calculated by adding the contents of the address register specified by the instruction to the signed twos complement offset that also forms part of the instruction. Figure 6.9 illustrates how the effective address is calculated.

In terms of register-transfer language, the operation:
MOVE d16(A0),D0 is written: $[D0]\leftarrow[MS(d16+[A0])]$. The number 'd16' is a 16-bit twos complement value in the range $-32K$ to $32K$, which indicates how far the operand is from the location pointed at by A0.

Now that we have defined address register indirect addressing, let's apply it to the addition of the hundred numbers:

```
NUM1      EQU     $002000
NUM2      EQU     NUM1+2
          ORG     $001000
          MOVEA   #0,A0       [A0]←0
          MOVE    NUM1,D0     [D0]←[MS(NUM1)]
LOOP      ADD     NUM2(A0),D0 [D0]←[D0]+[MS(NUM2+[A0])]
          ADDA    #2,A0       [A0]←[A0]+2
          CMPA    #198,A0     [A0]-198 note 99 words=198 bytes
          BNE     LOOP        IF Z≠0 THEN [PC]←LOOP
```

In the example above, we add to the contents of D0 the contents of the memory location whose address is NUM2 plus the number in the address register A0. Initially, [A0]=0, so that NUM2 is the first operand. When

MOVE $d16(A0),D0

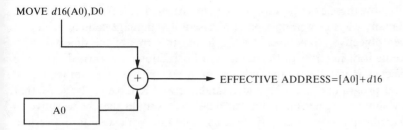

EFFECTIVE ADDRESS=[A0]+$d16$

Consider the instruction MOVE.B $25(A0),D0,
where the contents of address register A0 are $76.

Fig. 6.9 An illustration of address register indirect addressing with displacement.

MOVE.B $25(A0),D0

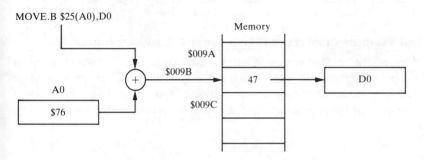

the loop is repeated a second time, the number in address register A0 is 2, and the operand at location NUM2 + 2 (i.e. NUM3) is picked up.

A real 68000 programmer would never write the above fragment of code because it is so inefficient! The following few lines of code demonstrate how the algorithm is more likely to be written. The effect of ADD (A0) + ,D0 is to add the contents of the memory location pointed at by A0 to the contents of D0 and then to increment the contents of A0 by the size of the item being accessed. In this case A0 is incremented by 2 since D0 is a word operand.

Each time this instruction is used, A0 is automatically modified to point to the next item in memory. We shall meet this addressing mode again. The instruction DBRA D1,LOOP subtracts 1 from the contents of D1 and branches back to the instruction labelled by 'LOOP'. If, however, D1 is decremented and goes from 0 to − 1, the loop is not taken and the next instruction in sequence is executed. DBRA is read as 'decrement and branch'. Because the branch terminates on − 1 rather than 0, loading Di with N causes DBRA Di,LOOP to execute $N + 1$ times. Note that the LEA NUM1,A0 instruction loads the address register with the specified effective address (i.e. NUM1). We can now add the sequence of numbers using only five instructions.

```
        LEA     NUM1,A0     A0 points at list of numbers
        CLR     D0          Clear the total
        MOVE    #99,D1      Set up the counter for 100 cycles
LOOP    ADD     (A0)+,D0    Add in a number and move pointer to next
        DBRA    D1,LOOP     Repeat until all numbers added
```

By now these examples will have demonstrated at least one thing: there are many ways of writing a piece of assembly-language code to achieve a given objective. Sometimes it is inefficient in terms of the time taken to execute it or in terms of the number of instructions. Be warned that pure efficiency is not always the only criterion by which a program is judged! Good programs should be understandable and reliable in the sense that they should not be full of hidden bugs. Nor should they be sensitive to particular patterns of data (i.e. they should not work well until a certain input causes them to fail and give unpredictable results). There are many large programs that cost more to maintain (i.e. fixing the bugs as they are discovered) than the hardware on which the programs run.

An example of address register indirect addressing

One of the most common of all mathematical calculations (because it crops up in many different areas) is the evaluation of the scalar product (or inner product) of two vectors. Suppose A and B are two n-component vectors, the inner product S, of A and B is given by

$$S = \sum_{i=1}^{n} a_i b_i = a_1 b_1 + a_2 b_2 + \cdots + a_n b_n.$$

Consider the case in which the components of A and B are 16-bit integers.

```
        TTL     SCALAR          Name of program
        ORG     $002000         Origin of data
S       DS      1               Reserve a word for the product
VEC1    DS      $10             Reserve 16 words for Vector₁
VEC2    DS      $10             Reserve 16 words for Vector₂
N       EQU     $10             16 components (n=16)
        ORG     $001000         Origin of program
        CLR     D0              [D0]←0
        SUBA    A0,A0           [A0]←0
LOOP    MOVE    VEC1(A0),D1     [D1]←[[A0]+VEC1]
        MULU    VEC2(A0),D1     [D1]←[D1]×[[A0]+VEC2]
        ADD     D1,D0           [D0]←[D0]+[D1]
        ADDA    #2,A0           [A0]←[A0]+2
        CMPA    #2*N,A0         [A0]-2N note N words=2N bytes
        BNE     LOOP            IF Z≠0 THEN [PC]←LOOP
        MOVE    D0,S            [S]←[D0]
```

Note that the instruction MULU ⟨ea⟩,Di has the effect of multiplying the 16-bit word at the effective address specified by ⟨ea⟩ by the 16-bit contents of Di(0:15). The 32-bit product is loaded into Di(0:31). MULU operates on unsigned values and is interesting because it uses two 16-bit source operands and yields a 32-bit destination operand. As the 68000 lacks any clear address register instruction, we are forced to use either MOVEA #0,A0 or the faster SUBA A0,A0 to clear A0. One last point of interest is that many assemblers permit expressions such as '2*N' which are automatically evaluated and the correct literal stored in the instruction.

Address register indirect addressing can also be used with jump instructions. For example, we can write JMP (A0) which means jump to the address whose value is in A0. In RTL terms, JMP (Ai) is defined as [PC]←[Ai]. This indirect jump instruction permits the programmer to specify a location dynamically (i.e. at run time) and is used in conjunction with jump tables.

Variations on a theme

The 68000 supports two important variations on address register indirect addressing. One variation is called *address register indirect addressing with autoincrementing* and the other is called *address register indirect addressing with autodecrementing*.

An important application of address register indirect addressing is the sequential accessing of tables of information. If we access an item of data by a MOVE (Ai),Dj instruction, the next item (i.e. word) in the table can be accessed by first updating the address pointer, Ai, by ADDA #2,Ai and then repeating the MOVE (Ai),Dj. Clearly, it would be sensible to combine these two instructions in order to reduce the size of the program. The 68000 supports an automatic post-increment mode which permits an address register to be incremented after it has been used in the address register indirect addressing mode. This addressing mode is indicated by writing a '+' after (Ai) to give (Ai)+. The following are examples of address register indirect addressing with post-incrementing:

```
ADD   (A2)+,D2        [D2]←[D2]+[MS([A2])]; [A2]←[A2]+2
MOVE  D0,(A1)+        [MS([A1])]←[D0]; [A1]←[A1]+2
CLR   (A0)+           [MS([A0])]←0; [A0]←[A0]+2
MOVE  (A2)+,A(3)+     [MS([A2])]←[MS([A3])]; [A2]←[A2]+2;
                      [A3]←[A3]+2
```

The pointer register is automatically incremented by 1 for byte operands, 2 for word operands and 4 for long-word operands. Consider the following examples:

```
MOVE.B (A0)+,D5       [D5(0:7)]←[MS([A0])]; [A0]←[A0]+1
MOVE.L (A0)+,D5       [D5(0:31)]←[MS([A0])]; [A0]←[A0]+4
```

Similarly, the 68000 also provides an automatic pre-decrementing mode. In this case the assembly-language form of the effective address is −(Ai), and the contents of Ai are decremented *before* they are used to access the operand at the address pointed at by Ai. As above, the pre-decrement is by 1, 2 or 4, depending on whether the operand is a byte, word or longword, respectively. Note that both pre-decrementing and post-incrementing addressing modes do not permit the use of an offset in the calculation of an effective address. To make this clear, we present some sample 68000 instructions below. Some of these represent legal and some represent illegal addressing modes:

```
ADD    (A2)-,D2       Illegal—post-decrementing not allowed
MOVE   D0,12(A1)+     Illegal—offset (i.e. 12) not allowed
MOVE   -(A2),(A3)+    Legal
SUB    D3,+(A4)       Illegal—pre-incrementing not allowed
CMP    (A6)+,D3       Legal
```

It should be noted that pre-decrementing and post-incrementing are complementary operations in the sense that 'one undoes the other'. For example, suppose we use MOVE D3, − (A2) to store the contents of D3 in a stack in memory. MOVE D3, − (A2) decrements A2 and then copies D3 to the top of the stack pointed at by A2. After this instruction has been executed, A2 is pointing to the top item on the stack. If later we wish to remove D3 from the stack and put it in D5, we can execute MOVE (A2) + ,D5. Note that we must use **post-incrementing** to leave A2 pointing to the new top item on the stack.

Indexed addressing

The 68000 has another variant on the address register indirect addressing mode called **indexed addressing**, which uses two registers to calculate the effective address of an operand. The assembly-language form of the effective address is written '$d8(Ai,Xj)$', where $d8$ is an eight-bit signed constant forming part of the instruction, Ai is one of the eight address registers, and Xi is either one of D0–D7 or A0–A7. The effective address is calculated from the expression $d8 + [Ai] + [Xi]$. A typical instruction using this addressing mode might look like CLR 28(A3,D6) and has the effect $[MS(28 + [A3] + [D6])] \leftarrow 0$ (i.e. clear the contents of the location whose address effective address is given by the contents of A3 plus the contents of D6 plus 28).

Although indexed addressing looks complex, it is really a modest variation on address register indirect addressing. All that has been changed is that the effective address is given by the contents of **two** modifier registers. An important application of indexed addressing is in the accessing of two-dimensional tables in which the location of an element is specified by its row position and its column position.

A simple example of indexed addressing is provided by a data structure representing the days of the week. Suppose the structure consists of a number of weeks, each of which is divided into seven days. An item of data is accessed by locating the head of the data structure, counting off the appropriate number of weeks and then accessing the required day. If the location of the array in memory is DIARY and we wish to access the location corresponding to Tuesday of week five, we need to access location DIARY + (5 − 1)*7 + Tuesday (where Tuesday = 2) = DIARY + 28 + 2 = DIARY + 30.

The data structure can be accessed using indexed addressing by loading A0 with DIARY, D0 with the location of the start of the desired week, and then using the desired day as a constant as demonstrated in the following fragment of code.

```
SUNDAY      EQU   0
MONDAY      EQU   1
TUESDAY     EQU   2
WEDNESDAY   EQU   3
  .
  .

            LEA   DIARY,A0              A0 points to head of structure
            MOVE  WEEK, D0             D0 contains week number
            SUB   #1,D0               Calculate (Week −1)*7
            MULU  #7,D0               D0 now contains number of days
            MOVE  TUESDAY(A0,D0),D1   Access the required item
```

6.4.5 Relative addressing

The relative addressing mode is similar to address register indirect addressing in the sense that the effective address of an operand is given by the contents of a register plus an offset. As before, the offset is part of the instruction and follows the op-code. However, in the case of relative addressing, the register used to calculate the effective address is the **program counter** itself. Thus, the location of the operand is specified relative to the current instruction. If we denote relative addressing by means of '(PC)', the operation **load data register D0 relative** is written:

MOVE $d16$(PC),D0

and is defined in RTL as: $[D0] \leftarrow [MS([PC] + d16)]$. As before, $d16$ is a 16-bit twos complement offset.

Figure 6.10 demonstrates the relationship between the PC, the instruction and the operand address.

Relative addressing is important because it allows the programmer to write position-independent code, PIC. That is, the machine-code version of a program is independent of the actual physical location of the program in memory. PIC enables programs to be moved about in memory

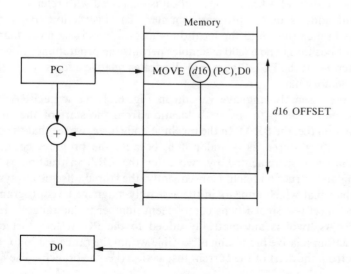

Fig. 6.10 Relative addressing.

(relocated) without modifications being made to them. For example, 'MOVE 36(PC),D0' means store the contents of D0 36 locations on from this instruction. It does not matter where the operation 'MOVE 36(PC),D0' lies in memory, because the data associated with it will always be stored in the 36th location following the instruction.

The 68000 permits the use of relative addressing for source operands, but not for destination operands! For example, MOVE $d16(PC)$,D3 or ADD $d16(PC)$,D2 are legal 68000 instructions, whereas MOVE D3,$d16(PC)$ and ADD D2,$d16(PC)$ are illegal instructions. Fortunately, we can get round the problem of writing completely position-independent code for the 68000 by loading the address of the operand into an address register using position-independent code and then using address register indirect addressing. To achieve this we use the LEA (load effective address) instruction that we defined earlier. That is, we can write the following:

```
LEA.L   VALUE_1(PC),A0   Calculate the relative address of
.                        VALUE_1 and store it in A0
.
.
.
MOVE    D2,(A0)          Store D2 at address pointed at by A0
.
MOVE    (A0),D3          Move the word pointed at by A0 to D3
.
.
.
VALUE_1 DS      1        Reserve one word of memory for data
```

It is important to note that when the instruction LEA VALUE_1(PC),A0 is assembled, the assembler takes the value of VALUE_1 and subtracts the current value of the program counter from it to evaluate the offset required by the instruction.

Virtually all microprocessors have a relative branching mode in which the destination of a branch instruction is expressed with reference to the current address in the program counter. The instruction 'BRA *+6' means branch (jump) to the location whose address is six more than the current position (The 68000 assembler permits the programmer to write a * to represent the PC). Figure 6.11 illustrates relative addressing in terms of a memory map.

In the assembly-language version in Fig. 6.11, we write BRA *+6, which means jump to the sixth location from the start of the current instruction (i.e. the BRA). In the machine-code form, we see that the offset (i.e. *+6) is stored as 4 and not 6, because the program counter is automatically incremented by two after the BRA instruction is read during an instruction fetch. Consequently, the stored offset is always two less than that which appears in the assembly-language level program.

The offset is a signed twos complement number in the range −128 to +127. As 'two' is automatically added to the PC at the start of an instruction, relative branching is possible within the range −126 to +129 bytes from the start of the current instruction (i.e. the branch). The 68000

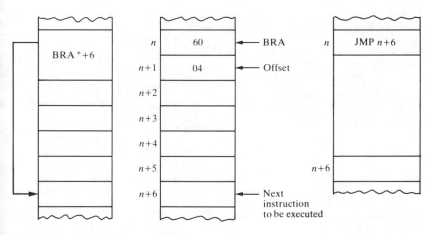

Fig. **6.11** Relative branching.

Assembly-language form. Offset=6 because the destination is 6 bytes from the start of the current instruction.

Machine-code form. Stored offset=4. because the destination is 4 bytes from the end of the current instruction.

Equivalent form without using the relative addressing mode. The JMP instruction uses the actual address of the destination $n+6$.

supports two modes of relative branching: a short branch with an 8-bit offset that provides a range of -126 to $+129$ bytes, and a long branch with a 16-bit offset that provides a range of $-32K$ to $32K$ bytes. Fortunately, the programmer does not usually have to worry too much about short and long branches! Most assemblers automatically provide the correct form. Two modes exist only because most branches are less than 128 bytes and the resulting short branch can be coded with less bits to make the program run faster.

Figure 6.11 also illustrates the importance of relative branching in the production of position-independent code. The program containing the instruction BRA *+6 can be relocated merely by moving it in memory, but the program containing JMP $N+6$ must be modified if it is relocated. An example of relative branching is provided by the program of Fig. 6.12 in which a block of data is moved from one region of memory to another. The first location of the block to be moved is 'FROM', and the first location of its destination is 'TO'. The number of words to be moved is given by 'SIZE'.

Remember that the programmer does not normally have to worry about the calculation of relative branch offsets as the assembler performs this process automatically. For example, in Fig. 6.12, the instruction 'BNE REPEAT' causes a branch backwards to instruction 'MOVE (A0)+,(A1)+' in the event of the zero bit in the CCR not being set. From the memory map of Fig. 6.12, we see that the address of the branch operation is $001010 and the address of the operation 'MOVE (A0)+,(A1)+' is $00100C. We therefore have to branch four locations from the start of the 'BNE', or 6 locations from the end of the 'BNE'. As the CPU always increments the PC by 2 at the start of a branch, the stored offset is -6. In twos complement form this is $FA.

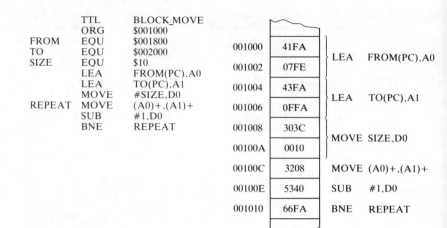

Fig. 6.12 An example of relative addressing.

6.4.6 Indirect addressing

In absolute, or direct addressing, the location of the operand required by an instruction is provided by the address following the op-code and this address is the effective address of the operand. In indirect addressing the effective address of the operand is given by the contents of the memory location pointed at by the address following the op-code. In other words, the instruction provides the address of the address of the data. Figure 6.13 illustrates this concept with the instruction MOVE [22],D0. Square brackets are frequently used by assemblers to denote the indirect addressing mode. The 68000 does not support indirect addressing, although the newer and more powerful 68020 does. Therefore, MOVE [22],D0 is a hypothetical 68000 instruction, introduced for teaching purposes.

The instruction MOVE [22],D0 causes the processor to read the contents of location 22 to get the address of the operand (i.e. 25). Location 25 contains the number 17, which is the actual value loaded into D0. MOVE [22],D0 is represented in RTL terms by

$$[D0]\leftarrow[MS([MS(22)])]$$
or $\qquad$ $[D0]\leftarrow[[22]]$

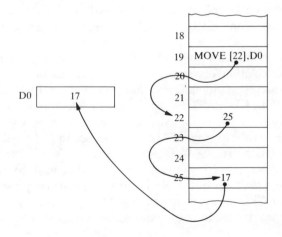

Fig. 6.13 Indirect addressing.

Indirect addressing may be thought of as part of a natural progression starting with immediate addressing. Below are the RTL definitions of immediate addressing, absolute addressing, and indirect addressing. I have also included 'indirect indirect addressing' to show that the process can be continued indefinitely.

Addressing mode	Assembly language form	RTL form
Immediate	MOVE #VALUE,DO	[DO] ← VALUE
Absolute	MOVE ADDRESS,DO	[DO] ← [ADDRESS]
Indirect	MOVE [ADDRESS],DO	[DO] ← [[ADDRESS]]
Indirect indirect	MOVE [[ADDRESS]],DO	[DO] ← [[[ADDRESS]]]
And so on		

From the above definition of indirect addressing, it should be apparent that indexed addressing is really a form of indirect addressing, because the index register contains the address of the operand. In fact, indirect addressing is not provided on all microprocessors because it is not absolutely necessary if indexed addressing is available. Of course, indirect addressing gives the programmer an almost unlimited number of index registers.

Indirect addressing allows the calculation of addresses at run-time during the execution of a program. The following program shows how indirect addressing is used to add together 100 numbers. Remember that this program cannot be run on a 68000 microprocessor, because the general form of indirect addressing is not available.

```
          TTL     EXAMPLE
          ORG     $002000           Data origin
POINTER   DC.L    NUMB              POINTER to address of list of numbers
NUMB      DS.W    100               Reserve 100 words for the numbers
          ORG     $001000           Origin of program
          CLR     D1                Clear total
NEXT_ONE  ADD     [POINTER],D1      Add in the number pointed at
          ADD.L   #2,POINTER        Increment the pointer
          CMP     #NUMB+200,POINTER Test for end of list
          BNE     NEXT_ONE          Continue until all added in
```

This program is intended only to illustrate the application of indirect addressing. I have assumed that the word length is sufficient to deal with the sum of the numbers without overflow. The only instruction in the above program not available on the 68000 is ADD [POINTER],D1.

In this program the variable called POINTER contains the address of the first number to be added to the total in D1. Initially, POINTER is set to $2004, the address of the first number in the list by means of the assembler directive POINTER DC.L NUMB, where NUMB is the address of the first item in the list of 100 numbers. After each number in the list is added to the total in D1 by 'ADD [POINTER],D1', the value of POINTER is incremented by two. When the contents of POINTER have increased by 200 (i.e. one hundred 2-byte words), the addition is complete.

6.4.7 68000 addressing modes summary

Addressing modes cause students more problems than any other aspect of assembly-language programming. These addressing modes are not really all that complex and simply tell the computer where to find the data it needs. Here, we are going to provide a short summary of the 68000's addressing modes to provide a unified picture of how they all fit together.

1. Data or address register direct

The address of an operand is specified by a data or address register. The data taking part in the operation is in the specified register. For example, MOVE D3,D4 means [D3]←[D4] and MOVEA.L D3,A2 means [A2]←[D3]. Main store is not accessed by this addressing mode.

2. Immediate addressing

The actual operand forms part of the instruction and is indicated to the assembler by a '#' symbol. For example, MOVE #123,D4 means [D4]←123. Immediate addressing is used to specify a constant that does not vary while the program is running.

3. Absolute addressing

In absolute addressing the operand is specified by its actual location in the main store. For example, MOVE D3,1234 means [MS(1234)]←[D3]. Absolute addressing is used to specify variables. In a real program, the address '1234' would normally be referred to by a symbolic name. Although programmers of early 8-bit microprocessors of the 8080 or 6800 vintage relied heavily on absolute addressing, today's 68000 programmers use it relatively infrequently. There is nothing intrinsically wrong with this addressing mode, but it does not permit position-independent code. Absolute addressing cannot be used to access elements in data structures such as arrays, lists, and tables.

4. Address register indirect addressing

In address register indirect addressing, the address of the desired operand is stored in one of the 68000's eight address registers. This addressing mode is indicated to the assembler by enclosing the register in round brackets (e.g. (A3) or (A0)). The instruction MOVE (A0),D3 means read the contents of address register A0, use the number found in A0 to access memory and then move the data at that address to D3. In terms of register-transfer language, MOVE (A0),D3 is defined as [D3]←[MS([A0])]. The 68000 supports a number of variations on address register indirect addressing.

(a) Address register indirect with an offset

We frequently wish to access data whose location is expressed with respect to some datum which is in an address register. That is, the effective address of the operand is given by the contents of the address register specified by the instruction plus an offset forming part of the instruction. For example, suppose A0 points to the start of a table with 20 entries and we wish to access the seventh entry. We could execute the following code to do this:

```
ADDA     #7,A0     Move A0 seven bytes onward
MOVE.B   (A0),D1   Get the desired entry
```

Unfortunately, there is a flaw in this scheme. After the operation has been carried out, the contents of A0 no longer point to the head of the data structure. A better approach is to use an offset to point to the desired entry in the data structure:

```
MOVE.B   7(A0),D1 Get the item seven bytes on from A0
```

In address register indirect addressing with offset, the effective address of an operand is written in assembly-language form as $d16(Ai)$, where $d16$ is a 16-bit twos complement offset and Ai is a pointer register. The location of the operand is given by $[MS([Ai] + d16)]$.

(b) Address register indirect with post-incrementing

Address register indirect with post-incrementing is identical to plain address register indirect addressing, except that the address register used to generate the effective address is incremented *after* it has been used to access the operand. Automatic post-incrementing allows us to step through a table of sequential elements *without* having to increment the pointer register 'manually'. The effect of the single instruction MOVE.B (A3)+,D2 and the pair of instructions MOVE (A3),D2 and ADDA #1,A3 is identical.

The amount by which the address register is incremented after it has been used is automatically selected as 1, 2, or 4, depending on whether the operand accessed was a byte, a word or a long word, respectively. In other words, the address register steps through the memory in units of a byte, word or long word according to the nature of the data.

In the next section, it is demonstrated that this addressing mode can be used to retrieve an item of data from the stack pointed at by the address register.

(c) Address register indirect with pre-decrementing

Address register indirect with pre-decrementing is identical to address register indirect with post-incrementing except that the address register is *decremented before* the operand is accessed.

For example, the instruction MOVE.B −(A0),D3 is identical to the instruction pair SUBA #1,A0 and MOVE (A0),D3. This addressing mode is used to step through tables in the *reverse* way from address register indirect with post-incrementing.

(d) Indexed addressing

Indexed addressing permits the programmer to specify the effective address of an operand as the contents of two registers and a constant offset. One of the register pair must be an address register and the other may be an address register or a data register. The assembly-language form of the effective address is written $d8(Ai,Aj)$ or $d8(Ai,Dj)$, where $d8$ is an 8-bit twos complement value in the range -128 to $+127$. The operand accessed by this addressing mode is expressed in RTL as $[MS([Ai]+[Xj]+d8)]$, where Xj is either Aj or Dj.

Indexed addressing can be used to access two-dimensional tables with one register being used to calculate a row position and the other a column position. Equally, one register can be used to point to a region of data and the other used to hold the address of the desired operand from the start of this table.

5. Relative addressing

Relative addressing or, more properly, program counter relative addressing permits the programmer to specify the address of an operand with respect to the current contents of the program counter. The assembly language form of a relative address is $d16(PC)$, where $d16$ is a 16-bit signed constant. The operand accessed by this addressing mode is $[MS([PC]+d16)]$.

Relative addressing is important to the 68000 programmers because it enables them to write position-independent code. As all operands are specified with respect to the PC, it means that a section of code can be located anywhere within memory *without* having to recalculate addresses. Relative addressing generally replaces the absolute addressing mode.

Strangely enough, the 68000 is not able to specify destination operands by means of relative addressing, which means that ADD 1234(PC),D3 is a legal instruction, while ADD D3,1234(PC) is not! Programmers may overcome this limitation by first calculating the relative address of an operand by means of a load effective address instruction (LEA), and then using address register indirect addressing with the effective address in the address register. That is, we can write LEA 1234(PC),A3 to get the relative address in A3 and then access the operand by means of ADD D3,(A3).

It is important to appreciate that all assemblers automatically calculate relative address offsets—the programmer does not have to evaluate the appropriate value of $d16$. For example, if a variable Day_2 were to be accessed by means of the instruction MOVE Day_2(PC),D2, the assembler would automatically calculate the difference between the contents of the program counter (i.e. the address following the instruction MOVE Day_2(PC),D2) and the address of 'Day_2'. The offset stored as part of the instruction would be this calculated value.

The 68000 permits conditional and absolute branches with relative addresses. All branches of the form Bcc $d8$ or Bcc $d16$ cause a branch to the address given by PC + $d8$ or PC + $d16$. A $d8$ branch permits a range of -126 to 129 bytes from the current instruction and the $d16$ branch permits a range of $-32K$ to $+32K$ bytes. The assembler automatically selects the appropriate form of the branch and calculates the offset ($d8$ or $d16$). Programmers merely have to write the Bcc label and the assembler evaluates ($[PC]-$label).

Figure 6.14 illustrates the action of the 68000's addressing modes.

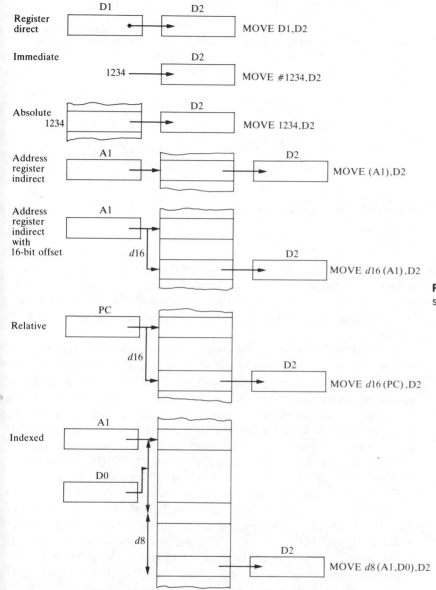

Fig. 6.14 68000 addressing modes summary.

6.5 The stack

A stack is an important type of data structure with the property that items are removed from the stack in the reverse order to which they are entered. For this reason a stack is often called a LIFO (last-in–first-out) queue. Figure 6.15 presents a series of diagrams illustrating the operation of a stack as items are added to it and removed from it.

It can be seen that the stack expands as items are added to it and contracts as they are removed. Note that unlike a conventional first-in–first-out, FIFO, queue, the stack has only one *end* and items are always

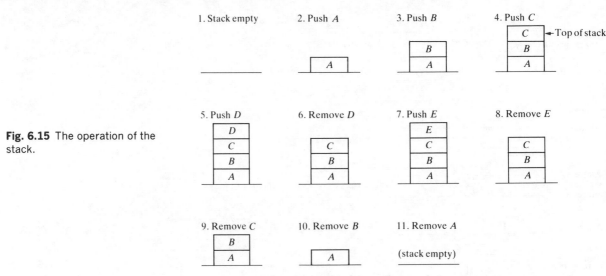

Fig. 6.15 The operation of the stack.

added or removed at this point. This special position is called the *top-of-stack* (TOS). The next position on the stack is referred to as next-on-stack (NOS). When an item is added to the stack it is said to be *pushed* on to the stack, and when an item is removed from the stack it is said to be *pulled* or *popped* off the stack.

The stack is a very important data structure in computer science and has applications in many different areas. Imagine a computer which is able to move data from memory to the stack (and vice versa), and to perform operations on the top item of the stack (monadic operators) or on the top two items of the stack (dyadic operators). When a dyadic operation (plus, multiply, AND, OR, etc.) takes place, the top two items on the stack are removed and the result of the operation takes their place. For example, ADD would read the TOS, the new TOS (i.e. the old NOS), add the two items pulled from the stack, and push the result on the stack.

The following example illustrates the evaluation of the expression $(A + B)(C - D)$ on a hypothetical stack-based computer. We will assume that the instruction PUSH pushes the contents of D0 onto the stack, ADD, SUB and MUL all act on the top two items on the stack, and PULL pulls the top item on the stack off the stack and places it in D0. Remember that a dyadic operation such as ADD pulls the top two operands off the stack, carries out the addition and then pushes the result on the stack.

```
1.  MOVE A,D0    Get A in D0
2.  PUSH         Push it on the stack
3.  MOVE B,D0    Get B in D0
4.  PUSH         Push it on the stack
5.  ADD          Pull the top two items off the stack,
                 add them, and push the result
6.  MOVE C,D0    Get C in D0
7.  PUSH         Push it on the stack
8.  MOVE D,D0    Get D
9.  PUSH         Push it on the stack
```

```
10.  SUB        Pull the top two items off the stack,
                subtract them, and push the result
11.  MUL        Pull the top two items off the stack,
                multiply them, and push the result
12.  PULL       Pull the result off the stack and put it in D0
```

Figure 6.16 represents the state of the stack at various stages in the above procedure. The number below each diagram in Fig. 6.16 corresponds to the line number in the program above. Although the 68000 and all other similar microprocessors do not permit operations on the stack in the form above (e.g. ADD, SUB, MUL), some special-purpose microprocessors have been designed to support stack-based languages like FORTH.

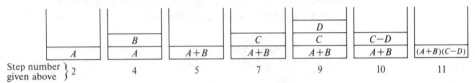

Fig. 6.16 The use of the stack in the evaluation of arithmetic expressions.

The 68000 stack

When a stack is implemented in hardware, the addition of a new item to the top of the stack causes all other items on the stack to be pushed down. Such a hardware stack is frequently implemented as a modified shift register. Similarly, when an item is removed from the stack, the NOS becomes TOS and all items are pulled up. When a stack is implemented by a microprocessor, the items on the stack are not moved themselves, but a pointer to the top of the stack is modified as the stack waxes and wanes. In some implementations, the stack pointer points to the next free location on the stack, while in others, it points to the current top of stack.

The 68000 has a 32-bit system stack pointer, which is the address register A7. We call A7 the *system* stack pointer because it is used by the CPU to store return addresses during subroutine calls (as we shall see later). Most 68000 assemblers permit the programmer to write either A7 or SP interchangeably. Unlike earlier 8-bit microprocessors, the 68000 is able to maintain up to seven other stacks simultaneously, because *all* its address registers can act as stack pointers. It is worth noting here that the 68000 has, in fact, two system stack pointers—that is, there are two A7s! As only one A7 is accessible at a time and the other A7 is hidden from view, this little detail should not cause the reader to lose any sleep. Two system stack pointers are provided and one is associated with the operating system. A stack pointer dedicated to the user is intended to prevent user programs accessing and possibly corrupting a stack belonging to the operating system.

In what follows, the 68000 system stack is used to illustrate the operation of a stack. Intuitively, one would expect the assembly-language form of the operation to push data register D0 on the stack to be

PUSH D0 and the corresponding mnemonic to pull an item from the stack and put it in D0 to be PULL D0. The manufacturers of the 68000 have decided not to define explicit PUSH and PULL instructions, but to resort instead to the address register indirect with pre-decrementing addressing mode and the address register indirect with post-incrementing addressing mode, respectively.

Figure 6.17 illustrates the effect of a PUSH D0, which is implemented by MOVE.W D0, − (SP) and PULL D0, which is implemented by MOVE.W (SP)+,D0. The stack in the 68000 grows 'backwards' in memory as data is pushed on it. That is, if the stack pointer contains, say, $80014C and a word is pushed onto the stack, the new value of the stack pointer will be $80014A. The way in which the stack grows, towards the 'higher' or 'lower' ends of memory, is entirely irrelevant. In this text we assume that the stack grows towards lower addresses.

For the 68000, MOVE.W D0, − (SP) is defined as

$$[SP] \leftarrow [SP] - 2$$
$$[MS([SP])] \leftarrow [D0]$$

and MOVE.W (SP)+,D0 is defined as

$$[D0] \leftarrow [MS([SP])]$$
$$[SP] \leftarrow [SP] + 2$$

These push and pull operations may be used with word or long word operands. A long word operand automatically causes the PC to be decremented or incremented by 4. Address registers A0–A6 may be used to push or pull byte, .B, operands—but not A7, the system stack pointer.

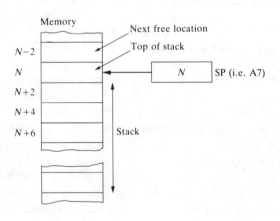

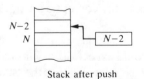

Stack after push

Fig. 6.17 The 68000's stack.

Note that the 68000 stack pointer is decremented before a push and incremented after a pull. Consequently, the stack pointer always points at the item at the top of the stack. Some microprocessors have stacks that point at the next free position on the stack (i.e. TOS-2). MOVE (SP),D3 *copies* the top item on the stack into D3 and does not affect the stack pointer, whereas MOVE (SP)+,D3 *pulls* the top item off the stack and deposits it in D3.

When the stack shrinks after MOVE.W (SP)+,D0 operations, the items on the stack are not physically deleted, they are still there in the memory until overwritten by a MOVE.W D0,-(SP) operation.

Some applications of the stack in computer science are quite esoteric and involve the manipulation and evaluation of algebraic expressions. Such uses are beyond the scope of this text. The stack has a rather more prosaic use as a temporary data store. Executing a MOVE.W D0,-(SP) saves the contents of D0 on the stack, and executing MOVE.W (SP)+,D0 returns the contents of D0. The application of the stack as a temporary storage location avoids storing data in explicitly named memory locations.

The 68000 has a special instruction MOVEM (move multiple registers) that can be used to save or retrieve an entire group of registers. For example MOVEM.L D0–D7/A0–A6,-(A7) has the effect of pushing all registers on the stack pointed at by A7. The register list used by MOVEM is of the form Di–Dj/Ap–Aq and specifies data registers Di–Dj inclusive and address registers Ap to Aq inclusive. Groups of registers are pulled off the stack by, for example, MOVEM.L (A7)+,D0–D2/D4/A4–A6.

The most important applications of the stack from the computer architecture point of view are in the implementation of subroutines (discussed in the following section), and in the implementation of interrupts (Section 7.2). Section 11.2 shows how the stack is used by the operating system to implement multiprogramming, a means of executing two or more programs at the same time.

6.5.1 The stack and subroutines

Suppose a particular sequence of operations is to be performed two or more times during the execution of a program. Writing out the same block of assembly-language instructions over and over again is both tedious to the programmer and wasteful of memory space. The subroutine provides a solution to this problem.

A subroutine is a piece of code that can be called or invoked from any point in a program. Here, the expression *calling a subroutine* means that a branch is made to the entry point of the subroutine (i.e. its first executable instruction). After the subroutine has been executed, a return must be made to the instruction following the point at which it was called. Figure 6.18 illustrates this concept. In high-level languages the subroutine is frequently known as a procedure. The subroutine is to computing what subcontracting is to the building trade.

The key to understanding subroutines is the *return mechanism.* If the same piece of code can be called from several points, some device must

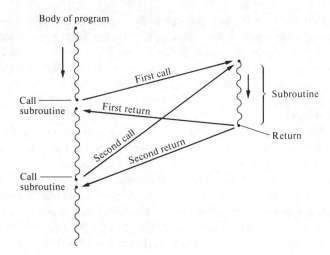

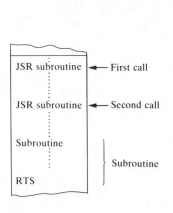

Fig. 6.18 The subroutine call.

exist to allow a return to the correct place. The Data General Nova minicomputer deposits the return address in accumulator A3 (it is a four-accumulator machine). At the end of the subroutine, the programmer simply executes a 'load program counter with the contents of A3' and a return is made. Unfortunately, there is a snag in this arrangement. A3 cannot readily be used by the programmer while a subroutine call is in progress. This is not entirely true as the contents of A3 may be saved in memory to make A3 available to the programmer, but, of course, at the cost of keeping track of the subroutine return address.

A much better way of handling the return addresses of subroutines is to store them on the stack. This is done by most microprocessors and minicomputers in the following way.

1. *Subroutine call*
   Push the contents of the PC on the stack.
   Jump to the subroutine.

2. *Return from subroutine*
   Pull the return address off the stack.
   Put the return address in the program counter.

The value of the PC pushed on the stack during a subroutine call is usually the **return** address (i.e. the address of the next instruction following a return from subroutine. The effect of these operations on the stack is illustrated by Fig. 6.19. Notice that the stack 'grows' when the subroutine is called and declines after a return. Since the last item stored on the stack is the first item to be removed from it, the stack is well-suited to nested subroutines. That is, a subroutine is able to call another subroutine, and this process repeated indefinitely. Actually, it can continue only until all the memory allocated to the stack is exhausted, at which time stack overflow is said to occur. An example of the behaviour of the stack when subroutines are nested is given in Fig. 6.20. Note that the stacks of figs.

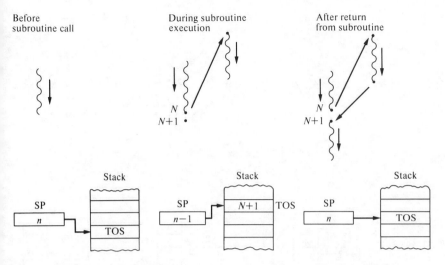

Fig. 6.19 The use of the stack to hold subroutine return addresses. Note: N is the address of the instruction that implements the subroutine call—$N+1$ is the address of the next instruction. In a 68000 system the actual address of the next instruction is $N+x$, where x is the number of bytes taken by the call instruction. Similarly, although we have shown the stack position as decremented by 1 from n to $n-1$, a 68000 would decrement it by four because an address takes 4 bytes on the stack.

6.19 and 6.20 have been simplified. 68000 return addresses take four bytes.

Writing a subroutine in assembly language is simplicity itself. All that needs to be done to turn a block of code into a subroutine is to append the instruction *return from subroutine*, RTS, to the end of the block. Suppose it is necessary to divide the 16-bit integer in data register D3 by two and add three several times during the course of a program (i.e. $[D3] \leftarrow [D3]/2 + 3$). The subroutine below will accomplish this:

```
DIV2PLUS3 ASR   #1,D3  Shift D3 one place right (divide by 2)
          ADD.W #3,D3  Add 3 to get [D3]←[D3]+3
          RTS          return
```

Subroutines are called by executing the instruction BSR ⟨label⟩ or JSR ⟨label⟩, where BSR means branch to subroutine and JSR means jump to subroutine. For our present purposes, the only difference between BSR and JSR is that BSR uses a relative address and JSR an absolute address. Remember that the programmer simply supplies the label of the subroutine and the assembler automatically calculates the appropriate relative or absolute address. To call the above subroutine, all we have to do is write 'BSR DIV2PLUS3'. We can use either the 68000's JSR (jump to subroutine) or its BSR to achieve the same effect. BSR is preferred because it permits the use of position-independent code, although the range of branching with BSR is $-32K$ bytes to $+32K$ bytes from the present instruction. JSR requires an absolute address and cannot therefore be used to generate position-independent code.

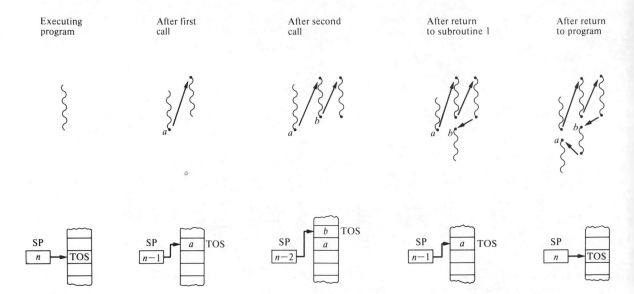

| Executing program | After first call | After second call | After return to subroutine 1 | After return to program |

Fig. 6.20 An example of nested subroutines.

We will now look at how subroutines are used in typical programs. The following program inputs text from the keyboard of a microcomputer until an '@' is typed. Then the text is printed out. As it would be very tedious to write a subroutine to input a character from the keyboard, a subroutine in the operating system at $013000 is pressed into use. Many computers provide the programmer with a list of suitable subroutines that they can call and thereby save much tedious work. In this case we will assume that calling the subroutine at $013000 by BSR $013000 will input data from the keyboard into D0. Similarly, a subroutine at $013800 outputs the character in D0. When the subroutine at $013000 is called, a return is made with the ISO/ASCII code of the key that was pressed stored in data register D0. Likewise, calling the subroutine at $013800 causes the character corresponding to the ISO/ASCII code of the data in data register D0 to be printed. In the program below, the BUFFER is a region of memory reserved for the data to be stored.

```
              TTL      PRINTOUT             Name the program
              ORG      $000400              Define the origin for data
BUFFER        DS.B     40                   Reserve 40 bytes of storage
GET_CHAR      EQU      $013000              Address of input routine
PUT_CHAR      EQU      $013800              Address of output routine
              ORG      $002000              Program origin
              LEA      BUFFER(PC),A0        Preset A0 as pointer register
NEXTIN        BSR      GET_CHAR             Get a character
              MOVE.B   D0,(A0)+             Store character and move pointer to next
              CMP.B    #'@',D0              IF character = '@' THEN print
              BNE      NEXTIN               ELSE repeat
PRINT         LEA      BUFFER(PC),A0        Reset pointer to start of buffer
```

```
NEXTOUT    MOVE.B    (A0)+,D0           Get a character and update pointer
           CMP.B     #'@',D0            IF character = '@' THEN EXIT
           BEQ       DONE
           BSR       PUT_CHAR                           ELSE print character
           BRA       NEXTOUT            Repeat
DONE       STOP      #$2700             Halt the 68000 (the STOP instruction
                                        provides a way of halting the 68000)
           END
```

In this example, I have introduced further assembler directives, whose meaning should be evident to the reader. The instruction CMP.B #'@',D0 means compare the contents of the lower-order byte of data register D0 with the byte whose ISO/ASCII code corresponds to the symbol '@'. Bracketing a character by apostrophes is often used by assemblers to denote that the following character should be replaced by its ISO/ASCII value. For example, MOVE.B #'A',D0 and MOVE.B #$41,D0 are equivalent. Note that the instruction LEA BUFFER(PC),A0 generates position-independent code because it calculates the address of the buffer relative to the program counter. If we had written LEA BUFFER,A0, we would have generated code that is not position independent.

When an RTS is encountered at the end of a subroutine, the long-word address on the top of the stack is pulled and placed in the program counter in order to force a return to the calling point.

6.5.2 Subroutines, the stack, and parameter passing

A subroutine exists to carry out some particular function. In order to do this, it is almost always necessary to transfer data between the subroutine and the program calling it. The only exception is the use of a subroutine in triggering some event. For example, a subroutine may be designed to ring a bell, or to sound an alarm. Simply calling it causes some predetermined action to take place, and no communication exists between the subroutine and the program calling it.

Consider now the use of subroutines in inputting or outputting data, Obtaining data from a keyboard (or transferring it to a display device or printer) is a complex operation. Consequently, input (and output) transactions are often dealt with by subroutines.

In our previous example, we used the subroutine 'GET_CHAR' at address $013000 to input a character from the keyboard. When the subroutine GET_CHAR is invoked by executing the operation BSR GET_CHAR, a branch to $013000 is made. This address is the entry point to the subroutine, and a branch to $013000 has the effect of reading the keyboard until a key is pressed. The subroutine scans the keyboard until the operator strikes a character. A return to the calling point is made with the ISO/ASCII-code of the character in data register D0.

In this case there is communication between the subroutine and the calling program. As only a single byte is passed from subroutine to calling program, a data register provides a handy vehicle to transfer the character.

The above method of passing data between subroutine and calling program employs registers to transfer data. In our example, the data was passed in D0, although there is no reason why the address registers could not have been used. It is interesting to note that the carry bit of the CCR is often chosen to pass information from a subroutine to its calling program. A single bit may not seem like an awful lot of information. However, problems sometimes arise within the subroutine and the calling program must be informed about them. Suppose a subroutine had been called to input data from a terminal and the terminal was faulty or not switched on. By setting the carry bit prior to a return from subroutine, the calling program can be informed that an error exists. The following fragment of a program illustrates this point.

```
BSR GETDATA    Call subroutine and return with data in D0
BCS ERROR      If carry set THEN something went wrong
  .
  .            } ELSE deal with the data
  .
ERROR          Recover from error condition
```

Apart from destroying old data that was originally in the registers, passing information via registers has no disadvantages. Unfortunately, it is not applicable to situations in which larger quantities of data have to be transferred. We will now look at an alternative method of passing data to a subroutine.

Suppose a subroutine were written to search a region of memory containing text for the first occurrence of a given string. In this case the subroutine must be informed of the starting and ending addresses of the region of memory to be searched, and the corresponding starting and ending addresses of the string of characters to be matched. The address map of Fig. 6.21 illustrates the arrangement of the two strings in memory.

The information required by the subroutine in this example is the four 32-bit addresses, $00801000, $0080100B, $00801051, and $00801054. The subroutine must return the value $00801008 (the starting point of the string 'text') to the calling program.

An alternative method of passing parameters to a subroutine involves passing information by specifying its *location* rather than its actual value. That is, instead of telling the subroutine the information it needs to know, we tell it where to find that information. Figure 6.22 shows how the parameters in the above example can be grouped into a block and the address of the start of the block passed to the subroutine.

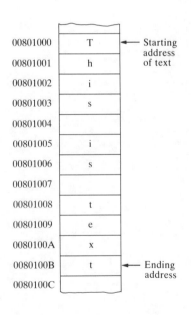

Fig. 6.21 Memory map of the string-matching problem.

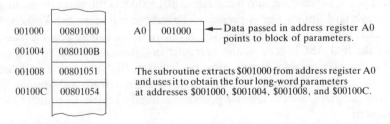

Fig. 6.22 Passing parameters by their address.

The fragment of code demonstrates how the pointer to the parameters is passed to the subroutine and how the parameters can be assessed by the subroutine.

```
        LEA       PARAM_BLOCK, A0   A0 points to parameters
        BSR       MATCH             Call the text match algorithm
        .
        .
MATCH   LEA       (A0),A1           A1 points at parameter 1
        LEA       4(A0),A2          A2 points at parameter 2
        LEA       8(A0),A3          A3 points at parameter 3
        LEA       $C(A0),A4         A4 points at parameter 4
        .
        .
        MOVE.B    (A1)+,D0          Get first item from string
        .
        RTS
```

Passing parameters by means of a common data area

It is possible to reserve a data area common to both the subroutine and calling program. A common data area removes the problem of passing parameters, because the variables required by the subroutine are the same as those in the calling program. For example, if we have variables P and Q in the calling program, the subroutine explicitly refers to P and Q. Such a solution is not popular, because the subroutine cannot be interrupted or called by another program. Any data stored in explicitly named locations could be corrupted by the interrupting program. Section 7.2 deals in detail with the interrupt mechanism and its implementation.

For the purposes of this chapter, a brief description of the interrupt will suffice. An interrupt is a method of diverting the processor from its intended course of action, and is employed to deal with input or output transactions (and certain other events) that must be attended to as soon as they occur. Whenever a processor receives an interrupt request from some device, it finishes its current instruction and then jumps to the program dealing with the cause of the interrupt. After the interrupt has been serviced, a return is made to the point immediately following the last instruction executed before the interrupt was dealt with. The return mechanism of the interrupt is almost identical with that of the subroutine—the return address is saved on the stack.

Suppose a subroutine is interrupted during the course of its execution. If the interrupt-handling routine also wishes to use the subroutine, any data stored in explicitly named memory locations will be overwritten (corrupted) by the re-use of the subroutine. If the data had been stored in registers and the contents of the registers pushed on the stack by the interrupt-handling routine, no data in the subroutine would have been lost by its re-use. After the subroutine has been re-used by the interrupt-handling routine, the contents of the registers stored on the stack are restored and a return from interrupt made with the state of the registers exactly the same as at the instant the interrupt was serviced.

Passing parameters on the stack

An ideal way of passing information between the subroutine and calling program is via the stack. Suppose three parameters, P1, P2, P3, are needed by the subroutine. The parameters are pushed on the stack immediately before the subroutine call.

```
MOVE  P1,-(A7)  Push the first parameter
MOVE  P2,-(A7)  Push the second parameter
MOVE  P3,-(A7)  Push the third parameter.
```

The state of the stack initially, prior to the subroutine call, and immediately after it, is given in Fig. 6.23. Note that the return address is a long word and takes up two words on the stack.

Fig. 6.23 Passing parameters on the stack. Note that P1, P2, P3 are each 2-byte values and therefore the stack is decremented by 2 after each parameter is pushed. The return address takes 4 bytes and is depicted as RET_H and RET_L.

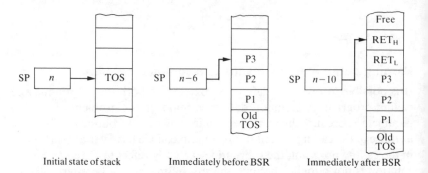

Initial state of stack   Immediately before BSR   Immediately after BSR

On entering the subroutine, the data may be retrieved in several ways. One possibility is to transfer the contents of the stack pointer to another address register by means of the instruction LEA (SP),A0. Now parameter P1 can be loaded into D1 by MOVE 8(A0),D1. Similarly, P2 can be loaded into D2 by MOVE.W 6(A0),D2 and P3 into D3 by MOVE.W 4(A0),D3.

The only difficulty presented by passing parameters on the stack is that after a return from the subroutine has been made by an RTS, the contents of the stack pointer are SP−6, where SP is the value of the stack pointer before P1, P2, and P3 were pushed on the stack. The stack pointer can be restored to its original value, or **cleaned up,** by executing three dummy pull operations (i.e. MOVE (A7)+,D0). However, a much more efficient way of cleaning up the stack is to execute the instruction LEA.L 6(SP), SP to move the stack pointer down by three words. P1, P2, P3 are, of course, still in the same locations in memory, but they will be overwritten as new data is pushed on the stack.

The advantage of using the stack to pass parameters to subroutines is that the subroutine may be interrupted and then used by the interrupting program without the parameters being corrupted. As the data is stored on the stack, it is not overwritten when the subroutine is interrupted because new data is added at the top of the stack, and then removed after the interrupt has been serviced.

A simple 68000 program

We will now put together some of the 68000's instructions and write a simple program to implement the type of text-matching algorithm described in the section on parameter passing. A region of memory contains a line of text whose starting address is $002000. The line is terminated by a carriage return, whose ISO/ASCII code is $0D. A text string is stored in a buffer at location $002100 onwards, and is also terminated by a carriage return. The program is to be written in the form of a subroutine, and the address of the first character in the line matching the first character of the string placed on the stack before the return. If the match is unsuccessful, the null address, $00000000, is pushed on the stack.

In what follows, the line of text will be referred to as 'LINE', and the text string as 'TEXT'. The problem can be solved by sliding the string along the line until each character of the string matches with the corresponding character of the line, as illustrated in Fig. 6.24. Note that all data values in this example are *byte* values.

```
*          MATCH matches the substring whose address starts at STRING
*          with the string whose address starts at LINE. Both strings are
*          terminated by a carriage return.
*          The match is carried out by comparing the first character of
*          the substring with each of the characters of the string, one by
*          one. If a match is found, the rest of the characters of the
*          substring are matched with the corresponding characters of the
*          string. If they all match up to the substring terminator, the
*          search is successful. As soon as a mismatch is found, we return
*          to matching the first character of the substring with a
*          character from the string.
*          If the terminator of the string is reached, the search has been
*          unsuccessful.
*
LINE       EQU        $002000      Location of line of text
STRING     EQU        $002100      Location of string to be matched
CRET       EQU        $0D          Carriage return
*
MATCH      MOVEA.L    (A7)+,A6     Pull long-word return address off stack
                                   A6 contains subroutine return address
           LEA        LINE,A0      A0 points to LINE
           LEA        STRING,A1    A1 points to STRING
*
NEXT       MOVE.B     (A0)+,D0     Get a character from LINE
           CMP.B      #CRET,D0     Is it a terminator (carriage return)?
           BEQ        FAIL         If carriage return then no match so exit
           CMP.B      (A1),D0      Match char from LINE with first char of
                                   STRING
           BNE        NEXT         If no match then move along LINE
*
*          We have to save the address pointers before performing the
*          submatch, in case we have to return to matching the pairs
*          of first characters
*
```

```
              MOVEA.L    A0,A3        Save A0 in A3 in case of no full match
              MOVEA.L    A1,A4        Save A1 in A4
              ADDA.L     #1,A1        Increment pointer to STRING to start
                                      character 2
*
LOOP          MOVE.B     (A1)+,D0     Perform submatch — get char of STRING
              CMP.B      #CRET,D0     If terminator found then success
              BEQ        SUCCESS
              CMP.B      (A0)+,D0     Else compare pair of chars
              BEQ        LOOP         Repeat while they match
*
*             No submatch found so prepare to continue matching pairs
*             of first characters
*
              MOVEA.L    A3,A0        Restore A0 and A1
              MOVEA.L    A4,A1         to their values before the submatch
              BRA        NEXT         Try again
*
SUCCESS       SUBA.L     #1,A3        Undo work of auto-increment
              MOVE.L     A3,-(A7)     Push address of match on stack
              JMP        (A6)         Return from subroutine
*
FAIL          MOVE.L     #0,-(A7)     Push null address on stack for fail
              JMP        (A6)         Return.
```

Fig. 6.24 Matching a string and a substring.

| THIS   THAT THEN THE OTHER | line | |
THEN THE	string	
THIS THAT THEN THE OTHER	Step	Matches
THEN THE	1	2
THEN THE	2	0
THEN THE	3	0
THEN THE	4	0
THEN THE	5	0
THEN THE	6	2
THEN THE	7	0
THEN THE	8	0
THEN THE	9	1
THEN THE	10	0
THEN THE	11	8 (All match)

6.6 Designing assembly-language programs

Now that we have gone through the operation of the CPU and have looked at the structure and instruction set of a typical high-performance microprocessor, the next step is to discuss the design of assembly-language programs. Of all the subjects I teach, I find that students have the greatest difficulty in understanding assembly language. I suspect that students' problems arise because they are often taught what instructions do and are then expected to build programs out of them. Such an approach to teaching assembly language is about as sensible as describing the manufacture and structural properties of bricks to architects and then expecting them to go away and design houses.

I do not intend to cover assembly-language programming in detail, as that would depart too far from the scope of this text. Equally, it is unreasonable to introduce the CPU and assembly language without at least indicating how assembly-language programs are put together. Most students will never write extensive assembly-language programs—not least because of the availability of so many high-level languages. However, computer users are often forced to write small assembly-language programs to link peripherals to, say, operating systems. Such programs are called *device drivers*.

6.6.1 Writing programs in pseudocode

A convenient way of transforming a requirement (e.g. for a word processor or a data base) into a program is to use pseudocode as an intermediate step. Pseudocode is so called because it is not a formal computer language, but offers programmers a way of expressing algorithms in a top-down and structured fashion without all the complexity of a real language like Pascal.

As an example of pseudocode, consider how we might express the sequence of actions involved in getting up and going to work. We can do this most easily by initially concentrating only on what we want to do and leaving the details of how we actually carry out individual actions until a later stage.

Our first-level pseudocode may be written in the form:

```
Go_To_Work
  Get_Up
  Wash
  Dress
  Have_Breakfast
  Drive_To_Work
End Go_To_Work
```

Notice how, at this stage, we have simply defined the major sequence of activities involved in getting up and going to work. As yet, we have not filled in any of the details. It is possible to use any of a large number of conventions to represent actions in pseudocode. Some use bold text to represent actions, some use underscores to link words (e.g. Drive_To_work) as I have done and some concatenate the words and start each new word with an upper-case character.

A second-level pseudocode elaborates on each of the individual actions. For example, Have_Breakfast can be elaborated as:

```
Have_Breakfast
  Make_Tea
  Boil_Egg
  Butter_Bread
  Eat_Breakfast
  Wash_Dishes
End Have_Breakfast
```

The process of elaboration may be continued until we reach the point at which each action at the pseudocode level can be replaced by a relatively small number of instructions in the appropriate computer language.

6.6.2 Conditional behaviour

In this section I am going to take a step backwards and go over material we have already introduced. I make no apology for this retrograde step because I find that year after year some of my students have great difficulty in converting a problem into assembly language. In particular they have more problems with conditional behaviour than with any other aspect of assembly-language programming (apart from addressing modes).

Conventional computers execute programs sequentially instruction-by-instruction. This is true of both low-level (assembly language) programs and high-level language programs. However, there are three occasions when a computer does not follow this pattern and executes instructions out of their natural sequence. The first is when an event originating in hardware affects the sequence of operations. For example, a disk drive may interrupt the flow of operation by demanding attention, because it is ready to receive new data.

A second case of non-sequential behaviour is caused by the unconditional branch or jump instructions. Examples are GOTO (in high-level languages) and BRA (branch) or JMP (jump) in low-level languages.

The third case of non-sequential behaviour is the conditional branch that forces the computer to take one of two or more courses of action, depending on the result of a prior action or calculation. We are going to show how conditional behaviour is implemented in a low-level language. But, before we do this, we look at conditional behaviour in a broader context.

Conditional behaviour is a part of everyday life. Consider the following example:

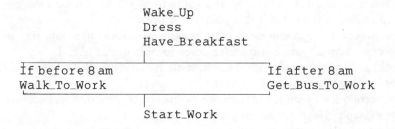

In this example, we have two possible activities that may take place after the activity 'Have_Breakfast'. Either we walk to work or we get a bus to work. Conditional behaviour requires that we test a variable (i.e. the time) and then execute one of two actions.

Typical high-level languages express conditional behaviour in the form of an IF THEN ELSE construct.

```
Wake_Up
Dress
Have_Breakfast
IF before 8 am THEN Walk_To_Work ELSE Get_The_Bus_To_Work
Start_Work
```

In more formal terms, we can write the expression in the form IF L THEN S1 ELSE S2, where L is a Boolean expression which has the value true or false and S1 and S2 are *executable actions*. Thus, if the Boolean expression L is true, action S1 is executed and, if L is false, action S2 is executed. In the above example, L is 'Is the time before 8 am', S1 is 'Walk_To_Work' and S2 is 'Get_The_Bus_To_Work'.

Note that there is a *joining up* after the conditional behaviour—it does not matter how we get to work; once there, we 'Start_Work'.

High-level languages permit quite complex expressions for the Boolean value L. For example, we may write:

$$\text{IF } x > 3.6 \text{ OR } x + 2 < \sin(p) \text{ THEN S1 ELSE S2.}$$

Low-level languages take a rather less subtle approach. As we discovered earlier all CPUs have some form of condition code register, CCR, that records certain things about the status of the CPU. For example, the format of the 68000's CCR is given by Fig. 6.25.

	Status word														
15	14	13	12	11	10	9	8	7	6	5	4	3	2	1	0
T	0	S	0	0	I_2	I_1	I_0	0	0	0	X	N	Z	V	C

Status byte ← | → CCR

Bit	Designation	Meaning	
0	C	Carry bit	
1	V	Overflow bit	
2	Z	Zero bit	
3	N	Negative bit	
4	X	Extend bit	CCR
5		Undefined	
6		Undefined	
7		Undefined	
8	I_0	Interrupt mask	
9	I_1	Interrupt mask	
10	I_2	Interrupt mask	
11		Undefined	Status byte
12		Undefined	
13	S	Status bit	
14		Undefined	
15	T	Trace bit	

Fig. 6.25 The format of the 68000's condition code register.

The bits of the 68000's CCR are updated each time the CPU carries out an operation (i.e. an assembly-language or machine-code instruction). A bit of the CCR may be set by an instruction, cleared by it or remain unaffected. It is important to note that the contents of the CCR are updated automatically by the CPU without any intervention by the programmer. In fact, it is also possible to modify deliberately the contents of the CCR by certain instructions that act directly on the bits of the CCR.

The relationship between the CCR and the CPU is unique in the sense that each CPU treats its CCR in a different way to other CPUs. Consequently, the assembly-language programmer must be aware of the relationship between the CCR and the instruction set. Table 6.3 indicates how the 68000 updates its CCR after each instruction is executed. For example, an exchange register instruction, EXG, has no effect on any bit of the CCR and the bits of the CCR remain in the state they were in before the EXG was executed. On the other hand, an add instruction, ADD, affects every bit of the CCR. The new values of the CCR bits depend on the *result* of the addition.

Table 6.3 Relationship between the CCR and the 68000's instructions

Mnemonic	Description	Operation	X	N	Z	V	C
ABCD	Add decimal with extend	$(Destination)_{10}+(source)_{10}+x\rightarrow destination$	●	U	●	U	●
ADD	Add binary	$(Destination)+(source)\rightarrow destination$	●	●	●	●	●
ADDA	Add address	$(Destination)+(source)\rightarrow destination$	—	—	—	—	—
ADDI	Add immediate	$(Destination)+immediate\ data\rightarrow destination$	●	●	●	●	●
ADDQ	Add quick	$(Destination)+immediate\ data\rightarrow destination$	●	●	●	●	●
ADDX	Add extended	$(Destination)+(source)+x\rightarrow destination$	●	●	●	●	●
AND	AND logical	$(Destination)\wedge(source)\rightarrow destination$	—	●	●	0	0
ANDI	AND immediate	$(Destination)\wedge immediate\ data\rightarrow destination$	—	●	●	0	0
ASL, ASR	Arithmetic shift	$(Destination)\ shifted\ by\ \langle count\rangle\rightarrow destination$	●	●	●	●	●
B_{cc}	Branch conditionally	If cc then $PC+d\rightarrow PC$	—	—	—	—	—
BCHG	Test a bit and change	$\sim(\langle bit\ number\rangle)\ OF\ destination\rightarrow Z$	—	—	●	—	—
		$\sim(\langle bit\ number\rangle)\ OF\ destination\rightarrow$ $\langle bit\ number\rangle\ OF\ destination$					
BCLR	Test a bit and clear	$\sim(\langle bit\ number\rangle)\ OF\ destination\rightarrow Z$	—	—	●	—	—
		$0\rightarrow\langle bit\ number\rangle\ OF\ destination$					
BRA	Branch always	$PC+displacement\rightarrow PC$	—	—	—	—	—
BSET	Test a bit and set	$\sim(\langle bit\ number\rangle)\ OF\ destination\rightarrow Z$	—	—	●	—	—
		$1\rightarrow\langle bit\ number\rangle\ OF\ destination$					
BSR	Branch to subroutine	$PC\rightarrow-(SP),\ PC+d\rightarrow PC$	—	—	—	—	—
BTST	Test a bit	$\sim(\langle bit\ number\rangle)\ OF\ destination\rightarrow Z$	—	—	●	—	—
CHK	Check register against bounds	If $D_n\langle 0\ or\ D_n\rangle$ then TRAP	—	●	U	U	U
CLR	Clear an operand	$0\rightarrow Destination$	—	0	1	0	0
CMP	Compare	$(Destination)-(source)$	—	●	●	●	●
CMPA	Compare address	$(Destination)-(source)$	—	●	●	●	●
CMPI	Compare immediate	$(Destination)-immediate\ data$	—	●	●	●	●
CMPM	Compare memory	$(Destination)-(source)$	—	●	●	●	●
DB_{cc}	Test condition, decrement, and branch	If $\sim_{cc}$ then $D_n-1\rightarrow D_n$; if $D_n\neq-1$ then $PC+d\rightarrow PC$	—	—	—	—	—
DIVS	Signed divide	$Destination/(source)\rightarrow destination$	—	●	●	●	0
DIVU	Unsigned divide	$(Destination)/(source)\rightarrow destination$	—	●	●	●	0
EOR	Exclusive OR logical	$(Destination)\oplus(source)\rightarrow destination$	—	●	●	0	0
EORI	Exclusive OR immediate	$(Destination)\oplus immediate\ data\rightarrow destination$	—	●	●	0	0
EXG	Exchange register	$R_x\leftarrow\rightarrow R_y$	—	—	—	—	—
EXT	Sign extend	$(Destination)\ sign\text{-}extended\rightarrow destination$	—	●	●	0	0
JMP	Jump	$Destination\rightarrow PC$	—	—	—	—	—
JSR	Jump to subroutine	$PC\rightarrow-(SP);\ destination\rightarrow PC$	—	—	—	—	—
LEA	Load effective address	$Destination\rightarrow A_n$	—	—	—	—	—
LINK	Link and allocate	$A_n\rightarrow-(SP);\ SP\rightarrow A_n;\ SP+displacement-SP$	—	—	—	—	—
LSL, LSR	Logical shift	$(Destination)\ shifted\ by\ \langle count\rangle\rightarrow destination$	●	●	●	0	0
MOVE	Move data from source to destination	$(Source)\rightarrow destination$	—	●	●	0	0

Table 6.3 —*continued*

Mnemonic	Description	Operation	X	N	Z	V	C
MOVE to CCR	Move to condition code	(Source)→CCR	•	•	•	•	•
MOVE to SR	Move to the status register	(Source)→SR	•	•	•	•	•
Move from SR	Move from the status register	SR→destination	—	—	—	—	—
MOVE USP	Move user stack pointer	USP→A_n; A_n→USP	—	—	—	—	—
MOVEA	Move address	(Source)→destination	—	—	—	—	—
MOVEM	Move multiple registers	Registers→destination (Source)→registers	—	—	—	—	—
MOVEP	Move peripheral data	(Source)→destination	—	—	—	—	—
MOVEQ	Move quick	Immediate data→destination	—	•	•	0	0
MULS	Signed multiply	(Destination)×(source)→destination	—	•	•	0	0
MULU	Unsigned multiply	(Destination)×(source)→destination	—	•	•	0	0
NBCD	Negate decimal with extend	$0-(Destination)_{10}-x$→destination	•	U	•	U	•
NEG	Negate	0-(Destination)→destination	•	•	•	•	•
NEGX	Negate with extend	0-(Destination)-x→destination	•	•	•	•	•
NOP	No operation	—	—	—	—	—	—
NOT	Logical complement	~(Destination)→destination	—	•	•	0	0
OR	Inclusive OR logical	(Destination) V (source)→destination	—	•	•	0	0
ORI	Inclusive OR immediate	(Destination) V immediate data→destination	—	•	•	0	0
PEA	Push effective address	Destination→-(SP)	—	—	—	—	—
RESET	Reset external devices	—	—	—	—	—	—
ROL, ROR	Rotate (without extend)	(Destination) rotated by ⟨count⟩→destination	—	•	•	0	•
ROXL, ROXR	Rotate with extend	(Destination) rotated by ⟨count⟩→destination	•	•	•	0	•
RTE	Return from exception	(SP)+→SR;(SP)+→PC	•	•	•	•	•
RTR	Return and restore condition codes	(SP)+→CC;(SP)+→PC	•	•	•	•	•
RTS	Return from subroutine	(SP)+→PC	—	—	—	—	—
SBCD	Subtract decimal with extend	$(Destination)_{10}-(source)_{10}-x$→destination	•	U	•	U	•
S_{cc}	Set according to condition	If cc then 1's→destination else 0's→destination	—	—	—	—	—
STOP	Load status register and stop	Immediate data→SR; STOP	•	•	•	•	•
SUB	Subtract binary	(Destination)-(source)→destination	•	•	•	•	•
SUBA	Subtract address	(Destination)-(source)→destination	—	—	—	—	—
SUBI	Subtract immediate	(Destination)-immediate data→destination	•	•	•	•	•
SUBQ	Subtract quick	(Destination)-immediate data→destination	•	•	•	•	•
SUBX	Subtract with extend	(Destination)-(source)-x→destination	•	•	•	•	•
SWAP	Swap register halves	Register [31:16]←→register [15:0]	—	•	•	0	0
TAS	Test and set an operand	(Destination) tested→CC: 1→[7] OF destination	—	•	•	0	0
TRAP	Trap	PC→-(SSP); SR→-(SSP); (vector)→PC	—	—	—	—	—
TRAPV	Trap on overflow	If V then TRAP	—	—	—	—	—
TST	Test on operand	(Destination) tested→CC	—	•	•	0	0
UNLK	Unlink	An→SP. (SP)+→A_n	—	—	—	—	—

⊕	Logical exclusive OR	•	Affected
∧	Logical AND	—	Unaffected
V	Logical OR	0	Cleared
~	Logical complement	1	Set
U	Undefined		

The Z bit is set if the result of an operation yields a zero result. The N bit is set if the most significant bit of the result is one. The carry bit is set if the carry-out of the most significant bit of the result is one. The V bit is set if the operation yields an out-of-range result when the operand(s) and result are all regarded as twos complement values. Remember that for the puspose of setting or clearing bits of the CCR, the term *most significant bit* refers to bit 7, 15, or 31, depending on whether the current operation is a byte, word, or long-word operation, respectively.

The conditional branch and 68000 assembly language

Although the conditional test performed by a high-level language can be quite complex (e.g. IF $X + Y \div Z > 3t$), the conditional test at the assembly-language level is rather more basic. In fact, the only test that can be carried out is one on the contents of the condition code register. Conditional branches generally have the form B_{cc}, where *cc* represents one of a number of possible conditions to be tested. Table 6.4 lists the 68000's conditional branches.

Table 6.4 The 68000's conditional branches

Mnemonic (*cc*)	Condition	Flags tested	Branch taken if
CC	Carry clear	C	C=0
CS	Carry set	C	C=1
NE	Not equal	Z	Z=0
EQ	Equal	Z	Z=1
PL	Plus	N	N=0
MI	Minus	N	N=1
HI	Higher than	C,Z	$\bar{C}.\bar{Z}=1$
LS	Lower than or same as	C, Z	C+Z=1
GT	Greater than	Z,N,V	$N.\bar{Z}+\bar{N}.\bar{V}.\bar{Z}=1$
LT	Less than	N,V	$N.\bar{V}+\bar{N}.V=1$
GE	Greater than or equal to	N,V	$N.\bar{V}+\bar{N}.V=0$
LE	Less than or equal to	Z,N,V	$Z+(\bar{N}.V+N.\bar{V})=1$
VC	Overflow clear	V	V=0
VS	Overflow set	V	V=1

A conditional instruction takes an argument (i.e. operand) which is the address of the statement to be taken if the conditional test is true. Practical assembly languages invariably express arguments in the form of labels. Consider the following example:

```
       ADD  D1,D2   Add D1 to D2 and branch if result minus
       BMI  ERROR
        .
        .            }  'ELSE' part
        .
        .
ERROR   .            }  'THEN' part
        .
```

The operation 'ADD D1,D2' adds the contents of D1 to D2, deposits the results in D2 and updates the condition code register accordingly.

When the BMI instruction is executed, the branch is taken (the 'THEN' part) if the N bit of the CCR is set (i.e. the result of the operation was negative). In this case, a branch to the line labelled by 'ERROR' is made and the intervening code between 'BMI ERROR' and 'ERROR . . .' is not executed.

If the branch is not taken because the result of ADD D1,D2 was not negative, the code immediately following the BMI ERROR is executed. This code corresponds to the 'ELSE' part of our IF . . . THEN . . . ELSE construction.

Unfortunately, there is an error in the above example. Suppose that the condition N = 1 is not met and the ELSE part is executed. Once this has been done we fall through to the THEN part, which is not what we want to do. After the ELSE part has been executed, it is necessary to skip round the 'THEN' part by means of an BRA instruction.

```
        ADD   D1,D2
        BMI   ERROR
        ·     ⎫
        ·     ⎬        'ELSE' part
        ·     ⎭
        BRA   EXIT    Skip past the 'THEN' part
ERROR   ·     ⎫
        ·     ⎬        'THEN' part
        ·     ⎭
EXIT
```

The BRA (branch) instruction is called an unconditional branch because it forces the computer to execute the next instruction indicated by the address following the BRA. In this case, the address provided is the symbolic address 'EXIT'.

Before continuing, there are two points worth making. The 68000 microprocessor, like most other computers, uses relative branching so that the operand following a B_{cc} represents the distance to be branched from the current instruction rather than the absolute address. Second, we said earlier that not all the 68000's instructions affect the CCR. For example, consider the following two examples:

```
        ADD   D1,D2
        BMI   ERROR
```

and

```
        ADD   D1,D2
        EXG   D3,D4
        EXG   D5,D6
        BMI   ERROR
```

Both these fragments of code have the *same* effect as far as the BMI ERROR is concerned. However, the second case might prove confusing to the reader of the program who may well imagine that the state of the CCR prior to the BMI ERROR is determined by the EXG D5,D6 instruction.

We will now look at a more extended example of conditional behaviour. A subroutine is to be designed to convert a 4-bit hexadecimal value into its ISO/ASCII equivalent. Table 6.5 illustrates the relationship between the internal binary value of a number (its hexadecimal representation) and its ISO/ASCII equivalent (expressed in hexadecimal form).

For example, if the internal binary value in a register is 00001010, its hexadecimal equivalent is A. In order to print the *letter* A on a terminal, it is necessary to transmit the ISO/ASCII code for the letter A (i.e. $41) to it. Once again, please note that there is a difference between the internal binary representation of a number within a computer and the *code* used to represent the *symbol* for that number. The *number six* is expressed in eight

Table 6.5 Relationship between ISO/ASCII characters and hexadecimal values

ASCII/ISO character	Hexadecimal value
0	30
1	31
2	32
3	33
4	34
5	35
6	36
7	37
8	38
9	39
A	41
B	42
C	43
D	44
E	45
F	46

bits by the binary pattern 00000110 and is stored in the computer's memory in this form. On the other hand, the *symbol* for a six (i.e. '6') is represented by the binary pattern 00110110 in the ISO/ASCII code. If we want a printer to make a mark on paper corresponding to '6', we must send the binary number 00110110 to it. Consequently, numbers held in the computer must be converted to their ISO/ASCII forms before they can be printed.

From Table 6.5 we can derive an algorithm to convert a 4-bit internal value into its ISO/ASCII form. A number in the range 0–9 is converted into ISO/ASCII form by adding hexadecimal 30 to the number. A number in the range A to F is converted to ISO/ASCII by adding hexadecimal 37. If we represent the number to be converted by HEX and the character code by ISO, we can write down a suitable algorithm in the form:

```
IF HEX < $A THEN ISO: = HEX + $30
              ELSE ISO : = HEX + $37
```

Alternatively, we can rewrite the algorithm as

```
ISO : = HEX + $30
IF ISO > $39 THEN ISO : = ISO + 7
```

The alternative algorithm can be translated into low-level language as

```
*        Note: D0.B holds HEX value on subroutine entry
*              D0.B holds the ISO equivalent on return
*        No other register is modified by this subroutine
         ADD.B   #$30,D0  ISO:=HEX+$30
         CMP.B   #$39,D0  IF ISO≤$39 THEN EXIT
         BMI     EXIT
         ADD.B   #7,D0                    ELSE ISO:=ISO+7
EXIT     RTS
```

Templates for control structures

We can readily represent some of the control structures of high-level languages as *templates* in assembly language. A template is a pattern or example that can be modified to suit the actual circumstances. In each of the following examples, the high-level construct is provided as a comment to the assembly-language template by means of asterisks in the first column. The condition tested is D0 = D1 and the actions to be carried out are Action1 or Action2. The templates can be used by providing the appropriate test instead of CMP D0,D1 and providing the appropriate sequence of assembly-language statements instead of Action1 or Action2.

```
*        IF D0=D1 THEN Action1
*
         CMP     D0,D1        Perform test
         BNE     EXIT         IF D0≠D1 THEN exit
Action1   ·                   ELSE execute Action1
          ·
EXIT                          Exit point for construct
```

```
*                 IF D0=D1 THEN Action1 ELSE Action2
*
                  CMP       D0,D1              Compare D0 with D1
                  BNE       Action2            IF D0≠D1 perform Action2
Action1           .                            Fall through to Action1 if D0=D1
                  .
                  BRA       EXIT               Skip round Action2
Action2           .                            Action2
                  .
EXIT                                           Exit point for construct
```

```
*                 FOR K=I TO J
*                 .
*                 .
*                 ENDFOR
*
                  MOVE      #I,D2              Load loop counter, D2, with I
Action1           .                            Perform Action1
                  .
                  ADD       #1,D2              Increment loop counter
                  CMP       #J+1,D2            Test for end of loop
                  BNE       Action1            IF not end THEN go round again
EXIT                                           ELSE exit
```

```
*                 WHILE D0=D1 DO Action1
*
Repeat            CMP       D0,D1              Perform test
                  BNE       EXIT               IF D0≠D1 THEN exit
Action1           .                            ELSE carry out Action1
                  .
                  BRA       Repeat             Repeat loop
EXIT                                           Exit from construct
```

```
*                 REPEAT Action1 UNTIL D0=D1
*
Action1           .                            Perform Action1
                  .
                  CMP       D0,D1              Carry out test
                  BNE       Action1            Repeat as long as D0≠D1
EXIT                                           Exit from loop
```

```
*                 CASE OF I
*                     I=0 Action0
*                     I=1 Action1
*                     I=2 Action2
*                     I=3 Action3
*                     .
*                     .
*                     I=N Action
*                     I>N Exception
*
                  CMP.B     #N,D0              Test for I out of range
                  BMI       EXCEPTION          IF I>N THEN exception
```

```
            MULU      #4,D0          Each address is a longword
            LEA       Table,A0       A0 points to table of addresses
            LEA       (A0,D0),A0     A0 now points to case I in table
            MOVEA.L   (A0),A0        A0 contains address of case I handler
            JMP       (A0)           Execute case I handler
*
Table       ORG       <address>      Here is the table of exceptions
Action0     DC.L      <address0>     Address of case 0 handler
Action1     DC.L      <address1>     Address of case 1 handler
Action2     DC.L      <address2>     Address of case 2 handler
    .
    .
ActionN     DC.L      <addressN>     Address of case N handler
EXCEPTION             . . .          Exception handler here
```

Note that the case number I (stored in D0) must be multiplied by four before it can be added to the address in A0. This action is necessary since the cases numbers are consecutive integers 0,1,2,3 while the addresses of the case handlers are consecutive long-word addresses (A0+0, A0+4, A0+8, ...).

6.6.3 An example of program design

We are now going to look at a more extended example of program design and construct a subroutine to add together two 32-bit IEEE format floating point numbers.

As we learned in Chapter 4, a 32-bit IEEE floating point number is expressed in the form

$$N = (-1)^S \times 1.F \times 2^{E-127}$$

where S is the sign bit, E is the 8-bit stored exponent and F is the stored 23-bit mantissa.

Before even attempting to generate an algorithm, we have to think for a moment about floating point numbers. In particular, we must be aware that the IEEE format stores packed floating point numbers that have been normalized. In their packed form, the leading '1' from the mantissa has been suppressed and must be inserted before we can perform calculations. Moreover, the IEEE format uses sign and magnitude to represent signed values. If we are going to use the 68000's twos complement facilities to carry out the addition/subtraction, it is necessary to convert negative numbers into their appropriate twos complement form. Unfortunately, this can cause a problem! The normalized twos complement value 1.000...0 cannot be converted to its positive form directly, because the range of valid twos complement numbers is $-2^{(n-1)}$ to $+2^{(n-1)}-1$. Therefore, the most negative number cannot be turned into its positive counterpart without first denormalizing it to 1.1000...0. We will look out for this exception.

In order to keep the complexity of this problem within reasonable bounds, we are going to consider only the process of addition. We will assume that on entry to the subroutine, the two numbers to be added are in D0.L and D1.L and that the result will be returned in D2.L with D0 and D1 unmodified. All other data registers must not be modified by this subroutine.

We can quickly express the sequence of actions to be performed by this program in pseudocode.

```
Module Floating_Point
  Unpack_D0 {to get first FP number}
  Unpack_D1 {to get second FP number}
  Add_The_Unpacked_Numbers_Together
  Pack_The_Result
  Put_The_Result_In_D2
End Floating_Point
```

The next step is to look more closely at how we are going to unpack the floating point numbers.

```
Unpack
  Save_Sign_Bit
  Save_Exponent {in Exponent register}
  Save_Mantissa {in Mantissa register}
  Insert_Leading_1_Before_Mantissa
  Convert_Mantissa_To_Twos_Complement_Form
End Unpack
```

Unpacking a packed 32-bit floating point number is tricky, because we have to decide what to do with the sign bit, the exponent and the mantissa. As the unpacked mantissa is a 24-bit value, we must hold it in a 32-bit register (there are no 24-bit registers in the 68000). The sign bit can be used to convert the mantissa from its sign and magnitude form to a twos complement form. Doing this avoids storing the sign bit explicitly and allows us to use the 68000's twos complement operations on the mantissa. Finally, the 8-bit exponent can be loaded into the lower-order byte of a data register. The following fragment of pseudocode allows us to represent the detailed unpacking of an IEEE floating point number by

```
Unpack
  Copy_FP_Number_To_Exponent_Register
  Shift_FP_Number_Seven_Places_Left {to align mantissa}
  Clear_Sign_Bit {msb=0 to make number temp +ve}
  Insert_Leading_1 {mantissa number now starts 01...}
  IF Sign_Of_FP_Number=1 THEN Negate_Mantissa
  Shift_Exponent_Left_23_Places {Align exponent as LB byte}
End Unpack
```

Now we have to consider how the addition is to be performed:

```
Add_The_Two_Floating_Point_Numbers
  Find_The_Larger_Number {by finding the larger exponent}
  IF Larger_Exponent<Smaller_Exponent+24
    THEN
```

```
                          BEGIN
                            WHILE Smaller_Exponent<Larger_Exponent
                               Shift_Smaller_Mantissa_Right
                               Add_1_To_Smaller_Exponent
                            ENDWHILE
                          Add_Mantissas
                      Renormalize_result
                      END
                        ELSE Result=Larger_Number {as difference so great}
                      End Add_The_Two_Floating_Point_Numbers
```

An important step in the addition of floating point numbers lies in the renormalization following the addition of the two mantissas. The two mantissas are initially 32-bit normalized twos complement values in the form $01XXX \ldots X$ (if they are positive) or $10XXX \ldots X$ (if they are negative). If two positive (or negative numbers) are added, we may get arithmetic overflow. Overflow can readily be detected and the resulting mantissa shifted one place right (and the exponent incremented) to bring it back into range. However, if a positive number is added to a negative number, the result may be denormalized or even zero. For example, we may get a positive mantissa of, say, $00001XXX \ldots XX$ or a negative mantissa of $11110XXX \ldots XX$. In these cases we must shift the mantissa left until we get either $01XXX \ldots XX$ or $10XXX \ldots XX$.

The final step is to repack the mantissa and exponent into the correct IEEE floating point format.

```
         Pack
           Clear_Destination_Register
           Copy_FP_number_to_Exponent_Register
           Align_Exponent                  {shift exponent 23 places left}
           Copy_FP_number_to_Mantissa_Register
           Align_Mantissa                  {shift mantissa 7 places right }
           IF mantissa negative THEN
                                 BEGIN
                                     Convert_Mantissa_To_Magnitude_Form
                                     Add_Sign_Bit_To_Destination_Register
                                 END
           Delete_Leading_Bit_Of_Mantissa
           Move_Mantissa_To_Destination_Register
           Move_Exponent_To_Destination_Register
         End Pack
```

At this stage we can now begin to write our 68000 assembly-language program.

```
*
*       FP addition adds two IEEE format 32-bit floating point
*       numbers in D0 and D1 together and returns with the result
*       in D2. The contents of data registers D3-D7 are not
*       modified by this subroutine.
*
*       Below is a list of the registers used by this subroutine
```

```
*          together with the structure of each of the registers.
*          FP1 arrives in D1 and is unpacked into D3, D4 and FP2 arrives
*          in D1 and is unpacked into D5, D6. The result is later
*          packed into D2.
*
*          31 30    23 22              0
*           ┌─┬──────┬─────────────────┐
*           │S│  E   │       M         │      D0=packed FP1
*           └─┴──────┴─────────────────┘      D1=packed FP2
*                                             D2=packed result
*
*          31                          0
*           ┌───────────────────────────┐
*           │            M              │     D3=unpacked 32-bit mantissa
*           └───────────────────────────┘     D5=unpacked 32-bit mantissa
*
*                                   7  0
*                                  ┌────┐
*                                  │ E  │        D4=unpacked 8-bit exponent
*                                  └────┘        D6=unpacked 8-bit exponent
*
*          31                          0
*           ┌───────────────────────────┐
*           │                           │     D7=temp working register
*           └───────────────────────────┘
*
*
*
*
*
*
*
*

FPADD      MOVEM.L    D3-D7,-(A7)       Save working registers on the stack
           MOVE.L     D0,D7             Copy source 1 to temp reg
           BSR        UNPACK              and unpack it into D5,D6
           MOVE.L     D5,D3             Put unpacked FP in D3, D4 pair
           MOVE.B     D6,D4             Exponent in D4, mantissa in D3
           MOVE.L     D1,D7             Now unpack D1
           BSR        UNPACK            Leave unpacked pair in D5, D6
*
*          Put the larger number in D3, D4 pair
*          We need to do this because we will have to denormalize
*          the larger number later.
*
           CMP.B      D6,D4             Compare exponents
           BCC        NoSwap            IF D6>D4 THEN carry set and swap
           EXG        D6,D4             Swap exponents
           EXG        D5,D3             Swap mantissas
*
*
*
NoSwap     EQU        *
*          IF larger exponent > smaller exponent +24 THEN EXIT
*          No need to do anything if one exponent exceeds other
*           by more than 24
*
*
*
*
```

```
          MOVE.B    D4,D7          D7=temp copy of larger exponent
          SUB.B     #24,D7         Reduce larger exponent by 24
          CMP.B     D7,D6          IF difference greater than 24
          BCS       REPACK             THEN skip addition
*
*         Add the mantissas together (result in D3)
*         Denormalize the number with the smaller exponent by
*         shifting its mantissa right (i.e. divide by 2) and adding 1
*         to its exponent (i.e. multiplying by 2) until both exponents
*         are equal.

ADD       CMP.B     D4,D6          Compare exponents
          BEQ       ADDM           IF exponents same THEN add mantissas
          ASR.L     #1,D5             ELSE divide smaller mantisa by 2
          ADD.B     #1,D6                and increment smaller exponent
          BRA       ADD            REPEAT
*
ADDM      ADD.L     D5,D3          Add mantissas with equal exponents
          BVC       ADD1           IF no overflow THEN EXIT
          ROXR.L    #1,D3                ELSE shift mantissa right
          ADD.B     #1,D4                   and increment exponent
ADD1      TST.L     D3             Test for zero mantissa (special case)
          BNE       RENORM         If mantissa not zero then renormalize
          CLR.L     D2             Else clear entire FP number
          BRA       EXIT              and exit
*
*         If a negative number has been added to a positive number,
*         it is possible that the result may not be normalized and
*         is not of the form 0.1XXX...XX or 1.0XXX...XX.
*         We must renormalize the result by shifting the mantissa
*         left and subtracting 1 from the exponent until it is
*         normalized.
*         However, we must look out for the exception 1.0000...00
*         and force it to the form 1.10000..00 to avoid the '-1'
*         anomaly.
*
RENORM    MOVE.L    D3,D7          Make temp copy of result mantissa
          AND.L     #$C0000000,D7  Mask to 2 ms bits (sign+leading)
          CMP.L.    #$40000000,D7  Look for 0.1XXX...X (for +ve result)
          BEQ       NO_NORM        If 01XXX...X then result OK
          CMP.L     #$80000000,D7  Look for 10XXX...X (for -ve result)
          BEQ       NO_NORM        If 10XXX...X then result OK
          ASL.L     #1,D3          Shift mantissa left (×2)
          SUB.B     #1,D4          Decrement exponent
          BRA       RENORM         Repeat while not normalized
NO_NORM   EQU       *
*
*         At this stage, the result is in the pair D3=mantissa and
*         D5=exponent. We must combine D3 and D5 into a packed
*         result in D2. Repacking the exponent is easy — it is
*         just moved from D5 to the correct position in D2. Repacking
*         the mantissa is more complex, because we must convert it
*         from twos complement to modulus form (saving the sign bit
*         in the msb position of D2), and then delete the leading 1
*         before moving it to the correct position in D2.
*
```

```
REPACK    CLR.L     D2                      Clear D2 before receiving D3,D4 pair
          MOVE.B    D4,D2                   Copy exponent to destination
          MOVE.L    #23,D7                  Set up D7 as a temp shift counter
          LSL.L     D7,D2                   Align exponent in correct position
          TST.L     D3                      IF mantissa negative THEN
          BNE       POS                     nothing more to do
          OR.L      #$80000000,D2           Else set sign bit of result in D2
          NEG.L     D3                      Convert mantissa to positive form
          CMP.L     #$80000000,D3           Test for -1 anomaly
          BPL       POS                     If mantissa not -1 then skip correction
          CLR.L     D3                      Else set mantissa to zero
          ADD.L     #$00800000,D2           and increment exponent in result (D2)
POS       AND.L     #$3FFFFE00,D3           Clear leading bits in unpacked mantissa
          LSR.L     #7,D3                   Align mantissa
          OR.L      D3,D2                   Add mantissa to result
EXIT      MOVEM.L   (A7)+,D3-D7             Restore working registers
          RTS                               and return
*
*         UNPACK takes a packed floating point number in D7 and packs
*         it into an 8-bit exponent in the LS byte of D6, and a 32-bit
*         twos complement mantissa in D5. Unpacking the exponent simply
*         involves shifting the packed floating point number 23 places
*         left to align the exponent's lsb with the register's lsb.
*         The exponent is unpacked by shifting it 7 places left (through
*         the exponent). The ms two bits of the unpacked mantissa
*         are used to hold a zero and the suppressed leading 1,
*         respectively. Finally, the mantissa is coverted to signed
*         twos complement form by testing the sign bit of the original
*         unpacked number.
*
UNPACK    MOVE.L    D7,D6                   Copy whole unpacked number to D6
          MOVE.L    #23,D2                  Set up D2 as a temp shift counter
          LSR.L     D2,D6                   Get exponent in LS byte of D6
          MOVE.L    D7,D5                   Copy whole FP number to D5
          ASL.L     #7,D5                   Align mantissa
          AND.L     #$7FFFFFFF,D5           Clear sign bit
          OR.L      #$40000000,D5           Insert leading 1 in mantissa
          TST.L     D7                      IF FP number +ve THEN
          BPL       UNPACK1                             RETURN
          NEG.L     D5                                  ELSE negate mantissa
          MOVE.L    D5,D7                   Take temp copy of mantissa
          AND.L     #$C0000000,D7           Mask to ms two bits YY000...000
          CMP.L     #$C0000000,D7           Test for 11XXX...XX mantissa
          BNE       UNPACK                  If not 11XXX...X then OK
          ASL.L     #1,D5                   Else shift mantissa left to get 10XXX..
          SUB.B     #1,D6                   and compensate exponent
UNPACK1   RTS                               Return
*
```

Summary

In this chapter we have both looked at the programming model of a modern microprocessor and introduced the way in which assembly-language programs can be constructed. Probably the most difficult aspect of any microprocessor's assembly language is its addressing modes. Although the 68000 has a larger range of addressing modes than earlier 8-bit devices, its addressing modes are not particularly difficult to understand since they follow a regular pattern. However, it is not just the addressing modes themselves that are difficult to understand but the way in which they are used. Perhaps one of the best ways of approaching addressing modes is to ask 'what problems do they solve?' Thus, instead of learning how indexed addressing operates, it is better to consider a problem such as accessing an element in an array that could not be solved easily without resorting to indexed addressing.

At the end of this chapter I have emphasized how conditional behaviour is implemented in assembly language, because it is this aspect of assembly-language programming that confuses some of my students when they attempt to map high-level algorithms onto a low-level language.

Problems

1. If you had to design a computer with a three-address instruction format, an addressing range of 30 000 bytes and 275 instructions, what is the minimum word length required?

2. What are the advantages and disadvantages of multi-length instructions?

3. Explain how the following assembler directives are used:
EQU
ORG
DC
DS

4. Draw a memory map corresponding to the following sequence of assembler directives.
ORG $001000
DS.B 12
DC.B 'The date is'
DC.L 1234
DS.L 2

5. What are the fundamental differences between the 68000's address and data registers?

6. What are the advantages and disadvantages of separate address and data registers in the way in which they are implemented in the 68000?

7. The 68000 implements negative addresses because the contents of address registers are treated as signed twos complement values. What is a negative address and how is it used?

8. The 68000 has addressing modes that are indicated by $-(Ai)$ and $(Ai)+$ in 68000 assemblers. What are they (i.e. what do they do?) and explain why one is used only with auto-incrementing and one with auto-decrementing?

9. What is the effect of the following sequence of 68000 instructions? Explain what each individual instruction does, and then explain what the overall effect of the three instructions is.

```
LEA     1234,A0
MOVE.L  (A0),A0
JMP     (A0)
```

10. The 68000 does not permit the operation CLR A0 (because address register direct is not a legal addressing mode for a CLR instruction). Write down two ways of clearing the contents of an address register (each using a single legal instruction from the 68000's instruction set).

11. The 68000 has the following condition code bits: C, V, X, N and Z. Which is the 'odd one out' and why?

12. What does the term 'effective address' mean and how is it used?

13. What is the meaning of the expression 'sign extension' and how is it related to the 68000?

14. Write a sequence of instructions to calculate the parity of the low-order seven bits of D0. If the parity is even, write zero into bit 7 of D0 and if it is odd write 1 into bit 7 of D0. For example if $D0(7:0) = X0111011$ (where $X = $ don't care), the routine yields the value 10111011.

15. Write suitable 68000 assembly instructions to perform the following operation:

$$[D1] \leftarrow [D0] \text{ and } [D1(0:15)] = 0.$$

16. Write a sequence of instructions to reverse the order of the bits of register D0. That is, $D0(0) \leftarrow D0(31)$; $D0(1) \leftarrow D0(30)$; ... $D0(31) \leftarrow D0(0)$.

17. Write a subroutine to move a block of memory from one location to another. Before entering the subroutine the following addresses are pushed on the stack (in this order): the starting address of the block to be moved, the ending address of the block to be moved, the starting address of the block's new location. By 'starting address' we mean the lowest address in the block.

Take care to consider all the possible cases (e.g. overlapping blocks). Your subroutine should return a carry bit = 0 if the routine is successful and a carry bit = 1 if there is an error (what are the possible errors that might be encountered?).

Input/output

So far we have examined the internal structure and operation of the central processing unit in a digital computer. However, if a computer is to be of real value to people it must have some way of communicating with them. After all, there's no point in creating a super computer the size of a shoe box that can solve the ultimate question of life, the universe, and everything, if it cannot tell us the answer. We are now going to look at some of the ways in which information is moved between the computer and external systems ranging from a simple on/off switch to a visual display unit.

Computer input/output (I/O) is quite a complex subject and is best subdivided into three areas:

1. The *strategy* by which data is moved into or out of the computer.

2. The *hardware* or *interface* that actually moves the data into or out of the computer.

3. The *input/output devices* themselves that convert data into a form that can be used by an external system or which take data from the outside world and convert it into a form that can be processed digitally. Data may be converted into an almost infinite number of representations, from a close approximation to human speech to a signal that opens or closes a valve in a chemical factory. Input/output devices are frequently called *peripherals*.

In this chapter we are going to examine each of these three aspects of I/O in turn.

The difference between the above three aspects of I/O is readily illustrated by means of examples. Consider first a small computer connected to a visual display unit (VDU or, in US terminology, a CRT terminal). The data is moved into or out of the computer by *programmed data transfers*. Whenever the computer has data for the CRT terminal, an instruction in the program writes data into the *output port* that communicates with the CRT terminal. Similarly, when the computer requires data, an instruction reads data from the *input port* connected to the keyboard. The term *port* indicates an interface between the computer and an external I/O device. Programmed data transfer or programmed I/O represents the *strategy* by which the information is moved but tells us nothing about *how* the data is moved. In this example the keyboard and CRT terminal are the actual I/O devices (i.e. peripherals).

To keep our example simple, let's just consider data output from the computer. When the computer sends data to the output port, the output port transmits that data to the CRT terminal. The output port is frequently a sophisticated integrated circuit whose complexity may even approach that of the CPU itself. Such a *semi-intelligent* device relieves the computer of the tedious task of actually communicating with the CRT terminal directly, and frees it to do useful calculations. In practice, the connection between a computer and a CRT terminal almost always consists of a *twisted-pair* (two parallel wires twisted at regular intervals). As the data written into the output port by the CPU is in parallel form (say eight bits), the output port must serialize the data and transmit it a bit at a time over the twisted pair to the CRT terminal. Moreover, the output port must supply *start* and *stop* bits to enable the CRT terminal to synchronize itself with the stream of bits from the computer. Chapter 10 deals in more detail with serial data transmission. We can now see that the output port is the device that is actually responsible for moving the data between the processor and the peripheral.

The CRT terminal is the output device proper. It accepts serial data from the computer, reconstitutes it into a parallel form and uses the data to select a character from a table of symbols. The symbols are then displayed on a television-style (raster-scan) screen. Sometimes the transmitted character is a control symbol (e.g. carriage return, line-feed, backspace) that affects the format (layout) of the display rather than adding a new character to it. Figure 7.1 illustrates the relationship between the concepts expressed in the above example.

As another example of the relationship between I/O strategy, I/O hardware and I/O peripherals, consider the writing of a block of data to a disk. It is often impractical to use programmed data transfers for disk I/O since they are either too slow or waste valuable computing time. The output strategy most frequently resorted to is *direct memory access (DMA)*, in which the data is transferred from the computer's main memory to a peripheral, or vice versa, without passing through the CPU's registers. The CPU simply tells the DMA hardware to move a block of

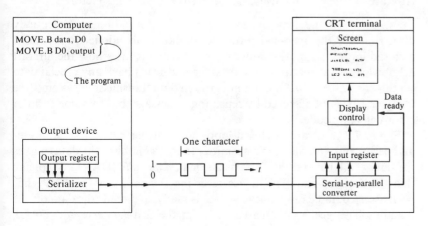

Fig. 7.1 The relationship between the CPU and CRT terminals.

data and the DMA hardware gets on with the task, allowing the CPU to continue its main function of information processing. Note that this strategy (i.e. DMA) requires specific hardware to implement it.

The DMA hardware is called a DMA controller (DMAC) and is responsible for actually moving the data between the memory and the peripheral. It must provide addresses for the source or destination of data in memory, and signal to the peripheral that data is needed or is ready. Furthermore, the DMAC must grab the computer's internal data and address buses for the duration of data transfer. Data transfer by DMA must be done while avoiding a conflict with the CPU for the possession of the buses. In this example the peripheral is a disk drive—a complex mixture of electronics and high-precision mechanical engineering designed to store data by locally affecting the magnetic properties of the surface of a disk rotating at a high speed.

Before dealing with input/output strategies, we must introduce the concept of *handshaking*, as it is fundamental to all exchanges of information.

Handshaking

Irrespective of the strategy by which data is moved between the processor and peripheral, all data transfers fall into one of two classes: open-ended or closed-loop. In an open-ended I/O transaction the data to be output is sent on its way and its safe reception assumed. Open-ended data transfers correspond to the basic level of service offered by the mail service. A letter is written and dropped into a mail-box. The sender believes that after a reasonable delay, it will be received.

Many systems, both human and computer, find open-ended data transfers perfectly satisfactory. The probability of data getting lost or corrupted is very small, and its loss may not be of any importance. If Aunt Mable doesn't get a birthday card, the world does not come to an end. Consider now the following exchange of information at an airport.

Approach control	'Golf Zulu Victor Cleared to Teesside for straight in approach. Runway 23. Wind 270 degrees 10 knots. QFE 1019 millibars. Report field in sight.'
Aircraft	'Runway 23. QFE 1019. Golf Zulu Victor.'

In such cases, the loss or corruption of information is potentially disastrous and the open-ended transfer of data is abandoned in favour of a closed-loop system. The above example demonstrates how the aircraft acknowledges the receipt of the message and reads back any crucial data (in this case 23 and 1019). Data integrity in data transmission systems (see Chapter 10) is not achieved by repeating a message, but by some form of error-detecting code.

Figure 7.2 illustrates a closed-loop data transfer between a computer and peripheral. Initially, the transmitter (i.e. originator of the data) makes the data available and then asserts a signal, *data valid* (DAV), to indicate that the data is valid. The device receiving the data sees that DAV has been asserted, indicating that new data is ready, and reads the data off the data bus. The receiver in turn asserts a signal called *data accepted* (DAC),

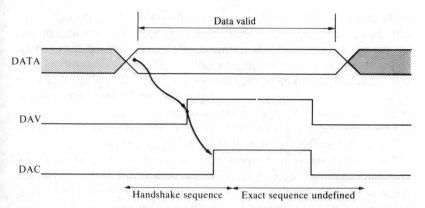

Fig. 7.2 An example of handshaking.

which is a reply to the transmitter, indicating the satisfactory reception of the data. The transmitter then de-asserts DAV to complete the data exchange. This sequence of events is known as *handshaking*. Apart from indicating the receipt of data, handshaking also caters for slow peripherals, because the transfer is held up until the device indicates its readiness by asserting DAC.

Figure 7.3 shows how the handshaking process may be taken a step further in which the acknowledgement is itself acknowledged, to create a fully interlocked data transfer. The term *fully interlocked* means that each stage in a handshaking procedure can continue only when the previous stage has been *acknowledged*. At point A in Fig. 7.3 the transmitter asserts DAV, indicating the availability of data. At B the receiver asserts DAC, indicating that DAV has been observed and the data accepted. So far this is the same procedure as in Fig. 7.2. The transmitter sees that DAC is asserted and de-asserts (i.e. negates) DAV, indicating that data is no longer valid and that it is acknowledging that the receiver has accepted the data. Finally, at D the receiver de-asserts DAC to complete the cycle, and to indicate that it has seen the transmitter's acknowledgement of its receipt of data. The difference between Figs. 7.2 and 7.3 (i.e. between

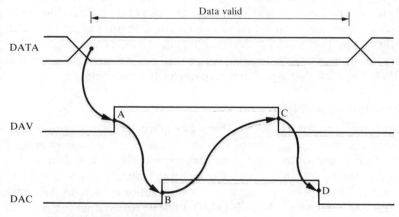

Fig. 7.3 Fully interlocking handshaking.

A transmitter asserts data valid
B receiver asserts data accepted
C transmitter de-asserts data valid in response to B
D receiver de-asserts data accepted in response to C

handshaking and fully interlocked handshaking) should be stressed again. Handshaking merely involves an acknowledgement of data, which implies that the assertion of DAV is followed by the assertion of DAC. What happens after this is undefined. In fully interlocked handshaking each action (i.e. the assertion or negation of a signal) takes place in a strict sequence, which ends only when all signals have finally been negated. Interlocked handshaking is a two-way process because the receiver acknowledges the assertion of DAV by asserting DAC while the transmitter acknowledges the assertion of DAC by negating DAV.

Many real systems employing closed-loop data transfers make the entire handshaking sequence automatic in the sense that it is carried out by special-purpose hardware. The computer itself does not get involved in the process. Only if something goes wrong does the processor take part in the handshaking.

In any data transfer involving handshaking, a problem arises when the transmitter asserts DAV, but DAC is not asserted by the receiver in turn (because the equipment is faulty or the receiver is not switched on). When the transmitter wishes to send data, it starts a timer concurrently with the assertion of DAV. If DAC is not asserted by the receiver after a given time has passed, the operation is aborted. The period of time between the start of an action and the declaration of a failure state is called a *time-out*. When a time-out occurs, an interrupt (see Section 7.2) is generated, forcing the computer to take action. In a poorly designed system without a time-out mechanism, the non-completion of a handshake causes the transmitter to wait for DAC forever and the system is then said to *hang up*.

7.1 Programmed I/O

In programmed I/O an instruction in the program initiates the data transfer. Some microprocessors (e.g. Intel 8080 or 8086) have explicit I/O instructions. For example, executing an 'OUT 123' with the 8080 causes the contents of its accumulator to be placed on the data bus, the number 123 to be placed on the eight least-significant bits of the address bus, and a pulse to be generated on the system's $\overline{\text{IOW}}$ (input/output write) line. Each of the I/O ports in a 8085 system monitors the address lines. When an I/O port sees its own address together with a read or write signal to a port (i.e. $\overline{\text{IOW}}$), it acts on that signal and executes an I/O data transfer.

Memory-mapped I/O

Many microprocessors lack any form of explicit I/O instruction. If these devices are to use programmed I/O, they must resort to *memory-mapped I/O*. That is, part of the normal memory space of the CPU is dedicated to I/O operations, and an I/O port is arranged to look like a normal memory location. These ports are accessed by conventional memory reference instructions such as MOVE D0,IO_PORT (to output data) and MOVE IO_PORT,D0 (to input data). A disadvantage of memory-mapped I/O is that part of the memory space available to programs and data is lost to the I/O system.

Consider a 68000 microprocessor with an output port located at $008000 connected to a CRT terminal. Storing data in memory location $008000 has the effect of sending it to the CRT terminal. As far as the processor is concerned, it is merely storing data in memory. The fragment of a program in Table 7.1 sends 128 characters (starting at $001000) to the CRT terminal. The system and its memory map is illustrated in Fig. 7.4.

The numbers in the right hand column give the time to execute each instruction in microseconds, assuming a clock rate of 8 MHz. To output the 128 characters takes approximately $128 \times (8 + 8 + 8 + 10)/8 = 544\ \mu s$, which is a little over half of a thousandth of a second. Data is transferred at a rate of one character per $4\frac{1}{4}\ \mu s$.

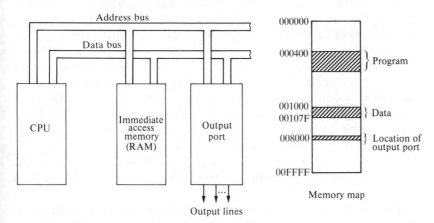

Fig. 7.4 Memory-mapped I/O.

Although the program in Table 7.1 looks as if it should work, it is unsuited to almost all real situations involving programmed output. Most peripherals connected to an output port are relatively slow devices and sending data to them at this rate would simply result in almost all the data being lost. Some interfaces are, however, able to deal with short bursts of

Table 7.1 Simple example of programmed output

```
*  FOR I = 1 TO 128
*        Move date from Table(I) to output_port
*  ENDFOR
*                                                                   Cycles

PORT      EQU      $008000       Location of memory-mapped port
          ORG      $001000       Origin for data area
TABLE     DS.B     128           Reserve 128 bytes for the table
COUNT     EQU      128           Size of block to be output
          ORG      $000400       Origin of program
          MOVE     #COUNT,D1     [D1]←128              Set up loop counter
          LEA      TABLE,A0      [A0]←TABLE            A0 points to the table
          LEA      PORT1,A1      [A1]←Port1            A1 points to the port
*
LOOP      MOVE.B   (A0)+,D0      [D0]←[MS([A0])]       Get data to be output        8
*                                [A0]←[A0]+1
          MOVE.B   D0,(A1)       [MS([A1])]←[D0]       Output the data              8
          SUB      #1,D1         [D1]←[D1] − 1         Decrement counter            8
          BNE      LOOP          IF Z ≠ 0 THEN [PC]←LOOP                           10
```

high-speed data because they store data in a buffer (a short-term memory arranged as a first-in first-out queue) while they are slowly processing it.

A solution to the problem of dealing with such a mis-match in speed between computer and peripheral is found by asking the peripheral if it is ready to receive or to transmit data, and not sending data to it until it is ready to receive it. That is, we introduce a type of handshaking procedure between the peripheral and the interface.

Almost all memory-mapped I/O ports occupy two or more memory locations. One location is reserved for the actual data to be input or output, and one holds a *status* byte associated with the port. For example, let $008000 be the location to which data is sent and $008002 be the location of the status byte. Suppose that bit 0 of the status is a 1 if the port is ready for data, and a 0 if it is busy. The fragment of program in Table 7.2 implements memory-mapped output at a rate determined by the peripheral.

The program in Table 7.2 is identical to the previous example except for lines 10–14 inclusive. In line 10 an address register, A2, is used to point to the status byte of the interface at address $008002. In line 12 the status byte of the interface is read into D2 and masked down to the least-significant bit (by the action of AND.B #1,D2 in line 13). If the lsb of the status byte is zero, a branch back to line 12 is made by the instruction in line 14. When the interface becomes free (as indicated by the lsb of the status byte being 1), the branch to WAIT is not taken and the program continues exactly as in Table 7.1.

The action of lines 12, 13, and 14 is called a *polling loop*, in which the

Table 7.2 Using the polling loop to control the flow of data

```
*       FOR I  =  1 TO 128
*                 REPEAT
*                     Read port_status_byte
*                 UNTIL Port_not_busy
*                 Move data from Table(I) to output_port
*       ENDFOR
*
1.      PORT_DATA    EQU      $008000        Location of memory-mapped port
2.      PORT_STAT    EQU      $008002        Location of port's status byte
3.                   ORG      $001000        Start of data area
4.      TABLE        DS.B     128            Reserve 128 bytes of data
5.      COUNT        EQU      128            Size of block to be output
6.                   ORG      $000400        Origin of program
7.                   MOVE     #COUNT,D1      Set up character counter in D1
8.                   LEA      TABLE,A0       A0 points to table in memory
9.                   LEA      PORT_DATA,A1   A1 points to data port
10.                  LEA      PORT_STAT,A2   A2 points to port status byte
11.     LOOP         MOVE.B   (A0)+,D0       Get a byte from the table
12.     WAIT         MOVE.B   (A2),D2        Read the port's status
13.                  AND.B    #1,D2          Mask all but lsb of status byte
14.                  BEQ      WAIT           IF Z = 0 THEN [PC] ← WAIT
15.                  MOVE.B   D0,(A1)        Store data in peripheral
16.                  SUB      #1,D1          Decrement loop counter
17.                  BNE      LOOP           Repeat until COUNT = 0
```

output device is continually *polled* (questioned) until it indicates it is free, allowing the program to continue. A typical low-cost printer operates at 30 characters/second, or approximately 1 character per 33 000 µs. As the polling loop takes about 3 µs, the loop is executed 11 000 times per character. Operating a computer in a polled I/O mode is a grossly inefficient thing to do, but a small microcomputer might have 'nothing better to do' while it is waiting for a peripheral to become free (i.e. not busy). Many of the first generation of personal computers were operated in this way. However, a more powerful computer working in a multiprogramming environment can attend to someone else's program during the time the I/O port is busy. In this case a better I/O strategy is to ignore the output peripheral until it is ready for a data transfer and then let the peripheral ask the CPU for attention. Such a strategy is called *interrupt-driven* I/O.

7.2 Interrupt-driven I/O

As we know, a computer executes instructions sequentially unless a jump or a branch is made. There is an important exception to this rule called an *interrupt*. An interrupt is an event that forces the CPU to modify the sequence of actions that would have occurred if the interrupt had not taken place. Here we deal entirely with hardware interrupts and omit the software interrupt which is, essentially, a programmed call (or jump) to the operating system. For the purposes of this introduction, we first deal with the interrupt structure of a primitive 8-bit microprocessor, the 6502, before we turn to the complexities of the 68000's interrupt-handling facilities.

Most microprocessors have one or more input pins called *interrupt request* inputs. The 6502 designates this pin $\overline{\text{IRQ}}$ (pronounced 'not interrupt request'). The bar above the 'IRQ' signifies that a low-level (logical zero) at the pin requests the interrupt. Note that the word *request* carries with it the implication that the interrupt request may or may not be granted. Bit 2 of the 6502's program status word, PSW, is an interrupt mask bit which, when set, causes interrupt requests to be ignored. Figure 7.5 illustrates the structure of the 6502's interrupt system.

When the 6502's $\overline{\text{IRQ}}$ pin goes low (assuming the interrupt mask bit of the PSW is clear) the following sequence of events takes place. First, the CPU is allowed to finish its current instruction. All 8-bit microprocessors and many large computers cannot be stopped in mid-instruction, as individual machine-code instructions are indivisible and must always be executed to completion. Second, the contents of the program counter and the program status word are pushed on to the stack. The PSW must be saved because the interrupt occurs at a time not controlled by the programmer and the interrupt routine will almost certainly modify the condition code bits. Third, the interrupt mask bit of the PSW is set to stop (disable) further interrupts. Finally, the program counter is loaded with the contents of memory locations $FFFE and $FFFF($FFFF holds the most significant byte of the address and $FFFE the LSB). The word

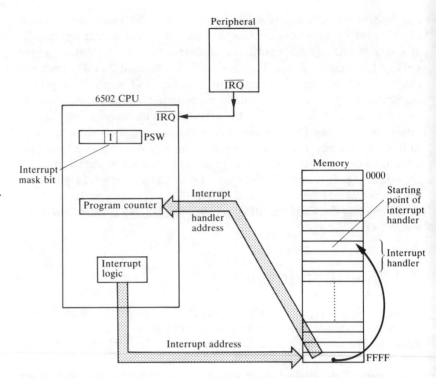

Fig. 7.5 6502's interrupt structure.

stored in these two bytes is the address of the procedure, called an *interrupt-handling routine*, that deals with the interrupt.

The CPU now executes the interrupt-handling routine pointed at by the contents of $FFFE, $FFFF. At the end of this routine, an RTI (return from interrupt) instruction is executed which takes the contents of the registers saved on the stack and returns them to the CPU's program counter and PSW, so that the CPU continues as if the interrupt had never happened. I like to think of an interrupt as a subroutine which is jammed or forced into a program by an external event ($\overline{IRQ}$ going low). The majority of CPUs deal with interrupts in the same way as the 6502 and we list the major actions that take place following an interrupt request.

1. recognize interrupt request;
2. complete the current instruction;
3. save the PC and processor status on the stack;
4. jump to the interrupt-handling routine;
5. execute the interrupt-handling routine;
6. execute a return from interrupt instruction;
7. restore the PC and processor status;
8. continue as before the interrupt.

Figure 7.6 illustrates the action of an interrupt in a 6502 system and an example of the hardware required to implement interrupt-driven I/O in a 6502 system given in Fig. 7.7. Here the $\overline{IRQ}$ input to the CPU is pulled up to a logical one state by a resistor. When any I/O device generates an interrupt, it pulls the $\overline{IRQ}$ pin down to a logical zero. Note the simplicity of Fig. 7.7—very few components are needed to implement interrupt-

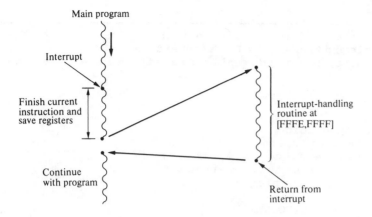

Fig. 7.6 The sequence of events taking place during an interrupt.

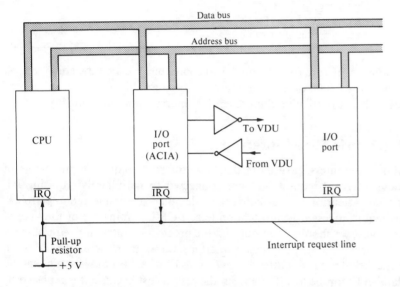

Fig. 7.7 Interrupt-handling logic in a 6502 system.

driven I/O in a small microprocessor system. This arrangement is analogous to the emergency cord in a train. When it is pulled, the driver knows only that attention is requested. The driver does not yet know who pulled the cord. Similarly the CPU does not know which peripheral caused the interrupt or why.

Interrupt-driven I/O requires a more complex program than programmed I/O, because the information transfer takes place not when the programmer wants or expects it, but when the data is available. That is, the software required to implement interrupt-driven I/O is frequently part of a complex operating system. A fragment of a hypothetical interrupt-driven output routine in 68000 assembly language is provided in Table 7.3. Each time the interrupt-handling routine is called, data is obtained from a buffer and passed to the memory-mapped output port at $008000. In a practical system some check would be needed to test for the end of the buffer.

Although the basic idea of interrupts is common to most computers, there are considerable variations in the precise nature of the interrupt-

Table 7.3 A simple interrupt handler

```
*              Pick up pointer to next free entry in the table (buffer)
*              Read a byte from the table and transmit it to the interface
*              Move the pointer to the next entry in the table and save the pointer in memory
*              Return from interrupt
*
*
*
               ORG      $001000        Data origin
BUFFER         DS.B     1024           Reserve 1024 bytes for the table
POINTER        DS.L     1              Reserve a long word for the pointer
OUTPUT         EQU      $008000        Location of memory-mapped output port
               ORG      $002000        Start of the program fragment
*
               MOVE.L   POINTER,A0     [A0]←[MS(POINTER)]
               MOVE.B   (A0)+,D0       [D0]←[MS([A0])]; [A0]←[A0]+1
               MOVE.B   D0,OUTPUT      [MS(OUTPUT)]←[D0]
               MOVE.L   A0,POINTER     [MS(POINTER)]←[A0]
               RTE                     return from interrupt
```

handling structure from computer to computer. We are now going to look at how the 68000 deals with interrupts because this particular microprocessor has a particular comprehensive interrupt-handling facility.

7.2.1 Prioritized interrupts

Many computers have more than one interrupt request input. Some of these interrupt-request pins are connected to peripherals requiring immediate attention (e.g. disk drive), while others are connected to peripherals requiring less urgent attention (e.g. a CRT terminal). For the sake of accuracy, we should point out that the processor's interrupt-request input is connected to the peripheral's interface, rather than the peripheral itself. If the disk drive is not attended to (serviced) when its data is available, the data will soon be lost. Data from the disk is lost because it is replaced by new data. In such circumstances, it is reasonable to assign a *priority* to each of the interrupt-request pins. For example, a processor may be provided with seven interrupt-request pins from $\overline{IRQ7}$ first (most important) to $\overline{IRQ1}$ last. If an interrupt is caused by the assertion of $\overline{IRQ3}$, and no other interrupts are pending, it will be serviced. If an interrupt at a level *higher* than $\overline{IRQ3}$ occurs, it will be serviced *before* the level 3 interrupt service routine is completed. However, interrupts generated by $\overline{IRQ1}$ or $\overline{IRQ2}$ will be stored pending the completion of $\overline{IRQ3}$'s service routine.

The 68000 does not have seven *explicit* $\overline{IRQ1}$ to $\overline{IRQ7}$ interrupt request inputs (simply because such an arrangement would require seven precious pins). Instead, the 68000 has a three-bit *encoded interrupt request* input, $\overline{IPL0}$ to $\overline{IPL2}$. The 3-bit value on $\overline{IPL0}$ to $\overline{IPL2}$ reflects the current level of interrupt request from 0 (i.e. no interrupt request) to 7 (the highest level corresponding to $\overline{IRQ7}$). Figure 7.8 illustrates some of the components involved in the 68000's interrupt-handling structure. Most applications of the 68000 employ a 74LS148 *priority encoder* chip to convert an interrupt request on $\overline{IRQ1}$ to $\overline{IRQ7}$ into a three-bit code in $\overline{IPL0}$ to $\overline{IPL2}$. The

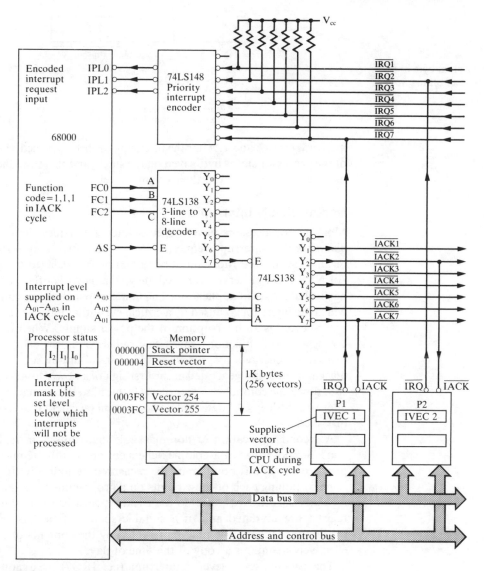

Fig. 7.8 The 68000's interrupt structure.

74LS148 automatically prioritizes an interrupt request and its output reflects the highest interrupt-request level asserted.

The 68000 does not **automatically** service an interrupt request. There is a three-bit interrupt mask field in the system byte of its processor status word illustrated in Fig. 7.9. The 68000 responds to an interrupt only if its level is greater than that of the interrupt mask. For example, if the interrupt mask has a current value of 4, only interrupt requests on $\overline{IRQ5}$ to $\overline{IRQ7}$ will be serviced. When the 68000 services an interrupt, the interrupt mask bits are reset to make them equal to the level of the interrupt currently being serviced. For example, if the interrupt mask bits were set to 2 and an interrupt occurred at level $\overline{IRQ5}$, the mask bits would be set to 5. Consequently, the 68000 can now be re-interrupted only by

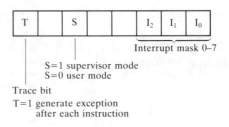

Fig. 7.9 The system byte of the 68000's processor status word.

interrupt levels 6 and 7. After the interrupt has been serviced, the old value of the processor status byte saved on the stack, and therefore the interrupt mask bits, are restored to their original level.

Non-maskable interrupts

Most microprocessors have a special interrupt request input, termed a *non-maskable* interrupt request, NMI. Here, the term non-maskable means that the interrupt cannot be turned off (i.e. delayed or suspended). An NMI must be serviced immediately. The NMI is often found in two particular classes of application. The first group includes circumstances in which the interrupt is caused by a critical event that must not be missed. A typical event is an interruption of the power supply. When this happens the system still functions for a few milliseconds on energy stored in capacitors (energy storage devices found in all power supplies). A non-maskable interrupt generated at the first sign of a power loss is arranged to shut down the computer in an orderly fashion, so that it may be re-started later with little loss of data and no corruption (accidental over-writing) of disk files.

A second application of non-maskable interrupts is in real-time systems. Suppose that in a complex chemical process the temperature and pressure at various points must be measured periodically. If this is not done by polling each of these points on a programmed basis, a stream of regularly spaced NMIs will do the trick. At each NMI the contents of a register are up-dated and, if a suitable span of time has elapsed, the readings are taken. The time represented by the contents of the register effectively maintains a copy of the time of day.

The 68000 uses a level 7 interrupt (i.e. $\overline{\text{IRQ7}}$) as a non-maskable interrupt, because an interrupt on $\overline{\text{IRQ7}}$ is *always* serviced by the 68000. If a level 7 interrupt is currently being serviced by the 68000, a further active transition on $\overline{\text{IRQ7}}$ (i.e. a high to low edge) results in the 68000 servicing the new level 7 interrupt.

7.2.2 Vectored interrupts

Early microprocessors of the 8085, 6800, and 6502 vintages resort to a simple method of locating their appropriate interrupt-handling routines following the detection and acceptance of an interrupt. These microprocessors read the contents of a particular memory location (determined by the designer of the chip) and jump to the address stored in that location. We have already said that the 6502 stores its interrupt-handling routine at address $FFFE. Consequently, first-generation microprocessor systems were forced to store the address of their interrupt handlers in read-only memory. A fixed and predetermined address that points to an interrupt-handling routine has several disadvantages. In particular, it is not possible to distinguish between interrupts originating from one of a number of different peripherals. Before we look at how the 68000 solves the problem of multiple interrupt sources, it is instructive to consider how typical 8-bit microprocessors perform the task of isolating the cause of an interrupt request.

The 6502 microprocessor has a single $\overline{IRQ}$ input and all interfaces capable of generating an interrupt have their $\overline{IRQ}$ output pin connected to the CPU's $\overline{IRQ}$ pin. When an interface generates an interrupt by pulling $\overline{IRQ}$ low, the CPU cannot immediately determine which interface was responsible. One way out of this difficulty is to poll each of the interface's status registers. Polling is, of course, done within the interrupt-handling routine. All interfaces have a status register containing one or more interrupt-request flag bits. If an interface caused the interrupt, its interrupt flag bit is set. As the programmer chooses the order in which the interfaces are polled following an interrupt, a limited measure of prioritization is built into the polling process. Polling can be very inefficient if there are many devices capable of causing an interrupt. It is a well-known law of the universe that when searching through a pile of magazines for a particular issue, the desired issue is always at the opposite end to the point at which the search was started. Incidentally, beginning the search at the other end of the pile does not defeat this law. Likewise, the device that generated the interrupt is the last device to be polled.

The 68000 and vectored interrupts

In a system with a CPU capable of implementing *vectored interrupts* the interface itself provides some means of identifying its associated interrupt-handling routine, thereby removing the need for polling. Whenever the 68000 detects an interrupt, the 68000 acknowledges it by transmitting an *interrupt acknowledge* to all the interfaces that might have originated the interrupt. The 68000 generates an interrupt acknowledge by putting out a code of 1,1,1 on its three *function code* outputs, FC0 to FC2 (see Fig. 7.10). The function code is used by the 68000 to inform external devices (i.e. memory or interfaces) about the nature of the current bus cycle. When FC0,FC1,FC2 = 1,1,1, the 68000 is acknowledging an interrupt request. However, as the 68000 has seven levels of interrupt request, it is necessary for the 68000 to acknowledge the appropriate level of interrupt. It would be terribly unfair if a level 2 and a level 6 interrupt occurred nearly simultaneously and the interface requesting a level 2 interrupt thought that *its* interrupt was about to be serviced. To avoid seven explicit interrupt acknowledge pins, the 68000 puts out the level of the interrupt being serviced on the three least-significant bits of its address bus (A_{01}–A_{03}).

When an interface issues an interrupt, it waits for an acknowledgement from the 68000 on its $\overline{IACK}$ input and then checks A_{01}–A_{03} to determine whether the 68000 is acknowledging the level of interrupt it is requesting. If the 68000 is acknowledging its interrupt, the interface puts out an *interrupt vector number* on data bits D_{00}–D_{07}. That is, the interface is able to respond with a number ranging from 0 to 255. When the 68000 receives the interrupt vector number, it multiplies it by *four* to get an entry into the 68000's interrupt vector table. For example, if an interface responds to an $\overline{IACK}$ cycle with a vector number of 100, the 68000 multiplies it by 4 to get 400. In the next step, the 68000 reads the contents of location 400 to get the *interrupt vector*. The interrupt vector points to the location of the interrupt-handing routine for the interface that initiated the interrupt and therefore the interrupt vector is loaded into the 68000's program counter to start interrupt processing.

As an interface can supply one of 256 different vector numbers, it is theoretically possible to support 256 unique interrupt-handling routines for 256 different interfaces. I say *theoretically*, because it is unusual for 68000 systems to dedicate all 256 vector numbers to interrupt handling. In fact, the 68000 itself uses vector numbers 0 to 63 for purposes other than handling *hardware* interrupts. The manufacturers of the 68000 *recommend* that only interrupt numbers 64 to 255 be used for interrupt handling.

Why does the 68000 multiply the vector number by four? The answer to this is easy: the interrupt *vector* loaded into the 68000's PC is a 32-bit value that occupies *four* bytes in memory. Therefore, each vector number is associated with a four-byte (i.e. long-word) block of memory. The interrupt vector table itself takes up $4 \times 256 = 1024$ bytes of memory. Figure 7.10 illustrates the way in which the 68000 implements vectored interrupts.

The above scheme of vectored interrupts seems to have an important flaw! Although there are $256 - 64 = 192$ interrupt vector numbers, the 68000 has only *seven* levels of interrupt. Why then do we need to cater for so many interrupt handlers? In the first case, it is not necessary for all interfaces to be active at the same time. We could envisage a scheme with, say, 20 interfaces with 20 interrupt handlers. It is perfectly possible to program the interfaces so that only seven of them can issue an interrupt at any instant.

There is, however, a better way of expanding interrupt levels beyond the seven provided by the 68000. Figure 7.11 shows how interrupt requesters at a given priority level can be prioritized by *daisy chaining*. Each peripheral has an $\overline{IACK\_IN}$ input on its left and an $\overline{IACK\_OUT}$ output on its right. The $\overline{IACK\_OUT}$ pin of each peripheral is wired to the $\overline{IACK\_IN}$ pin of the peripheral on its right. Thus, the $\overline{IACK\_OUT}/\overline{IACK\_IN}$ pins constitute a daisy chain (i.e. a head-to-tail connection). Suppose an interrupt request at level 6 is issued and acknowledged by the 68000. The interface at the left-hand side of the daisy chain closest to the 68000 receives the $\overline{IACK}$ signal first from the CPU. If this interface generated the interrupt, it responds with and interrupt vector. If the interface did not request service, it passes the $\overline{IACK}$ signal to the device on its right. That is, $\overline{IACK\_IN}$ is passed out on $\overline{IACK\_OUT}$. The $\overline{IACK}$ signal ripples down the daisy chain until a device responds with an interrupt vector.

Daisy chaining interfaces permits an unlimited number of interfaces to share the same level of interrupt and each interface to have its own interrupt vector number. Individual interfaces are prioritized by their

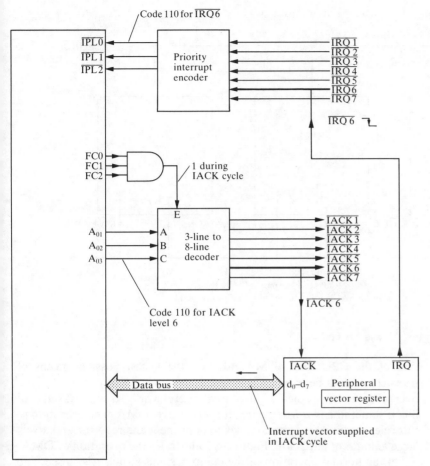

Fig. 7.10 Responding to a vectored interrupt.

position with respect to the CPU. The closer to the CPU an interface is, the more chance it has of having its interrupt request serviced in the event of multiple interrupt requests at this level

Interrupts considered harmful

Each aspect of life can be divided into one of two categories: a good thing or a bad thing. There are those who are firmly convinced that interrupts are a bad thing. A single interface generating the occasional interrupt causes few headaches. But imagine a system with many interfaces, all generating their interrupts asynchronously (i.e. at random). The entire system no longer behaves in a deterministic way but becomes stochastic (non-deterministic) and is best described by the mathematics of random processes. This system is analogous to a large group of people in a bar— there is always someone who never seems to get served.

7.3 Direct memory access

Direct memory access, DMA, is an input/output strategy that moves data between a peripheral and the CPU's memory without the direct interven-

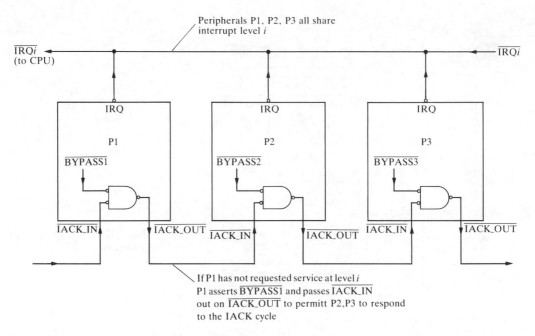

Fig. 7.11 Daisy-chaining interrupts at the same level of priority.

tion of the CPU itself. DMA provides the fastest possible means of transferring data between an interface and memory, as it carries no CPU overhead and leaves the CPU free to do useful work. As in most walks of life, if something is worth having, it is expensive. DMA is no exception to this rule, because it is quite complex to implement and requires a relatively large amount of hardware. Figure 7.12 illustrates the operation of DMA.

During normal operation of the computer, bus switch 1 is closed, and bus switches 2 and 3 are open. The CPU controls the buses, providing an address on the address bus and reading data from memory or writing data to memory via the data bus. When a DMA transfer takes place, bus switch 1 is opened, and switches 2 and 3 closed. The DMA controller (DMAC) provides an address to the address bus and hence to the memory. At the same time, it provides a DMA grant (DMAG) signal to the peripheral which is then able to write to, or read from, the memory directly. When the DMA operation has been completed, the DMAC hands back control of the bus to the CPU.

A real DMA controller is a very complex device. It has several internal registers, at least one to hold the address of the next memory location to access and one to hold the number of words to be transferred. Many DMACs are able to deal with several interfaces, which means that their registers must be duplicated. Each interface is referred to as a **channel** and typical single-chip DMA controllers handle up to four channels (i.e. peripherals) simultaneously.

DMA normally operates in one of two modes: burst mode or cycle stealing. In the **burst mode** the DMA controller seizes the system bus for the duration of the data transfer operation (or at least for the transfer of a large number of words). Burst mode DMA allows data to be moved into

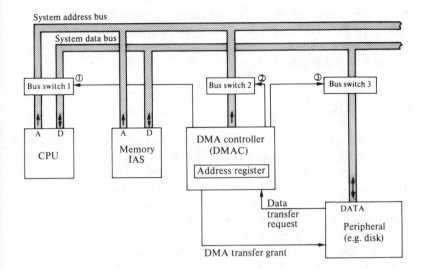

Fig. 7.12 Input/output by means of DMA.

memory as fast as the weakest link in the chain memory/bus/interface will permit. Unfortunately, in the burst mode the CPU is effectively halted because it cannot use its data and address buses.

In the **cycle steal mode**, DMA operations are interleaved with the normal memory accesses of the computer. As the computer does not require access to the system buses for 100 per cent of the time, DMA can take place when they are free. In many microprocessor systems, this **free time** occurs while the CPU is busy generating an address ready for a memory read or write cycle. Figure 7.3 illustrates cycle stealing.

When the system clock is low, the CPU does not need the use of the buses, so the DMAC grabs them and carries out a data transfer. When the clock goes high the CPU carries out its normal memory access cycle. DMA by cycle stealing is said to be transparent because the computer does not 'see' it. That is, the transfer is invisible to the computer and no processing time is lost. A DMA operation is initiated by the CPU writing a start address and the number of words to be transferred into the DMAC's registers. When the DMA operation has been completed, the

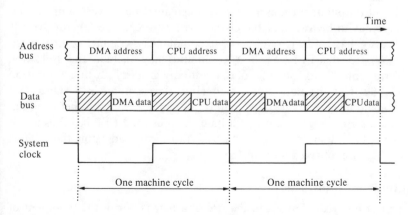

Fig. 7.13 DMA by cycle stealing.

Note: The shaded region indicates invalid data

DMAC generates an interrupt, indicating to the CPU that the data transfer is over, and that a new one may be initiated or results of the current transfer made use of. Small microprocessor systems frequently do not make use of DMA facilities.

7.4 Channel I/O

As computers have become more and more powerful and an increasing number of I/O devices attached to them, even DMA has proved insufficient to cope with the volume of I/O traffic. When people become overloaded, they delegate responsibility for certain tasks to other people. Computers have been forced to do the same and have given the job of dealing with large quantities of I/O to other computers.

Channel I/O is implemented by placing a small computer between the main computer and its peripherals. This computer is frequently called a front end processor (FEP), because it processes the data being input to, or output from, the main processor. It is interesting to note that as mainframe computers get more powerful, so do their FEPs. I have even heard people boast about the power of their mainframes by quoting the type of computer used as an FEP. The implication is, if that's the power of the FEP, just imagine what the mainframe can do.

The FEP is known by other names. IBM uses the term *channels* to describe the streams of data handled by the FEP, and CDC have renamed the FEPs *peripheral processing units* (PPUs). Because of the widespread influence of IBM, the concept of I/O channels is now standard throughout the computer industry. Note that *FEP* or *PPU* denotes what the I/O system is, while *channel* describes the facility it provides.

When an FEP handles a mainframe's I/O transactions, two types of I/O need be considered. There is the I/O as seen by the mainframe, and the I/O as seen by the FEP. The FEP deals with the peripherals themselves and may employ any of the techniques described earlier (polled, interrupt-driven, DMA) to actually move the data between itself and a peripheral. Clearly, the FEP must know the characteristics of each peripheral it services.

Input/output operations as seen by the mainframe are very simple. It no longer has to be aware of the characteristics of each peripheral. All the processor has to do is send a single command, a channel control word (CCW), to the FEP. Such a command may include the following information. 'Read 256 bytes of data into my memory starting at location $002F00. Get the data from channel B, device number 4.' Once this command has been issued, the mainframe can deal with another program while the FEP is getting on with its task. When the FEP has finished, it interrupts the mainframe and returns a status word indicating the success, or otherwise, of the data transfer.

Intelligent interfaces

The last few years have seen the rise of a new factor in the treatment of I/O—the introduction of the so-called intelligent peripheral or intelligent interface. Once upon a time, peripherals (e.g. disk drives, CRT controllers, keyboards) were all different in the way they were interfaced to a computer. Each peripheral required a particular sequence of signals to be exchanged between it and the processor to ensure an orderly flow of data. This sequence varied widely from peripheral to peripheral. Today microprocessors are being embedded in all but the most primitive of peripherals. The embedded microprocessor can deal with some of the complexities of interfacing, with the result that peripherals can now be bought with standard interfaces. One such example is the IEEE-488 bus. Any device sold as being compatible with the IEEE-488 bus can be connected to all other devices displaying the same compatibility, allowing new devices to be plugged into systems without any changes in hardware, and few (if any) changes in software.

7.5 Interfaces

We are now going to look at two chips that have been created to simplify the interface between a microprocessor and an external system. Both of these are relatively basic first-generation interfaces intended for applications involving eight-bit microprocessors. I have selected these particular devices because they are widely used and are not as difficult to explain as the current crop of interfaces optimized for high-performance 16/32-bit microprocessors. The first interface to be described is the PIA which transfers data between an external system and a processor via an 8-bit highway, and the second interface is the ACIA which transfers data on a single-bit serial highway.

7.5.1 The parallel interface

The 6821 peripheral interface adapter, PIA, is a 40-pin chip containing all the logic necessary to move data between the CPU's registers and one of two 8-bit I/O ports. The eight pins making up a port may be programmed individually to act as inputs or outputs. For example, a port may be configured as two inputs and six outputs. Figure 7.14 gives a block diagram of the 6821 from which it can be seen that the I/O ports, referred to as the *A side* and the *B side*, appear symmetrical. In general they are, but small differences in the behaviour of these ports are described when necessary. Each port has two control pins assocated with it that can transform the port from a simple I/O latch into a device capable of performing a handshake or initiating interrupts, as required.

The interface between the PIA and the CPU is quite conventional, as Fig. 7.14 demonstrates. Fifteen of the PIA's *CPU-side* pins make the PIA look to the CPU like a block of four locations in RAM. These pins comprise a data bus and its associated control circuits. The two register-select pins (RS_0 and RS_1) are used by the CPU to discriminate between the PIA's internal registers and are normally connected to the lower-order two bits of the CPU's address bus (A_{01}, A_{02} in the case of the 68000). In addition to the PIA's register select lines, it has a clock input, E, that is

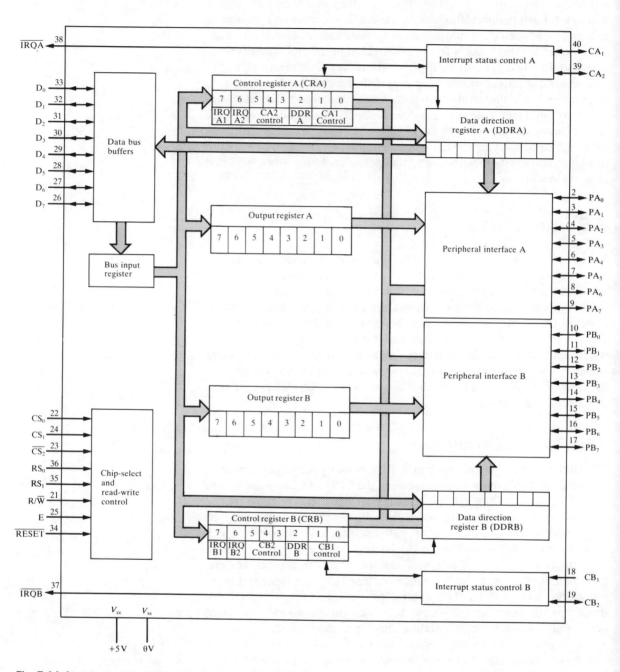

Fig. 7.14 Structure of the 6821 PIA and its interface to a CPU.

used for internal synchronization, a read/write control input, a reset input that can be used for force it into a known state when the system is first powered up, three chip-select inputs, and two interrupt request outputs. The chip-select inputs $CS_0, CS_1, \overline{CS_2}$ must be 1,1,0 to enable the PIA. Modern peripherals rarely have more than a single active-low chip-select input.

The PIA has two interrupt outputs: $\overline{IRQA}$ that can be used to signal an interrupt generated by the PIA's A side and an $\overline{IRQB}$ output that can be used to indicate an interrupt generated by side B. In practice, many users of the PIA simply wire $\overline{IRQA}$ and $\overline{IRQB}$ together and poll the PIA's status registers to determine which side generated the interrupt. When the PIA is first powered up, a pulse is applied to its $\overline{RESET}$ input to force the contents of all its internal registers into a zero state. In this mode the PIA is in a 'safe' state with all its programmable pins configured as inputs. It would be highly dangerous to permit the PIA to assume a random initial configuration, since any random output signals might cause havoc elsewhere.

In order to understand how the PIA operates and hence how it can be used, it is necessary to understand the function of its six internal registers. The PIA has two peripheral data registers (PDRA and PDRB), two data-direction registers (DDRA, DDRB), and two control registers (CRA and CRB). A location within the PIA is addressed by accessing the PIA with the appropriate two-bit address on RS_0, RS_1. However, as RS_0 and RS_1 can distinguish between no more than *four* of the *six* internal registers, some mechanism must be provided to obtain the necessary discrimination. Such a mechanism is implemented by making bit 2 of the control registers (written CRA_2 or CRB_2) act as a pointer to either the data register or the data-direction register. Table 7.4 shows how this works.

From Table 7.4 it can be seen that RS_1 determines which of the two sides of the PIA is selected, while RS_0 determines whether the control register or one of the *pair of registers* formed by the peripheral data register and the data register, is selected. Thus, the control registers can always be unconditionally accessed when $RS_0 = 1$, but to select a per-

Table 7.4 The register selection scheme of the PIA

RS_1	RS_0	CRA_2	CRB_2	Location selected	Address
0	0	1	X	Peripheral data register A	BASE
0	0	0	X	Data direction register A	BASE
0	1	X	X	Control register A	BASE+2
1	0	X	1	Peripheral data register B	BASE+4
1	0	X	0	Data direction register B	BASE+4
1	1	X	X	Control register B	BASE+6

X = don't care
BASE = base address of PIA
RS_0 = register select 0 (usually A_{01})
RS_1 = register select 1 (usually A_{02})
CRA_2 = bit 2 of control register A
CRB_2 = bit 2 of control register B

ipheral data register or a data-direction register, bit 2 of the appropriate control register must be set or cleared, respectively.

From the programmer's point of view, the peripheral data registers act as the interface between the PIA and the outside world. When one of the PIA's I/O pins is acting as an *input*, data is moved from the relevant pin through the peripheral data register onto the CPU's data bus during a read cycle. Conversely, when acting as an *output*, the CPU latches a 1 or 0 into the appropriate bit of the peripheral data register which determines the state of the corresponding output pin of the PIA.

The data-direction registers determine the direction of data transfer on the PIA's 16 I/O pins. If a logical zero is written into bit i of DDRA, then bit i of the A-side peripheral data register is configured as an input. Conversely, writing a one into bit i of DDRA configures bit i of the A-side peripheral data register as an output. In this way the I/O pins of the PIA's A-side or B-side ports may be defined as inputs or outputs by writing an appropriate code into DDRA or DDRB, respectively. Consequently, the PIA's 16 I/O pins can be defined dynamically and, if necessary, altered during the course of a program. The example in Table 7.5 demonstrates how side A is configured as an input, and side B as an output. The PIA is assumed to be located at PIA_BASE which is the base address of the PIA's memory-mapped registers. Accesses to the PIA are made via the pointer to the base address stored in address register A0.

Once the procedure in Table 7.5 has been carried out, data can be read from side A of the PIA into D0 by reading from the PIA with a MOVE.B (A0),D0 instruction, and data may written into side B by writing to the PIA with a MOVE.B D0,4(A0) instruction.

Table 7.5 Configuring a PIA

```
PIA_BASE     EQU    <address of memory-mapped PIA>
PDRA         EQU    0
DDRA         EQU    0
CRA          EQU    2
PDRB         EQU    4
DDRB         EQU    4
CRB          EQU    6
                                 LEA       PIA_BASE,A0
BEGIN
  Select DDRA
    {by setting CRA2 to 0}       CLR.B     CRA(A0)
  Select DDRA as input
    {by writing 0s into DDRA}    MOVE.B    #0,DDRA(A0)
  Select DDRB
    {by setting CRB2 to 0}       CLR.B     CRB(A0)
  Select DDRB as output
    {by writing 1s into DDRB}    MOVE.B    #%11111111,DDRB(A0)
  Select PDRA as input port
    {by setting CRA2 to 1}       ORI.B     #%00000100,CRA(A0)
  Select PDRB as output port
    {by setting CRB2 TO 1}       ORI.B     #%00000100,CRB(A0)
  END
End module
```

Table 7.6 CA_1 control

CRA_1	CRA_0	Transition of CA_1 control input	$IRQA_1$ interrupt flag status	Status of PIA IRQA output
0	0	negative edge	set on −ve edge	masked (remains high)
0	1	negative edge	set on −ve edge	enabled (goes low)
1	0	positive edge	set on +ve edge	masked (remains high)
1	1	positive edge	set on +ve edge	enabled (goes low)

For example, if CRA_1,CRA_0 is set to 0,1, a negative (falling) edge at the CA_1 control input sets the $IRQA_1$ status flag in control register CRA to one and the PIA's $\overline{IRQA}$ interrupt request output is asserted to interrupt the host processor. Note that CRA_1 determines the sense of the transition on CA_1 that sets the interrupt flag status, and CRA_0 determines whether the PIA will interrupt the host processor when the interrupt flag is set.

Table 7.7. CA_2 Configured as an input with $CRA_5=0$

CRA_5	CRA_4	CRA_3	Transition of input line CA_2	IRQ_2 interrupt flag status	Status of PIA IRQA output
0	0	0	negative edge	set on −ve edge	masked (remains high)
0	0	1	negative edge	set on −ve edge	enabled (goes low)
0	1	0	postive edge	set on +ve edge	masked (remains high)
0	1	1	postive edge	set on +ve edge	enabled (goes low)

Table 7.8 CA_2 as an output when $CRA_5=1$

Case	CRA_5	CRA_4	CRA_3	Output CA_2 Cleared	Set
1	1	0	0	Low on the falling edge of E after a CPU read side A data operation	High when interrupt flag bit CRA_7 is set by an active transition of CA_1 input.
2	1	0	1	Low on the falling edge of E after a CPU read side A data operation	High on the negative edge of the first E pulse occurring during a deselect state of the PIA.
3	1	1	0	Low when CRA_3 goes low as a result of a CPU write to CRA.	Always low as long as CRA_3 is low. Will go high on a CPU write to CRA which changes CRA_3 to a 1.
4	1	1	1	Always high as long as CRA_3 is high. Will be cleared on a CPU write to CRA that clears CRA_3	High when CRA_3 goes high as a result of a CPU write to CRA.

Note that the E clock is an external clock input to the PIA which is required for internal synchronization.

Controlling the PIA

In addition to determining whether a data-direction register or a peripheral data register can be directly accessed from the data bus, the two control registers are responsible for controlling the two special-purpose pins associated with each port of the PIA. Side A has CA_1 (an input only pin) and CA_2 (an input or output pin). Similarly, pins CB_1 and CB_2 are associated with side B. In general the operation of CA_1, CA_2 and CB_1, CB_2 are similar, but important differences do exist. A description of control register A and CA_1 and CA_2 is given, and any difference in the behaviour of the corresponding B-side pins are dealt with as necessary.

Here we should point out that the CA_1, CA_2 (or CB_1, CB_2) pins are used to control the flow of information between the peripheral and the PIA by providing any required handshaking procedure.

The structure of control register A, CRA, is illustrated in Fig. 7.15 and the function of CRA's control bits described below. Bits CRA_0–CRA_5 are control bits that are selected by the programmer to set up the operating mode of the PIA. Bits CRA_6 and CRA_7 are *status* bits that are set or cleared by the PIA itself. CRA_6 is interrupt-request flag 1, $IRQA_2$, and is set by an active transition at the CA_2 input pin. Similarly, CRA_7 corresponds to the interrupt request flag, $IRQA_1$, and is set by an active transition at the CA_1 input pin.

CA_1 control (CRA_0, CRA_1).   The four possible combinations of these two bits can be used to detect transitions on the CA_1 control input and generate an interrupt if required. That is, CRA_0 and CRA_1 can be programmed to interrupt the host processor following an active transition at the CA_1 input. Whenever an interrupt is caused by an active transition on CA_1, the interrupt flag in the control register, $IRQA_1$ is set and the $\overline{IRQA}$ output pin goes low. After the CPU has read the contents of peripheral data register A, $IRQA_1$ is automatically reset. The relationship between the CA_1 control input, CRA_0, CRA_1 and the interrupt flag ($IRQA_1$) is described in Table 7.6.

From Table 7.6 it can be seen that the value of CRA_1 determines the sense of the transition on CA_1 that causes CRA_7 (i.e. $IRQA_1$) to be set. However, if CRA_0 is clear, no interrupt request is generated to the CPU. Thus CA_1 can be used as an auxiliary input if bit CRA_0 is clear, or as an interrupt request input if bit CRA_0 is set. In a typical application of the PIA, CA_1 is connected to a peripheral's ready output so that the peripheral can request attention when it is ready to take part in a data transfer. When the processor receives the interrupt, it can then read data from (or write data to) the PIA.

Data direction access control (CRA_2).   The data-direction access control bit determines whether data-direction register A or peripheral data register A is selected. When the PIA is reset, $CRA = 0$ so that the data-direction register is always available after a reset.

CA_2 control (CRA_3, CRA_4, CRA_5).   The CA_2 input may be programmed to generate an interrupt request (in a similar way to CA_1), or it may be programmed to act as an output. Bit 5 of the control register determines the functions of CA_2. If bit $5 = 0$, CA_2 behaves as an interrupt-request input (Table 7.7) and if bit $5 = 1$, CA_2 behaves as an output (Table

bit	7	6	5	4	3	2	1	0
function	$IRQA_1$	$IRQA_2$	CA_2 control			DDRA	CA_1 control	

CRA_1	CRA_0	Transition of input line CA_1	IRQA1 interrupt flag status	*Status* of PIA $\overline{IRQA}$ output
0	0	negative edge	set on ↓ edge	masked (remains high)
0	1	negative edge	set on ↓ edge	enabled
1	0	positive edge	set on ↑ edge	masked (remains high)
1	1	positive edge	set on ↑ edge	enabled

CRA_5	CRA_4	CRA_3	Transition of input line CA_2	IRQA$_2$ interrupt flag status	*Status* of PIA IRQA output
0	0	0	negative edge	set on ↓ edge	masked (remains high)
0	0	1	negative edge	set on ↓ edge	enabled
0	1	0	positive edge	set on ↑ edge	masked (remains high)
0	1	1	positive edge	set on ↑ edge	enabled

Fig. 7.15 The PIA's side A control register, CRA.

				Output CA_2	
Case	CRA_5	CRA_4	CRA_3	Cleared	Set
1	1	0	0	Low on the falling edge of E after CPU read side A data operation.	High when interrupt flag bit CRA_7 is set by an active transition of CA_1 input.
2	1	0	1	Low on the falling edge of E after CPU read side A data operation	High on the negative edge of the first E pulse occurring during a deselect state of the PIA.
3	1	1	0	Low when CRA_3 goes low as a result of a CPU write to CRA.	Always low as long as CRA_3 is low. Will go high on a CPU write to CRA which changes CRA_3 to a 1.
4	1	1	1	Always high as long as CRA_3 is high. Will be cleared on a CPU write to CRA that clears CRA_3.	High when CRA_3 goes high as a result of a CPU write to CRA.

7.8). From Table 7.7 it can be seen that the behaviour of CA_2, when acting as an interrupt-request input, is entirely analogous to that of CA_1.

When CA_2 is programmed as an output with $CRA_5 = 1$ it behaves in the manner defined in Table 7.8. It is in this mode that sides A and B of the PIA differ—a separate table (Table 7.9) describes the behaviour of CB_2 as a function of CRB_4 and CRB_3 when $CRB_5 = 1$. As the significance of the

Table 7.9 CB_2 as an output when $CRB_5 = 1$

Case	CRB_5	CRB_4	CRB_3	Output CA$_2$	
				Cleared	Set
1	1	0	0	Low on the rising edge of the first E pulse following a CPU write side B data operation	High when the interrupt-flag bit CRB_7 is set by an active transition of transition of the CB_1 input.
2	1	0	1	Low on the rising edge of the first E pulse following a CPU write side B data operation.	High on the positive transition of the next E pulse following a deselect of the PIA.
3	1	1	0	Low when CRB_3 goes low as a result of a CPU write to CRB.	Always low as long as CRB_3 is low. Will go high on a CPU write to CRB which changes CRB_3 to a 1.
4	1	1	1	Always high as long as CRB_3 is high. Will be cleared on a CPU write to CRB that clears CRB_3.	High when CRB_3 goes high as a result of a CPU write to CRB.

entries in Table 7.8 is not immediately apparent, further explanation is given case by case.

Case 1 $CRA_5 = 1$, $CRA_4 = 0$, $CRA_3 = 0$. This is known as the ***handshake mode*** and is used when a peripheral is transmitting data to the CPU via the PIA. A timing diagram of the action of the handshake mode of CA_2 is given in Fig. 7.16, together with an explanation of the steps involved. In the handshake mode CA_2 goes high whenever a peripheral has data ready for reading, and remains high until the CPU has read the data from the PIA's data register.

Case 2 $CRA_5 = 1$, $CRA_4 = 0$, $CRA_3 = 1$. This mode is sometimes called the pulsed mode, input-programmed handshaking mode, or ***autohandshaking*** mode and is illustrated in Fig. 7.17. Essentially, CA_2 automatically produces a single pulse at a logical 0 level after the peripheral data register of side A has been read by the CPU. Since the peripheral receives a pulse on CA_2 after the CPU has read the PIA, the peripheral knows that its data has been received and that the PIA is ready for new data.

Case 3 $CRA_5 = 1$, $CRA_4 = 1$, $CRA_3 = 0$. In this mode CA_2 is set to a logical zero and remains in that state until CRA_3 is set. That is, CA_2 is cleared under program control. Consequently, in these modes CA_2 is nothing more than a simple output pin that can be set or cleared as required.

Case 4 $CRA_5 = 1$, $CRA_4 = 1$, $CRA_3 = 1$. Now CA_2 is set to a logical one and remains in that state until CRA_3 is cleared. Cases 3 and 4 demonstrate the use of CA_2 as an additional output, set or cleared under program control.

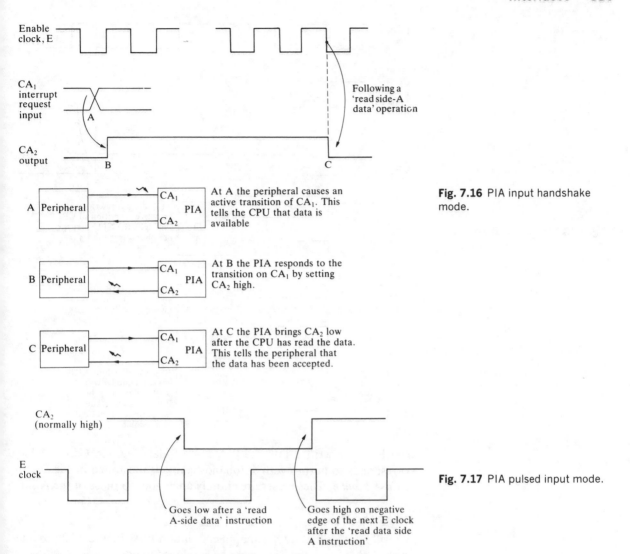

Fig. 7.16 PIA input handshake mode.

Fig. 7.17 PIA pulsed input mode.

Differences between side A and side B ports

The significant differences between side A and B occurs in the behaviour of CA_2 and CB_2 when programmed in the handshake or autohandshake modes. Side A performs handshaking operations when data is read from the PIA by the CPU. Side B performs handshaking operations when data is written into the PIA from the CPU. This difference becomes apparent when the cases of CB_2 programmed as an output are considered (i.e. $CRB_5 = 1$). See Table 7.9.

Case 1 $CRB_5 = 1$, $CRB_4 = 0$, $CRB_3 = 0$. In this handshaking mode CB_2 goes high whenever a peripheral is ready to receive data, and remains high until the CPU has written data into the PIA's side B data register. Figure 7.18 gives the timing diagram of this mode of operation.

Case 2 $CRB_5 = 1$, $CRB_4 = 0$, $CRB_3 = 1$. In this mode the PIA tells the peripheral that data is available by putting a pulse on the CB_2 pin after

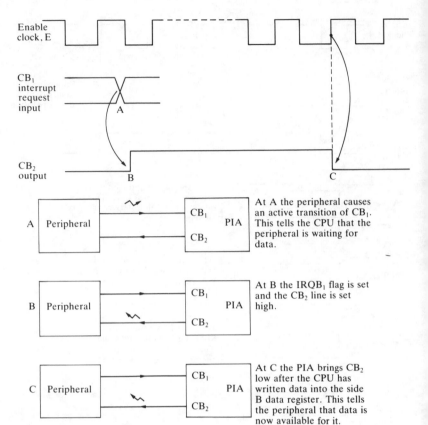

Fig. 7.18 PIA handshake output mode.

data has been written into the PIA's side B data register. Case 2, which corresponds to output with autohandshaking is illustrated in Fig. 7.19.

Case 3 and 4. These cases are entirely analogous to those of the A side.

Using the PIA

We will now look at a typical application of a PIA. Figure 7.20 provides an example of how the PIA might be employed to interface a 68000-based system to a printer. The printer receives data from the host processor via its data bus, d_0–d_7. When the printer is ready to receive a new character, it asserts its active-low $\overline{RDY}$ output and when a valid character is on d_0–d_7, the host processor must assert the active-low strobe input to the printer, $\overline{STB}$.

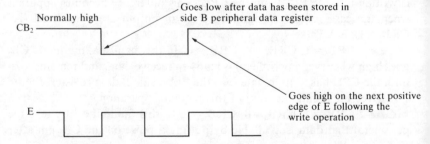

Fig. 7.19 PIA side B pulsed output mode.

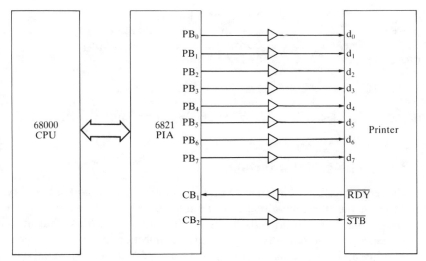

Fig. 7.20 An application of the PIA.

Since the host processor is being used to send data *to* the printer, it is reasonable to employ side B of a PIA to interface the printer, as side B provides an output handshake facility. If the printer's $\overline{\text{RDY}}$ line is connected to the PIA's CB_1 control input, the PIA can interrupt the host processor whenever the printer is ready. Similarly, by connecting the PIA's CB_2 control output to the printer's $\overline{\text{STB}}$ input, a autohandshaking procedure can be implemented.

```
Module Printer control
    Setup_PIA {CR=IRQB₁,IRQB₂,CB₂ control,DDR/DR select,CB₁ control}
             {     X    ,X    ,101         ,0             ,00        }
                {output handshake, select DDR, CB₁ -ve sensitive }
    Configure Side B as output
            {Load DDRB with all one's}
    Select data register
            {Set bit 2 of control register CRB}
    End-setup

    Poll PIA
            {by testing IRQB₁}
    UNTIL Printer RDY
            {RDY asserted causes IRQB₁←1}
    Transmit data to PIA
End module
```

```
PIA      EQU        <address of PIA>          Location of memory mapped PIA
PDRB     EQU        4                         Offset for peripheral data reg B
DDRB     EQU        4                         Offset for data direction register B
CRB      EQU        6                         Offset for control register B
IRQB     EQU        7                         IRQ1=bit 7 of CRB
CRSET    EQU        %00101000                 Data to setup control register
CRB2     EQU        4                         Bit 2 of CRB controls DDRB/PDRB
*
```

```
        LEA       PIA,A0                          A0 points to PIA
        MOVE.B    #CRSET,CRB(A0)                  Set up control register B
        MOVE.B    #%11111111,DDRB(A0)             Configure side B as output
        OR.B      #CRB2,CRB(A0)                   Select PDRB
*
Poll    BTST.B    #IRQB,CRB(A0)                   Test CB₁ (RDY) status
        BEQ       Poll                            Until RDY asserted
        MOVE.B    D0,PDRB(A0)                     Transmit a byte to the printer
:
```

7.5.2 The serial interface

The serial interface transfers data into and out of the CPU and its memory system a bit at a time along a single line. Serial data transfer is much slower than the parallel data transfer offered by a PIA, but it is inexpensive as it requires only a single connection between the serial interface and the external world (apart from a ground-return). Serial data transmission is used by all data transmission systems that operate over distances greater than a few metres and Chapter 10 will have much more to say on the subject of data transmission. Here we are more interested in the interface that connects a CPU to a serial data link.

We are going to look at the 6850 asynchronous communications adaptor, ACIA. We are not interested in fine details about the ACIA's internal operation, but rather in what it does and how it is used to transmit and receive serial data. Note that when referring to serial transmission we often use the term *character* to refer to a unit of data rather than *byte* because many transmission systems are designed to transmit information in the form of ISO/ASCII-encoded characters.

A character is transmitted bit by bit (i.e. a bit at a time) and Fig. 7.21 demonstrates the possible structure of a single 7-bit character. It will be seen later that the 6850 ACIA is able to transmit or receive data in a variety of formats. During a period in which no data is being transmitted from an ACIA, the serial output of the ACIA is at a logical 1, which is called the *mark* condition. When a character is to be transmitted, the output of the ACIA is brought low (a mark-to-space transition) for a period of one bit time. The bit time is the reciprocal of the rate at which successive serial bits are transmitted and is measured in *Baud*, which, for a binary signal, corresponds to bits/s. The initial bit is called the *start* bit and tells the receiver that a stream of bits, representing a character, is about to be received.

During the next seven time slots (each of the same duration as the start bit) the output of the ACIA depends on the value of the character being transmitted. This format is called non-return to zero (NRZ). After the character has been transmitted, a further two bits (a *parity* and a *stop* bit) are appended to the end of the character. At the receiver, the parity bit is generated locally from the received data and then compared with the received parity bit. If the received and locally generated parity bits differ, an error in transmission is assumed to have occurred. A simple parity bit cannot correct an error once it has occurred, nor detect a pair of errors in

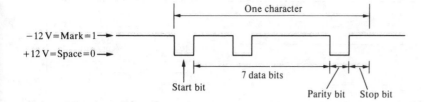

Fig. 7.21 Format of an asynchronous serial character.

a character. The stop bit (or optionally two stops bits) signals the end of the character. At the end of the stop bit(s), the transmitter output is once more in its mark state and is ready to send the next character. Note that the whole character is composed of ten bits but contains only seven bits of useful information. Some serial data transmission systems do not employ a parity bit as an error detector.

The key to asynchronous data transmission is that once the receiver has detected a start bit, it need maintain synchronization only for the duration of a single character. The receiver examines successive received bits by sampling the incoming signal at the centre of each pulse. Because the clock at the receiver is not synchronized with the clock at the transmitter, each received data bit will not be sampled exactly at its centre.

The internal arrangement of the 6850 ACIA is given in Fig. 7.22. This chip is a highly programmable interface whose parameters can be defined under software control. The ACIA has a single receiver input and a single transmitter output. The *CPU side* of the ACIA is very much the same as that of the PIA, as Fig. 7.21 demonstrates. Note that the 6850 does not have a $\overline{\text{RESET}}$ input (due to a lack of pins) and must be reset by a software command after the initial power-up sequence.

The peripheral side pins of the ACIA

The ACIA employs seven pins to communicate with a peripheral. These seven pins may be divided into three groups: receiver, transmitter, and modem control.

Receiver. The receiver has a clock, RX clock, and a serial data input RXD. The receiver clock input is used to sample the incoming data bits. The signal at the clock input to the ACIA may be 64, 16, or 1 times that of the bit rate of the received data. The receiver's serial data input receives data from the peripheral to which the ACIA is connected via, typically, RS232C (V24), RS422, RS423 or RS485 interfaces. These interfaces match the TTL levels at the ACIA to the signal levels found on popular data links.

Transmitter. The transmitter has a clock input from which it generates the timing of the transmitted data pulses. As in the case of the receiver, the transmitter clock may be operated at 64, 16, or 1 times the rate of the data. In many cases the transmitter and receiver clocks are derived from the same oscillator. The transmitter data output TXD, provides a serial signal at a TTL level.

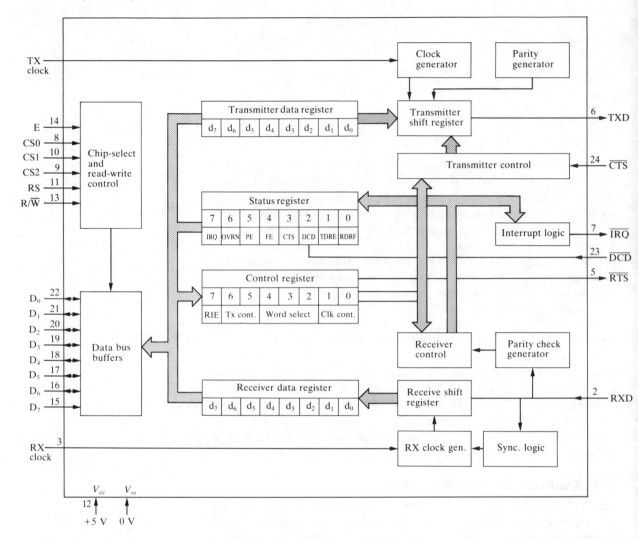

Fig. 7.22 Internal arrangement of the ACIA. Note: TX clock, RX clock are external clocks that determine Tx, Rx baud rates. RXD, TXD: serial input/output. $\overline{\text{CTS}}$, $\overline{\text{RTS}}$, $\overline{\text{DCD}}$: signals used to control a modem. Their use is optional.

Modem control. The ACIA has three pins (two inputs and one output) with which it can communicate with a modem or similar equipment. We will look at the modem in more detail in Chapter 10. At this point, all we need say is that the modem is a black box that interfaces a digital system to the public switched telephone network and therefore permits digital signals to be transmitted across the telephone system. The *request to send* ($\overline{\text{RTS}}$) output of the ACIA may be set or cleared under software control and is used by ACIA to tell the modem that it is ready to transmit data to it.

The two active-low inputs to the ACIA are *clear-to-send* ($\overline{\text{CTS}}$) and *data-carrier-detect* ($\overline{\text{DCD}}$). The $\overline{\text{CTS}}$ input is a signal from the modem to the ACIA and inhibits the ACIA from transmitting data if the modem is not ready for the data (because the telephone connection has not been established or has been broken). If the $\overline{\text{CTS}}$ input is high, a bit is set in the ACIA's status register, indicating that the modem (or other terminal equipment) is not ready for data.

The $\overline{\text{DCD}}$ input of the ACIA is employed by the modem to indicate to the ACIA that the carrier has been lost (i.e. a signal is no longer being received) and that valid data is no longer available at the receiver's input. A low-to-high transition at the $\overline{\text{DCD}}$ input sets a bit in the status register and may also initiate an interrupt if the ACIA is so programmed. In many simple applications of the ACIA that do not use a modem, the $\overline{\text{CTS}}$ and $\overline{\text{DCD}}$ inputs are not used and are connected to ground (i.e. logical zero = asserted level).

The ACIA's internal registers

The ACIA has four internal registers: a transmit data register (TDR), a receive data register (RDR), a control register (CR), and a status register (SR). Since the ACIA has a single register-select input, only two internal registers can be directly accessed by the CPU. As, however, two of the registers (RDR and SR) are always read from and two of the registers (TDR and CR) are always written to, the $R/\overline{W}$ input of the ACIA is used to distinguish between the two pairs of registers. The addressing arrangements of the ACIA are given in Table 7.10.

Table 7.10 The register selection scheme of the ACIA

RS	$R/\overline{W}$	Type of register	ACIA register
0	0	Write only	Control register
0	1	Read only	Status register
1	0	Write only	Transmit data
1	1	Read only	Receive data

The control register is a write only register and defines the operational properties of the ACIA, particularly the format of the transmitted or received data. The format of the control register is given in Table 7.11. The *counter division* field, CR_0 and CR_1 determines the relationship between the transmitter and receiver bit rates and their respective clocks (Table 7.12).

When CR_1 and CR_0 are both set to one, the ACIA is reset and all internal status bits, with the exception of the CTS and DCD flags, are cleared. The CTS and DCD flags are entirely dependent on the signal level at the respective pins. The ACIA is initialized by writing ones into bits

Table 7.11 The format of the control register

Bit	7	6	5	4	3	2	1	0
Function	Receiver interrupt enable	Transmitter control		Word select			Counter division	

Table 7.12 The relationship between CR_1, CR_0 and the division ratio

CR_1	CR_0	Division ratio
0	0	$\div 1$
0	1	$\div 16$
1	0	$\div 64$
1	1	master reset

CR_1 and CR_0 of the control register and then writing one of the three division ratio codes into these positions. In the majority of systems $CR_1 = 0$ and $CR_0 = 1$ for a divide by 16 ratio.

The *word select* field, CR_2, CR_3, CR_4 defines the format of the received or transmitted characters. These three bits allow the selection of eight possible arrangements of number of bits per character, type of parity, and number of stop bits (Table 7.13).

The *transmitter control* field, CR_5 and CR_6, determines the level of the request to send ($\overline{RTS}$) output, and the generation of an interrupt by the transmitter portion of the ACIA. Table 7.14 gives the relationship between these controls bits and their functions. $\overline{RTS}$ can be employed to tell the modem that the ACIA has data to transmit.

The transmitter interrupt can be enabled or disabled depending on whether the CPU is operating in an interrupt-driven or in a polled-data mode. If the transmitter interrupt is enabled, a transmitter interrupt is generated whenever the transmit-data register (TDR) is empty, signifying the need for new data from the CPU. Note that if the ACIA's clear-to-send input is high, the TDR empty flag bit in the status register is held low, inhibiting any transmitter interrupt.

The effect of setting both CR_6 and CR_5 to a logical one requires some

Table 7.13 The word select bits

CR_4	CR_3	CR_2	Data word length	Parity	Stop bits	Total bits
0	0	0	7	Even	2	11
0	0	1	7	Odd	2	11
0	1	0	7	Even	1	10
0	1	1	7	Odd	1	10
1	0	0	8	None	2	11
1	0	1	8	None	1	10
1	1	0	8	Even	1	11
1	1	1	8	Odd	1	11

Table 7.14 The function of transmitter control bits CR_5 and CR_6

CR_6	CR_5	$\overline{RTS}$	Transmitter interrupt
0	0	Low	Disabled
0	1	Low	Enabled
1	0	High	Disabled
1	1	Low	Disabled—a break level is put on the transmitter output

explanation. If both of these bits are high a *break* is transmitted until the bits are altered under software control. That is, the transmitter output of the ACIA is held at its space level. A break may be used to generate an interrupt at the receiver because the asynchronous format of the serial data precludes the existence of a space level for more than about ten bit periods.

The *receiver interrupt enable* field consists of bit CR_7 which, when clear, inhibits the generation of interrupts by the receiver portion of the ACIA. Whenever bit CR_7 is set, a receiver interrupt is generated by the receiver data register (RDR) flag of the status byte going high, indicating the presence of a new character ready for the CPU to read. A receiver interrupt can also be generated by a low-to-high transition at the data-carrier-detect ($\overline{DCD}$) input, signifying the loss of a carrier. Note that CR_7 is a composite interrupt enable bit. It is impossible to enable either an interrupt caused by the RDR being empty or an interrupt caused by a positive transition at the $\overline{DCD}$ pin alone.

Setting up the ACIA

The following pseudocode and 68000 assembly-language listing demonstrates how a 6850 ACIA is initialized before it can be used to transmit and receive serial data.

```
Module ACIA_set-up
  Perform a software reset
   {By writing 1,1 to CR₁,CR₀}
  Select counter division ratio
   {clk/16=CR₁,CR₀=0,1}
  Select character format
   {CR₄,CR₃,CR₂=1,0,1}
  Select operating mode
   {CR₆,CR₅=0,1=assert RTS, enable transmitter interrupt}
  Select receiver interrupt mode
   {CR₇=1 to enable Rx interrupt}
Code part

ACIA_BASE    EQU       <address>           Location of ACIA in memory
CR           EQU       0                   Control register offset
             LEA       PIA_BASE,A0         A0 points to ACIA
             MOVE.B    #%00000011,CR(A0)   Reset ACIA
             MOVE.B    #%10110101,CR(A0)   Set up ACIA
             RTS
End module
```

The status register

The status register has the same address as the control register, but is distinguished from it by being a read-only register. The format of the status register is given in Table 7.15. Below is a description of the eight bits of the control register.

Table 7.15 The format of the status register

7	6	5	4	3	2	1	0
IRQ	PE	OVRN	FE	CTS	DCD	TDRE	RDRF

Bit 0 Receiver data register full (RDRF). When set the RDRF bit indicates that the receiver data register is full and a character has been received. Whenever RDRF is set, the interrupt request flag, bit 7, is also set if the receiver interrupt is enabled. The RDRF bit is cleared by reading the data in the receiver data register. Whenever the $\overline{DCD}$ input is high, the RDRF bit remains at a logical zero, indicating the absence of any valid input.

The RDRF bit is frequently used to detect the arrival of a character when the ACIA is operated in a polled input mode.

```
Module Receive_char
 REPEAT
  Read ACIA status
 UNTIL RDRF = 1
 Read ACIA data

Code part
ACIA_BASE      EQU      <address of ACIA>      ;
RDRF           EQU      0                      Rx data ready = bit 0 of SR
SR             EQU      0                      Offset for status register
DR             EQU      2                      Offset for data register
               LEA      ACIA_BASE,A0           A0 points to ACIA
POLL           BTST.B   #RDRF,SR(A0)           Test Rx status bit
               BEQ      POLL                   Until byte received
               MOVE.B   DR(A0),D0              Move input from ACIA to D0
               RTS
End module
```

Bit 1 Transmitter data register empty (TDRE). This is the transmitter counterpart of RDRF. A logical 1 in TDRE indicates that the contents of the transmit data register (TDR) have been transmitted and the register is now ready for new data. The IRQ bit is also set whenever the TDR flag is set if the transmitter interrupt is enabled. The TDRE bit is at a logical zero when the TDR is full, or when the $\overline{CTS}$ input is at a logical 1, indicating that the terminal equipment is not ready for data. The fragment of code below demonstrated how the TDRE flag is used when the ACIA is operated in a polled output mode.

```
Module Transmit_char
 REPEAT
  Read ACIA status
 UNTIL TDRE = 1
 Write data to ACIA

Code part
ACIA_BASE      EQU      <address of ACIA>
```

```
TDRE           EQU         1                 Tx data register empty=bit 1
SR             EQU         0                 Offset for status register
DR             EQU         2                 Offset for data register
               LEA         ACIA_BASE,A0      A0 points to ACIA base
POLL           BTST.B      #TDRE,SR(A0)      Test Tx for empty state
               BEQ         POLL              Repeat until Tx ready
               MOVE.B      D0,DR(A0)         Move byte from D0 to ACIA
               RTS
End module
```

Bit 2 Data carrier detect (DCD).   The DCD bit is set whenever the $\overline{DCD}$ input is high, indicating that a carrier is not present. The $\overline{DCD}$ pin is normally employed only in conjunction with a modem. When the signal at the $\overline{DCD}$ input makes a low-to-high transition, the DCD bit is set and the IRQ bit is set if the receiver interrupt is enabled. The DCD bit remains set even if the $\overline{DCD}$ input returns to a low state. To clear the DCD bit, the CPU must read the contents of the ACIA's status register and then the contents of the data register.

Bit 3 Clear to send (CTS).   The CTS bit directly indicates the status of the ACIA's $\overline{CTS}$ input. A low level on the $\overline{CTS}$ input indicates that the modem is ready for data. If the CTS bit is set, the transmit data register empty bit is inhibited (clamped at zero), and no data may be transmitted by the ACIA.

Bit 4 Framing error (FE).   The framing error bit is set whenever a received character is incorrectly framed by a start bit and a stop bit. A framing error is detected by the absence of the first stop bit, and indicates a synchronization (timing), error, faulty transmission, or a break condition. The framing error flag is set or cleared during receiver data transfer time and is present throughout the time that the associated character is available.

Bit 5 Receiver overrun (OVRN).   The receiver overrun flag bit is set when a character is received, but is not read by the CPU before a subsequent character is received, over-writing the previous character which is now lost. Consequently, the receiver overrun bit indicates that one or more characters in the data stream have been lost. Synchronization is not affected by an overrun error—the error is caused by the CPU not reading a character, rather than by a fault in the transmission process. The overrun bit is cleared after reading the data from the RDR or by a master reset.

Bit 6 Parity Error (PE).   The parity error is set whenever the received parity bit does not agree with the parity bit generated locally at the receiver from the preceding data bits. Odd or even parity may be selected by writing the appropriate code into bits 2, 3, and 4 of the control register. If no parity is selected, then both the transmitter parity generator and the receiver parity checker are disabled. Once a parity error has been detected and the parity error bit set, it remains set as long as a character with a parity error is in the receiver data register.

Bit 7 Interrupt Request (IRQ).   The interrupt request bit is a composite interrupt request flag because it is set whenever the ACIA wishes to interrupt the CPU, for whatever reason. The IRQ bit may be set by any of the following:

1. receiver data register full (SR bit 0 set);
2. transmitter data register empty (SR bit 1 set);
3. DCD bit set (SR bit 2).

Whenever IRQ = 1 the $\overline{\text{IRQ}}$ pin of the ACIA is pulled low. The IRQ bit is cleared by a read from the RDR, or a write to the TDR.

Programming the ACIA

We are now going to look at a more complete program that uses some of the ACIA's error detecting facilities when receiving data.

```
ACIA          EQU      $<ACIA address>     Base address of ACIA
ACIAD         EQU      ACIA+2              Address of data register
RDRF          EQU      0                   Receiver_data_register_full
TDRE          EQU      1                   Transmitter_data_register_empty
DCD           EQU      2                   Data_carrier_detect
CTS           EQU      3                   Clear_to_send
FE            EQU      4                   Framing_error
OVRN          EQU      5                   Over_run
PE            EQU      6                   Parity_error

INPUT         MOVE.B   ACIA,D0             Get status from ACIA
              BTST.B   #RDRF,D0            Test for received character
              BNE      ERROR_CHECK         If char received then test SR
              BTST.B   #DCD,D0             Else test for loss of signal
              BEQ      INPUT               Repeat loop while DCD clear
              BRA      DCD_ERROR           Else deal with loss of signal
ERROR_CHECK   BTST.B   #FE,D0              Test for framing error
              BNE      FE_ERROR            If framing error, deal with it
              BTST.B   #OVRN,D0            Test for overrun
              BNE      OVRN_ERROR          If overrun, deal with it
              BTST.B   #PE,D0              Test for parity error
              BNE      PE_ERROR            If parity error deal with it
              MOVE.B   ACIAD,D0            Load the input into D0
              BRA      EXIT
*
DCD_ERROR     Deal with loss of signal
              BRA          EXIT
*
FE_ERROR      Deal with framing error
              BRA          EXIT
*
OVRN_ERROR    Deal with overrun error
              BRA          EXIT
*
PE_ERROR      Deal with parity error
EXIT          RTS
```

7.6 Input/output devices

So far we have examined how information in digital form is read by a computer, processed in the way dictated by a program and then output in digital form. We have not yet considered how information is converted between real-world form and digital form.

In the first part of this section we describe two of the most frequently used computer interfaces: the CRT terminal and the printer. As microprocessor systems are now being connected to a wide variety of interfaces, from speech synthesizers to robots, a short section is also devoted to the direct control of electronic devices and the conversion of information between analogue and digital form.

7.6.1 The keyboard

The CRT terminal or VDU has now become the principal input/output device for the majority of microcomputer (not to mention minicomputer and mainframe) systems. The CRT terminal is so popular because it is an almost entirely electronic device and is inexpensive to produce. It is cheap because it relies on semiconductor technology for its electronics and on television technology (tried and tested) for its display. All printers are electromechanical devices and are inherently more expensive. A CRT terminal can logically be separated into two parts: an input device (the keyboard), and an output device (the display). Note that the terms *input* and *output* refer here to the device as seen from the CPU. That is, a keyboard provides an output which in turn becomes the CPU's input. We look first at the way in which a keyboard operates and then at the display part of a CRT terminal.

The switch

A keyboard is composed of two parts, a set of keys that detect the pressure of a finger and an encoder that converts the output of a key into a unique binary code representing that key.

The keyswitch that detects the pressure of a finger, a *key stroke*, is normally a mechanical device (see Fig. 7.23). A typical keyswitch contains a plunger which is moved by a finger against the pressure of a spring. At the end of its travel the plunger forces two wires together, making a circuit. Note that the output of this device is inherently binary (on or off). Between the plunger and wires is a small stainless steel *snap-disk* which, when bowed downwards by the plunger, produces an audible click. A similar click is made when the plunger is released. Consequently, the act of depressing a keyswitch has a positive feel because of its tactile feedback. In fact, one of the differences between low-cost and *professional* keyboards is the presence, or otherwise, of this feedback.

Another form of mechanical switch employs a plunger with a small magnet embedded in one end. As this magnet is pushed downwards, it approaches two gold-plated iron contacts in a glass tube (a reed relay). These contacts become magnetized by the field from the magnet, attract each other and close the circuit. Because the contacts are in a sealed tube,

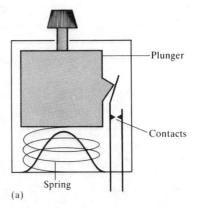

(a)

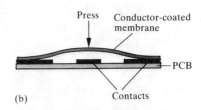

(b)

Fig. 7.23 The mechanical switch: (a) the basic switch; (b) the membrane switch.

the reed relay is one of the most reliable types of mechanical switches. Figure 7.23 also describes the *membrane* switch that provides a very low-cost mechanical switch for applications such as microwave oven control panels. A thin plastic membrane is coated with a conducting material and spread over a printed circuit board. Either by forming the plastic membrane into slight bubbles or by creating tiny pits in the PCB, it is possible to engineer a tiny gap between contacts on the PCB and the metal-coated surface of the membrane. Any pressure on the surface of the membrane due to a finger pushes it against a contact to close a circuit. The membrane switch is very cheap to produce, and can be hermetically sealed for ease of cleaning and application in hazardous environments. Equally, it suffers all the disadvantages of other types of low-cost mechanical switch.

Although the mechanical switch has excellent ergonomic properties, it has rather less good electrical properties. In particular, the contacts get dirty and make intermittent contact, or they tend to bounce when brought together, producing a series of pulses rather than a single clean make.

Non-mechanical switches

In order to overcome some of the problems inherent in the design of mechanical switches, a number of non-mechanical switches have been devised. Three of the most commonly used types are the Hall-effect switch, the elastometric switch, and the capacitive switch. The Hall-effect switch consists of a magnet that is pushed against the force of a spring towards a *Hall cell*. The Hall cell is a semiconductor device through which a steady current flows. When a magnetic field is applied at right angles to the current, a voltage is produced across the terminals of the cell at right angles to both the magnetic field and the current flow. Figure 7.24 illustrates the operation of such a switch. By detecting the Hall-effect voltage due to the magnetic field, it is possible to generate a digital output corresponding to switch-open or switch-closed. The Hall-effect switch does not suffer from contact bounce, but is relatively expensive.

The *capacitive* switch relies on the change in capacitive coupling between two metallic contacts when a finger is pressed against them. The great advantage of a capacitive switch keyboard is its extremely low cost and small size—it is often nothing more than a printed-circuit board, the contacts being simply etched on the surface. Some capacitive switches use

Fig. 7.24 The Hall-effect switch.

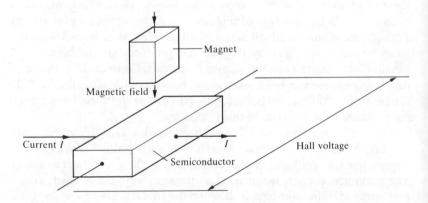

Magnet

Magnetic field

Current I

I

Hall voltage

Semiconductor

a single contact to sense a key stroke and rely on the capacitive coupling between the contact and ground via the finger.

Unfortunately, the capacitive switch keyboard has no tactile feedback and is rather unpleasant to use. Designers get round the lack of tactile feedback by providing audio feedbacks. Each time a keystroke is made, a short audio bleep is sounded from a loudspeaker. The capacitive switch is found in some very low-cost personal computers, television *touch-sensitive* tuners, and in professional equipment which must be hermetically sealed for operation in hazardous environments.

Elastometric switches employ certain types of material that change their electrical resistance when subjected to pressure. When a finger is pressed against the material, the drop in its electrical resistance is detected by a suitable interface. As above, this type of switch lacks any tactile feedback and its feel is said to be 'mushy and ill-defined'.

Because of the influence of the typewriter, the layout of most electronic keyboards closely follows that of the QWERTY keyboard. QWERTY is not a mnemonic; it is the order of letters on the back row of characters (from left to right) on a typewriter. Historically, the QWERTY layout was devised to minimize the probability of keys jamming together on a mechanical keyboard when certain letter combinations were struck nearly simultaneously. Not all keyboards have a QWERTY layout as languages other than English were prone to jamming due to entirely different sequences of characters.

The QWERTY layout is no longer relevant to electronic keyboards and the keys should, ideally, be repositioned to suit the typist. Unfortunately, it would be expensive to retrain a whole generation of typists and therefore it appears that we are stuck with the QWERTY layout for the immediate future.

Small keyboards have a separate numeric keypad containing the digits 0–9, decimal point, and some cursor control characters (backspace, line-feed, carriage-return, etc.). Modern keyboards are often fitted with so-called *function keys* (e.g. F0, F1, . . . , F11 in the case of the IBM PC), that carry out special actions depending on the application program being run.

In order to reduce the total number of keys, and hence the size and cost of the keyboard, many of the keys have two, three, or even four different functions. Multifunction keys are implemented by the introduction of three special keys, shift, control and alternate, whose purpose is to modify the meaning of the other keys. The shift key behaves in a fashion entirely analogous to the corresponding key on a typewriter and either converts a lower-case character into its upper-case equivalent, or selects between one of two alternative symbols (e.g. ':' or '*'). The action of the control key is to permit the normal alphanumeric keys to be used to generate the non-printing ISO/ASCII control characters. The alternate key, ALT, permits new functions to be specified that are not covered by the shift and control functions. Indeed, some of today's computers use combinations of these modifier keys (e.g. shift and control simultaneously) to create even more special functions. In Table 4.1 (Chapter 4) the first two columns depict the control characters. The control characters are normally intended for the control of a data link between a computer and a remote device.

The keyboard encoder

The conversion of a keystroke into its ISO/ASCII-encoded equivalent is frequently performed by a special-purpose LSI chip called a *keyboard encoder*. Figure 7.25 illustrates the operation of such a chip, which contains all the circuitry necessary to convert a signal from one of an array of switches into a binary code together with a key-pressed strobe. It is perfectly possible to design a keyboard encoder with a PIA of the type described early in this chapter. Software inside the computer can be used to scan the keyboard (as described later).

An eight-bit output port has a wire connected to each of its output pins. These wires run horizontally in Fig. 7.25. Similarly, an eight-bit input port has eight wires connected to it, and these run vertically in Fig. 7.25. At each of the $8 \times 8 = 64$ cross-points is a switch which, when depressed, makes a connection between the vertical line and the corresponding horizontal line. As long as no key is pressed, there is no connection between any vertical and any horizontal line. Clearly, if any switch is pressed we can determine which key it was by determining its row and its column.

The eight vertical input lines are each terminated in a resistor connected to $+5$ V, so that these lines are *pulled up* to a logical one. That is, if a byte were read from the input port, it would be 11111111. Suppose now the output port puts the binary word 11111110 onto its eight output lines, as illustrated in Fig. 7.26. If the CPU reads from its input port with, say, the

Fig. 7.25 The keyboard encoder.

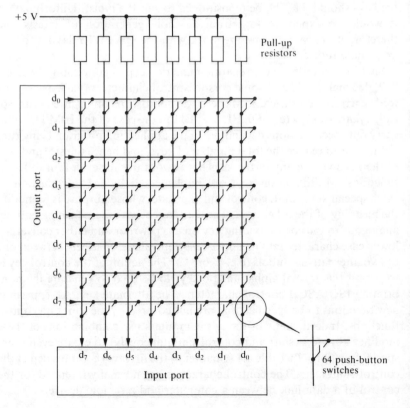

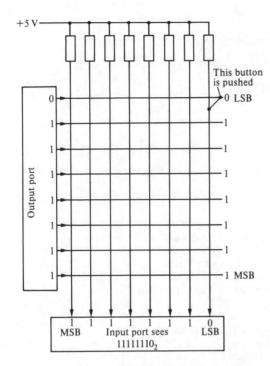

Fig. 7.26 The state of the keyboard with one key pressed.

top right-hand key pressed, it will see 11111110. If the next key to the left is pressed it will see 11111101. Pressing a key on the topmost row will cause a zero to be read into the vertical position corresponding to that key. Pressing a key in any other row has no effect on the data read.

The CPU next outputs the byte 11111101 and reads the input lines to interrogate the second row of keys. This process is continued cyclically with the CPU outputting 11111011 to 01111111, as the zero is shifted one place left each time. In this way all eight rows are interrogated one by one. The assembly-language program in Table 7.16 gives an idea of the software necessary to operate the keyboard.

7.6.2 The CRT display

We are now going to describe how the CRT display operates. At the heart of most display systems lies the cathode-ray tube (CRT), which is operated in one of two modes: point-plotting or raster-scan. A CRT is little more than a special type of the vacuum tube ('valve' in the UK) that was once used in all radios and TVs before they were replaced by transistors. A block diagram of the display part of a point-plotting display is given in Fig. 7.27.

When the temperature of the *cathode* of a CRT is raised to about 600°C by a heating element, it gives off negatively charged electrons. The sides of the far end of the CRT are coated with a conductive material connected to a very high positive voltage with respect to the cathode. This terminal is called the *anode*. The potential difference between the cathode and anode is normally in the range 3000–20 000 V. At such a large potential difference between cathode and anode, the electrons are accelerated down

Table 7.16 Reading data by scanning a keyboard

```
* Set X to 01111111
* Set X_counter to -1
* REPEAT
*   Rotate X left
*   Increment X_counter
*   Output X
*   Read Y
* UNTIL Y ≠ 11111111 (i.e. a key is pressed)
*
* Set Y_counter to 0
* WHILE Y ≠ 11111110
*   Shift Y right
*   Increment_Y counter
* ENDWHILE
* Concatenate X and Y to get 6-bit value of key location
*
```

	ORG	$002000	Subroutine origin
XLINES	EQU	$008000	Output port for horizontal lines
YLINES	EQU	$008002	Input port for vertical lines
*			
	MOVE.B	#%01111111,D0	Preset initial value of X
	MOVE.B	#-1,D1	Preset X_counter to -1
XLOOP	ROL.B	#1,D0	Rotate value of X one place left
	ADD.B	#1,D1	Increment X_counter in step
	AND.B	#%00000111,D1	X_counter is modulo 8 (range 0–7)
	MOVE.B	D0,XLINES	Send value of X to output port
	MOVE.B	YLINES,D2	Read value of Y from input lines
	CMP.B	#%11111111,D2	Has a key been pressed?
	BEQ	XLOOP	Repeat if Y is all ones
*			
	CLR.B	D3	Preset Y_counter to 0
YLOOP	CMP.B	#%11111110,D2	Test for Y=0
	BEQ	CONCAT	Exit to concatenate X and Y counts
	ROR.B	#1,D2	Rotate value of Y one place right
	ADD.B	#1,D3	Increment Y_counter
	BRA	YLOOP	Repeat
*			
CONCAT	LSL.B	#3,D2	Shift value of Y_counter 3 places left
	OR.B	D2,D1	Add in X_counter
	RTS		Return with key value in D1

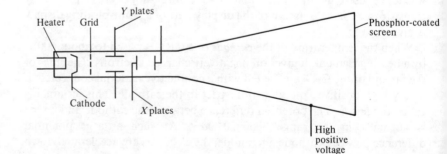

Fig. 7.27 The cathode ray tube.

the CRT to strike its front surface (face) with considerable kinetic energy. The face is coated with a *phosphor* that glows when bombarded by high-energy electrons. Since the stream of electrons is focused into a narrow beam by focusing electrodes (not shown), a small bright spot is created on the front of the screen.

In front of the cathode lies a fine wire mesh, called the *grid*, which, when negatively charged, repels electrons from the cathode, reducing the intensity of the spot. The beam passes between two pairs of plates, one in the *X* plane and one in the *Y* plane. By putting an electrostatic charge on these plates, the beam can be deflected to any point on the face of the tube. Modern CRT terminals and televisions operate on a slightly different principle. They deflect the beam magnetically by passing a current through a pair of coils oriented at right angles to each other, outside the CRT. It is easier to deflect a beam of electrons through a wide angle magnetically than electrostatically.

Two binary inputs, X,Y, are applied to the inputs of two digital-to-analog converters that transform the binary number into a voltage proportional to its digital value. These analog voltages are conveyed, via amplifiers, to the *X* and *Y* deflection plates (or deflection coils) of a CRT. The beam is deflected in both the *X* and *Y* axes to a position determined by the X and Y digital inputs. An additional input is applied to the grid to turn on, or turn off (blank), the beam. To operate this type of display, a table of *X,Y* values is maintained in the computer's memory, and pairs of values are fed to two output ports sequentially. The ports are connected to two digital-to-analog converters which provide the voltages needed to deflect the beam. The points are plotted rapidly to avoid flicker, as the image soon fades. It is necessary to display all points at least 50 times a second in an operation called *refreshing* the display.

The raster-scan display

An alternative form of display operates in a raster-scan mode (a raster is the path of the beam over the surface of the screen), in which the beam of electrons is periodically swept across the screen, line by line, so that the entire surface of the display is covered. In the raster-scan mode, the CRT controller does not have to specify explicit *X* and *Y* coordinates of the point it wishes to plot. Instead, the CRT controller brightens up the display, to produce a dot, when the beam is at the appropriate *X,Y* location. The detailed operation of a raster-scan display, which forms the principle of the television picture, is as follows.

A linearly rising sawtooth voltage is applied to the *X* deflection circuits of the CRT (see Fig. 7.28), causing the beam of electrons to trace out a horizontal line across the display. In a domestic television receiver the intensity of the beam is modulated by the received signal to form the picture, whereas in a CRT terminal the beam is switched on or fully off to generate a pattern of dots. When the beam reaches the right-hand edge of the display it is turned off and rapidly returned to its horizontal starting position (flyback), ready for the next scan. While the beam is scanning in the horizontal plane, it is also scanned in the vertical plane at a much lower rate. In this way each horizontal scan (a line) falls below the

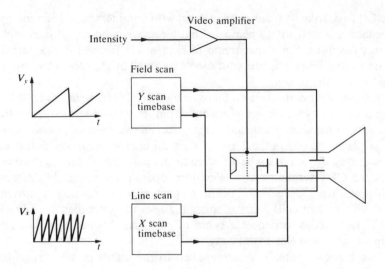

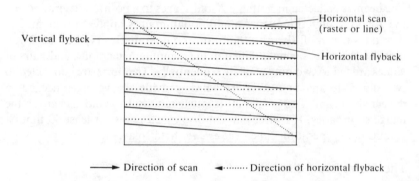

Fig. 7.28 The structure of a raster-scan display.

preceding scan. In Europe there are 50 vertical scans a second and each vertical scan (called a field) is composed of $312\frac{1}{2}$ lines. A frame is made up of two consecutive fields containing $312\frac{1}{2}$ odd-numbered lines and $312\frac{1}{2}$ even-numbered lines. The total number of lines per frame is $2 \times 312\frac{1}{2} = 625$ in Europe and $2 \times 262\frac{1}{2} = 525$ in the USA.

The reason for displaying odd-numbered and even-numbered lines in consecutive fields stems from the difficulty of scanning all 625 lines in one fiftieth of a second. Such an arrangement is called *interlacing*. Interlacing is used in some CRT terminals to give 625 lines of vertical resolution, but many CRT terminals do not employ it and are left with $312\frac{1}{2}$ pairs of lines. We will soon see that the number of lines displayed affects the number of rows of characters that can be fitted onto a screen.

A CRT screen is divided into a matrix of rows and columns, defining the display format. Typical display formats are 80×24, 40×24, 64×16, and 32×16. The first figure in each pair gives the number of *columns* per line, and the second figure the number of *rows* per frame. Figure 7.29 provides the format of a typical display. Each character is displayed as a 5×7 dot-matrix, called a font, within a block of 6 dots by 8 lines. To avoid

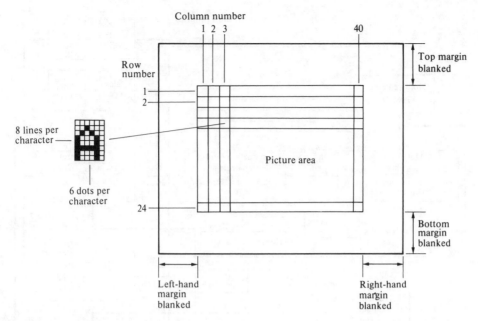

Fig. 7.29 Format of a raster-scan display.

confusion when describing CRT terminals, we will employ the term *line* to mean a single horizontal raster-scan and *row* to mean a row of characters that is itself made up of a number of consecutive rasters.

Displaying data on a CRT

The block diagram of a simple 40 column by 24 row display generator is given in Fig. 7.30. The output of this circuit is called *composite video* and is fed to the video circuits of a raster-scan display (i.e. a television screen). In other words, this block diagram represents the additional logic needed to enable a television to display digital data. The key to the operation of the circuit is a clock generator, which provides pulses at a rate of 5.76 MHz. The *dot clock* is the rate at which successive dots are displayed and is divided by six to produce a character clock at 0.960 MHz or 960 kHz. The divisor is six because there are five dots per character plus a blanked dot space between adjacent characters. We will see that much of the logic of a display generator is concerned with successively dividing the dot clock by integers to get a character clock, a row rate and a field rate.

The character clock (i.e. one pulse per character) is divided by 60 to get 60 character positions, or time slots, per line. Only 40 characters are to be displayed; the remaining 20 time slots form the left- and right-hand margins of the display, and allow time for the flyback. That is, the column counter counts from 0 to 59 as a line is scanned from left to right and columns 0 to 39 are used to display text on the screen while columns 40 to 59 are blanked. A simple circuit can be used to detect the 40th column and to blank the screen until the column counter is reset to 0 on the next line.

After dividing the character clock by 60, a frequency of 960 kHz/60 (i.e. 16 kHz) is obtained, which is the line rate and is also used to generate a

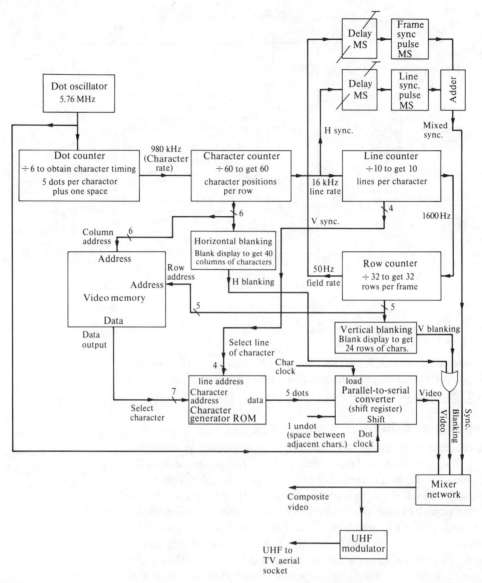

Fig. 7.30 A display generator.

line-synchronizing signal called the line sync. It is this synchronizing signal that informs the television when to start a new line. The line clock is then divided by ten to give ten vertical lines per row of characters. Seven lines are needed to build the character and three lines to form a space between adjacent rows of characters.

The output of the line counter, $16\,\text{kHz}/10 = 1.6\,\text{kHz}$, is divided by 32 to give 32 row slots per field. Of these 32 slots only 24 display characters, the remaining eight form the top and bottom margins. The output of the row counter is $1.6\,\text{kHz}/32 = 50\,\text{Hz}$, which is the field rate found in the UK. The field rate is also used to generate field sync pulses to keep the television display in step with the display generator.

Having set up the dividers, or *timing chain*, it is a simple matter to generate the display itself. As the character and row counters sequentially step through all $40 \times 24 = 960$ character positions, the binary outputs of these counters interrogate a block of random access memory to produce an ISO/ASCII-encoded word for each character position. That is, the row and column counts act as address inputs to the memory and the data from the memory represents the code of the character to be displayed. This block of memory may be part of the CRT terminal circuitary or it may be part of the CPU's own memory space. The output of the random access memory is fed to the address input of a special-purpose read only memory called a *character generator*, that converts the character code into the actual pattern of dots forming that character. The ROM has an additional address input which selects one of the seven lines of the character currently being displayed. This address comes from the divide-by-10 line counter.

The output of the ROM consists of a 5-bit word forming one of the seven lines of the character. The bits are zero for a blank dot or one for a displayed dot, and are fed to a 6-bit shift register (one bit is permanently set to 0 to give the inter-character spacing). The shift register is loaded by the character clock at the start of each new character, and the dots are shifted out by the dot clock. These dots are then fed to the circuits which generate the signal to be fed to the television receiver. Other parts of the circuit are the display blanking, which sets the video output to zero when characters are not being displayed, and the mixing circuit, which combines the video signal with the synchronizing (sync) pulses. The output waveform is called the composite video signal, and is illustrated in Fig. 7.31.

If the display generator above is to be turned into a CRT terminal, additional circuitry is needed to write characters into the RAM, sometimes called video RAM or display memory. Counters, either in hardware or software are also needed to keep track of where the next character is to go. Special arrangements are necessary to cater for control characters. For example, when a carriage return is received by the CRT terminal, it does not display it, but uses it to reset to zero the column position counter. Similarly, a new line simply increments the row position counter.

Virtually all CRT terminals have a cursor. A cursor is a special symbol (sometimes flashing) displayed on the screen to indicate the position into which the next character is to go. To generate a cursor the contents of the display generator's row and column counters are compared with the pointers to the next free position on the screen. When the two values are equal, the beam of the CRT must be at the position of the next free character and may therefore be turned on to produce a cursor.

The above description of a CRT terminal is, of necessity, rudimentary, with much fine detail omitted. However, most CRT terminals do operate on these principles. Today, much of the logic of a display generator is available on a single integrated circuit costing a few pounds. In general, the cost of CRT terminals is dropping as their internal circuitary uses fewer and fewer components.

The CRT controller chip

Few designers would now build a display system around discrete logic (i.e.

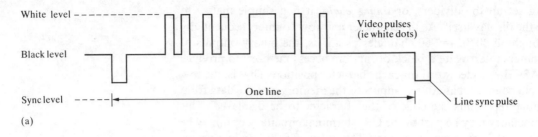

(a)

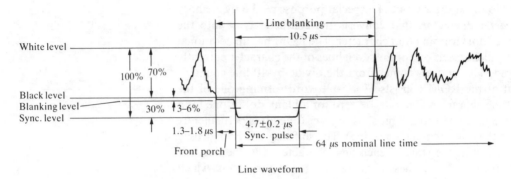

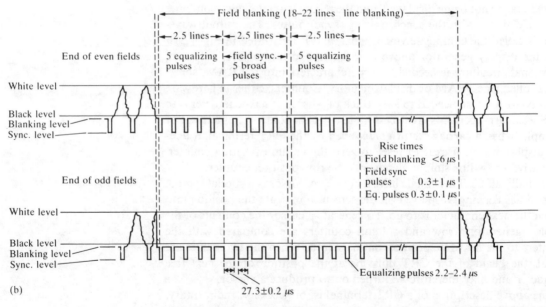

(b)

Fig. 7.31 The composite video signal: (a) Conceptual signal; (b) CCIR standard video format.

SSI and MSI chips). Instead they can save about 20–50 packages by employing a special **CRT controller** chip, the CRTC. The CRTC is interfaced to a CPU exactly like any other interface (e.g. a PIA or an ACIA). Its purpose is to generate all the timing and control signals required to create a video signal. Figure 7.32 illustrates how its display is constructed around a CRTC.

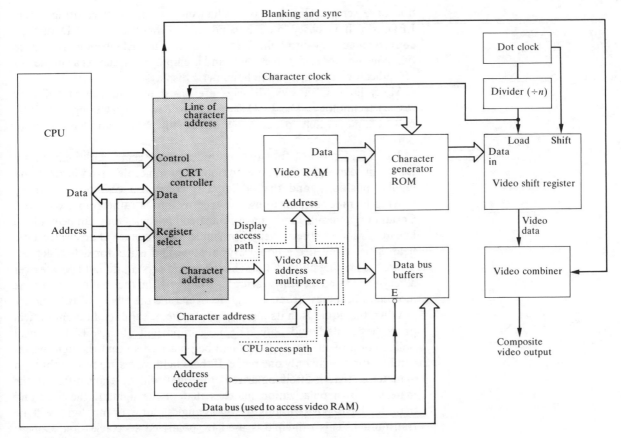

Fig. 7.32 The CRT controller.

In normal display operation, the CRTC generates an address of the next character to be displayed, which it uses to access the video RAM containing the character codes (usually ISO/ASCII). The output from the video RAM is fed to the ROM containing the bit patterns of the character set. A second address output from the CRTC selects the current line of character. A certain amount of user-supplied logic is necessary to convert the output of the character-generator ROM into the serial signal required by the CRT.

The address inputs of the video RAM are connected to a *multiplexer* which enables the CPU to access the video RAM. We do not need to go into details here, but when the CPU generates an address that falls within the video RAM's memory space, the output of the address decoder connects the video RAM's address lines to the CPU's address lines and enables the tri-state buffers between the video RAM's data bus and the CPU's data bus. In this state, the CPU can update the display memory.

7.6.3 The liquid crystal display

The cathode ray tube is a rather large bulky and power-hungry device which is unsuited to applications requiring miniaturization and portability. Fortunately, there are several other ways of displaying information on a screen. One display mechanism uses the light emitting diode, LED, which is based on semiconductor technology. A LED directly converts a current into light. Unfortunately, the LED is an active device that consumes considerable power and is employed largely as a simple on/off indicator or in modest alphanumeric displays.

Many large CRT-style displays are based on liquid crystal display (LCD) technology. The LCD is a passive device consuming very little power, is moderately low cost (but not exactly cheap), and lends itself to portability.

The liquid crystal is not the contradiction it seems. Although we are taught in school that a solid is composed of molecules fixed in rigid and regular positions, and that a liquid is composed of molecules freely moving in random directions, the true picture is rather more complex. Certain organic substances have elongated molecules that can be made to line up (or modify their orientation) under the influence of an electrostatic field. This is called the liquid crystal state and exists for a few degrees above the melting point of the solid (i.e. liquid crystals do not operate over a very wide range of temperatures—eventually the thermal motion of the molecules becomes strong enough to overcome the effects of the field).

When the liquid is in its liquid crystal state, it exhibits different optical properties to its liquid state. The most important of these is the optical polarization of the liquid. Light can be polarized so that the light waves exhibit vibration in only one plane. If these light waves are passed through a material that is itself polarized, the light will be transmitted if the material's own polarization matches that of the light. If the light and material have polarizations at right angles, little or no light will be transmitted. This principle is used by polarized spectacles and camera filters to cut down glare from reflected light.

There are three groups of liquid crystal that display a relationship between polarization and electrostatic field. The most important group employs 'twisted nematic' liquid crystals whose polarization rotates as the electrostatic field is applied (see Fig. 7.33(a)). More importantly, the amount of rotation is 90° for an applied voltage of below 3 V.

A display is constructed by sandwiching the liquid crystal between two layers of glass. An electrostatic field can be applied to each cell by means of electrodes deposited on the surface of the glass. The glass is coated with materials that cause the orientation of the liquid crystal to take up a preferred state in the absence of an external field. Of course, it is necessary to deposit transparent conductors onto the glass. Since a direct current would cause electrolysis of the liquid crystal (thereby destroying it), the field is provided by an alternating current in the range 25–500 Hz. The liquid cell is placed between two polarizers so that light hitting the surface will either be reflected back from the far surface or not reflected back, depending on the polarization of the liquid (Fig. 7.33(b)).

LCDs consume very tiny currents, although their response time is rather slow (up to 100 ms). The contrast ratio (i.e. ratio of light reflected in the on state to light reflected in the off state) of LCDs is rather poor. Moreover, the technological difficulties of creating arrays of many pixels has held up their development. Fortunately, the introduction of the laptop

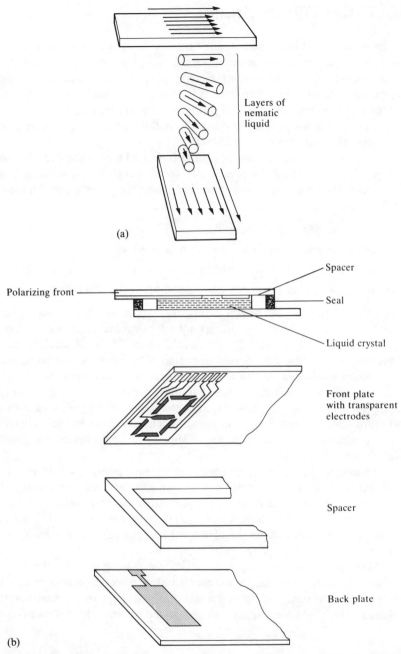

(a)

Layers of
nematic
liquid

Polarizing front

Spacer

Seal

Liquid crystal

Front plate
with transparent
electrodes

Spacer

Back plate

(b)

Fig. 7.33 The liquid crystal display: (a) direction of polarization rotated through 90° when charge applied; (b) construction of a simple LCD seven-segment display.

portable in the late 1980s had led to renewed research into the high-resolution LCD. Many high quality laptop portables do not rely on reflected light but employ a cold cathode fluorescent panel behind the LCD to illuminate it. It is possible to create 'shades' (i.e., a grey scale between fully on and fully off) by modulating the time for which the cell is on and off.

7.7 The impact printer

The printer produces a permanent **hard copy** output from a computer by converting digital information into marks on paper. Because printers rely on precisely machined, moving mechanical parts, they tend to be more expensive than purely electronic CRT terminals and are often less reliable. Moreover, the range of prices of printers is much greater than that of CRT terminals. A low-cost printer costs about $100 while a high-volume line printer may cost more than $20 000.

There is a very wide variety of printer types and mechanisms, each being a particular trade-off between cost, speed, reliability, and quality of printing. However, all printers must perform the same basic functions. These are

1. move the paper to a given line;
2. move the **print-head** to a given point along a line;
3. select a character to be printed;
4. make a mark on the paper corresponding to that character.

The first and last of the above functions are relatively easy to explain, and are dealt with first. Depending on the application, paper is available in single-sheet, continuous roll, or fan-fold form. The feed mechanism of printers is not radically different from that of typewriters. The paper may be moved by **friction feed**, in which the paper is trapped between a motor-driven roller and pressure rollers that apply pressure to the surface of the paper. As the roller (or platen) moves, the paper is dragged along with it. Figure 7.34(a) shows the operation of a friction feed drive. Such a drive is not perfect and may allow paper to slip, or at least prevent the precise alignment of the paper.

An alternative paper-feeding mechanism is the **tractor feed** or **sprocket-feed** (Fig. 7.34(b)). Here a number of conical pins form a ring round the ends of the platen. The edges of the paper (invariably fan-fold paper) are perforated with holes on the same pitch (spacing) as the pins. The pins fit through the holes and, as the platen rotates, the paper is accurately and precisely pulled through the printer.

Making a mark on paper is intimately connected with the way a character is formed, but a number of fundamental principles can be identified. The most widespread method of marking paper is based on the impact of a hard object against an ink-coated ribbon, which is then forced

Fig. 7.34 Mechanisms for feeding the paper through a printer: (a) the pressure or friction feed; (b) the tractor feed.

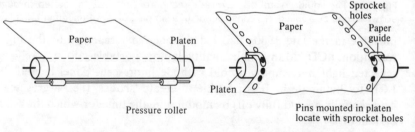

(a) The pressure feed

(b) The tractor feed

onto the paper to make a mark in the shape of the object. This is how most office typewriters operate. Printers are often referred to by the way in which the mark on the paper is made. Popular arrangements using impact printing are the golf-ball, the cylinder, the daisy-wheel, the line-printer, and the drum printer.

Some printers form characters on paper without physically striking the paper and are therefore known as **non-impact** printers. One group of non-impact printers employs special paper, coated with a material that turns black (or blue) when heated to about 110°C. Such printers are called thermal printers and form a character by heating a particular combination of dots within a matrix of, typically, 7 by 5 points (like the CRT terminal). Thermal printers are often very cheap (until you think about the cost of the special paper), and are relatively silent in operation. Another mechanism involves paper coloured black but surfaced with a thin film of shiny aluminium. If a needle electrode is applied to the surface and a large current passed through it, the aluminium film is locally vaporized to reveal the dark coating underneath.

Another method of printing involves spraying a fine jet of ink at the paper. As this technique also includes the way in which the character is selected and formed, it will be dealt with in more detail later. Later we will describe the laser printer.

The hardware that actually prints the character is called the print head. There are two classes of print head: the single print head and the multiple print head found in line printers. Typewriters employ a fixed print head and the paper and platen move as each new character is printed. A fixed print head is unsuitable for high-speed printing, as the platen and paper have a high mass and hence a high inertia, which means that the energy required to perform a high-speed carriage return would be prohibitive. Since the mass of the print head is very much less than that of the platen, most printers are arranged so that the paper stays where it is and the print head moves along the line.

One way of moving the print head is to attach it to a nut on a threaded rod (the lead screw). At the end of the rod is a stepping motor, which can rotate the rod through a fixed angle at a time. Each time the rod rotates the print head is moved left or right (depending on the direction of rotation). In another arrangement the print head is connected to a belt, moved by the same technique as the paper itself. The belt passes between two rollers, one of which moves freely and one of which is controlled by a stepping motor.

As the way in which the character is formed is so fundamental to the type of printer, a number of printer types are described as follows.

7.7.1 The dot matrix printer

A dot matrix printer forms individual characters from a matrix of dots in much the same way as a CRT terminal forms its characters. The dots are formed by a number of wires (called needles) pressing an inked ribbon onto the paper, or the needles may be used with spark erosion techniques, or may be replaced by heating elements in a thermal printer. Dot matrix printers have relatively few moving parts and are moderately low-cost.

Most printers found in personal computer systems employ dot matrix techniques and cost in the range $100–1000. Figure 7.35 illustrates the operation of a dot matrix print head. Seven solenoids individually control seven wires. The solenoid is a coil which, when energized by a current, creates a strong magnetic field inside it. Because the wires are made of iron they can be moved in or out of the solenoid by passing a current through it. The seven wires are brought together by a ruby guide plate to form a column of seven dots. By energizing a particular combination of solenoids, that group of needles is propelled towards the ribbon producing a pattern of dots on the paper. After each column of dots has been printed, the head is moved one dot position to print another column. After five (or seven) columns have been printed a complete character has been formed. Because the character is made up of small dots, it is possible to program the dot matrix printer for any character set, and some printers also allow the use of dot graphics. Unfortunately, the print quality of a dot matrix printer is unacceptably poor in business applications where image is everything.

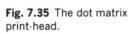

Fig. 7.35 The dot matrix print-head.

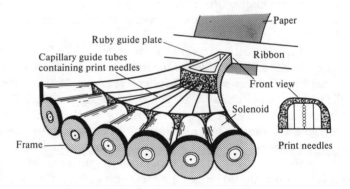

First-generation dot matrix printers sometimes had no more than seven dots per column and the quality of their output was rather poor. Today's 24-dot print heads can produce remarkably high quality output that is almost up to the quality of the office typewriter. Many matrix printers are able to operate in an NQL (near letter quality) mode by merging and overlapping dots to produce letters that look as if they were made by daisy-wheel printers (provided, of course, you have poor sight).

Since dot matrix printers work by forming characters out of patterns of dots, there is no reason why they cannot be directed to print *any* pattern of dots and therefore draw pictures (i.e. operate in a graphics mode). Most of today's dot matrix printers have an in-built processor that interprets the incoming characters from the host computer as printing characters or as control characters. Certain sequences of control character force the printer to print specified sequences of dots (rather than ISO/ASCII characters). As much of the work in generating graphics has been led by companies making printers, it should come as no surprise to learn that not all printers use the same code sequence to describe graphics. Indeed, when you buy one of today's complex word processors, you usually get dozens of printer driver programs and must select the appropriate driver for your printer. Fortunately, many printers use codes developed by Epson, and some printers can be forced to abandon their 'own' codes and to *emulate* another printer.

7.7.2 The cylinder and golf-ball printers

Figure 7.36 illustrates the operation of both the cylinder print-head and the golf-ball. The operation of these print-heads is very similar. The cylinder print-head is found in teletype machines and is a metallic cylinder with four rows of sixteen symbols embossed around it. The ribbon and paper are positioned immediately in front of the cylinder, and the hammer is located behind it. The cylinder is rotated about its vertical axis and is moved up or down until the desired symbol is positioned next to the ribbon. A hammer, driven by a solenoid, then strikes the back of the cylinder, forcing the symbol at the front onto the paper through the ribbon.

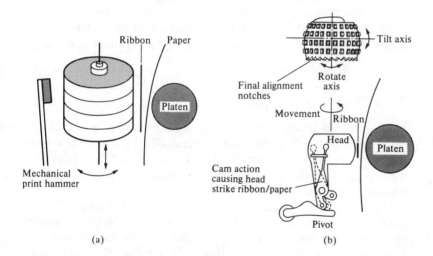

Fig. 7.36 (a) Cylinder and (b) golf-ball print-heads.

The golf-ball head was originally used in IBM typewriters, but is now found in a wider range of printers. Characters are embossed on the surface of a metallic sphere. For a given volume the sphere has more usable space than the cylinder. The golf-ball rotates in the same way as a cylinder, but is tilted rather than moved up or down to access different rows of characters. Unlike the cylinder, the golf-ball is propelled towards the ribbon and the paper by a cam mechanism, rather than by a hammer striking it at the back.

Although there is no conceptual difference between the cylinder and the golf-ball, the cylinder mechanism currently in use provides only the upper-case 64 character subset of the ISO/ASCII code. The golf-ball provides both upper and lower case characters and is interchangeable. This means that by changing golf-balls different type faces may be obtained. The golf-ball printer is said to produce *correspondence quality* printing.

7.7.3 The daisy-wheel printer

Like its namesake, the daisy-wheel printer has a disk with a large number of slender petals arranged around its periphery. At the end of each of these *petals* or spokes is an embossed character. The wheel is made of plastic or metal and is very light-weight, giving it a low inertia. A typical daisy wheel has 96 spokes, corresponding to the upper- and lower-case subsets of the ISO/ASCII code. Figure 7.37 illustrates the daisy-wheel.

The daisy-wheel rotates in the vertical plane, at high speed, in front of the ribbon. As the wheel rotates, each of the characters passes between a solenoid-driven hammer and the ribbon. When the desired character is at a print position, the solenoid is energized and the hammer forces the spoke against the ribbon to mark the paper. It should be appreciated that a considerable amount of (microprocessor controlled) electronics is needed to carry out the complex timing required by a daisy-wheel printer. Some printers even control the amount of current in the solenoid (and hence the force of the hammer) according to the size of the character. This gives each character a uniform density. Some impact printers put so much force into a period that a tiny hole is made in the paper! Daisy-wheel printers are often used in conjunction with word processors because of their high-quality printing. However, the introduction of the laser printer has provided users with a more versatile high-quality printer than the daisy-wheel.

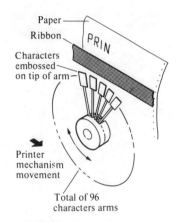

Paper
Ribbon
Characters embossed on tip of arm
Printer mechanism movement
Total of 96 characters arms

Fig. 7.37 The daisy-wheel printer.

7.7.4 The line-printer

A line-printer is so-called because it prints a whole line of text at one go, rather than by printing characters sequentially. Line-printers are expensive, often produce low-quality output, and are geared to high-volume, high-speed printing. One of the common forms of line-printer, the drum printer, is illustrated in Fig. 7.38.

In front of the ribbon is a drum extending along the entire width of the paper. Along the circumference of the drum is embossed the character set to be printed. This character set is repeated, once for each of the character positions, along the drum. A typical line printer has 132 character positions and a set of 64 characters. Consequently, there are

Fig. 7.38 The line printer.

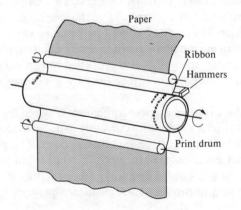

Paper
Ribbon
Hammers
Print drum

$132 \times 64 = 9448$ characters embossed on the drum. As the drum rotates, the rings of characters pass over each of the 132 print positions, and a complete set of characters passes each printing point once per revolution. Unlike some other printers, a mark is made on the paper by a hammer hitting the paper and driving it into the head through the ribbon. By controlling the instant at which the hammer is energized, any particular character may be printed. As there is one hammer per character position, a whole line may be printed during the course of a single revolution of the drum.

Suppose the line to be printed contains the single word ALAN, and that in each ring of characters the first character is A followed by B etc. The paper is assumed to have been advanced to the current line by a tractor mechanism. As the drum rotates, a timing signal is generated and sent to the electronics controlling the hammers. When a synchronizing pulse is produced by the first letter (i.e. A), hammers one and three are energized and the pattern A A is printed. After the drum has stepped to its twelfth position, the second hammer is energized and the line now contains ALA. Another two steps of the drum and the fourth hammer is energized to generate the finished line ALAN. After the drum has completed a full revolution, the paper is advanced one line and the sequence repeated.

A drum printer operates in the speed range of 100–400 lines per minute. As there are up to 132 hammers striking the paper in a very short time, the drum printer is a fairly noisy machine. In fact, it is possible to create a sequence of characters that will play a tune on the line printer. It is also a very good way of annoying the computer room operators.

The chain or belt printer is another realization of a line-printer and is illustrated in Fig. 7.39. A continuous belt is made up of links, each containing an embossed character. The belt rotates in the horizontal plane, and the ribbon is positioned between the belt and the paper. A number of hammers (one per character position) are located behind the belt. As the appropriate character moves in front of a hammer, the hammer is energized and the character forced onto the paper through the ribbon.

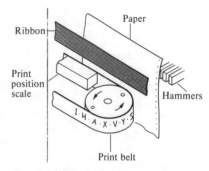

Fig. 7.39 The belt printer.

7.7.5 The ink-jet printer

The ink-jet printer is an unusual type of printer owing more to the CRT for its operation than the impact printer. The basic features of an ink-jet printer are illustrated in Fig 7.40. A fine jet of ink is emitted from a tiny nozzle to create a high-speed stream of ink drops. The nozzle is vibrated ultrasonically so that the ink stream is broken up into individual drops. As each drop leaves the nozzle it is given an electrical charge, so that the stream of drops can be deflected electrostatically, just like the beam of electrons in a CRT. By moving the beam, characters can be written on to the surface of the paper. The paper is arranged to be off the central axis of the beam, so that when the beam is undeflected, the ink drops do not strike the paper and are collected in a reservoir for reuse.

Ink-jet printers are high-speed devices and are almost silent in operation. Until recently, the ink-jet printer was very expensive and was

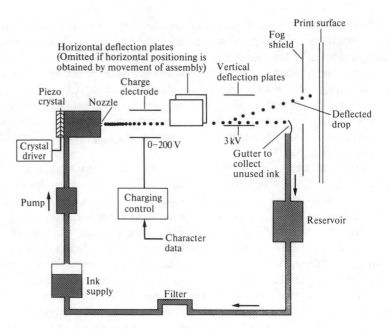

Fig. 7.40 The ink-jet printer.

regarded with suspicion because it had suffered a number of 'teething problems' during its development. In particular, it was prone to the clogging of the nozzle. Many of the early problems have now been overcome. For example, at least one ink-jet printer combines the printhead that generates the ink-jet with the ink reservoir. When the ink supply is exhausted after about 1000 pages, the head assembly is thrown away and a new head inserted. Although this looks wasteful, it costs little more than a conventional ribbon and both reduces maintenance requirements and increases reliability.

Many ink-jet printers now use a rather different technique to print characters. They operate as a dot matrix printer by employing a head with multiple nozzles (one for each of the dots in a dot matrix array). This head usually comes into intimate contact with the paper and there is no complex ink delivery and focusing system. The holes through which the ink flows are too small to permit the ink to leak out. Ink is forced through the holes by using a piezo-electric crystal. When a piezo-crystal has an electronic field applied to it, it flexes. By applying an electronic pulse to such a crystal, it flexes and forces a single drop of ink through one of the holes onto the paper (there is a separate crystal for each of the holes in the print head). Some ink-jet printers use an even simpler technique for ejecting a drop of ink out of the head. They employ a fine wire behind the nozzle to instantaneously heat the ink to boiling point and therefore force out a tiny drop. Such printers provide a print quality almost as good as a laser printer (i.e. 300 dots per inch) for the cost of a dot matrix printer.

It is possible to design colour ink-jet printers by using several sets of nozzles where each set is connected to a reservoir with a different ink colour. Such colour printers are remarkably inexpensive. Colour dot matrix printers are also produced which operate by using a ribbon with coloured bands and moving the selected colour in front of the print-head by mechanical means.

7.7.6 The laser printer

The laser printer has now brought the ability to produce high-quality text and graphics to those who, only a few years ago, could afford no more than a medium quality dot-matrix printer. In fact the quality of the laser printer is sufficiently high to enable a small office to create artwork similar to that once produced by the professional typesetter. This activity is now known as desktop publishing, DTP, because anyone with about $7,000 can now set themselves up as a typesetter.

Laser printing technology is not quite as new as it might appear. In fact, the laser printer is no more than the photocopier specially modified to accept input from a host computer. The principle of the photocopier and the laser printer is both elegant and simple but its practical implementation is very complex. At the heart of a laser printer lies a precisely machined metal drum, which is as wide as the sheets of paper to be printed. The secret of the drum lies in its coating (selenium) which is an electrical insulator with an important property. When selenium is illuminated by light, it becomes conductive. Modern laser printers use organic chemicals instead of selenium.

A photocopier works by first charging up the surface of the drum to a very high electrostatic potential (typically 1000 V with respect to ground). By means of a complex arrangement of lenses and mirrors, the original to be copied is scanned by a very bright light and the image projected onto the rotating drum. After one rotation, the drum contains an invisible image of the original document. If the image is invisible we are entitled to ask ourselves, 'What form does this image take?' Black regions of the document reflect little light and corresponding regions of the drum receive no light. The selenium coating in these regions is not illuminated, does not become conducting and therefore it retains its electrical charge.

White regions of the document reflect light onto the drum, causing the selenium to become conducting and to lose its charge. In other words, the image on the drum is in terms of electrostatic charge, ranging from high voltage (black) to zero voltage (white).

In the next step the drum is rotated in close proximity to a very fine black powder called the *toner*. One of the effects of an electrostatic charge is its ability to attract nearby light objects. Consequently, the toner is attracted to those parts of the drum with a high charge. Now the drum contains a true positive image of the original. The image is a positive image because black areas on the original are highly charged and pick up the black toner.

The drum is then rotated in contact with the paper which is given an even higher electrostatic charge. The charge on the paper causes the toner to transfer itself from the drum to the paper. In the final stage, the surface of the paper is heat treated to fix the toner on to it. Unfortunately, not all toner is transferred from the drum to the paper. Residual toner is scraped off the drum by rotating it in contact with a very fine blade. Eventually, the drum becomes scratched or the selenium no longer functions properly and it must be replaced. In contrast with other printers, the laser printer requires the periodic replacement of some of its major components.

Unlike the photocopier, the laser printer has no optical imaging system. The image is written directly onto the drum by means of an electromechanical system. As the drum rotates, an image is written onto it line by line in very much the same way that a television picture is formed in a cathode ray tube.

Figure 7.41 illustrates the basic principles of the laser scanner. A low-power semiconductor laser and optical system produces a very fine spot of laser light. By either varying the intensity of the current to the laser or passing the beam through a liquid crystal, whose opacity is controlled electronically (i.e. modulated), the intensity of the light spot falling on the drum can be varied.

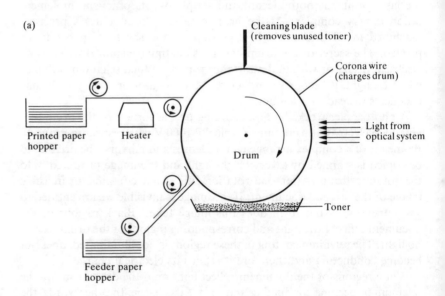

(a)

Fig. 7.41 The laser scanner: (a) basic structure; (b) optical arrangement.

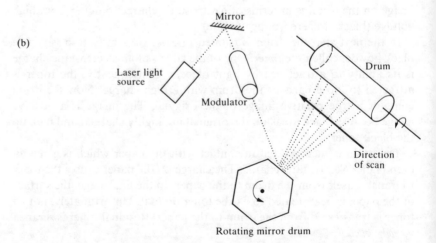

(b)

The light beam strikes a multi-sided rotating mirror. As the mirror turret rotates, the side currently in the path of the light beam sweeps the beam across the surface of the selenium-coated drum. By modulating the light as the beam sweeps across the drum, a single line is drawn. Note that this process is rather like a raster–scan in a CRT display. After a line has been drawn, the next mirror in the rotating turret is in place and a new line is drawn below the previous line, because the selenium drum has moved by one line.

Thus, the combined motions of the rotating mirror turret and the rotating selenium drum allow the laser beam to scan the entire surface of the selenium drum. Of course, the optical circuits required to perform the scanning are very precise indeed. The resolution imposed by the optics and the laser beam size permits a resolution of about 300 dots per inch. Such a resolution is suitable for moderately high-quality text but is not entirely suitable for high-quality graphics. It has been suggested that a dot density of up to 800 dots/inch is required for the highest quality image. There is little point in increasing dot density beyond 800 dots/inch as the human eye cannot resolve any further increase in picture quality. Interestingly enough, the first television system due to Logie Baird used a purely mechanical scanning system which was rather like the optical arrangement now found in a laser printer or photo-copier.

Not all later printers employ the same optical arrangements, because the rotating mirror turret is complex and requires careful alignment. One alternative technique designed by Epson uses an incandescent light source behind a stationary liquid crystal shutter. The liquid crystal shutter has a linear array of 2000 dots, each of which can be turned on and off the build up a single line across the drum. Because a complete line is written in one operation, the only major moving part involved in the scanning process is the photosensitive drum itself.

Other ways of avoiding the complex rotating drum mirror turret are a linear array of light emitting diodes (LEDs) in an arrangement similar to the liquid crystal shutter, or a CRT projection technique that uses a CRT to project a line onto the photosensitive drum (Fig. 7.42).

Later printers generate images (i.e. the arrangement of dots) electronically by converting the codes for characters into suitable patterns of dots stored in read-only memories. By changing the character generator ROMs (often housed in user insertable/removable cassettes), it is possible to change font types.

Many laser printers are able to print dot-map pictures. That is, each pixel of the picture is assigned a bit in the printer's memory. A linear resolution of 300 dots/inch requires $300 \times 300 = 90\,000$ dots/square inch. A sheet of paper measuring 11 inches by 8 inches (i.e. 88 square inches) can hold up to $88 \times 90\,000 = 7\,720\,000$ dots or just under 1 M bytes of storage.

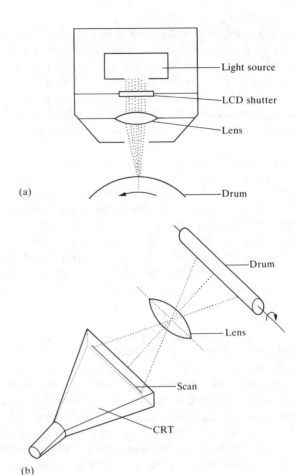

(a)

(b)

Fig. 7.42 The print drum: (a) LCD shutter; (b) CRT scanner.

7.8 User-oriented interfaces

So far we have described the conventional computer input/output devices: the keyboard, CRT terminal, and printer. There is, however, an immense range of other input/output devices, each designed for some specific application. For example, a cartographer uses a digitizer to enter a map into a computer and a graph-plotter to draw the map after it has been processed. On the other hand, an automatic-baggage handling system at an airport may get its input in the form of human speech (a varying air pressure) and use its output to control the hydraulic devices needed to move the baggage from one conveyor to another.

As the topic of special-purpose input/output devices can be expanded without limit, we will give only a broad overview here. There are two fundamental classes of I/O device: digital and analog. Devices whose inputs or outputs can be directly represented in a binary form are classified as digital devices (including those already discussed). Devices whose inputs or outputs are in the form of a continuously varying signal, which may have an infinite number of values, are classified as analog devices. For example, the microphone, loudspeaker, and thermometer are all intrinsically analog devices.

Digital input

All that is needed to implement digital input is some form of switch to select between a logical one and a logical zero. The electronic aspect of most mechanical switches is utterly trivial; two conductors are either pushed together to make a circuit, or pushed apart to break it. Conventional toggle switches, push-buttons and rotary switches (found on volume controls in some radios and televisions) are part of everyday life. We have already come across some of the many forms of switch in Section 7.6.1. While many switches are in full view some are kept hidden.

Consider the humble *limit switch*, designed to detect the extreme motion of a moving device. If the control electronics of an elevator fail and the winding gear attempts to pull the carriage up beyond the highest floor the possibility of an accident exists. If a switch connected to a lever is mounted above the normal upper limit of the carriage, any unwanted upward movement will push the lever, close a circuit, and enable the safety devices to take over.

Another form of mechanical switch called a *pressure-activated* switch is illustrated in Fig. 7.43. It is often necessary to know whether the pressure of fluid or gas in a pipe is above or below a given value. The fluid is allowed to come into contact with a thin, flexible diaphragm which is bowed outwards by the pressure. Clearly, the degree of movement by the diaphragm is a function of the pressure of the fluid. By virtue of a contact attached to the diaphragm, a fixed contact closes the circuit when the pressure is sufficiently high. In addition to the purely mechanical switch there are two-state switches that respond to other stimuli such as light or heat. All the above digital inputs force the computer to take some action when a particular event takes place—the opening or closing of the switch.

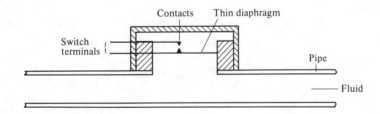

Fig. 7.43 The pressure-sensitive switch.

Digital output

The basic output of almost all digital computers is one or more binary values, each represented as signals in the range 0–0.4 V for a logical zero, and 2.8–5 V for a logical one. The simplest way of exploiting these signals to turn on (or off) some device, is to use a relay. Figure 7.44 shows the construction of a typical reed relay. When a current passes through the coil, a magnetic field is induced in the iron core. At a sufficiently high value the magnetic field is strong enough to attract a piece of iron, whose

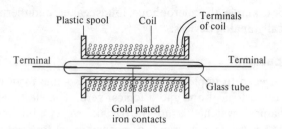

Fig. 7.44 The relay.

movement opens (or breaks) a contact. The coil can be connected directly between the output of the computer and ground. An output of 0.4 V is too low to energize the coil, while an output of 2.8 V is enough to operate the switch. In a real system some additional electronics would probably be needed to boost the output of the computer to a sufficient level, as all but the smallest relays require moderately large currents to energize the coil. The relay performs exactly the same function as a mechanical switch, and therefore anything that can be operated by a human pushing a button or throwing a switch can also be done by a computer.

We are now going to look at how the analog signals can be converted into digital values and vice versa.

7.8.1 The analog interface

It is often said that we live in an analog world, where the vast majority of measurable quantities have an infinite number of values within a given range. The temperature of a room is an analog quantity because it changes from one value to another by going through an infinite number of infinitesimal increments on its way. Similarly, air pressure, speed, sound intensity, weight, and time, are all analog quantities. Figure 7.45 illustrates a varying analog value as a function of time.

Fig. 7.45 An analog quantity as a function of time.

At first sight it might appear that the analog and digital worlds are mutually incompatible. Fortunately there exists a gateway between the analog and digital worlds called quantization. The fact that an analog quantity can have an infinite range of values is irrelevant. If somebody says they will arrive at 9.0 a.m. they are not telling the truth: 9.0 a.m. exists for an infinitesimally short period, so no event can be said to take place at 9.0 a.m. Of course what they really mean is that they will arrive at 9.0 a.m. plus or minus an unspecified amount of time. In other words, if we measure an analog quantity and specify it to a precision sufficient for our purposes, the error between the actual analog value and its measured value is unimportant. Once the analog value has been measured, it exists in a numeric form which can be transformed into a binary value and fed into a computer.

Figure 7.46 illustrates the equipment necessary to convert an analog quantity into a digital value. The transducer is a device which converts an analog quantity (temperature, pressure etc.) into an electrical signal whose level is a well-defined function of the property being measured. The output of most transducers is very small and must be increased to a suitable level by an amplifier. The output from the amplifier is then converted into digital form by an analog-to-digital converter (ADC). The output of the ADC is often in binary form and is fed in to the computer by means of a normal digital interface.

Fig. 7.46 Reading analog quantities.

Consider a digital system designed to read the temperature of the air. The transducer may operate in one of several ways, all of which involve some change in the electrical properties of matter with a change in temperature. Suppose the transducer generates an output from 0 V to 1 V as the temperature varies from $-10°C$ to $+40°C$. The output of the transducer is connected to an 8-bit analog-to-digital converter producing an output of \$FF for an input of 1 V. Therefore, the 50 degree range, $-10°C$ to $+40°C$, generates a binary output in the range 00000000 to 11111111. Each bit of the output corresponds to $50/256 = 0.2°C$. This figure is known as the resolution of the converter, and is the smallest change in temperature that can reliably be detected.

Because analog quantities are continuous, there is always an error equal to the difference between the actual signal being measured and its quantized value. This error is less than, or equal to, the resolution of the converter (at least in theory—all ADCs have small imperfections called non-linearities and do not behave perfectly). Usually the error inherent in the ADC is less than one half of the least significant bit. When designing an analog input for a computer, it is necessary to choose an ADC with the required resolution. This is easier to say than to do. Although 8-bit single-chip ADCs cost very little, the price of a DAC or ADC rises exponentially with resolution. The most precise DACs and ADCs that are normally available (we are excluding very special DACs and ADCs that might be found in special laboratories) have 18 bits of resolution and are used in high-quality sound processing. The digital-to-analog converters in CD players usually have 14 or 16 bits resolution. It is possible to relate the resolution of a DAC or ADC to its **dynamic range** and its **signal-to-noise ratio**. These terms are figures of merit and provide (on a logarithmic scale) an indication of the effect of quantization. The unit of these figures of merit is the **decibel**, which is used to specify the figure of merit of audio amplifiers or cassette decks. Table 7.17 provides the relationship between

Table 7.17 Relationship between resolution and signal-to-noise ratio

Resolution bits n	Discrete states 2^n	Binary weight 2^{-n}	Value of Q for 10 V FS	S/N ratio (dB)	Dynamic range (dB)
4	16	0.0625	0.625 V	34.9	24.1
6	64	0.0156	0.156 V	46.9	36.1
8	256	0.00391	39.1 mV	58.1	48.2
10	1024	0.000977	9.76 mV	71.0	60.2
12	4096	0.000244	2.44 mV	83.0	72.2
14	16384	0.0000610	610 µV	95.1	84.3
16	65536	0.0000153	153 µV	107.1	96.3

ADC and DAC resolution and dynamic range and signal-to-noise ratio for various bit lengths.

Having quantized a signal in value, we must also quantize it in time. It is impossible to sample a varying analog signal continuously. In any case, it takes up to several microseconds for a typical microprocessor to read an input. So how often do we have to sample a signal? The answer can be found from everyday experience. A television picture appears to be moving, yet it is (like a cine film) made up of a sequence of still pictures. Clearly, viewing a rapid sequence of stills (i.e. samples) gives the impression of continuous motion. Now consider sampling the temperature of a swimming pool. As such a large body of water has a high thermal inertia its temperature changes very slowly, so that a sample taken every few minutes would probably be adequate. These two examples demonstrate that the rate at which an analog quantity must be sampled is related to the rate at which it is changing.

There is a theorem stating that a signal can be completely reconstructed if it is sampled at more than twice the frequency of the maximum frequency component in the signal. If speech is being sampled for processing by a computer, and the maximum frequency component in the speech signal is 3000 Hz, then it must be sampled at least 6000 times a second. This is the theoretical minimum, and a higher sampling rate (say 10 000 Hz) would be needed in a real system. This corresponds to a sample every 0.1 ms (i.e. 100 µs). Once a signal has been sampled and input to a computer, it can be processed digitally in the same way as any other numeric value.

Digital-to-analog conversion

Conceptually the digital-to-analog converter, DAC, is a very simple device. If a binary value is to be converted into analog form, all we have to do is to generate an analog value proportional to each bit of the digital word and then add these values to give a composite analog sum. Figure 7.47 illustrates this process. An m-bit digital signal is latched by m D flip-flops and held constant until the next value is ready for conversion. The flip-flops constitute a digital sample-and-hold circuit! Each of the m bits operates a switch that passes either zero or V_i volts to an analog adder, where V_i is the output of the ith switch. The output of this adder is

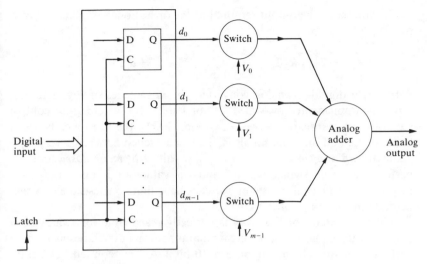

Fig. 7.47 The basic digital-to-analog converter.

If $d_i = 0$ 0 is passed to the analog adder;
if $d_i = 1$ V_i is passed to the analog adder.

$$V = d_{m-1}V_{m-1} + d_{m-2}V_{m-2} + \ldots + d_0V_0.$$

Note that the $\{d_i\}$ in this equation represents binary values zero or one and the $\{V_i\}$ represents binary powers of the form $(1, \frac{1}{2}, \frac{1}{4}, \frac{1}{8}, \ldots)$.

A possible implementation of a digital-to-analog converter is given in Fig. 7.48. The total current flowing into the inverting terminal of the operational amplifier is equal to the linear sum of the currents flowing through the individual resistors. As each of the resistors can be connected to ground or to a precisely maintained reference voltage, V_{ref}, the current flowing through each resistor is either zero or $V_{ref}/(2^iR)$, where $i = 0,1,2,\ldots,$ $m-1$. The total current flowing into the operational amplifier is given by

$$\frac{2V_{ref}}{R[d_{m-1}2^{-1} + d_{m-2}2^{-2} + \ldots + d_02^{-m}]}$$

where d_i represents the state of the ith switch.

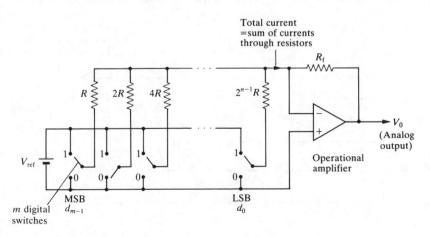

Fig. 7.48 Implementing the digital-to-analog converter.

The voltage at the output terminal of the operational amplifier is given by

$$V_0 = -2\frac{V}{R^{\text{ref}}} R_{\text{f}}[d_{m-1}2^{-1} + d_{m-2}2^{-2} + \ldots + d_0 2^{-m}].$$

In a real digital-to-analog converter, the m switches of Fig. 7.48 are, typically, implemented by MOSFETs or JFETs. By switching the control gate of these transistors between two logic levels, the resistance between their source and drain terminals is likewise switched between a very high value (the *off* or *open* state) and a very low value (the *on* or *closed* state). A perfect transistor switch has off and on values of infinity and zero, respectively. Practical transistor switches have finite on-resistances which degrade the accuracy of the DAC.

While the circuit of Fig. 7.48 is perfectly reasonable for values of m below about six, larger values create manufacturing difficulties associated with the resistor chain. Suppose a 10-bit DAC is required. The ratio between the largest and smallest resistor is 2^{10}:1 or 1024:1. If the device is to be accurate to one lsb, the precision of the largest resistor must be at least one half part in 1024, or approximately 0.05 per cent. Manufacturing resistors to this absolute level of precision is difficult and costly with thin-film technology, and virtually impossible with integrated circuit technology.

The *R–2R* ladder

An alternative form of digital-to-analog converter is given in Fig. 7.49, and DAC relies on the $R-2R$ ladder so called because all resistors in the ladder have the value either R or $2R$. While it is difficult to produce highly accurate resistors over a wide range of values, it is much easier to produce pairs of resistors with a precise 2:1 ratio in resistance.

As the current from the reference source flows down the ladder (from left to right in Fig. 7.49), it is divided at each junction (i.e. the node between the left R, right R and $2R$ resistors) into two equal parts, one flowing along the ladder to the right and one flowing down the $2R$ shunt resistor. The network forms a linear circuit and therefore the superposition theorem, which states that 'in a linear system the effect is the sum of

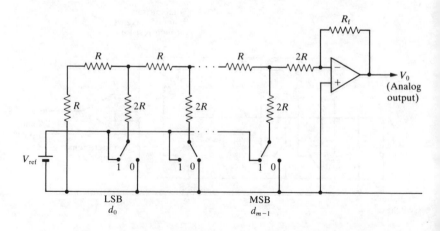

Fig. 7.49 The $R–2R$ digital-to-analog converter.

all the causes' can be applied. Consequently, the total current flowing into the inverting terminal of the operational amplifier is equal to the sum of all the currents from the shunt (i.e. $2R$) resistors, weighted by the appropriate binary value.

A digital-to-analog converter based on the R–$2R$ ladder has three advantages over the type described in Fig. 7.4:

1. All resistors have a value of either R or $2R$, making it easy to match resistors and to provide a good measure of temperature tracking between resistors. Furthermore, the residual *on* resistance of the transistor switches can readily be compensated for.

2. By selecting relatively low values for R in the range 2.5–10 kilohms, it is both easy to manufacture the DAC and to achieve a good response time because of the low impedance of the network.

3. Due to the nature of the R–$2R$ ladder, the operational amplifier always sees a constant impedance at its input, regardless of the state of switches in the ladder, which improves the accuracy of the operational amplifier circuit.

The R–$2R$ ladder forms the basis of many, if not the majority, of commercially available DACs. Real circuits are arranged slightly differently to that of Fig. 7.49 to reduce still further the practical problems associated with a DAC.

Analog-to-digital conversion

While converting a digital value into an analog signal is relatively easy, at least for word lengths up to 12 bits, the inverse process of converting an analog quantity into a digital value is frequently rather more involved. In fact, apart from one special type of A/D converter, analog-to-digital conversion is performed in a roundabout way.

The feedback analog-to-digital converter

The feedback analog-to-digital converter, paradoxically, uses a digital-to-analog converter to effect the required conversion. Figure 7.50 illustrates the basic principle behind this class of converter. A local digital-to-analog converter transforms a digital value, $D = d_0, d_1, \ldots, d_{m-1}$, into an analog

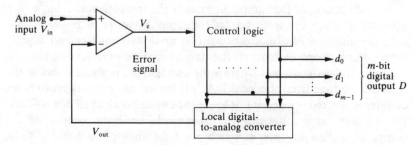

Fig. 7.50 The feedback analog-to-digital converter.

$V_e = A\,(V_{in} - V_{out})$ where A = gain of operational amplifier voltage, V_{out}. The value of D is determined by the block labelled *control logic* in one of the ways to be described later.

V_{out} from the DAC is applied to the inverting input of an operational amplifier and the analog input to be converted is applied to its non-inverting input. The output of the operational amplifier corresponds to an error signal, and is equal to A times $(V_{in}-V_{out})$, where A is the gain of the amplifier. The error signal is used by the logic network to modify the digital data, D, in such a way as to minimize the error signal $A(V_{in}-V_{out})$. When the difference between V_{in} and V_{out} is less than that between two quantized signal levels (i.e. Q), the conversion process is complete. In plain English, the digital output is varied by trial and error until the locally generated analog voltage is as close to the analog input as it is possible to achieve. The next step is to examine ways of implementing this *trial and error* process.

The ramp converter

The simplest possible feedback ADC is the ramp converter (see Fig. 7.51), which uses a binary counter to generate the digital output, D. At the start of a conversion, the binary counter is cleared to zero. A new conversion process starts with the resetting of the RS flip-flop. When $\bar{Q}$ goes high following a reset, the AND gate is enabled and clock pulses are fed to the counter causing the output of the counter, D, to increase monotonically from zero (i.e. $0,1,2,\ldots,2^{m-1}$).

The output from the counter is applied to both an m-bit output latch and a DAC. As the counter is clocked, the output of the local DAC ramps upward in the manner shown in the timing diagram of Fig. 7.51(b). The locally generated analog signal is compared with the input to be converted in a digital comparator, whose output is the sign of the local analog voltage minus the input (i.e. $\text{sign}(V_{out}-V_{in})$). When this value goes positive, the flip-flop is set. At the same time, its $\bar{Q}$ output goes low, cutting off the stream of clock pulses to the counter, and its Q output goes high, providing an End_of_conversion (EOC) output and latching the contents of the binary counter into the output latches.

The ramp feedback ADC has a variable conversion time. If the analog input is close to the maximum (i.e. full-scale) value, a total of 2^m clock pulses are required. For an 8-bit ADC the maximum conversion time is 256 times the settling time of the DAC plus associated delays in the comparator and counter. The advantage of the ramp ADC is its great simplicity and low hardware cost.

A modification of the ramp converter is the tracking converter, which operates in much the same way as the ramp converter of Fig. 7.51, but with the addition of a bidirectional (i.e. up/down) counter and slightly more complex control logic. At the start of each new conversion process, the comparator determines whether the analog input is above or below the feedback voltage from the local DAC. If the analog input is greater, the counter is clocked up, and if it is lower the counter is clocked down. Thus, the counter ramps upwards or downwards until the output of the comparator changes state, at which point the analog input is said to be acquired by the converter.

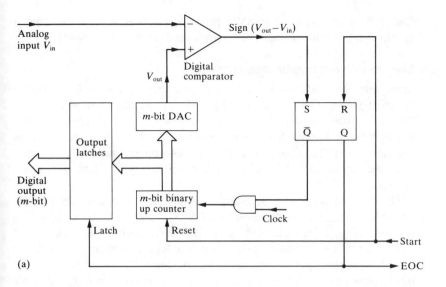

(a)

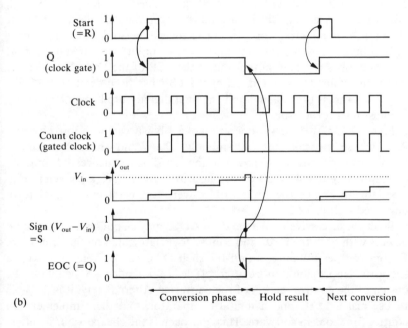

(b)

Fig. 7.51 The ramp analog-to-digital converter.

If the analog input is constant, the conversion time of the counter is effectively zero, once the input has been initially acquired. As long as the input changes slowly with respect to the rate at which the output of the local DAC can ramp upwards or downwards, the tracking counter faithfully converts the analog input into the appropriate digital output. If, however, the analog input rapidly changes its level, the local analog voltage may not be able to track the input, acquisition is lost and the digital output becomes invalid.

The tracking ADC is most useful when the input is changing slowly and his highly autocorrelated. Human speech represents such a signal. If the converter is subject to essentially random inputs (e.g. it is fed from a multiplexer), it offers little or no advantage over a ramp converter.

The successive-approximation converter

Intuitively, it would seem reasonable to take very large steps in increasing the analog signal from the local DAC early in the conversion process, and then to reduce the step size as the conversion proceeds and the local analog voltage approaches the analog input. Such an ADC is known as the successive approximation ADC and uses a binary search algorithm to guarantee an m-bit converstion in no more than m iterations (i.e. clock cycles).

The structure of a successive-approximation DAC is adequately illustrated by the generic converter of Fig. 7.50. It is only the strategy by which the control logic generates successive steps that interests us here. At the start of a new conversion process, the digital logic sets the most significant bit (MSB) of the input of the local DAC to a logical one level and all other bits to zero. In other words, the first guess is equal to one half the full-scale output of the converter. If the analog is greater than half the full-scale output from the local DAC, the MSB is retained at a logical one level, otherwise it is cleared. On the second iteration, the next most significant bit (i.e. d_{m-2} in an m-bit word) is set to a logical one and retained at one if the output of the DAC is less than the analog input, or cleared if it is not. This process is repeated m times until the LSB of the DAC has been set and then retained or cleared. After the LSB has been dealt with in this way, the process is at an end and the final digital output may be read by the host microprocessor.

Figure 7.52 illustrates the operation of a 4-bit successive-approximation ADC whose full-scale input is nominally 1.000 V and whose analog input to be converted is 0.6400 V. All the possible sequences of outputs corresponding to a 4-bit successive-approximation DAC are given in Fig. 7.53, together with the results of converting 0.6400 into digital form described in Fig. 7.52.

Practical successive-approximation ADCs may be bought as single-chip devices with both the DAC and control logic fabricated on the same chip. For greater performance, an off-the-shelf DAC can be combined with a successive-approximation register, a device intended to facilitate the design of the control section of the converter. Alternatively, it is possible to use just a DAC and a digital comparator, and then implement all control functions in software. This approach is the cheapest but it suffers from a relatively slow conversion rate.

7.8.2 The mouse

Since the introduction of the personal computer, there has been a considerable growth in the range and type of 'pointer devices'. A pointer device is a two-dimensional input mechanism that can be used to move a cursor to any point on the surface of a CRT display. Pointer devices are employed in three broad roles. First they are used by computer games to move an object to any part of the screen. Entering such information by

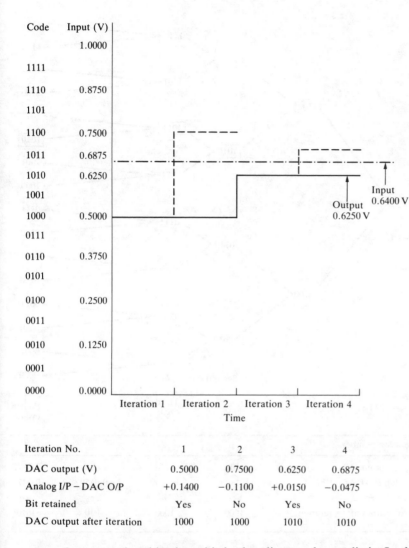

Iteration No.	1	2	3	4
DAC output (V)	0.5000	0.7500	0.6250	0.6875
Analog I/P − DAC O/P	+0.1400	−0.1100	+0.0150	−0.0475
Bit retained	Yes	No	Yes	No
DAC output after iteration	1000	1000	1010	1010

Fig. 7.52 Operation of the successive-approximation converter.

means of a conventional keyboard is both tedious and unrealistic. In this application, pointer devices provide an 'arcade style' environment at home.

A second use of pointer devices is in user-friendly operating systems like Windows. The operator does not have to learn (i.e. remember) a complex operating system command syntax. Instead, the user is presented with a series of self-explanatory images or icons and then employs the pointer device to select the desired operation by moving the cursor to the appropriate icon. The operation is activated by clicking the pointer (some pointers have a button on their top that can be pushed without moving the hand from the pointer).

The third application of pointer devices is in user packages such as desktop publishing, computer-aided design, artwork and graphics.

There are various types of pointer device with a remarkably wide range of price/performance parameters. Three of the simplest pointer devices are the joystick (used largely in games applications), the mouse (used as an

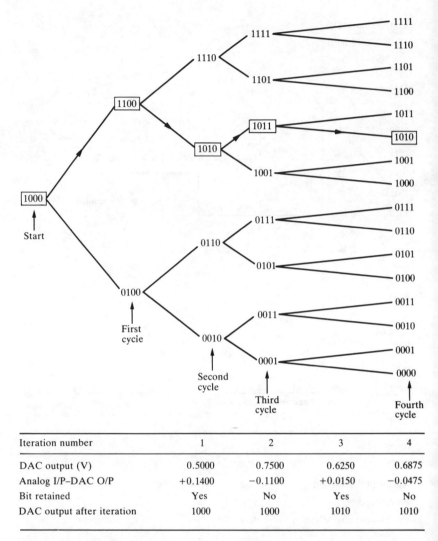

Fig. 7.53 Example of successive approximation.

Iteration number	1	2	3	4
DAC output (V)	0.5000	0.7500	0.6250	0.6875
Analog I/P–DAC O/P	+0.1400	−0.1100	+0.0150	−0.0475
Bit retained	Yes	No	Yes	No
DAC output after iteration	1000	1000	1010	1010

operating system interface and for CAD-like applications) and the trackball.

The trackball is a pointer device very much like the mouse and differs from the mouse only in its ergonomics. The mouse is dragged along a surface such as a table, while a trackball is really an 'upside down mouse' which users control by rotating a ball in a fixed housing. Trackballs are often integrated into the computer equipment and are located on the operator's keyboard. A typical application of a trackball might be in a radar controller's console. Operators can rapidly rotate the trackball with their hand to move the cursor to an aircraft under their control. The computer might then display the distance and bearing of the aircraft from the airport.

Another pointer device is the more expensive graphics tablet that is able to determine the X,Y coordinates of a 'pen' when it is placed on the tablet. The graphics tablet is often referred to as a 'digitizer' and a state-of-the-art digitizer might be able to resolve the position of the pointer to an accuracy of ± 0.1 mm (0.004 in).

There are many ways of converting the motion of a mouse into a signal that can be fed into a computer. One technique is to use optical sensing. Figure 7.54 demonstrates the principle of an optical mouse. As the ball rotates (due to the friction between itself and the desk), its motion is resolved into two axes by means of the rollers located at right angles to each other. If the mouse is moved upwards or from left to right, only one roller rotates. If the mouse is moved diagonally both rollers rotate and their relative speed is a function of the diagonal angle.

Each roller is connected to a shaft which rotates an optical encoder (i.e. an opaque disc with holes in its surface). When the encoder rotates, it interrupts a beam of light between an LED and a detector. Each pulse is

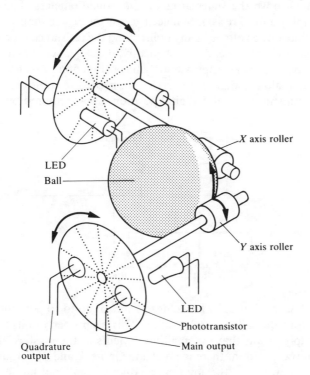

Fig. 7.54 Optimal mouse.

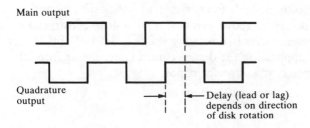

fed to the computer and by adding up the number of pulses received, it is possible to determine how far the mouse has moved along that axis. In practice, two beams of light are necessary because a single beam would make it impossible to determine whether the mouse was moving in a positive or a negative direction. A second detector is required to produce a quadrature signal that is out of phase with the main signal. If the ball is rotated one way, the quadrature signal leads the main signal and if the rotation is reversed the quadrature signal lags the main signal.

The joystick is usually a low-cost, low-resolution input found in games applications. Its principal advantage over the mouse/trackball is that it can provide four axes (the conventional left/right up/down axes, plus a twist or rotate axis and a fourth pseudo-axis can be incorporated as a push button on the joystick's top.

Figure 7.55 illustrates the operation of the joystick. Mechanical linkages move the slider arms of two potentiometers. The potentiometers employ a fixed resistance placed across the power supply. If the resistance is linear, the voltage at any point along the resistance is proportional to its distance from its end. Consequently, the slider supplies an analog voltage output that is an approximately linear function of its position. Note that two analog-to-digital converters are needed to transform the two analog outputs into X and Y digital position inputs required by the computer.

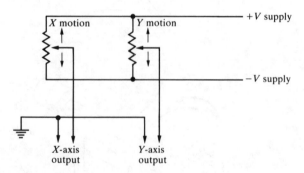

Fig. 7.55 The joystick.

A joystick usually has a 'dead zone' of up to 10 per cent of its full scale output about its neutral position. This is a property of its construction and simply means that for small movements of the joystick about its central neutral position, there is no change in its X and Y outputs. This has the advantage that the joystick produces a null output in its 'hands off' neutral position and is unaffected by small movements. Its disadvantage is that it is more difficult to use the joystick to make precision movements when it is near to its neutral position.

It is perfectly possible to construct a joystick with an optical encoding system as described above, just as it is possible to construct a mouse with potentiometers on its two rotating shafts instead of optical encoders. In any given application the designer must select the appropriate compromise between cost and performance.

Summary

In this chapter we have looked at the way in which computers perform their input and output operations. Since this topic is so large, we have divided it into three regions: the strategy by which data is moved into and out of the computer, the interface chips that actually move the data and the devices or peripherals that generate or make use of the data.

Problems

1. What is an input/output strategy, as opposed to an input/output device?

2. What is the difference between an intelligent and an unintelligent input/output device?

3. What is DMA and why is it so important in high performance computer systems?

4. What examples of 'handshaking' can you find in everyday life?

5. The 68000 supports only memory-mapped I/O since it has no dedicated I/O bus or I/O instructions. What are the disadvantages of memory-mapped I/O?

6. What is a prioritized vectored interrupt?

7. To what extent are interrupts and subroutines the same and to what extent do they differ?

8. How are the individual characters of an asynchronous serial interface divided into individual bits (assuming that the receiver has no knowledge of the transmitter's clock frequency)?

9. What is an interlaced picture (i.e. raster scan display), and why may it give poor results when used to display text (as opposed to TV style images)?

Computer memory

In this chapter we are going to look at the various ways in which information is stored inside a computer. Memory systems are divided into two distinct classes: immediate access main stores and secondary stores. We examine first the high-speed main store and then look at the secondary stores that hold data not currently being processed by the CPU. Before we consider storage devices proper, we introduce some of the terminology and underlying concepts associated with memory systems.

Every one knows what memory is, but it is rather more difficult to define it. *Memory* can be defined as the long- or short-term change in one or more of the physical properties of matter caused by some *event*. That is, after the event has taken place, the change remains. For example, ice forms on a pond during a spell of cold weather and lingers when the weather gets warmer. The water has changed state from a liquid to a solid under the influence of a low temperature and now *remembers* that it has been cold, even though the temperature has risen above freezing point. To create a computer memory, it is necessary to find some property of matter that can be modified and, at a later time, the modification be detected.

Without memory we would not be able to follow a film, because anything that happened prior to the current point in time would have vanished. As the film is watched, the optical signal from the eye causes actual changes within the brain—the event has passed but its effect remains. The film itself is a memory device. The photons of light once produced by a scene alter the chemical structure of a thin coating of silver halides on a sheet of plastic.

Both human memory and photographic film share a property called *forgetfulness*. Human memory may gradually fade unless it is *refreshed* by repetition or a reminder. Even colour film slowly fades when exposed to bright sunlight. At least one type of computer memory, called dynamic memory, also forgets its stored data unless it is periodically refreshed.

A computer needs two types of memory: immediate access store (which we have called main store throughout this text) and secondary storage. The whole concept of the Von Neumann stored program computer is founded on the sequential execution of a series of operations. Clearly, the program must be stored (remembered) if the individual instructions are to be carried out sequentially. A memory would not be necessary if all instructions were executed simultaneously. Furthermore, as the results of these instructions yield temporary or intermediate results, some memory is needed to hold them. Such memory falls in a class called *immediate access* because it must be able to access its contents at the same rate the CPU executes instructions.

Since computers normally execute many different programs, those programs not currently being used must be stored somewhere. In addition to programs themselves there are often large quantities of data to be retained until needed. *Secondary storage* devices are able to hold large quantities of information cheaply but cannot access their data at anything like the speed a computer can execute instructions.

Because much of computer technology (e.g. the CPU) is associated with binary arithmetic and Boolean algebra, it is reasonable to expect computer memories to follow this trend. Most memory systems store information in binary form by exploiting some two-valued property of the storage medium. Humans sometimes do this in non-computer applications. For example, consider the proverbial knot in a piece of string. The information is stored as one bit; knot or no-knot. I've always wondered why people don't tie different types of knot and thereby increase the information-carrying capacity of the piece of string.

The most important requirements of a binary memory element is that two stable (at least over a short period of time) states exist, and that these states are separated by an energy barrier. If there were no energy barriers separating the states, it would be possible for a stored binary value to change its state at the least provocation. In the case of our piece of string, it requires a considerable energy input either to tie a knot or to untie it.

Memory terminology

As there are many different types of memory device, each with its own characteristics, a vocabulary must be devised to describe them. Below are a few of the terms found most frequently in literature dealing with memory technology.

Memory cell. A memory cell is the smallest unit of information storage and can hold a single logical zero or logical one. Memory cells are often grouped together to form words. The location of each cell in the memory is specified by its address, which is called a *physical address* to distinguish it from the logical address of an operand generated by the computer.

Access time. The access time is one of the most important parameters of any memory component and is the time taken to read data from a given memory location, measured from the start of a read cycle. The access time is made up of two parts: the time taken to locate the required memory cell and the time taken for the data to become available from the memory cell. Strictly speaking, we should refer to read cycle access time, but because many semiconductor memories have identical read and write access times, the access time is normally taken to mean the read or write access time. This is not true of all forms of memory, because some devices have quite different read and write access times. Some memories are also specified in terms of cycle time, which is the time that must elapse between two successive read or write accesses. Access time and cycle time are often identical. However, this is not true for either semiconductor dynamic memories or ferrite cores.

Random access. When I first came across this term I naively thought it meant that a memory cell was selected at random and that if it was not the desired cell another random access was made. This is not so. When a memory is configured so that the access time of any cell within it is constant (or effectively constant) and is independent of the actual location of the cell, the memory is then said to be random access memory (RAM). That is, the access time of random access memory is constant and does not depend on the location of the data being accessed. In practice, this means that the CPU does not have to worry about the time taken to read a word from memory because all read cycles have the same duration.

If a memory is random access for the purpose of read cycles, it is invariably random access for the purpose of write cycles. It is unfortunate that the term RAM is often employed to describe read/write memory (as opposed to read only memory) where data may be read from the memory or written into it. This usage is incorrect, because the term random access indicates only the property of constant access time and has nothing to do with the memory's ability to modify (i.e. write) its data. Another term for random access is *immediate access*. In everyday life the closest analog of random access memory is the dialled telephone system. The time taken to connect with (access) any subscriber is constant and independent of their physical location.

Serial access. In a serial access memory, the time taken to access data is dependent on the physical location of the data within the memory and can vary over a wide range for any given system. Usually, the data moves past some read/write device so that in accessing any given memory cell, the waiting time depends on the time taken for the memory cell to move to the read/write device. Examples of serial access memories are magnetic tape transports, disk drives, shift registers and magnetic bubble memories. Serial access is also referred to as *sequential* access.

Volatile memory. Volatile memory loses its contents when the source of power is removed. This term applies to most types of semiconductor memory in which data is stored as a charge on a capacitor or as the state of a transistor (on or off) in a bistable circuit. Memories based on magnetism are generally non-volatile because their magnetic state does not depend on a supply of power.

Read only memory (ROM). Read only memory can have its contents read but not (under normal operating conditions) modified. True read only memories are, by definition, non-volatile. Read only memory is frequently used to hold operating systems, interpreters, assemblers and other system software in microprocessor systems.

Static memory. Once data has been written into a static memory cell, it remains there until it is either altered by over-writing it with new data or by removing the source of power if the memory is volatile. Static semiconductor memory cells usually employ cross-coupled transistors (i.e. a flip-flop) to hold the data.

Dynamic memory. Dynamic memories store data in the form of a charge on the inter-electrode capacitance of a field effect transistor. Because the capacitor is not perfect the charge gradually leaks away, discharging the capacitor and losing the data. Whenever dynamic memories are used (they are much cheaper than static memories) some additional circuitry is needed periodically (every 2 ms) to restore the charge on the capacitors in an operation known as *memory refreshing*.

Memory technology

There are many ways of storing binary information and each technique has its advantages and disadvantages (cost, speed, power consumption, size etc.). Some of the most widely used properties of matter used to store information are as follows:

Electrical with feedback. An electronic switch is held in a given logical state because its output is fed back to its input, holding it in a fixed state. A flip-flop or bistable is such a memory element.

Electrical with a stored charge. An electrical charge (a surfeit or deficit of electrons) is stored on a conductor which is electrically insulated from its surroundings to stop the charge draining away. Information is stored as a charge or as no charge. This memory element corresponds to the *capacitor* and is the basic storage element in semiconductor dynamic memory chips.

Magnetic. Individual atoms have a magnetic field caused by the spin of electrons. The spin has one of two values (up or down), creating two possible magnetic states. As the orientation of the spin of the electrons in most matter is random, due to the much stronger thermal vibrations of the atoms, there is no overall magnetic effect. However, a class of materials exhibit *ferromagnetism*, in which the interactions between the spins of adjacent electrons cause them to align themselves parallel with one another. Under these circumstances all the atoms in the bulk material are oriented with their spins in the same direction and the material is *magnetized*. As we can magnetize material with its electron spins in one of two states and detect these states, magnetic materials may be used in computer memories.

Structural. By modifying the structure, shape, or the dimensions of some object we can represent a very large number of possible states. In practice, real systems use the 'there/not-there' principle in which holes are made or not made in paper. This rapidly disappearing form of memory is found in punched cards and paper tape. The phonogram record is a structural memory that stores analog information by deforming the spiral groove cut into the surface of a plastic disk. At any instant the analog information is a function of the depth of the cut in the side of the groove.

Spatial. In a spatial memory data is stored as a moving wave that travels through some medium. Superman has a neat trick enabling him to see into the past. He just zooms away from earth at a speed faster than light and then simply views the past event from its light, which has been streaming away from the earth at a constant speed of 300 000 km/s. The memory of the event is represented by a stream of photons moving in space. Early computers converted information into sound pulses travelling down tubes filled with mercury. When the train of pulses representing the stored binary sequence has travelled from one end of the tube to the other end, it is detected, amplified and recirculated. This type of memory is called a delay-line memory and is no longer found in digital computers. The magnetic bubble memory described in Section 8.5 is a modern form of spatial memory.

8.1 Semiconductor memory

Semiconductor random access memory is fabricated on silicon chips by a process that is effectively identical to the process used to manufacture microprocessors and their related support chips. Were it not for the availability of low-cost semiconductor memory, the microprocessor revolution would have been seriously delayed if microprocessors had been constrained to use the ferrite core memory of 1960s and 1970s mainframes.

The principle features of semiconductor memory are its low cost, high density (measured in bits per chip), and ease of use. There are two major classes of semiconductor memory: static and dynamic.

8.1.1 Static memory

Static semiconductor memory is easiest to use from the designer's or engineer's point of view and is generally found in small and medium-size memories. Some larger computer memory systems do use the less economic static semiconductor memory devices because of their greater reliability than dynamic memory. However, large memories are generally built with dynamic memory because of its lower cost. A typical semiconductor memory chip, the 62256 256K CMOS RAM, is illustrated in Fig. 8.1. The acronym **CMOS** indicates the technology used to manufacture it (cf. TTL), and the **256K** denotes the capacity of the memory in bits. All semiconductor memories are specified in terms of their capacity (e.g. 1K, 4K, 16K, 64K, 256K, 1M, 4M, 16M bits) and their **organization**.

The organization of a memory component is an expression of the way in which its storage locations are internally arranged. Memory components are said to be organized as n word by m bits (the total capacity is defined as mn). Some memory components are bit-organized, so that a bit-organized 256K chip is arranged as 256K locations, each of one bit. Others are nybble organized with, for example, a 16K chip arranged as 4K locations, each containing 4 bits. The 62256 is byte-organized as 32K words of 8 bits. Such **byte-wide** chips are suited to small memories in microprocessor systems in which one or two chips may be sufficient for all the processor's read/write memory requirements.

The pin-out of the 62256 is illustrated in Fig. 8.1 and has 28 pins, of which 15 are the address inputs needed to select one of $2^{15} = 32\,768$ unique locations. Eight data lines transfer data from the 62256 during a CPU read cycle, and receive data from the processor during a CPU write cycle. Electrical power is fed to the chip via two pins. The following three control pins determine the operation of the memory component:

$\overline{CS}$	chip select	low to select chip for read or write access
$R/\overline{W}$	read/write	low to write data when chip selected
$\overline{OE}$	output enable	low to output data when chip selected for read.

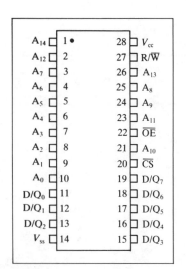

A_{14} ☐	1 •	28	☐ V_{cc}
A_{14} ☐	1 •	28	☐ V_{cc}
A_{12} ☐	2	27	☐ $R/\overline{W}$
A_7 ☐	3	26	☐ A_{13}
A_6 ☐	4	25	☐ A_8
A_5 ☐	5	24	☐ A_9
A_4 ☐	6	23	☐ A_{11}
A_3 ☐	7	22	☐ $\overline{OE}$
A_2 ☐	8	21	☐ A_{10}
A_1 ☐	9	20	☐ $\overline{CS}$
A_0 ☐	10	19	☐ D/Q_7
D/Q_0 ☐	11	18	☐ D/Q_6
D/Q_1 ☐	12	17	☐ D/Q_5
D/Q_2 ☐	13	16	☐ D/Q_4
V_{ss} ☐	14	15	☐ D/Q_3

PIN NAMES	
A_0–A_{14}	Address
$R/\overline{W}$	Write Enable
$\overline{OE}$	Chip Enable
$\overline{CS}$	Output Enable
D/Q_0–D/Q_7	Data Input/Output
V_{cc}	+5 V Power Supply
V_{ss}	Ground

Fig. 8.1 The 62256 32K×8 static RAM.

In order for the chip to take part in a read or wr. operation, its $\overline{CS}$ pin must be in a logical zero state. Whenever $\overline{CS}$ is inactive high, the memory component ignores all signals at its other pins. Disabling the 62256 by turning off its internal tri-state bus drivers permits several 62256s to share the data bus as long as only one 62256 is enabled at a time. The $R/\overline{W}$ input determines whether the chip is storing the data at its eight data pins ($R/\overline{W} = 0$), or is transferring data to these pins ($R/\overline{W} = 1$). The $\overline{OE}$, output enable, pin is used to turn on the memory's tristate bus drivers during a CPU read cycle and off at all other times. Not all memory chips have a separate $\overline{OE}$ control input. Many save a pin by combining $\overline{OE}$ with $\overline{CS}$ (i.e. the output data buffers are automatically enabled when $\overline{CS} = 0$ and $R/\overline{W} = 1$).

Data is stored in this and other static RAM chips in flip-flops, each composed of four or six transistors. Figure 8.2 shows the internal arrangement of this type of chip. It is fortunate that all the address decoding and read/write electronics is located on the chip, greatly simplifying the design of the memory system. Figure 8.3 demonstrates how the 62256 can be connected to a 68000 CPU. As the 68000 has a 16-bit data bus, it is necessary to connect two 62256s in parallel to provide 32K words of storage. However, as the 62256 has only 15 address inputs and the 68000 has 23 address outputs, it is necessary to map the memory's 32K word address space onto the 68000's 8M word address space. That is, the chip must be made to respond only to addresses falling in one of the CPU's 2^8 blocks of 32K words. In Fig. 8.3 a simple logic subsystem, called an *address decoder*, decodes the 68000's eight higher-order address lines, A_{16}–A_{23}, to generate a $\overline{CS}$ input for the 62265 static RAM chips.

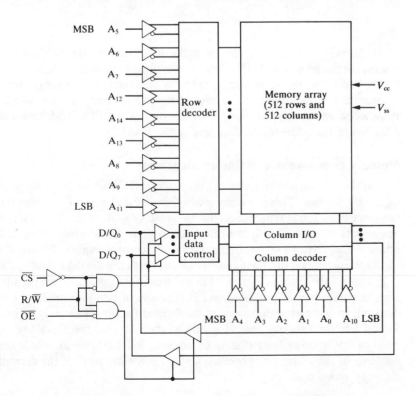

Fig. 8.2 The internal arrangement of a static RAM.

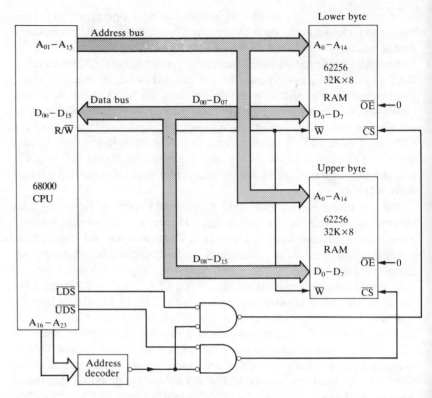

Fig. 8.3 Connecting the 62256 static RAM to a 68000 CPU.

Note: $\overline{LDS}$ selects the lower byte ($D_{00}-D_{07}$)
$\overline{UDS}$ selects the upper byte ($D_{08}-D_{15}$)

At this point we do not intend to make an excursion into the design of system memories and their interface to microprocessors and will return to address decoding when we discuss memory organization. We simply wish to provide an illustration of the ease of the use of memory chips. Apart from a few gates, it is necessary only to connect the CPU's address and data bus to the address and data bus of the RAM.

Memory component and timing diagrams

One of the parameters of a memory chip of most interest to the designer is its *timing diagram*. This is a *cause and effect* diagram which illustrates the sequence of actions taking place during a read or write cycle. The systems designer is concerned with the relationship between information on the address and data buses, and the memory's control inputs. Figure 8.4 shows the simplified timing diagram of a memory chip during a read cycle.

In Fig. 8.4 the timing diagram of the address bus appears as two parallel lines crossing over at points A and B. The use of two parallel lines is a convention and means that some of the fourteen address lines may be in a logical zero state and some in a logical one state. It is not the actual logical state of the address lines that is of interest, but the time at which the contents of the address bus become stable for the duration of the current memory access cycle.

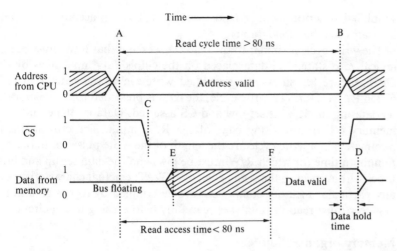

Fig. 8.4 The read-cycle timing diagram of a static RAM.

At point A in Fig. 8.4, the contents of the address bus have fully changed from their previous value and are now stable. This point is taken as a reference for some of the memory's timing parameters. Because logic transitions are never instantaneous, it is usual to show all changes of state by a sloping line.

Between points A and B the address bus contains the address of the memory location currently being read from. During this time the address from the CPU must not change. The time between A and B is the minimum cycle time of the memory. A quoted value of 80 ns means that another memory access cannot begin until at least 80 ns after the current cycle. The $R/\overline{W}$ line must be at a logical one state for the duration of the entire read cycle.

Consider now the operation of the memory component in a read cycle. The CPU puts out an address on its address bus corresponding to a location within the memory. The higher-order address lines from the CPU, A_{15}–A_{23}, cause the output of the address decoder to be asserted and to select the memory components as described in Fig. 8.3. At point C in Fig. 8.4 the chip select input, $\overline{CS}$, goes low, which has the effect of turning on the three-state bus driver outputs connected to the data pins. Up to point E the contents of the data bus are represented by a single line midway between the two logic levels. This convention indicates that the data bus is floating, and is disconnected from the data output circuits of the memory.

When the three-state output circuits are turned on by $\overline{CS}$ going low at point E, the data bus stops floating and data appears at the output terminals. Unfortunately, sufficient time has not yet elapsed for the addressed memory word to be located and its contents retrieved. Consequently, the contents of the data bus between points E and F are not valid and cannot be used. At point F the data is valid and the time between points A and F is called the read access time of the chip.

At the end of the read cycle designated by point B, the contents of the address bus begin to change. Because of propagation delays in the chip, the data at its output pins does not change until some guaranteed minimum time has elapsed. This delay is called the data hold time, and is the duration between points B and D. The above description is a rather simplified description of a read cycle. For a fuller account of timing diagrams see the bibliography.

The write cycle is similar to the read cycle except that R/$\overline{W}$ must be in a logical zero state, and data placed on the chip's data input lines by the CPU. Figure 8.5 shows the simplified write-cycle timing diagram of a 62256 RAM. During a write cycle, the data is presented to the memory at its data inputs, R/$\overline{W}$ is set low and $\overline{CS}$ asserted. Data is latched into the memory cell by the rising edge of the R/$\overline{W}$ input. The critical timing parameters in a write cycle are the length of the write pulse width (i.e. the minimum time for which R/$\overline{W}$ must be low) and the data set up and hold times with respect to the rising edge of R/$\overline{W}$. The actual characteristics of any particular memory component are determined by its design and the engineer must read its data sheet carefully before using it in a circuit.

Memory organization

We will now look at how the various semiconductor memory components that constitute a memory subsystem are arranged with respect to the microprocessor. Readers who are not interested in microprocessor systems design may skip this section.

The uniquely addressable locations (e.g. 16M bytes for the 68000) that form the memory of a microprocessor system are often imagined as being laid out, side by side, in a column of locations, numbered sequentially from 00 . . . 0 to 11 . . . 1. This imaginary column is often referred to as an *address space*. Because various regions of the address space can be grouped together into blocks of consecutive locations, the resulting grouping is usually called a *memory map*. The blocks forming the memory map refer to hardware devices (i.e. blocks of RAM, ROM), or they may refer to logical entities (i.e. programs, subroutines, editors, etc.). Figure 8.6 illustrates these concepts. For the purpose of our discussion of address decoding, we are going to consider, unless stated otherwise, 8-bit microprocessors with a 16-bit address bus spanned by A_0–A_{15} (i.e. 64K bytes

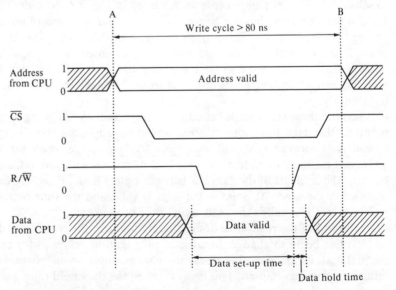

Fig. 8.5 The write-cycle timing diagram of a static RAM.

memory space). We do this because the 68000 has a 23-bit address which unnecessarily complicates our task of explaining how address decoding works.

Address decoders

If the memory of an 8-bit microprocessor system were constructed from memory components with 64K uniquely addressable locations, the problem of address decoding would not exist. Each of the microprocessor's address output lines, A_0–A_{15}, would simply be connected to the corresponding address input lines of the memory component. However, in the majority of microprocessor systems, not only do the actual memory components have fewer than 64K uniquely addressable locations, but the type and size of the memory components is often mixed (e.g. 8K × 8 RAMs and 16K × 8 ROMs). It is this wide range of memory components that frequently causes problems for the designer of microprocessor systems.

Consider the situation illustrated by Fig. 8.7, in which two 1K × 8 memory components are connected to a system address bus, consisting of 16 lines. The ten system address lines A_0–A_9 are connected to the corresponding address inputs of the two memory components, M_1 and M_2. Whenever a location (one of $2^{10} = 1024$) is addressed in M_1, the corresponding location is addressed in M_2. The data outputs of M_1 and M_2 are connected to the system data bus. Because the data outputs of both M_1 and M_2 are connected together, it is necessary that the data bus drivers in the memory components be tri-state devices. That is, only one of the memory components at a time may put data onto the system data bus. This is done by including a chip-select input in each of the memory devices. Whenever the chip-select input of M_1 or M_2 is inactive (i.e. in a logical 1 state) the appropriate data bus drivers are turned off, and no data is put on the data bus.

Let $\overline{CS_1}$ be made a function of the address lines A_{10}–A_{15}, so that

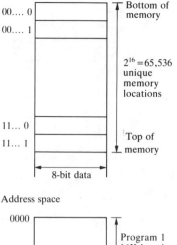

Address space

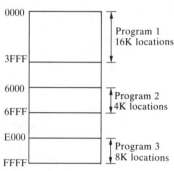

Fig. 8.6 Address space and the memory map.

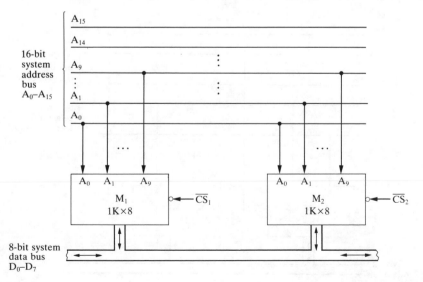

Fig. 8.7 Connecting two 1K×8 memories to a 16-bit address bus.

$\overline{CS_1} = f_1(A_{15}, A_{14}, A_{13}, A_{12}, A_{11}, A_{10})$. Similarly, let $\overline{CS_2}$ be a function of the same address lines, so that $\overline{CS_2} = f_2(A_{15}, A_{14}, A_{13}, A_{12}, A_{11}, A_{10})$. Suppose we choose f_1 and f_2 subject to the constraint that there are no values of A_{15}, $A_{14}, \ldots, A_{10}$ that cause $\overline{CS_1}$ and $\overline{CS_2}$ to be low simultaneously. Under these circumstances, the conflict between M_1 and M_2 is resolved, and the memory map of the system now contains two disjoint 1K blocks of memory. There are several different strategies for decoding A_{10}–A_{15} (i.e. choosing f_1 and f_2). These strategies may be divided into three groups: partial address decoding, full address decoding, and block address decoding.

Partial address decoding

Partial address decoding is the simplest, and consequently the most inexpensive form of address decoding to implement. Figure 8.8 demonstrates how two 1K blocks of memory can be connected to a system address bus in such a way that both blocks of memory are never accessed simultaneously. The conflict between M_1 and M_2 is resolved by connecting $\overline{CS_1}$ directly to A_{15} of the system address bus and by connecting $\overline{CS_2}$ to A_{15} via an inverter. In this way M_1 is selected whenever $A_{15} = 0$, and M_2 is selected whenever $A_{15} = 1$. Although we have succeeded in distinguishing between M_1 and M_2 for the cost of a single inverter, a heavy price has been paid. Because $A_{15} = 0$ selects M_1 and $A_{15} = 1$ selects M_2, it follows that either M_1 or M_2 will always be selected. Thus, although the system address bus can specify 64K unique addresses, only 2K different locations can be accessed. In this case, the address lines A_{10}–A_{14} take no part in the address-decoding process and consequently have no effect on the selection of a location within either M_1 or M_2. Figure 8.9 gives the memory map of the above system, from which it can be seen that M_1 is repeated 32 times in the lower half of the memory space, and M_2 is repeated 32 times in the upper half of the memory space.

Partial address decoding is widely used in dedicated microcontroller systems where low cost is of paramount importance. The penalty paid

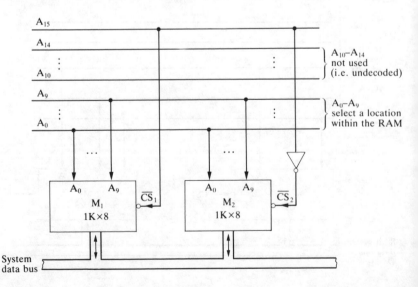

Fig. 8.8 Resolving contention by partial address decoding.

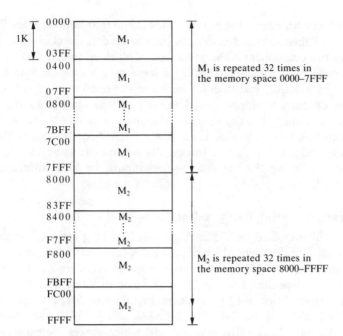

Fig. 8.9 The memory map corresponding to Fig. 8.8.

when a partial address-decoding system is employed is that it prevents full use of the microprocessor's address space and frequently makes it difficult to expand the memory system at a later date.

Full address decoding

A microprocessor system is said to have full address decoding when each addressable location within a memory component responds to a single address on the system's address bus. That is, all the microprocessor's address lines, A_0–A_{15}, are used to access each physical memory location, either by specifying a given device or by specifying an address within it. Full address decoding represents the ideal but is sometimes impractical as it may require an excessive quantity of hardware to implement it. For example, a memory-mapped peripheral in a 68000 system may have just a control and data register (selected by A_{01}). If the component is to be decoded fully, address lines A_{02}–A_{23} have to be decoded. If partial address decoding is used, the peripheral can be mapped onto a, say, 32K word block which leaves the simpler task of decoding A_{16}–A_{23}. Remember that if the two-word peripheral is mapped onto a block of 32K words, the two memory locations are repeated $32K/2 = 16K$ times.

Block address decoding

Block address decoding is a compromise between partial address decoding and full address decoding. It avoids the inefficient memory usage of partial address decoding, by dividing the memory space into a number of blocks. These blocks are sometimes referred to as pages.

In a typical application of block address decoding, a microprocessor's 64K memory space is divided into 16 blocks of 4K. We can do this with nothing more than a relatively inexpensive component to decode the four high-order address lines, A_{12}–A_{15}, into 16 lines. Each of these 16 lines is associated with one of the binary states of the four address lines. The 16 outputs of this address decoder can then be used as the chip-select inputs of memory components. The advantage of block address decoding is that no memory component can occupy a memory space larger than a single block. In practice, real microprocessor systems often employ a combination of partial address decoding, full address decoding, and block address decoding. For example, a system may have block address decoding with 16K blocks, in which case $16K \times 1$ RAMs or $16K \times 8$ ROMs will be fully address decoded. If several PIAs share the same 16K block of memory by using the PIAs' chip-select inputs, we have an example of partial address decoding within a block of memory.

Address decoding using m-line to n-line decoders

The problems of address decoding can often be greatly diminished by means of data decoders which decode an m-bit binary input into one of n outputs, where $n = 2^m$. The three most popular decoders are the 74LS154 4-line to 16-line decoder, the 74LS138 3-line to 8-line decoder, and the 74LS139 dual 2-line to 4-line decoders. Figures 8.10–8.12 give the pin-outs and truth tables for the 74LS154, 74LS138, and 74LS139 respectively. All three decoders have active-low outputs, which makes them particularly suitable for address-decoding applications, because the majority of memory components have active-low chip-select inputs.

The 74LS154, in addition to its four inputs A,B,C and D, has two active-low $\overline{\text{ENABLE}}$ inputs ($\overline{E}_1, \overline{E}_2$). Unless both of these $\overline{\text{ENABLE}}$ inputs are in a zero logic state, the binary code at the input of the 74LS154 ignored, and all outputs remain in the logical one state. This important facility may be employed in one of three ways. Firstly, the $\overline{\text{ENABLE}}$ input may be used to strobe the outputs, allowing them to be synchronized with a control signal. For example, the 68000 asserts its active-low $\overline{\text{AS}}$ (address strobe) output when it is accessing its memory space.

The 74LS138 3-line to 8-line decoder is one of the most popular address-decoding devices found in microprocessor systems. It has a smaller package than the 74LS154 (16 pins as opposed to 24). Because the 74LS138 has three enable inputs (two active-low and one active-high) it is particularly useful when decoders are to be connected in series, or when the enable inputs are to be connected to address lines in order to reduce the size of the block of memory being decoded.

Consider now an example of address decoding using the 74LS138 3-line to 8-line decoder. As stated above, the example will use an 8-bit microprocessor with a 16-bit address bus. The microprocessor system is to be designed with, initially, 8K bytes of static RAM in the range 0000–1FFF and with provision for the addition of further 4K blocks of RAM up to a maximum of 32K bytes. The read/write memory is provided by $4K \times 8$ devices, which have 12 address lines. The microprocessor is to have a 2K EPROM monitor in the range F800–FFFF. Provision must be made for at least eight memory-mapped peripherals in the 512 byte range E000–E1FF.

Table 8.1 gives the address table of the above system and demonstrates how three 74LS138s divide the memory space into blocks of suitable size for the RAM, ROM, and peripherals. Figure 8.13 gives a circuit diagram

$\overline{E}_1$	$\overline{E}_2$	Inputs D	C	B	A	0	1	2	3	4	5	6	Outputs 7	8	9	10	11	12	13	14	15
0	0	0	0	0	0	0	1	1	1	1	1	1	1	1	1	1	1	1	1	1	1
0	0	0	0	0	1	1	0	1	1	1	1	1	1	1	1	1	1	1	1	1	1
0	0	0	0	1	0	1	1	0	1	1	1	1	1	1	1	1	1	1	1	1	1
0	0	0	0	1	1	1	1	1	0	1	1	1	1	1	1	1	1	1	1	1	1
0	0	0	1	0	0	1	1	1	1	0	1	1	1	1	1	1	1	1	1	1	1
0	0	0	1	0	1	1	1	1	1	1	0	1	1	1	1	1	1	1	1	1	1
0	0	0	1	1	0	1	1	1	1	1	1	0	1	1	1	1	1	1	1	1	1
0	0	0	1	1	1	1	1	1	1	1	1	1	0	1	1	1	1	1	1	1	1
0	0	1	0	0	0	1	1	1	1	1	1	1	1	0	1	1	1	1	1	1	1
0	0	1	0	0	1	1	1	1	1	1	1	1	1	1	0	1	1	1	1	1	1
0	0	1	0	1	0	1	1	1	1	1	1	1	1	1	1	0	1	1	1	1	1
0	0	1	0	1	1	1	1	1	1	1	1	1	1	1	1	1	0	1	1	1	1
0	0	1	1	0	0	1	1	1	1	1	1	1	1	1	1	1	1	0	1	1	1
0	0	1	1	0	1	1	1	1	1	1	1	1	1	1	1	1	1	1	0	1	1
0	0	1	1	1	0	1	1	1	1	1	1	1	1	1	1	1	1	1	1	0	1
0	0	1	1	1	1	1	1	1	1	1	1	1	1	1	1	1	1	1	1	1	0
0	1	X	X	X	X	1	1	1	1	1	1	1	1	1	1	1	1	1	1	1	1
1	0	X	X	X	X	1	1	1	1	1	1	1	1	1	1	1	1	1	1	1	1
1	1	X	X	X	X	1	1	1	1	1	1	1	1	1	1	1	1	1	1	1	1

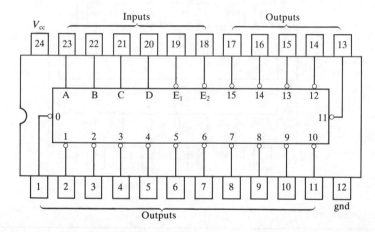

Fig. 8.10 Truth table and pin-out of the 74LS154.

of the address decoding circuitry and Fig. 8.14 illustrates the memory map of this system. It is easy to see the advantages of this form of address decoding (i.e. block decoding). Firstly, RAM, ROM or peripheral devices can be added without further alterations to the address-decoding circuitry, simply by employing the unused outputs of the three decoders. Secondly, the system is flexible. By modifying the connections between the decoder circuits and the memory components they select, the effective address of those memory components may be altered.

Address decoding with the PROM

Address decoding is the art of extracting the chip-select signal of a memory component from a number of address lines. The techniques of address decoding described earlier in this section employ either random logic or m-line to n-line decoders (which are themselves collections of random logic elements in a single package) to decode address lines. An alternative approach is to use a field-programmable read-only memory to generate the signals needed to select the memory components. The PROM

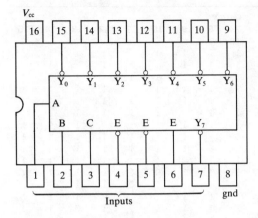

$\bar{E}_1$	$\bar{E}_2$	E_3	C	D	A	$\bar{Y}_0$	$\bar{Y}_1$	$\bar{Y}_2$	$\bar{Y}_3$	$\bar{Y}_4$	$\bar{Y}_5$	$\bar{Y}_6$	$\bar{Y}_7$
1	1	0	X	X	X	1	1	1	1	1	1	1	1
1	1	1	X	X	X	1	1	1	1	1	1	1	1
1	0	0	X	X	X	1	1	1	1	1	1	1	1
1	0	1	X	X	X	1	1	1	1	1	1	1	1
0	1	0	X	X	X	1	1	1	1	1	1	1	1
0	1	1	X	X	X	1	1	1	1	1	1	1	1
0	0	0	X	X	X	1	1	1	1	1	1	1	1
0	0	1	0	0	0	0	1	1	1	1	1	1	1
0	0	1	0	0	1	1	0	1	1	1	1	1	1
0	0	1	0	1	0	1	1	0	1	1	1	1	1
0	0	1	0	1	1	1	1	1	0	1	1	1	1
0	0	1	1	0	0	1	1	1	1	0	1	1	1
0	0	1	1	0	1	1	1	1	1	1	0	1	1
0	0	1	1	1	0	1	1	1	1	1	1	0	1
0	0	1	1	1	1	1	1	1	1	1	1	1	0

Figure 8.11 Truth table and pinout for the 74LS138

Figure 8.12 Truth table and pinout for the 74LS139

Inputs			Outputs			
$\bar{E}$	B	A	$\bar{Y}_0$	$\bar{Y}_1$	$\bar{Y}_2$	$\bar{Y}_3$
1	X	X	1	1	1	1
0	0	0	0	1	1	1
0	0	1	1	0	1	1
0	1	0	1	1	0	1
0	1	1	1	1	1	0

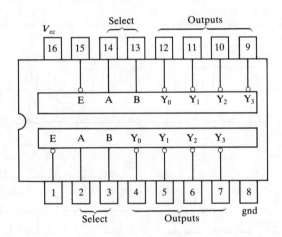

Table 8.1 Address table of a microprocessor system

Device	Address range	A_{15}	A_{14}	A_{13}	A_{12}	A_{11}	A_{10}	A_9	A_8	A_7	A_6	A_5	A_4	A_3	A_2	A_1	A_0
RAM 1	0000–0FFF	0	0	0	0	X	X	X	X	X	X	X	X	X	X	X	X
RAM 2	1000–1FFF	0	0	0	1	X	X	X	X	X	X	X	X	X	X	X	X
''																	
''																	
''																	
RAM 8	7000–7FFF	0	1	1	1	X	X	X	X	X	X	X	X	X	X	X	X
		decoded by IC_1															
P_1	E000–E03F	1	1	1	0	0	0	0	0	0	0						
P_2	E040–E07F	1	1	1	0	0	0	0	0	0	1						
.																	
.																	
.																	
P_8	E1C0–E1FF	1	1	1	0	0	0	0	1	1	1						
							decoded by IC_3										
ROM	F800–FFFF	1	1	1	1	1	X	X	X	X	X	X	X	X	X	X	X
		decoded by IC_2															

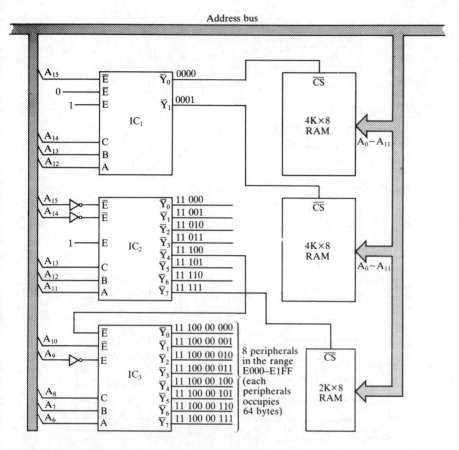

Fig. 8.13 Circuit of an address decoder for Table 8.1.

is, in fact, serving as a function generator with its address lines acting as inputs and its data lines as outputs.

The n address inputs of a PROM select one of 2^n unique locations within it. Each of these locations, when accessed, puts a word on to the PROM's m data lines. Whereas random logic generates chip-select signals directly, the PROM looks up their values in a table. The bipolar PROM is a popular form of address decoder, particularly in professional microprocessor systems. The access time of a PROM is in the region of 10–50 ns, which is comparable with the delay incurred by two low-power Schottky TTL m-line to n-line decoders connected in series. Furthermore, it is sometimes possible to perform all the address decoding required by a small microprocessor system with a single PROM. The PROM address decoder saves valuable space on the microprocessor board and makes the debugging or modification of the system easier.

Consider the example of a PROM address decoder illustrated by Fig. 8.15 and Table 8.2. A microprocessor system is to have 16K bytes of RAM at 0000–3FFF, 2K bytes of memory-mapped I/O at 8000–87FF, 2K bytes of RAM at A000–A7FF, 4K bytes of ROM at E000–EFFF, and 4K bytes of ROM at F000–FFFF. As the smallest block of memory to be

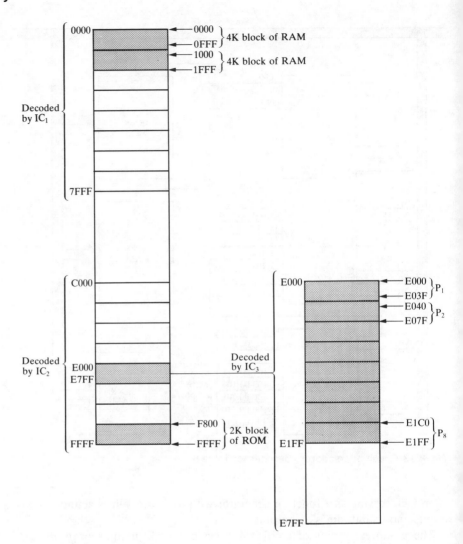

Fig. 8.14 Memory map for the system of Table 8.1 and Fig. 8.13.

selected is 2K bytes (i.e. 2^{11}), any address-decoding arrangement must decode the five address lines A_{11}–A_{15}. There are five blocks of memory to be decoded, so the PROM must have at least five data outputs. In Fig. 8.15 a 32×8 PROM decodes the five highest-order address lines. Although the PROM has eight data outputs, only five of them are needed in this application, leaving the remaining three unconnected. These three outputs may be used to expand the system at a later date. In this example the PROM is enabled by connecting its active-low chip-select input to $\overline{S}$, which is an active-low strobe derived from the microprocessor's control signals. Unfortunately, whenever the PROM's chip-select input, $\overline{CS}$, is high, the data output lines of the PROM are left floating. This situation occurs whether the PROM has tri-state or open-collector outputs. If the outputs of the PROM are allowed to float, there is a danger that a memory component may be enabled spuriously and data corrupted.

Table 8.2 The PROM as an address decoder

	System address lines					PROM data outputs							
	A_{15} A_{14} A_{13} A_{12} A_{11}												
Address range	PROM address inputs												
	A_4	A_3	A_2	A_1	A_0	D_7	D_6	D_5	D_4	D_3	D_2	D_1	D_0
0000–07FF	0	0	0	0	0	1	1	1	1	0			
0800–0FFF	0	0	0	0	1	1	1	1	1	0			
1000–17FF	0	0	0	1	0	1	1	1	1	0			
1800–1FFF	0	0	0	1	1	1	1	1	1	0			
2000–27FF	0	0	1	0	0	1	1	1	1	0			
2800–2FFF	0	0	1	0	1	1	1	1	1	0			
3000–37FF	0	0	1	1	0	1	1	1	1	0			
3800–3FFF	0	0	1	1	1	1	1	1	1	0			
4000–47FF	0	1	0	0	0	1	1	1	1	1			
4800–4FFF	0	1	0	0	1	1	1	1	1	1			
5000–57FF	0	1	0	1	0	1	1	1	1	1			
5800–5FFF	0	1	0	1	1	1	1	1	1	1			
6000–67FF	0	1	1	0	0	1	1	1	1	1			
6800–6FFF	0	1	1	0	1	1	1	1	1	1			
7000–77FF	0	1	1	1	0	1	1	1	1	1			
7800–7FFF	0	1	1	1	1	1	1	1	1	1			
8000–87FF	1	0	0	0	0	1	1	1	0	1			
8800–8FFF	1	0	0	0	1	1	1	1	1	1			
9000–97FF	1	0	0	1	0	1	1	1	1	1			
9800–9FFF	1	0	0	1	1	1	1	1	1	1			
A000–A7FF	1	0	1	0	0	1	1	0	1	1			
A800–AFFF	1	0	1	0	1	1	1	1	1	1			
B000–B7FF	1	0	1	1	0	1	1	1	1	1			
B800–BFFF	1	0	1	1	1	1	1	1	1	1			
C000–C7FF	1	1	0	0	0	1	1	1	1	1			
C800–CFFF	1	1	0	0	1	1	1	1	1	1			
D000–D7FF	1	1	0	1	0	1	1	1	1	1			
D800–DFFF	1	1	0	1	1	1	1	1	1	1			
E000–E7FF	1	1	1	0	0	1	0	1	1	1			
E800–EFFF	1	1	1	0	1	1	0	1	1	1			
F000–F7FF	1	1	1	1	0	0	1	1	1	1			
F800–FFFF	1	1	1	1	1	0	1	1	1	1			
						a	*b*	*c*	*d*	*e*			

unused in this application and hence left unprogrammed

a: 4K ROM$_1$ F000–FFFF
b: 4K ROM$_2$ E000–EFFF
c: 2K RAM$_1$ A000–A7FF
d: 2K I/O 8000–87FF
e: 16K RAM$_2$ 0000–3FFF

Floating chip-select outputs can be avoided by connecting pull-up resistors between the PROM's data outputs and the positive supply rail to force them into a logical one state whenever the PROM is de-selected.

In the circuit in Fig. 8.15 an 8-bit byte is put on the PROM's data output whenever $\overline{S}$ is low, otherwise the outputs are pulled up into the logical one state. Table 8.2 gives the relationship between A_{11}–A_{15} of the system address bus (connected to A_0–A_4 of the PROM), and the outputs

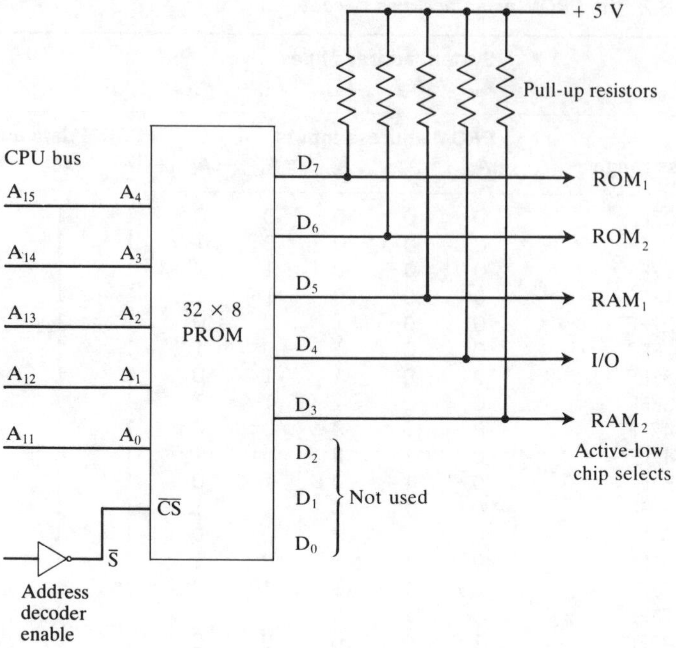

Fig. 8.15 An address decoder using a PROM.

of the PROM D_0–D_7. In order to understand the action of the PROM, consider the behaviour of D_7. There are 32 entries in the D_7 column, of which 30 are high and two are low. The two low entries occur at $A_{15}.A_{14}.A_{13}.A_{12}.A_{11}$ and $A_{15}.A_{14}.A_{13}.A_{12}.\overline{A_{11}}$, and select the 4K block of ROM at F000–FFFF. Note that A_{11} does not affect the selection of this ROM, and the state of A_{11} therefore represents a don't care condition.

Now consider the behaviour of the PROM's D_5 output. In Table 8.2 the column corresponding to D_5 has a single, logical zero entry at $A_{15}.\overline{A_{14}}.A_{13}.\overline{A_{12}}.\overline{A_{11}}$. In this case all five address lines take part in the selection of the 2K block of RAM at A000–A7FF. One important distinction between the PROM and the m-line to n-line decoder should now be clear. The m-line to n-line decoder decodes n equal-sized blocks of memory while the PROM can decode blocks of memory of varying size. The selection of the 16K block of RAM at 0000–3FFF is performed by D_3. In the column corresponding to D_3 there are eight logical zero entries. By inspecting Table 8.2 it can readily be seen that these zeros span all the 8 possible combinations of A_{11}, A_{12}, A_{13} for which $A_{14}=0$ and $A_{15}=0$. Therefore, the 16K block of RAM is selected whenever $A_{15}=0$ and $A_{14}=0$, irrespective of the values of A_{11}–A_{13}.

As we have just observed, the PROM can select blocks of memory of different size. In a system with a 16-bit address bus, a PROM with n address inputs (i.e. 2^n bytes) can fully decode a block of memory with a minimum size of $2^{16}/2^n = 2^{16-n}$ bytes. Larger blocks of memory can be decoded by increasing the number of active entries (in our case, zeros) in the data column of the PROM's address/data table. The size of the block of memory decoded by a data output is equal to the minimum block size multiplied by the number of active entries in the appropriate data column. For example, in Table 8.2 $n=5$ and therefore gives a minimum block size of $2^{16-5} = 2^{11} = 2K$ bytes. In the column corresponding to D_3, there are eight active entries, indicating a total block size of $8 \times 2K = 16K$ bytes. Today the systems designer can use programmable logic elements such as PALs and PLAs to implement address decoders.

The structure of memory systems

To conclude the section on memory organization, we look at how a bank of memory components may be connected to a microprocessor. In this case we will use the 68000. There are really two ways of organizing semiconductor memory: one is to use byte-wide memory components and the other is to use bit-wide memory components. For example, a 64K byte block of memory can be organized as eight 8K-byte × 8 devices or as eight 64K-byte × 1 devices. Both solutions require eight chips but the 64K-byte × 1 solution is invariably preferred. Why? Because the loading on the data bus is reduced to one chip per data line, while the 8K-byte × 8 bit solution requires eight connections per data line. Furthermore, byte-wide memory components are usually physically larger than bit-wide devices. However, the use of byte-wide components can result in lower power dissipation because fewer memory chips are selected at any one time. Figure 8.16 demonstrates the circuit of a byte-organized memory and Figure 8.17 a bit-organized memory.

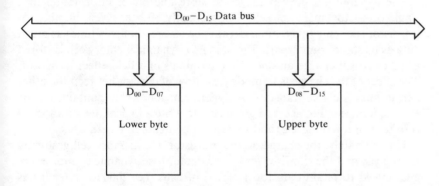

Fig. 8.16 An example of byte-organized memory.

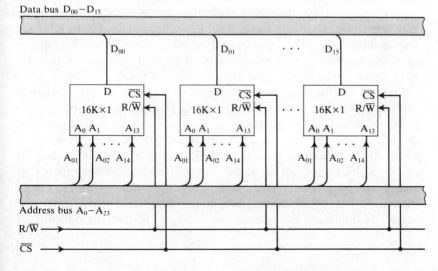

Fig. 8.17 An example of bit-organized memory.

8.1.2 Dynamic memory

Dynamic random access read/write memory (DRAM) or, more simply, dynamic memory, is the most compact and low-cost form of semiconductor memory available today. Currently, the industry standard dynamic RAM chip has a capacity of $1M \times 1$ bits, 4M bit chips are in full production and 16M bit chips represent the current state of the art. Not only is the dynamic RAM both cheaper and denser in terms of bits/chip than static memory, DRAM chips consume less power than some of their static memory counterparts. This statement is true for NMOS DRAM versus NMOS static RAM—but not for CMOS static RAM which has a very low-power consumption. What then is the difference between static RAM and dynamic RAM? The classical answer to this question is 'static RAM works and dynamic RAM doesn't'. Behind this remark lies the fact that dynamic memory systems, unlike static memories, need a considerable amount of circuitry to control them. Moreover, the operation of this control circuitry is quite critical.

The static RAM stores data in the form of the state of two cross-coupled transistors acting as an RS flip-flop. One of the transistors in the pair is *on* and the other is *off*. The typical static memory chip requires an additional four transistors per flip-flop making a total of six transistors per bit of stored information.

The dynamic memory manages to store one bit of information in a single-transistor memory cell. Consequently, for a given number of transistors per chip, a dynamic memory can store about six times as much data as its static counterpart. The data in a dynamic memory cell is stored as an electrical charge on one of the terminals of a field-effect transistor. The effect of the charge is to modify the flow of current between the other two terminals of the transitor. A dynamic memory chip contains all the electronics needed to access a given cell, to write a logical one or a logical zero to it in a write cycle, and to read its contents in a read cycle.

Unfortunately, the charge on the transistor in a memory cell gradually leaks away and the transitor forgets its data. Most dynamic memories are guaranteed to retain data for a period of 2 ms (i.e. 2000 μs) after it has been written. In order to retain data for longer than 2 ms, the dynamic memory requires that the data be rewritten into every cell periodically in an operation is called *refreshing*. Refreshing dynamic memories is largely responsible for the difficulty in using dynamic memory. In practice, simply accessing a memory cell refreshes it and, as we shall soon see, it is possible to refresh a group of 128, 256, 512 etc. cells at a time.

Figure 8.18 illustrates the arrangement of a typical $265K \times 1$ dynamic memory chip, which is available in a 16-pin DIL package. By putting the 256K RAM in a 16-pin package the semiconductor manufacturers have created another problem for the designer. A 256K memory space is spanned by 18 address lines ($2^{18} = 256K$), so that a 16-pin package is clearly unable to cater for the address inputs, data lines, power supply pins and control lines. The apparent lack of pins is overcome by multiplexing the address bus—the address is fed into the chips as two consecutive 9-bit values. Multiplexing the address bus increases further the difficulty of

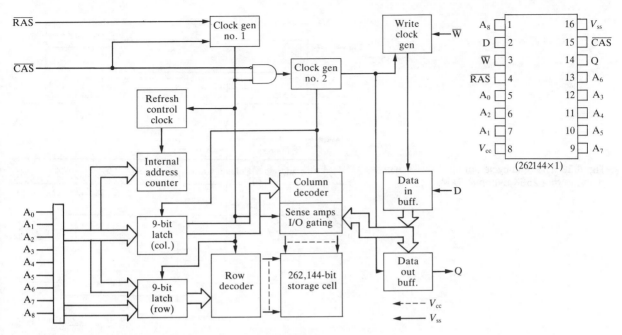

Fig. 8.18 The internal organization of a 256K dynamic RAM.

using dynamic RAM. As the 256×1 memory component contains only a single bit in each of its 256K addressable locations, sixteen of these chips are required to construct a 16-bit wide memory module.

The DRAM read cycle

Reading data from a DRAM chip is far more complex than accessing a static RAM chip. The simplified timing diagram of a dynamic RAM read cycle is given in Fig. 8.19. The cells are accessed by specifying the column and the row of a given cell.

The read cycle starts with the 9-bit row address of the current memory location being applied to the address inputs of the RAM. The $\overline{RAS}$ (row address strobe) of the chip is then brought to a logical zero state and the row address latched into flip-flops inside the chip. The next step is to apply the 9-bit column address to the chip and then bring the column address strobe ($\overline{CAS}$) low. The data in the cell accessed by the 18-bit address then appears on the data-output line after a delay of typically 80–150 ns from the point at which $\overline{RAS}$ went low.

A write cycle, described in Fig. 8.20, is essentially similar to a read cycle except that the write input must go low before $\overline{CAS}$ goes low and the data to be stored in the addressed cell must be applied to the data-in line.

There are several ways of performing the refresh operation, but one of the simplest is known as an RAS-only refresh cycle and is illustrated in Fig. 8.21a. The row-refresh address is applied to the address input of the chip, and the $\overline{RAS}$ input brought low for a specified period. After each refresh operation, the row-refresh address is incremented by one, so that

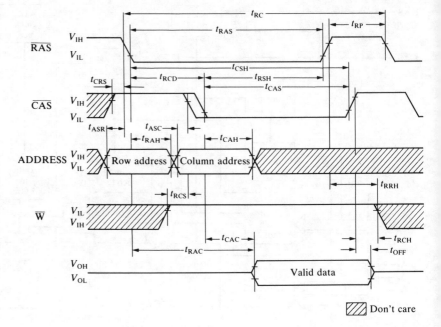

Fig. 8.19 The read-cycle timing diagram of a 256K dynamic RAM.

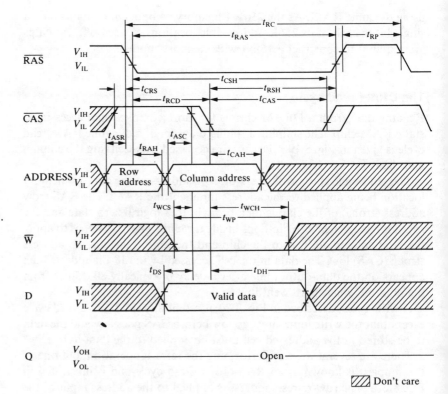

Fig. 8.20 The write-cycle timing diagram of a 256K dynamic RAM.

all 256 rows are eventually refreshed. The refresh address must be supplied by logic external to the chip. Many of today's DRAM chips now include *internal* refresh address generators and all that need be done to refresh them is to assert $\overline{CAS}$ while $\overline{RAS}$ is high. Of course, $\overline{CAS}$ must be pulsed low once for each row address to be refreshed. This refresh mode is called 'CAS before RAS' (Fig. 8.21b).

Unlike the static RAM, which has an access time equal to its cycle time, the dynamic RAM has a cycle time longer than its access time. This is because certain internal operations must take place within the DRAM before another access can begin. A typical chip has an access time of 100 ns and a cycle time of 150 ns.

An indication of the logic needed to control a dynamic memory is given in Fig. 8.22. The dynamic memory control must carry out the address multiplexing and generate the necessary $\overline{RAS}$ and $\overline{CAS}$ signals. It must also perform 256 row refresh cycles ever 2 ms (some DRAMs need refreshing only every 4 or 8 ms). To do this it has to send a refresh request to the CPU and await a refresh grant from the CPU. When the refresh is granted, the controller sends a row refresh address to the memory and forces $\overline{RAS}$ low. The refresh address counter is automatically

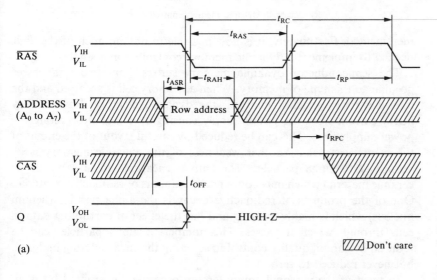

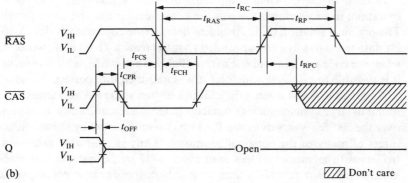

Fig. 8.21 The DRAM refresh cycle. (a) The RAS-only refresh; (b) the CAS-before-RAS refresh.

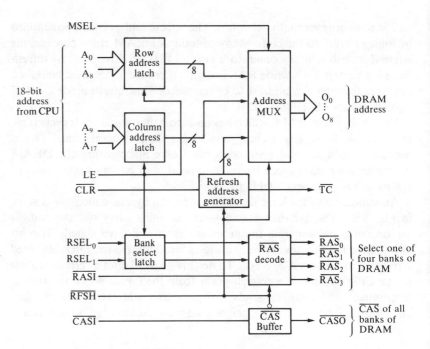

Fig. 8.22 Controlling the dynamic memory. LE=latch enable (i.e. capture CPU address); RSEL$_0$, RSEL$_1$=select bank of DRAM (one of four); RASI, CASI=$\overline{\text{RAS}}$ and $\overline{\text{CAS}}$ inputs from timing generator.

Am 2964B Dynamic memory controller

incremented. Fortunately, it is now possible to obtain much of the logic needed to implement a dynamic memory controller on a single chip.

The semiconductor dynamic memory suffers from two weaknesses peculiar to this type of memory. When a memory cell is accessed and the inter-electrode capacitor charged, the dynamic memory draws a very heavy current from the power supply causing a voltage drop along the power-supply lines. This can be reduced by careful layout of the circuit of the memory system. Another weakness of the dynamic memory is its sensitivity to alpha particles. The chip is encapsulated in a plastic or ceramic material which may contain tiny amounts of radioactive material. One of the products of radioactive decay is the alpha particle (helium nucleus) which is highly ionizing and has the effect of corrupting data in cells through which it passes. The number of alpha particles can be reduced by careful quality control in selecting the encapsulating material, but never reduced to zero.

In most of the personal computers an occasional corrupted bit is an irritation; in professional systems the consequences may be more severe. The practical solution to this problem lies in error-correcting codes. A 16-bit data word has five bits appended to it to create a 21-bit code word. If, when the code word is read back from the dynamic RAM, a bit is in error, it is possible to calculate which bit it was and therefore correct the error.

As dynamic RAM is more difficult to use than static RAM it tends to be found in large systems such as minicomputers and mainframes. However, over the last few years dynamic RAM has been adopted by the manufacturers of many of the personal computers. Only single-board microcontrollers with memories of less than about 64K bytes, systems that place more emphasis on reliability than cost, or high-speed computers, use static memory devices today. A few larger microprocessor systems do employ the more expensive static memory because of its greater reliability than the dynamic RAM.

8.1.3 Other types of semiconductor memory

ROM. Semiconductor technology is eminently well suited to the production of high-density, low-cost, read only memories. There are several types of ROM; mask-programmed, PROM, EPROM, and EEPROM being the most frequently encountered types. In general, semiconductor ROM, unless stated otherwise, is of the mask-programmed type, which is programmed during the manufacture of the chip. Mask-programmed ROM is available in sizes from 8K to 1M bits organized as $1K \times 8$ and $256K \times 8$, respectively, in 24- or 28-pin DIL packages. The application of ROM is even easier than semiconductor static RAM. As the ROM is never written to, a ROM chip requires nothing more than the address of the location to be accessed and a chip-select (or chip-enable) signal to operate the output circuits of the chip's data bus. Figure 8.23 shows how ROM (or EPROM) is connected to a processor's address and data buses.

As much as any other component the ROM has been responsible for the growth in personal and other similar low-cost computers. A typical operating system and BASIC interpreter requires approximately 8K to 512K bytes of memory, and is therefore able to fit into (typically) two or four ROMs. Without such large ROMs, system software would have to be stored on floppy disks (usually $100 or more for a disk drive and its associated power supply and controller). Although ROMs cannot be reprogrammed or modified, it is not excessively expensive to remove the ROMs containing the system software of a computer, and to replace them with an updated version.

Another application of the ROM is in dedicated microprocessor-based controllers. When a microcomputer is assigned to a particular fixed task, say an ignition control system in an automobile, the software is fixed for the lifetime of the device. A ROM provides the most cost-effective way of storing this form of software.

EPROM. The EPROM is an erasable programmable read-only memory. It shares some of the basic features of the mask-programmed ROM and many EPROMs can even be plugged into a socket designed for a mask-programmed ROM. The EPROM can be programmed by the user by means of a special programming machine costing from a hundred dollars upwards. Data is stored in an EPROM in the form of electrostatic charges on highly insulated conductors. The charges can remain for periods in excess of ten years without leaking away.

The EPROM costs several times as much as a mask-programmed ROM of the same density, but has the advantage that small-scale productions of microprocessor systems with their operating systems in EPROM are feasible. Although mask-programmed ROMs are relatively cheap, the manufacturer normally charges several thousand dollars for setting up the mask. The EPROM can be used several times because the data stored in it is erased by illuminating the silicon chip with untraviolet light. The silicon

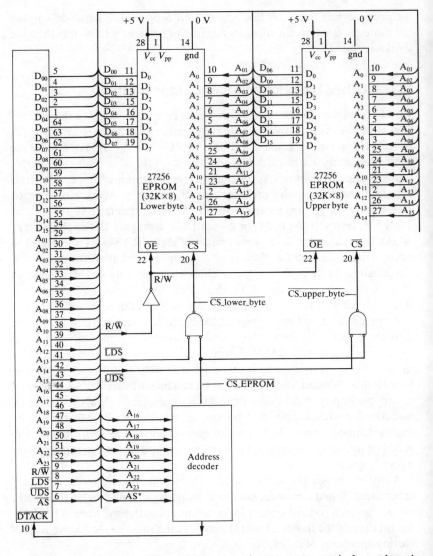

Fig. 8.23 The organization and application of a semiconductor EPROM.

chip is located in a DIL package under a quartz window that is transparent to ultraviolet light. Ultraviolet light causes the stored charge to drain away through the insulator.

As EPROMs can be programmed, erased and reprogrammed, they are suitable for both small-scale projects and for development work in laboratories. Once a program has been written and debugged in EPROM, it can later be committed to mask-programmed ROM if necessary. A mistake in EPROM costs less than the same mistake in mask-programmed ROM.

EEPROM. A recent development of the EPROM is the electrically erasable programmable ROM that can be programmed and *erased* electrically. Consequently it can be programmed *in situ* and does not have to be removed and placed under an ultraviolet light. The reader might be forgiven for asking what the difference between a read/write RAM and an EEPROM is. The EEPROM is non-volatile, unlike the typical semiconductor RAM. Unfortunately, it is much more expensive than semiconductor RAM, often requires non-standard sources of power, and has a relatively long access time. The EEPROM is found in special applications where data must be retained when the power is off. A typical application is in a radio receiver that can store a number of different frequencies and recall them when the power is re-applied.

PROM. The PROM (programmable read-only memory) can be programmed by the user just like the EPROM. However, the PROM is programmed by fusing tiny metallic links in the chip by passing such a large current through them that they melt. A continuous link represents a logical one and a broken (fused) link a logical zero. Clearly, a PROM can be programmed once and once only. Because of the way it is made, the PROM has a very low access time (10–50 ns) and is largely used as a logic element rather than as a means of storing a program.

Pseudo-ROM. Until recently the majority of LSI chips including the 68000 were fabricated by an NMOS process and require a current in the range of several tens to several hundred milliamperes for normal operation. Another process for the manufacture of LSI chips is called CMOS and produces chips with a very much lower power consumption. Although CMOS technology has been around for some time, the cost of CMOS was prohibitively high for all but special-purpose devices until the 1980s. When CMOS memories are not being accessed, their current consumption is so tiny that a small battery producing approximately 2.8 V is sufficient to supply enough current to retain the stored data while the mains power is disconnected. Such memory is strictly read/write memory, but, because it is effectively non-volatile, has some of the characteristics of ROM.

8.2 Ferrite core memory

Ferrite core memories belong to the adolescence of the computer industry and are no longer widely used (except in very old computers or in highly specialized applications). The reader may omit this section—I have included it for three reasons: the first is that ferrite core memory systems were, until recently, very important. The second reason is that the *principles* of ferrite core memory operation are the same principles that govern the operation of disk and tape storage systems. The third reason is that ferrite cores provide an excellent example of the two-state nature of the digital computer.

In the very early days of computing immediately after the Second World War, all manner of weird and wonderful devices were used to store digital data. For example, in 1849 Williams employed a cathode ray tube to store data in the form of an electrostatic charge on the face of the tube at a density of up to ten bits per square centimetre. In 1953 the ferrite core was first introduced in the MIT Whirlwind computer. The ferrite core is a small toroid of magnetic material that stores data in the form of a clockwise or anticlockwise internal magnetic field.

Until quite recently the size, cost, and speed of ferrite cores made them the logical choice as the basis of the computer's main immediate access store. As semiconductor memory has plummeted in price while offering higher densities (bits per chip), greater speeds (lower access times), and a much reduced power consumption, the ferrite core has become obsolete.

Since ferrite cores are non-volatile and consume no power when they are not being accessed (unlike semiconductor memory), there are still a few areas in which their use continues. With the advent of CMOS semiconductor memory and its tiny current consumption, even these applications of ferrite core will soon disappear. Having said this, I should point out that ferrite core memories are still popular in certain industrial applications because they are regarded as being more robust than other types of memory and are therefore better suited to harsh environments (e.g. regions with high levels of ionizing radiation). Plated-wire memory, an offshoot of core memory, largely replaced ferrite core memory in the late 1970s.

A ferrite core or toroid is a small ring-shaped piece of magnetic material with a diameter normally in the range 0.75–0.125 mm (0.03–0.005 inches). When magnetized, the field inside the core lies in the plane of the core and runs clockwise or anticlockwise as shown in Fig. 8.24.

Magnetic field clockwise (logical state 0)   Magnetic field anti-clockwise (logical state 1)

Fig. 8.24 The ferrite core.

Writing data into a ferrite core

In order to use ferrite cores in a practical memory two things are necessary. It must be possible to magnetize a core in a required state to store data, and it must be possible to determine the direction of a core's magnetization to read (retrieve) the data.

Writing data into a core is accomplished by generating a magnetic field within the core. When a current, I, flows through a wire, it generates a vector magnetic field, H, in the surrounding space. Figure 8.25 shows a wire carrying a current I passing through a ferrite core.

The current I creates a magnetic field H around the wire, where H is proportional to I. Inside the core a magnetic field, B, is produced by the combined effects of the external field, H, and the internal magnetization of the core material. A graph of the relationship between the internal magnetic field B and the external magnetic field H for a square-loop ferrite material is given in Fig. 8.26. The curve is called a *hysteresis loop*.

Before considering the implications of a hysteresis curve, it is helpful to examine the nature of ferromagnetic materials. It has already been stated that the origin of magnetism lies in the motion of electrons in their orbits. In most matter the magnetic effects of electron spin are entirely overcome by the stronger forces generated by the thermal vibration of the atoms,

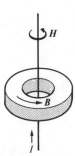

Fig. 8.25 The relationship between I, H, and B.

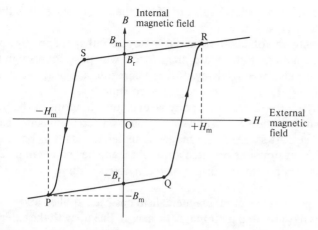

Fig. 8.26 The hysteresis curve.

which has the effect of stopping any magnetic interaction between adjacent atoms. In ferromagnetic materials such as iron and some of its compounds, there is a strong interaction between electron spins, resulting in the alignment of electrons over a region of the material called a domain. These domains range from one micrometre to several centimetres in size. Because the electron spins are aligned within a domain, the domain exhibits a very strong spontaneous magnetization and behaves like a tiny magnet.

Within a large piece of ferromagnetic material, the individual domains have their magnetic axes arranged at random. Because of the random orientations of the domains, there is no overall magnetic field in the bulk material. We will now describe the hysteresis curve and then relate it to the above model of ferromagnetism.

Suppose that the external field is zero. That is, $H = 0$ because $I = 0$. There are two possible values of B, $+B_r$ representing a logical state one, and $-B_r$ representing a state zero. The suffix r in B_r stands for remnant, and refers to the magnetism remaining in the core when the external field is zero. Like the flip-flop, the ferrite core has two stable states and can remain in either of the states indefinitely. Unlike the flip-flop, the ferrite core is a non-volatile store and requires no power source to retain data.

Assume that initially the core is magnetized in a logical zero state. If a negative external field is applied (i.e. negative I, therefore negative H), the value of B goes slightly more negative than $-B_r$ and we move towards point P in Fig. 8.26. If H is now reduced to zero the remnant magnetization returns to $-B_r$. In other words, there is no net change in the state of the core.

Now consider applying a small positive value of H. We move along the curve towards Q. If the external magnetization is reduced we move back to $-B_r$. However, if H is increased beyond $+H_m$, the magnetization of the core flips over at Q, and we end up at R. Now, when we reduce H to zero, we return to $+B_r$ and not $-B_r$. That is, if the core is initially in a negative state, increasing the external magnetization beyond H_m causes the core to assume a positive state. A magnetic field of less than H_m is insufficient to change the core's state.

Similarly, if the core is in a one state ($+B_r$), a positive value of H has little effect, but a negative value of H less than $-H_m$ will switch the core to a zero state $(-B_r)$.

The switching of a core from one state to another is done by applying a pulse with a magnitude greater than I_m to a wire passing through the core. A current pulse of $+I_m$ always forces a core into a logical one state, and a pulse of $-I_m$ forces it into a logical zero state.

The hysteresis curve can readily be explained in terms of the behaviour of domains. Figure 8.27 shows a region of a ferromagnetic material at three stages. At stage (a) the magnetic material is said to be in its virgin state with the domains oriented at random, and has no net magnetization. This corresponds to the origin of the hysteresis curve, where $H=0$ and $B=0$.

At stage (b) an external magnetic field has been applied and some of the domains have rotated their magnetic axes to line up with the external field. As the external field is increased, more and more domains flip over, and there comes a point where the domains already aligned with the external field reinforce it, causing yet more domains to flip over. This process soon develops into an avalanche as the internal field rapidly builds up, and all domains are aligned with the external field. At this point (c) the bulk material is fully magnetized and is said to be saturated.

The hysteresis curve of Fig. 8.26 is also called a B–H curve, and differs from one magnetic material to another. In general, the best B–H curve for the purpose of storing data is square, so that the transition from one state to another (i.e. from $-B_r$ to $+B_r$) takes place for an infinitesimally small change in H. Such a magnetic material is said to have a square-loop B–H characteristic. Magnetic materials displaying strong hysteresis effects are called **hard**, while those displaying little or no hysteresis are called **soft**.

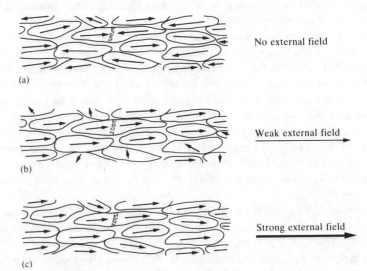

Fig. 8.27 The magnetization of a ferromagnetic material.

Reading a core

Having magnetized a core, it is necessary to determine its state in order to find out whether it was storing a logical one or zero. Unfortunately, it is effectively impossible to directly determine which state a core is in. However, we can determine the state indirectly.

Consider a second wire passing through the core called a *sense wire*, so-called because it senses the core's state. When a current pulse of $-I_m$ is passed through the core, one of two things may happen. If the core was originally in a zero state $(-B_r)$, it will remain in that state. If, however, the core was in a one state $(+B_r)$, it will be switched to a zero state by the pulse. Figure 8.28 shows the effect of these two operations on the voltage induced into the sense line.

In Case 1 the core does not change state and the voltage on the sense line consists of two small pulses (the differential of the switching pulse). In Case 2 there is a much larger pulse on the sense line caused by the change in magnetic flux as the core changes state. The two hysteresis diagrams in Fig. 8.28 illustrate the paths taken by the cores in these two cases.

It should be apparent that the effect of reading a core is to destroy its data. For this reason ferrite cores are said to be destructive read-out (DRO) devices. After a read cycle has taken place all cores which have been interrogated are left in a zero state so that a read cycle must be followed by a write cycle to restore the data. For this reason, the read access time of a ferrite core is less than its cycle time, because a new access cannot begin until after the data has been re-written following a read operation.

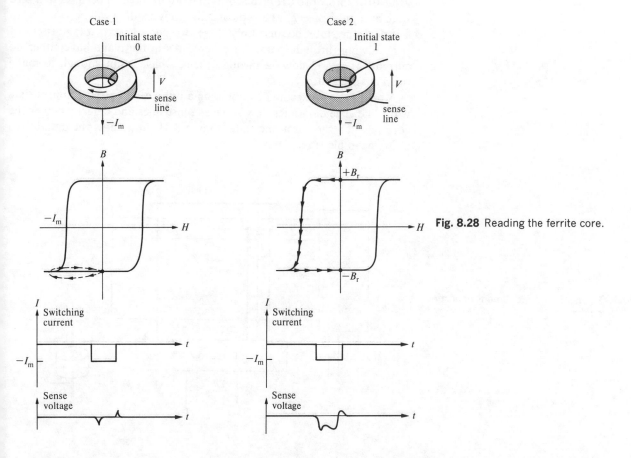

Fig. 8.28 Reading the ferrite core.

8.2.1 The core memory plane

So far we have looked at the characteristics of a single core representing one memory cell. In a practical arrangement of a ferrite core memory n words by m bits must be catered for. A possible system is illustrated in Fig. 8.29.

The key to the operation of memory planes is the coincident-current selection technique. The current needed to switch a core is at least I_m and may be provided by a single pulse on one wire or as a number of pulses on separate wires. That is, two wires each carrying $I_m/2$ will do as well as one wire carrying I_m. Consider now the writing of data into the ith word of the array. The address decoder uses the p-bit word address to select one of the n word lines ($n=2^p$). If a pulse of $-I_m$ is applied to the ith word line (horizontally), all m cores threading that line are forced into a zero state.

To write a logical one into the ith word, a current pulse of $+I_m/2$ is applied to the appropriate word line. This current is, of course, not enough to alter the magnetization of the cores alone. If a pulse of $+I_m/2$ is applied to one of the m data lines, the total current flowing through the core threaded by that word and data line is now $+I_m$, sufficient to switch it into a logical one state. It should now be clear why this is called a coincident-current selection technique.

Figure 8.30 illustrates how a 4-word by 4-bit memory writes the data value 0101 into word 01. If the cores in word 01 have all been set to a zero state by a pulse of $-I_m$, the two cores in heavy shading will be switched to a logical one state, because only these two cores have a total current of $+I_m$ flowing through them. All other cores in the plane have either no current, or $+I_m/2$ flowing through them, which is not enough to make them change state.

A read cycle is executed by applying a pulse of $-I_m$ to the appropriate word line. The data lines now serve as sense lines and detect whether the core was in a zero or a one state. Figure 8.31 shows how the data in the above example is read.

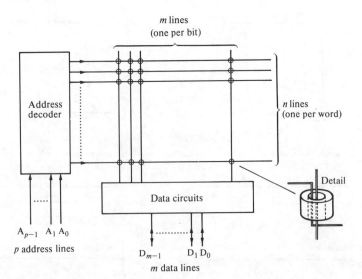

Fig. 8.29 The two-dimensional core store.

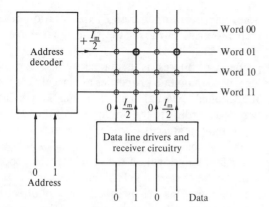

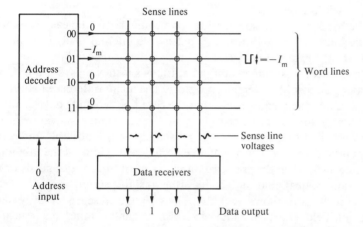

Fig. 8.30 An example of the two-dimensional core store in a write cycle. Data 0101 is written into word 01 by applying a current pulse of $+I_m/2$ to the word line corresponding to address 01, and current pulses of 0, $I_m/2$, 0, and $I_m/2$, respectively, to the four data lines.

Fig. 8.31 Reading the two-dimensional core memory. A current pulse of $-I_m$ is applied to word line 01 forcing all four cores threaded by this line into a logical zero state. The cores are read by sensing the voltage on the four data lines.

Once more it should be noted that the read cycle has destroyed the data and a write cycle is needed to restore it so that the access time of a ferrite core is shorter than the cycle time. The cycle time is the minimum time which must elapse between the two consecutive read accesses of the core store.

8.2.2 Thin-film memory

Thin-film memory is a logical extension of ferrite core memory in which the ferrite core is replaced by either a thin film of magnetic material, or a coating of magnetic material along a conductor. The latter arrangement is called a plated-wire memory.

Two disadvantages of ferrite core memory have led to the search for a better alternative. These are the relatively slow switching speed of the core (typically 3 µs to less than 500 ns), and the manufacturing difficulties of threading them.

Very thin films of nickel–iron are deposited on an inert substrate. These films, having a thickness of approximately 1 µm, exhibit two important magnetic properties. They do not have the same domain structure as ferrite materials, and the switching of the direction of magnetization takes place at the molecular level rather than by the rotation of the individual domains. For all practical purposes the thin film behaves like a single domain.

The other property of interest is its magnetic anisotropy. Unlike many ferrite materials whose magnetic properties are largely independent of the direction of the applied external field, the thin film exhibits different magnetic properties according to the orientation of the field. Anisotropy is a characteristic of many materials—wood, for example, is easier to chop along the grain than across it.

When the film is first laid down on the substrate, the deposition is done in the presence of a steady external field. This has the effect of creating two magnetic axes in the film. One axis is called the easy direction and lies in the direction of the external field present during the film's manufacture. The thin-film displays a square-loop $B–H$ characteristic in the easy axis, very much like the ferrite core.

The hard axis of magnetization, perpendicular to the easy axis, has a nearly linear $B–H$ relationship. That is, the internal field, B, is proportional to the external field H, and little hysteresis is exhibited.

Readers can best understand what follows if they regard a thin film as behaving almost like a ferrite core store. The major difference between the thin film and the ferrite core is that the core is a two-state device, and the thin film a four-state device. Two of the thin film's states are stable, corresponding to a logical one or zero, and two are unstable and cannot be maintained in the absence of an external field. Think of the thin film as a coin which, when dropped, can land in one of three ways: heads or tails (the stable states), and on its edges (the unstable state).

Figure 8.32(a) shows two thin films in the absence of an external magnetic field. One is in a logical zero state, and the other in a logical one state. In Fig. 8.32(b) an external field has been applied parallel to the hard axis, causing the field in the thin film to be rotated as shown. The internal field is the vector sum of the fields in the hard and easy axes. If the external field is reduced to zero, the magnetization of the film returns (or relaxes) to its initial state as in Fig. 8.32(a).

If the external field in the hard direction is increased to the level in Fig. 8.32(c), the magnetization of the film aligns itself parallel to the hard direction. Note that both samples are now in neither a logical one nor a logical zero state. Once the film is in this state a small magnetic field parallel to the easy axis will determine the state of the film when the field in the hard direction is removed. This is analogous to a coin balanced on its edge; it needs only a very small force to topple it in one direction or the other.

Figure 8.33 shows how a two-dimensional, word-organized thin-film store is constructed. Digit lines run parallel to the hard axis of magnetization of the thin films. Perpendicular to the digit lines run the word lines, arranged as hairpin loops running over digit lines and then back under them.

To read data from a film, a word current is passed down a word line to create a magnetic field along the hard axis of the films. This causes all the thin films traversed by the selected word line to rotate their internal fields

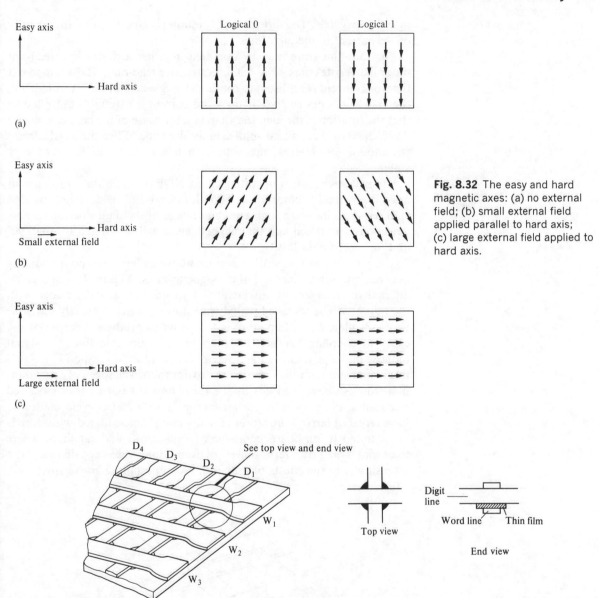

Fig. 8.32 The easy and hard magnetic axes: (a) no external field; (b) small external field applied parallel to hard axis; (c) large external field applied to hard axis.

Fig. 8.33 The two-dimensional thin-film store.

through 90° from their stable axis. The rotating magnetic field causes a voltage to be induced in each of the digit lines passing over the film. The direction of rotation determines the polarity of the induced voltage, and hence indicates whether the film was in a zero state or a one state.

Data is written into the bits of a word by applying a word pulse to force the films representing the bits of the chosen word to be magnetized along the hard axis. Then a current is applied to the digit lines to produce magnetic fields either up or down the easy axis. When the word current is removed, the magnetization of the films rotate clockwise or anticlockwise into the easy axis. The direction of rotation is determined by the polarity of the current in the digit lines

The thin-film store may be operated in either a destructive read-out mode like ferrite cores, or in a non-destructive read-out (NDRO) mode. If the word current is sufficient to rotate the magnetization fully through 90°, the read-out is destructive. If the word current is carefully controlled so that the rotation is through less than 90°, the sense of the core can still be determined by the induced voltage in the digit line. When the word current is removed, the internal magnetization relaxes to its undisturbed easy state.

Unfortunately, when operating in an NDRO mode, the word current must be carefully controlled. Too little and the field is not rotated sufficiently to induce a high enough voltage in the digit line for reliable detection. Too much and the magnetization will be rotated through 90° and the stored data lost.

The planar thin-film store described above suffers from poor coupling between the sense line and the magnetic films. Figure 8.34 shows an alternative arrangement in which the digit lines are actually coated with the thin film. The so-called plated-wire store operates in exactly the same way as a planar thin-film store but is easier to produce. Because of the excellent coupling between the digit line and the thin film, the signal induced in the digit line is 100 times greater than the corresponding signal in a planar store, for the same word-drive current. The speed of a real thin-film store is determined not by the thin film itself but by the associated electronics. Plated-wire stores are available with 250 ns cycle times and have replaced ferrite core stores in many mainframes. Plated-wire store is often found in on-board computers in spacecraft and satellites, where their non-volatility, zero power consumption when not in use, and insensitivity to the effects of radiation are important characteristics.

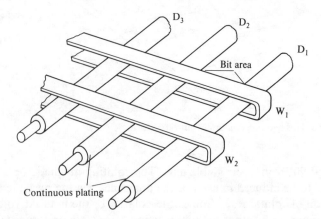

Fig. 8.34 The plated-wire store.

8.3 Memory hierarchy

In any real computer system there are many ways of storing information. For example, there are the internal registers within the CPU itself—the accumulator/data registers, stack pointer, index/address registers and program counter. Then there is the main store ranging in size from 32K bytes to 32M or more bytes with an access time of 80 ns to about 500 ns. Even this is sometimes partitioned into a high-speed *cache* memory and a slower main store. The cache memory will be discussed in Chapter 10. Next we have the much slower disk drives followed by tape transports. If all these devices store data, why do we need so many of them?

The answer to this question is the same as to that to the question 'Why do I travel by rail instead of air?' As in every aspect of life, economics play a dominant role. The characteristics a computer designer would like to see in a memory device are often mutually exclusive. The ideal memory has the following characteristics:

1. *High speed.* Its access time should be low, preferably 1 ns, or less.

2. *Small size.* It should be physically small. Ten thousand megabytes per cubic centimetre is ideal.

3. *Low power consumption.* The entire memory system should run off a watch battery for ten years.

4. *Robustness.* The memory should not be prone to errors—a logical one spontaneously turning into a logical zero or vice versa. It should also be able work at temperatures of $-60°C$ or at $200°C$. (The military are very keen on this.)

5. *Low cost.* The memory should cost nothing and should, ideally, be given away free with software.

Now let us look at the characteristics of real memory devices.

Internal CPU memory. Registers in CPUs have very low access times as they are built with the same technology as the CPU itself. They are very expensive and consume much power, limiting the number of internal registers and scratchpad memory within the CPU itself. This is especially true when the CPU is fabricated on a silicon chip, although the number of registers that can be included on a chip has inceased dramatically in recent years.

Main store. Main store or immediate access store memory holds the programs and data during their execution and is relatively fast (20–150 ns and about 300 ns for some EPROMS). It is normally implemented as semiconductor static or dynamic memory. In the past the main store was implemented as ferrite core storage (plated wire memories are a variation on ferrite core store). Magnetic memory systems are costly, consume relatively high power, and are physically bulky.

Magnetic disk. The magnetic disk stores large quantities of data in a small space and has a very low cost per bit. Unfortunately it is a serial access device and its access time, although fast in human terms, is orders of magnitude slower than immediate access store. A typical disk drive can store 300 megabytes and has an access time of 18 ms.

Magnetic tape. Magnetic tape is an exceedingly cheap serial access device and can store over 100 megabytes on a low-cost tape. Unfortunately, its average access time is abysmally long and therefore it is largely used for archival purposes.

By combining all these types of memory in a single computer system, the computer engineer can get the best of all worlds and build a relatively low-cost memory system with a speed performance only a few per cent lower than that of a large main memory. The key to computer memory design is having the right data in the right place at the right time.

A very large computer system may have thousands of programs and even millions of data files, but only a few programs and files are required by the CPU at any one time. By designing an operating system that tries to move data from disks and tapes into the main store so that the CPU always (or nearly always) finds the data it wants in the main store, the system has the speed of a giant high-speed store at a tiny fraction of the cost. Such an arrangement is called a *virtual memory* because the memory appears to the user as, say, a 1000 metabyte main store, when in reality there may be a real main memory of only ten megabytes and 1000 megabytes of disk storage. Chapter 10 provides further details on virtual memory systems.

8.4 Secondary storage

We have already seen that a computer's memory is partitioned into a high-speed, high-cost, low-capacity main store and a low-speed, low cost, high-capacity secondary store. The term *secondary store* is synonymous with tape transports and disk drives, although magnetic bubble memories have sometimes challenged the disk drive as a secondary storage device. The late 1980s have seen the rise of optical memory, which is replacing disk and tape drives in certain applications.

8.4.1 Magnetic surface recording

The operation of both disk drives and tape units is virtually the same: one records data on a flat platter coated with a magnetic material, while the other records data on a thin band of flexible plastic coated with magnetic material. Figure 8.35 illustrates the generic recording process (I have called it *generic* because the model serves both disk and tape systems).

The *write head* used to write data consists of a ring of high-permeability soft magnetic material with a coil wound round it. High-permeability means that the material offers a low resistance to a magnetic field. Notice the similarity between a write head and a ferrite core with a write line passing through it. The material of the write head is magnetically soft and

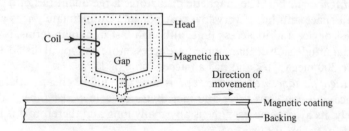

Fig. 8.35 The read/write head.

does not have the same square-loop hysteresis property of the ferrite core. Consequently it does not exhibit residual or remnant magnetization.

A very important feature of the write head is a tiny air gap in the ring. When a current flows in the coil a magnetic flux is created within the ring. This flux flows round the core, but when it encounters the air gap, it spreads out as illustrated in Fig. 8.36.

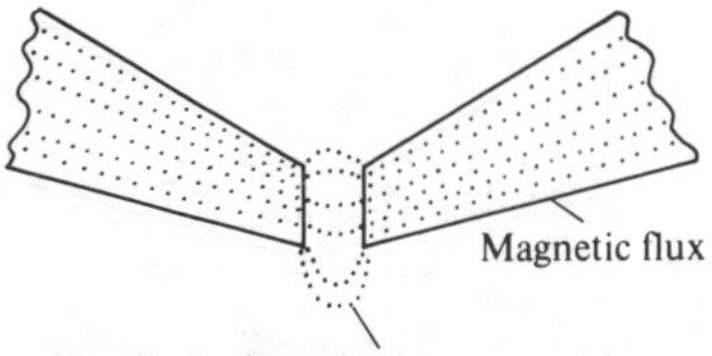

As the head is either close to, or in contact with, the recording medium, the magnetic field round the air gap passes through the magnetic material coating the backing. If this field is strong enough, it causes the magnetic particles (domains) within the coating to become aligned with the field. Since the magnetic surface is moving, a continuous strip of surface is magnetized. If the direction of the current is changed, the field reverses and the magnetic particles in the coating are magnetized in the opposite direction.

Having recorded data in the form of a magnetized band along a track, we have to reverse the process to retrieve the data. A read head is essentially the same as a write head (sometimes the same head serves as both read and write head). When the magnetized material moves past the gap in the read head, a magnetic flux is induced in the head. The flux, in turn, induces a voltage across the terminals of the coil which is proportional to the rate of change of the flux, raher than the absolute value of the magnetic flux itself. Figure 8.37 shows the waveforms associaed with writing and reading. The voltage from the read head is given by

$$V = K \frac{d\Phi}{dt},$$

where K is a constant depending on the physical parameters of the system, and Φ is the flux produced by the moving magnetic medium. Since the derivative of a constant is zero, only *transitions* of magnetic flux can be detected. The output from a region of the surface with a constant magnetization is zero, making it difficult to record digital data directly on tape or disk, as we shall soon see.

As time has passed, engineers have produced greater and greater packing densities (up to about 300 000 bits per square centimetre—two million bits per square inch). Using vertical recording (see later) recording densities of over $2\frac{1}{2}$ million bits per square centimetre (15 million bits per square inch) are possible. One of the main sources of improvement has been in the composition of the magnetic medium used to store data. The size of the particles has been reduced and their magnetic properties improved. Some tapes employ a thin metallic film rather than individual

Magnetic flux

Flux 'bulges' out (in air) to extend into the surface of the tape

Fig. 8.36 The head–air gap.

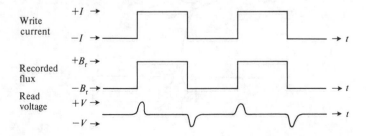

Write current

$+I \rightarrow$
$-I \rightarrow$

Recorded flux

$+B_r \rightarrow$
$-B_r \rightarrow$

Read voltage

$+V \rightarrow$
$-V \rightarrow$

Fig. 8.37 Read/write waveforms.

particles. Metal oxide coatings are typically 0.9 μm (35 μin) thick with oxide particles approximately 0.25 μm by 0.6 μm (10 μin by 25 μin) with an ellipsoidal shape. A thin film coating is typically only 0.1 μm (4 μin) thick.

Vertical recording

The basic recording process we have just described uses *horizontal recording*, in which the magnetic domains on the surface of the recording medium are magnetized in the *horizontal* plane, which is the same plane as the medium itself.

Unfortunately, as the packing density of bits is increased by reducing the size of the magnetized domains, a phenomenon called *demagnetization* makes it harder to read the stored data. Figure 8.38 illustrates the effects of demagnetization. When the tiny magnets representing the domains are placed end to end with North pole to North pole, the magnetic fields from the magnets tend to cancel each other out.

An alternative form of recording employs *vertical* magnetization in which the domains are magnetized in the plane perpendicular to the surface of the medium (see Fig. 8.39). Vertical recording requires a special magnetic medium and a special read/write head. However, not only can we use vertical recording to create very tiny domains, the effects of demagnetization are reduced and there is a very sharp change of field at cell boundaries, making it easier to read back the recorded data. Unfortunately, it is not quite as easy to design magnetic media suitable for vertical recording as it is to design media for conventional horizontal recording.

Thin film heads

The conventional read/write head uses a ring of magnetic material with a tiny air gap. In 1978 IBM developed the thin film head, Fig. 8.40, which

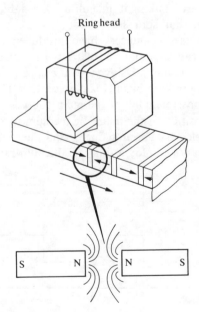

Fig. 8.38 Horizontal recording and demagnetization.

employs a permalloy head (permalloy is a magnetically soft material composed of a mixture of nickel and iron) around which is wound a spiral of copper. Thin film heads are constructed by the same type of technology used in the manufacture of semiconductors. Consequently, the thin film read/write head can now be made with great precision, mass produced at relatively low cost, and made as small as necessary. When not energized (i.e. no current flowing in the coil), the magnetization of the permalloy is parallel to the surface of the recording medium. When a write current flows through the coil, the magnetic field from the head is rotated through 90° and therefore magnetizes the surface. A thin film head permits data to be recorded and played back at a higher speed than a conventional read/write head.

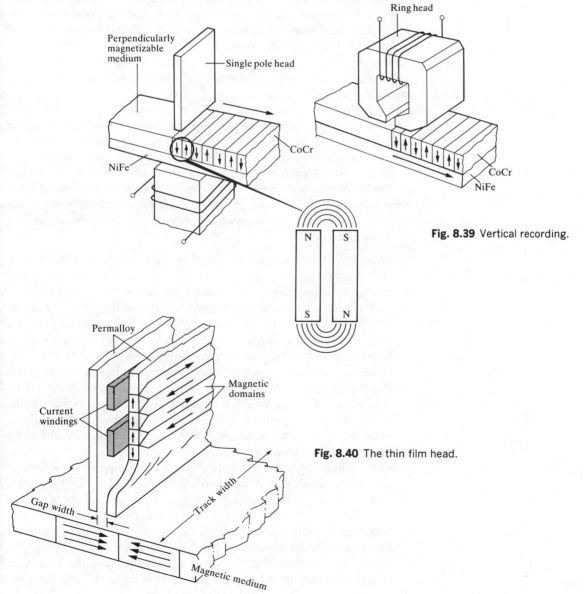

Fig. 8.39 Vertical recording.

Fig. 8.40 The thin film head.

Data encoding techniques

Now that we have described the basic process by which information is recorded on a magnetic medium, we are going to look at some of the ways in which digital data is encoded before it is recorded. All magnetic secondary stores record data serially, a bit at a time, along the path described by the motion of the magnetic medium under the write head. Tape transports have multiple parallel read/write heads and record a number of parallel tracks simultaneously across the width of the tape. However, the data recorded along each track is recorded serially.

It is not possible to transmit the logical ones and zeros to be recorded directly to the write head. A process called *encoding* or *modulation* must first be used to transform the data pattern into a suitable format. Similarly, when the information is read back from the tape it must be *decoded* or *demodulated* to extract the original digital data. The actual encoding/decoding process chosen is a compromise between the desire to pack as many bits of data as possible into a given surface area while preserving the reliability of the system and keeping its complexity within reasonable bounds.

When various encoding techniques are compared, the comparison is done on the basis of a number of properties associated with all recording methods. Interestingly, these are roughly the same criteria involved in the selection of a system for transmitting digital data over long distances. In what follows the term *flux reversal* is used frequently. It indicates a *change of state* in the recorded magnetic field in the coating of the tape or disk. Simply reversing the direction of the current in the write head causes a flux reversal. Some of the criteria by which a recording code may be judged are as follows:

1. *Efficiency*. The storage efficiency of any code is defined as the number of stored bits per flux reversal and is expressed as a percentage. The maximum value is 100% and corresponds to one bit per flux reversal.

2. *Inter-symbol correlation*. The symbols representing the data to be stored should be as unlike each other as possible. By doing this we make it easy to distinguish between the symbols even if they are badly distorted due to defects in the recording/playback process. In a two-valued digital system, the symbols should be identical but of opposite sign (i.e. inverted). This is defined as 100 per cent correlation.

3. *Bandwidth*. The bandwidth occupied by a signal is a measure of its rate of change. According to a theory due to the French mathematician Fourier, any arbitrary waveform can be expressed as an infinite series of sinewaves and cosinewaves with frequencies of f, $2f$, $3f$, $\ldots$, etc. The bandwidth occupied by a signal is the range of frequencies over which it extends. Bandwidth is measured in units called hertz (Hz) which correspond to the old 'cycles per second'. For example, the telephone network has a bandwidth of 300–3000 Hz. Frequencies above and below these limits are not transmitted by the telephone network. As real human speech has a wider bandwidth, the telephone distorts it by cutting off low and high frequencies. Consequently, the quality of telephone speech is rather poor. In engineering terms, very low and

very high frequencies are difficult to handle. A recording code with a narrow bandwidth is preferable to one with a wide bandwidth. In particular, very low frequencies approaching d.c. (direct current or zero frequency) should be avoided.

4. *Self clocking*.   The encoded data must ultimately be decoded and separated into individual bits. A code that provides a method of splitting the bits off from one another is called self-clocking and is highly desirable. A non self-clocking code makes it difficult to separate the data stream into individual bits.

5. *Complexity*.   The simpler the encoding and decoding processes are the less they cost. Because the recording and playback processes involve time-varying analog signals, the precision and tolerance of the circuitry should not be so great that its cost is prohibitive. Although the signals involved in digital recording are nominally digital (i.e. two-state), in practice the signal read off the tape or disk has all the properties of an analog signal.

6. *Noise immunity*.   An ideal code should have the largest immunity to extraneous signals (i.e. noise). Noise in magnetic recording systems is caused by imperfections in the magnetic coating leading to **drop-outs** and **drop-ins**. A drop-out is a loss of signal caused by missing magnetic material, and a drop-in is a noise-pulse. Another source of noise is **cross-talk**, which is the signal picked up by the head from adjacent tracks. Cross-talk is introduced because the tracks are very close together and because the read/write head might not be perfectly aligned with the track on the surface of the recording medium. Noise can also be caused by imperfect erasure. Suppose a track is recorded and later erased. If the erase head did not pass exactly over the centre of the track, it is possible that the far edge of the track might not have been fully erased. When the track is re-recorded and later played back, a spurious signal from the unerased portion of the track will be added to the wanted signal.

The characteristics of a number of possible encoding/decoding techniques are presented below. The list is by no means exhaustive but does include those found in many tape transports and disk drives.

Return-to-zero encoding

In its pure form, return-to-zero, RZ, recording requires that the surface be unmagnetized for a logical zero and magnetized by a short pulse for a logical one. Unfortunately, because no signal is applied to the write head during a zero, any logical ones already on the tape or disk are not erased or overwritten. A modification of RZ recording is return to bias recording, RB, in which a logical zero is recorded by saturating the magnetic coating in one direction, and a logical one by saturating it in the opposite direction by a short pulse of the opposite polarity.

Figure 8.41 illustrates RB reading. The actual pulse width used depends on the characteristics of the head and the magnetic medium. A wide pulse reduces the maximum packing density of the recorded data and is wasteful

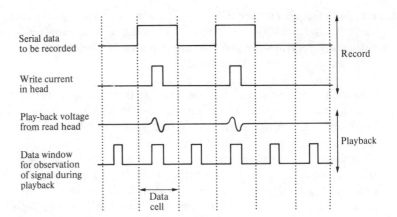

Fig. 8.41 Return-to-bias recording.

of tape or disk surface but is easy to detect, while a very narrow pulse may be difficult to detect.

Data is read from the disk/tape by first generating a **data window**, which is a time-slot during which the signal from the read head is to be sampled. Then the signal from the read head is sampled at the centre of this window. Unfortunately, a sequence of zeros generates no output from the disk/tape, and there is no simple way of making sure that the data window falls exactly in the middle of a data cell. For this reason return-to-bias is said to be non-self-clocking. The efficiency of RB recording is 50 per cent, the correlation fair, but the noise sensitivity poor. A low-frequency response is needed to handle the signal from the disk/tape. For all these reasons, RB recording is not popular and is seldom employed.

Non-return-to-zero encoding

One of the widely used data-encoding techniques is called modified non-return-to-zero or NRZ1. Each time a logical one is to be recorded, the current flowing in the head is reversed. When reading data each change in flux is interpreted as a logical one. Figure 8.42 illustrates NRZ1 recording. NRZ1 requires a maximum of one flux transition per bit of stored data, and represents the optimum packing density of 100 per cent. NRZ1 has a

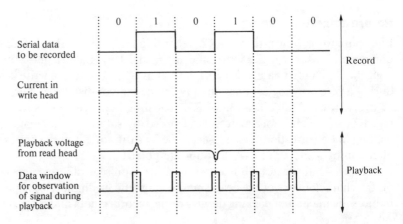

Fig. 8.42 Non-return to zero one recording (NRZ1).

poor correlation, requires a low frequency bandwidth and has fair sensitivity to noise. The greatest drawback of NRZ1 is that it is not self-clocking.

Phase encoding

The majority of high-density magnetic tape transports employ phase encoding or Manchester encoding to record data. At the centre of each and every bit cell is a flux transition: a low-to-high transition indicates a logical one and a high-to-low transition a logical zero. As there is always a transition at the centre of each data cell, a clock signal can be derived from the recorded data, and therefore the encoding technique is self-clocking. A stream of alternate ones and zeros requires one flux transition per bit, while a stream of ones or zeros requires two flux changes per bit.

Figure 8.43 illustrates phase encoding. Phase encoding has a low efficiency of 50 per cent because a maximum of two transitions per bit are required. The correlation is 100 per cent because there is a maximum difference between ones and zeros. The bandwidth requirements are good because there is no low-frequency component in the recorded signal. However, as there are two flux transitions per bit, the maximum recorded frequency is twice that of NRZ1 at an equivalent bit density. The circuit complexity is greater than that of NRZ1, although suitable encoder/decoders are available as single chips. Finally, phase encoding has a good immunity to noise. Because of these attributes phase encoding is widely used in digital data transmission systems as well as magnetic recording systems.

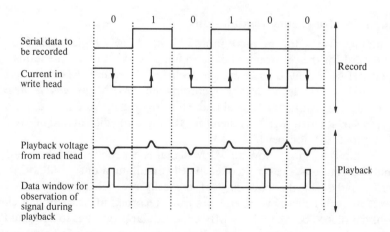

Fig. 8.43 Phase-encoded recording.

Frequency modulation

Frequency modulation, FM, is widely used to encode data in floppy disk systems. Like PE, this encoding technique is self-clocking. The encoded waveform is created by marking the boundary of each data cell with a clock pulse. A pulse is then placed at the centre of a cell to denote a logical one, otherwise the cell is left empty. Figure 8.44 shows the clock pulses, data pulses and combined clock and data pulse waveform. This waveform is then used to record the information by reversing the current flowing in

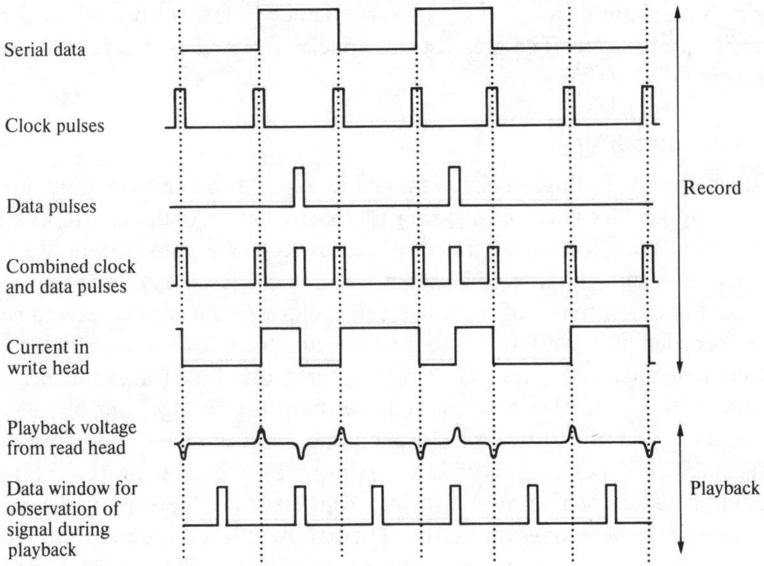

Fig. 8.44 Frequency modulaton.

the write head (and therefore the flux in the magnetic medium) at each pulse. FM recording is identical to PE in all its properties except that a one or zero is recorded by the presence or absence of a transition at the centre of a cell rather than by the direction of the transition. Frequency modulation is somewhat a misnomer. True frequency modulation is described in Chapter 9 when we deal with data transmission.

Modified frequency modulation

Modified frequency modulation, MFM, has largely replaced FM as the standard for the recording of data on floppy disks. In fact, the terms FM and MFM are little used outside technical literature. FM is generally referred to as *single density* recording and MFM as *double density* recording, because MFM is able to store twice the amount of data for a given surface area. MFM is therefore 100 per cent efficient and needs only one flux transition per bit.

Figure 8.45 shows how an MFM signal is encoded. As in FM, a data pulse is placed at the centre of each cell containing a one. Unlike FM the clock pulses at the boundary of the cells are deleted, but with one exception. Whenever two zeros are to be recorded in succession, a clock pulse is placed between them. MFM has similar properties to FM and PE, although its correlation is lower. Because the maximum gap between flux transitions is no more than $2T$, where T is the width of a data cell, MFM is self-clocking. Although it is the most complex of the codes described so far, there are a number of chips designed to encode and decode MFM signals. Some chips will deal with both FM and MFM, so that both systems may be used to record and playback data without modification of the hardware. Figure 8.46 shows FM and MFM modulation on the same time-scale to demonstrate that MFM packs in twice the number of bits per unit time.

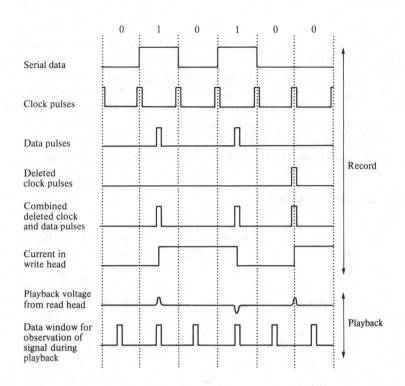

Fig. 8.45 Modified frequency modulation (MFM).

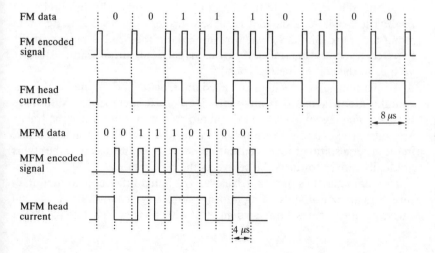

Fig. 8.46 FM and MFM drawn to the same time-scale.

Group codes

Another encoding technique found in both magnetic disk and tape secondary stores is the *group code*, which began to gain popularity in the early 1970s when it was first adopted by IBM for one of their tape systems. Other coding schemes assign a particular waveform to each bit to be recorded which proves incompatible with some of the requirements of an optimum code in terms of bandwidth, inter-symbol correlation, and flux density. A group code takes n bits to represent an m-bit *source* word.

Table 8.3 Example of group code recording

Data to be encoded	GCR 4/5 code to be recorded
0000	11001
0001	11011
0010	10010
0011	10011
0100	11101
0101	10101
0110	10110
0111	10111
1000	11010
1001	01001
1010	01010
1011	01011
1100	11110
1101	01101
1110	01110
1111	01111

Thus, although there are 2^n possible *code* words, only 2^m of these 2^n values are used to create 2^m *different* waveforms for recording on the tape or disk. This means that waveforms with poor recording and playback characteristics can be removed from the code words to be stored on the tape or disk. For example, the 4/5 group code in Table 8.3 uses *five* bits to encode *four* bits of data. The algorithm that maps the four bits of data onto the 5-bit group code to be recorded avoids the occurrence of more than two zeros in succession. Therefore, this group code guarantees at least one flux transition per three recorded bits, making the code self-clocking.

8.4.2 The disk drive

A disk used in magnetic recording is a flat, circular, rigid sheet of aluminium coated with a thin layer of magnetic material. The disk rotates continually about its central axis in much the same way as an audio disk rotates in a gramophone record player. Information is stored along concentric tracks round the disk, and a read/write head is positioned above the track currently being written to, or read from. Here we shall consider only the movable-head disk, in which one head can move from one track to another rather like the tone-arm of a gramophone record player. Figure 8.47 illustrates the operation of such a disk drive. A major difference between the audio and magnetic disks is that the groove on the audio disk is physically cut into its surface. The tracks on a magnetic disk are simply the circular path traced out by the motion of the disk under the read/write head. As a current is passed through the head it writes data along the track. Similarly, when reading data, the head is moved to the required track and the motion of the magnetized surface induces a tiny voltage in the coil of the read head.

A precision servo-mechanism called an *actuator* moves the head horizontally along a radial from track to track. Remember the difference between the magnetic disk and the audio record: in the former the tracks are concentric and it is necessary for the head to step from track to track; in the latter a spiral groove is cut into the surface of the disk and the stylus gradually moves towards the centre as the disk rotates.

The characteristics of disk drives vary from manufacturer to manufacturer and are continually being improved on. A typical disk drive has 200 tracks per inch, stores data at a density of 2200 bits per inch, and rotates at

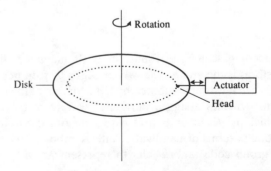

Fig. 8.47 The magnetic disk.

2400 rpm. The storage capacity of disk drives is expressed in megabytes and ranges from 20 to more than 1000M bytes.

Disk drives are very expensive items and in some installations their cost may exceed that of the CPU and main memory. The cost of a disk drive lies in its complex and precise mechanical structure. For this reason manufacturers have reduced the effective cost per megabyte of disk drives by stacking the disks and using more than one head. Figure 8.48 illustrates this arrangement.

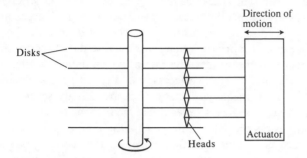

Fig. 8.48 The multi-disk drive.

A drive might have 11 disks with 22 surfaces, of which 20 are used for storing data (the top- and bottom-most surfaces are not used). The 20 heads move together and are driven by a common actuator. The motion of the heads describes a *cylinder*. That is, the corresponding tracks on each of the surfaces are collectively known as a cylinder.

The heads themselves are quite complex. They must not only have the correct electrical and magnetic properties (the air-gap in the read/write head may be only 50-μm wide—0.002 inch), but also the correct mechanical properties. If the head were actually in physical contact with the disk surface, the abrasive magnetic coating would soon wear it out as its velocity over the surface of the disk is of the order of 100 km/h^{-1} (60 m.p.h). The head is mounted in a holder called a *slipper* which is positioned above the disk at about 0.5–2.5 μm (20–100 μin) from the surface. Such a level of precision is not possible by current engineering standards. However, giving the slippers some of the properties of an aerofoil (i.e. like an aeroplane's wings) causes them to float in the moving layer of air just above the surface of the disk.

When an object moves, the layer of air (boundary layer) at its surface moves with it. At some distance from the surface the air is still. Consequently there exists a velocity gradient between the surface and the still air. At a certain point above the disk's surface, the velocity of the air flowing over the head generates enough lift to match the pressure of the spring pushing the head towards the disk. At this point, the head is in equilibrium and floats above the disk. Modern slippers fly at below 0.5 μm (20 μin) and have longitudinal grooves cut in them to dump some of the lift. The precision of a modern slipper is so great that the acid in a fingerprint caused by careless handling can destroy its aerodynamic contour.

Occasionally, the head does hit the surface and is said to crash. A crash

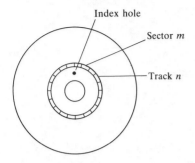

Index hole

Sector *m*

Track *n*

Fig. 8.49 The floppy disk.

usually damages part of a track and this track must be labelled 'bad' and the lost data rewritten from a back-up copy of the file.

Tracks are subdivided into units called sectors and the sectors are themselves divided into blocks of data (Fig. 8.49).

The disk controller (i.e. the electronic system that controls the operation of a disk drive) specifies a track and sector and either reads its contents into a buffer (i.e. temporary store) or writes the contents of the buffer to the disk. The ability to step to a given track leads to disks being regarded as random access devices by some, although strictly speaking disk drives are sequential access devices because it is necessary to wait until the desired sector moves under the head before it can be read.

The user of a disk drive is often most interested in three parameters: the total capacity of the system, the rate at which data is written to or read from the disk, and its average access time. Typical storage capacities range from 20 to 1000 megabytes, data rates are usually several megabytes/ second and average access times range from 15 ms to 60 ms. The average access time is composed of three parts: the time required to step to the desired track (seek time), the time taken for the disk to rotate so that the sector to be read is under the head (latency), and the time taken to actually read the data. In practice, the reading time is often left out of published access times.

The average time to step from track to track is quite difficult to obtain because the head does not always step at constant velocity and considerations such as head **settling time** need to be taken into account. The head settling time is the time taken for the head to stop bouncing after it has been loaded (pushed against the surface of the disk) and refers to floppy disk drives (see later). Moreover, the average number of steps per access depends very much on the arrangement of the data, and on what happens to the head between successive accesses. If the head is **parked** at the periphery of the disk, it must move further on average than if it is parked at the centre of the tracks.

In the absence of any other information, a crude estimate of the average stepping time is one third the number of tracks multiplied by the time taken to step from one track to the adjacent track. This figure is based on the assumption that the head moved a random distance from its current track to its next track each time a seek operation is carried out. If the head were to be retracted to track 0 after each seek, the average access time would be **half** the total number of tracks multiplied by the track-to-track stepping time.

If the head were to be parked in the middle of the tracks after each seek, the average access time would be one quarter of the number of tracks multiplied by the track-to-track stepping time. The average time for a given sector to move to a head, **rotational latency**, is easier to calculate. It is simply one half of a period of revolution. For a disk operating at 3600 rpm, it is

$$\frac{1}{2} \times \frac{60}{3600} = \frac{1}{120}\,\text{s} = 8.33\,\text{ms}.$$

A worked example on the operation of a disk drive is given later in this section.

A short glossary of disk drive terminology

There is insufficient space in this introductory text to cover all the various aspects of disk drives in any detail, so the following glossary is provided to help the reader.

Moving-head disk. A single read/write head scans the surface of a disk by stepping from track to track. This is the type of disk drive already covered and should be contrasted with the fixed-head disk drive described below.

Fixed-head disk. A separate read/write head is employed for each track. The heads are permanently positioned over the tracks and the unit is normally pressurized with an inert gas to keep out dust. Such an arrangement is found where a very low access time is required because, of course, the access time is equal to the rotational latency.

Exchangeable disk pack. Some moving head disk drives are sealed and the disks themselves cannot be taken out. Others have exchangeable disk packs so that the disks may be removed and replaced.

Hard-sectored disk. Hard-sectored disks have a physical means of identifying the beginning of the sectors forming a track. Typically, these take the form of holes or slots in the disk which may be detected optically.

Soft-sectored disk. A soft-sectored disk is formatted before any data can be written on it. This involves writing the track and sector number of each sector onto the disk. Soft-sectored disks allow more flexibility in that various sector sizes may be created under software control. Hard-sectored disks are more efficient because no space is wasted labelling the start of a sector. Figure 8.52 in the following section provides and example of a soft-sectored floppy-disk.

The floppy disk drive

The floppy disk drive bears the same relationship to the hard disk drives previously described as a microlight does to a jumbo jet. This is not intended to be a disparaging comparison because the floppy disk brings to the microcomputer the ability to create and manipulate files at a reasonable price.

The floppy disk drive was developed by IBM in the late 1960s as a low-cost alternative to the conventional hard disk drive. The floppy disk is made of plastic coated with a magnetic material and is enclosed in a 20 cm (8 in) square protective envelope. The floppy disk is a removable medium, and can be transported from one system to another. Figure 8.50 shows the arrangement of the floppy disk, with a central hub aperture, a cut-out to allow the head to access the disk, and an index hole. The floppy disk is so-called because the sheet of plastic of which it is composed is very thin and is therefore not rigid. A floppy disk can readily be bent and (probably) destroyed. They should therefore be handled with great care.

Today, the 20 cm (8 in) floppy disk is rarely seen as it has been replaced by the minifloppy disk 13.3 cm ($5\frac{1}{4}$ in) and the 8.9 cm ($3\frac{1}{2}$ in) floppy disk which is not only very small but comes in a robust rigid plastic case. Although the typical capacity of an 8 inch floppy disk in the mid 1970s was about 300K bytes and the capacity of a $5\frac{1}{4}$ inch floppy disk was 80K

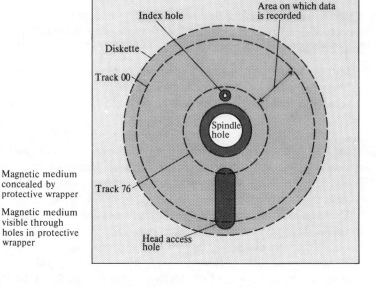

Fig. 8.50 The floppy disk.

bytes, the high-density $5\frac{1}{4}$ inch floppy disks of today can hold 1.2M bytes of data (rendering the cumbersome 8 inch system obsolete).

The disk drive is invariably mounted so that its mouth is at the front of the equipment in which it is located in contrast with the traditional hard disk drive, which is a large item and stands alone from the computer. The mouth that receives the floppy disk is covered by a flap which is opened to insert the disk and then closed to clamp it in place. A tapered drive hub fits through the central hole in the disk. The disk is clamped in place by a second spring-loaded hub forced against the opposite surface of the disk.

The floppy disk rotates at 360 r.p.m., or about one tenth the speed of a hard disk drive. Such a low speed simplifies the drive mechanism and reduces the frictional heating of the disk in its envelope, but at the cost of increasing the rotational latency to 83 ms.

A small hole, the ***index hole***, is cut in the disk to provide a method of detecting the start of a track. Whenever the hole passes between a light source on one side of the disk and a photoelectric cell on the other, an electrical pulse is generated, informing the disk controller that the start of a track has been located. A hard-sectored 8 inch disk has 26 holes spaced round the circumference because the start of each sector must be indicated by a pulse. All $5\frac{1}{4}$ and $3\frac{1}{2}$ inch mini-floppy disks now use soft-sectoring.

The read/write head of a floppy disk is moved to the desired track by a stepping mechanism which we shall describe shortly. The head is positioned over the disk and is able to access its surface through a cut-out in the cardboard envelope. During a read or write access, the head is loaded by applying a pressure pad to the back of the disk and pushing it against the head. Note that the head comes into intimate contact with the disk and does not fly above it. Some systems permanently load the read/write head against the surface of the disk. In order to prevent undue wear on the head and the surface of the disk, the motor may be stopped after a period of disk inactivity.

Figure 8.51a shows one of the head-positioning mechanisms. A stepper motor is connected to a lead screw which rotates as the motor rotates. A nut is threaded on the screw and attached to the head carriage. As the screw rotates, the nut moves in or out, carrying the head assembly with it. The motor is a stepping motor which, unlike conventional motors, does not rotate smoothly but moves in a jerky fashion a few degrees at a time. Short electrical pulses are applied to the motor causing it to step a precise number of degrees, moving the head assembly to the selected track. There are several other ways of moving the read/write head, some of which are described when we look at the hard disk drive.

Because the floppy-disk drive is a relatively low-precision device and makes extensive use of low-cost plastic parts, the track-to-track spacing is much greater than that found in hard disks. The first generation of 8 inch floppy disks had 77 tracks at a density of 48 tracks/inch. The tracks were divided into 26 sectors to give an overall capacity of 300K bytes. A more modern IBM compatible $5\frac{1}{4}$ inch floppy disk has 80 tracks on **both sides** to give a capacity of 1.2M byte. This value expresses the formatted capacity and represents the data available to users. It does not include data which perform housekeeping tasks such as labelling the track and sector number of each sector stored on the disk. In hard disk terms this capacity is tiny indeed. But in terms of the capacity of typical microcomputers it is large enough for many applications—especially when it is remembered that the floppy disk costs only a few cents.

The amount of data stored on both standard and mini-floppy disks has increased since the early 1970s. Many systems now employ double density, MFM, encoding with two-sided, 80 track disks. The most dense recording systems use twice the data rate for a given disk speed (i.e. 360 r.p.m.), which doubles the recorded density to achieve a storage capacity of 1.2M bytes. These systems require special high-density floppy disks to cope with the increased number of flux reversals per inch. All the measures used to increase disk capacity yield a combined sixteenfold increase in capacity.

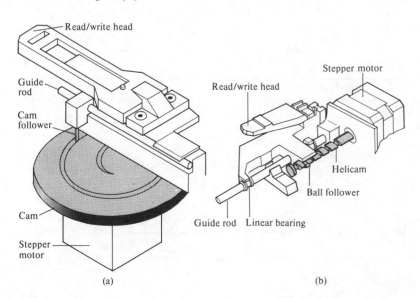

Fig. 8.51 Two head-positioning mechanisms: (a) spiral cam positioner; (b) lead-screw positioner.

Unfortunately, it has also made it more difficult to transfer programs between computers because there are now two recording methods (single or double density), single or double-sided disks and two different track densities.

The recording format

IBM not only provided the floppy disk drive, they also created a ***de facto*** recording standard, the IBM 3740 format. The major semiconductor manufacturers have made a number of single-chip floppy disk controllers implementing this and other formats. Figure 8.52 shows how data is written on a disk formatted according to the IBM 3740 standard.

The Winchester disk drive

One of the growth areas of computer technology in the early 1980s was in compact, low-cost, hard disk drives for use in minicomputers and high-performance microprocessor systems. Such disk drives are generally called Winchester disks. The term *Winchester* is generic and describes a wide range of small disk drives—there appears to be no single feature that makes a system a Winchester. The term is associated with IBM and is said to be related to the Winchester rifle by some, and to the town of Winchester by others. Early Winchester disks had capacities of 5M–10M bytes, but by the late 1980s low-cost Winchesters with capacities of 20M–200M bytes became commonplace.

As the recording density has increased and the inter-track spacing reduced, it has become more and more necessary to find ways of making

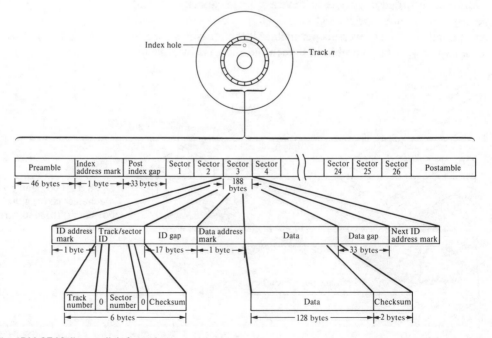

Fig. 8.52 The IBM 3740 floppy-disk format.

sure that a head flies exactly over the track it is accessing. This has led to increasingly complex head-positioning mechanisms and their associated electronics. Winchester technology solves the problem of head tracking by making the disks, read/write heads, and positioner an integral unit. The disks cannot be changed, so the problem of trying to follow a track on a disk written by another unit does not arise. Because the ***head disk assembly*** requires no head alignment, the track spacing can be reduced and the storage density increased.

The Winchester disk drive is a sealed chassis which stops the entry of dirt and dust. Most drives have a small hole in the unit protected by an air filter to equalize internal and external air pressures. As the disk rotates in a clean environment, the flying height of the head can be reduced, and the recording density increased.

Unlike conventional hard disk drives, it is not necessary to retract the heads beyond the outer rim of the disks when the unit is not in use. As the heads fly only when the disks are rotating, and are not retracted when the disk is stationary, it is necessary to make a portion of the surface of the disks available to the heads as a 'landing area'. That is, the heads are permitted to land (come in contact with) a part of the disk where data is not stored. In order to make this possible it is necessary to lubricate the surface of the disk. A consequence of this arrangement is that the disks must be brought up to speed (and stopped) as quickly as possible to reduce the time for which the heads are in contact with the disks.

Some, but not all, Winchester disk drives use a rotary head positioner to move the read/write heads rather than the linear (in and out) positioners found on conventional hard disk drives. Figure 8.53 shows how a voice-coil actuator rotates an arm about a pivot, causing the head assembly to track over the surface of the disks. A voice coil is so called because it works like a loudspeaker. A current is passed through a coil positioned within a strong magnetic field provided by a permanent magnet. The current in the coil generates a magnetic field, causing the coil to be attracted to, or repulsed by, the fixed magnet, moving the pivoted arm. This represents just one of the many head assembly actuators currently in use.

Winchester technology was originally applied to 35 cm (14 in) disks. It has been extended to 8 inch disks and the $5\frac{1}{4}$ and $3\frac{1}{2}$ in mini-Winchester are

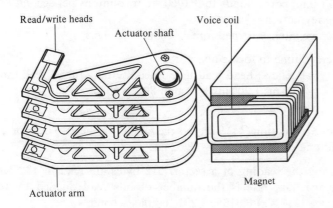

Read/write heads   Actuator shaft   Voice coil

Actuator arm   Magnet

Fig. 8.53 The Winchester head assembly positioning mechanism.

now available. A mini-Winchester costs as little as $200 and can store 20M bytes. There are a vast number of Winchester disk drives on the market, each with its own particular parameter. However, the typical rotational speed is 3600 r.p.m., the data transfer rate 5M bits/sec, the capacity 100M bytes, and the access time 20 ms. It is not unreasonable to believe that the floppy disk drive will come under ever-increasing pressure from the Winchester.

A worked example

A $5\frac{1}{4}$ inch floppy disk drive uses two-sided disks and records data on 80 tracks per side. Each track has 9 sectors and holds 512 bytes of data. The disk rotates at 360 r.p.m., the seek time is 10 ms track-to-track, the head settling time is 10 ms, and the head-load time is 200 ms. From the above information calculate the following.

1. The total capacity of the floppy disk in bytes.

2. The average rotational latency.

3. The average time to locate a given sector assuming that the head is initially parked at track 0, and is in an unloaded state. The head is loaded after the required track has been located.

4. The time taken to read a single sector once it has been located.

5. The average rate at which data is moved from the disk to the processor during the reading of a sector. This should be expressed in bits per second.

6. Estimate the packing density of the disk in terms of bits per inch around a track located at 3 inches from the centre.

Solution

1. Total capacity
   $$= \text{sides} \times \text{tracks} \times \text{sectors} \times \text{bytes/sector}$$
   $$= 2 \times 80 \times 9 \times 512$$
   $$= 737\,280 \text{ bytes (called 720K bytes).}$$

2. Average rotational latency $= \frac{1}{2}$ period of revolution.
   360 r.p.m. corresponds to $360/60 = 6$ revolutions per second.
   One revolution $= \frac{1}{6}$ second.
   Average latency is therefore $\frac{1}{12}$ second $= 83.3$ ms.

3. Average time to locate a sector
   $$= \text{latency} + \text{head load time} + \text{head settling time} + \text{seek time}$$
   $$= 83.3 \text{ ms} + 200 \text{ ms} + 10 \text{ ms} + 80/2 \times 10 \text{ ms}$$
   $$= 693.3 \text{ ms.}$$

4. In one revolution ($\frac{1}{6}$ s) 9 sectors pass under the head. Therefore, time to read one sector is $\frac{1}{6} \times \frac{1}{9}$ s $= 18.52$ ms.

5. During the reading of a sector, 512 bytes are read in 18.52 ms. The average data rate is the number of bits read divided by the time taken $= (512 \times 8)/0.01852 = 221\,166$ bits/second.

6. Packing density

    = total number of bits divided by track length

    $= 9 \times 512 \times 8/(2 \times 3.142 \times 3)$

    = 1955.4 bits/inch

8.4.3 The tape transport

In a tape storage system information is recorded on a thin strip of polyester tape coated with a magnetic material. The tape is $\frac{1}{2}$ inch wide and is stored in (typically) 27 cm (10.5 in) reels of 730 m (2400 feet). The construction of a tape transport (or tape drive) for digital data is not greatly different from a high-quality domestic reel-to-reel recorder. One possible arrangement of a digital tape deck is given in Fig. 8.54.

    The basic function of a tape transport is to move tape at a constant speed past a read/write head. When searching for a particular block of data, the tape is moved at a relatively high speed and stopped when the start of the block is found. Because of their inertia, the tape spools cannot be halted instantaneously. Consequently, if a simple tape transport were used, the tape would be broken, or at least stretched, every time it were stopped. In high-quality tape transports the movement of the tape past the heads is decoupled from the motion of the give-out and take-up spools. How this is actually achieved is described shortly.

    Tape is pulled past the read/write head(s) by a *capstan* and *idler-wheel* arrangement. A capstan is a cylinder of precisely machined and polished hard metal rotating at a constant speed. As the tape passes the capstan, it is pushed against the capstan by an idler-wheel (or pinch roller). Friction between the capstan, tape and idler causes the tape to be pulled. The idler-wheel rotates because of the motion of the tape against it—it is not driven

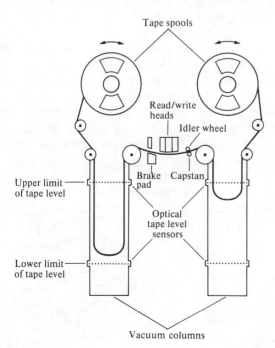

Fig. 8.54 The tape transport.

by any mechanism itself. When the tape is stopped, a solenoid pulls the idler-wheel away from the tape. Brake pads are also applied to the tape to stop it.

The tape between the capstans and spools hangs in a loop in the two vacuum columns below each of the tape spools. By sucking air out of the bottom of the column, the tape loop is kept hanging down. At the top and bottom of the vacuum columns photoelectric sensors are located to detect the presence or absence of the tape loop. By the use of these sensors to control the speed of the spool motors, the length of the loop in the vacuum column can be kept approximately constant. For example, if the left-hand reel is paying out tape too fast, the loop grows downwards. When it reaches the lower sensors the motion of the left-hand spool is slowed down and the loop starts to shorten.

The purpose of the vacuum columns is to allow the almost instantaneous stopping of the tape as it moves past the tape heads. When the idler wheel disengages from the capstan, the tape brakes are applied and the spool motors stopped. The tape under the heads stops almost instantaneously, but the spools momentarily continue either to pay out tape or take it up. This simply leads to one of the tape loops growing and the other shrinking. Vacuum column buffers have their disadvantages. A power failure can lead to tape spillages when the power is re-applied. Vacuum column buffers also consume considerable power and are regarded as being error prone. They cannot be used in aircraft because of the low ambient air pressure. The vacuum system sucks dust from the air and deposits it where it is least wanted—on the tape. Finally, the constant hiss of the air into the vacuum columns sometimes annoys the operators.

Early tape transports used *tension arms* to buffer the tape—a technique still widely found on domestic tape transports. Figure 8.55 illustrates the tension arm, which takes up slack tape or pays out tape when the tape tension increases. This arrangement proves satisfactory for low to medium tape speeds up to 18 cm/s (45 in/s).

The tension arm has been developed to allow tape speeds of 30 cm/s (75 in/s) in an arrangement called the *floating shuttle*, and is illustrated in Fig. 8.56. It was observed that the tension arms tend to work in unison, with one taking up slack and the other paying out tape. By combining the two loops in a freely moving shuttle, an improved performance is possible because the shuttle can be kept light (15 g). The shuttle is a small block with two pulleys, around which are routed the take-up and pay-out loops

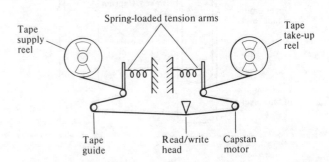

Fig. 8.55 The tension arm tape buffer.

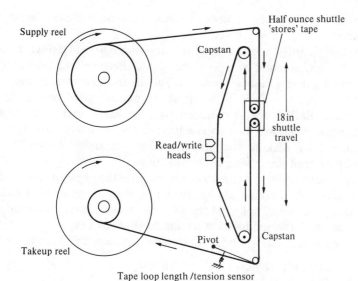

Fig. 8.56 The floating shuttle.

from the reels. A sophisticated motor control system is needed to keep the shuttle within two or three inches of its centre position.

Parameters of tape transport mechanisms

Tape unit parameters vary widely in terms of both tape speed and recording format. Typical speeds vary from 32 to 640 cm/s (12.5 to 250 in/s). The details of a popular recording format (nine-track phase-encoded data) are given in Fig. 8.57.

The read/write heads have nine tracks, of which eight record a byte at a time across the width of the tape. The ninth track contains an odd parity bit. That is, if the nine tracks are considered to form a column of data, the bit in the parity track is chosen to make the total number of ones in the column odd. A single parity bit helps to detect errors because if a column

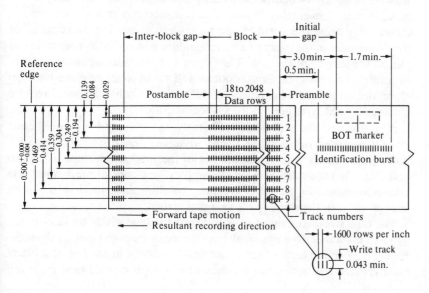

Fig. 8.57 The format of data on a tape.

with an even number of ones is found at least one error must have occurred.

Data is recorded in blocks since it is impossible to read a single byte at a time by starting and stopping the tapes. Between the blocks is an interblock gap (typically 19 mm—$\frac{3}{4}$ in) giving the tape time to stop after a read/write operation and to accelerate to normal speed before the next operation. Each block is preceded by a preamble and followed by a postamble, which are used to synchronize the electronics during a read operation. By making the preamble and postamble symmetric it is possible to read the tape in either direction.

Tapes have markers at their ends to indicate the physical start and end of the tape. The markers take the form of a piece of metallic foil attached to the tape, or small holes. There are also software markers recorded on the tape, BOT (beginning of tape) and EOT (end of tape).

The parameters of a UNIVAC 16 tape transport are given below:

Data rate (bytes)	96 000
Density (bits/in)	1 000
Tape speed (in/s)	125
Interrecord gap (in)	0.75
Interrecord gap time (ms)	12
Rewind time (min)	2

The streaming tape drive

The types of tape transport we have already discussed are the classic secondary stores of mini- and mainframe computers. Their parameters, performance, and cost belong to the world of the mainframe. By the early 1970s tape transports were using recording densities of 6250 bytes/in, speeds of 500 cm/s (200 in/s), a 0.75 cm (0.3 in) inter-record gap, and were able to start and stop within 1 ms.

Today low-cost, high-performance microcomputers are freely available with Winchester hard disks providing the high-speed secondary store. Since Winchesters employ fixed media, it is necessary to find some way of transferring programs between computers and preserving the contents of the Winchester in the event of a system failure leading to the corruption of part of the surface of the disk. The floppy disk provides a convenient way of transporting programs, but is not as well suited to the role of a back-up store, due to its limited capacity. A 40M byte Winchester would require almost 33 1.2M byte floppy disks to back it up.

A solution to the problem of efficiently and cheaply backing up hard disks is provided in the shape of the *streaming tape* drive. The cost of a highe-performance tape transport lies in the mechanism needed to stop and start the tape quickly. Such a complex tape control mechanism has been abandoned in the tape streamer, resulting in a mechanism small enough to fit in the same space as a disk drive.

The tape streamer cannot stop and start the tape within an inter-block gap and must therefore use an alternative mechanism to position the tape. Figure 8.58 shows how a tape is nominally stopped at the end of a block but overshoots it because of the lack of any sophisticated tape buffering

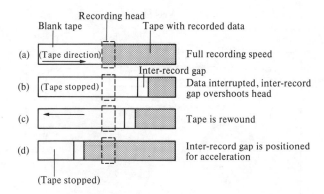

Fig. 8.58 Re-positioning the type in a streamer.

mechanism. The tape must then be rewound and positioned before the interblock gap so that when the tape is re-started it will come up to speed by the time the next block is passing the read/write head. This process takes approximately one second and is a thousand times slower than a vacuum-buffered tape transport.

The inability to stop and start on an inter-block gap is not as bad as it sounds. The tape streamer is frequently used to store large blocks of data from the disk and therefore runs continuously, rather than by skipping from one data block to another. Modern tape streamers solve the stop/ start problem by providing a 'massless buffer'. As the cost of semiconductor memory is now so low, it is possible to read a large chunk of data from the tape into memory local to the streamer. The host computer then reads data not from the tape directly, but from the semiconductor memory. In this way it is possible to skip almost instantaneously from block to block, because the data is now held in random access memory.

Some manufacturers have pressed the ordinary domestic video cassette recorder (VCR) into service as a tape streamer. The VCR is not only remarkably cheap, it can record as much as 100M bytes on a single video cassette. Because the VCR was never designed to store digital data reliably, it is necessary to record each data block six or more times for added security.

Tape cassettes and cartridges

The digital cassette recorder is the most inexpensive form of magnetic tape transport and is comparable in size with the domestic cassette player. The cassettes themselves are identical to those used to record music except that they are made to a much higher standard, and are free from imperfections such as drop-out. Figure 8.59 shows the structure of a cassette drive which hardly differs from the domestic version. Indeed, the only major difference is that all the controls are operated electronically by solenoids instead of the piano-key controls found on some domestic units.

A typical cassette recorder records digital data at a density of 630 bits/ cm (1600 bits/in). Note that a cassette drive records data along one track serially, unlike the nine-track reel-to-reel tape transport. The data is phase encoded. In fact, the recorder has a two-track head, but the tracks are not

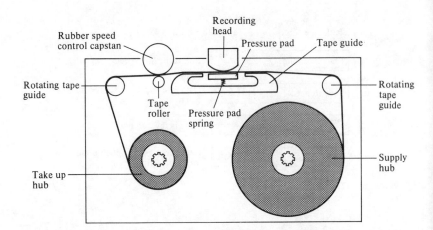

Fig. 8.59 The cassette drive.

used concurrently. They merely double the effective length of the tape by allowing one head to access the upper surface, and one head the lower. The tape moves at 76 cms (30 in/s) in the read or write modes, and data is transferred at 24K bits/s. The total capacity of the cassette is 40M bytes. The major parameters of the cassette recorder are given in Table 8.4.

The read/write head has a dual gap allowing simultaneous reading and writing. A combined read/write head permits the recorded data to be read back immediately after it has been recorded and any record errors detected. If an error is found, the writing of the current block may be aborted, the tape backed-up, and the block rewritten.

The cost of a cassette drive and its associated electronic subsystem is a little more than that of one of today's 100 M byte Winchester drives. The main applications of the cassette are the exchange of data between computers, numerical control and data logging. Data logging is the term used to describe a system dedicated to the gathering of information. For example, a cassette mechanism and a microprocessor system can be encapsulated in a small sealed unit, and left at the side of a busy road to

Table 8.4 Details of a typical cassette transport

Parameter	Value
Data format	10 000 flux reversals/in NRZ1 modulation
Tape speed (read/write)	76 cm/s (30 in/s)
(rewind)	230 cm/s (90 in/s)
Start time (30 ips)	100 ms
(90 ips)	300 ms
Data transfer rate	24K bits/s
Recording density	8000 bits/inch
MTBF	35 000 hours
MTTR	0.5 h
Error rate (soft)	1 in 10^8
Error rate (hard)	1 in 10^{10}

record the timing and density of traffic. After several days, an engineer will come and unlock the box, replace the cassette, and take away the old cassette for analysis, usually on a minicomputer.

The cartridge is merely an up-market version of the cassette. A typical cartridge uses 6 mm ($\frac{1}{4}$ in) magnetic tape, holds ten times as much data as a cassette, and generally exceeds the performance of a cassette drive in all respects.

8.5 Magnetic bubble memory

The magnetic bubble memory is a small high-density serial access secondary store with a very low latency. When I first encountered magnetic bubble memories in the late 1960s, I was told that they represented the future form of secondary store. In the 1990s the bubble memory is still awaiting its call to fame. Although they are now in commercial production and are very useful in a few applications, they have never achieved a dominant position in the memory market. In fact, some semiconductor companies have stopped producing them. The magnetic bubble memory has been squeezed from two sides—there has been a steady reduction in the cost and size of disk drives, while at the same time there has been an even more dramatic drop in the price of semiconductor random access memory, together with a massive increase in the number of bits per chip.

The discovery of magnetic bubble technology is associated with Andrew Boback at Bell Laboratories in 1968. Magnetic bubbles are cylindrical domains within a thin layer of a special magnetic material. The most common material used to create magnetic bubble devices is gadolinium gallium garnet, referred to as GGG (for obvious reasons). Like the thin films we have discussed earlier, GGG exhibits uniaxial magnetic anisotropy, and is easier to magnetize in one plane than another. A thin film of GGG has its easy axis oriented perpendicular to its plane. Figure 8.60 shows the structure of a sheet of GGG under the effect of varying degrees of external magnetization.

In Fig. 8.60(a) there is no external field and the domains are arranged at random in a striped or serpentine fashion. If a bias field, H_b, is applied at right angles to the film in the plane of easy magnetization, the domains not magnetized in the same direction as the external field begin to shrink. The magnetization of the bulk material is parallel to the external field and is in the down direction. The magnetization of the anti-parallel domains is said to be in the up direction. Figure 8.6(b) shows the effect of small values of H_b.

As the external field is increased (Fig. 8.60(c)), the irregularly shaped islands of up magnetization shrink further and become bubble shaped when 'viewed' from above. The bubbles are very small, ranging from 100 μm to 0.01 μm. Typical bubbles have a diameter of approximately 10 μm. If the external magnetic field is increased to the point illustrated in Fig. 8.60(d), the bubbles become unstable and disappear.

Because a bubble is inherently two-state (there or not-there) it can be used to represent binary data. Typical magnetic bubble devices store 1M

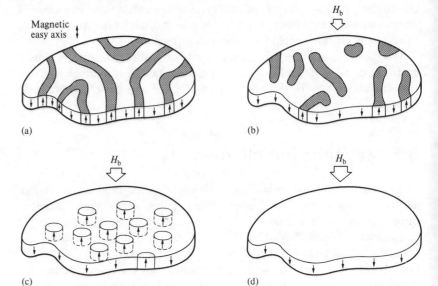

Fig. 8.60 Magnetic bubbles.

bits. All that is needed is a method of generating bubbles at will, detecting them, addressing them, and removing (annihilating) them.

The bubbles are very mobile under the influence of a magnetic field in the plane of the material and can wander about within the film. Although the bubbles move laterally through the film, there is no actual physical movement involved, it is the orientation of the atoms in the crystal that changes.

Structure of bubble memories

Once the GGG film has been deposited on some inert substrate, a layer of silicon dioxide is placed on top to provide a carrier for the next layer and to act as a barrier between layers. On top of the silicon dioxide is deposited a layer of an alloy of copper and aluminium, deposited by photolithographic techniques to produce the structures that generate, transfer, replicate, detect, and annihilate the bubbles. On top of this is a second silicon dioxide layer, followed by a permalloy layer also deposited by photolithography. Permalloy is a magnetic material that reacts with the magnetic bubbles. A magnetic bubble memory is sandwiched between two permanent magnets to generate the constant (static) field, H_b, needed to maintain the bubbles.

Figure 8.61 shows how the permalloy patterns deposited on the surface of the film are used to guide the movement of bubbles through the film. In this diagram we are looking down on the film. The permalloy patterns take the form of rows of 'T' and 'I' bars (although there are other possible structures). If a polarizing magnetic field, H_p, is applied in the plane of the film, the permalloy Ts and Is are magnetized. Note that the polarizing field is at right angles to the bias field, H_b, which serves only to maintain the bubbles. H_p is a variable (rotating) field, and serves to move the bubbles through the film.

In Fig. 8.61(a) the direction of magnetization is along the top of the Ts from right to left, causing the top of the Ts to be magnetized and to behave as if they were tiny bar magnets. The north pole is at the left of the T. Remember that the bubbles are really columns of magnetization with their poles at the top and bottom. Suppose that the bubbles have their south poles at the top. Initially the magnetic bubble in Fig. 8.61(a) is attracted to the north pole of a T. As everyone knows, 'like poles repel, unlike poles attract'.

The in-plane magnetic field, H_p, is rotated 90° clockwise to produce the situation of Fig. 8.61(b). Here the vertical sections of the Ts and Is are magnetized. The base of the I to the left of the bubble's former position becomes a south pole, repelling the bubble. The centre of the T becomes a north pole attracting it. Consequently, it moves to the centre of the T.

In Fig. 8.61(c) the magnetic field has been rotated a further 90° clockwise and the magnetization of the Ts and Is is that of Fig. 8.61(a), but with north and south reversed.

A further 90° rotation of H_p produces the situation shown in Fig. 8.61(d). The bubble is repelled by the South pole of its T, and attracted to

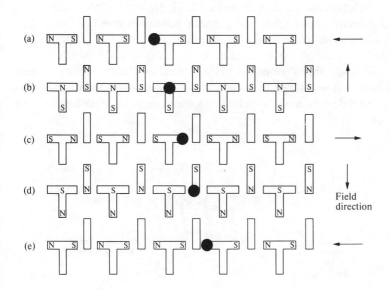

Fig. 8.61 Moving the bubbles.

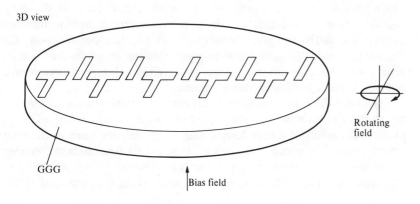

the north pole of the I to its right. The bubble leaves the T and moves to the I. The bubble has now moved from a T to an I, representing a small step for bubblekind, but a giant leap for memory technology.

In Fig. 8.61(e) the field has rotated through a further 90° (360° in total). The magnetization of the Ts and Is is now identical to the starting position of Fig. 8.61(a). The bubble leaves the I and is attracted to the north pole of the T to its right. The bubble has now moved from one T to the next T.

The structure of Fig. 8.61 behaves like a shift register, with one full rotation of the in-plane magnetic field corresponding to a clock pulse in a conventional shift register built from flip-flops.

Continuing the analogy with the shift register, data is shifted into the least significant position of the shift register on each clock pulse. In magnetic bubble memory terms, a bubble is created at the entry to a row of Ts and Is for a logical one, or not created for a logical zero. The bubble is created by passing a current pulse through a tiny conducting loop in the copper–aluminium layer. This generates a magnetic field in the easy direction of magnetization, reversing the bulk magnetization of the film to create a bubble. If a sufficiently large current is passed through the loop in such a direction as to enhance the bias field, H_b, the bubble is destroyed.

The detection mechanism for magnetic bubbles is given in Fig. 8.62. A series of chevron elements (i.e. **V** shaped) have the effect of stretching a bubble into a rod shape, increasing the intensity of the bubble's external magnetic field. The effect of the bubble's field on the chevrons is to alter their electrical resistance to a current flowing through them, and hence permit the detection of a bubble by measuring the resistance of the chevrons.

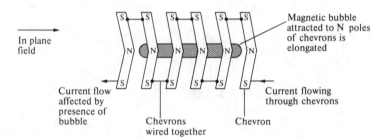

Fig. 8.62 The bubble detector.

We have now described how the bubbles are created, shifted, detected, and destroyed. The actual details of a real magnetic bubble memory module are fairly complex, particularly its physical construction, the electronics needed to generate its in-plane rotating magnetic field and its generation/detection circuitry. Figure 8.63 shows the construction of a typical magnetic-bubble memory module

The major difference between a real magnetic-bubble memory and the above description is in the arrangement of the shift register. A single large loop would result in a very long access time, and any fault in the loop would render the entire chip useless. Figure 8.64 illustrates the major–minor loop organization of a typical device. A number of minor loops (say 156 each containing 513 bits) store the data. Data is transferred to the

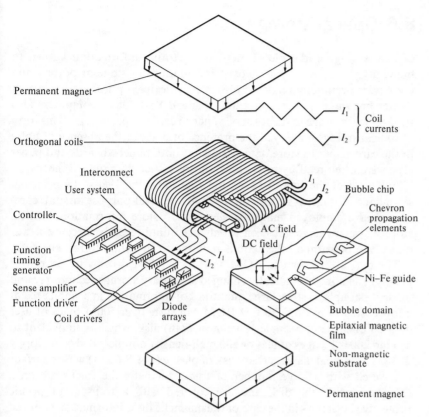

Permanent magnet

Orthogonal coils

Interconnect

User system

Controller

Function timing generator

Sense amplifier

Function driver

Coil drivers

Diode arrays

I_1

I_2

Coil currents

I_1

I_2

Bubble chip

Chevron propagation elements

AC field

DC field

Ni–Fe guide

Bubble domain

Epitaxial magnetic film

Non-magnetic substrate

Permanent magnet

Fig. 8.63 The construction of a magnetic bubble memory module.

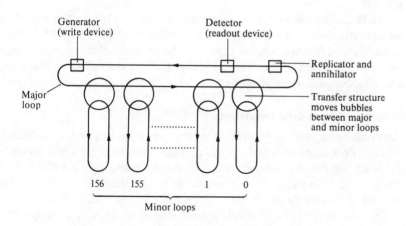

Generator (write device)

Detector (readout device)

Replicator and annihilator

Major loop

Transfer structure moves bubbles between major and minor loops

156   155   1   0

Minor loops

Fig. 8.64 Major–minor loop organization.

desired minor loop via the major loop linking all minor loops with the bubble generate/detect circuitry. Modern devices have access times of approximately 4 ms, transfer rates of 0.1 Mbits per second, and capacities of 1 Mbits.

8.6 Optical storage

Optical storage is the oldest method of storing information known to humanity. Early systems employed indentations in stone or pottery and these were eventually rendered obsolete by flexible optical storage media (better known as papyrus and later paper). Yesterday's computers also used optical storage in the form of punched cards or paper tape. This form of optical storage employed the presence of holes or the absence of holes in the card/paper to store data. However, both punched cards and paper tape were often read by mechanical means rather than optical means.

For most of the time between the 1950s and the 1980s, the principal secondary storage systems employed by general-purpose digital computers have employed magnetic elements to store information. Optical storage systems have not been widely used until recently, because it was difficult to perform all the actions required to store and to retrieve data.

The optical disk or CD-ROM and the WORM disk (write once read mostly) has now dramatically changed secondary storage technology and made it possible to store large quantities of information in a small area at a low cost. For example, a CD-ROM can store over 500M bytes of user data on one side of a single 120 mm (4.72 in) disk, which is equivalent to around 200 000 pages of text or 500 high-density double-sided $5\frac{1}{4}$ in floppy disks. The optical disk is a rigid disk of plastic (Fig. 8.65(a)) whose surface is covered with a large number of tracks (actually the tracks are on a substrate inside the disk and are covered with a transparent plastic protective layer). As in the case of the magnetic disk, information is stored along a track in binary form. However, unlike the magnetic disk, the track of an optical disk is a continuous spiral (like that of a gramophone record).

While the principles of the optical disk are almost trivial, the details of its operation are very complex. The fundamental problems of optical storage are as follows: reliably detecting the presence of tiny bumps called pits on the surface of the disk, optically tracking the reflective elements, and encoding/decoding the data.

Storing and reading information

An optical disk stores information by means of reflecting or non-reflecting metallic dots along the track. A beam of light produced by a semiconductor laser is focused onto the surface of the track and light reflected from the surface is detected by a photosensitive transistor or diode. Figure 8.65(b) illustrates the structure of the surface of the optical disk.

Data is recorded as a series of variable-length pits along a spiral track at a constant pitch (1.6 μm). The 'pits' and 'land' are coated onto a substrate and covered with a protective transparent layer. The disk itself is produced by stamping from a master disk which is, itself, produced by the same type of technology employed to fabricate microprocessors. Consequently, it is very expensive to make one CD-ROM, but very cheap to make thousands.

Light from the laser is focused first through an objective lens and then

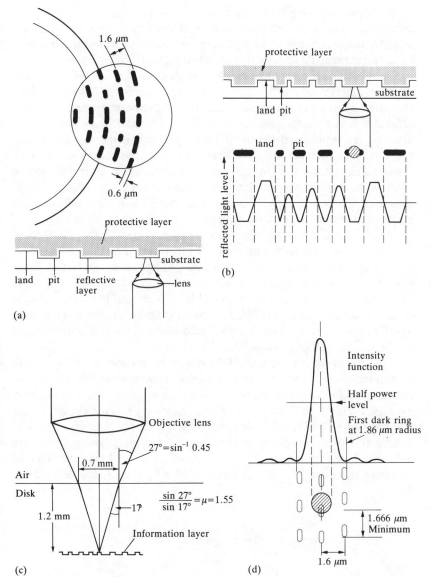

Fig. 8.65 The optical disk: (a) how tracks are arranged; (b) structure of surface (the optical system receives low light levels from the pits (scattering) and high light levels from the land (reflecting)); (c) optical focusing; (d) distribution of light intensity.

by the air:disk interface onto the pits as Fig. 8.65(c) demonstrates. Note that this arrangement means that the spot of light on the surface is very much larger (by three orders of magnitude) than the pits and therefore surface imperfections and dust particles do not interfere with the read-back process.

Light from the area between the pits (i.e. the land) is reflected back, while light from the pits is scattered. The scattering is caused because the height of the pit is approximately 0.13 μm above the land and light reflected from the pit and the surrounding land destructively interfere with each other (i.e., they cancel each other out since 0.13 μm is one quarter of the wavelength of the light in the plastic medium and therefore the light from the pit and the land differ by one half-wavelength). Figure 8.65(b) demonstrates how the relative intensity of the light is modulated by the pits. A change in the level of light intensity reflected from the surface of the disk represents a change from land to pit or from pit to land.

The resolution (i.e. the smallest element that can be 'seen') of the optical system is determined by the wavelength of the laser light (700 nm) and the numerical aperture of the objective lens (0.45). Numerical aperture, NA, is defined as lens diameter/focal length and the value of 0.45 is a compromise between resolution and depth of focus (increasing the resolution and hence storage capacity makes it harder to focus the beam on the disk). These values of wavelength and NA provide a minimum resolution of 1 μm. Note that there is sometimes confusion about the wavelength of the laser light. The wavelength is 780 nm in air, but when it travels through the plastic material of the disk its wavelength is reduced to 500 nm).

Figure 8.65(d) shows the distribution of light intensity from a beam of light falling on a pit within an array of pits (formed by adjacent tracks). Note that at the microscopic level, a beam of light does not have a 'hard edge' but instead displays an intensity distribution. The sizes of the pits are such that half the energy of the spot falls on a pit and half falls onto the land. The reflected energy is ideally zero if the light from the pits and land interfere destructively. The optimum separation of the pits is determined by the wavelength of the light used by the laser.

The data stored on the CD-ROM has to be encoded to achieve both maximum storage density and freedom from errors. Moreover, the encoding technique must be self-clocking to simplify the data recovery circuits. Figure 8.66 illustrates the basic encoding scheme chosen by the designers of CD-ROM. The length of the pits themselves is modulated and the transition of a pit to land (or from land to pit) is a one. The source data is in byte form and each byte is encoded into a 14-bit code. That is, although there are $2^{14} = 16\,384$ possible 14-bit patterns, only $2^8 = 256$ of

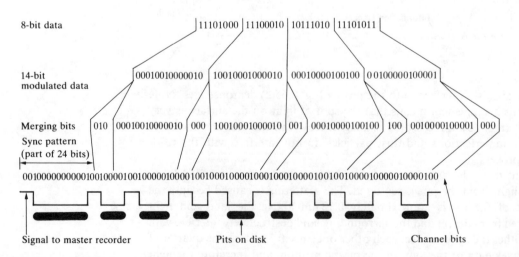

Fig. 8.66 Encoding of data.

these patterns are actually used. The encoding algorithm chooses 14-bit code words that do not have two consecutive ones separated by less than two zeros. Moreover, the longest permitted run of zeros is ten. These two restrictions mean that the 14-bit code has 267 values that meet the criteria, of which 256 are actually used. The 14-bit codes corresponding to the first ten 8-bit codes are given in Table 8.5.

The groups of 14-bit code words are not simply joined 'end to end', but are separated by three 'merging bits'. The function of the merging bits is to ensure that the encoding rules are not violated when the end of one group is taken in conjunction with the start of the next. These merging bits carry no useful data and are simply separators. The example below demonstrates the need for merging bits.

Table 8.5 Part of the 8- to 14-code conversion table

	Data bits	Channel bits
0	00000000	01001000100000
1	00000001	10000100000000
2	00000010	10010000100000
3	00000011	10001000100000
4	00000100	01000100000000
5	00000101	00000100010000
6	00000110	00010000100000
7	00000111	00100100000000
8	00001000	01001001000000
9	00001001	10000001000000
10	00001010	10010001000000

Forbidden pattern 101

. . . . 0010   1000 . . . .

End of first code ↑   ↑ Start of next code

Merging pattern ensures no illegal bit pattern

. . . . 00100001000 . . . .

There is, in fact, another constraint on the choice of these merging bits. Another factor in the choice of the pattern of bits to be used as the merging bits is the need to keep the lengths of the track and land along the surface of the tracks equal (when averaged). This restriction is necessary because the average energy reflected from the surface is used by the focusing and tracking mechanism, and therefore it is necessary to avoid changes in average energy due to data dependency.

The channel clock derived from the signal recovered from the pits and land is 4.3218 MHz because this is the maximum rate of change of signal from the pits and land at the standard CD scanning speed of 1.3 m/s. The bit density is 1.66 bits/μm or 42K bits/inch. At a track pitch of 1.6 μm this corresponds to 6×10^8 bits/in^2 or 10^6 bits/mm^2.

So far, we have talked about the encoding of the data to achieve a maximum density of bits. Due to the way in which pits are laid down and to the unbelievably high precision required by the system, it is impossible to avoid large numbers of errors. Since it is impossible to realistically reduce the number of errors, it is necessary to employ powerful error-correcting codes to nullify the effect of the errors. Due to the complexity of these codes (not to mention the mathematical background), all we can do is to report their characteristics.

The cross interleaved Reed–Solomon code (CIRC) takes groups of 24 bytes of data and encodes them into groups of 32 bytes. Information is interleaved (spread out) so that a burst of errors at one location affects several code groups. These groups can be individually corrected. If all the errors fell into a single group, it would be impossible for the code to repair the damage (i.e. correct all the errors). One of the differences between the CD used to store audio information and the CD-ROM is that the latter employs an extra layer of encoding to reduce further the undetected error rate to one in 10^{13} bits. Moreover, the sophisticated CIRC encoding makes it possible to correct an error burst of up to 450 bytes (which would take up 2 mm of track length). The capacity of a CD-ROM is 553 megabytes of user data.

The spiral track of the CD-ROM is divided into sectors and each sector is individually addressable. The address of a sector is expressed absolutely with respect to the start of the track and is in the form of minutes, seconds and blocks from the start (this format is the same as that of the CD). A sector or block is composed of 12 synchronizing bytes (for clock recovery), a 4 byte header that identifies the sector, a block of 2048 bytes of user data and 288 auxiliary bytes largely made up of the error-correcting code.

Since the size of the pits is constant and they are recorded along a spiral on a disk, the number of pits per revolution must vary between the inner and outer tracks. Contrast this with the magnetic disk, in which the bit density changes between inner and outer tracks because the 'bits' must be smaller on inner tracks if there are to be the same number as in outer tracks.

A consequence of constant size pits is that the speed of the disk depends on the location of the sector being read (i.e. the disk moves with a constant linear velocity, rather than a constant angular velocity). Think about it. If the pits are of constant length, there are more pits around an outer track and therefore the disk must rotate slowly to read them at a constant rate. As the read head moves in towards the centre, the disk must speed up since there are less pits around the circumference. The disk spins at between about 200 and 500 r.p.m. As you might imagine, this arrangement severely restricts the access time of the system. Moreover, the relatively heavy read head assembly also reduces the maximum 'track-to-track' stepping time. These factors together limit the average access time of a CD-ROM to in the region of 100–200 ms (an order of magnitude worse than some hard disks). Note that I said 'track-to-track' stepping, even though the track is really a continuous spiral. When in the seek mode, the head steps across the spiral and reads an address block to determine whether it has reached the correct part of the spiral.

Tracking and focusing

We have described how data is stored on a CD but have said little about the mechanism used to read it from the surface of the disk. Figure 8.67 demonstrates how data is read. Coherent light from the laser at a wavelength of approximately 700 nm is focused onto the surface of the disk. The light is passed through a 'quarter-wave' plate which rotates the plane of its polarization by 45°. Light from the surface of the disk is reflected back along the same axis as the incident light and is reflected by a polarizing prism, which rotates its polarization by 45° to the detector. Since the polarization of the light has now been rotated by 90° with respect to the light from the laser, it is possible to ensure that only the light reflected from the disk's surface reaches the detector.

Because the optical system requires a degree of positioning that is

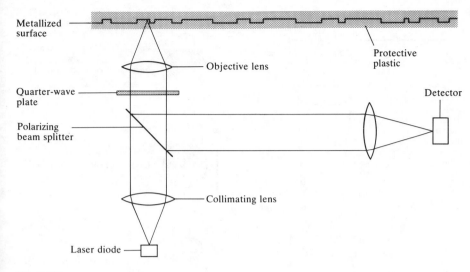

Metallized surface

Protective plastic

Objective lens

Quarter-wave plate

Detector

Polarizing beam splitter

Collimating lens

Laser diode

Fig. 8.67

accurate to within a wavelength of light, a precise positioning mechanism is necessary. The horizontal position of the read head is determined by precision servo-motors and its position from the surface of the disk is determined by a coil in a magnetic field (changing the current in the coil changes the force between the coil and the magnet). Figure 8.68(a) illustrates the principle of the vertical positioning (i.e. focusing) mechanism. Light from the surface is split into two equal halves by an optical wedge and there beams are focused onto a pair of photodiodes.

When the beam is correctly focused on to the surface (position B in Fig. 8.68(a)), the two beams are focused on the centre of each of the photodiode pairs. Each diode produces an equal output and no position correction is necessary. However, if the head moves towards the disk surface (position C), the reflected beam is wider and the optical wedge causes the split beams to focus behind the photodiodes in position C_1. As a result of this, inner diodes D_2 and D_3 receive less light than the outer diodes. If the head moves away from the surface, the converse situation arises. It is possible to derive a focusing signal from

$$F_{error} = (D_1 + D_4) - (D_2 + D_3).$$

Radial focusing (i.e. making sure that the beam falls exactly in the centre of the track) is performed in a similar way to focusing in the vertical plane. Figure 8.68(b) demonstrates the effect of a beam focused exactly on the pits and beams that are offset to the left and to the right. When a beam is correctly focused, both pairs of diodes D_1, D_2 and D_3, D_4 receive equal amounts of light. If the beam wanders off track, one pair will receive more light than the other. A radial error can be obtained by comparing the outputs from the pairs of detectors:

$$R_{error} = (D_1 + D_2) - (D_3 + D_4).$$

The radial error can be used to move the head to the left or the right. I

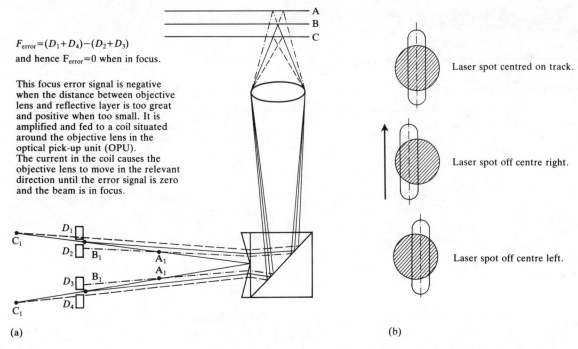

$F_{error} = (D_1 + D_4) - (D_2 + D_3)$

and hence $F_{error} = 0$ when in focus.

This focus error signal is negative when the distance between objective lens and reflective layer is too great and positive when too small. It is amplified and fed to a coil situated around the objective lens in the optical pick-up unit (OPU).
The current in the coil causes the objective lens to move in the relevant direction until the error signal is zero and the beam is in focus.

Laser spot centred on track.

Laser spot off centre right.

Laser spot off centre left.

(a)   (b)

Fig. 8.68

hope that you appreciate the elegance of the above arrangement which employs the same hardware to focus in two dimensions simultaneously.

The received data rate is compared with an accurate crystal clock and any difference is used to speed up or to slow down the disk's drive motor.

Unfortunately, optical disks will not completely replace magnetic disks in the near future. As we said above, optical disks rotate at a relatively low speed and the laser head has a much greater mass than a flying thin-film magnetic read/write head. Taken together these make the access time of optical disks relatively slow. Furthermore, it is relatively difficult to write to optical disks, which means that low-cost systems are read-only and are best suited to information retrieval systems (e.g. encyclopaedias, literature surveys, legal, and medical information). The considerable cost of producing a CD-ROM commercially suggests that only information that will sell large numbers of copies or information for which users are willing to pay a high premium will appear on CD-ROM.

Writable CDs

As it is easier to write information than to erase it, many optical storage systems operate in write-once, read-mostly mode called 'WORM'. Because the 550M byte capacity of a CD is so large, it is convenient to add a new file each time an existing file is updated. Typical WORMs store about 400M bytes of data (single sided), have an access time of the order of 100 ms, cost about $3000 (the cost of the medium is $100 double-sided).

There is no single leading WORM technology and the various manufacturers employ different techniques to write to the CD (the principles of reading and tracking are the same as the CD-ROM). Some WORMs employ organic dyes that are vaporized when subjected to write pulses from the laser (the write laser uses pulses of much higher energy than the read laser). Some WORMs simply ablate the surface of a non-reflecting layer of material above a reflecting background to create a pit. Some WORMs employ a powerful laser to melt a region of a coating of tellurium to create a pit.

It is possible to create true read/write optical storage systems that are able to write data onto the disk, read it and then erase it in order to write over it. Clearly, any laser technology that burns or ablates a surface cannot be used in an erasable system. Erasable CDs employ a rather complex technology that brings together several fundamental principles in physics.

Figure 8.69 illustrates the principle of the erasable CD. The CD substrate is pre-stamped with the track structure and the track or groove coated with a number of layers (some are for the protection of the active layer). The active layer uses a material like tellurium iron cobalt (TeFeCo) which changes the polarization of the reflected laser light. The magnetization of the TeFeCo film determines the direction of the reflected light's polarization.

Initially (a) the film is subjected to uniform magnetic field to align the TeFeCo molecules and therefore provide a 'base' direction for the polarization of the reflected light. This base can be thought of as a continuous stream of zero bits. During the read phase a short pulse of

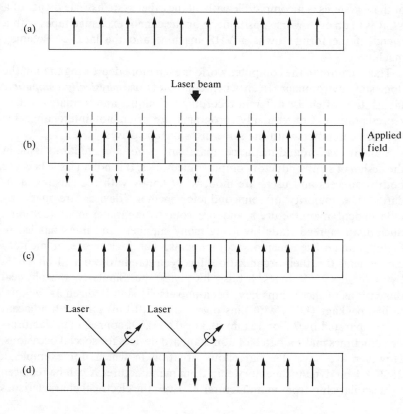

Fig. 8.69 Optical storage: (a) virgin coating (no data stored); (b) write operation—apply reverse field and locally heat surface with laser; (c) post-write—heated region cools and magnetic field frozen; (d) read operation—the polarization of the reflected light is rotated by the magnetization. The direction of rotation depends on that of the magnetization.

laser light hits the surface and heats the film changing its magnetic properties (b). By simultaneous activation of an electromagnet under the surface of the disk, the direction of the film's magnetization can be reversed with respect to the base direction. This creates a one (c). When the spot cools down, the drop in temperature fixes the new direction of magnetization.

The disk is read by focusing a much weaker polarized beam on the disk and then detecting whether the reflected beam was rotated clockwise or counterclockwise (d).

To erase a bit, the area that was written to is pulsed once again with the low-power laser and the direction of the magnetic field from the electromagnet reversed to write a zero.

8.7 Standards and magnetic media

We are going to look at the relationship between magnetic recording media and standardization because media incompatibility is one of the most important sources of frustration to the systems integrator. 'Media incompatibility' is as much an everyday domestic issue as it is an issue in the world of computing. Many households now have a record player, a cassette recorder, a video recorder (VCR) and a compact disc player. Each of these devices replays data, representing sound or vision, recorded on some physical medium. Unfortunately, the medium associated with each of these systems is incompatible with all the other systems. The owner of a VCR is in an even worse position: he or she cannot exchange tapes with a friend, if the former owns a VHS machine and the latter a Betamax machine.

The situation in the computer world is even more depressing than in the domestic environment. Even when computers use *physically compatible* media, they often use different recording techniques and formats for data representation. Consequently, programs are often not interchangeable between computers with the same disks or tape drives.

Standardization and media compatability is not a contentious issue in the design of semiconductor computer memories. It is not an issue because both producers and users are moderately happy with the existing standards. The majority of semiconductor memory devices are made by independent manufacturers and are sold to computer manufacturers. Such a widespread trade involving many suppliers and users has led to highly standardized memory components. The logical size of memory components (i.e. their organization) has been standardized as: 1 bit × 64K bytes, 1 bit × 256K bytes, 8 bits × 8K bytes, etc. Similarly, the physical dimensions of these chips have been universally standardized as the dual in line package (DIL) with pins on a 2.5 mm (0.1 in) grid with adjacent rows separated by 7.5 or 15 mm (0.3 or 0.6 in). Of course, manufacturers do sometimes make a batch of non-standard devices for special occasions. However, we have the marvellous situation in which, for example, a 256K × 1 bit dynamic memory chip from manufacturer X can be replaced by a similar chip from manufacturer Y. Even the electrical characteristics and the pin-out of these chips have been standardized. The vast majority of today's digital components operate with the so-called TTL voltage ranges (i.e. a logical-zero output is a voltage between 0 V and 0.4 V and a logical-one output is a voltage greater than 2.8 V).

The standardization of magnetic media is in a terrible mess. In order to understand why this is so, it is necessary to look at an example. We will consider the ISO standard ISO 3788–1976 (E) for '9-track, 12.7 mm wide magnetic tape recorded at 1600 r.p.i., phase encoded'. What we are up against is a recording/playback process which, ultimately, has so many options that it can be very difficult to move data from one place to another on tape (or disk) without a great deal of effort.

Figure 8.70 shows the physical arrangement of magnetic tape. Information is stored by magnetizing the surface, with the magnetic domains pointing either up the tape or down the tape. We have to specify the physical dimensions of the tape if it is to be interchangeable. At this level there are relatively few options. Tape is generally 12.7 mm (0.5 in) wide or 6.30 mm (0.25 mm) wide. Having specified the most important dimension of the tape, we have also to consider the tape housing (the reel or the cassette). Various standards have been devised for their dimensions.

Magnetic tape systems record data in parallel along a number of tracks. For example, ISO 3788–1976 (E) specifies the nine parallel tracks illustrated in Fig. 8.71. Nine tracks are used because most data is byte-oriented (i.e. arranged in multiples of 8 bits) and a 9-track format provides a byte of data plus a parity track. The parity track is used to aid the detection of an error in the other 8 bits. Some earlier tape mechanisms recorded data along seven tracks (6 bits plus parity).

A glance at Fig. 8.71 shows that the position of the tracks along the surface have been standardized and that data is arranged into blocks. It is not enough just to record information on tape, but the information has to be ***arranged*** in a meaningful fashion. ISO 3788–1976 (E) specifies a block structure which consists of between 18 and 2048 rows of data and is preceded by a preamble and succeeded by a postamble. The forming of

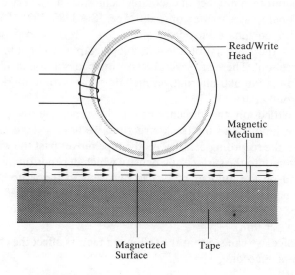

Read/Write Head

Magnetic Medium

Magnetized Surface

Tape

Fig. 8.70 The physical arrangement of magnetic tape.

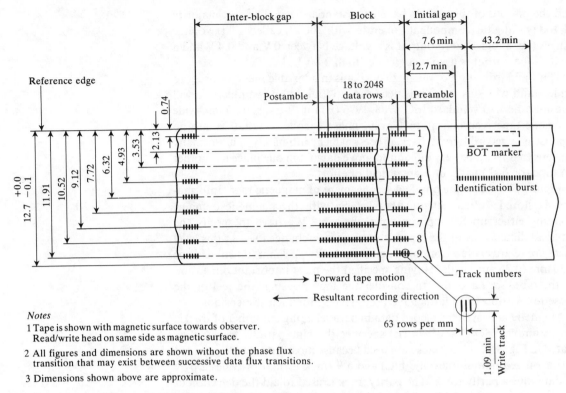

Fig. 8.71 Recording data on magnetic tape.

data into units called **blocks** (blocking) is necessary, because the tape drive cannot read or write a single row of bits efficiently. Each block is separated from its neighbours by an inter-block gap which is nominally 15 mm (0.6 in) long.

Because of the way in which the magnetic record/playback process operates, it is not possible to store binary ones and zeros on the tape directly. Therefore, a number of encoding techniques have been devised to encode data before it is written onto the tape. ISO 3788–1976 (E) specifies that the data be 'phase encoded' and a one bit is defined as 'a flux transition to the polarity of the interblock gap when reading in the forward direction'. There are several recording codes in use in addition to phase encoding. Popular alternatives include non-return to mark (NRZ1) zero and group codes.

Having settled on the dimensions of the tape, the recording (i.e. encoding) technique and the track structure, we have at least one major variable left: the recording density. As the tape moves past the write head, data is written onto the surface at a density which depends on the speed of the tape and on the number of bits/second sent to the write head. The greater the packing density (in bits per inch), the greater the efficiency of data storage. ISO 3788–1976 (E) specifies a packing density of 1600 bits per inch (63 per mm).

At this stage, we can see that the following factors affect the choice of a magnetic tape recording:

1. tape dimensions (including the tape spool);

2. tape recording (encoding mechanism);

3. data format (tracks, block size);

4. recording density (bits per inch).

Various combinations of the above parameters have been standardized, so that there are not as many options as the readers might fear. Even so, it is a lucky programmer that can take a tape from machine A and immediately run it on machine B in a different installation.

Up to now, we have said nothing about the information stored on the tape, other than to say that it is recorded in blocks of 8-bit columns with an inter-block gap between blocks.

ISO 3788–1976 (E) prescribes that the data be recorded in the form of ISO 7-bit character codes or, optionally, the 8-bit extended ISO code. The structure of files on magnetic tape is rather dependent on the operating system that created them. However, ISO 1991–1979 (E) does specify the file structures necessary for data interchange on magnetic tape.

As another example of the success and failure of standardization, let's consider the floppy disk. The floppy disk drive was originally devised by IBM and its associated standards were therefore *de facto* IBM standards. The original IBM floppy disk had a diameter of approximately 8 inches. The lower cost $5\frac{1}{4}$ in floppy disk drive soon brought interchangeable magnetic media to the world of the microcomputer.

The vast majority of floppy disks have information written on them in accordance with IBM's standards for both 8 and $5\frac{1}{4}$ in floppy disks. Here standardization was imposed partly because of the weight of IBM but more because the first generation of floppy disk controller interface chips were internally designed to support IBM formats. A few companies, like Apple, did not adopt IBM formats, with the result that a floppy disk created on an Apple cannot even be read by most other computers.

Although most floppy disks are compatible with IBM formats, there are still quite a few options to be considered. There are 8, $5\frac{1}{4}$, $3\frac{1}{2}$ and 3 in disks. There are single-density and double density disks (the density refers to the type of recording code where FM = single density and MFM = double density). There are single-sided and double-sided disks. There are disks with *regular* track spacing and disks with half-track spacing. In all, there are currently at least 32 valid options for floppy disk recording systems and each option is a recognized standard! Sometimes it is vital not only to standardize something, but to limit the available number of options to prevent the concept of standardization becoming farcical. To be fair, the growth in the options of floppy disk standards has been driven by the rapid improvements in technology. The single-density, single-sided $5\frac{1}{4}$ in floppy disk of 1976 with its 80K byte capacity looks silly in comparison with today's $3\frac{1}{2}$ in disks with a capacity of 1.4 M bytes.

Even though there are quite a few different physical formats for floppy disks, things become much worse at the software level. The various software houses have designed their own file structures, which means that a file recorded under, say, the FLEX operating system cannot be read on a computer running CP/M—even though both disks share the same physical block structure. That is, the operating systems are both able to read the binary information off the disk, but they interpret its meaning differently. Figure 8.72 illustrates the number of options available to the user of floppy disks. Such incompatibility has led to a small cottage industry where entrepreneurs have devised schemes which read one format and produce a new disk with another format.

It is a pity that no standard file structure has emerged for the floppy disk user. To a considerable extent, software houses are not entirely unhappy with the situation. They are able to produce a number of versions of the same software, one version for each disk format. In this way, they can select an optimum pricing policy. For example, a program running on, say, the Apple IIe or the BBC microcomputer may be sold for, say, $80. The same program formatted for the IBM PC might sell for $500. To be fair, it must be stated that the two versions of the same program differ not only in terms of their file structure, there are differences in the way they relate to the operating system of the computer on which they run and differences in the source languages in which they are written. Even allowing for this, the large pricing difference can only be explained in terms of what the market will support than in development costs.

The lack of universal standards for the storage of information on magnetic media has had a powerful and negative influence on microcomputing. Because programs cannot readily be exchanged, time is wasted on converting between standards. Some institutions have delayed their entry into microcomputing simply because of the lack of standardization in media, language, operating systems and interfaces.

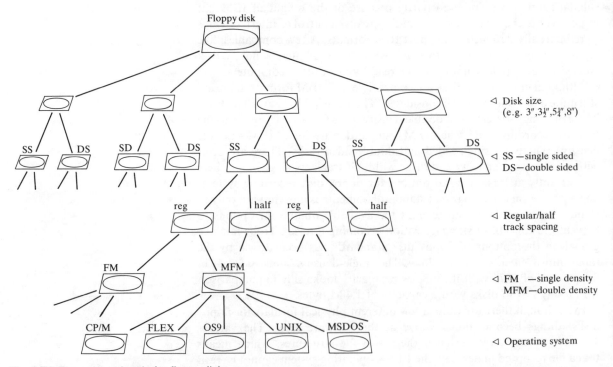

Fig. 8.72 The options jungle for floppy disks.

The relationship between magnetic media and standardization seems to encompass all the advantages and disadvantages of standardization. It is not always possible to design a single standard to cater for both today's systems and tomorrow's. The original Philips audio cassette could not have been used for video recording and it was therefore necessary to develop new standards for video recording (e.g. VHS and Betamax). In order to bring out video recording systems as soon as possible, commercial considerations led to two major standards for domestic VCRs. These standards were entirely incompatible with each other.

Few members of the public would applaud this situation, as they were the losers in the long term. They suffered an economic penalty for this state of affairs. Anyone with a VCR using the minority standard (Betamax) could not acess the wide range of pre-recorded VHS tapes.

The supplier of non-standard equipment reduces the danger of competition from other suppliers. However, this is a dangerous path to take, because the potential user often avoids equipment which is not standard and which uses non-standard media.

Summary

In this chapter we have looked at some of the aspects of a computer's memory system. We began with a description of the characteristics of fast semiconductor memory and then moved on to characteristics of slower but much cheaper secondary storage. Today, there is a bewildering number of memory technologies. We have briefly covered some of them: from semiconductor dynamic memory to devices based on magnetism to optical storage technology. Memory technology is important because, to a great extent, it determines the way in which we use computers. Faster CPUs make it possible to process data rapidly, enabling us to tackle problems like high-speed, real-time graphics. Faster, denser and cheaper memories make it possible to store and process large volumes of data. For example, the optical disk makes it possible to implement very large on-line databases. Low-cost high-capacity hard disks now enable people to carry up to 100M bytes of data in a portable computer. This corresponds to approximately 200 000 pages of printed text.

Problems

1. A dynamic RAM chip costs $1 and is organized as 65536×4 bits. A memory composed of 4 megawords is to be built with these chips. If each word of the memory is 48 bits wide, how many chips are required? What will the cost of the memory be, if the cost of the other components is estimated to be 20 per cent of the cost of the memory chips themselves? Note that one megaword is 2^{20} words.

2. A magnetic tape has a packing density of 800 characters per inch, an interblock gap of $\frac{1}{2}$ in, and is filled with records. Each contains 400 characters. Calculate the fraction of the tape containing useful data if the records are written as:

(a) single record blocks

(b) blocks containing four records.

3. A moveable-head disk drive has 10 disks and 18 surfaces available for recording. Each surface is composed of 200 concentric tracks and the disks rotate at 2400 r.p.m. Each track is divided into 8 blocks of 256 32-bit words. There is one read/write head per surface and it is possible to read the 18 tracks of a given cylinder simultaneously. The time to step from track to track is 1 ms (10^{-3} s). Between data transfers the head is parked at the outermost track of the disk.

Calculate:

(a) the total capacity of the disk drive;

(b) the maximum data rate in bits/second;

(c) the average access time in milliseconds;

(d) the average transfer rate when reading 256 word blocks located randomly on the disk.

(e) Given that the disk has a 12 in diameter and the outermost track comes to 1 in from the edge of the disk, calculate the recording density (bits/inch) of the innermost and the outermost tracks. The track density is 200 tracks/in.

4. As video cassette recorders have dropped in price an engineer proposes to use them to store digital data. What is the storage capacity of a one-hour tape (in bits), and at what rate is data transferred?

A TV picture is transmitted as 625 lines, repeated 25 times per second. The useful portion of each line can be used to store 256 bits.

5. The assumption about head movement in Problem 3 is, in general, incorrect. Assume that a disk drive has N concentric cylinders numbered from 0 to $N-1$. The innermost cylinder is numbered 0.

Derive an expression for the average random move from one cylinder to another (in terms of the number of head movements). Assume that when seeking the next cylinder, all cylinders have an equal probability of being selected. Hence, or otherwise, show that the average movement approaches $N/3$ for large values of N.

Hint: Consider the Kth cylinder and calculate the number of steps needed to move to the Jth cylinder, where J varies from 0 to $N-1$.

6. How does the price and performance of memory determine the way in which computers are used (in contrast with the price and performance of CPUs)?

7. Define the meaning of the following terms:

(a) access time;

(b) random access;

(c) serial access;

(d) static memory;

(e) dynamic memory.

8. Design and address decoder to be used in a 68000-based system (which has address lines A_{01} to A_{23}) to provide 2M bytes of static read–write memory starting at address $10\,000_{16}$, 512K bytes of read-only memory starting at address $C0\,0000_{16}$, and 64K bytes of I/O space starting at address $FF\,0000_{16}$.

9. What are the advantages and disadvantages of partial address decoding as opposed to full address decoding?

10. What is the advantage of the PROM as an address decoder over the three-line to eight-line decoder?

11. What factors make DRAM harder to use than static RAM (from the point of view of the systems designer)?

12. Why is it impossible to record long strings of 1s or 0s on magnetic disk or tape without first modulating the recording signal?

13. Magnetic bubbles are said to move from point to point in a crystal of GGG. What actually moves?

14. What is the difference between the track of a CD-ROM and the track of a magnetic disk?

15. How is the location of data on a CD-ROM specified (i.e. what is its address)?

Computer communications

9

Two of the greatest technologies of our age are telecommunications and computer engineering. Telecommunications is concerned with moving information from one point to another point or from one point to many other points. I think it is no exaggeration to say that the telecommunications industry is largely taken for granted by the vast majority of people. If you were to ask the average person what the greatest technological feat of 1969 was, they would probably reply 'The first manned landing on the moon'. A much more magnificent achievement was the ability of millions of people half a million kilometres away to watch what was taking place on the moon in their own homes. However, if most people are not aware of the great developments in the telecommunications industry, they will not have missed the microprocessor revolution. In the last few years powerful computers have become even more powerful and minicomputers and microprocessors have spread to industry, education, research, and the home.

It is hardly surprising that these two technologies with their widely differing origins, histories, and traditions should now be brought together to allow computers physically separated from each other to communicate and share resources. Computer networks are part of a general trend towards distributed computing that can be seen in multicomputer systems, in distributed data bases, and in the use of intelligent terminals.

This chapter examines the way in which computers communicate with each other. 'Why should one computer wish to communicate with another?', I hear you ask. Computers communicate with each other for the same reason that people cooperate with each other—efficiency. By sharing skills and resources a group of n people can achieve more than n times that of one person alone. We sum up this philosophy in the phrase 'The whole is greater than the sum of its parts.'

The first part of Chapter 9 introduces the idea of a **protocol**, which is a vital component of any communications system. Simply moving data from one point to another is not the whole story. Protocols are the mutually agreed rules or procedures enabling computers to exchange data in an orderly fashion. Protocols make sure that the data gets to its correct destination and deal with the problems of lost or corrupted data.

Following protocols we go on to look at how data is moved from one point to another. Two examples of data path are examined, the telephone network and the RS232C interface that links together computers and peripherals. All the data paths considered here move digital data from one point to another, a bit at a time.

Two important protocols for the transmission of serial data are briefly examined. These are a character-oriented protocol that treats data as blocks of ISO/ASCII encoded characters, and a bit-oriented protocol that treats data as a continuous stream of bits.

The final part of this chapter is devoted to local area networks, and describes the features of some of the LANs in current use. An important aspect of LANs is the way in which the computers and peripherals are able to share the same network without apparent conflict.

Linking computers

As a simple demonstration of the advantage of linking computers together to form a network, consider the following example. A scientist is using a minicomputer to control an experiment. One day the scientist has to perform a numerical calculation so complex that it will require all the minicomputer's time for several days. During the time that the minicomputer is devoted to number crunching, it may be necessary to shut down the experiment. If the equipment must be run continuously, the scientist can buy a new and more powerful computer capable of handling both experiment and calculation. Unfortunately, this approach is terribly wasteful as, once the calculation has been completed, the new computer is under-used. A much better solution is to buy time on a large mainframe and pay only for the work actually done. The scientist can obtain access to the computational facilities he or she needs in one of two ways. One is to physically take the problem to the mainframe on magnetic tape or disk. The other is to transmit the problem over some data-carrying network from the minicomputer to the mainframe, and then receive the results from the mainframe.

Because it is very expensive to lay down physical connections between computers, the existing public switched telephone network, PSTN, is often used to link them. In many cases the telephone network does not provide an ideal solution to the linking of computers, as it was never designed to handle high-speed digital data. Such networks connecting computers together over considerable distances (say more than 1 km) are called wide area networks (WANs).

Over the last few years a considerable change in the pattern of computer use has taken place. The flood of low-cost microcomputers and minicomputers has led to a corresponding increase in the number of peripherals capable of being controlled by a computer. It is now commonplace to connect together many different computers and peripherals on a given site (e.g. a factory), enabling data to be shared, control centralized, and efficiency improved. Such a network is called a local area network (LAN).

Consider a typical example of a LAN in a university. Figure 9.1 shows how clusters of computers and peripherals are connected to NIUs (network interface units), and the NIUs interlinked by an Ethernet, one of

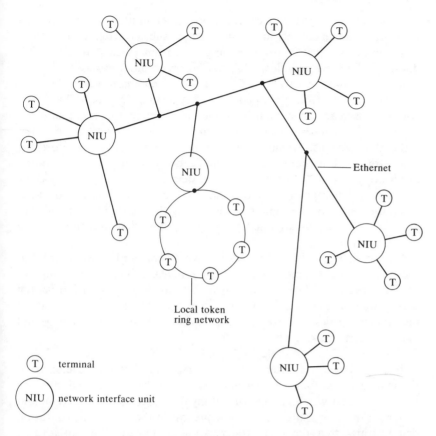

Fig. 9.1 A typical local area network in a large organization.

the types of LAN widely available from several suppliers. The NIUs each have their own microprocessor and serve to link a group of devices with each other and the network. Conceptually, they perform the same function as a telephone exchange. A VDU is located in each lecturer's room, allowing him or her to communicate with a mainframe on an adjacent site, one of the university's minicomputers or one of the many microprocessors and their peripherals. In the near future, it is envisaged that the automated office will become commonplace. For example, when the university introduces the technology of the automated office, lecturers will be able to consign memos to a file store making them available to those who need them. A user who accesses the memory will be able to ask for those memos relevant to him or her. Memos can be displayed on a VDU and a hard copy printed in the unlikely event of it being important.

9.1 Protocols and computer communications

Before we look at protocols for computer communications, I must make an important point. In the descriptions of systems that follow, I use analogies in order to illustrate difficult or abstract concepts. In general, these are analogies with only limited application and cannot be extended too far.

To an outsider or a novice, the world of computer communications must seem like an entirely hardware-oriented subject. After all, computer communications just involves moving data from place A to place B—doesn't it? It therefore follows that computer communications is all about data-transmission hardware. Consequently, communication between computers is possible provided that they employ standard hardware conforming to agreed standards. In fact, much of computer communications is largely concerned with how computers go about exchanging data, rather than with just the mechanisms used to transmit data. Therefore, the standards used in computer communications relate not only to the hardware parts of a communication system (i.e. the plugs and sockets connecting a computer to a transmission path, the transmission path itself, the nature of the signals flowing along the transmission path), but also to the procedures (called protocols) followed in transmitting the information.

Most readers will have some idea of what is meant by a standard, but they may not have come across the term *protocol* as it is used in computer communications. When any two *parties* communicate with each other (be they people or machines), they must both agree to abide by a set of unambiguous rules. For example, they must speak the same language and one may start speaking only when the other indicates a readiness to listen.

Consider another example. Suppose I have a bank overdraft and I send a cheque to cover it. If after a few days I receive a threatening letter from the manager, what am I to conclude? Was my cheque received after the manager's letter was sent? Has one of my debits reached my account and increased the overdraft? Was my cheque lost in the post? This confusion demonstrates that the blind transmission of information can lead to unclear and ill-defined situations. It is necessary for both parties to know exactly what messages each has and has not received. What we need is a set of rules to govern the interchange of letters.

Such a set of rules is called a protocol and, in the case of people, is learned as a child. When computers communicate with each other, the protocol must be laid down more formally. If many different computers are to communicate with each other, it is necessary that they adhere to standard protocols that have been promulgated by national and international standards organizations, trade organizations, and other related bodies.

Over the last few years, the number of computers, computer users, and the volume of data to be exchanged between computers (or between computers and their peripherals) has increased dramatically. Unfortunately, manufacturers have been slow to agree on and to adopt standard protocols for the exchange of data, which has led to incompatibility between computers. To add insult to injury, it is often difficult to transfer data between computers that are nominally similar. Not only do computers frequently employ different dialects of the same high-level language, they format data in different ways, they encode it in different ways, and they transmit it (or store it on disk or tape) in different ways. Even the builders of the Tower of Babel had only to contend with different languages.

By demonstrating how protocols are used in computer communications, it is hoped to make the reader appreciate the role of standards in computer communications and take them into account when he or she specifies, purchases, or designs such equipment. It is a sad fact that many working hours are lost in both manufacturing and service industries simply because engineers have to waste time interfacing non-standard equipment to computers or providing for communications between incompatible systems.

The issue of standardization arises not only in the world of computer communications. Standardization is an important part of all aspects of information technology. For example, the lack of suitable standards or the non-compliance with existing standards has a dampening effect on the progress of information technology. Independent manufacturers do not wish to enter a chaotic market that demands a large number of versions of each product or service produced to cater for all the various non-standard implementations. Similarly, users do not want to buy non-standard equipment or services which do not integrate with their existing systems.

9.1.1 Basic reference model for open systems interconnection (OSI)

It is impossible to read any book today on computer communications without encountering the so-called *International Standards Organization Basic Reference Model for Open Systems Interconnection* or, more mercifully, the *ISO model for OSI* (ISO 7498). A system, in the ISO context (and jargon), is defined as 'a set of one or more computers together with the software, peripherals, terminals, human operators, physical processes and means of data transfer that go with them, which make up a single information processing unit.'

The reference model for OSI is not a set of protocols for a communications system. It is a *framework* for the identification and design of protocols for existing or for future communications systems. It enables engineers to identify and to relate together different areas of standardization. Note that OSI does not imply any particular technology or method of implementing systems. In other words, the reference model helps engineers to design protocols for computer communications systems.

The expression *open system* simply means a system which is open to communication with other open systems. A system is open only if it employs agreed (i.e. standardized) protocols when it communicates with the outside world. Of course, it does not have to employ standard protocols for communications within the system itself. An analogy with an open system is a television receiver because it is open to the reception of sound and pictures from transmitters using the agreed protocol (e.g. 625 lines/frame, 50 fields/s, PAL colour in the UK or 525 lines/frame, 60 fields/s, NTSC colour in the USA). A pocket calculator can be regarded as a closed system because it is unable to receive an input from another system.

Before the development of the ISO reference model and the allocated protocol standards, many communications systems were designed by equipment manufacturers on an *ad hoc* basis. That is, the manufacturers produced a package of hardware and software that would provide communications facilities between two points in their network. The purpose of the ISO reference model is to **compartmentalize** or to **isolate** the specific functions performed by the communications system from all other aspects of the system. Once these functions have been isolated, it is possible to devise standards for them. In this way, equipment or software that performs a given standard function can be produced by any manufacturer. If designers use hardware and software conforming to well-defined standards, they can create an information transmission system by putting together all the necessary parts. These parts may be obtained from more than one source. As long as their functions are clearly defined and the way in which they interact with other parts is explicitly stated, they can be used as the building blocks of a system. Alternatively, a manufacturer can produce these building blocks for incorporation in other people's systems.

It should be appreciated that ISO 7498, which describes the reference model, is not an easy document to understand. The standard was written for the implementer of standards and is addressed to them. This document provides a formal and precise framework for the description of standards related to computer communications and identifies the set of standards needed to allow open computer communications to take place.

Figure 9.2 illustrates the structure of the ISO reference model for OSI, where two parties, A and B, are in communication with each other. A

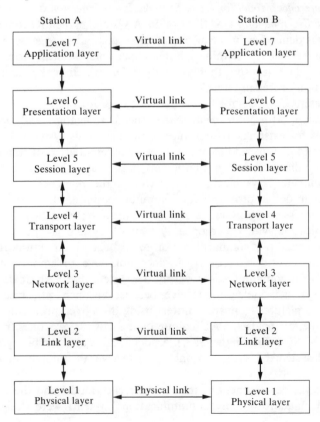

Fig. 9.2 The basic reference model for open systems interconnection.

most important feature of the ISO model is the way in which it divides the task of communicating between two points between a number of *layers* of protocol. Each layer carries out an action or service required by the layer above it. The actions performed by any given layer of the reference model are precisely defined by the service for that layer and require an appropriate protocol for the layer between the two points that are communicating. Note that this conforms to current thinking about software and is strongly related to the concept of modularity. In everyday terms, consider an engineer in one factory who wishes to communicate with an engineer in another factory. The engineer in the first factory describes to an assistant the nature of some work that is to be done. The assistant then dictates a letter to a secretary who, in turn, types the letter and hands it to a courier. Here, the original task (i.e. communicating the needs of one engineer to another) is broken down into subtasks, each of which is performed by a different person. Note that the engineer does not have to know about the actions carried out by other people involved in the exchange of data. Indeed, it does not matter to the engineer how the information is conveyed to his or her counterpart.

In the ISO model, communication *between* layers within a system takes place between a layer and the layers *immediately* above and below it. Layer X in System A communicates only with layers $X+1$ and $X-1$ in System A (see Fig. 9.2). Layer 1 is an exception, as there is no layer below it. Layer 1 communicates only with layer 2 in A and with the corresponding layer 1 in B at the other end of the communications link. In terms of the descriptive analogy used above, the secretary who types the letter communicates only with the assistant who dictates it and with the courier who transports it. Figure 9.3 illustrates the above example in terms of ISO layers. Of course, this rather simple example does not correspond exactly to the ISO model. In particular, layers 3–6 are represented by the single layer called 'assistant'.

Another characteristic of the ISO model is the *apparent* or *virtual* link between corresponding layers at each end of the communication channel. Two corresponding layers at two points in a network are called *peer*

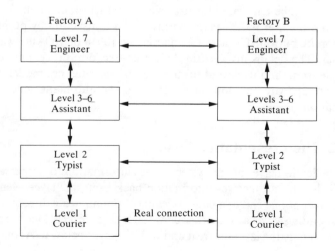

Fig. 9.3 Illustrating the concept of layered protocols.

subsystems and communicate using layer protocols. Therefore, a message sent by layer X at one end of the link is in the form required by the corresponding layer X at the other end. It appears that these two layers are in direct communication with each other, as they are using identical protocols. In fact, one layer X is using the layers below it to transmit the message across the link. At the other end, layer 1 and higher layers process the message until it reaches layer X in the form it left layer X at the other end of the link. Returning to our analogy, the secretary at one factory appears to communicate directly with the secretary at the other factory, because the language used in the letter is appropriate to the task being performed by the two secretaries.

We now look at the functions performed by the seven layers of the ISO reference model for open systems interconnection, starting with the uppermost layer, the application layer.

9.1.2 The application layer

The highest layer of the ISO reference model is the *application* layer which is concerned with protocols for application programs (e.g. file transfer, electronic mail). This layer represents the interface with the end-user, but since, strictly speaking, the OSI reference model is concerned only with *communications*, it does not necessarily represent the way in which the end-user employs the information. The protocol observed by the two users in the application layer is determined entirely by the nature of the application. For example, consider the communication between two lawyers when they are using the telephone. The protocol used by the lawyers is concerned with the semantics of legal jargon. Note that although one lawyer appears to be speaking directly to another, he or she is using another medium involving other protocols to transport the data. In other words, there is no *real* person-to-person connection but a virtual person-to-person connection built upon the telephone network.

Another example of an application process is the operation of an automatic teller at a bank. The operator is in communication with the *bank* and is blissfully ignorant of all the technicalities involved in the transaction. The bank asks the user what transaction he or she wishes to make and the user indicates the nature of the transaction by pushing the appropriate button. The actual bank may be 100 m or 100 km away from the user. The details involved in the communication process are entirely invisible from (and irrelevant to) the user; in the reference model the user is operating (with the control program in the automatic teller) at the applications level.

9.1.3 The presentation layer

The application layer in one system passes information to the *presentation* layer below it and receives information back from this layer. Remember that a layer at one end of a network cannot communicate directly with the corresponding layer at the other end. Each layer (except one) communicates with only the layer above it and with the layer below it. At one end of the communications system the presentation layer translates data between the local format of data required by the application layer above it and a format (agreed with the other end) for transfer. At the other end the format for transfer is translated (if necessary) into the local format of data for the application layer. To take another analogy, a Soviet diplomat can phone a Chinese diplomat at the UN even though neither speaks the other's language. Suppose the Soviet diplomat speaks to a Russian-to-English interpreter who speaks to an English-to-Chinese interpreter at the other end of a telephone link, who, in turn, speaks to the Chinese diplomat. The diplomats represent the applications layer process and talk to each other about political problems (i.e. the processing by the application procedures). However, they are not speaking to each other directly, but are employing a presentation layer to format the data before it is transmitted between them. In this example, the Chinese-to-English and English-to-Russian translators represent the presentation layer. The analogy can also illustrate an important characteristic of the reference model. The English-to-Chinese translator may be a human or a machine. Replacing one with the other has no effect on the application layer above it or on the information transfer layers below it. All that is needed is a mechanism that translates English to Chinese, subject to specified performance criteria.

The major function of the presentation layer is the translation of data from one code to another. However, important additional functions may be data encryption and text compression.

9.1.4 The session layer

Below the presentation layer sits the *session* layer. The session layer organizes the dialogue between two presentation layers. It establishes, manages and synchronizes the channel between two application processes. It provides dialogue control of the type 'Roger, over' in radio communications, and protocol mechanisms to synchronize application communications (but synchronization actions must be initiated at the application layer). Thus the session layer controls the setting of synchronization points and resolves collisions between synchronization requests. An example is: '. . . did you follow that? . . .' '. . . then I will go over it again'.

9.1.5 The transport layer

The four layers below the session layers are responsible for carrying the message between the two parties in communication. The *transport* layer isolates the session (and higher) layers from the network itself. At first sight, it may seem surprising that as many as four layers are needed to perform such an apparently simple task as moving data from one point in a network to another point. However, we are talking about establishing and maintaining connections across interlinked LANs and wide area networks (WANs) with, possibly, major differences in technology and performance—not just communications over a simple wire. The reference model has been designed to include both LANs and WANs which may involve communication paths across continents and include several different communications systems. Figure 9.4 shows how the ISO model for OSI caters for communications systems with intermediate nodes.

The transport layer is responsible for the reliable transmission of messages between two application nodes of a network and for ensuring that the messages are received in the order in which they were sent. The transport layer isolates higher layers from the characteristics of the real networks that actually carry the data by providing the reliable economic transmission required by an application independent of the characteristics of the underlying facilities (for example, error detection/correction, multiplexing to reduce cost, splitting to improve throughput, and message reordering). In brief, the transport layer does not have to know anything about how the actual network is organized.

As an example of a transport function, it should be appreciated that some systems (e.g. packet switching networks) divide information into units called packets and then send them across a complex network of circuits. Some packets take one route through the network and others take another. Consequently, it is possibe for packets to arrive at their destination *out of sequence*. In this case, the transport layer must assemble packets in the correct order, which involves storing the received out-of-sequence packets until the system is ready for them.

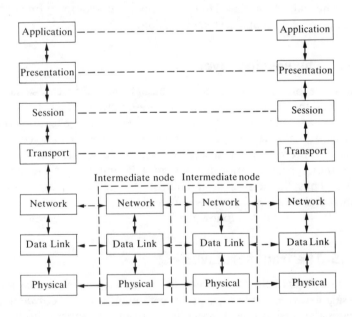

Fig. 9.4 Networks with intermediate node between end stations.

9.1.6 The network layer

The *network* layer serves the transport layer above it by conveying data between the local transport layer and the remote transport layer. Consequently, the network layer is system dependent unlike the layers above it. Remember that complex communications systems may have many paths between two points. The network layer chooses the optimum path for a message to cross the network or for the establishment of a *virtual connection*. As an analogy, consider the postal system. Mail which is sent to a nearby sorting office may be directed to a more distant sorting office if the local office is congested and cannot cope with the volume of traffic. Similarly, in a data transmission network, transmission paths are chosen to minimize the transit time of packets and the cost of transmission (the cost of each link must be paid for).

9.1.7 The data-link layer

The *data-link* layer establishes an error-free (to a given probability) connection between two adjacent points in a network. Information may be transmitted from one end of a network to the other end *directly*, or it may be transmitted from point to point via intermediate nodes in a series of hops. The data-link layer at one node receives a message from the network layer above it and sends it via the physical layer below it to the data-link layer at the adjacent node. The data-link layer also detects faulty messages and automatically asks for their retransmission. Protocols for the data-link layer and the physical layer below it were the first protocols to be developed and are now widely adopted. They cover many different technologies: LANs (for example Ethernet-type networks using CMSA/CD), and WANs (for example X.25).

9.1.8 The physical layer

The lowest layer is called the *physical* layer and is unique because an actual physical connection between any two points in a network exists only at this level. The physical layer is responsible for receiving the individual bits of a message from the data-link layer and for transmitting them over some physical medium to the adjacent physical layer which detects the bits and passes them to the data-link layer above it.

The physical layer does not guarantee reliable delivery of its messages! The service offered by this layer is known as a *best effort service*. Information sent on the physical medium may be lost or corrupted in transit because of electrical or electromagnetic noise interfering with the transmitted data. On some channels (e.g. radio or telephone) the error rate may be very high (one bit lost in 10^3 transmitted bits), while on others (e.g. fibre optic links) it may be very low (one bit lost in 10^{12}). It is the responsibility of layers on top of the physical layer to make up for imperfections in this layer. The physical communication paths themselves may be copper wires, optical fibres, microwave links, or satellite links.

Remember that the ISO reference model permits modifications to one layer without changing the whole of a network. For example, the physical layer between two nodes can be switched from a coaxial cable to a fibre-optic link without any alterations whatsoever taking place at any other level. After all, the data-link layer is interested only in giving bits to, or receiving them from, the physical layer. It is not interested in how the physical layer goes about its work.

Figure 9.5 shows how standards for the layers of the reference model

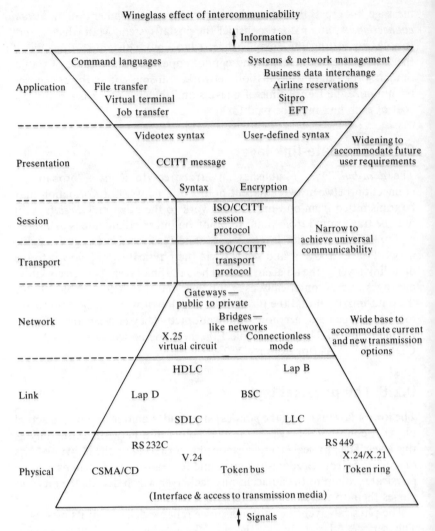

Fig. 9.5 Standards for the layers of the basic reference model.

have grown. Note that the figure is **hour-glass** shaped. The bottom is broad to cater for the many low-level protocols introduced to deal with diverse types of channel, technology, and network, while the middle is narrow because it is desirable to have as few protocols as possible to move information around a network. The top is wide because it reflects the great range of applications of LANS.

Since this is a text devoted to the hardware aspects of computers, we are now going to look more closely at the bottom two layers of the reference model: the physical layer and data-link layer.

9.2 The physical layer of a communications link

Figure 9.6 illustrates the physical link that connects together with stations or nodes. A **station** is a point in a network that communicates with

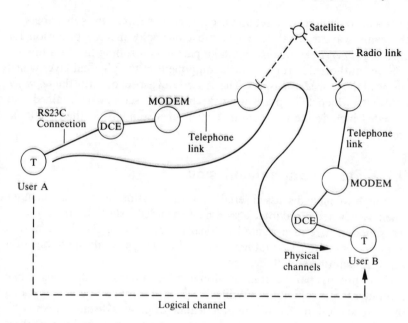

Fig. 9.6 The physical channel.

another point in the network. Alternative words for station are **node** and **receiver** or **transmitter**. Before we can consider the factors influencing the design of a physical channel, it is necessary to look at the function it performs. The reader may find the repetition of the word **physical** a little boring. I employ this word to distinguish between two very different entities—a physical channel and a logical channel. A physical channel is the **actual** transmission path connecting two stations and may be a wire link, a radio link, or any other suitable medium. A logical channel is an **apparent** transmission path linking two stations but which may not actually exist. Of course, a logical channel is made up of one or more physical channels operating in tandem. However, the characteristics of a logical channel may be very different from those of the physical channels of which it is composed.

We can describe a physical channel under three headings: the signal path itself, the mechanical interface to the signal path, and the functionality of the channel. Clearly, the physical layer link must carry data from one node to another. Assuming that the data is to be transmitted electronically over a binary **baseband channel** (see later), the nature of the signal flowing across the channel must be defined. That is, we must ask what signal levels constitute logical ones and logical zeros.

A second and less obvious consideration concerns the mechanical arrangement of the link. What type of plugs and sockets does it use to connect the node with the transmission path? Standard connectors are as vital as standard signal levels, if the equipment at the end of a link is to be readily interchangeable with equipment from several different manufacturers.

The third aspect of a physical layer link of importance is its **functionality**. In other words, what does it do (apart from transmit data)? For example, consider the telephone channel. It not only permits voice signals to be sent from one subscriber to another, but it also transmits the dialling pulses or tones needed to set up the connection between the subscribers. In the same way, a serial data link must normally include provision for carrying **supervisory signals** that take part in controlling the data link.

Some authors describe a fourth component of the physical layer which they call the **procedural aspect**. The procedural aspect governs the **sequence** of events which take place when a channel is set up, maintained and closed. I include the procedural element of a standard in the functional element.

9.2.1 Serial data transmission

Although we have discussed serial data transmission in an earlier chapter when we covered serial interfaces, I have included a short section on serial transmission here as a reminder. Ideally, information should be moved from one computer to another a word at a time, with all the m bits of a word transmitted simultaneously.

Conceptually, parallel transmission involves linking the data bus of one computer to that of another. While this is feasible for computers separated by up to several metres, it is impracticable for greater distances. An m-bit parallel data highway requires m wires to carry the data, and two or three aditional wires to control the flow of information.

Almost all networks transmit data from point to point serially a bit at a time. A serial data link requires only two lines, one to carry the data and one to be the ground return. Note that a voltage has a meaning only when specified with respect to some reference point such as the ground or the earth. If two points are linked by a single path, data can be moved in only one direction at a time.

There are three types of transmission path between stations. The most basic transmission path is called **simplex** and permits the transmission of information in one direction only. That is, there is a single transmitter at one end of the transmission path and a single receiver at the other end. There is no reverse flow of information. The other two arrangements are more interesting and are called **half-duplex** and **full-duplex**, respectively. These are illustrated by Fig. 9.7(a) and (b). In a half-duplex data link, information is transmitted in only one direction at a time (e.g. from A to B or from B to A). Two-way transmission is achieved by **turning round** the channel. For example, the radio found in a taxi represents a half-duplex system. Either the driver speaks to the base station or the base station speaks to the driver. They cannot have a simultaneous two-way conversation. When the driver has finished speaking, he or she says 'over' and switches the radio from transmit mode to receive mode. On hearing 'over', the base station is switched from receive mode to transmit mode. In a full-duplex system, simultaneous transmission in both directions is possible. The telephone channel is an example of a full-duplex system, because it is possible to both speak and listen at the same time. However, some data transmission systems use the telephone network in a half-duplex mode.

Serial data transmission brings with it two problems. First, how is the stream of data divided up into individual bits and how are the bits divided into separate words? Second, how is the data physically transmitted over

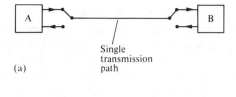

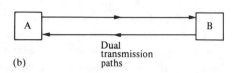

Fig. 9.7 (a) Half-duplex and (b) full-duplex transmission.

long distances? The division of the data stream into bits and words is handled in one of two ways: asynchronously and synchronously. These are treated separately.

9.2.2 Asynchronous serial transmission

We have already met asynchronous serial systems in Chapter 7. The following introduction is included here for the sake of completeness. In an asynchronous serial transmission system the clocks at the transmitter and receiver responsible for dividing the data stream into bits are not synchronized. Figure 9.8 shows the waveform corresponding to a single 7-bit character. The output from the transmitter sits at a logical one state whenever data is not being transmitted and the line is idle, which corresponds to a *mark* condition and is represented by a -12 V in many systems operating over short distances.

In what follows, a bit period is the shortest time for which the line may be in a logical one or a logical zero state. When the transmitter wishes to transmit a word, it places the line in a logical zero (space) state for one bit period. A logical zero is represented by $+12$ V. When the receiver sees this logical zero, called a start bit, it knows that a character is about to follow. The incoming data stream can then be divided into seven bit periods and the data sampled at the centre of each bit. The receiver's clock is not synchronized with the transmitter's and the bits are not sampled exactly in the centre. However, if the receiver's clock is within approximately 4 per cent or so of the transmitter's clock, the system works well.

After seven data bits have been sent, a parity bit is transmitted to give a measure of error protection. If the receiver finds that the received parity does not match the calculated parity, an error is flagged, and the current character rejected.

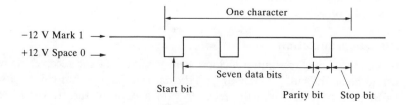

Fig. 9.8 Asynchronous serial transmission.

Following the parity bit are one (or optionally two) stop bits at a logical one level. The stop bit carries no information and serves only as a spacer between consecutive characters. After the stop bit has been transmitted, a new character may be sent at any time. Asynchronous serial data links are used largely to transmit data in (ISO/ASCII-encoded) character form.

If the duration of a single bit is T seconds, the length of a character is given by start bit + seven data bits + parity bit + stop bit = $10T$. Asynchronous transmission is clearly inefficient, since it requires ten data bits to transmit seven bits of useful information. There are several formats for asynchronous data transmissions in common use. Some transmit seven bits of data per character, others eight. Some have odd parity bits, some even, and some have no parity.

The speed at which a serial data link operates is expressed in bits per second and is typically in the range 110 to 9600 bits/s. For a binary (i.e. two-level) signal, one bit per second is called one baud, so that a VDU transmitting data at 2400 bits/s is said to operate at 2400 baud. The baud-rate of a transmission system is defined as the number of changes of state of the signal per second, and is also called the signalling speed. If the data were transmitted in the form of an eight-level signal at 2400 baud, the bit rate would be 7200 bits/s, as each signal element is equivalent to three bits $(8 = 2^3)$ of information.

Once the receiver has assembled all the bits of a character, the character is read by the computer using any of the techniques discussed in Chapter 7. In fact, because the transmission and reception of serial data is performed entirely by special-purpose integrated circuits, the computer itself does not have to worry about the fine details of serial data transmission.

9.2.3 Synchronous serial transmission

Asynchronous data links are largely used to link peripherals (VDUs, printers, modems, etc.) with computers. When information has to be passed between the individual computers of a network, synchronous serial transmission is generally employed. In a synchronous serial data transmission system, information is transmitted continuously with no gap between adjacent groups of bits. I use the expression *groups of bits* because synchronous systems often transmit entire blocks of pure binary information at a time, rather than a sequence of ISO-encoded characters.

There are two problems facing the designer of a synchronous serial system. One is how to divide the incoming data stream into individual bits, and the other is how to divide the data bits into meaningful groups. We briefly look at the division of serial data into *bits* and return to the division of serial data into *blocks* when we introduce character-oriented and bit-oriented protocols.

Bit synchronization

If a copy of the transmitter's clock were available at the receiver there would be no difficulty in breaking up the data stream into individual bits. Unfortunately, providing the receiver with a copy of the transmitter's

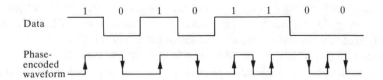

Fig. 9.9 Phase-encoded synchronous serial transmission.

clock would require an additional transmission path for the clock and thereby increase the cost of the data link. A better solution is found by encoding in such a way that a synchronizing signal is included with the data signal. In Chapter 8 ways of encoding digital data for recording on magnetic media were introduced. Some of these techniques can readily be applied to data transmission. If the data stream is phase encoded, a separate clock can be derived from the received signal and the data extracted. Figure 9.9 shows a phase-encoded signal.

9.2.4 Modulation and data transmission

We are now going to look at a topic called *modulation*, which is a method of modifying signals to make them suitable for transmission over a particular channel. Before we introduce various modulation methods, it is instructive to take a short look at the history of data transmission.

The transmission of digital data predates the electronic digital computer by over a century. As early as 1809 King Maximilian asked the Bavarian Academy of Sciences to suggest a scheme for high-speed communication over long distances because he had seen how the French visual semaphore system had helped Napoleon's military campaigns. As a result, Sommering designed a crude telegraph which used 35 conductors (one for each character). Sommering's telegraph relied on the fact that the passage of electricity along a conductor can be detected by passing the electricity through acidified water in a glass tube. The electric current breaks down the water into oxygen and hydrogen and the appearance of bubbles in the tube inform the operator that a particular character is being received. Sommering's telegraph was not well suited to high-speed transmission.

Shortly after the connection between electricity and magnetism had been established, the telegraph was invented and became well established in the 1830s. Figure 9.10 illustrates the operation of the telegraph. When the key is depressed, a current flows in the circuit and energizes the solenoid (i.e. magnetizes the iron core inside the coil). This produces an audible click as a small iron plate is attracted to the iron core. In 1843 Morse sent his assistant A. Vail to the printer's to count the relative frequencies of the letters they were using to set up their press. The resulting code consisted of four symbols: the dot, the dash (= 3 dots), the

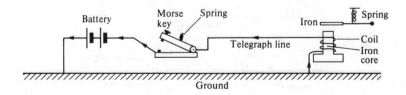

Fig. 9.10 The telegraph.

space between dots and dashes, and the space between words. Frequently occurring letters such as 'E' were given short codes ('E' = '·'), and infrequently occurring letters were given long symbols ('Q' = '– – . –'). It is interesting to note that the Morse code is relatively close to the optimum Huffman code for the English language. We met variable-length Huffman codes in Chapter 4.

As transmission paths increased in length with the advances in technology during the nineteenth century, it became apparent that signals suffer distortion during transmission. A sharply rising pulse at the transmitter is received at the far end as a highly distorted pulse with long rise and fall times. Figure 9.11 illustrates the effect of this so-called telegraph distortion. The sponsors of the transatlantic cable project were worried by the effect of this distortion and the problem was eventually handed to Lord Kelvin. In 1855 Kelvin presented a paper to the Royal Society analysing the effect of pulse distortion. Kelvin's paper is the corner-stone of what is now called transmission-line theory.

The cause of the problems investigated by Kelvin lies in the physical properties of electrical conductors. At its simplest, the effect of a transmission line is to reduce the speed at which signals can change state.

The very first long-distance telecommunications networks were designed to transmit *digital* information from point to point. Indeed, very few people realize that the first digital data-transmission system linking North America with England was in use as early as 1866! Information was transmitted in binary form using two signal levels (no current = mark, current = space). The transmitter was the Morse key and the receiver the Morse telegraph.

In 1872 a Scotsman who had recently emigrated to the USA started work on a method of transmitting several signals simultaneously over a single line. The man was Alexander Graham Bell and the project was his *harmonic telegraph*. Bell's harmonic telegraph project failed, but it did lead to a spin-off in 1876 called the telephone. In one real sense the invention of the telephone was a disaster for the future of data-transmission systems, because the telephone network that sprang up in the 1880s was intended to transmit only speech signals in analog form.

A network designed to transmit intelligible speech (as opposed to hi-fi) must transmit analog signals in the frequency range 300–3300 Hz (i.e. the so called voice-band). Consequently, the telephone network now linking millions of subscribers across the world cannot be used to directly transmit digital data which requires a bandwidth extending to zero

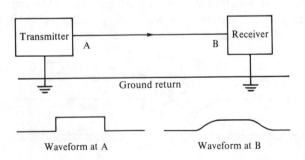

Fig. 9.11 Telegraph distortion.

frequency (i.e. d.c.). If the computer had been invented before the telephone, we would not have had this problem! Transmission paths that transmit or pass signals with frequency components from d.c. to some upper limit are called **baseband** channels. Transmission paths that transmit frequencies between a lower and an upper frequency are called **bandpass** channels.

Digital information from computers or peripherals must be converted into analog form before it is transmitted across a bandpass channel such as the PSTN. At the receiving end of the network, this analog signal is converted into digital form. Ironically enough, some of the links on modern long-haul telephone networks now transmit digital data, which means that the analog signals derived from the digital data must be converted to digital form before transmission over these links. In the future, it is possible that the PSTN will become entirely digital (as it was in the 1830s) and speech will be converted to digital form within the subscriber's own telephone.

Signals and modulation

The fundamental waveform of electronics is the sinewave of Fig. 9.12. Any transmission system can be characterized by drawing a graph of the attenuation (i.e. reduction in power) experienced by a sinewave transmitted across the network as a function of frequency. Figure 9.13 shows the frequency response of a telephone channel, where frequencies in the range 300–3000 Hz are transmitted with little attenuation. Frequencies above or below these limits are severely attenuated.

A digital signal is not a sinewave and the simple analytical techniques

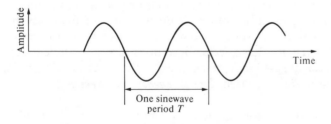

Fig. 9.12 The sinewave.

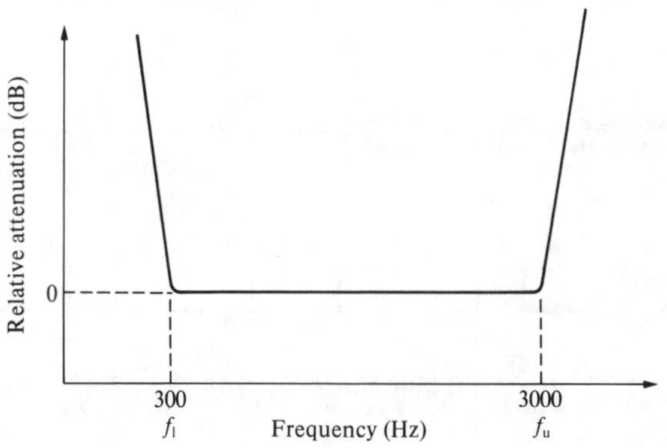

Fig. 9.13 The characteristics of the telephone network.

employed to design linear circuits cannot be used to determine what happens when a digital pulse train is transmitted across a linear network. It can, however, be shown that a digital pulse is made up of a series of sinewaves with frequencies of f, $2f$, $3f$, ..., where f is related to the width of the pulse. In theory the sinewaves extend up to infinite frequencies.

If a sequence of binary signals were presented to the transmitting end of a telephone network, the various sinewaves making up the binary pulses would be attenuated. Since the telephone network does not attenuate each frequency component equally, the sinewaves at the receiving end of the network would not add up to produce the same waveform that was presented to the transmitting end. In fact, the digital signals would be so severely distorted that they would be unrecognizable at the receiving end of the circuit. Distortion is introduced because both the high- and low-frequency sinewaves that make up the pulse are not transmitted by the network.

As the telephone network can transmit voice-band signals in the range 300–3000 Hz, various ways of converting digital information into speech-like signals have been investigated. Figure 9.14 shows how the digital data can be used to change, or *modulate*, the amplitude of a sinewave in sympathy with the digital signal. This is known as amplitude modulation (AM). The equipment needed to generate such a signal is called a *modulator* and that needed to extract the digital data from the resulting signal is called a *demodulator*. The interface between a computer and a telephone system is called a *modem* (modulator–demodulator). Because AM is more sensitive to noise (i.e. interference) than other modulation techniques, it is not widely used in data transmission.

Instead of modulating a sinewave by changing its amplitude, it is possible to vary its frequency in sympathy with the digital data. In a binary system, one frequency represents one binary value, and a different frequency represents the other. Figure 9.15 shows a frequency modulated (FM) signal. FM is widely used because it has a better tolerance to noise than AM (i.e. it is less affected by various forms of interference). As two frequencies are used to represent the two binary states, frequency modulation is sometimes referred to as *frequency-shift keying*, FSK.

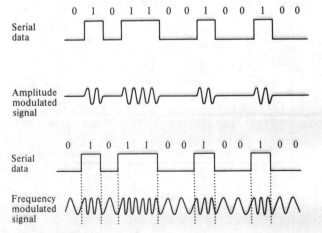

Fig. 9.14 Amplitude modulation.

Fig. 9.15 Frequency modulation.

Another form of modulation illustrated in Fig. 9.16 is *phase modulation* (PM). In this case, the phase of the sinewave is changed in sympathy with the digital signal. PM is widely used and has fairly similar characteristics to FM. If the phase change corresponding to a logical one is 180° and 0° (no change) corresponds to a logical zero, one bit of information can be transmitted at each time slot (Fig. 9.16). If, however, the phase is shifted by multiples of 90°, two bits at a time can be transmitted (Fig. 9.17).

Modems operate over a wide range of bit rates from 300 to 9600 bits/s (or even higher). In general, low bit rates are associated with the switched telephone network where some lines are very poor and signal impairments reduce the data rate to 2400 bits/s or below. The higher rates of 4800 bits/s and 9600 bits/s are generally found on privately leased lines where the telephone company offers a higher grade of service.

Today it is possible to transmit data at 19 200 bits/s over ordinary telephone lines by using very sophisticated transmission and reception

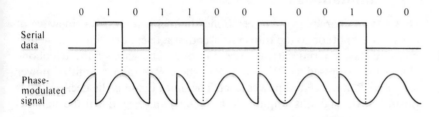

Fig. 9.16 Phase modulation.

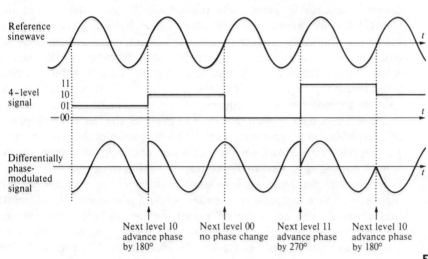

Fig. 9.17 Differential phase modulation.

Transmitted bits	Phase change (degrees)
00	0
01	90
10	180
11	270

techniques. By simultaneously changing the amplitude and phase of a signal, it is possible to transmit several bits of information at once in an arrangement called quadrature amplitude modulation (QAM). Typically, 16-point QAM uses sixteen different waveforms to transmit four bits at one go, and therefore the data rate is four times the signalling rate.

9.3 Data transmission across the PSTN

The most widely used transmission path for wide area digital data networks is the telephone system. We are going to discuss some of the characteristics of the telephone network and then describe a few of the modems used to interface digital equipment to the network.

9.3.1 Channel characteristics, impairments, and limitations

One way of characterizing a telephone channel is to apply a sinewave of constant amplitude to the transmitter end of a telephone link and then to measure its amplitude at the receiving end. The gain of the telephone channel is expressed as $10 \log_{10}(P_o/P_i)$, where P_i is the transmitted power level and P_o the received power level. The unit of gain is the decibel and is positive if the signal is amplified (i.e. $P_o > P_i$) and negative if the signal is attenuated (i.e. $P_o < P_i$).

By varying the frequency of the sinewave and recording the gain of the channel for each frequency, the relationship between the gain of the channel and the transmitted frequency can be derived. Such a graph is called the amplitude–frequency distortion characteristic of the channel (see Fig. 9.13). Note that the frequency axis (the horizontal axis) is invariably plotted on a logarithmic scale. An ideal channel should display a flat frequency response over all the frequencies of interest. That is, the gain should not vary with frequency. A similar type of graph is used to characterize hi-fi equipment. Figure 9.13 provides the frequency response of a hypothetical telephone channel. The attenuation of the channel in its passband is referred to a 0 dB level (i.e. a gain of unity) and attenuation at other frequencies is measured with respect to this value.

Figure 9.13 demonstrates how some frequencies are transmitted with little attenuation and how frequencies below f_1 (the lower cut-off point) and above f_u (the upper cut-off point) are rapidly attenuated, as the frequency moves away from the respective cut-off point. Most telephone channels are not as well behaved as the ideal channel of Fig. 9.13. The passband (between f_1 and f_u) is not usually so flat and the passband may sometimes be very much less than 300–3300 Hz. Because the attenuation against frequency plot is not flat, we call this characteristic the channel's amplitude–frequency *distortion*.

Unfortunately, the graph of Fig. 9.13 does not tell the whole story. Signals suffer not only from attenuation distortion but from *phase distortion*. Unless the reader has a knowledge of signal theory, he or she is unlikely to be familiar with this concept. Phase distortion is related to the time delay experienced by the various sinewaves making up a particular digital sequence. That is, if each sinewave from which a particular pulse sequence is composed suffers a different delay in travelling through the network, the series of sinewaves at the receiving end of the network will add up to produce a waveform with a very different shape to the one that was originally transmitted. All that need be said here is that the phase distortion introduced by a telephone channel distorts the **shape** of transmitted pulses, making it difficult to distinguish between signals representing a logical zero and those representing a logical one. Equipment can be designed to overcome some of the effects of the amplitude and phase distortion introduced by a telephone channel. Such equipment is called an **equalizer** and is associated with high-speed transmission systems where the effects of distortion are more severe.

Figure 9.18 defines the limits of acceptance of attenuation–frequency distortion for a telephone channel between a single transmitter and receiver. The shaded area represents the forbidden region of unacceptable attenuation. If a real telephone channel has an amplitude–frequency distortion characteristic that falls outside the envelope of Fig. 9.18, the telephone company should try to correct the faulty line or equipment.

The reader might now be tempted to think that any signal can be transmitted across a telephone channel, as long as it falls within the envelope described by Fig. 9.18. We shall soon see that although it is technically possible to do this, there are other factors.

An analog channel provided by the PSTN is a linear channel in the sense that the output of the channel is the **linear** sum of all the inputs to the channel. This means that it is possible to transmit two signals in different parts of the channel's bandwidth and then to split them up at the receiver. Digital systems do not have this property—it is not generally possible to add two digital signals together at one end of a channel and then separate them at the other end.

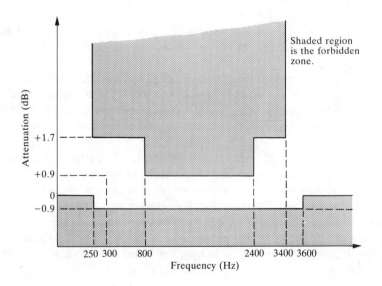

Fig. 9.18 Limits of acceptance for attenuation–frequency distortion.

Because analog channels have the ability to transmit more than one signal at once, the PTTs (in many countries PTT = post, telegraph and telecommunications body) have allocated certain parts of the telephone channel's bandwidth to signalling purposes. Human speech does not contain appreciable energy within these signalling bands and a normal telephone conversation does not affect the switching and control equipment using these frequencies.

A consequence of the use of certain frequencies for signalling purposes is that data transmission systems must not generate signals falling within specified bands. Figure 9.19 shows the internationally agreed restriction on signals transmitted by equipment connected to the PSTN. Note that any signals transmitted in the ranges 500–800 Hz or 1800–2600 Hz must have levels 38 dB below the maximum in-band signal level.

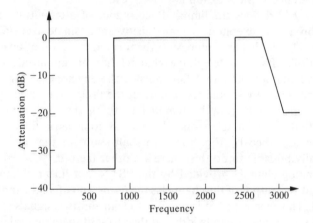

Fig. 9.19 Restriction on energy content of transmitted signals.

9.3.2 Noise and telephone channels

A perfect telephone channel would deliver to the receiver an exact copy of the signal presented at the transmitter. We have just seen that the amplitude–frequency characteristics of the channel distort the shape of the transmitted signal. Another source of signal impairment is called *noise*. Noise is the generic term for unwanted signals that are added to the received signal.

The most common form of noise is called *thermal noise* and is caused by the random motion of electrons in matter. Thermal noise appears to human listeners as the background hiss on telephone, radio, and television circuits. Thermal noise is frequently referred to as *Gaussian noise* because of its particular statistical properties. There is no way in which thermal noise can be removed once it has been added to a signal. The amount of thermal noise depends on the temperature of the system and its bandwidth. Only by cooling the system or by reducing its bandwidth can we reduce the effects of thermal noise. Receivers designed to pick up the weak signals received from distant space vehicles are cooled in liquid nitrogen to minimize the effects of thermal noise on a received signal. In general, the contribution of thermal noise to all other forms of noise is not usually the limiting factor in switched telephone networks.

Telephone channels are prone to many sources of man-made (i.e. avoidable) forms of noise that are far more harmful than thermal noise. *Cross-talk* is noise picked up from other circuits due to unwanted electrical, capacitive, or magnetic coupling. In everyday terminology, we can think of cross-talk as 'crossed lines'. Careful shielding of cables and isolation of circuits can reduce cross-talk. Another form of noise is *impulsive noise*, which produces the clicks and crackles on telephone circuits. Impulsive noise is caused by transients when heavy loads are switched near telephone circuits, lightning, dirty and intermittent electrical connections. Impulsive noise accounts for the majority of transmission errors in telephone networks and is worse in switched circuits than in private leased lines.

Yet another form of noise is caused by *echoes*. When the transmitted signal reaches the receiver, none of it should be echoed back to the transmitter. Sometimes the *echo cancellors* at each end of a telephone channel may be poorly adjusted and permit a transmitted signal to be echoed from the receiver back to the transmitter and then back again to the receiver. When this happens, the receiver gets the transmitted signal plus a time-delayed and attenuated version of the transmitted signal. The echo can be sufficiently large to affect the operation of the receiver.

The above forms of noise are called *additive* because they are added to the received signal. Another class of noise is called *multiplicative* noise and is caused by *multiplying* the received signal by a noise signal. The most common form of multiplicative noise is called *phase jitter* and is caused by random errors in the phase of the clock used to sample the received signal.

9.4 Modems

We are now going to look at some of the modems used to transmit digital data over the PSTN.

If digital data is to be transmitted from one point to another across a telephone channel, it is necessary that the modems at each end of the transmission path be compatible. Because of the variation in the quantity of telephone channels and the economics (i.e. cost) of modems, there are a number of different types of modem. Generally, as the speed of a modem goes up, so does its price. A 9600 bits/s modem may cost many times more than a modem operating at 300 bits/s.

There are, unfortunately, two sets of standards for modems. In the USA the scene has been dominated by the Bell System, which has devised a series of *de facto* standards for modems. Outside the USA, modem standards have been determined by the International Consultative Committee on Telegraphy and Telephony (CCITT). Both these organizations have produced standards for the same transmission rates, but the modulation techniques employed by Bell are not compatible with those of the CCITT. For example, a CCITT modem operating at 1200 bits/s uses FSK (i.e. frequency-shift keying) with a 1300 Hz signal representing a logical one and a 2100 Hz signal representing a logical zero. The Bell 202C modem operates with frequencies of 1070 Hz and 1270 Hz.

Like almost everything else associated with computer technology, the modem is essentially a simple device with so many variants that its simplicity is obscured by a mass of details. Before describing actual modems, we list some of their parameters.

Transmission rate.　The transmission rate of a modem is a measure of the speed at which it transmits or receives digital information. A modem's transmission rate should not be confused with the frequency or frequencies used in the modulation process. Typical transmission rates are 75, 300, 600, 1200, 2400, 4800, and 9600 baud. Unfortunately, baud rates of more than 2400 are not available over switched telephone channels. Higher rates are possible on private channels which are rented from the PTT (e.g. Bell Northern, AT and T in the USA and British Telecom in the UK).

Modulation method.　Most low- and medium-speed modems use frequency modulation to transport information. However, the frequencies chosen to represent a logical one or a logical zero vary with a number of factors. High-speed modems employ phase modulation and various types of QAM (quadrature amplitude modulation) in an attempt to raise the baud rate without increasing the modulation frequency.

Channel type.　Some modems operate in a half-duplex mode, permitting a communication path in only one direction at a time. Others support full-duplex operation with simultaneous, two-way communication. Note that full-duplex operation does not necessarily imply two *equal* channels. Some systems permit a relatively high data rate (e.g. 1200 baud) in one direction and a low data rate in the other, or reverse, direction (e.g. 75 baud).

Originate/answer modems.　Whenever information is exchanged between two modems, one modem is called the *originating* modem because it is at the end of the end of the channel that carried out the dialling and set up the channel. The *answer* modem is at the end of the channel that receives the call. Many modems can both originate calls and answer calls, but some modems are answer only and cannot originate a call. Originate and answer modems employ different frequencies to represent ones and zeros (when using frequency modulation).

Modem standards.　As stated above, modem standards fall into two groups—those standardized by the CCITT and those standardized by the Bell Telephone Company.

Asynchronous/synchronous.　An asynchronous data transmission system transmits information in the form of, typically, 8-bit characters with periods of inactivity between characters. A synchronous system transmits a continuous stream of bits without pauses, even when the bits are carrying no actual user information. Modems are designed to operate with either asynchronous or synchronous data streams. Low-speed transmission system usually adopt asynchronous transmission system and high-speed transmission systems (over 2400 baud) are invariably synchronous.

Typical modem standards

The parameters of four modems are given below.

Bell 103
Mode: 300 baud, full-duplex, asynchronous, FSK

Transmit frequency (originate)	Space = 1070 Hz, Mark = 1270 Hz
Receive frequency (originate)	Space = 2025 Hz, Mark = 2225 Hz
Transmit frequency (answer)	Space = 2025 Hz, Mark = 2225 Hz
Receive frequency (answer)	Space = 1070 Hz, Mark = 1270 Hz

Bell 202
Mode: 1200 baud, half-duplex, asynchronous, FSK

Transmit frequency	Space = 2200 Hz, Mark = 1200 Hz
Receive frequency	Space = 2200 Hz, Mark = 1200 Hz

CCITT V21
Mode: 300 baud, full-duplex, asynchronous, FSK

Transmit frequency (originate)	Space = 1180 Hz, Mark = 980 Hz
Receive frequency (originate)	Space = 1850 Hz, Mark = 1650 Hz
Transmit frequency (answer)	Space = 1850 Hz, Mark = 1650 Hz
Receive frequency (answer)	Space = 1180 Hz, Mark = 980 Hz

CCITT V23 Mode 2
Mode:1200 baud, half-duplex, asynchronous, FSK

Transmit frequency	Space = 2100 Hz, Mark = 1300 Hz
Receive frequency	Space = 2100 Hz, Mark = 1300 Hz.

The frequency spectra of these four modem standards are illustrated in Figs. 9.20–9.23. Note that both half-duplex systems have a narrow-band *back channel* or reverse channel. A reverse channel is a low-speed communication path in the opposite direction to the main channel. For example, the Bell 202 1200 baud modem has a 5 baud reverse channel and the CCITT V23 mode 2, 1200 baud, modem has a 75 baud reverse channel. The reader might be forgiven if he or she wonders what the difference is between a full-duplex modem and a half-duplex modem with

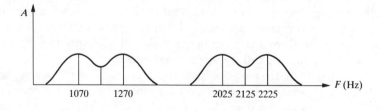

Fig. 9.20 Bell 103 full-duplex frequency spectrum.

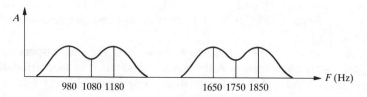

Fig. 9.21 CCITT V.21 full-duplex frequency spectrum.

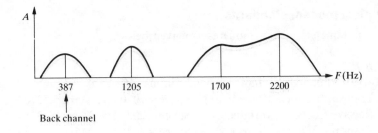

Fig. 9.22 Bell 202 half-duplex frequency spectrum.

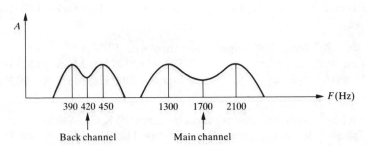

Fig. 9.23 CCITT V.23 mode 2 half-duplex frequency spectrum.

a reverse channel! The answer is that a full-duplex channel is able to transmit equally in both directions. Modems with reverse channels are able to transmit only limited information across the reverse channel. A reverse channel offers an excellent mechanism for error control because requests to retransmit lost data can be made via the reverse channel. Another application of reverse channels is in accessing data bases or similar software. The forward or main channel is used by the computer to terminal link to display data on the user's screen. The reverse channel is used by the terminal-to-computer link because the user is sending relatively little data to the computer.

9.4.1 Modems and equalization

One of the effects of the distortion introduced by the attenuation–frequency and phase–frequency characteristics of a transmission path is to cause the *time dispersion* of a transmitted signal element. Time dispersion simply means that a signal is spread out in time and has a longer duration at the receiver than it had at the transmitter. Despite its fancy name, time dispersion is a commonplace event. When you go to a concert in a large hall, the music from the instruments suffers time dispersion. When it happens to sound, we call the effect *reverberation*.

If an infinitely narrow unit pulse is applied to one end of the telephone channel, it appears at the other end as a continuous rounded waveform with a duration greater than about $\frac{1}{3}$ ms (Fig. 9.24). The value of $\frac{1}{3}$ ms is given by the reciprocal of the bandwidth of the channel (i.e. 1/3000 Hz). The waveform of Fig. 9.24 is known as the *impulse response* of the channel.

Tests over telephone circuits have shown that the time dispersion of a digital signal does not normally exceed 6 ms, but it can occasionally be very much greater. Even at a relatively low signal element rate of 600

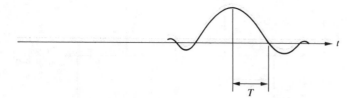

Fig. 9.24 The received signal from a single transmitted pulse.

baud, an individual signal element is likely to be lengthened so that it overlaps up to five of its immediately neighbouring elements. This overlap is called **inter-symbol interference**. Fortunately, the dispersed signal energy represents usually only a fraction of the energy of the signal in the correct time slot, so that the effect of the inter-symbol interference is negligible. At higher transmission rates, inter-symbol interference becomes the limiting factor in correctly decoding the received data.

We will demonstrate the effect of inter-symbol interference on the transmission of a simple pulse train. Suppose a data-transmission system produces pulses with an interval T seconds between adjacent pulses. Assume that each of these pulses may have an amplitude of $+1$ or -1 units.

If we are concerned only with the amplitude of the pulse at integer multiples of T seconds, then the received pulse can be represented by the sequence of Fig. 9.25, or numerically by the vector $0, -\frac{1}{4}, \frac{1}{4}, 1, \frac{1}{4}, -\frac{1}{4}, 0$, which is called the **sampled impulse response** of the channel. Suppose a message consisting of the bits $-1,1,1,1,-1,1$, is transmitted. The received signal is given by the waveform of Fig. 9.26 and is made up of the sum of six time-shifted impulse responses, each of which is multiplied by $+1$ or -1 depending on the polarity of the transmitted signal element.

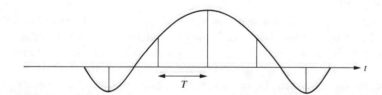

Fig. 9.25 The sampled impulse response of a channel.

From Fig. 9.26 it can be seen that the original message is **recoverable** simply by sampling at the **correct** instant (i.e. sampling the received signal when the component due to a transmitted signal element is -1). Where the inter-symbol interference is worse than this, simple circuits alone cannot recover the transmitted data.

t	2t	3t	4t	5t	6t	7t	8t	9t	10t	11t	12t
−1(0	−0.25	0.25	1	0.25	−0.25	0)					
	1(0	−0.25	0.25	1	0.25	−0.25	0)				
		1(0	−0.25	0.25	1	0.25	−0.25	0)			
			1(0	−0.25	0.25	1	0.25	−0.25	0)		
				−1(0	−0.25	0.25	1	0.25	−0.25	0)	
					1(0	−0.25	0.25	1	0.25	−0.25	0)
0.00	0.25	−0.50	−1.00	0.75	2.00	0.50	−0.75	0.50	0.50	−0.25	0.0

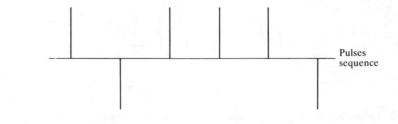

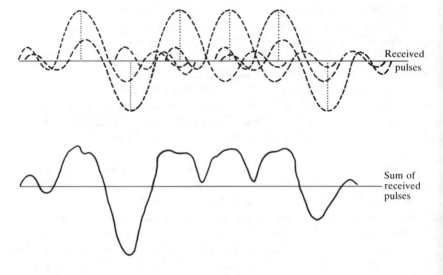

Fig. 9.26 The received signal due to a sequence of six pulses.

Equalization

Equalization is a process whereby some of the effects of the distortion introduced by a transmission path may be nullified or, at least, reduced. Conceptually, an equalizer may be thought of as a filter, whose attenuation–frequency and group-delay–frequency responses are the inverse of those of the channel. Equalization is carried out on the line or is performed within the modem. Another term for equalization is *line conditioning*. In fact, the equalization of a telephone channel is analogous to the use of a graphic equalizer in a hi-fi system to correct the frequency distortion introduced by loudspeaker and the acoustics of the room.

On a fixed line (i.e. a non-dialled line), it is possible to set up the equalizer once and for all and then to forget it. Unfortunately, on a switched line (especially at high data rates) every time a channel is obtained by dialling a new path through the telephone network, a different transmission is set up requiring a unique form of equalization. For this reason, automatic adaptive equalizers exist which adapt to any changes in the nature of the distortion introduced by the channel.

It is difficult to describe the equalizer in any detail without resorting to discrete mathematics and the Z-transform. One of the simplest forms of equalizer is implemented by means of a *linear transversal filter* which consists of a series of delay units and attenuators and an adder as illustrated in Fig. 9.27. Conceptually, you can think of an equalizer as

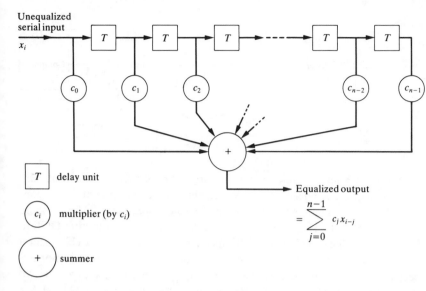

Unequalized
serial input

x_i

c_0 c_1 c_2 c_{n-2} c_{n-1}

$+$

$\boxed{T}$ delay unit

c_i multiplier (by c_i)

$+$ summer

Equalized output

$$= \sum_{j=0}^{n-1} c_j x_{i-j}$$

Fig. 9.27 The linear transversal equalizer.

undoing the effects of time dispersion by cancelling out the effects of neighbouring pulses on a received pulse.

9.5 The RS232C physical layer protocol

The first really universal standard for the physical layer was published in 1969 by the Electronic Industry Association (EIA) in the USA and is known as RS232C (Recommended Standard 232 version C). Because 1969 is such a long time ago in the world of electronics and predates the microprocessor revolution, RS232C could not have been developed for today's world. It was intended for a specialized purpose but has now been adapted by many manufacturers to suit modern data links. The development of such an early standard is good because RSC232C was there ready to be used when today's new microcomputer equipment first appeared. Unfortunately, it was not optimized for such a role.

Early in the development of data transmission systems, RS232C was created as a standard for the connection between computer equipment and modems. Any manufacturer's computer equipment can be simply plugged into another manufacturer's modem, as long as both systems conform to RS232C. Such a standard allows one manufacturer to produce equipment for a different manufacturer's computers. Although it is sometimes said that standards limit progress by enforcing a rigid conformity, the reverse is true. Without agreed standards, a manufacturer is very wary of entering a new market. Who would produce LP gramophone records if there were twenty different speeds instead of the standard speed of $33\frac{1}{3}$ r.p.m.?

RS232C specifies the plug and socket at the modem and the digital equipment (i.e. their mechanics), the nature of the transmission path and the signals required to control the operation of the modem (i.e. the functionality of the data link).

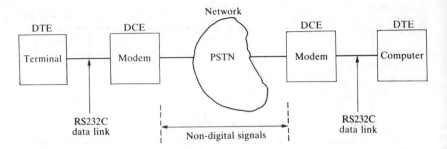

Fig. 9.28 Linking DTE to DCE with RS232C data link.

From the point of view of the standard, the modem is known as **data communications equipment** (DCE) and the digital equipment to be connected to the modem is known as **data terminal equipment** (DTE). Figure 9.28 illustrates the role played by the RS232C standard in linking DCE to DTE. A corollary is that RS232C specifies a link between a DTE and a DCE rather than a link between two similar devices. This is important because the RS232C standard is now largely used to link together two similar pieces of equipment (i.e. both ends of the data link are DTEs). We will soon see the significance of this.

Because RS232C was intended for DTE–DCE links, its functions are very largely those needed to control a modem. Unfortunately, the control functions provided by RS232C data links are not always suited to, or needed by, links between two DTEs. In practice, this means that a computer manufacturer and a printer manufacturer may both supply equipment with interfaces sold as **conforming to** RS232C. Yet each manufacturer may choose to implement a subset of the many functions provided by RS232C, as not all the functions are required by their particular applications. Unfortunately, they may choose slightly different subsets, making it impossible to plug the printer into the computer with a cable and connector conforming to RS232C.

9.5.1 Basic RS232C control lines

The next step in our examination of the RS232C standard is to describe the *functions* carried out by the RS232C signals flowing between the DTE and the DCE. It is this aspect of RS232C that causes all the trouble when printer X is connected to computer Y.

The absolute minimum service provided by an RS232C data link is the point-to-point transmission of data without any associated control functions. Figure 9.29 illustrates such a subset. Information is transmitted between DTE and DCE (or DTE and DTE) in a single direction (half-duplex) or in two directions (full-duplex) providing the four variations in Fig. 9.29.

Note that when DTE is connected to DCE (Fig. 9.29(c)), the corresponding pins of the DTE and DCE are connected together (i.e. pins 2 to 2, 3 to 3). This is because the data-out pin of the DTE is the corresponding data-in pin of the DCE. When DTE is connected to DTE (Figs. 9.29(b) and 9.29(d)), it is necessary to *cross over* pins 2 and 3 as shown.

Relatively few data links use the absolute minimum subset of functions (a)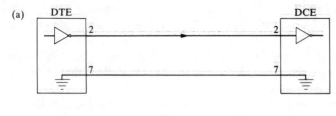

(b)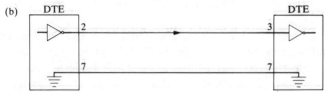

Fig. 9.29 The RS232C minimal subset: (a) DTE connected to DCE half-duplex; (b) DTE connected to DTE half-duplex; (c) DTE connected to DCE full-duplex; (d) DTE connected to DTE full-duplex.

(c)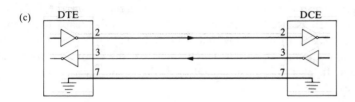

(d)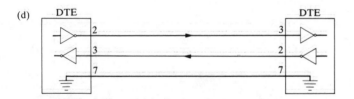

provided by the connection in Fig. 9.29. However, even modest peripherals such as printers require some form of control. Figure 9.30 illustrates the most widely used control lines. The arrows at the end of signal lines show the direction of data transmission with respect to the DTE. The function of these control lines is described below. Here we reintroduce two terms: asserted and negated. When a signal is said to be asserted, it is placed in the state which causes its *named* action to take place. Conversely, when a signal is negated, it is placed in the state that stops or defeats its named action. For example, when *request to send* is asserted, it indicates that a device is ready to transmit data. When it is negated, it indicates that the transmitter is unable to send data. These terms have been adopted because they remove the need to remember whether a logical one or a logical zero causes some action to take place. Asserted simply means *place in the active state*, irrespective of whether that state is electrically high or low. RS232C control signals are asserted by placing them in an electrically high state.

We met some of the RS232C control signals in Chapter 7 when we introduced the ACIA—the asynchronous communications adaptor that interfaces a computer to a serial data link. Note that the ACIA uses active-low control signals (e.g. $\overline{\text{RTS}}$), while the RS232C link uses active-high

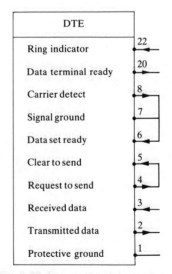

Fig. 9.30 The most widely used lines of RS232C.

control signals (e.g. RTS). For this reason, the control inputs and outputs of the ACIA are interfaced to RS232C lines via inverting buffers.

Request to send (RTS).   This is a signal from the DTE to the DCE. When asserted, RTS indicates to the DCE that the DTE wishes to transmit data to it.

Clear to send (CTS).   This is a signal from the DCE to the DTE and, when asserted, indicates that the DCE is ready to receive data from the DTE.

Data set ready (DSR).   This is a signal from the DCE to the DTE which indicates the readiness of the DCE. When this signal is asserted, the DCE is able to receive from the DTE. DSR indicates that the DCE (usually a modem) is switched on and is in its normal functioning mode (as opposed to its self-test mode).

Data terminal ready (DTR).   This is a signal from the DTE to the DCE. When asserted, DTR indicates that the DTE is ready to accept data from the DCE. In systems with a modem, it maintains the connection and keeps the channel open. If DTR is negated, the communication path is broken. In everyday terms negating DTR is the same as hanging up a phone.

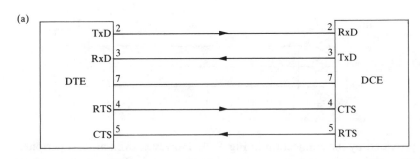

Fig. 9.31 Connecting RTS to CTS
(a) DTE to DCE; (b) DTE to DTE;
(c) locally.

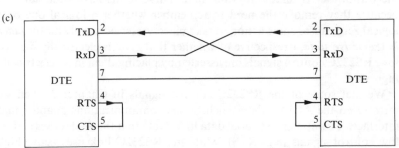

The way in which the RTS and CTS pair of control signals is applied is illustrated by Fig. 9.31. In Fig. 9.31(a), DTE is connected to DCE without any lines being crossed over. In Fig. 9.31(b), DTE is connected to DTE and pins 4 (RTS) and 5 (CTS) are crossed over. CTS and RTS must be crossed over because the RTS output of one side of the data link serves as the CTS input at the other side.

Sometimes, DTE is connected to a DCE or a DTE and the RTS/CTS handshaking procedure between the pair is not required (or is not implemented), *but* the DTE requires a response to the assertion of its RTS output. Figure 9.31(c) shows how this situation can be handled. The RTS output is connected *directly* to the CTS input at the connector so that the DTE automatically receives a handshake whenever it asserts its RTS output. Of course, in this mode the DTE may 'think' that the remote DCE/DTE is ready to receive data when it is not.

9.6 Other physical channels

The majority of transmission paths are composed of twisted pairs, coaxial cable, radio links or fibre optic links.

A *twisted pair* is nothing more than two wires that are twisted around each other (as opposed to running parallel to each other). Twisted pairs are used to transport low-frequency signals over relatively short distances. For example, twisted pairs are used to connect a telephone to its local exchange or a computer to a modem a few metres away.

Coaxial cable is, essentially, the type of cable used to connect televisions to antennas and consists of an inner conductor entirely surrounded by an outer conductor. Between the two conductors lies an insulating material, called a dielectric. Sometimes the outer conductor is *braided* or woven from fine copper wire and sometimes it is a solid conductor. Figure 9.32 illustrates the structure of coaxial cable (often abbreviated to co-ax), whose thickness may vary between 5 and 25 mm. Coaxial cables are able to operate at high data rates (greater than 100M bits/s) and are used over

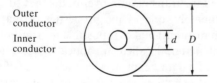

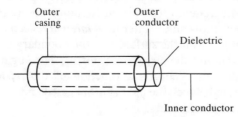

Fig. 9.32 Coaxial cable.

short to medium distances. Coaxial cable is used to transmit voice-band telephone signals (permitting up to 10 000 channels per cable), television signals (as in cable television) and digital signals in certain classes of local area network. Transmission over distances greater than 1 km is achieved by feeding the signal into an amplifier (called a repeater) and regenerating it before sending it on its way down the coaxial cable.

Radio links permit data to be transmitted over medium to long distances without a physical connection between adjacent stations (apart from the 'ether' or 'free space' that separates all objects). Fibre optic links use a cable similar to coaxial cable, but which can transmit much higher rates of data over longer distances without regeneration. We look at fibre optic links first and then return to radio links.

9.6.1 Fibre optic links

The very first signalling systems used optical technology: the signal fire, the smoke signal and later the semaphore. Such transmission systems were limited to line-of-sight operation and could not be used in fog. The ability to transmit electrical signals over wires independently of weather conditions and to process the signals electronically made the direct electronic circuit of the telegraph and the telephone the preferred method of data transmission for a long time.

Today, the confluence of a number of different technologies has, once again, made it possible to use light to transmit messages. Semiconductor technology has given us the laser and the LED (light emitting diode) that can directly convert pulses of electricity into pulses of light in both the visible and infra-red (IR) parts of the spectrum. Similarly, semiconductor electronics has created devices that can turn light directly into electricity so that we can detect the pulses of light from the laser or LED. The relatively new science of materials technology has given us the ability to create a fine thread of transparent material called an *optical fibre*. The optical fibre provides a simple method of piping light from its source to its detector just as the coaxial cable pipes electronic signals from one point to another.

As every one knows, light can be transmitted only in a straight line and therefore cannot be used for transmission over paths that turn corners or go round bends. Fortunately, one of the properties of matter (i.e. the speed of light in a given medium) makes it possible to transmit light down a long thin cylinder of material called an optical fibre. Figure 9.33(a) demonstrates the effect of a light beam striking the surface of an optically dense material in a less dense medium such as air. Light rays within the dense material striking the surface at nearly right angles to the surface pass from the material into the surrounding air. Light rays striking the surface at a shallow angle suffer *total internal reflection* which means they are reflected just as if the surface (i.e. the boundary between the optically dense material and the air) were a mirror. The angle (θ_c) at which total internal reflection occurs is a function of the *refractive index* of the material through which the light is propagated and the surface material at which the reflection occurs.

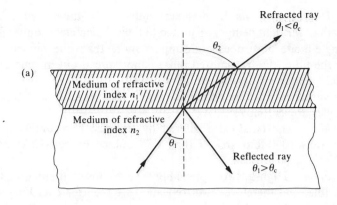

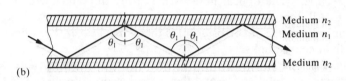

Fig. 9.33 Total internal reflection.

By drawing out a single long thread of a transparent material such as plastic or glass, we can create an optical fibre as illustrated in Fig. 9.34. The optical fibre consists of three parts, the core itself that transmits light, a *cladding* that has a different index of reflection to the core and hence causes total internal reflection at its interface with the core, and a sheath that provides the optical fibre with protection and mechanical strength. It should be noted that the diameter of the optical fibre is very small indeed—often less than 100 μm. Sometimes there is an abrupt junction between the core and cladding (a step-index fibre) and sometimes the refractive index of the material varies continuously from the core to the cladding (a graded index fibre). Graded index fibres are difficult to produce and therefore more expensive than step-index fibres, but they offer lower attenuation and a higher bandwidth.

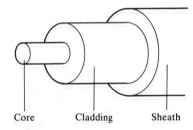

Fig. 9.34 The optical fibre.

Light entering at one end of the fibre is transmitted along the fibre by bouncing of the sides due to the internal reflections at the fibre surface. Figure 9.33(b) demonstrates this effect. Fibre optic links can be created from many materials but a fibre drawn from high-quality fused quartz has the least attenuation and the greatest bandwidth (e.g. the attenuation can be less than 1 dB/km). The bandwidth of fibre optic links can range from 200 MHz to over 10 GHz (10^9 Hz) which represents very high data rates indeed.

There are several types of optical fibre, each with its own special properties (e.g. attenuation per km, bandwidth and cost). Two generic classes of optical fibre are multimode and single mode fibres. *Multimode* fibres operate as described by bouncing the light from side to side as it travels down the fibre. Since a light beam can take many paths down the cable, the transit time of the beam is spread out and a single pulse of light is received as a considerably broadened pulse. Consequently, a multimode fibre cannot be used at very high pulse rates.

A *single-mode* fibre has a diameter only a few times that of the wavelength of the light being transmitted (a typical diameter is only 5 μm). As a single-mode fibre does not support more than one optical path through the fibre, the transmitted pulse is not spread out in time and a very much greater bandwidth can be achieved.

The advantages of a fibre optic link (Fig. 9.35) over more conventional technologies are as follows:

Bandwidth. The bandwidth offered by the best fibre optic links is approximately 1000-fold greater than that offered by coaxial or radio links.

Attenuation. High-quality optical fibres have a lower attenuation than coaxial cables and therefore fewer repeaters are required over long links (e.g. undersea cables).

Mechanics. The optical fibre itself is truly tiny and therefore light-weight. All that is needed is a suitable sheath to prevent it from mechanical damage or corrosion. It is therefore cheaper to lay fibre optic links than coaxial links.

Immunity to EM interference. Fibre optic links are not affected by electromagnetic interference and therefore they do not suffer the effect of noise induced by anything from nearby lightning strikes to cross-talk from adjacent cables. Furthermore, since they do not use electronic signals to convey information, there is no signal leakage from an optical fibre and therefore it is much harder for unauthorized persons to eavesdrop.

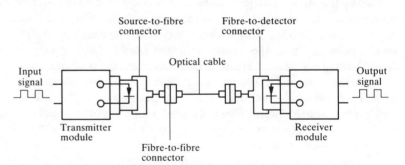

Fig. 9.35 The fibre optic link.

9.6.2 Radio links

Radio links transmit information through the ether and do not require a physical medium to be laid down between the transmitter and receiver. Radio links can be characterized by the frequency of the radio signals used to transport data and whether or not they are terrestrial or satellite links. Figure 9.36 illustrates a portion of the electromagnetic spectrum used to transmit information.

Radio signals in the frequency range 100 kHz to about 400 MHz are used for conventional purposes—terrestrial radio and television broadcasting. Frequencies above 1 GHz are called **microwaves** and are used for many applications ranging from radar to information transmission to heating. Microwaves have two important properties. They travel in straight lines and they can be modulated at high frequencies to carry high

Figure 9.36 The radio frequency spectrum

Frequency band*	Name	Typical uses
3–30 kHz	Very low frequency (VLF)	Long-range navigation; sonar
30–300 kHz	Low frequency (LF)	Navigational aids; radio beacons
300–3000 kHz	Medium frequency (MF)	Maritime radio; direction finding; distress and calling; commercial AM radio
3–30 MHz	High frequency (HF)	Search and rescue; aircraft comm. with ships; telegraph; telephone; and facsimile; ship-to-coast
30–300 MHz	Very high frequency (VHF)	FM radio; land transportation; air traffic control; taxi cab; police; navigational aids
0.3–3 GHz	Ultra high frequency (UHF)	UHF television channels; radiosonde; navigational aids; surveillance radar; satellite comm.; radio altimeters;
3–30 GHz	Super high frequency (SHF)	microwave links; airborne radar; approach radar; weather radar; common carrier land mobile
30–300 GHz	Extremely high frequency (EHF)	Railway service; radar landing systems; experimental

* Abbreviations: kHz=kilohertz=10^3 Hz; MHz=megahertz=10^6 Hz; GHz=gigahertz=10^9 Hz.

data rates. As microwaves travel in straight lines it is necessary to transmit them from tower to tower and few industrial cities are without some landmark festooned with microwave dishes (e.g. Telecom Tower in London). Because of the earth's curvature, microwave repeaters are needed every 100 km or so (depending on the terrain and the height of the transmitter and receiver dishes).

Since the late 1960s satellite microwave links have become increasingly more important. A satellite placed in *geostationary* orbit 35 785 km above the equator takes 24 hours to orbit the earth. As the earth itself rotates once every 24 hours, a satellite in a geostationary orbit *appears* to hang motionless in space and remain over the same spot. Such a satellite can be used to transmit messages from one point on the earth's surface to another point up to approximately 12 000 km away, as illustrated in Fig. 9.37. Theoretically three satellites each separated by 120° could completely cover a band around the earth. However, receivers at extreme limits of reception would have their dishes pointing along the ground at a tangent to the surface of the earth. As the minimum practical angle of elevation is about 5°, satellites should not be more than about 110° apart for reliable operation. Data is transmitted up to the satellite on the up-link frequency, regenerated and transmitted down again at the down-link frequency. Suitable microwave or coaxial links transmit data from a local source to and from the national satellite terminals.

Satellites are used to transmit television signals, telephone traffic and

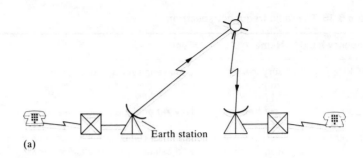

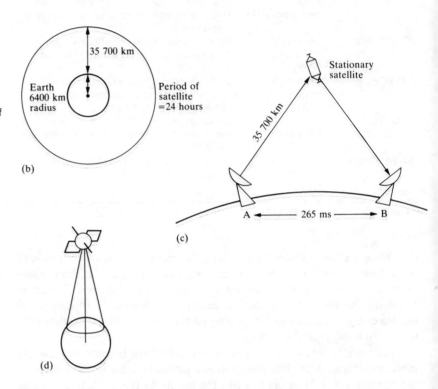

Fig. 9.37 The satellite link:
(a) structure of the link; (b) the
orbit; (c) transmission delay;
(d) geostationary orbits; (e) field of
view is approximately one third of
the surface of the Earth.

data signals. Data signals can be transmitted at rates greater than 50M
bits/s which is many times faster than that offered by the public switched
telephone network but rather less than that offered by the fibre optic link.
Some believe that many satellite links will ultimately be replaced by fibre
optic links. The only real advantage of the satellite is its ability to
broadcast from one transmitter to many receivers. It may well be that in
years to come, satellites will be used almost exclusively for domestic
broacasting purposes.

Satellite systems are generally very reliable. The sheer size of the
investment in the satellite and its transport vehicle means that engineers
have spent much time and energy in designing reliable satellites. Unfortunately, a satellite does not have an infinite lifespan. Its solar power panels
gradually degrade due to the effect of the powerful radiation field

experienced in space, and it eventually runs out of the fuel required by its rocket jets to keep it pointing accurately at the surface of the earth.

Satellites operate in the 1–10 GHz band since frequencies below 1 GHz are subject to interference from terrestrial sources of noise, and frequencies above 10 GHz are attenuated by the atmosphere. Satellite users have to take account of a problem imposed by the length of the transmission path (about 70 000 km). Microwaves travelling at the speed of light (300 000 km/s) take approximately 265 ms to travel from the source to their destination (Fig. 9.37c). Consequently it is impossible to receive a reply from a transmission in under 0.5 s. Data transmission modes using half-duplex become difficult to operate due to the long transit delay and the large turn around time. Satellite data links are better suited to full-duplex operation.

9.7 The data-link layer

Now that we have looked at some of the ways in which data is moved from one point to another by the physical layer, the next step is to examine the data-link layer. Here we are going to look at two popular protocols for the data-link layer—a character-oriented protocol and a bit-oriented protocol.

9.7.1 Character-oriented protocols

One of the tasks of the data link layer is to divide the stream of bits (or characters) it receives from the physical layer into blocks. At first sight, it might appear that dividing a continuous stream of bits or characters into meaningful units is a difficult task. Infactitisquiteaneasytasktoformbitsintowords. Here I have removed inter-word spacing in plain English text making it harder, but not impossible to read. Readers are able to make sense of the above sequence of characters by looking for recognizable groups corresponding to words. A similar technique can be applied to streams of characters (character-oriented protocols) or to streams of bits (bit-oriented protocols).

In character-oriented transmission the data to be transmitted is encoded in the form of (usually) ISO/ASCII characters. For example, the string 'Alan' is sent as the sequence of four seven-bit characters below. The individual letters are coded in hexadecimal form as: 'A' = 41, 'l' = 6C, 'a' = 61, 'n' = 6E.

Data stream = 1000001001101110000110111011

This string of bits is read from left to right, with the first bit (i.e. leftmost bit) representing the least significant bit of the 'A'.

What is needed is some method of identifying the beginning of a message. Once this has been done, the bits can be divided into groups of seven (or eight if a parity bit is used) for the duration of the message.

The ISO/ASCII code has a number of special characters specifically designed to control a data link. The *synchronous idle* character SYN ($16 or 0010110) is used to denote the beginning of a message. The receiver reads the incoming bits and ignores them until it sees a SYN character. Unfortunately, this simple scheme is flawed; the end of one character together with the beginning of the next may by chance look like a SYN character. To avoid this problem, two SYN characters are transmitted sequentially. If the receiver does see a SYN, it reads the next character. If this is also a SYN the start of a message is assumed to have been located, otherwise a false synchronization is assumed and the search for a valid SYN character continued.

Character-oriented protocols provide point-to-point communication between two stations. Like all data-link layer protocols, they both control the flow of information (message sequencing and error recovery) and they set up and maintain the transmission path.

Character-oriented protocols employ an alphabet of characters to represent data supplied from (or delivered to) higher levels and to carry out control functions. These are also called byte control oriented protocols (BOPs). A consequence of reserving special characters for control functions is that the transmitted data stream must not contain certain combinations of bits, as the will be interpreted as control characters. Fortunately, there are ways of getting round this problem. Note that character-oriented protocols may employ either synchronous or asynchronous serial transmission techniques.

Functions of the ISO/ASCII control characters

The most commonly used character set for character-oriented protocols is the ISO/ASCII set. ASCII stands for American Standard Code for Information Interchange and uses an 8-bit code. Seven bits define one of 128 characters and the eighth bit is an (optional) parity bit. The ISO/ASCII code has become an international standard and is also known as the 'CCITT Alphabet Number 5'. British standard BS 4730:1974 specifies the UK version of the ASCII code. Table 9.1 lists the 128 characters of the ISO/ASCII character code, thirty-two of which are dedicated to system control functions. The meaning of some of these control characters is given below. Readers with more important things to do may skip ahead to BiSync.

NUL (null). This is a fill-in character which may be added to or removed from a data stream without affecting the information content of the data stream.

SOH (start of heading). This is the first character of a heading of an information message.

STX (start of text). A character which precedes a text and which is used to terminate a heading.

ETX (end of text). A transmission control character which terminates a text.

EOT (end of transmission). A transmission control character which indicates the conclusion of the transmission of one or more text.

Table 9.1 The ISO coded character set for information interchange

					b_7	0	0	0	0	1	1	1	1
					b_6	0	0	1	1	0	0	1	1
					b_5	0	1	0	1	0	1	0	1
				column		0	1	2	3	4	5	6	7
b_4	b_3	b_2	b_1	row									
0	0	0	0	0		NUL	TC$_7$ (DLE)	SP	O	@	P	`	p
0	0	0	1	1		TC$_1$ (SOH)	DC$_1$	!	1	A	Q	a	q
0	0	1	0	2		TC$_2$ (STX)	DC$_2$	''	2	B	R	b	r
0	0	1	1	3		TC$_3$ (ETX)	DC$_3$	#	3	C	S	c	s
0	1	0	0	4		TC$_4$ (EOT)	DC$_4$	$	4	D	T	d	t
0	1	0	1	5		TC$_5$ (ENQ)	TC$_5$ (NAK)	%	5	E	U	e	u
0	1	1	0	6		TC$_6$ (ACK)	TC$_6$ (SYN)	&	6	F	V	f	v
0	1	1	1	7		BEL	TC$_{10}$ (ETB)	´	7	G	W	g	w
1	0	0	0	8		FE$_0$ (BS)	CAN	(	8	H	X	h	x
1	0	0	1	9		FE$_1$ (HT)	EM	)	9	I	Y	i	y
1	0	1	0	10		FE$_2$ (LF)	SUB	*	:	J	Z	j	z
1	0	1	1	11		FE$_3$ (VT)	ESC	+	;	K	[	k	{
1	1	0	0	12		FE$_4$ (FF)	IS$_4$ (FS)	,	<	L	\	l	|
1	1	0	1	13		FE$_3$ (CR)	IS$_3$ (GS)	–	=	M	]	m	}
1	1	1	0	14		SO	IS$_2$ (RS)	.	>	N	^	n	-
1	1	1	1	15		SI	IS$_1$ (US)	/	?	O	_	o	DEL

ENQ (enquiry).   A transmission control character used as a request from a remote station.

ACK (acknowledge).   A transmission control character transmitted by a receiver as an affirmative response to the sender.

BEL (bell).   A control character that rings a bell signalling the need for attention.

BS (backspace).   A format effector which moves the active position (the position at which the next character is to be printed) one character position backwards on the same line.

HT (horizontal tabulation).   A format effector which advances the active position to the next predetermined character position on the same line.

LF (line feed).   A format effector which advances the active position to the same character position of the next line.

VT (vertical tabulation).   A format effector which advances the active position to the same character position in the next predetermined line.

FF (form feed).   A format effector which advances the active position to the same character position on a predetermined line of the next form or page.

CR (carriage return).   A format effector which moves the active position to the first character position in the same line.

SO (shift out).   A control character used in conjunction with shift in and escape to extend the graphic set of the code. It may alter the meaning of the bit combinations which follow it until a shift in character is reached. The characters space and delete are not affected by shift out.

SI (shift in).   A control character which is used in conjunction with shift out and escape to extend the graphic character set of the code. It may reinstate the standard meaning of the bit combinations which follow it.

DLE (data link escape).   A transmission character which changes the meaning of a limited number of consecutively following characters. It is used exclusively to provide supplementary data transmission control functions. Only graphic characters and transmission control characters can be used in DLE sequences.

DC1 (device control 1).   A device control character primarily intended for turning on an ancillary device. It may also be used to restore a device to its basic mode of operation.

DC2 (device control 2).   A device control character primarily intended for turning on an ancillary device. It may also be used to set a device mode of operation (in which case DC1 is used to restore the device to the basic mode), or for any other device control function not provided by other DCs.

DC3 (device control 3).   A device control character primarily intended for turning off or stopping an ancillary device. This function may be a secondary-level stop, e.g. wait, pause, stand-by or halt (in which case DC1 is used to restore normal operation). If not used in this mode it may be used for any other device control function.

DC4 (device control 4).   A device control character primarily intended for turning off, stopping or interrupting an ancillary device. If not required for this purpose it may be used for any other device control function not provided by other DCs.

NAK (negative acknowledge).   A transmission control character transmitted by a receiver as a negative response to the sender.

SYN (synchronous idle).   A transmission control character used by a synchronous transmission system in the absence of any other character (the idle condition) to provide a signal from which synchronism may be achieved or retained between data-terminal equipment.

ETB (end of transmission block).   A transmission control character used to indicate the end of a transmission block of data where data is divided into such blocks.

CAN (cancel).   A character, or the first character of a sequence, indicating that the data item preceding it is in error. As a result this data item must be ignored.

EM (end of medium).   A control character that may be used to identify the physical end of a medium, or the end of the used portion of a medium, or the end of the wanted portion of data recorded in a medium. The position of this character does not necessarily correspond to the physical end of the medium.

SUB (substitute character).   A control character used in place of a character that has been found to be invalid or in error. SUB is intended to be introduced by automatic means.

ESC (escape).   A control character used to provide an additional control function. It alters the meaning of a limited number of consecutively following bit combinations which constitute the escape sequence.

FS	(file separator)	Control characters used to qualify data logically – the specific meaning of any character has to be defined for each application. These characters delimit information in the form of a file, group, record and unit respectively.
GS	(group separator)	
RS	(record separator)	
US	(unit separator)	

9.7.2 An example of a byte-oriented protocol

One of the most widely used character-oriented protocols is the binary synchronous, or BiSync, protocol originally devised by IBM. Information at the physical layer is transmitted *synchronously*. However, the BiSync protocol transmits information in the form of individual characters and the data-link layer is responsible for dividing the data from the physical layer into separate characters and the stream of characters into individual blocks or frames.

The BiSync message format is presented in Fig. 9.38. BiSync uses special characters in the ISO/ASCII code to perform certain control functions. Two synchronizing characters, SYN, denote the start of the message. The next field is the *header field* that begins with the SOH (start of header) character. The header field is really a control field and can be used to regulate the flow of data by means of special ISO/ASCII characters. After the header field comes the *text field* preceded by an STX (start of text) character. Following the text field is an ETX (end of text) character and error-detecting code (BCC).

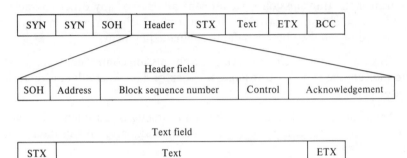

Fig. 9.38 The format of a BiSync frame.

Figure 9.39 shows an exchange of messages between two systems, A and B, can be presented graphically. The vertical axis represents increasing time so that the diagram is read from top to bottom. Initially computer A sends a message, Block 1, to computer B. A's message is acknowledged by B, which sends an acknowledge message, ACK, to A.

The second block from A is corrupted by noise and B sends a negative acknowledge message, NAK, inviting A to repeat its transmission. Block 3 is received satisfactorily by B, but B's acknowledgement gets lost. If nothing were done, the system would hang up, with A waiting for a reply forever. To get out of this deadlock, A starts a timer when it sends a message. If a reply is not received within a reasonable interval, a *time-out* is generated, forcing A to send a reply-request or enquiry (ENQ) message to B. Then B will reply with an ACK or a NAK depending on whether it received the last message.

Unfortunately, the above scheme contains a potential ambiguity. If A sends a message which is entirely lost in transmission, computer B will receive no ACK or NAK from B, and after a time-out it will send a reply-request. When B gets the reply-request, it sends an acknowledgement to the last message it received. This is not A's most recent message but the one before it. The last message sent by A has been lost and neither A nor B is aware of this. When A receives the ACK from B it sends its next message instead of repeating the last message.

A way round this ambiguity is to resort to numbered acknowledgements. The simplest arrangement employs two acknowledgement codes, ACK-0 and ACK-1. These codes are used alternately. Figure 9.40 demonstrates how the two ACKs resolve this ambiguity.

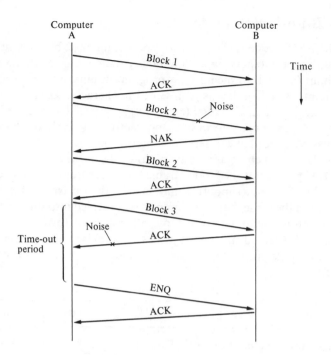

Fig. 9.39 Two-way communication with BiSync. Block 2 from A is corrupted by noise. This is detected by B which then sends a negative acknowledge (NAK) to A, inviting A to retransmit its message. Block 3 is received correctly by B but its acknowledgement is lost on the way to A. After a suitable delay A sends an enquiry request (ENQ), and B repeats its acknowledgement. As we shall see, this arrangement is not reliable and contains an ambiguity.

The above treatment of a character-oriented protocol is intended only to give an idea of how messages are exchanged in an órderly fashion. The setting up of calls and their *clearing-down* after a transmission are not included here. Readers wishing to pursue this further should consult the bibliography. Housley, in particular, provides a very clear introduction to protocols.

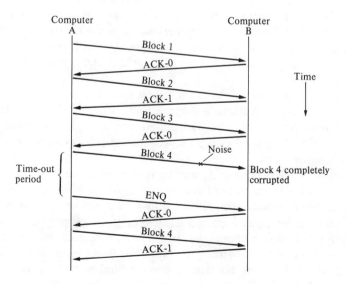

Fig. 9.40 The use of ACK-0 and ACK-1. In this case two alternate values for the acknowledgement message are used. These are ACK-0 and ACK-1, and are always sent alternately ACK-0, ACK-1, ACK-0, ACK-1, ACK-0, ... After receiving an ACK-0, A sends Block 4 which is severely corrupted and is not received by B. After a time-out, A sends an enquiry request and receives ACK-0 as a response. A knows that ACK-0 is a response to Block 3. If Block 4 had been received, A would have seen an ACK-1.

9.7.3 Bit-oriented protocols

The ISO/ASCII code is excellent for representing text, but is ill-fitted for representing pure binary data. Pure binary data can be anything from a core dump (a block of memory), a program in binary form, to floating point numbers. When data is represented in character form, it is easy to choose one particular character (e.g. SYN) as a special marker. When the data is in a pure binary form it is apparently impossible to choose any particular data word as a reserved marker or flag.

As in the case of character-oriented protocols, the key to understanding the HDLC protocol is the HDLC frame format. A frame is a single entity and HDLC does not support a unit smaller than a frame. Frames are indivisible in the sense that they cannot be subdivided into smaller frames, just as an atom cannot be divided into other atoms. However, a frame is composed of several distinct parts just as an atom is made up of neutrons, protons, and electrons. Figure 9.41 illustrates the HDLC format of a single frame.

Fig. 9.41 The HDLC frame format.

Flag					Flag
01111110	Address	Control	Information (optional)	FCS	01111110

Each frame begins and ends with a unique 8-bit flag, 01111110. Whenever a receiver detects the sequence 01111110, it knows that it has located the start or the end of a frame. Of course, an error in transmission may generate a spurious flag by converting (say) the sequence 01·101110 into 01111110. In such cases, the receiver will lose the current frame. Due to the unique nature of the flag, the receiver will automatically re-synchronize when the next opening flag is detected.

One of the key features of HDLC is its ability to transmit information entirely *transparently*. When we say that information is transparent, we mean that it is invisible to the data-link layer and has no special *tag* or code associated with it to indicate that it is data and not something else. Remember that character-oriented protocols employ some characters to carry user-supplied data while other characters are reserved for system functions. HDLC puts no restrictions *whatsoever* on the nature of the data carried acrosss the link. Consequently, higher levels of the reference model can transmit any bit sequence they wish without affecting the operation of the data-link layer.

I hope that by now you have noticed an apparent contradiction in what I have said above. 'A frame is delimited by a *unique* flag (01111110)' and '*any* binary pattern may be transmitted as data'. This contradiction is resolved by a delightfully simple scheme called *zero insertion and deletion* or *bit-stuffing*.

Figure 9.42 shows how bit-stuffing is used to make data transparent. Data from the block marked *data source* is passed to an encoder marked *zero insertion*, which operates according to a simple algorithm. A bit appearing at its input is passed *unchanged* to its output unless the five preceding bits have all been ones. In the latter case, two bits are passed to the output: a zero followed by the input bit. As an example consider the sequence 0101111110 containing the forbidden flag sequence (Fig. 9.42(b)). The first bit in the sequence is the left-most bit.

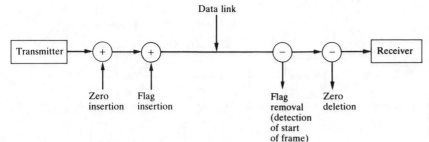

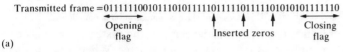

(a)

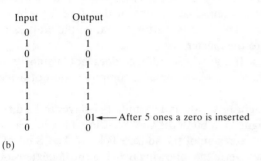

(b)

Fig. 9.42 (a) Bit insertion and deletion; (b) an example of zero insertion.

The sequence at the output of the decoder is now 01011111010. Note that the flag pattern is broken up and cannot interfere with the operation of the data link. Flags intended as actual frame delimiters are appended to the data stream (in Fig. 9.42) *after* the zero insertion block.

At the receiving end of the link, opening and closing flaps are detected and removed from the data stream by the flag removal circuit. The data stream is then passed to the block marked *zero deletion* for decoding, which operates in the reverse way to zero insertion: if five ones are received in succession, the next bit (which *must* be a zero) is deleted. For example, the received sequence 01011111010111111000 is decoded as 01011111101111100.

From Fig. 9.41, it can be seen that the information in an HDLC frame is divided into five logical fields: an address field, a control field, an information field and a frame check sequence (FCS). Of these, the information field is *optional* and need not form part of every frame.

The address field

The data-link protocol can be configured to operate in one of several modes and Fig. 9.43 illustrates the widely used *master–slave* mode. In this mode, one station is designated as the *master* station and all the other stations connected to the master are called *slaves*. Such an arrangement may be found in a bank where a central master communicates with a slave station at each teller position. A characteristic of the master–slave mode is that only the master may send messages when it wishes. A slave is not permitted to transmit until it is invited to do so by the master.

In a master–slave arrangement, the address field provides the address of

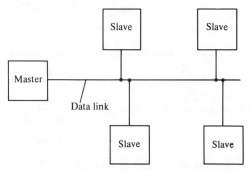

Fig. 9.43 Master–slave
transmission with HDLC.

Note: All communication is between a slave and the
master. Direct slave-to-slave communication is not allowed.

the slave (even if there is only one slave in the system). The master does
not need an address as there is a unique master. When a master sends a
frame, the address field contains the address of the slave for which the
frame is intended. If the slave is transmitting a frame, the address is its
own, identifying itself to the master.

Any slave receiving a frame whose address does not match its own
address ignores the message. Unlike humans, computers do not listen to
third-party traffic.

The address field is eight bits wide and permits 127 slaves to be directly
identified. If the least-significant bit of the address field bit is a logical zero,
the following byte is an extension of the address field. If the LS bit of the
extension address is also a zero, the following byte is a further extension of
the address. Clearly, this arrangement permits an infinitely extensible
address field.

Two special-purpose addresses have been defined. The address
11111111 is a global address indicating that the frame is a broadcast frame
and is intended for all stations on the network. The special address
00000000 (null) causes the frame to be ignored by all stations! A null
address is included for test purposes.

The control field

The real power of the HDLC protocol lies in its 8-bit control field, which
defines the type of the frame being transmitted and controls the flow of
messages across the data-link layer. Table 9.2 defines the three types of
control field used by an HDLC frame. Note that the control field bits are

Table 9.2 The format of the HDLC control field

Frame type	1	2	3	4	5	6	7	8
I frame	0		$N(S)$		P/F		$N(R)$	
S frame	1	0	S	S	P/F		$N(R)$	
U frame	1	1	M	M	P/F	M	M	M

$N(S)$ = send sequence number
$N(R)$ = receive sequence number
P/F = poll/final bit
SS = two supervisory bits
MMMMM = five modifier bits.

numbered 1–8 (bit 1 is the least significant bit) and are written with the LSB on the left. This contradicts the conventional numbering of bits from 0 to $m-1$ with the LSB on the right. I have used the format of Table 9.2 because *that* is the format used by the standard.

Life becomes confusing when a standard employs notation which is not conventional. If an author adopts (by rewriting the standard) conventional notation, the reader may find it difficult to read other documentation relating to the standard. If the author uses the same notation as that of the standard without warning the reader, he or she may misinterpret the information.

The two least-significant bits of a C field define one of three types of frame: I frame, S frame or U frame. An I frame or *information* frame contains an information field and is used to transport data from a higher-level layer than the data-link layer.

The S-frame or *supervisory* frame is used to control the flow of information on the link. Typical functions include acknowledging I-frames or requesting the retransmission of frames lost during transmission. There are four types of S frame; the actual type is indicated by the two bits labelled 'S' in Table 9.2. We shall look more closely at the S frame later.

The *unnumbered* frame (U frame) provides control functions not available with the I or C frames. U frames perform functions like setting up or changing the operating mode of the data link layer and connecting or disconnecting two stations.

All three types of control fields have a poll/final (P/F) bit, which is a dual-purpose bit. When transmitted by a master station, it is called a *poll* bit (P-bit) and indicates that the master is polling (i.e. asking) the secondary station for a response. Remember that in the master–slave mode, the secondary station cannot transmit until it is invited to do so by the master. A control field with P/F = 1 sent by the master indicates such an invitation.

When a control field is sent by a secondary station, the P/F bit is defined as a *final* bit and, when set, indicates that the current field is the last frame of the series. In other words, a slave sets P/F = 1 when it has no more frames to send.

Much of the power of the control field lies in two state variables $N(S)$ and $N(R)$. They are called state variables because they define the state of the system at any instant. Both are three-bit numbers in the range zero to seven. $N(S)$ is called the *send sequence number* and $N(R)$ is called the *receive sequence number*.

Only I frames contain a send sequence number, $N(S)$, which uniquely labels the current information frame. For example, if $N(S) = 101$ the frame is numbered 5. When this frame is received the value of $N(S)$ is examined and compared with the previous value. If the previous value was 4, the message is received in sequence. But if the value was not 4, there is a gnashing of teeth and grieving over a lost message. Note that the sequence count is modulo 8, so that it goes 67012345670 ...... Consequently, if eight messages are lost, the next value of $N(S)$ will apparently be correct.

The receive sequence number, $N(R)$, is available in both S and I control fields. $N(R)$ indicates the number of the *next* I frame that the receiver expects to see. That is, an $N(R)$ acknowledges I frames up to and including $N(R) - 1$. Suppose A is communicating with B and is sending to B an information frame with $N(S) = 3$, $N(R) = 6$. The interpretation of this frame is that A is sending frame number 3, and has safely received frames up to 5 from B. It is saying that it expects to see an information frame from B with its value of $N(S)$ equal to 6. By means of the $N(R)$ and $N(S)$ state variables, it is impossible to lose a frame without detecting an error, as long as there are not more than seven out-standing I frames that have not been acknowledged. If eight or more frames are sent, it is impossible to tell whether a value of $N(R) = i$ refers to frame i or to frame $i - 8$. It is up to the system designer to ensure that this situation never happens. We will soon look at how $N(S)$ and $N(R)$ are used in more detail.

The FCS field

We have already said that the data-link layer is built on top of an *imperfect* physical layer. Bits transmitted across a physical medium may become corrupted by noise with a one being transformed to a zero or vice versa. The error rate over point-to-point links in a dedicated local area network may be of the order of one bit lost in every 10^{12} bits. Error rates over other channels may be very much worse than this. Section 9.7.5 looks at some of the ways in which errors can be detected and their effects made good. Here we simply describe the FCS field for completeness.

HDLC chooses its message coding and decoding scheme to provide the maximum possible error protection. At the receiver, the bits of the address field, control field and I field are treated as the coefficients of a long polynomial, which is divided by a special polynomial called a generator. The HDLC protocol uses the CCITT generator 10001000000100001 or $x^{16} + x^{12} + x^5 + 1$. The results of the division yields a quotient (which is thrown away) and a 16-bit remainder, which is the 16-bit FCS appended to the frame.

At the receiver, the message bits forming the A, C, and I fields are also divided by the generator polynomial to yield a locally calculated remainder. The calculated remainder is compared with the received remainder in the FCS field. If they match, the frame is assumed to be valid. Otherwise the frame is rejected.

The reader may wonder how the FCS is detected, because the I field, when present, may be of any length and no information is sent to indicate its length directly. In fact, the FCS field cannot be detected. The receiver assembles data until the closing flag is detected and then works backwards to obtain the FCS and the I field.

9.7.4 HDLC message exchange

The HDLC protocol caters for several configurations and operating modes. Here we consider only the unbalanced normal response mode (NRM). A data link is unbalanced when it is operated in a master–slave mode. In the NRM mode, a secondary station (i.e. slave) may initiate transmission only as a result of receiving explicit permission from the primary station (i.e. master). That is, a master can send data to a slave at any time, but a slave may respond only when invited to do so by the master.

Before we continue, it is necessary to define the four messages associated with a supervisory frame. Table 9.3 shows how the four S frames are encoded.

Table 9.3 The format of the S-frame

Control bit								S-frame type
1	2	3	4	5	6	7	8	
1	0	0	0	P/F	←—$N(R)$—→			RR (receiver ready)
1	0	0	1	P/F	←—$N(R)$—→			REJ (reject)
1	0	1	0	P/F	←—$N(R)$—→			RNR (receiver not ready)
1	0	1	1	P/F	←—$N(R)$—→			SREJ (selective reject)

The RR (receiver ready) frame indicates that the station sending it is ready to receive information frames and is equivalent to saying, 'I am ready'. The REJ (reject) frame indicates an error condition and usually implies that one or more frames have been lost in transmission. The REJ frame rejects **all** frames, starting with the frame numbered $N(R)$. Whenever a station receives an REJ frame, it must must go back and retransmit all messages after $N(R) - 1$. Sending all these messages is sometimes inefficient, because not all frames in a sequence may have been lost.

The RNR (receiver not ready) frame indicates that the station is temporarily unable to receive information frames. RNR is normally used to indicate a busy condition (the receiver's buffers may all be full). The busy condition is cleared by the transmission of an RR, REJ or SREJ frame. An I frame sent with the P/F bit set will also clear the busy condition.

The SREJ (selective reject) frame rejects the single frame numbered $N(R)$ and is equivalent to 'please retransmit the frame $N(R)$'. The use of SREJ is often more efficient than REJ, as the latter requests the retransmission of all frames after $N(R)$ as well as $N(R)$. The REJ command is necessary when either a number of frames have been lost, or the receiver is not capable of storing frames.

One way of demonstrating the HDLC protocol is provided by the frame exchange sequence of Fig. 9.44, which shows an exchange of messages between A (the master) and B (the slave) operating in half-duplex mode. Each frame is denoted by 'type, $N(S)$, $N(R)$, P/F', where type is I (for an information field), RR, REJ, RNR, or SREJ. Typical HDLC frames are:

I,5,0   means I frame, $N(S) = 5$, $N(R) = 0$
I,5,0,P   means I frame, $N(S) = 5$, $N(R) = 0$, Poll bit set by master
REJ,,4,F means S frame, $N(R) = 4$, Reject, Final bit set by slave

Note that a double comma indicates the absence of an $N(S)$ field.

Initially (Fig. 9.44), the master station sends three I frames, the last of which has its poll bit set to force a response from the slave. The slave responds by sending two I frames which are terminated by setting the F bit of the C field. If the slave had no I frames to send, it would have responded

Fig. 9.44 An example of an HDLC message exchange sequence. A message is denoted by type, $N(S)$, $N(R)$, P/F. For example, I,3,0,P indicates an information frame numbered 3, with an $N(R)$ count of 0, and the poll bit set indicating that a response is required. Note that message 3 from A (i.e. I,3,2) is lost. Therefore, when A sends the message I,4,2,P with the poll bit set, B responds with REJ,,3,F. This indicates that B is rejecting all messages from A numbered 3 and above, and that the F bit is set denoting that B has no more messages to send to A.

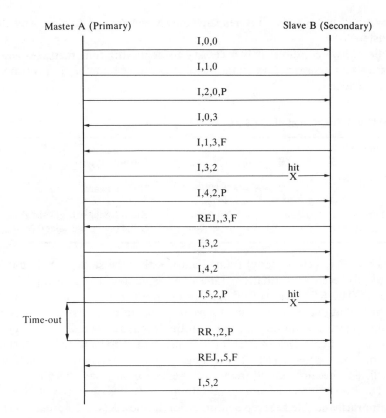

with RR,,3,F. Note that the values of $N(S)$ and $N(R)$ in a frame are those appropriate to the *sender* of the frame.

The master sends a further two I frames, terminated by a poll bit. However, the first frame in this pair (I,3,2) is corrupted by noise and rejected by the receiver (slave). Thus, when the slave responds to the poll from the master, it sends a supervisory frame, REJ,,3,F, rejecting the I frame numbered 3 and all succeeding frames. This causes the master station to repeat the two frames numbered $N(S) = 3$ and $N(S) = 4$.

When the master station sends an I frame numbered I,5,2,P, it is corrupted in transmission and rejected by the receiver. Now the secondary station cannot respond to this polled request. When the master sends a message with $P = 1$, it starts a timer. If a response is not received within a certain period, the time-out, the master station must take action. In this case, it sends a supervisory frame (RR,,2,P) to force a response. The secondary station replies with another supervisory frame (REJ,,5,F) and the master then repeats the lost message.

Students are often confused by the provision of both REJ and SREJ supervisory frames. A selective reject frame, SREJ,,$N(R)$, rejects only the message whose send sequence count is $N(R)$. Therefore, SREJ,,$N(R)$ is equivalent to 'please repeat your message with $N(S) = N(R)$'. If a sequence of messages are lost, it is better to use REJ,,$N(R)$ and have $N(R)$ and all messages following $N(R)$ repeated.

However, even if only one message is lost, it is sometimes necessary to use a REJ. Suppose that the current value of $N(S)$ is 6 and that and the message $N(S) = 3$ has been lost. If a response REJ,,3 is received, messages with $N(S) = 3,4,5$, and 6 must be repeated. Although this process is inefficient and time consuming, it has a valid application. If the receiver cannot store incoming messages, an error will always force it back to the lost message. Remember that HDLC was designed *before* low-cost microprocessor systems had become available. By having the REJ procedure, it is not necessary to build 'intelligence' into the slave part of the data link.

Figure 9.45 shows the operation of an HDLC system operating in full-duplex mode, permitting the simultaneous exchange of messages in both directions.

We have explained only part of the HDLC data-link layer protocol. Unnumbered fields are used to perform operations related to the setting up or establishing of the data-link layer channel and the eventual clearing down of the channel.

Before we move on to local area networks, we are going to examine the way in which errors introduced by the physical layer can be detected and corrected.

9.7.5 Error detection and correction at the data-link layer level

A transmission error occurs whenever one or more bits in a message are so severely corrupted by noise that they are incorrectly detected at the receiver. As a data-transmission system is intended to convey information from one point to another reliably, some mechanism must be introduced to deal with the errors that inevitably occur on any real physical channel. Although we have introduced error-detecting and error-correcting code in Chapter 4 when we were looking at coding techniques, we will cover this

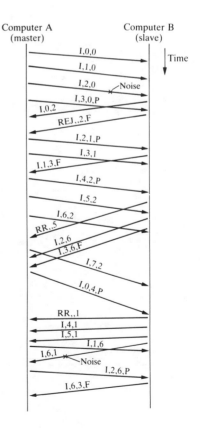

Fig. 9.45 HDLC full-duplex transmission.
In this case messages can be transmitted between A and B in both directions simultaneously. Consider the first seven messages. (1) *A sends* a frame I,0,0 (information frame numbered 0, A is expecting a frame from B numbered 0). (2) *A sends* frame I,1,0 (information frame numbered 1, A is still expecting a frame from B numbered 0). (3) *A sends* frame I,2,0. This frame is corrupted by noise and is not correctly received by B. (4) *B sends* frame I,0,2 (information frame numbered 0, B is expecting a frame from A numbered 2). Note that because A's frame I,2,0 has been lost, B is still expecting to see a frame from B labelled with $N(S)=2$. (5) *A sends* I,3,0,P (information frame numbered 3, A is expecting a frame numbered 0 from B). A is also polling B for a response. At this point A does not know that its previous message has been lost, and A has not yet received B's last message. (6) *B sends* a reply to A's poll. This is REJ,,2,F indicating that all A's messages numbered 2 and above have been rejected. The final bit, F, is set indicating that B has nothing more to send at the moment. (7) *A now sends* I,2,1 (information frame 2, and A is expecting to see a frame from B numbered 1). This frame is a repeat of A's information frame numbered 2 which was lost earlier.

topic again here with a somewhat different emphasis. Error detection is a process that determines whether or not an error has occurred in the transmission of a message. For example, if I receive the message 'My birthday falls on February 30', I know that a transmission error has occurred because February 30 is not a valid date. However, I do not know what the correct message should have been.

Once we know that a message is in error, we can deal with the situation in one of two ways. Either we must request a retransmission of the faulty message or we must *repair* the damage done to the message. Data-transmission codes which derive a correct message from a faulty message are known as error-correcting codes, ECCs.

The best way of illustrating the concepts involved in error-detecting and error-correcting codes is to introduce some examples. Consider four codes:

Code 1 The input sequence is copied to the output sequence without modification.

Code 2 Each input element is duplicated. Inputting a one causes a 11 to be output and inputting a zero causes a 00 to be output.

Code 3 Each input element is repeated three times. Inputting a one causes a 111 to be output and inputting a zero causes a 000 to be output.

Code 4 This is similar to Code 3 because each input element is triplicated. However, in this case the order of the output sequence is rearranged so that the three output bits corresponding to each input are spread out over three groups of three. For example, if the input sequence is *a,b,c*, the output sequence is *a,b,c, a,b,c, a,b,c*.

The codes introduced here serve only for illustrative purposes and do not represent practical codes used by real data-transmission systems. Suppose that the bit pattern 100 is applied to the transmitter and that the third received bit is corrupted. The four codes defined above can be represented as follows:

Coder	Input sequence	Transmitted sequence	Received sequence
1	100	100	101
2	100	110000	111000
3	100	111000111	110000111
4	100	100100100	101100100

The data received from Coder 1 is in error, but there is no way of detecting the error. Any received code is as valid (i.e. legal) as any other code.

The data received from Coder 2 is in error because the second group is 10, which is an illegal bit pattern as only the patterns 00 and 11 are valid. Clearly, we have detected an error but we cannot correct it because there is no way of telling which bit has been corrupted.

When we examine the data from Coder 3, it is clear that the first group, 110, is in error as it is not one of the two valid codes (000 and 111). If we make the assumption that one error is much more likely than two errors, we can say that the transmitted code was probably a 1. Now we have both detected **and** corrected an error.

The output of Coder 4 can be rearranged to yield the sequence 111 000 100 and the offending error detected and corrected. That is, Coder 4 behaves exactly like Coder 3 under these circumstances.

Now let's consider the effect of two errors in the transmitted sequence. Assume that both the second and third transmitted bits are corrupted:

Coder	Input sequence	Transmitted sequence	Received sequence
1	100	100	111
2	100	110000	101000
3	100	111000111	100000111
4	100	100100100	111100100
			(ie 111,100,100)

In this case, the two errors go undetected by Coder 1, but both errors are detected by Coder 2. Coder 3 detects that an error has taken place but makes an incorrect attempt to correct the error because the received code, 100, is assumed to represent 0.

Because Coder 4 scrambles the order of the bits, the two errors falling in adjacent groups and can be both detected **and** corrected.

These examples teach us that some codes detect errors and others both detect and correct errors. Moreover, they tell us that multiple errors may entirely defeat error correcting codes. The most important thing to note is that an error-detecting or error-correcting code adds bits to the data to be transmitted.

Single-bit parity error-detecting codes

The principle behind any error-correcting code is quite simple. A message word is transformed into a code word by the addition of **redundant** bits which are a function of the message. These bits are called redundant because they carry no new information, as they are derived from the message according to some algorithm. All they do is to help detect errors.

Consider a source (i.e. unencoded) message with a length m bits. There are 2^m possible valid messages of m bits. Now suppose that we create an n-bit code word by adding r redundant bits to the message. That is, $n = m + r$.

Although the code word has $2^n = 2^{m+r}$ possible values, only 2^m of these values are valid. When a code word is received, it is checked to see whether it represents a valid message. If it is valid, no error is assumed to have occurred.

The simplest error-correcting code is the single-bit parity check code. In this case, $r = 1$. In an even parity code, a parity-bit, P, is appended to the message. P is chosen to make the total number of ones in the code word even. For example, the 4-bit messages 0010 and 0110 would be coded as 00101 and 01100 respectively (the parity bit is at the right). When a code word is received, the total number of ones are counted. If the result is even, no error is assumed. Otherwise the message is rejected as faulty. Note that a single parity bit will always detect a single or an odd number of errors but will fail to detect an even number of errors.

Single-bit parity error checking is frequently associated with character-oriented codes, where a parity bit can be conveniently attached to a 7-bit character to yield an 8-bit code word. Single-bit parity error-detecting codes are quite useful when the error rate is relatively low and great reliability is not required.

Cyclic redundancy check codes

Modern data transmission systems require more sophisticated error-detecting codes than that offered by the simple parity bit. Like most of today's error-correcting or -detecting codes, the cyclic redundancy check code requires a certain amount of mathematical knowledge before its operation can be understood.

The stream of ones and zeros of a message can be regarded as the coefficients of a polynomial. For example, the message 1101 may be represented by the polynomial

$$1101 \rightarrow 1x^3 + 1x^2 + 0x^1 + 1x^0 = x^3 + x^2 + 1.$$

Suppose we take a polynomial of order m, representing an m-bit message. The polynomial is first multiplied by x^r and then divided by an r-bit polynomial G. The result obtained is $x^r M(x) = Q(x)G(x) + R(x)$, where $M(x)$ is the message polynomial and $R(x)$ is the r-bit remainder polynomial. The remainder polynomial, $R(x)$ is the cyclic check code and is appended to the message before transmission.

At the receiver, the m bits of the message are divided by the same generator polynomial, $G(x)$, and a locally calculated remainder is obtained. This is compared with the received CRC and an error flagged if they are not the same.

The power of the cyclic redundancy check error-detecting code is twofold. It is very easy to implement in hardware and it detects a very large fraction of all possible errors.

The standard generator polynomial specified by CCITT X.25 is

$$G(x) = x^{16} + x^{12} + x^5 + 1.$$

This polynomial detects any burst error with a length less than or equal to r bits. Burst errors with a length greater than r bits will be detected with a probability of $1 - 2^{-r}$.

Error-correcting codes

Most communication systems rely entirely on error-detecting codes to deal with physical channel impairments. Whenever the receiver detects that a message is in error the receiver asks the transmitter to repeat the lost message. Such a system is called ARQ—automatic repeat request. An alternative approach is to use a forward error-correcting code, FEC, which provides the receiver with a means of correcting transmission errors without incurring the delay associated with ARQ. Such a delay may be vital in real-time applications or in deep space communications links.

We have already looked at a very primitive error-detecting and -correcting code. Simply triplicating each transmitted bit enables us to detect and correct a single error. Such a scheme is grossly inefficient and requires two check bits for each message bit. In any case, it cannot deal with multiple errors. There are many practical error-detecting and -correcting codes in use today, although they are too complex to cover here. One of the simplest practical error-detecting and -correcting codes is the Hamming code introduced in Chapter 4.

The vast majority of data transmission systems do not employ forward error-correcting codes, but rely on the very powerful error-detecting properties of the CRC codes and request the retransmission of any faulty messages. Sometimes both FECs and ARQ codes are combined. By using an FEC with a cyclic redundancy check code, it is possible to automatically correct single-bit errors in the received data and to request the retransmission of messages that are then found to have incorrect CRCs.

9.8 Local area networks

It is not an exaggeration to say that local area networks (LANs) are changing the face of computing today. The impact of LANs is due to their high performance and low cost, making it feasible for even the smallest organizations to link together all their computers and allied digital equipment.

As long as only modest quantities of data were being transmitted over long, often intercontinental, distances, the overall impact of data transmission on computing was essentially minimal. With the advent of low-cost microprocessor and minicomputer systems together with the clustering of a number of such devices in a relatively small area (an office, polytechnic, university or laboratory), a need for a specialized form of inexpensive communications network was felt. Because of this pressure, a branch of data transmission dealing with the transfer of large quantities of information at high speed between *geographically distributed computers* arose. This new field is, of course, known as local area networks. Data transmission systems operating over much greater areas than LANs (and using public communications facilities) are called wide area networks (WANs).

We begin this section by defining LANs in terms of their *properties* and then introduce the concept of *LAN topology* which is a measure of the way in which the nodes of a LAN are connected together. Finally, we look at particular types of LAN in use today and show how they pass messages between the various nodes of the LAN.

What is a LAN?

Local area networks and beauty have at least one thing in common: they both exist only in the eye of the beholder. There is no absolute definition of a local area network! Equally, everybody knows (or thinks they know) what is meant by a LAN. Writers avoid the problem of trying to define a LAN by listing its properties. I will follow in their footsteps.

1. A LAN is local. Here is where the difficulty of defining a LAN begins. What is local to one person is frequently distant to another. In the UK, a trip of 100 km is sometimes regarded as a major excursion. In the USA, it is often no more than a hop to your nearest neighbour. The sense of *local* in local area network carries with it the idea of a single site—even if the site is very large. That is, a local area network links the computing facilities on a single site. The site may be a laboratory, a factory or an entire complex of factories. In recent years the term metropolitan area network (MAN) has been coined to indicate a network extending over a relatively large area such as a number of separate sites or even part of a city.

2. A LAN is private. A LAN belongs to the owner of the site on which it is operated and does not use public data transmission equipment such as the telephone network. Therefore, the owner of the LAN does not have to comply with the very complex legal restrictions and obligations associated with a public network. This goes hand-in-hand with point 1 above. The LAN extends over a single site because public carriers are not necessary. As soon as separate sites are linked, they invariably require the use of a public network. Note that a LAN on one site can be connected to a LAN on another site by means of the PSTN. The interface between the LAN and the PSTN is called a *gateway*. A gateway is an interconnection between two or more separate networks. In everyday terms, the Leicester Square underground station is a gateway because it allows travellers on the Northern Line to move on to the Piccadilly Line.

3. A LAN offers a high data rate. The rate at which information can be transmitted across a physical channel depends on the length and the electrical properties of the transmission path. LANs have relatively short transmission paths and often use coaxial cable or a twisted pair, permitting data rates up to and, well beyond, 10M bits/s, which is very much greater than the 300–9600 bits/s supported by most telephone channels.

4. A LAN is reliable. Most LANs are relatively simple systems with a coaxial cable connecting the various nodes of the network. There are no complex switching systems like those associated with the telephone exchange. LANs are reliable because they link systems over relatively short distances and are not subject to the forms of interference that plague the long-haul transmission paths of the telephone network. Furthermore, the LAN does not employ the fault- and noise-prone mechanical or electronic message-switching associated with the telephone system. Consequently, a well-designed LAN should offer a very long MTFB (mean time between failure) and a short MTTR (mean time to repair) when it does fail. A repair may involve little more than replacing one of the nodes that has failed. LANs are normally designed so that the failure of a single node has little effect on the performance of the system.

5. A LAN is cheap. It has been devised to connect low-cost systems and therefore the use of expensive technology or transmission media cannot be tolerated. Typical LANs link their nodes by means of twisted pairs or coaxial cables. LANs are not only cheap, but require little labour in their installation. One of the most clearly defined trends to emerge from the microprocessor world is the tendency for the price of anything associated with microprocessors to fall dramatically as time passes. We have already witnessed remarkable drops in the price of secondary storage (floppy and hard disk drives) and of peripherals (printers and modems). If low-cost microprocessor systems are to be linked, the local area network chosen to do this must be cost-effective. Nobody is going to pay $20 000 to link together two $1000 microcomputers—not even in California.

6. *A LAN is fair to the users.* A LAN should offer all its nodes *full connectivity*, which means that any given node should be able to communicate with any other node. Equally, each node should have the same access rights to the transmission medium, so that all nodes have the same probability that their message will be delivered across the network. The fairness criterion exists only at levels 1 and 2 of the ISO model for OSI. A higher level may limit the scope of a particular node's access rights.

7. *The nodes of a LAN should be equal.* This criterion is, perhaps, a little more tendentious than the others and is not a characteristic of every LAN. When we say that all nodes should be *equal* we mean that they should have the *same* software and the *same* hardware. A corollary of this statement is that it should be possible to add new nodes to an existing system without modifying the software at all the other nodes.

9.8.1 Network topology

The topology of a network describes the way in which the individual users of the network are linked together. There are four basic topologies suitable for use in a LAN: the unconstrained topology, the star network, the bus, and the ring.

The unconstrained network

The most general topology is the unconstrained network of Fig. 9.46(a). The individual nodes are connected together in an arbitrary fashion. Its advantage is that additional links can be provided to reduce bottlenecks where heavy traffic passes between a group of nodes. Further nodes and links can readily be added without disturbing the hardware of the existing system. The road network of most countries is an unconstrained topology, with new roads being added when and where necessary.

The disadvantage of the unconstrained topology is that a decision must be made at each node on the best way to route a message on the way to its destination. In terms of the analogy with the road system, the driver must have a road map to enable him or her to drive from one place to another. A message cannot just be transmitted from one node to each other node to which it is connected as this would lead to the message being multiplied at each node and propagated round the network forever. Instead, each node must have its own *road map* and make a decision on which link the message is to be transmitted on the way to its destination. Calculating the

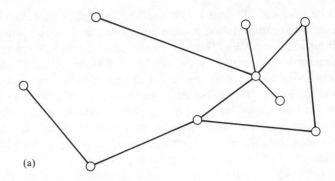

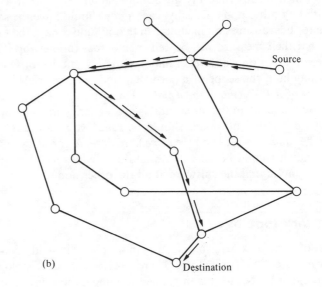

Fig. 9.46 (a) The unconstrained topology; (b) routeing a message through an unconstrained topology.

best route through the network for each message has the computational overhead of working out routeing algorithms. Furthermore, whenever a new link or node is added to the network, the routeing information must be changed at each node. Figure 9.46(b) shows how a message may be routed through an unconstrained topology.

The star network

Figure 9.47 shows how the star network eliminates the need for nodes to make routeing decisions, by routeing all messages from source to destination via one central node. The star has a simple topology and has advantages when the physical topology of the network matches its logical topology. Clearly, there are circumstances where the nodes are distributed in such a way that the links between some of the nodes and the central node are economically unviable.

The star network has two obvious disadvantages. As all messages pass through the central node, the loss of the central node totally wrecks the network. Other networks may offer a degraded but useful service if part of the network fails. Furthermore, because all traffic passes through the central node, it must be capable of working at sufficiently high speed to handle all nodes to which it is connected.

The bus topology

The bus topology is illustrated in Fig. 9.48. The bus (and also the ring) are attempts to minimize the complexity of a network by removing both a special-purpose central node and the need for individual nodes to make routeing decisions.

In a bus topology all nodes are connected to a common data highway, which may be a single bus linking nodes or it may be a number of buses with branches linking the individual buses. Such a topology is called an **unrooted tree**. When a message is put on the bus by a node, it flows outwards in all directions and eventually reaches every point in the network. The bus has one topological and one practical restriction. Only one path may exist between any two points; otherwise there would be nothing to stop a message flowing round a loop forever. The practical limitation is that the bus cannot normally exceed some maximum distance from end to end.

The principal problem faced by the designers of a bus is how to deal with a number of nodes wanting to use the bus at the same time. This is called bus contention and is dealt with later.

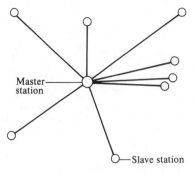

Fig. 9.47 The star.

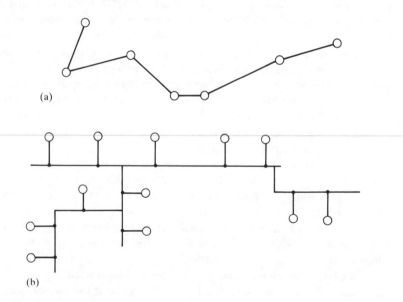

(a)

(b)

Fig. 9.48 The bus: (a) the simple bus; (b) the more general form of bus.

The ring topology

Figure 9.49 illustrates the ring topology, in which the nodes are connected together in the form of a ring. Like the bus this leads to a decentralized structure, as no central node is needed to control the ring. Each node simply receives a message from one neighbour and passes it on to its other neighbour. Messages flow in one direction round the ring.

The only routeing requirement placed on each node is that it must be able to recognize a message intended for itself. The ring does not suffer

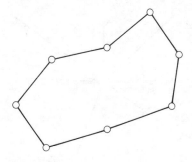

Fig. 9.49 The ring topology.

from contention like the bus topology. However, a node on the ring has the problem of how to inject a new message into the existing traffic flow.

In the early days of LANs, the ring was considered prone to failure. A broken link makes it impossible to pass messages all the way round the ring. There are now a number of *double ring* structures with two links between each of the nodes. If one of the links is broken it is possible for the ring to reconfigure itself and bypass the failure.

9.8.2 Flow-control mechanisms in buses

One of the earliest local area networks and one which has had a profound effect on the development of today's LANs is ALOHA. ALOHA was designed to link remote terminals spread out over the Hawaiian islands with central processing facilities at Honolulu on the island of Oahu. The central processor was called the *Menahune* which is an Hawaiian name for an imp. The word *imp* is a reference to the IMPs (interface message processors), which formed the nodes of the ARPANET wide area network. ARPANET was, possibly, the first true computer network.

From a topological viewpoint, ALOHA has a star structure with a central master, the Menahune, surrounded by slaves. The physical link layer was implemented by UHF radio channels. Full-duplex operation was achieved by using a frequency of 407.35 MHz for slave-to-master communication, and 413.75 MHz for master-to-slave communication.

Communication between the master (Menahune) and a slave (i.e. a user terminal) is entirely straightforward: the master simply transmits a packet of information. A packet consists of a 32-bit header plus a 16-bit header parity check field, and up to 80 bytes of data followed by a 16-bit parity check field. The maximum packet size is therefore 88 bytes (i.e. 704 bits) and it takes 73 ms to transmit at a baud-rate of 9600 bits/s. A packet from the master is received by all slaves, but only the slave whose own address matches that in the packet's header responds to it.

Things are very different from the point of view of the reverse channel from a slave to the master. Although the network's topology is arranged like a star, it behaves as a bus as far as slave-to-master traffic is concerned! The reason for this is quite simple. Each slave uses the same medium (radio at 407.35 MHz) and all slaves are linked together by the *ether*. Consequently, whenever a slave transmits, its message spreads out to *all* other slaves, as well as to the master.

Such a bus network introduces the problem of *contention*. No two nodes can access the same channel simultaneously, without the messages interfering destructively with each other. When two messages do overlap in time, the event is called a collision and both messages are lost.

ALOHA deals with the problem of contention in a rather simple but crude fashion. Any slave wishing to communicate with the master just goes ahead and transmits its message. Of course, if another slave is transmitting at the same time or joins in before the message is finished, the message is lost. The loss of a message is detected by an equally crude technique: if the slave does not receive an acknowledgement within a time-out period, it assumes that its message has been corrupted in transmission.

When one message from a slave node collides with another, both messages are lost. If the duration of a message is T seconds and two messages just collide, the total time lost is $2T$ seconds. One way of improving the efficiency of ALOHA is to confine the transmission of packets to discrete time-slots.

Assuming that the probability of a station wanting to transmit a packet has a Poisson distribution, it can be shown that the maximum throughput of this system approaches 18 per cent of the maximum channel capacity. To make this clearer, consider revolving doors. If people arrive at the doors at random, and the maximum capacity of the doors is 1000 people per hour when all the people follow one after the other (polite behaviour without contention), then with people using a random wait every time they collide, the maximum throughput cannot exceed 180 people per hour.

Dividing the channel time into fixed slots of a duration equal to the maximum packet length (so-called slotted ALOHA), and permitting the transmission of a packet only at the start of a time slot, much reduces the chance of collision and increases the maximum efficiency to 35 per cent. If packets are transmitted at random, the beginning of one packet can collide with the end of another and a period of time equal to two packet lengths is lost. If all packets are transmitted in fixed time slots, a collision cannot affect two adjacent slots, and a time equal to only one packet length is lost. Of course, this arrangement requires that all transmitters have access to an accurate clock in order to schedule their messages to fall within the time slots.

In a *contention net* any node wishing to transmit just goes ahead and puts its message on the bus. As there is no control over when a node may transmit, there is nothing to prevent two or more nodes transmitting simultaneously. If this does happen, all messages being transmitted are irretrievably scrambled and lost. The simplest form of contention control would be to let the transmitters retransmit their messages. Unfortunately, such a scheme would not work, as the competing nodes would keep retransmitting the messages which would keep getting scrambled. There are two things to note here. The technical term for two or more messages being lost due to overlapping transmission is a collision. The problem of collisions in a bus network is identical to that of two people approaching the same revolving door together: they cannot both get in, they step back, and advance together causing a collision, so they step back again, advance together, collide, ...

A better strategy on detecting a collision is to *back off* or wait a random time before trying to retransmit the frame. Under these circumstances it is less likely that the competing nodes would reschedule the transmissions for the same time. In terms of our revolving door, as soon as the two people collide, they each immediately throw a dice, and then wait the number of seconds the dice shows before trying again. It is unlikely that they would each get the same number, so they can go through the door separately. Networks operating under this form of contention control are well suited to bursty traffic. That is, the arrangement works as long as the average traffic is very low (much less than the maximum capacity of the bus). If the amount of traffic rises, there comes a point where collisions generate repeat messages that generate further collisions and further repeats, and the system eventually collapses.

A better form of contention control is to allow the node to listen to the bus before trying to send its frame. Obviously, if one node is already in the process of sending a message, other nodes are not going to attempt to transmit. A collision will now occur only if two nodes attempt to transmit at nearly the same instant. Once a node has started transmitting and its signal has propagated throughout the network, no other node can interrupt. For almost all systems this danger zone, the propagation time of a message from one end of the network to the other, is very small and is only a tiny fraction of the duration of a message.

A further modification of this arrangement is to allow the transmitters to listen to the bus while they are transmitting. Suppose a transmitter, thinking the bus was free, had started transmitting, and at the same time another transmitter had done likewise. After a very short time both transmitters become aware that the bus is in use and abort their messages. In this way the effect of a collision is reduced, because the transmitters stop as soon as they detect the collision. In the absence of a listen-while-transmitting mechanism, a collision is detected indirectly by the absence of any acknowledgement to the message.

Ethernet

One of the most popular derivatives of ALOHA is Ethernet, which is supported by DEC, Xerox and Intel. The physical layer of Ethernet uses a baseband coaxial cable with phase-encoded data transmitted at 10M bits/s. The term baseband means that the digital data is transmitted directly without the need for modems. The contention mechanism adopted by Ethernet is called carrier sense multiple access with collision detect (CSMA/CD). When an Ethernet station wishes to transmit a packet, it first listens to the state of the bus. If the bus is in use, it waits for the bus to become free. In Ethernet terminology this is called *deference*. Once a station has started transmitting it acquires the channel, and after a delay equal to the end-to-end round trip propagation time of the network, a successful transmission without collision is guaranteed.

Before the packet has propagated throughout the network, a *collision window* exists during which two stations may begin transmitting unknown to each other. When a station realizes that its packet is being corrupted by another packet, it reinforces the collision by transmitting a *jam* packet. If it stopped transmitting immediately, the other transmitter might not detect the collision. The collision would be detected indirectly much later by the error-detecting code that forms part of the transmitted frame. This process is inefficient and wastes time. The sending of a short jam packet makes the collision obvious to all listeners. After the jam has been sent, another attempt is made after a *random delay*. If repeated attempts fail, the random delay is increased as the sender tries to adapt to a busy channel.

9.8.3 Flow control in rings

A ring network connects all stations to each other in the form of a continuous loop. Unlike the stations of a bus network, which listen passively to data on the bus unless it is meant for them, the stations of the ring must take an active part in all data transfers. Basically, when receiving incoming data they must test it and decide whether to keep it for themselves or to pass it on to their next neighbour. In general, the mechanisms used to determine which station may gain access to the ring are more varied than those for buses. Three popular control techniques are token passing, register insertion, and slotted rings. Contention control in the sense of bus networks is not found in rings.

Token rings

One of the fascinating things about LANs is the way in which many of their seemingly abstract technological aspects can be related to everyday life. A classic railway problem is the control of trains on a single line. Collisions occur if two trains travel in opposite directions from the ends of a single line. These collisions tend to be more harmful than those on data networks. One of the early solutions was to provide a metal ring or token for the stretch of line. Only the driver in possession of the token has a right to use the line. If a driver arrives at one end of the line and the token is not there the train must wait; if it is there the driver can pick it up, enter the line, and hang up the token as its other end. As long as the driver has the token, no one can enter the line behind the train or ahead of it. After the driver has hung up the token, another train can take it and go back down the line.

Token rings pass a special bit pattern (the token) round the ring from station to station. The station currently holding the token is the station that can transmit data if it so wishes. If it does not wish to take the opportunity to send data itself, it passes the token on round the ring. For example, suppose the token has the special pattern 11111111, with zero stuffing used as in the case of HDLC to keep the pattern unique. A station on the ring wishing to transmit monitors its incoming traffic. When it has detected seven ones it inerts the last bit of the token and passes it on. Thus, a pattern called a **connector** (11111110) passes down the ring. The connector is created to avoid sending the eighth '1' and thereby passing on the token. The station holding the token may now transmit its data. After it has transmitted its data, it sends a new token down the ring. As there is only one token, contention cannot arise on the ring unless, of course, a station becomes antisocial and sends out a second token. In practice, a practical system is rather more complex, because arrangements must be included for dealing with lost tokens.

Register insertion rings

The structure of a node in a **register insertion ring** is illustrated in Fig. 9.50. A message to be transmitted is first loaded into a shift register. This shift register is, initially, not part of the ring. When the station notices that the ring is either idle or is at a point between two separate messages, it breaks

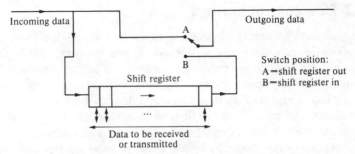

Fig. 9.50 The register insertion ring.

the loop and inserts the shift register. The message to be transmitted is clocked out of its shift register at the same rate data is moved round the ring. As the message leaves the shift register at one end, any data on the ring is shifted in at the other end. In effect, the register has *lengthened* the ring. Since the shift register is now part of the ring, it can neither be removed nor used to send other messages.

When the message has moved round the ring it eventually arrives in the originating shift register. At this instant the register can be switched out of the circuit, and the message *swallowed*. If the message is ever damaged on its journey round the ring, the sender must wait for the ring to become idle before the shift register can be switched out.

Slotted rings

In a slotted ring one or more packet *carriers* (the slots) are passed round the ring. A carrier is not a physical entity like a railway carriage. It is just a special type of packet whose bits can be modified by the nodes through which it passes. Up to now we have considered that all packets (i.e. frames) are only generated or received but never modified. Each carrier has a header, a tail, and a full/empty bit. Whenever an empty carrier passes a station wishing to transmit data, the station fills the packet with data and marks the carrier as full by setting the full/empty bit. At its destination the data is *removed* from the carrier and the full flag is cleared. The Cambridge ring operates on this principle.

Figure 9.51 shows the format of the packet used by the Cambridge ring. The first bit is a synchronization bit and denotes the start of the packet—rather like the start bit of asynchronous systems. The second bit is the full/empty bit. The third bit is used by a master station called the monitor. A ring structure is moderately democratic but it needs a special station, the monitor, to generate empty packets on power-up, and to ambush corrupted packets.

The packet includes an eight-bit destination address, followed by a 16-bit field. Following the data field are a two-bit control field and a single parity bit. Compared to the HDLC format or the Ethernet format, the packets flowing round the Cambridge ring are relatively crude.

There are many published papers on the relative advantages and disadvantages of the various types of local area network. Some prefer the Ethernet, others the token ring. Some like the bus because it is very easy to extend, others say that they would not use it because it cannot guarantee the receipt of a message within a finite period as it is theoretically possible

1	2	3	4		11	12		19	20		27	28		35	36		37	38	39	40

Fig. 9.51 The format of data on the Cambridge ring. 1: Leader or slot framing bit (always 1); 2: full/empty bit (1=full); 3: monitor control bit; 4–11: destination address; 12–19: source address; 20–27: data byte 1; 28–35: data byte 2; 36: type bit A; 37: type bit B; 38–39: see table; 40: even parity bit.

Response bits

38	39	Response
0	0	BUSY—destination node cannot deal with packet
0	1	ACCEPT—destination node accepts packet
1	0	NOT SELECTED
1	1	IGNORE—no node has read the packet

for a message to suffer an infinite sequence of collisions. Other (wiser) engineers say that the actual form of a LAN is often unimportant as the interface between the user program and the LAN (i.e. the operating system) is normally much slower than the most primitive forms of LAN.

9.8.4 Standards and LANs

During the late 1970s, it became apparent that LANs were going to become a major area of growth and that the introduction of a large number of *ad hoc* protocols for LANs would have, ultimately, a bad effect on the computer industry. In 1980 the IEEE established its Standards Project 802 to provide a framework for LAN standards. The 802 committee set itself the goal of designing a standard for the new LANs that would take account of existing and prospective technology, and the needs of the various LAN users. The 802 committee did not intend to produce standards for all seven layers of the ISO/ASCII basic reference model, but limited themselves to standards for the physical and data-link layers.

At the time that the IEEE was organizing its 802 project, the Ethernet LAN was rapidly becoming a *de facto* standard for contention buses and therefore the IEEE had to incorporate it in their work. At the same time, engineers were involved in an often violent debate about the relative merits of buses and rings as LAN topologies. The IEEE 802 committee had little choice but to reflect the nature of the real world, so they devised a set of standards that took account of both bus and ring topologies. They wanted the greatest happiness of the greatest number of people. The IEEE 802 draft standard includes standards for a CSMA/CD bus (i.e. Ethernet), a token ring and a token bus. Figure 9.52 illustrates the scope of the 802 standards.

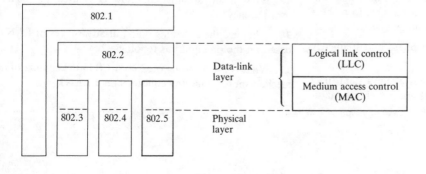

Fig. 9.52 Scope of the IEEE 802 standards for LANs.

Summary

In this chapter we have taken a brief look at some of the aspects of interest to those involved with computer communications networks. Computer networks is a subject that is advancing as rapidly as, if not faster than, any other branch of computer science, because it increases the power of computer systems and exploits many of today's growing technologies. It is all too easy to think of computer communications as a hardware-oriented discipline centred almost exclusively on the transmission of signals from point A to point B. Modern computer communications networks have software components that far outweigh their hardware components in terms of complexity and sometimes even cost. In this chapter we have introduced the ideas behind the seven layers of the ISO basic reference model for open systems interconnection and have described protocols for the bottom two layers.

Problems

1. If today the cost of a computer is so relatively low, why is the field of computer communications expanding so rapidly?

2. What is the meaning of a protocol and why are protocols so important in the world of communications?

3. What is the difference between a WAN and a LAN?

4. What is an open system?

5. Why has the ISO model for OSI proved so important in the development of computer communications?

6. What are the differences between the transport and network layers of the ISO reference model?

7. Why is the physical layer of the OSI model different to all the other layers?

8. What is a virtual connection?

9. What are the differences between half-duplex and full-duplex transmission modes? How is it possible to make a half-duplex system look like a full-duplex system?

10. What is the difference between phase and frequency modulation?

11. What are the types of noise that affect a data link? Which types of noise are man made and which are 'natural'? If you were comparing a satellite link and a telephone link, what do you think are the effect, type and consequences of noise on each link?

12. If a channel has a sampled impulse response of 0.3 1.0 0.3 0.3, and the vector 1,1,1,0,0,0,1,0 is transmitted over this channel, what is the received vector?

13. Why cannot users transmit any type of signal they wish (i.e. amplitude, frequency characteristics) over the PSTN?

14. What is the difference between DTE and DCE?

15. What are the advantages and disadvantages of the following communications media: fibre optic link, twisted pair, satellite link?

16. Why is a SYN character required by character-oriented data link, and why is a SYN character not required by a bit oriented data link?

17. What is bit stuffing and how is it used to ensure transparency?

18. What are the advantages and disadvantages of LANs based on the ring and bus topologies?

19. What is the meaning of CSMA/CS in the context of a mechanism for handling collisions on a LAN?

Operating systems

In this concluding chapter we take a break from the hardware of a computer and look at its operating system. We begin with an overview of operating systems and then concentrate on two areas in which hardware meets software. These are *multitasking*, which permits a computer to run several programs at the same time and *memory management* which translates addresses from the computer into the actual addresses of data within the CPU's memory system.

It could be argued that a section on operating systems in an introductory hardware course is a little out of place. My reasons for including this topic here are twofold. The first is that the operating system is intimately connected with the hardware. It both controls the operation of the hardware and allocates hardware facilities to user programs. Secondly, most students following a course in computer hardware also take a parallel course in high-level languages, data processing, and data structures, removing any need for me to deal with these topics here. However, the formal treatment of operating systems is not normally encountered by students until much later in their course. I have therefore provided this short introduction and overview of operating systems.

The relationship between an operating system (frequently abbreviated to OS) and a computer is almost identical to the relationship between a conductor and his or her orchestra. The great conductor is an international celebrity who gets invited on all the talk shows on television and is showered with society's highest awards. And yet a conductor does not add a single note to a concert. The importance of conductors is well known. They co-ordinate the players. Moreover, a good conductor knows the individual strengths and weaknesses of players and can therefore apply them in such a way as to optimize their collective performance.

An operating system is frequently the most important piece of software in a computer system, and yet it solves no user-oriented problems and performs no useful calculations. Its role is to co-ordinate the work of all the functional parts of the computer (including its software), and hence maximize the efficiency of the system. Here efficiency may be taken as the fraction of time for which the CPU is actually executing user programs. It would be more accurate if we were to say that the operating system is designed to remove inefficiency from the system. For example, suppose a program requires a document to be printed on a line-printer. While the line-printer is busy printing the document, the CPU is idling with nothing to do. The operating system normally intervenes to give the CPU something else to do while it is waiting for the printer to finish.

A second and equally important role of the operating system is to act as the interface between user and computer. By means of a job control language, JCL, the user is able to ask the computer to perform a number of tasks (e.g. to edit a program, load and execute it) without having to know about the detailed operation of the system. First-generation operating systems used JCLs that looked rather like any other conventional computer language. Operating systems running on some of today's personal computers have rejected such JCLs in favour of graphically oriented operating systems such as Microsoft's Windows or GEM. These operating systems which make use of WIMP (windows, icons, mouse, pointer) environments, are well suited to people who are not full-time professional computer programmers. Operating systems can be very large programs indeed—the Multics operating system (the forerunner of Unix) is reported to require over 20M bytes of storage.

In fact, from the user's point of view, the operating system should behave like the perfect bureaucrat. It should be efficient, helpful, and (like all the best bureaucrats) should remain in the background. For example, a poorly designed operating system, when asked to edit a file, may reply 'ERROR 53'. The programmer now has to find the operating system manual to look up ERROR 53. It's all a waste of time really because the last user ripped out the page with the translation of error messages because he or she got fed up with having to refer to them.

A really good operating system would have replied 'Hi there, Sunshine. Sorry about this, but my disks are full. Tell you what, I've noticed you've got a lot of back-up copies of your program, so if you delete a couple I think we'll be able to find room for your file. Have a nice day'. Finkel, in his book *An operating systems vade mecum*, calls this aspect of an operating system the **beautification principle** which he sums up by '... an operating system is a collection of algorithms that hides the details of the hardware and provides a more pleasant environment.'

As we have seen, the operating system is not simply a large program but a conglomeration of programs that carry out a multitude of widely different tasks. Figure 10.1 attempts to show how the various components of the operating system relate to each other and to the many other programs run under the control and supervision of the operating system. The diagram is depicted as a series of concentric circles for several good reasons. First, the programs at the centre of the circle such as the scheduler that switches from one task to another in a multitasking environment are physically smaller than programs such as the data base manager in one of the outer rings. Second, the nearer operating system components are to the centre, the more important they are. By important we mean crucial to the operation and performance of the CPU. Third, operating system components closer to the centre are better protected than components and user programs away from the centre.

The more sophisticated of today's operating systems employ hardware and software protection mechanisms to protect the important inter rings

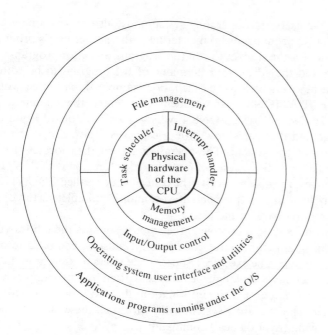

Fig. 10.1 The structure of a typical advanced operating system.

from illegal access or accidental access by other components. After all, if a user program corrupts part of the kernel, the operating system may well collapse and the system grind to a halt.

Not all computers have an operating system. When the computer is acting as a controller or is dedicated to a single task, there is no need for an operating system. The code that executes the task is simply held in memory (usually ROM) in machine-code form. Whenever functions normally performed by an operating system are required, they are incorporated into the task itself. A few personal computers that fall somewhere between the dedicated controller and the general-purpose computer have a range of operating-system facilities built into their high-level languages.

General-purpose operating systems were once found only on large computers but are now available on most personal computers. Some computer manufacturers call their operating system an *executive*, others call it a *monitor* or a *supervisor*. Before looking at the details of an operating system it is necessary to present an illustration of what an operating system actually does.

Consider the following example. A student wishes to edit a program and then run it. We will assume that the computer is a mainframe or a mini. The student goes to a terminal and logs on. By logging on he or she makes their presence known to the computer (a request for service), and at the same time the operating system is able to verify the user's identity and (if necessary) password. The logging-on sequence prevents unauthorized users from gaining access to the system, and may also perform an accounting function by measuring the total resources consumed.

If we assume that the computer has several terminals, another function of the operating system is to allocate processing time and memory space to each of the users. The operating system must also prevent one user from accidentally (or maliciously) interfering with another user's programs.

In order for the student to edit the program, an editor program must be invoked and the editor told the name of the program to be edited and what the new version is to be called. For example, if the source program is called EQUATIONS.3, the student may enter the command EDIT EQUATIONS.3,EQUATIONS.4, which is an example of a job control language and illustrates how little a user need know about the internal operation of the system. The operating system then locates the editor, transfers it from disk to the computer's main store, loads EQUATIONS.3 and prepares the disk to receive the edited version called EQUATIONS.4. If at any time one of these activities cannot be completed, the operating system reports back to the user.

When the editing is complete, the student submits the job for running. As the program is in source-code form, it must be compiled into object code before it can be executed. Source code refers to a program in a high-level or assembly-level language form as written by a programmer. Object code is the actual binary information that will be executed by the computer. The operating system will perform all these tasks by means of the following (hypothetical) command:

RUN PASCAL,EQUATIONS.4

It is then the job of the operating system to locate the Pascal compiler and the source program EQUATIONS.4, to perform the compilation, load the compiled version of EQUATIONS.4, and execute it. What's more, the operating system must decide where the program is to go in memory and to calculate all addresses of instructions and data accordingly.

At the end of the session the student logs off, freeing the terminal and the resources allocated to the current job. The operating system returns all these resources to its pool and prepares the necessary accounting information and statistics for the student's job. These statistics include the time for which he has been connected to the terminal, the actual CPU processing time used, the amount of disk space allocated, and the number of lines of output generated.

The situation today

A few years ago most operating systems were either designed for large mainframe computers or cut-down versions of mainframe operating systems intended to run on minicomputers or microcomputers. These operating systems used typical line-oriented job control languages not unlike UNIX or MS-DOS. Now that powerful microcomputers have spread into almost every working environment, a new generation of operating systems has been developed to take account of the new users. In particular, operating systems have been developed for users without great expertise in computer systems programming. Some of these operating systems employ *icons* and, possibly, a *mouse* to facilitate communication between the user and the operating system.

Instead of waiting for the operator to type in a command in an appropriate JCL, an icon-based operating system presents a list of alternative classes of action (e.g. edit, file, compile, execute, print, communicate with another computer, etc.). These *classes* are sometimes represented by *pictures* or *icons* indicating their action graphically (e.g. a picture of a hammer represents operating-system tools). Alternatively, the classes may be represented by a menu in words. The operator selects a class either by using the cursor control keys to move the cursor to the appropriate icon, or by using a mouse to move the cursor to the icon. The operating system may respond by expanding the class. For example, if the class is *file* (represented by the icon of a folder), the operating system may then display icons corresponding to retrieve a file, archive a file, delete a file or create a file. As you might expect, the icon invariably used to indicate file deletion is a trash can. Once again the operator uses the mouse or cursor to select the appropriate operation.

The purpose of these icon-based operating systems is to enable a naive user to operate a complex computer from the first moment it is plugged in without having to learn the vocabulary and syntax of an operating system. Moreover, icon-based operating systems frequently provide copious amounts of help if the operator runs into problems. By selecting a particular icon (which may be a picture of a book) or by hitting a particular key, the user can be provided with details of any particular command and how to use it. A few computer operators who have been exposed to conventional operating systems do not like icon-based operating systems. There are two reasons for this. The first is the 'I had to learn how to use a complex operating system so why shouldn't you' syndrome and the second is the delay introduced by an icon-based system. Clearly, it is faster to type EDIT file1,file2 than to move through a sequence of options offered by the operating system.

Note that the great change in operating systems over the past few years has been in the way in which they relate to the user rather than in the way in which they control resources. In fact it is possible to take a conventional JCL-based operating system such as MS-DOS or Unix and then write a 'front end processor' that takes commands from a WIMP environment and converts them into a form appropriate to the operating systems. Output from the operating system is converted into the appropriate WIMP display.

10.1 Types of operating system

Operating systems can be divided into many different categories. However, for the purpose of this introduction we will force operating systems into four classes: single-user, batch-mode, demand-mode, and real-time. Like many other computer concepts, the distinction between operating system classes is rather vague and any real operating system may have attributes common to several classes.

The *single user* operating system is the most primitive type found on many microprocessor systems (e.g. CP/M, OS9, MS-DOS) and allows one user to access the system at a time.

First generation operating systems worked in the *batch mode*. The jobs to be executed are fed into the computer, originally in the form of punched cards. Each user's job begins with a number of job control cards telling the operating system which of its facilities are required. The operating system then schedules the jobs according to the resources they require and their priority, and eventually generates the output—usually on a line-printer. Batch-mode operation is analogous to a dry cleaning service. Clothes are handed in and are picked up at some later date after they have been cleaned. The disadvantage of batch mode systems is their lengthy turn-around time. It's very frustrating to wait five hours for a print-out only to discover that the job did not run because of a simple mistake in one of the cards. Although punched cards are a thing of the past (but not in all countries), batch-mode operation is still implemented in some systems by creating a file consisting of a sequence of operating system commands. The batch is activated by telling the operating system to execute the sequence of commands to be found in a certain file. MS-DOS, for example, uses the extension '.BAT' to a file to indicate to the operating system that the contents of the file are to be treated as a sequence of commands.

Demand-mode operating systems permit a user to access the computer from a terminal. This is a great improvement over batch-mode because the user can complete each step before going on to the next one. Such an arrangement is also called *interactive* because the operating system and the user are engaged in a dialogue. Each time the user correctly completes an operation (say editing a file), he or she is informed of its success and invited to continue by some form of prompt message. If a particular command results in an error, the user is informed of this by the operating system and can therefore take the necessary corrective action.

A *real-time* operating system belongs, largely, to the world of process control in industry. The primary characteristic of a real-time operating system is that it must respond to an event within a well defined time. Consider a computer-controlled petrochemical plant. The computer running it invariably has a real-time operating system. The conditions at many parts of the plant are measured and reported to the computer on a regular basis. It is obvious that control actions must be taken as the conditions in the plant change. A sudden build-up of pressure in a reaction vessel cannot be ignored. The computer must either respond to an interrupt generated by the event, or poll the measuring equipment sufficiently often. Real-time operating systems are found wherever systems are computer controlled and the response time of the computer must closely match that of the system it is controlling.

Real-time operating systems are so called because the computer is synchronized with what people call *clock time*. Non-real-time systems operate in computer time. A job is submitted, and its results delivered after some elapsed time. There is no particular relationship between the elapsed time and the time of day. The actual elapsed time is a function of the loading of the computer and the particular mix of jobs it is running. In a real-time system the response time of the computer to any stimulus is guaranteed.

10.2 System software

The system software is a collection of programs designed to make the user's life an easier, if not an actually happy one. Some of the system programs to be briefly described are: the operating system utilities, the editor and the text processor, the assembler, the debugger, and the compilers.

10.2.1 Operating-system utilities

The operating-system utilities are those functions provided by the operating system that the user is able to access explicitly. These facilities allow the creation of files that may later be manipulated by other system software such as editors, assemblers, and compilers.

Each operating system has its own particular set of utilities. As an example of a typical system, I have chosen the MS-DOS utilities that run on IBM PC microcomputers and their clones. In many ways OS9 (a 68000 operating system) or UNIX would have been a better choice. However, more students will have encountered MS-DOS than these other operating systems. In what follows, *filename* is the name of a file and consists of up to eight characters. A filename may take an optional extension which can be up to three characters long. The extension is appended to the filename by a period (e.g. filename.ext) and is used to indicate the type of the file. For example, the extension .TXT indicates that the file is a text file, .BAT indicates a batch file, and .EXE indicates a binary file that can be loaded and executed.

As files are often stored on disk, it is sometimes necessary to indicate to the operating system the particular disk on which the file is located. MS-DOS does this by preceding the filename with ⟨disk⟩:, where ⟨disk⟩ may be A, B, C, or D. In order to simplify things, MS-DOS assumes a *working disk* and expects files to be located on that disk unless it is explicitly told otherwise. Consequently, it is necessary only to indicate the disk when a disk other than the working disk is to be accessed. In other words, if the working disk is C, it is not necessary to type C:myfile.txt, as myfile.txt will do just as well. The filename is formally defined as

[⟨drive⟩:]⟨name⟩[.⟨extension⟩]

The '⟨ ⟩' characters enclose a field that is supplied by the user. The '[' and ']' delimiters enclose an optional parameter. If no disk drive is specified, the operating system assumes the default drive (initially drive A). Typical filenames are

C:Pascal.TXT
RunJob.exe
TEST.TXT
A:READ.ME

Hierarchical files

The first generation of microcomputer operating systems were very crude and forced the user to group all files together in a single collection called a *flat* directory. While such an arrangement is adequate for ten or even forty files, it is cumbersome for systems with much larger numbers of files. Almost all today's operating systems support a ***hierarchical*** file structure that attempts to group like files together. The collection of all files is called a ***directory*** and a subgroup of files is called a ***subdirectory***. For example, I can group all my personal letters in a subdirectory called mail_slf and my professional letters in a subdirectory called mail_wrk.

MS-DOS implements a hierarchical or tree-structured filing system with a ***root*** directory at the top of the tree. A user with just a few files might be happy to keep all his or her working files in the root directory (along with the operating system itself). A more reasonable approach is to locate a number of subdirectories in the root directory. Each of these subdirectories may contain files or it may itself hold subdirectories. Figure 10.2 illustrates the file structure of a possible MS-DOS system. The various subdirectories of Fig. 10.2 are referred to as ***nodes*** of the tree. The relationship between two nodes in a hierarchical file system is frequently called *parent:child* if a subdirectory (the child) is a member of another directory (the parent).

Whenever a file is specified in a hierarchical system it must be specified in terms of its ***name*** and its ***path***. A file path is a representation of the way in which the file is reached from the root directory. For example, the file C:\TEXT\OUP\CHAP1 represents a file called 'CHAP1' which is in a

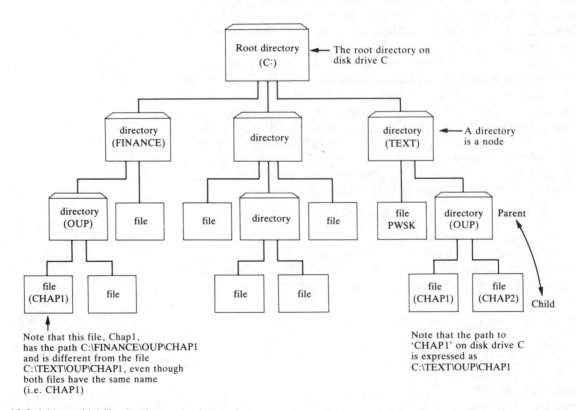

Fig. 10.2 A hierarchial file structure.

subdirectory called 'OUP'. The subdirectory 'OUP' is, itself, in a sub-directory called 'TEXT', and 'TEXT' is a subdirectory within the root directory on disk drive C. Figure 10.2 demonstrates this file structure. Note that a hierarchical structure permits more than one file to exist with the *same* name, as long as the like-named files are in different subdirectories.

We are now going to look at some of MS-DOS's utilities. It should be noted that most of these utilities are provided by other operating systems. Even operating systems based on windows or special function keys use the same utilities. The real difference between operating systems lies in the way in which the computer user accesses these facilities (e.g. by means of a formal job control language or simply by moving a pointer to a picture of the activity to be carried out).

Directory manipulation

MS-DOS implements a series of commands designed to operate on directories and subdirectories. Some of these commands are as follows.

1. MKDIR ⟨name⟩. Create a new subdirectory called ⟨name⟩ within the current directory.

2. CHDIR ⟨path⟩. Change the current directory to a new directory using the stated path. For example, CHDIR \LANGS\Pascal has the effect of making the current directory 'Pascal', which is in the subdirectory 'LANGS', which is in the root directory.

3. DIR. The directory command lists all the files and subdirectories in the current directory. Files are listed by MS-DOS with their name, extension and date of creation, and size. Other operating systems may include other attributes such as when the file was last accessed for a write operation and for a read operation.

4. RMDIR ⟨name⟩. Remove the subdirectory ⟨name⟩ from the current directory.

File manipulation

File manipulation commands apply operations to the files themselves rather than to the directories.

1. COPY ⟨source⟩,⟨destination⟩. The copy command copies a file from one place to another (without modifying the original copy). The effect of the COPY command is to copy *source* into a new file called *destination*. For example, COPY C:PROGRAM7.TXT A:PROG7 has the effect of copying a file called PROGRAM7 on disk C to a file which will be named PROG7 on disk A. The COPY command is frequently used to transfer a file from a floppy disk to a hard disk (to import a file), or from a hard disk to a floppy disk (to export a file or to create a back-up copy). MS-DOS supports an XCOPY command that is able to copy groups of files including the directory structure.

2. DEL ⟨name⟩. The delete command permits the removal of unwanted files. Entering DEL C:PROG7.TXT has the effect of deleting

PROG7.TXT from the directory on disk C. Note that it is not necessary to physically delete (i.e. overwrite) the file. Simply removing its name from the directory causes it to become an un-file.

3.   TYPE ⟨name⟩.   The type (sometimes called 'list') command has the effect of printing the contents of the named file on the terminal.

3.   ATTRIB [+R|−R][+A|−A]⟨filename⟩.   The attribute command permits a minimal level of file protection. The option list contains one or more of the following parameters: +R, −R, +A, −A. A plus adds the attribute and a minus removes it from the file. An 'R' write-protects the file and has the effect of stopping any further information being written into the file. It also stops the file from being deleted. The A attribute is used to specify whether the back up version of a file should also be copied by the XCOPY command. A +A parameter tells the operating system to copy the back up file and a −A parameter tell the operating system not to copy back up file.

Some operating systems provide further measures of protection. For example, a directory-protect operation stops a file appearing in the list of contents whenever the DIR function is used. A directory-protected file becomes *invisible* (i.e. secret) to the user unless he or she already knows that it is there! Another form of protection is to associate the file with a password. Whenever the file is to be accessed, the operating system asks the user to type in the password. If the password does not match the value stored in memory, the operation is abandoned and a message similar to 'insufficient access rights' passed to the user.

10.2.2 The editor

The editor is a program designed to manipulate text files and to format the text in the way desired by the operator. Today's editors are intended for on-line operation, rather than batch-mode operation. Before CRT terminals and on-line operation became so popular, information was often submitted to the computer in punched card form. Editing consisted largely of throwing away unwanted cards and replacing them by new cards. Editing punched paper tape involved cutting and splicing the punched tape and did not lead to that goal known as job satisfaction.

Traditional editors regard the text they are operating on as a sequence of lines, as if the text were printed on cards. All operations apply to a line of text, although they may be repeated and applied to a number of lines. Such an editor is known as a *line editor*. More modern editors operate on the page of text currently displayed on a CRT terminal. These editors are called *screen* editors and are rapidly replacing line editors, since they can manipulate entire paragraphs or columns of text in one operation.

Today there are a vast number of editors available to the computer user. They vary from computer to computer and any given computer often has a number of different editors, varying in sophistication. This is bad news for computer users who have to learn the syntax of each new editor they encounter. The basic functions of most editors are similar, but their commands vary just enough from editor to editor to be more than a trap for the unwary. Once, when changing from one editor to another, I typed D50, which was meant to delete line number 50. Instead it deleted the next 50 consecutive lines. I should have entered D#50, the '#' sign meaning 'line number'.

Although most editors have a host of sophisticated facilities, only the basic functions are described here. Five of the most important operations provided by an editor are as follows:

I   insert
D   delete
R   replace
F   find
C   change

The ***insert*** command allows text to be inserted into the current file. Screen editors permit insertion simpy by typing in the new text which is inserted at the current cursor position. Existing text is moved along as new text is inserted.

The ***delete*** command allows the removal of one or more unwanted lines. In a typical line editor, D deletes the current line, D3 deletes the next 3 lines and D#3 deletes the line whose number is 3. A screen editor provides a DEL key to delete the character at the current cursor position. Special character sequences (e.g. pressing the control key together with a particular letter) makes it possible to delete to the end of the current line or the end of the current paragraph.

The ***replace*** command causes one line to be replaced by another. Its use is equivalent to a delete followed by an insertion. Replace commands are found in line editors but are unnecessary in screen editors as text can be replaced by deletion followed by insertion at the current cursor position.

The ***find*** command enables the operator to search through the text for a given string of characters. A ***string*** is the term given to any sequence of consecutive characters. Without this command the programmer would either have to know all the line numbers or have a listing of the program (with line numbers) in front of him or her. For example, if the operator wishes to locate the line containing 'MOVE.B D3,DATA7' he or she enters the command

F/MOVE D3,DATA7/

The slash characters, /, form a delimiter for the string. The editor may replay by displaying the following line.

0023 START MOVE D3, DATA7   get 'DATA '

Now line 23 is the current line and may be edited as required. The 'change' function allows one string to be replaced by another avoiding the need to replace an entire line. In the above example it may be necessary to replace DATA7 by VAL9, in which case C/DATA7/VAL9/ is entered.

Editors often allow global commands which operate on a number of lines. For example, the change command is used to alter all occurrences of DATA7 within the next 12 lines of the text file in a single operation by means of the command C/DATA7/VAL9/12.

10.2.3 The word processor

The text processor, or word processor, takes over from where the editor left off. In fact, almost any of today's screen editors can reasonably be called a text processor or a word processor. An editor is employed to create other programs and other structured data forms, or to create text just as it is typed. For example, this book has been generated and manipulated by an editor. The function of the text processor is to operate globally on the text file created by the editor to produce a form suitable for printing. The text processor is able to perform left- and right-hand justification, which means that both the left- and right-hand margins of the text are straight. This enables people to produce letters and other text similar to that found in books or newspapers.

A screen editor produces processed text directly and is often referred to as 'WYSIWYG—what you see is what you get', because the text on the screen is an accurate representation of the text when it is printed. Some of the older systems (i.e. non-WYSIWYG editors) use special commands embedded in the text to carry out text formatting functions. For example, the command *.skip 4* might mean leave four blank lines when the document is printed.

Text processors also handle the heading and numbering of pages, and deal with footnotes.

Ten years ago the major split between different types of text processor was between the line editor and the screen editor. Today the situation has changed and all but the most primitive editors are screen based and include many sophisticated text processing options. The major split today is between word processors and desk-top publishing packages. High-speed processors coupled with low-cost main stores and large hard disk drives have given rise to DTP or desk-top publishing packages that permit text and graphics to be manipulated to create an output similar to that produced by publishers. Desk-top publishing brings an ability to handle a wide range of type fonts and to produce first-class output (on a laser printer) to the smallest of businesses.

10.2.4 The assembler

An assembler is a program that takes an assembly-language program, consisting of assembly directives and executable instructions, and converts them into machine-code form. The machine code created by the assembler may be saved as a file on disk, or loaded into the computer's memory for immediate execution.

As we have already dealt with assemblers, only a few details will be added here. An assembler frequently generates machine code for the machine on which the code is to be executed. However, it is sometimes more convenient to assemble a program on one machine to generate the code for another. For example, an IBM PC can be employed to assemble a program for later running on a 68000-based computer. Such an assembler is called a cross-assembler.

Closely associated with the assembler is the emulator. An emulator is a program which executes (i.e. interprets) machine code in software. For example, a 68000 program may be assembled on an IBM PC and the resulting 68000 machine code interpreted, line by line. That is, a program in 8086 machine code reads the 68000 op-codes, and then executes them. These operations are performed on 'synthetic' 68000 registers, which are, of course, locations in the PC's memory. Interpreting machine code in this way is relatively slow and inefficient, but it provides a way of checking the code for errors before it is actually run on the machine for which it is intended.

The linker, library, and loader

High-performance assemblers do more than simply translate assembly language into machine code. Programmers who write extensive amounts of assembly language soon find that they are using the same routines over and over again. Accordingly it makes sense to place these routines in a *library* for future use. However, as assembly-language programs operate on data in specific memory locations it is not easy to tack on a library program to a program being written. Why? Because the variables and memory allocation of the library routine will differ from those of the program being written. The *linker* has the job of resolving these problems and linking library routines into a program. Once the program has been linked, it must be loaded into the system's main store. The loader is responsible for making certain that the addresses generated by the linker are modified to suit the actual location of the program.

The debugger

A debugger is a program designed to monitor the running of another program. Here we shall concern ourselves with the debugger of machine-level programs. Once a program has been assembled, it can be executed. Sometimes the program does not work, or does not achieve the expected results. When this happens a debugger is often needed to help find the problem. Note that the debugger and the program being tested must be in memory at the same time. A debugger is so called because it *removes bugs (errors) from a program*. The basic functions of a debugger are to examine memory locations, to set breakpoints, and to trace the execution of a program.

The *display memory* function is employed to examine the contents of specified memory locations and to check if the data has changed in the way expected. It can also be used to preset the contents of memory locations prior to the running of a program. This enables a program to be tested with known data.

A *breakpoint* is a marker inserted in a program which, when encountered during the course of executing the program, causes predetermined event to take place. The breakpoint takes the form of a machine-code instruction. The 68000 calls the breakpoint a TRAP instruction, although many other microprocessors call it a software interrupt. Suppose a program is not behaving as expected. By inserting a breakpoint in the region where the problem is thought to lie, a check on the program's operation may be made. When the program is run, normal operation proceeds until the breakpoint is encountered. Then the execution of the program is halted and the contents of all the CPU's internal registers are printed. This provides the programmer with a snapshot of the state of the computer immediately preceding the breakpoint. After the breakpoint has been encountered it is (sometimes) possible to continue execution.

The *trace* function of a debugger is rather like an automatic breakpoint which is slowly moved through the program. After each instruction has been executed, the state of all registers is displayed. In this way, it is possible to monitor exactly what is happening while the program is being run.

10.2.5 The compiler

A compiler is a program (often as complex as, or more complex than, the operating system) that takes a source program in a high-level language, and compiles it into machine code suitable for execution. The operation of compilers is well beyond the scope of this book.

10.3 Multiprogramming

Multiprogramming is the ability of a computer to handle more than one job at once. Students often ask me in a slightly surprised tone, 'But how can a computer execute more than one program at a time? After all, it has only one program counter and one ALU.' The answer I give is that they are, strictly speaking, correct: a computer cannot execute two or more programs *simultaneously*, but it can give the impression that it is running several programs concurrently. The following example demonstrates how such an illusion is possible.

Consider a game of simultaneous chess. A first class player is pitted against a number of weaker opponents and moves from board to board making a move at a time. As the master player is so much better than his or her opponents, one of the master's moves takes but a fraction of the time they take. Consequently, each player shares the illusion that he or she has a single opponent of their own.

The organization of a game of simultaneous chess may readily be applied to the digital computer. All that is needed is a periodic signal to force the CPU to switch from one job to another and a mechanism to tell the computer where it was up to when it last executed a particular job. The jobs are normally referred to as *tasks* or *processes*, and the concepts of executing several tasks together is called concurrent programming or multiprogramming.

Before looking at the implementation of multiprogramming, its advantages should be pointed out. If each task required nothing but CPU time, then multiprogramming would have little advantage over running tasks consecutively (at least in terms of the efficient use of resources). If we re-examine the example of simultaneous chess, we find that its success is based on the great speed of the master player when compared with that of his or her opponents. While each player is laboriously pondering his or her next move, the master player is busy making many moves.

A similar situation exists in the case of computers. While one user is busy reading information from a disk drive and loading it into memory or is busy printing text on a printer, another user can take control of the CPU. A further advantage of multiprogramming is that it enables several users to gain access to a computer at the same time. This is very important today when 40 or more students wish to have access to a mainframe or mini at any given instant.

Figure 10.3 illustrates the advantages of multiprogramming by considering two tasks, A and B. Each of these tasks requires a number of different activities (e.g. CRT terminal input/output, disk access, etc.) to be performed during the course of its execution. The sequence of activities carried out by each of these two tasks as they are executed is given in Fig. 10.3(a).

If task A were allowed to run to completion before task B were started, valuable processing time would be wasted while activities not involving the CPU were carried out. Figure 10.3(b) shows how the tasks may be scheduled to make more efficient use of resources. The boxes indicate the period of time for which a given resource is allocated to a particular task. For example, after task A has first used the CPU, it accesses the disk. While the disk is being accessed by task A, task B is able to gain control of the processor.

The fine details of multiprogramming operating systems are far beyond the scope of an introductory book. However, the following principles are involved:

1. The operating system has algorithms built into it enabling it to schedule a job in the most efficient way, and to make best use of the facilities available. The algorithm may adapt to the type of jobs it is running, or the operators may feed system parameters into the computer

Task A	VDU 1	CPU	Disk	CPU	VDU 1

Time ⟶

Task B	VDU 2	CPU	Disk	VDU 2	CPU

(a)

Resource	Activity				
VDU 1	Task A			Task A	
VDU 2	Task B			Task B	
Disk			Task A	Task B	
CPU		Task A	Task B	Task A	Task B

(b)

Fig. 10.3 An example of multiprogramming: (a) two tasks in terms of the sequential activities they require; (b) the scheduling of the two tasks.

to maximize efficiency. When the parameters are adjusted by human operators, this is called *tuning* the operating system.

2. Possibly the greatest problem faced by the operating system is that of memory management. If more than one task is to be run, the operating system must allocate memory space to each of them. Moreover, the operating system should locate the tasks in memory in such a way as to make best possible use of the memory. Clearly, large gaps in memory should not be left between tasks.

3. If the CPU is to be available to one task while another is accessing a disk or using a printer, then these devices must be capable of autonomous operation. That is, they must either be able to take part in DMA operations without the active intervention of the CPU, or they must be able to receive a chunk of high-speed data from the CPU and process it at their leisure.

4. One of the principal problems a complex multitasking operating system has to overcome is that of *deadlock* or the *deadly embrace*. Suppose task A and task B both require CPU time and a printer to complete their activity. If task A has been allocated the CPU and the printer by the operating system, all is well and task B can proceed once task A has been completed. Now imagine the situation that occurs if task A requests CPU time and the printer but receives only the CPU, and task B makes a similar request and receives the printer but not the CPU. In this situation both tasks have one resource and await the other. As neither task will give up its resource, the system is deadlocked and hangs up indefinitely. Much work has been done on operating-system resource allocation algorithms to deal with this problem.

10.3.1 Switching tasks

It has already been pointed out that this book cannot go into the inner workings of an operating system. However, it is possible to outline the way in which task switching takes place. An important reason for including task switching is that it involves two hardware mechanisms described earlier—the interrupt and the stack.

Suppose an electronic pulse generator (i.e. a clock) were to be connected to a CPU's NMI (non-maskable interrupt which is equivalent to the 68000's $\overline{IRQ7}$) input and the clock set to generate a pulse every 0.01 s. Whenever the NMI line is asserted at each 0.01 s interval, the CPU is forced to respond to the interrupt. At the moment the interrupt occurs all the information that defines the task is in the CPU, the processor status word and any working registers currently being used by the task. This information is called the task's *context* or the task's *volatile* portion. An interrupt results in the program and machine status (e.g. CCR) being saved on the stack, and a jump made to the interrupt-handling routine. If at the end of the interrupt-handling routine an RTE (return from exception) is executed, the program counter and machine status are restored and execution of the program continues from the point at which it was interrupted.

Suppose now that the interrupt-handling routine does a devilishly cunning thing—it modifies the stack pointer before the RTE is executed. Now, when the RTE is executed, the value of the program counter retrieved from the stack is not that belonging to the program being executed just before the interrupt. Suppose that we arrange things so that the value of the PC loaded by a return from exception is the value of the PC that was saved when *another* program was interrupted. That is, it is the act of modifying the stack pointer that effects the task switching. Task switching is sometimes called *context* switching because it involves switching from the volatile portion of one task to the volatile portion of another task. The component of the operating system that is responsible for switching tasks is called the 'first level interrupt handler, FLIH' or the scheduler.

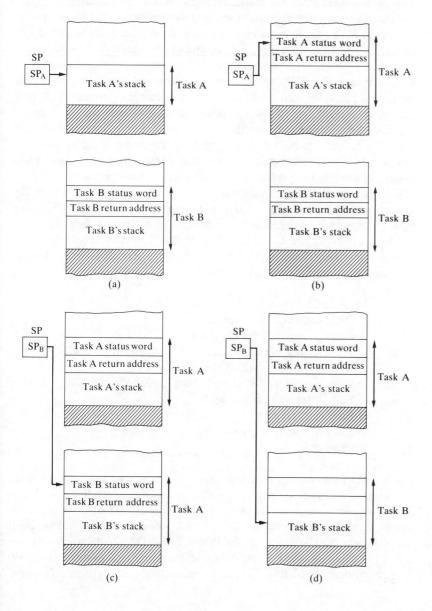

Fig. 10.4 Task switching: (a) Task A running; (b) Task A interrupted; (c) SP modified by operating system; (d) Task B running.

Figure 10.4 demonstrates how task switching works. Two tasks, A and B, are located in memory. To keep things simple, the regions of memory allocated to the tasks do not change during the course of their execution. Each task has its own stack, and at any instant the system stack pointer may be pointing to either A's stack or B's stack. In Fig. 10.4(a) task A is running. In Fig. 10.4(b) a task-switching interrupt has occurred and the contents of the program counter and machine status have been pushed onto the stack (i.e. A's stack). For the sake of simplicity Fig. 10.4 assumes that all items on the stack take a single word.

In Fig. 10.4(c) the operating system has changed the contents of the system stack pointer so that it is now pointing at task B's stack. Finally, in Fig. 10.4(d) the operating system executes an RTE, and task B's program counter is loaded from the stack causing task B to be executed.

Thus, at each interrupt, the operating system swaps the stack pointer before the RTE, causing the task to be switched. In a realistic system the operating system maintains a table of tasks to be executed. In addition to the stack pointer, each entry in the table contains further information about the task. Typically, this includes details about the task's priority, its maximum run time, and whether or not it is currently runnable. A task can be in one of the following three states. The task can be running (actually being executed), waiting its turn to be run, or blocked (not runnable as it is waiting for some resource to become available before it can be run). Tasks can be prioritized so that a task with a high priority will always be executed in preference to a task with a lower priority. A task is said to be runnable if it is executed when its turn arrives (subject to the limitations of priority). If the task is not runnable (i.e. blocked), it remains in the computer but is bypassed each time its turn comes. When the task is needed its run flag is set, and it will be executed next time round.

The behaviour of the part of an operating system that switches tasks can readily be expressed as pseudo code.

```
Module TaskSwitch
    Disable all further interrupts
    Push all registers on the stack
    Transfer registers from stack to TaskControlBlock(i)
    Locate the next task to run {i.e. Task(j)}
    Copy registers of next task from TaskControlBlock(j) to stack
    Pull all registers from stack
    Enable interrupts
    Return from exception
End module
```

Note that in this example all the registers (apart from the stack pointer) are saved following an interrupt, as the operating system does not know which registers constitute the task's volatile portion. A 68000-based kernel might employ the instruction MOVEM.L D0-D7/A0-A6,-(A7) to push the registers on the stack. A MOVEM.L D0-D7/A0-A6,-(A7) has the effect of pushing D0 to D7 and A0 to A6 onto the stack pointed at by A7. The mnemonic 'MOVEM' is read as 'move multiple registers'. The next step would be to copy these registers from the stack to the task's entry in the task control block. The next task can be restarted by loading the task's registers from the TCB to the stack and then pulling the registers off the stack immediately before executing a RTE instruction.

10.4 Memory management

Up to now we have assumed that the central processing unit of a computer generates the address of an instruction or data, and that this address corresponds to the actual location of the data in memory. Thus, if the computer executes MOVE \$1234,D0, the source operand is found in location number \$1234 of the computer's main random access memory. While this is true of most simple microprocessor systems, it is not true of many minicomputers and mainframes. The address generated by the CPU does not always correspond to the actual location of the data. Why this is so is the subject of this section.

Memory management is a general term that includes all the various techniques by which an address generated by a CPU is translated into the actual address of the data in memory.

We are going to show how memory management is used to permit computers with small main stores to execute programs that are far larger than the main store. We are also going to demonstrate how memory management is used in multitasking operating systems and how memory management can be employed to protect one task from being corrupted by another task.

Before looking at the reasons for memory management it is necessary to examine some of the concepts underlying the relationship between the location of data within the memory and the address of the data generated by the CPU. The conventional concept of memory is depicted in Fig. 10.5, where an address, p, is applied to the memory's address input to yield a data word, q, in a read cycle. An n-bit address allows up to 2^n unique locations to be specified and these locations can be represented as a linear list from 0 to $2^n - 1$. All these locations can also be mapped onto an n-dimensional space called *memory space*. Memory space is just a mathematical abstraction that enables us to visualize the arrangement of data in a memory just as a map enables us to visualize the structure of a country. We are interested in memory space because there are two types of memory space: the memory space seen by the CPU and the memory space implemented by the actual memory system. In fact, memory management is nothing more than the process of translating addresses in the CPU's memory space into addresses in the memory system's memory space.

The memory space of the memory system is called a *physical* memory space because each point in the memory space corresponds to a unique location in the actual memory. Figure 10.5 illustrates the concept of physical address space and provides an example for the case $n = 3$.

Physical address space is a general concept and is not restricted to any particular type of memory. It may even be spread over several devices,

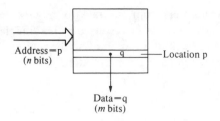

Fig. 10.5 Physical address space.

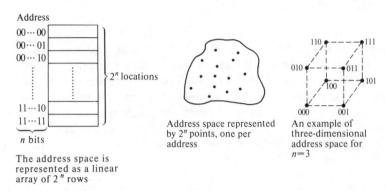

from high-speed RAM to low-speed magnetic tape. For our purposes, we will assume that physical memory includes only the main store, and that secondary store is excluded because of its vastly different characteristics. Later we shall see that *virtual memory* systems allow the secondary store to appear as part of the random access logical memory space.

Programmers are not concerned with physical address space. They are more interested in *logical* address space, the address space made up of the names of memory locations. The following analogy illustrates the difference between logical and physical addresses. A doctor has a filing cabinet in which the patient's records are stored. These records are stored in logical order by filing them alphabetically. They are never stored in the order of the physical addresses of the patients (i.e. the street names in which they live).

As an example of logical address space consider the address space made up of the eight names: ALICE, BRON, CINDY, DAN, EDNA, FRED, GEMMA, and HENRY. Figure 10.6 illustrates this logical address space both as a linear list and a three-dimensional space. Suppose these names have to be mapped onto a physical address space. One way of doing this is to generate a physical address for each of the names by adding together the ASCII codes for the first three letters of each name. Thus, ALICE is given the physical hexadecimal address $D6 = 41 + 4C + 49$. From Figure 10.7 we can see that each of the eight names has a unique location (not guaranteed by this address-generating algorithm), and that the order is not the same as the order of the logical name list. Moreover, the physical addresses of the names are not contiguous.

The address generated by the CPU is a logical address because it represents the name of a location somewhere in physical memory.

It's a nice academic exercise to distinguish between logical and physical address space, but how does it actually affect the programmer or the

(a)

Alice
Bron
Cindy
David
Edna
Fred
Gemma
Henry

(b)

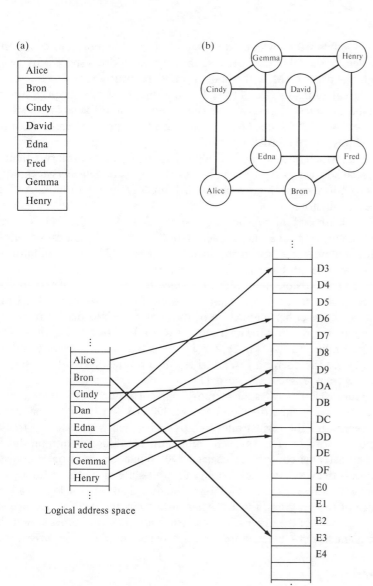

Fig. 10.6 Logical address spaces: (a) as a list; (b) in three dimensions.

Fig. 10.7 The relationship between physical and logical address space.

engineer who designs computers? Suppose I bought a microcomputer with an 8086 CPU (which has a 20-bit address bus) and 64K bytes of memory. I would be able to run programs of up to 64K bytes, but not larger programs. In other words, although the logical address space of the computer allows 1M locations to be uniquely addressed, the physical address space is limited to only 64K locations. Similarly, I may be able to afford a block of 256K bytes of dynamic RAM for a 6502-based computer but cannot address each physical memory location because the logical address space is limited to 64K.

The purposes of these analogies is to demonstrate that there is a difference between logical and physical addresses. The next step is to explain why this difference is important.

In today's world where addresses of 20 bits or more are common, a problem frequently arises because the physical address space provided by the high-speed RAM in the main store is frequently very much less than the logical address space of the CPU, limiting the size of the program that can be executed. For example the computer may be able to address $2^{32} = 4\,294\,967\,296$ bytes (4G bytes) of memory space, whereas the physical address space consists of only $2^{23} = 8M$ bytes of high-speed RAM. The problem which results when the logical address space is far larger than the physical address space is solved by resorting to *virtual memory* techniques, in which low-speed, high capacity disk units are made to look like high-speed main store.

A 68000-based microprocessor system has a 24-bit address bus, corresponding to a logical address space of 16M bytes. In a practical system 1M bytes of main store may be provided together with 20M bytes of hard-disk memory. The problem is how can we run programs greater than 1M bytes? One possible solution is to *widen* the immediate access memory space to include the disk space. That is, an address from the CPU can be used to access either main store or the contents of the disk, directly. For example, suppose that the instruction MOVE D0,DATA1 has the op-code corresponding to MOVE D0,DATA1 located in main store at address $1234, and the operand DATA1 is located on the disk with the physical address track 7, sector 5, word 11.

Figure 10.8 illustrates the memory map corresponding to this situation. The CPU reads the instruction MOVE D0,DATA1 from the main store, and generates the logical address DATA1 which is decoded as track 7, sector 5, word 11. The hardware must now read this location on the disk and transfer its contents to register D0. While this read operation is in progress the CPU must be frozen in a wait-state or halted. Although the physical address space is now large enough to deal with the logical address space of the program, the arrangement is unworkable. The average disk access time is of the order of 20 ms, which is a thousand times slower than the main store. A better approach is provided by the use of *overlays*.

Overlays

The programmer writes programs in the form of a *main part* and a number of chunks called *overlays*. These overlays are mutually exclusive in the sense that only one overlay is needed by the main part of the program at

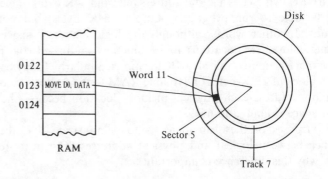

Fig. 10.8 Widening the address space to include disk space.

any instant. When a program using overlays is to be run, the operating system loads the main part into the main store, leaving the overlays on disk. The various overlays are written into a region of the main store reserved for overlays, as and when they are required by the main program. Because no two overlays are needed simultaneously, each new overlay is written over the old one. Figure 10.9 shows the relationship between the main store and disk store when using overlays.

The idea behind overlays is sometimes called the 80/20 rule because of the empirical observation that 80 per cent of the processing is often done by only 20 per cent of a program. Consequently, the active 20 per cent of a program can be loaded in main store for the whole time the program is running, and the remaining 80 per cent divided into overlays and loaded as required.

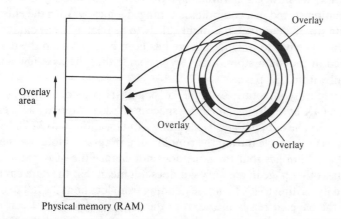

Physical memory (RAM)

Fig. 10.9 Disk overlays.

Overlaying solves the problem of the logical address space being greater than the available physical address space by permitting the physical address space of the overlay area to share several logical address spaces. Any ambiguity between logical addresses is resolved since only one overlay at a time occupies the overlay region. You can regard an overlay as a hotel room. Although it has a unique physical address, it is occupied by a constant stream of people with different logical addresses.

The use of overlays has the advantage of simplicity; no additional hardware is required to implement overlayed memory. Unfortunately, it puts great pressure on the programmer to write programs in a particular way, and, in any case, is applicable only to certain types of program. A good example of this is the operating system where some operations (e.g. DELETE, LIST, RENAME) can be treated as overlays and loaded only when they are actually required. Other parts of the operating system (e.g. the disk file manager) cannot be overlaid as they are constantly in use. A better, and more general, solution to the problem of limited physical address space is provided by *paging*.

Paging

When dealing with the CPU and addressing techniques earlier in this book, we saw how memory could be divided into a number of units called pages, just as a book is divided into pages. For example, a 24-bit address can be split into an 8-bit page number, and a 16-bit location within a page to provide 256 pages of 64K bytes. The same concept can be applied to the problem of limited physical address space by dividing the physical address space of both the main store and the secondary store into pages. Some of these pages are stored in main memory and some are stored in the secondary storage. We will see how paging can be used to try to keep the data that is accessed by the CPU in main store.

Only the programs actually being executed fill the pages in the main store, all other programs and data remain on disk. Whenever the CPU requires data which is not currently in a page in the main store, the page containing this data is moved from disk to the main store. At first sight this may seem an irrational thing to do. Instead of getting a single word from disk, we now get a whole page of words. Fortunately, most of the information stored in a computer is arranged logically, with the effect that the data stored at address q is highly likely to be related to the data located at addresses close to q. Once a page has been brought from the disk and installed in the main store, it is very probable that the next few accesses will fall within this page.

A simple hypothetical example of paging is provided by Fig. 10.10 where a 64K byte physical memory space is divided into two pages each of 32K bytes. The data in Page 0 extending from locations 0 to 32 767 is fixed and does not change during the running of a program. Note that here the term 'fixed' implies that the page does not change (i.e. it is not swapped with any other page in memory—it does not mean that the data cannot be altered by writing to it). Page 1, extending from locations 32 768 to 65 535, holds the page currently in use from the disk. That is, Page 1 can hold a 32K byte unit of data that has been transferred from the disk. A process called adddress mapping or address translation converts the logical address from the CPU into the physical address of the data in the main store. The relationships between the logical and physical addresses can be expressed as follows:

```
IF  LogicalAddress   < 32768
    THEN PhysicalAddress : = Logical Address
    ELSE PhysicalAddress : = LogicalAddress mod 32768 + 32768
ENDIF
```

For example, if the CPU refers to a logical address $001234, then it is translated into the physical address $001234. If, however, the CPU refers to logical address $011234, then $011234 is divided by 32 768 (i.e. $8000) to get the page number (i.e. 2), and the remainder (i.e. $1234) is added to $8000 to yield the location of the data (i.e. physical address $9234) in the main store. Note that we assumed that Page 2 of the logical address space is currently in main store.

At some point in the execution of the program the processor may generate a logical address falling outside the range of the pages currently in main store. In this case, a new page must be brought from disk and loaded into the physical memory from locations 32 768 to 65 535. The moving of pages is carried out by the operating system. The address mapping algorithm can now be expanded to include the detention of addresses not currently in main store.

```
IF LogicalAddress < 32768
   THEN PhysicalAddress : = LogicalAddress
   ELSE IF Currentpage = PhysicalAddress div 32768
           THEN PhysicalAddress : = LogicalAddress mod 32768 + 32768
           ELSE BEGIN
                   Get Newpage
                   PhysicalAddress : = LogicalAddress mod 32768 + 32768
                   END
         ENDIF
   ENDIF
```

It should now be clear that the physical page containing the memory location currently being accessed is stored in main store, and that the logical address generated by the processor is automatically translated into the address of the required data in main store. This translation is done by high-speed hardware. The process of moving data from disk to main store is called *swapping-in* and is carried out by the operating system. The converse operation is called swapping-out and takes place when a page in random access memory is to be overwritten by a new page swapped-in from disk. The page swapped-out is rewritten to disk (if it has been written to since it was swapped-in).

Whenever a logical address corresponds to a location within a page not currently in main store, the address translator generates an interrupt, forcing the operating system to intervene. Of course, paging is effective only as long as the number of memory references causing a page to be swapped into main store are few compared to the number of accesses within a page. Clearly, pages should be as large as possible and data well ordered. Unfortunately, in many real systems the data is not well ordered and the pages are relatively small—often 2 or 4K bytes.

The reader may be tempted to think that paging and overlaying are almost identical. This is not true for two reasons. There is often only one overlay area, while the paging technique is normally extended to a large number of pages. Moreover, when programmers write overlays they choose the addresses of programs and data to fall within the range provided by the overlay area. But when paging is used, the logical addresses generated by the program and its data are automatically modified to correspond to the physical address of the information in a main store. The simple scheme we have described above can be extended to a more general type of memory management called *virtual memory*.

Virtual memory

In a virtual memory system the programmer sees a large array of physical memory (the virtual memory) which appears to be entirely composed of high-speed main store. In reality, the physical memory is composed of a small high-speed RAM and a much slower sequential access disk store. Virtual memory has two advantages. It allows the execution of programs

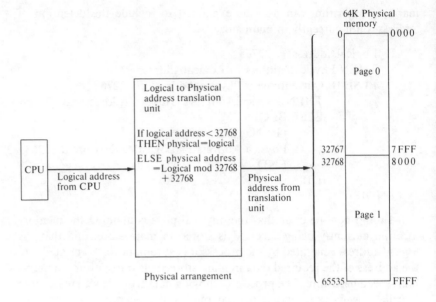

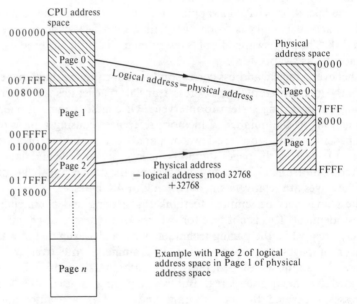

Fig. 10.10 A simple example of paging.

much larger than the physical memory would normally permit, and frees the programmer from worrying about choosing logical addresses falling within the range of available physical addresses. Programmers are at liberty to choose any logical address they desire for their program and its variables. The actual addresses selected by a programmer do not matter, since the logical addresses are automatically mapped into the available physical memory space as the operating system sees fit.

Practical virtual memory systems divide the physical random access memory space into pages of, typically, 512–4096 bytes. This allows several fragments of a virtual program to be in main store at any instant. Obviously, it is sensible to retain frequently used data in main store in order to avoid retrieving it from disk every time it is needed.

Figure 10.11 shows the relationship between virtual memory space and physical address space for a hypothetical processor with an 18-bit address bus. The virtual memory space, corresponding to the logical address space of the processor, spans a total of 256K bytes for a CPU with an 18-bit address bus. This virtual address space (i.e. logical address space) is divided into 64 pages of 4K bytes. The processor's main store, the physical memory of 64K bytes, is divided into 16 pages of 4K. Each of these 4K blocks is called a *page-frame* because it holds one page from the virtual memory. We now have a situation in which the processor can directly address data anywhere in one of its 64 pages, but only 16 of these pages can be in high-speed main store at the same time. The rest are stored on disk.

At any given time up to 16 pages of the virtual address space may be in main store. An example should make this diagram more clear. Suppose that the CPU executes MOVE D0,DATA1 where DATA1 has the logical address $02AED (see Fig. 10.11). The 4K bytes corresponding to logical addresses from $02000 to $02FFF are actually stored in physical memory from $D000 to $DFFF. Consequently the logical operand address $02AED must be translated into the physical address $DAED.

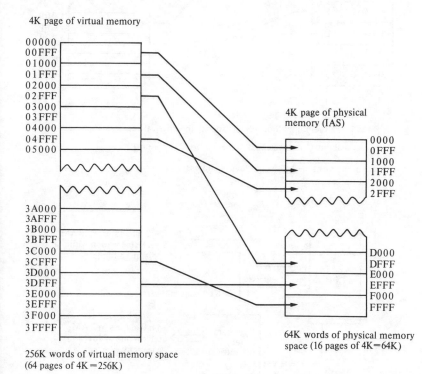

Fig. 10.11 The relationship between virtual address space and physical address space.

The arrangement in Fig. 10.11 raises two questions. When the CPU generates a logical address of an operand, how is this address translated into the physical address of the operand in main store? Secondly, what happens if the logical address has no corresponding physical address because the appropriate page is not in main store?

The processor maintains a page table, Fig. 10.12, which maps the pages in main store onto the processor's own logical address space. The logical address generated by the processor consists of two fields, a 12-bit address which selects a location within a page and a 6-bit page address which selects a particular page. Note that the 12-bit and 6-bit addresses together span the 18-bit virtual (logical) memory space. From Fig. 10.12 it can be

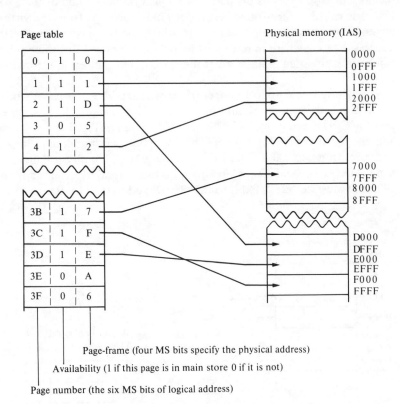

Fig. 10.12 The page table corresponding to Fig. 10.11.

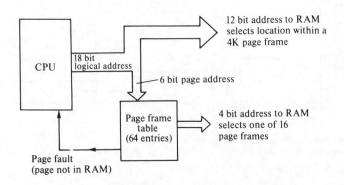

seen that the logical address, 000010 101011101101, causes entry two (i.e. 000010) of the page-table to be interrogated. This yields a page-frame address 13 (i.e. $D), and the data is accessed from location 1101 101011101101 in the main store.

As only a fraction of a large virtual program can be in main store at any time, a virtual address will sometimes be generated and the page on which the data lies will not be in main store. That is, when a page address is applied to the page table, the availability bit corresponding to that page will be zero. This situation is called a *page fault*, and the operating system must now intervene. As soon as a page fault is generated, the operating system fetches the missing page from the secondary store, loads it in main store, and updates the page table accordingly.

This process is called *demand paging* because a new page is not brought until needed. Once the main store is full of pages, each new page must overwrite an old one. One possible way of proceeding is to sacrifice the least recently used page every time a new page is brought from disk. The algorithm that implements this page replacement policy is called the LRU (least recently used algorithm). There are many other page replacement algorithms available, each with its own performance:complexity parameters. For example, the LRU algorithm requires that each page record the time at which it is accessed. Obviously, the memory management system must know when each page was last accessed if it is going to throw away the oldest page to make room for a new page. A much simpler algorithm is called NRU (not recently used) and simply marks each page when it is accessed with a binary flag from a clock. When the operating system wishes to reject a page it chooses a page with a flag that is different to the current state of the flag (i.e. the page must be old).

Real virtual memory systems are very complex and require both sophisticated hardware and software. One problem we have not yet considered is the duplication of memory space. Whenever a page is copied from the secondary store into the immediate access store, it exists in two places. If the CPU never modifies the page in its main store, there is no problem and the page can be overwritten by a new page at any time. However, if the CPU writes to this page, there is a divergence between the page in main store and the corresponding page on disk. Under these circumstances the operating system cannot swap-out the page in main store without writing the updated version on disk. In most systems each page has a *dirty bit* associated with it. When a word in the page is modified by the processor, the dirty bit is set, reminding the operating system that this page must be re-written to disk when it is swapped-out.

So far we have regarded virtual memory techniques as a solution to the problem of limited main store. Their ability to translate logical into physical addresses has two other important implications. The programmer is entirely free from having to think about where programs and data are going to be located in physical memory. Any logical addresses used by the programmer will be translated automatically into their address in main store by the page table. Similarly, in a multiprogramming environment new programs do not have to be located in contiguous blocks of main store, the page-table address translation permits a program to be located in main store with its pages scattered at random.

Memory management and multitasking

In a multitasking system, several tasks may be loaded into physical memory at the same time. A reasonably secure system must ensure that each task cannot access the resources belonging to another task. Equally, it seems sensible to avoid the duplication of programs.

Suppose task A requires a Pascal compiler and task B also requires a Pascal compiler. There should be only one copy of the compiler in physical address space to avoid needless waste of memory space. Memory management solves both the problems of task security and resource duplication.

Figure 10.13 demonstrates how memory management deals with the above problems. A protection mechanism is implemented by using the logical address generated by a task to interrogate information in the page table. Suppose the operating system is currently running task A. It sets a marker in the memory management unit to indicate that task A is

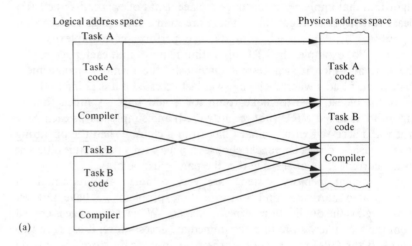

Fig. 10.13 Memory management and multitasking: (a) logical to physical mapping; (b) address translation unit.

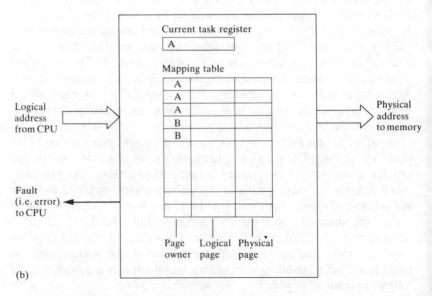

currently active. Each page in the page table belonging to task A has a marker indicating its ownership. When the CPU generates a logical address, the MMU (memory management unit) checks that the current logical page belongs to task A by matching the marker with the current page marker. If they are the same, a logical to physical address translation takes place. If they are not, a page error is signalled and the CPU interrupted.

Sharing a software resource between two programs is easily accomplished with memory management. All the operating system need do is to map two distinct logical addresses onto the same physical address space. Figure 10.13 demonstrates how this is done. Tasks A and B both wish to use the same compiler. Although we have shown separate compilers in the logical address space, these are mapped onto the same region of the physical address space.

At this point we should indicate that memory management is a complex subject and we have simply outlined some of the principles here. The memory management units for most of today's high performance microprocessors are often more complex than the CPU's themselves. Some microprocessors (e.g. 8086 and 68000) require external memory management chips, while a few microprocessors include on-chip memory management (such as the 68030 and the 80286/80386).

Virtual memories and microprocessors

Virtual memory techniques are not readily applicable to conventional 8-bit microprocessors with 16-bit address buses, because of the microprocessors' limited logical address space of 64K. However, it is exceedingly difficult to apply virtual memory techniques (as opposed to simple paging) to many conventional microprocessors. If an access is made to a location currently within the main store, automatic hardware address translators convert the logical address of the operand to its physical address in a few nanoseconds. This process is entirely transparent to the CPU. So far, so good.

Now suppose the logical address of an operand not currently in main store is generated. When the address translation hardware sees this address, it signals a 'not in main store condition' (i.e. a page fault) and the appropriate page must be brought from disk. Behind this seemingly simple remark lurk two problems. What happens to the current instruction and how is the new page moved from disk to main store? Whenever an operand not in RAM is accessed, the current instruction must either be aborted and re-run, or suspended until the operand is in main store.

If the current operation is aborted, the CPU itself can fetch the page before re-running the aborted instruction. But if the instruction is suspended by the CPU entering a wait state, another CPU must fetch the page. Figure 10.14 illustrates this sequence of events.

The majority of microprocessors do not have facilities for aborting instructions and then re-running them. This is because once an instruction has begun its path through the processor's execution unit, information about the machine's status prior to the instruction (e.g. CCR and PC) is lost. Consequently, it is impossible to abort an instruction and to 'wind

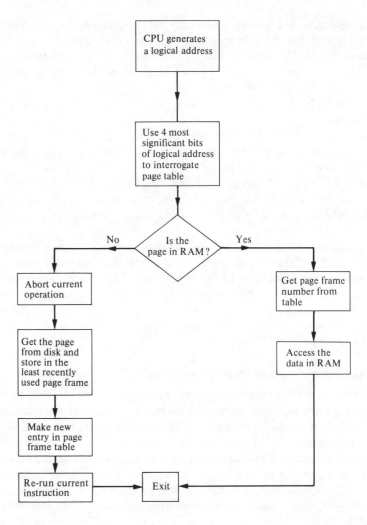

Fig. 10.14 The page-fault.

back' the processor to the exact state it was in immediately before the aborted instruction. If virtual memories were to be applied to most microprocessors it would be necessary to freeze the state of the CPU whenever an operand was not in main store and to use a second microprocessor to get a new page from disk. Once the page has been installed in main store, the second processor can 'go back to sleep' and the main processor allowed to complete its frozen instruction now that its operand is in main store.

Some 16-bit microprocessors such as the 68010 (but not the 68000) are more amenable to virtual memory techniques than their predecessors. For example, when the 68010 receives a page fault (called a bus error) which halts the current instruction, all the information necessary to re-run the current instruction is saved on the stack. After the operating system has dealt with the page fault, a return-from-exception instruction restores all the information stored on the stack and the aborted instruction is re-run. Now the instruction should be executed to completion since it will no longer generate a page fault when its operand is accessed.

The 68000 and memory management

The 68000 does not directly support memory management and requires an external MMU to implement memory management. However, the 68000 has two features that make it relatively easy to implement memory management systems. The first is the 68000's function code outputs on pins FC0–FC2, and the second is the 68000's ability to support two operating modes (user and supervisor). Whenever the 68000 accesses memory it puts a code on pins FC0–FC2 to indicate the type of memory cycle (data or instruction access, supervisor mode or user mode access). A memory management unit can examine the state of the function code pins to determine whether the current access is valid. For example, a data access can be denied to a region containing code (i.e. instructions) that should not be modified. Similarly, any access by a user program to a region of code containing the operating system can be trapped by the MMU and aborted.

The 68000 has an S bit in its system status byte that indicates whether it is in the user mode (S = 0) or in the supervisor mode (S = 1). For most practical purposes, there is no difference between these modes! However, each mode has its own address register A7. Consequently, whenever the 68000 is operating in its supervisor state it uses one A7 and whenever it is operating in its user mode it uses a different A7. As the supervisor mode is invariably dedicated to the operating system, it follows that the operating system has its *own* stack pointer that cannot be accessed by tasks running in the user mode. This feature makes 68000 systems much more robust than those with only a single stack pointer. Certain instructions that affect the operating mode of the 68000 cannot be executed while it is in the lower privileged user state.

When the 68000 is in the supervisor state, a change of state to user state can be made by simply setting the S bit to zero. The converse action is not permitted (a user program cannot set the S bit to one), because user programs must not be permitted to access the supervisor state. A change from user state to supervisor state is executed by means of an *exception* which may be a hardware interrupt, a software interrupt/trap or a page fault (i.e. bus error). Once an exception has occurred, the 68000 runs in the supervisor mode under the control of the operating system. One implication of this is that all input and output resources can be allocated to the operating system and user programs granted access to I/O only through operating system calls.

The 68000 has eight operating system calls, or traps, TRAP #0 to TRAP #7, each of which results in a software exception. When a TRAP #n is executed, the 68000 sets its S bit, saves the PC and status word on the stack pointed at by the supervisor stack pointer, A7, and calls the routine associated with TRAP #n. At the end of the exception-handling routine, the RTE instruction pulls the PC off the stack together with the 68000's status word and a return is made to the state that the 68000 was in before the TRAP was executed.

Why is such a complex behaviour necessary? Because all input/output activity is carried out via the operating system, applications programmers do not have to know how the I/O is actually implemented. For example, all they need to know is, say, that a TRAP #4 will cause the contents of D0 to be sent to the console. Moreover, no user program can actually access I/O devices directly and, possibly, carry out illegal actions. For example, the user cannot directly access a disk drive and therefore cause untold damage by accidentally corrupting large sections of the disk.

Cache memories

The basic concepts underlying virtual memory can be extended to any hierarchical memory structure. We are now going to look at the cache memory, which can dramatically raise the performance of a computer system at relatively little cost.

Cache memory provides system designers with a way of exploiting high-speed processors without incurring the cost of large high-speed memory systems. The word 'cache' is pronounced 'cash' or 'cash-ay' and is derived from the French word meaning 'hidden'. Cache memory is hidden from the programmer and appears as part of the system's memory space. There is nothing mysterious about cache memory. It is simply a quantity of very high-speed memory that can be accessed rapidly by the processor. The element of magic comes from the ability of systems with cache memory to employ a tiny amount of high-speed memory (e.g. 64K bytes of cache memory in a system with 4M bytes of DRAM) and expect the processor to make over 95 per cent of its accesses to the cache rather than the slower DRAM.

Cache memory can be understood in everyday terms by its analogy with a diary or notebook used to record telephone numbers. A telephone directory contains hundreds of thousands of telephone numbers and nobody carries a telephone directory around with them. However, most people have a diary or a note book with a hundred or so telephone numbers which they keep with them. Although the fraction of all possible telephone numbers in someone's notebook may be less than 0.01 per cent, the probability that their next call will be to a number in the notebook is high. Cache memory operates on exactly the same principle by locating frequently accessed information in the cache memory rather than in the much slower main memory. Unfortunately, unlike the personal notebook, the computer cannot know, *a priori*, what data is most likely to be accessed. Computer caches operate on a learning principle. By experience they learn what data is most frequently used and then transfer it to the cache.

The general structure of a cache memory is provided in Fig. 10.15. A block of cache memory sits on the processor's address and data buses in parallel with the much larger main memory. Note that the implication of *parallel* in the previous sentence is that data in the cache is also maintained in the main memory. To return to the analogy with the telephone notebook, writing a friend's number in the notebook does not delete their number in the directory.

The cache memory relies on the same principle as the notebook with telephone numbers. The probability of accessing the next item of data in memory is not simply a random function. Because of the nature of programs and their attendant data structures, the data required by a

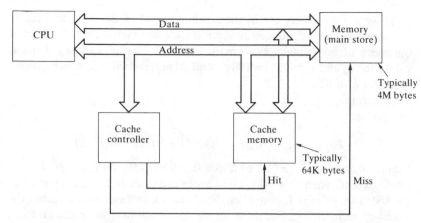

Fig. 10.15 Structure of a cache memory.

processor is often highly clustered throughout memory. This aspect of memories is called the *locality reference* and makes the use of cache memory possible.

A cache memory requires a cache controller to determine whether or not the data currently being accessed by the CPU resides in the cache or whether it must be obtained from the main memory. When the current address is applied to the cache controller, the controller returns a signal called 'hit', which is asserted if the data is currently in the cache. Before we look at how cache memories are organized, we will demonstrate their effect on a system's performance.

The principal parameter of a cache system is its hit ratio, H, which defines the ratio of hits to all accesses. The hit ratio is determined by statistical observations of the operation of a real system and cannot readily be calculated. Furthermore, the hit ratio is dependent on the actual nature of the programs being executed. It is possible to have some programs with very high hit ratios and others with very low hit ratios. Fortunately, the effect of locality of reference usually means that the hit ratio is very high—often in the region of 98 per cent. Before calculating the effect of a cache memory on a processor's performance, we need to introduce some terms.

Access time of main store	t_m
Access time of cache memory	t_c
Hit ratio	H
Miss ratio	M
Speed-up ratio	S

The speed-up ratio is defined as the ratio of the memory system's access time without cache to its speed with cache. For N accesses to memory the total access time of a memory without cache is given by: Nt_m.

For N accesses to a memory with cache the total access time is given by $N(Ht_c + Mt_m)$. We can express M in terms of H as $M = 1 - H$, since if an access is not a hit it must be a miss. Therefore the total access time for a system with cache is given by: $N(Ht_c + (1-H)t_m)$.

The speed-up ratio is therefore given by

$$S = \frac{Nt_m}{N(Ht_c + (1-H)t_m)} = \frac{t_m}{(Ht_c + (1-H)t_m)}.$$

As we are not interested in the absolute speed of the main and cache memories, we can introduce a new parameter, k, which defines the ratio of the speed of cache memory to main memory. That is, $k = t_c/t_m$. Typical values for t_m and t_c might be 100 ns and 20 ns, respectively, which gives a value for k of 0.2.

Therefore,

$$S = \frac{t_m/t_m}{Ht_c/t_m + (1+H)t_m/t_m} = \frac{1}{Hk + (1-H)} = \frac{1}{1 - H(1-k)}$$

Figure 10.16 provides a plot of S as a function of the hit ratio, H. As you might expect, when $H = 0$ (i.e. all accesses are made to the main memory) the speed-up ratio is 1, and when $H = 1$ (i.e. all accesses to the cache) the speed-up ratio is $1/k$. The most important conclusion to be drawn from Fig. 10.16 is that the speed-up ratio is a sensitive function of the hit ratio. Only when H approaches about 90 per cent does the effect of the cache memory become really significant. This result is consistent with common sense. If H drops below about 90 per cent, the accesses to main store take a disproportionate amount of time and fast accesses to the cache have little effect on system performance.

Cache organization

There are at least three ways of organizing a cache memory, each with its own performance:cost trade-off (i.e. direct-mapped, associative mapped and set associative mapped).

Direct-mapped cache

The simplest way of organizing a cache memory employs direct mapping, which relies on a simple algorithm to map data block i from the main memory into data block i in the cache. For the purpose of this section we will regard the smallest unit of data held in a cache as a **block** (sometimes

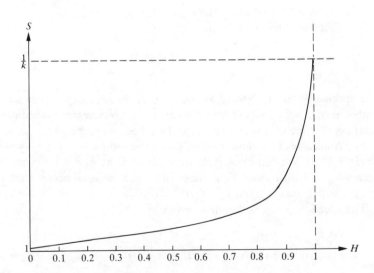

Fig. 10.16 Speed-up as a function of hit ration H.

called a 'line') which is made up of typically two or four consecutive words.

Figure 10.17 illustrates the structure of a highly simplified direct-mapped cache. The memory is composed of 32 words and accessed by a 5-bit address bus. For the purpose of this discussion we need only consider the set and block (as it does not matter how many words there are in a block). The address in this example has a 2-bit set field, a 2-bit block field and a 1-bit word field. The cache memory holds $2^2 = 4$ blocks. When the processor generates an address, the appropriate block in the cache is accessed. For example, if the processor generates the 5-bit address 01110, block 3 is accessed.

A glance at Fig. 10.17 reveals that there are four possible blocks numbered three—a block 3 in set 0, a block 3 in set 1, a block 3 in set 2 and a block 3 in set 3. In this example the processor accessed block 3 in set 1. The obvious question is 'how does the system know whether the block 3 accessed in the cache is the block 3 from set 1 in the main memory?'

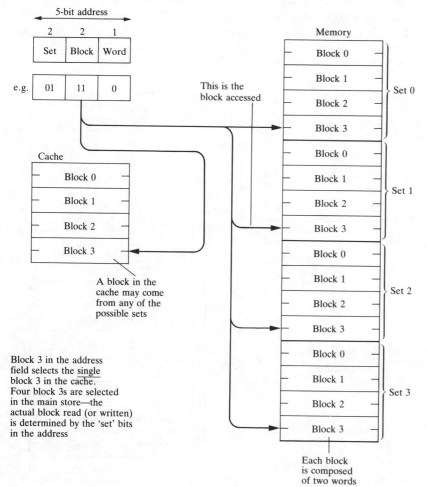

Fig. 10.17 A highly simplified direct-mapped cache.

Figure 10.18 demonstrates how the contention between blocks is resolved by direct-mapped cache. Associated with each block in the cache memory is a *tag* or label that identifies which set that particular block belongs to. When the processor accesses block 3, the tag belonging to block 3 in the cache is sent to a comparator. At the same time the set field from the processor is also sent to the comparator. If they are the same, the block in the cache is the desired block and a hit occurs.

If they are not the same, a miss occurs and the cache must be updated. The old block 3 from set 1 is either simply discarded or rewritten back to main memory, depending on how the updating of main memory is organized.

Figure 10.19 provides a skeleton structure of a direct-mapped cache memory system. The cache memory itself is nothing more than a block of very high-speed random access read/write memory. The cache tag RAM is a fast combined memory and comparator that receives both its address and data inputs from the processor's address bus. The address input is the block address from the processor which is used to access a unique location (one for each of the possible blocks). The data in the cache tag RAM at this location is the tag associated with that block. The cache tag RAM also has a data input which is the tag field from the processor's address bus. If the tag field from the processor matches the contents of the tag (i.e. set) field being accessed, the cache tag RAM returns a hit signal.

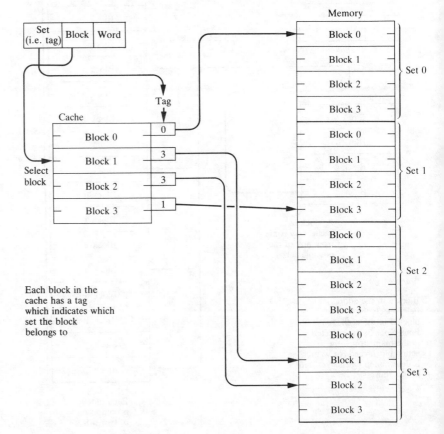

Fig. 10.18 Direct-mapped cache—resolution of contention between blocks.

Each block in the cache has a tag which indicates which set the block belongs to

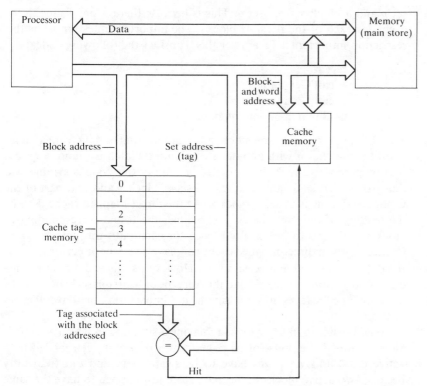

Fig. 10.19 Structure of direct-mapped cache.

The block address accesses the cache tag RAM. The accessed location returns the tag (i.e. set) corresponding to the accessed block. The tag is compared with the set address on the address bus. If they match, the block being accessed is in the cache

As Fig. 10.19 demonstrates, the cache tag RAM is nothing more than a simple high-speed random access memory with a built-in data comparator. Some of the major semiconductor manufacturers have implemented single-chip cache tag RAMs.

The advantage of the direct-mapped cache is almost self-evident. Both the cache memory and the cache tag RAM are widely available devices that, apart from their speed, are no more complex than any other mainstream integrated circuit. Moreover, the direct-mapped cache requires no complex block replacement algorithm. If block x in set y is accessed and a miss takes place, block x from set y in the main store is loaded into the frame for block x in the cache memory. That is, there is no decision concerning which block from the cache is to be rejected when a new block is to be loaded.

Another important advantage of direct-mapped cache is its inherent parallelism. Since the cache memory holding the data and the cache tag RAM are entirely independent, they can both be accessed simultaneously. Once the tag has been matched and a hit has occurred, the data from the cache will also be valid (assuming the cache data and cache tag memories have approximately equal access times).

The disadvantage of direct-mapped cache is almost a corollary of its advantage. A cache with n blocks has one restriction: at any instant it can hold only one block numbered x. What it cannot do is hold a block x from set p and a block x from set q. This is because there is one frame in the cache for each of the possible blocks. The important question is, 'is this restriction important?' To answer this, consider the following code:

```
repeat
    call Get_data
    call Compare
until match or end_of_data
```

The above innocuous fragment of code reads a string of data from a buffer and then matches it with another string until a match is found. Suppose that by purely bad luck the compiled version of this code is arranged so that part of the Get_data routine is in set x, block y and that part of the Compare routine is in set z, block y. As the direct-mapped cache permits the loading of only one block y at a time, the frame corresponding to block y will have to be reloaded twice for each path through the loop. Consequently, a direct-mapped cache can have a very poor performance if the data is arranged in a certain way. However, statistical measurements on real programs indicate that the very poor worst-case behaviour of direct-mapped caches has no significant impact on their average behaviour.

To add insult to injury, you can imagine a situation in which a cache is almost 'empty' (i.e. most of its page frames have not been loaded with active data) and yet pages have to be swapped in and out frequently because two active blocks in the main store just happen to have the same block numbers. In spite of these objections to direct-mapped cache, it is very popular because of its low cost of implementation and high speed.

Associative mapped cache

An excellent way of organizing a cache memory that overcomes the limitations of direct-mapped cache is described in Fig. 10.20. Ideally we would like a cache that places no restrictions on what data it can contain. The *associative* cache is such a memory.

An address from the processor is divided into two fields: the tag and the word. Like the direct-mapped cache, the smallest unit of data transferred into and out of the cache is the block. Unlike the direct-mapped cache, the associative cache displays no relationship between the number of blocks in the cache and the number of blocks in the main memory. For example consider a system with 1M bytes of main store and 64K bytes of associatively mapped cache. If the size of a block is four 32-bit words, the main memory is composed of $2^{20}/16 = 64K$ blocks and the cache is composed of $2^{16}/16 = 4K$ blocks. An associative cache permits any block in the main store to be loaded into one of its page frames. In this case, block i in the associative cache can be loaded with any one of the 64K possible blocks in the main store. Therefore, block i requires a 16-bit tag to uniquely label it as being associated with block j from the main store.

When the processor generates an address, the word bits can be used to select a word location in both the main memory and the cache. There is no block address that can be used to address a block in the cache (unlike the

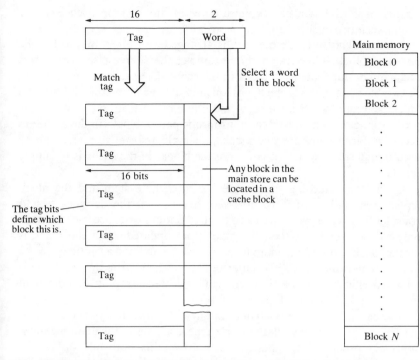

Fig. 10.20 Associative cache.

The tag field is matched with all tags in the cache simultaneously. If there is a match, the corresponding block is in the cache and there is a hit. If there is no match, the corresponding block is in main store.

direct-mapped cache memory). Why? Because the direct-mapped cache reserves each block in the cache for one of a set of possible blocks in the main store (the tag resolves which of the blocks is actually present). As the associative memory can store any of the 64K memory blocks in one of its page frames, it requires a 16-bit tag (assuming that there are 2^{16} possible blocks in the main memory) for each of its page frames. More importantly, as the cache's page frames (i.e. blocks) are not ordered, the tags are not ordered and cannot be stored in a simple look-up table like the direct-mapped cache.

Associative cache systems require a special type of memory called 'associative' memory. An associative memory has an n-bit input but not necessarily 2^n unique internal locations. The n-bit address input is a tag that is matched with a tag field in each of its locations simultaneously. If the input tag matches a stored tag, the data associated with that location is output. Otherwise the associative memory produces a miss output. In other words, an associative memory is not addressed in the same way that a computer's main store is addressed.

Associative cache memories are efficient because they place no restriction on the data they hold. Unfortunately, associative memories are very expensive and large associative memories are not available. Moreover, once the cache is full, a new block can be brought in only by overwriting a current block. As in the case of virtual memories, cache memories must use some page (i.e. block) replacement policy. Because of the high cost of fully associative memories, computer designers frequently employ an arrangement that is a compromise between direct-mapped caches and fully associative caches called set associative caches.

A set associative cache memory is arranged as a direct-mapped cache but each block is replicated. For example, the simplest set associative cache might duplicate each block in the cache. For example, there would be two block 5s in the cache. Consequently, it is now possible to hold two block 5s, one block 5 from set x and one block 5 from set y. When the processor accesses memory, the appropriate pair of blocks in the cache are accessed. Since there are two blocks, a simple associative match can be used to determine which (if either) of the blocks in the cache is to supply the data.

Apart from choosing the structure of a cache system and the block replacement policy (if it is an associative cache), the designer has to consider how write cycles are to be treated. Should write accesses be made only to the cache and then the main store updated when the block is written back? Should the main memory also be updated each time a word in the cache is modified? The latter policy is called 'write through' and is relatively efficient because the cache can be written to rapidly and the main memory updated over a longer span of time.

Another of the concepts often found in texts on cache systems is 'cache coherency'. As we know, data in the cache also lives in the main memory. When the processor modifies data it must modify both the copy in the cache and the copy in the main memory (although not necessarily at the same time). There are circumstances when the existence of two copies (which can differ) of the same item of data cause problems. For example, an I/O controller using DMA may attempt to move an old block of data from the main store to disk without 'knowing' that the processor has just updated the copy of the data in the cache but has not yet updated the copy in the main memory. Cache coherency is also known as data consistency.

Summary

In this short chapter we have introduced the operating system. Although you might think that the operating system deserves no space in a text devoted to computer architecture, there are several ways in which CPU and operating system concepts overlap. For example, the CPU's interrupt processing mechanism (and its stack) make it easy for the operating system to implement multitasking. In a similar way, the processor hardware and its operating system work together to implement virtual memory systems that automatically manage the storage of data.

Problems

1. What is the difference between a JCL and an operating system?

2. What is Finkel's 'beautification principle'?

3. Under what circumstance is an operating system unnecessary?

4. Why is multiprogramming a 'con-trick'?

5. How does multiprogramming make use of the stack to achieve efficient task switching?

6. What is a task's 'volatile portion'?

7. Write a 68000 program to perform task switching. You must design a task status block (one for each task) and use the task handler to switch tasks.

8. What is the difference between logical and physical addresses (a) from the point of view of the programmer, and (b) from the point of view of the (hardware) systems designer?

9. What is an overlay and why is it a poor solution to the problems of memory management?

10. What is the 80/20 rule and do you think it always holds good?

11. What is the difference between the LRU and NRU page replacement algorithms?

12. A cache memory may be operated in either a serial or a parallel mode with respect to the main memory. In the serial access mode, the cache is examined for data and if a miss occurs the main store is then accessed. In the parallel access mode both the cache and the main store are accessed simultaneously. If a hit occurs, the access to the main store is aborted.

Assume that the system has a hit ratio h and that the ratio of cache memory access time to main store access time is k ($k < 1$).

Derive expressions for the speed-up ratio of both a parallel access cache and a serial access cache.

If a serial mode cache is to be used and a 10 per cent penalty in speed-up ratio over the corresponding parallel access cache can be tolerated, what must the value of h be to achieve this? Assume that the main store access time is 150 ns and that the cache access time is 30 ns.

13. Describe the structure of a direct-mapped cache memory for use in a 68000 microprocessor system.

14. What are the advantages and disadvantages of direct-mapped cache memories when compared with other cache mapping systems?

Bibliography

This bibliography has been included to provide the student with a guide to further study.

Bartee, Thomas C. (1985). *Digital Computer Fundamentals* (6th edn). McGraw Hill, New York. Bartee provides a traditional and extensive approach to digital computers. This book provides a very comprehensive coverage of digital design and the logical structure of the CPU. The hardware emphasis would make this book more suitable for electronic engineers than computer scientists.

Clements, Alan (1987). *Microprocessor systems design: 68000 hardware, software and interfacing*. PWS-Kent, Boston. This book describes the 68000 microprocessor in detail and concentrates on the design of 68000-based microprocessor systems.

Deitel, Harvey M. (1984). *An introduction to operating systems*. Addison Wesley, New York. Deitel provides a very readable coverage of operating systems. Several operating systems are described in some detail.

East, Ian (1990). *Computer architecture and organization*. Pitman, London. A good introduction to computer architecture and logic design. East takes a modern approach to computer architecture and includes a description of three major processors (the 68000, the National Semiconductor 32000 and the Inmos transputer). An excellent appendix made of up fully worked solutions to problems is provided.

Gibson, J. R. (1979). *Electronic logic circuits*. Edward Anold, London. This book is devoted entirely to Boolean algebra and is written at an introductory level. It contains only 114 pages but is very well written and presented.

Gorsline, G. W. (1986). *Computer organization: hardware/software*. Prentice-Hall, New Jersey. Computer organization is devoted largely to the architecture of computers and looks at a wide range of computer architectures from the DEC LSI 11 to parallel processors and RISC machines. The level of this book makes it a suitable follow on from *The principles of computer hardware*.

Hill, Frederick J. and Peterson, Gerald R. (1984). *Digital logic and microprocessors*. Wiley, Chichester/New York. In many ways this is a conventional text that covers Boolean algebra, logic design and basic computer architecture (based on 8-bit microprocessors). However, Hill and Peterson provide an excellent and extensive introduction to register transfer language as a formal means of defining the action of digital systems. For example, they describe the operation of the 6502 microprocesser in RTL.

Housley, T. (1987). *Data communications and teleprocessing systems* (2nd edn). Prentice-Hall, New Jersey. Housley provides a very readable introduction to data communications and manages to cover a subject that is all too frequently either left to very advanced texts or treated at a very superficial level. This book provides an excellent introduction to the topic of protocols and is more oriented towards wide area networks based on the modem than towards local area networks.

Lane, Malcolm G. and Mooney, James D. (1988). *A practical approach to operating systems*. Boyd and Fraser, Boston. Lane and Mooney provide a comprehensive coverage of all aspects of operating systems (including 'modern' aspects like security, portability, and standards).

Lee, Graham (1982). *From hardware to software: an introduction to computers*. Macmillan, London. This large (454 pages) volume covers much of the material in my book. The two major differences are that Lee builds his book around 'a simple digital computer', a hypothetical computer designed for teaching purposes, and also includes considerable detail on software (assembly language, high level languages, and compiling).

Lister, A. M. (1988). *Fundamentals of operating systems*. Macmillan, London. Lister's short text on operating systems has become a classic because it provides a very readable account of operating systems. This text focuses on the core of the operating system, rather than the user interface. In particular, it covers CPU-related topics such as interrupt handling, task-switching, and memory management.

Prosser, Franklin P. and Winkel, David E. (1987). *The art of digital design*. Prentice-Hall, New Jersey. Prosser and Winkel cover digital logic and digital design together with an introduction to the CPU. Although there are many texts on logic design, this is of particular interest because it takes a formal top-down approach to the design of digital systems.

Stallings, William (1988). *Data and computer communications*. Macmillan, London. Stallings provides a comprehensive, and beautifully presented, overview of digital communications. All levels of digital data transmission are covered, from transmission media to protocols. This is a good introduction to data transmission because it does not include the high-level mathematics frequently associated with data transmission. A section is provided on the ISDN (integrated services digital network) which seeks to combine traditional analog communications facilities with modern digital data transmission.

Tanenbaum, Andrew S. (1988). *Computer networks*. Prentice-Hall, New Jersey. Tanenbaum provides extensive coverage of both wide area and local area networks in this 517 page book. This is an advanced book aimed at third-year students and postgraduates. It is well written and is a definitive work on computer communications. The hardware and electronics aspects of data transmission are not included.

Tanenbaum, Andrew S. (1984). *Structured computer organization* (2nd edn). Prentice-Hall, New Jersey. Tanenbaum provides a similar course to *The principles of computer hardware*. Tanenbaum's strength lies in his coverage of microprogramming and virtual systems. Tanenbaum takes a 'big systems approach' rather than viewing the computer world from the perspective of the microprocessor.

Ullmann, Julian R. (1982). *Micro-computer technology: an introduction*. Pitman, London. Although the title *Micro-computer technology* hints at the fabrication of the silicon chips themselves, this book deals entirely with Boolean algebra, sequential circuits, microcomputers, and assembly language programming. The Z80 microprocessor is chosen as an example throughout. Many of the examples are presented in terms of Pascal as are the assembly language programs. Professor Ullmann even describes assembly language as 'Destructured Pascal'. This is a superb book and is pitched at a somewhat higher level than mine. It includes a wealth of worked examples. I would recommend this to anyone wishing to go further into the principles of computer architecture than the majority of introductory texts.

van de Goor, A. J. (1989). *Computer architecture and design*. Addison-Wesley, New York. This book provides a second course in computer architecture. Unlike older and more conventional authors, van de Goor approaches computer architecture from a software standpoint (e.g. data structures) instead of a more traditional machine-based standpoint. That is, van de Goor begins by looking at the requirements of software and then showing how real machines fulfil these requirements. Several interesting topics are included in this work, ranging from an excellent coverage of cache memory systems to an introduction to non-von Neumann architectures.

Ward, Stephen A. and Halstead, Robert H. (1990). *Computation structures*. MIT Press, Massachusetts. This is a massive, large format text of 789 pages, although its title is rather misleading. The material covered by this magnificent work ranges from gates and Boolean algebra to machine architecture (memory technology and peripherals are not included). Rather than concentrating on a typical commercial microprocessor, the authors develop their own architecture and explore it in great detail. Although Ward and Halstead go into greater detail than many of their contemporaries, their work is very readable. This book will appeal to anyone who wishes to look beneath the surface of computer architecture.

Wilkinson, Barry and Horrocks, David (1982). *Computer peripherals*. Hodder and Stoughton. Devoted entirely to input and output devices, backing stores, and (in less detail) computer communications. All these topics are treated at an introductory level. This book is strongly recommended to those who wish to learn more about the structure, operation, and characteristics of peripherals.

Appendix: The 68000 instruction set

Use of the appendix

Each instruction is listed by its mnemonic in alphabetical order. The information provided about each instruction is: its assembler syntax, its attributes (i.e., whether is takes a byte, word or longword operand), its descriptions in words, the effect its execution has on the condition codes, and the addressing modes it may take.

The conditions code bits, X, N, Z, V, C, are updated after certain instructions. The effect of an instruction on a given bit of the CCR is specified by the following codes:

U The state of the bit is undefined (i.e., its value cannot be predicted)
– The bit remains unchanged by the execution of the instruction
* The bit is set or cleared according to the outcome of the instruction

Unless the addressing modes are implicit in the instruction (e.g., NOP, RESET, RTS etc.), both the legal source and destination addressing modes are specified by their assembly language syntax. Examples of source addressing modes are given below.

Dn, An	Data and address register direct
(An)	Address register indirect
(An)+, -(An)	Address register with auto-incrementing or auto-decrementing
d(An),d(An,Xi)	Address register indirect with displacement and address register indirect with indexing and a displacement
ABS.W, ABS.L	Absolute addressing with a 16-bit or 32-bit address
d(PC),d(PC,Xi)	Program counter relative addressing with a simple offset, or with an offset plus the contents of a register
imm	An immediate value (i.e., literal) which may be 16 or 32 bits, depending on the operand

Note that we employ the notation [X] to mean the contents of the X-bit of the CCR, rather than the more formal [CCR(X)]. The same applies to the other bits of the SR.

I have decided to make this appendix reasonably complete in the sense that it describes all the 68000's instructions, even though we have introduced only a tiny fraction of these in chapter 6. Many of these instructions are self-explanatory. However, the following concepts (related to exception processing and the 68000's user/supervisor states) should be mentioned:

The 68000 classifies both hardware and software interrupts as 'traps' or 'exceptions'. Although we could write a chapter on the 68000's exception processing mechanism, the essential points are:

1. The 68000 saves the return address and its status word on the stack before processing an exception. The status word includes the condition code register and a status byte that defines the level of the interrupt mask (0 to 7), the S-bit and the trace bit.

2. The 68000 takes the exception's vector number (0 to 255), multiplies it by four and uses the result to look up the address of the exception's handler (i.e. the code that handles the exception). For example, if a certain exception is associated with a vector number N, the 68000 performs the action:

```
N     ← N × 4      Multiply N by four
Temp ← [MS(N)]     Read the contents of 4N
[PC] ← Temp        Jump to the exception handler
```

3. After the exception has been processed, the instruction RTE (return from exception) restores the original value of the program counter and status word.

4. The 68000 operates in one of two 'states' or 'modes': user and supervisor. In simple 68000 systems without an operating system, the 68000 operates in its supervisor state—and that's that. In more complex systems, the 68000 operates in its supervisor state when running the operating system and in its user state when running user programs under the operating system. The S-bit of the status word determines whether the 68000 is in its user state ($S = 0$) or in its supervisor state. The S-bit is set after a hardware reset (i.e. on switch-on) and can be cleared by one of several instructions.

5. The 68000 has two A7 address registers; one for the user mode and one for the supervisor mode. Consequently, a user program may corrupt its own stack pointer but cannot corrupt the operating system's stack pointer. Note that the user's stack pointer can be accessed from the supervisor state but that the supervisor's stack pointer is invisible to the user state.

6. All exceptions force the S-bit to 1 which means that all exception processing is carried out in the supervisor state. That is, user programs are not allowed to process exceptions. In this way, the user can request operating system functions by means of a software interrupt (a TRAP instruction).

7. The 68000 has a trace bit (T-bit) in its status register. When the T-bit is set, the 68000 generates an exception following the execution of each instruction. The exception handler can be used to print the contents of each register on the screen and therefore permit the user to step through a program instruction by instruction (useful in a debugging mode).

8. Certain instructions are said to be privileged. These instructions can be executed only when the 68000 is operating in the supervisor state. That

is, a user program may not execute a privileged instruction. Any attempt to do so will cause a 'privilege violation exception' and control will be passed to the operating system. Privileged instructions are (generally) those that modify the state of the 68000's processor status byte (not the CCR). As you can imagine, user programs are not permitted to set the trace or status bits and the interrupt mask level.

The 68000's status word

15	14	13	12	11	10	9	8	7	6	5	4	3	2	1	0
T		S			I_2	I_1	I_0				X	N	Z	V	C

← Status byte → ← CCR →

Note: T=trace bit, S=supervisor bit, I_2, I_1, I_0=interrupt mask.

ABCD

Add decimal with extend

Operation: [destination] ← [source] + [destination] + [X]

Assembler syntax:
```
ABCD  Dy,Dx
ABCD  -(Ay),-(Ax)
```

Attributes: Size = byte

Description: Add the source operand to the destination operand along with the extend bit, and store the result in the destination location. Addition is performed using BCD arithmetic. The only legal addressing modes are data register direct and memory to memory with address register indirect using auto decrementing.

Application: The ABCD instruction is used in chain arithmetic to add together strings of BCD digits. Consider the addition of two nine-digit numbers. Note that the strings are stored so that the least significant digit is at the high address.

```
          LEA    Number1,A0     A0 points at first string
          LEA    Number2,A1     A1 points at second string
          MOVE   #$0,CCR        Clear X bit of CCR
          MOVE   #8,D0          Nine digits to add
LOOP ABCD  -(A0),-(A1)          Add a pair of digits
          DBRA   D0,LOOP        Repeat until 9 digits added
```

Condition codes:
```
X N Z V C
* U * U *
```
Z: Cleared if result is non-zero. Unchanged otherwise. The Z bit can be used to test for zero after a chain of multiple precision operations.

ADD

Add binary

Operation: [destination] ← [source] + [destination]

Assembler syntax:
```
ADD  <ea>,Dn
ADD  Dn,<ea>
```

Attributes: Size = byte, word, longword

Description: Add the source operand to the destination operand and store the result in the destination location.

Condition codes:
```
X N Z V C
* * * * *
```

Source operand addressing modes
```
Dn, An
(An)
(An)+, -(An)
d(An), d(An,Xi)
ABS.W, ABS.L
d(PC), d(PC,Xi)
imm
```

Destination operand addressing modes
```
Dn
(An)
(An)+, -(An)
d(An), d(An,Xi)
ABS.W, ABS.L
```

ADDA

Add address

Operation:	[destination] ← [source] + [destination]
Assembler syntax:	ADDA <ea>, An
Attributes:	Size = word, longword
Description:	Add the source to the destination address register store the result in the destination address register. Note that the source is sign-extended before it is added to the destination. For example, if we execute ADDA.W D3,A4 where A4 = 00000100 and D3.W = 8002, the number to be added is sign-extended to FFFF8002 and added to 00000100 to give FFFF102 which is stored in A4.
Application:	To add to the contents of an address register and not update the CCR. Note that ADDA D0,A0 is the same as LEA (A0,D0),A0.
Condition codes:	X N Z V C
	– – – – –
Source operand addressing modes	Dn, An
	(An)
	(An)+, −(An)
	d(An), d(An,Xi)
	ABS.W, ABS.L
	d(PC), d(PC,Xi)
	imm

ADDI

Add immediate

Operation:	[destination] ← <literal> + [destination]
Assembler syntax:	ADDA #<data>, <ea>
Attributes:	Size = Byte, word, longword
Description:	Add the immediate data to the destination operand. Store the result in the destination operand. Note that ADDI can be used to add a literal directly to a memory location. For example, ADDI.W #$1234,$2000 has the effect [M(2000)] ←1234.
Condition codes:	X N Z V C
	* * * * *
Destination operand addressing modes	Dn
	(An)
	(An)+, −(An)
	d(An), d(An,Xi)
	ABS.W, ABS.L

ADDQ

Add quick

Operation:	[destination] ← <literal> + [destination]
Assembler syntax:	ADDQ #<data>, <ea>
Attributes:	Size = Byte, word, longword
Description:	Add the immediate data to the destination operand. The immediate data must be in the range 1 to 8. Word and longword operations on address registers do not affect condition codes.

Condition codes:	Z N Z V C
	* * * * *
Destination operand	Dn, An
addressing modes	(An)
	(An)+, −(An)
	d(An), d(An,Xi)
	ABS.W, ABS.L

ADDX

Add extended

Operation:	[destination] ← [source]+[destination]+[X]
Assembler syntax:	ABCD Dy,Dx
	ABCD −(Ay),−(Ax)
Attributes:	Size = byte, word, longword
Description:	Add the source operand to the destination operand along with the extend bit, and store the result in the destination location. The only legal addressing modes are data register direct and memory to memory with address register indirect using auto decrementing.
Application:	The ADDX instruction is used in chain arithmetic to add together strings of bytes (words or longwords). Consider the addition of two 128-bit numbers, each of which is stored as four consecutive longwords.

```
          LEA    Number,A0      A0 points at first number
          LEA    Number2,A1     A1 points at second number
          MOVE   #$0,CCR        Clear X bit of CCR
          MOVE   #3,D0          Four longwords to add
LOOP ADDX  −(A0),−(A1)     Add pair of numbers
          DBRA   D0,LOOP        Repeat until all added
```

Condition codes:	X N Z V C
	* * * * *

Z: Cleared if result is non-zero. Unchanged otherwise
(Z bit can be used to test for zero after a chain of multiple precison operations).

AND

AND logical

Operation:	[destination] ← [source].[destination]
Assembler syntax:	AND <ea>,Dn
	AND Dn,<ea>
Attributes:	Size = byte, word, longword
Description:	AND the source operand to the destination operand and store the result in the destination location.
Condition codes:	X N Z V C
	− * * 0 0

Source operand addressing modes	Dn
	(An)
	(An)+, −(An)
	d(An), d(An,Xi)
	ABS.W, ABS.L
	d(PC), d(PC,Xi)
	imm

Destination operand addressing modes	Dn, An
	(An)
	(An)+, −(An)
	d(An), d(An,Xi)
	ABS.W, ABS.L

ANDI | AND immediate

Operation:	[destination] ← [literal].[destination]
Assembler syntax:	ANDI #<data>, <ea>
Attributes:	Size = byte, word, longword
Description:	AND the immediate data to the destination operand. Store the result in the destination operand. The ANDI operation permits a literal operand to be ANDed with a destination other than a data register. For example, ANDI #$FE00,$1234 or ANDI.B #$F0,(A2)+
Condition codes:	X N Z V C
	– * * 0 0
Destination operand addressing modes	Dn
	(An)
	(An)+, −(An)
	d(An), d(An,Xi)
	ABS.W,ABS.L

ANDI to CCR | AND immediate to condition code register

Operation:	[CCR] ← <data>.[CCR]
Assembler syntax:	ANDI #<data>, CCR
Attributes:	Size = Byte
Description:	AND the immediate data to the condition code register (i.e. the least significant byte of the status register).
Application:	Used to clear selected bits of the CCR. For example, ANDI #$FA,CCR will clear the Z and C bits
Condition codes:	X N Z V C
	* * * * *
	X: cleared if bit 4 of data is zero
	N: cleared if bit 3 of data is zero
	Z: cleared if bit 2 of data is zero
	V: cleared if bit 1 of data is zero
	C: cleared if bit 0 of data is zero

ANDI to SR

AND immediate to status register

Operation:
```
IF [S]=1
    THEN
    [SR] ← <literal> . [SR]
    ELSE TRAP
```

Assembler syntax: ANDI #<data>, SR

Attributes: Size = Word

Description: AND the immediate data to the status register and store the result in the status register. All bits of the status register are affected.

Application: Can be used to clear interrupt, S and T bits of the SR. Note that ANDI #<data>,SR affects both the status byte of the SR and the CCR. For example, ANDI #$3FFF,SR will clear the trace bit(s) of the status register. ANDI #$3FFE will clear the trace bit(s) and also clear the carry bit of the CCR.

Condition codes:
```
X N Z V C
* * * * *
```
X: cleared if bit 4 of data is zero
N: cleared if bit 3 of data is zero
Z: cleared if bit 2 of data is zero
V: cleared if bit 1 of data is zero
C: cleared if bit 0 of data is zero

ASL, ASR

Arithmetic shift left/right

Operation: [destination] ← [destination] shifted by <count>

Assembler syntax:
```
ASL  Dx,Dy
ASR  Dx,Dy
ASL  #<data>,Dy
ASR  #<data>,Dy
ASL  <ea>
ASR  <ea>
```

Attributes: Size = byte, word, longword.

Description: Arithmetically shift the bits of the operand in the specified direction (i.e., left or right). The shift count may be specified in one of three ways. The count may be a literal, the contents of a data register, or the value 1. An immediate count permits a shift of 1 to 8 places. If the count is in a register the value is from 1 to 64. If no count is specified, one shift is made (i.e., ASL <ea> shifts the contents of <ea> one place left).

Application: An ASL has the effect of multiplying a two's complement number by 2. Note that ASL is almost identical to the corresponding logical shift, LSR. The only difference between ASL and LSL is that ASL sets the V bit of the CCR if overflow occurs while LSL clears the V bit to zero. An ASR has the effect of dividing a two's complement number by 2.

Condition codes:
```
X N Z V C
* * * * *
```

Destination operand addressing modes
(An)
(An)+, −(An)
d(An), d(An,Xi)
ABS.W, ABS.L

Bcc

Branch on condition cc

Operation: If $cc = 1$ THEN [PC] ← [PC] + d

Assembler syntax: Bcc <label>

Sample syntax: BEQ Loop4

Attributes: BEQ takes an 8-bit or a 16-bit offset

Description: If the specified condition is met, program execution continues at location [PC] + displacement d. The displacement is a two's complement value. The value in the PC corresponds to the current location plus two. Note that a short branch to the next instruction is impossible, since the branch code 0 is used to indicate a long branch with a 16-bit offset. The range of the branch is -126 to $+129$ bytes with an 8-bit offset and $-\$32K$ to $+32K$ bytes with a 32-bit offset.

BCC	branch on carry clear	$\overline{C}$
BCS	branch on carry set	C
BEQ	branch on equal	Z
BGE	branch on greater than or equal	$N.V + \overline{N}.\overline{V}$
BGT	branch on greater than	$N.V.Z + \overline{N}.\overline{V}.\overline{Z}$
BHI	branch on higher than	$\overline{C}.\overline{Z}$
BLE	branch on less than or equal	$Z + \overline{N}.V + N.\overline{V}$
BLS	branch on lower than or same	$C + Z$
BLT	branch on less than	$N.\overline{V} + \overline{N}.V$
BMI	branch on minus (i.e, negative)	N
BNE	branch on not equal	$\overline{Z}$
BPL	branch on plus (i.e., positive)	$\overline{N}$
BVS	branch on overflow clear	$\overline{V}$
BVS	branch on overflow set	V

Condition codes: X N Z V C

     − − − − −

BCHG

Test a bit and change

Operation: [Z] ← NOT<bit number>OF[dest]

     <bit number>OF[dest] ←NOT<bit number>OF[dest]

Assembler syntax: BCHG Dn,<ea>

     BCHG #<data>,<ea>

Attributes: Size = byte, longword

Description: A bit in the destination operand is tested and the state of the specified bit is reflected in the condition of the Z condition code. After a test, the state of the specified bit is changed in the destination. If a data register is the destination then the bit numbering is modulo 32 allowing bit manipulation of all bits in a data register. If a memory location is the destination, a byte is read from that location, the bit operation performed using bit number modulo 8, and the byte written back to the location with zero referring to the least significant bit. The bit number for this operation may be specified either by an immediate value or dynamically by the contents of a data register.

Application:	If the operation BCHG #4,$1234 is carried out and the contents of memory location $1234 is 10101010, bit 4 will be tested. It is a 0 and therefore the Z bit of the CCR will be set to 1. Bit 4 of the destination operand will be changed and the new contents will be: 10111010.
Condition codes:	X N Z V C – – * – – Z: set if the bit tested is zero, cleared otherwise
Destination operand addressing modes	Dn (An) (An)+, –(An) d(An), d(An,Xi) ABS.W, ABS.L Note that data register direct (i.e., Dn) addressing uses a longword operand, while all other modes use a byte operand.

BCLR — Test a bit and clear

Operation:	[Z] ← NOT<bit number>OF[destination] <bit number>OF[destination] ←0
Assembler syntax:	BCLR Dn,<ea> BCLR #<data>,<ea>
Attributes:	Size = byte, longword
Description:	A bit in the destination operand is tested and the state of the specified bit is reflected in the condition of the Z condition code. After a test, the state of the specified bit is cleared in the destination. If a data register is the destination, then the bit numbering is modulo 32 allowing bit manipulation of all bits in a data register. If a memory location is the destination, a byte is read from that location, the bit operation performed using bit number modulo 8, and the byte written back of the location with zero referring to the least significant bit. The bit number for this operation may be specified either by an immediate value or dynamically by the contents of a data register.
Application:	If the operation BCLR #4,$1234 is carried out and the contents of memory location $1234 is 11111010, bit 4 will be tested. It is a 1 and therefore the Z bit of the CCR will be set to 0. Bit 4 of the destination operand will be cleared and the new contents will be: 11101010.
Condition codes:	X N Z V C – – * – – Z: set if the bit tested is zero, cleared otherwise
Destination operand addressing modes	Dn (An) (An)+, –(An) d(An), d(An,Xi) ABS.W, ABS.L Note that data register direct (i.e., Dn) addressing uses a longword operand, while all other modes use a byte operand.

BRA

Branch always

Operation:	[PC] ← [PC]+d
Assembler syntax:	BRA <label>
	BRA <literal>
Attributes:	Size = byte, word
Description:	Program execution continues at location [PC]+d. The displacement is a two's complement value. The value in the PC corresponds to the current location plus two. Note that a short branch to the next instruction is impossible, since the branch code 0 is used to indicate a long branch with a 16-bit offset.
Application:	A BRA is an unconditional relative jump (or goto)
Condition codes:	X N Z V C
	– – – – –

BSET

Test a bit and set

Operation:	[Z] ← NOT<bit number>OF[destination]
	<bit number>OF[destination]←1
Assembler syntax:	BSET Dn,<ea>
	BSET #<data>,<ea>
Attributes:	Size = byte, longword
Description:	A bit in the destination operand is tested and the state of the specified bit is reflected in the condition of the Z condition code. After the test, the specified bit is set in the destination. If a data register is the destination then the bit numbering is modulo 32 allowing bit manipulation of all bits in a data register. If a memory location is the destination, a byte is read from that location, the bit operation performed using bit number modulo 8, and the byte written back to the location with zero referring to the least significant bit. The bit number for this operation may be specified either by an immediate value or dynamically by the contents of a data register.
Condition codes:	X N Z V C
	– – * – –
	Z: set if the bit tested is zero, cleared otherwise
Source operand addressing modes for BSET Dn,<ea> form	Dn
	(An)
	(An)+, –(An)
	d(An), d(An,Xi)
	ABS.W, ABS.L
	Note that data register direct (i.e., Dn) addressing uses a longword operand, while all other modes use a byte operand.

BSR

Branch to subroutine

Operation:	[SP] ← [SP] – 4; [M([SP])] ←[PC]; [PC]+d

Assembler syntax:	`BSR <label>` `BSR <literal>`
Attributes:	Size = byte, word
Description:	The longword address of the instruction immediately following the BSR instruction is pushed onto the system stack. Program execution then continues at location [PC]+displacement. The displacement is a two's complement value. The value in the PC corresponds to the current location plus two. Note that a short branch to the next instruction is impossible, since the branch code 0 is used to indicate a long branch with a 16-bit offset.
Condition codes:	X N Z V C – – – – –

BTST — Test a bit

Operation:	`[Z] ← NOT<bit number>OF[destination]`
Assembler syntax:	`BTST Dn,<ea>` `BTST #<data>,<ea>`
Attributes:	Size = byte, longword
Description:	A bit in the destination operand is tested and the state of the specified bit is reflected in the condition of the Z condition code. The destination is not modified by a BTST instruction. If a data register is the destination, then the bit numbering is modulo 32 allowing bit manipulation of all bits in a data register. If a memory location is the destination, a byte is read from that location, the bit operation performed using bit number modulo 8, and the byte written back to the location with zero referring to the least significant bit. The bit number for this operation may be specified either by an immediate value or dynamically by the contents of a data register.
Condition codes:	X N Z V C – – * – – Z: set if the bit tested is zero, cleared otherwise
Destination operand addressing modes for `BTST Dn,<ea>` form	Dn (An) (An)+, −(An) d(An), d(An,Xi) ABS.W, ABS.L Note that data register direct (i.e., Dn) addressing uses a longword operand, while all other modes use a byte operand.

CHK — Check register against bounds

Operation:	`IF [Dn] <0 OR [Dn] > [<ea>] THEN TRAP`
Assembler syntax:	`CHK <ea>,Dn`
Attributes:	Size = word
Description:	The contents of the low order word in the data register specified in the instruction is examined and compared with the upper bound. The upper

bound is a two's complement integer. If the register value is less than zero or greater than the upper bound contained in the operand word, then the processor initiates exception processing.

Application:	Consider the following fragment of code:

```
MOVE.W subscript,D0    Get subscript to test
CHK    #max_bound,D0    Test against 0 and upper bound
                       TRAP on error ELSE continue
```

Condition codes:	X N Z V C
	– * U U U
	N: set if [Dn] <0; Cleared if [Dn] > [<ea>].
	N: undefined otherwise
Destination operand addressing modes	Dn
	(An)
	(An)+, −(An)
	d(An), d(An,Xi)
	ABS.W, ABS.L
	d(PC), d(PC,Xi)
	imm

CLR

Clear an operand

Operation:	[destination] ← 0
Assembler syntax:	CLR <ea>
Attributes:	Size = byte, word, longword
Description:	The destination is loaded with all zeros. Note that CLR cannot be used to clear an address register. SUBA.L A0,A0 will clear A0. Note that a side effect of the CLR's implementation is a read from the specified effective address before the clear (i.e., write) operation is executed. Under certain circumstances this may cause a problem (e.g., with write-only memory).
Condition codes:	X N Z V C
	– 0 1 0 0
Destination operand addressing modes	Dn
	(An)
	(An)+, −(An)
	d(An), d(An,Xi)
	ABS.W, ABS.L

CMP

Compare

Operation:	[destination] − [source]
Assembler syntax:	CMP <ea>,Dn
Attributes:	Size = byte, word, longword
Description:	Subtract the source operand from the destination operand and set the condition codes accordingly. The destination must be a data register. The destination is not modified by this instruction.
Condition codes:	X N Z V C
	– * * * *

Source operand addressing modes	Dn, An
	(An)
	(An)+, −(An)
	d(An), d(An,Xi)
	ABS.W, ABS.L
	d(PC), d(PC,Xi)
	imm

CMPA

Compare address

Operation:	[destination] – [source]
Assembler syntax:	CMPA <ea>,An
Attributes:	Size = word, longword
Description:	Subtract the source operand from the destination address register and set the condition codes accordingly. The address register is not modified. The size of the operation may be specified as word or longword. Word length operands are sign extended to 32 bits before the comparison is carried out.
Condition codes:	X N Z V C
	− * * * *

Destination operand addressing modes	Dn, An
	(An)
	(An)+, −(An)
	d(An), d(An,Xi)
	ABS.W, ABS.L
	d(PC), d(PC,Xi)
	imm

CMPI

Compare immediate

Operation:	[destination] – immediate data
Assembler syntax:	CMPI #<data>,<ea>
Attributes:	Size = byte, word, longword
Description:	Subtract the immediate data from the destination operand and set the condition codes accordingly. The destination is not modified by this instruction.
Condition codes:	X N Z V C
	− * * * *

Destination operand addressing modes	Dn
	(An)
	(An)+, −(An)
	d(An), d(An,Xi)
	ABS.W, ABS.L
	d(PC), d(PC,Xi)
	imm

CMPM

Compare memory with memory

Operation: [destination] - [source]

Assembler syntax: CMPM (Ay)+,(Ax)+

Attributes: Size = byte, word, longword

Description: Subtract the source operand from the destination operand and set the condition codes accordingly. The destination is not modified by this instruction. The only permitted addressing mode is address indirect with postincrementing for both source and destination operands.

Application: Used to compare the contents of two blocks of memory. For example:

```
        LEA     Source,A0       A0 points to source
        LEA     Destination,A1  A1 points to destination block
        MOVE.W  #Count-1,D0     Compare 'Count' words
    RPT CMPM.W  (A0)+,(A1)+     Compare pair of words
        DBF     D0,RPT          Repeat until all done
        EXIT    ...
```

Condition codes:
```
X  N  Z  V  C
-  *  *  *  *
```

DBcc

Test condition, decrement and branch

Operation:
```
IF (condition false)
    THEN [Dn] ← [Dn] -1
       IF [Dn] ≠ -1
          THEN [PC] ← [PC]+d
    ELSE [PC] ← [PC]+2 {fall through to next inst.}
```

Assembler syntax: DBcc Dn,<label>

Attributes: Size = word

Description: The DBcc instruction provides an automatic looping facility and replaces the usual decrement counter, test and branch instructions. Three parameters are required by the DBcc instruction: a branch condition (specified by 'cc'), a data register that serves as the loop down-counter, and a label that indicates the start of the loop. The DBcc first tests the condition 'cc', and if 'cc' is true the loop is terminated and the branch back to <label> not taken. The fourteen branch conditions supported by Bcc are also supported by DBcc, as well as DBF and DBT (F = false, and T = true). Note that many assemblers permit the mnemonic DBF to be expressed as DBRA (i.e. decrement and branch back). Note that the DBcc works in the opposite sense to a Bcc (conditional branch) instruction. BCC means branch on carry clear, while DBCC means continue on carry clear. That is, the DBcc condition is a loop terminator. If the termination condition is not true, the low-order 16 bits of the specified data register are decremented. If the result is −1, the loop is not taken and the next instruction is executed. If the result is not −1, a branch is made to 'label'. Note that the label respresents a 16-bit signed value, permitting a branch range of −32K to +32K bytes. Since the value decremented is 16 bits, the loop may be executed up to 64K times.

Application:

Suppose we wish to input a block of 512 bytes of data (the data is returned in register D1). If the input routine returns a value zero in D1, an error has occurred and the loop must be exited.

```
        MOVE.W  #511,D0      512 bytes to be input
AGAIN   BSR     INPUT        Get the data in D1
        MOVE.B  D1,(A0)+     Store it
        DBEQ    D0,AGAIN     REPEAT until D1=0 or 512 times
```

Condition codes:

```
X N Z V C
- - - - -
```

DIVS, DIVU

Signed divide, unsigned divide

Operation:

[destination] ← [destination]/[source]

Assembler syntax:

```
DIVS  <ea>,Dn
DIVU  <ea>,Dn
```

Attributes:

Size = word

Description:

Divide the destination operand by the source operand and store the result in the destination. The destination is a longword operand and the source is a 16-bit value. The result (i.e., destination register) is a 32-bit value arranged so that the quotient is the lower order word and the remainder is the upper order word. DIVU performs division on unsigned values and DIVS performs division on two's complement values. An attempt to divide by zero causes an exception. For DIVS, the sign of the remainder is always the same as the sign of the dividend (unless the remainder is zero).

Application:

Consider the division of D0 by D1. The instruction is DIVU D1,D0. The operation results in:

```
[D0(0:15)] ← [D0(0:31)]/[D1(0:15)]
[D0(16:31)] ← remainder
```

Condition codes:

```
X N Z V C
- * * * 0
```

Source operand addressing modes

Dn
(An)
(An)+, −(An)
d(An), d(An,Xi)
ABS.W, ABS.L
d(PC), d(PC,Xi)
imm

EOR

Exclusive OR logical

Operation:

[destination] ← [source]⊕[destination]

Assembler syntax:

```
EOR  Dn,<ea>
```

Attributes:

Size = byte, word, longword

Description:

EOR the source operand with the destination operand and store the result in the destination location. Note that the source must be a data register and that the operation EOR <ea>,Dn is not permitted.

Condition codes:	X N Z V C
	– * * 0 0
Destination operand	Dn
addressing modes	(An)
	(An)+, –(An)
	d(An), d(An,Xi)
	ABS.W, ABS.L

EORI   EOR immediate

Operation:	[destination] ← <literal> ⊕ [destination]
Assembler syntax:	EORI #<data>,<ea>
Attributes:	Size = byte, word, longword
Description:	EOR the immediate data with the destination operand. Store the result in the destination operand.
Condition codes:	X N Z V C
	– * * 0 0
Destination operand	Dn
addressing modes	(An)
	(An)+, –(An)
	d(An), d(An,Xi)
	ABS.W, ABS.L

EORI to CCR   Inclusive EOR immediate to CCR

Operation:	[CCR] ← <literal> ⊕ [CCR]
Assembler syntax:	EORI #<data>,CCR
Attributes:	Size = byte
Description:	EOR the immediate data with the condition code register (i.e. the least significant byte of the status register).
Application:	Used to toggle bits in the CCR. For example, EORI #$0C,CCR toggles the N and Z bits of the CCR.
Condition codes:	X N Z V C
	* * * * *

X: = toggled if bit 4 of data one; unchanged otherwise
N: = toggled if bit 3 of data one; unchanged otherwise
Z: = toggled if bit 2 of data one; unchanged otherwise
V: = toggled if bit 1 of data one; unchanged otherwise
C: = toggled if bit 0 of data one; unchanged otherwise

EORI to SR

Inclusive EOR immediate to status register

Operation:

```
IF [S]=1
    THEN
    [SR] ← <literal>⊕[SR]
    ELSE TRAP
```

Assembler syntax: `EORI #<data>,SR`

Attributes: Size = word

Description: EOR the immediate data with the status register and store the result in the status register. All bits of the status register are affected.

Condition codes:
```
X N Z V C
* * * * *
```
X: = toggled if bit 4 of data = 1; unchanged otherwise
N: = toggled if bit 3 of data = 1; unchanged otherwise
Z: = toggled if bit 2 of data = 1; unchanged otherwise
V: = toggled if bit 1 of data = 1; unchanged otherwise
C: = toggled if bit 0 of data = 1; unchanged otherwise

EXG

Exchange registers

Operation: `[Rx] ← [Ry]; [Ry] ← [Rx]`

Assembler syntax: `EXG Rx,Ry`

Attributes: Size = longword

Description: Exchange the contents of two registers. The size of the instruction is long as the entire contents are exchanged. The instruction permits the exchange of address registers, data registers and address and data registers.

Application: One application of EXG is to load an address into a data register (for the purpose of processing) the address using instructions that act on data registers. Then the reverse operation can be used to return the result to the address register. Doing this preserves the original contents of the data register.

Condition codes:
```
X N Z V C
– – – – –
```

EXT

Sign extend a data register

Operation: `[Destination] ← sign-extend[destination]`

Assembler syntax: `EXT Dn`

Attributes: Size = word, longword

Description: Extend the sign bit of a data register from a byte to a word or from a word to a longword. If the operation is word sized, bit 7 of the designated data register is copied to bits (8:15). If the operation is longword sized, bit 15 is copied to bits (16:31).

Application: If [D0]=$12345678, EXT.W D0 results in 12340078
                If [D0]=$12345678, EXT.L D0 results in 00005678

Condition codes:
```
X N Z V C
- * * 0 0
```

ILLEGAL

Illegal instruction

Operation: `[SSP] ← [SSP] -4; [M([SSP])] ← [PC];`
                `[SSP] ← [SSP] -2; [M([SSP])] ←[SP];`
                `[PC] ← Illegal instruction vector`

Assembler syntax: `ILLEGAL`

Attributes: None

Description: The bit pattern of the illegal instruction causes the illegal instruction trap
                to be taken.

Application: Any 'unknown' pattern of bits read by the 68000 during an instruction
                read phase will cause an illegal instruction trap. The ILLEGAL instruction
                can be thought of as an 'official' illegal instruction. It can be used to test
                the illegal instruction trap and will always be an illegal instruction in any
                future enhancement of the 68000.

Condition codes:
```
X N Z V C
- - - - -
```

JMP

Jump (unconditionally)

Operation: `[PC] ← destination`

Assembler syntax: `JMP <ea>`

Attributes: Unsized

Description: Program execution continues at the effective address specified by the
                instruction.

Application: Apart from a simple unconditional jump to an address fixed at compile
                time (i.e., JMP label), the JMP instruction is useful for the calculation of
                dynamic or computer jumps. For example, JMP (A0,D0.L) jumps to the
                location pointed at by the contents of A0, offset by the contents of D0.

Condition codes:
```
X N Z V C
- - - - -
```

Source operand   (An)
addressing modes   d(An), d(An,Xi)
                    ABS.W, ABS.L
                    d(PC), d(PC,Xi)

JSR

Jump to subroutine

Operation:	$[SP] \leftarrow [SP] -4; [M([SP])] \leftarrow [PC]; [PC] \leftarrow destination$
	JSR <ea>
Assembler syntax:	Unsized
Attributes:	
Description:	Pushes the longword address of the instruction immediately following the JSR instruction onto the system stack. Program execution then continues at the address specified in the instruction.
Application:	JSR (Ai) jumps to the address in Ai. JSR (Ai,Dj) jumps to the location [Ai] + [Dj] which permits dynamically computed addresses.
Condition codes:	X N Z V C
	– – – – –
Source operand addressing modes	(An)
	d(An), d(An,Xi)
	ABS.W, ABS.L
	d(PC), d(PC,Xi)

LEA

Load effective address

Operation:	$[An] \leftarrow <ea>$
Assembler syntax:	LEA <ea>, An
Attributes:	Size = longword
Description:	The effective address is computed and loaded into the specified address register. The difference between LEA and PEA is that LEA calculates an effective address and puts it in an address register, while PEA calculates an effective address in the same way but pushes it on the stack.
Application:	LEA is a very powerful instruction used to calculate an effective address. In particular, the use of LEA facilitates the writing of position independent code. For example, LEA TABLE(PC),A0 calculates the effective address of 'TABLE' with respect to the PC and deposits it in A0.

```
     LEA    Table(PC),A0      Compute the address of Table with respect to the PC
     MOVE   (A0),D1           Pick up the first item in table
                              Do something with this item
     MOVE   D1,(A0)           Put it back in the table
     .
     .
  Table DS.B   100
```

Source operand addressing modes	(An)
	d(An), d(An,Xi)
	ABS.W, ABS.L
	d(PC), d(PC,Xi)
Condition codes:	X N Z V C
	– – – – –

LINK

Link and allocate

Operation:

$[SP] \leftarrow [SP] - 4; [M([SP])] \leftarrow [An]; [An] \leftarrow [SP];$
$[SP] \leftarrow [SP] + d$

Assembler syntax:

LINK An,#<displacement>

Example syntax:

LINK A0,#-12

Attributes:

Unsized

Description:

The contents of the specified address register are pushed onto the stack. After the push, the address register is loaded with the updated stack pointer. Finally, the 16-bit sign-extended displacement is added to the stack pointer. The contents of the address register occupy two words on the stack. A negative displacement must be used to allocate stack area to a procedure. At the end of a LINK instruction, the old An has been pushed (i.e, saved) on the stack and the new An is pointing at the base of the stack frame. The stack pointer itself has been moved up by d bytes and is pointing at the top of the stack frame. The register An is called the frame pointer because it is used to reference data on the stack frame.

Application:

The LINK and UNLK pair are used to create local workspace on the top of a procedure's stack. Consider the code:

```
Subrtn LINK  A6,#-4    Create a 4-byte workspace
       .
       MOVE  D3,(A6)   Access stack frame via A6
       .
       UNLK A6         Collapse the workspace
       RTS             Return from subroutine
```

Condition codes:

```
X N Z V C
- - - - -
```

LSL, LSR

Logical shift left/right

Operation:

[destination] ← [destination] shifted by <count>

Assembler syntax:

```
LSL  Dx,Dy
LSR  Dx,Dy
LSL  #<data>,Dy
LSR  #<data>,Dy
LSL  <ea>
LSR  <ea>
```

Attributes:

Size = byte, word, longword

Description:

Logically shift the bits of the operand in the specified direction (i.e., left or right). A zero is shifted into the input position and the bit shifted out is copied into both the C and the X bit of the CCR. The shift count may be specified in one of three ways. The count may be a literal, the contents of a data register, or the value 1. An immediate count permits a shift of 1 to 8 places. If the count is in a register the value is from 1 to 64. If no count is specified, one shift is made (i.e., LSL <ea>).

Application:

If [D3] = 1100110010101110, the instruction LSL.W #5,D3 produces the result 1001010111000000.

Condition codes:

```
X N Z V C
* * * 0 *
```

Destination operand addressing modes	(An) (An)+, −(An) d(An), d(An,Xi) ABS.W, ABS.L

MOVE

Copy (i.e. move) data from source to destination

Operation:	[destination] ← [source]
Assembler syntax:	MOVE <ea>,<ea>
Attributes:	Size = byte, word, longword
Description:	Move the contents of the source to the destination location. The data is examined as it is moved and the condition codes set accordingly. Note that this is a copy command because the source is not affected by the move. The move instruction has the widest range of addressing modes of all the 68000's instructions.
Condition codes:	X N Z V C − * * 0 0
Source operand addressing modes	Dn, An (An) (An)+, −(An) d(An), d(An,Xi) ABS.W, ABS.L d(PC), d(PC,Xi) imm
Destination operand addressing modes	Dn (An) (An)+, −(An) d(An), d(An,Xi) ABS.W, ABS.L

MOVEA

Move address from its source to an address register

Operation:	[An] ← [source]
Assembler syntax:	MOVEA <ea>,An
Attributes:	Size = word, longword
Description:	Move the contents of the source to the destination location. The destination is an address register. The source must be a word or longword. If it is a word, it is sign-extended to a longword. The condition codes are not affected.
Application:	The MOVEA instruction is used to load an address register (some assemblers simply employ the MOVE mnemonic for both MOVE and MOVEA). Note that the instruction LEA can often be used to perform the same operation (e.g., MOVEA #$1234,A0 is the same as LEA $1234,A0). However, MOVEA (Ai),An cannot be implemented by a LEA operation, since MOVEA (Ai),An performs a memory access to obtain the source operand, as the following RTL demonstrates.

```
LEA    (Ai),An=[An] ←[Ai]
MOVEA (Ai),An=[An] ←[M([Ai])]
```

Condition codes:

```
X  N  Z  V  C
-- -- -- -- --
```

Source operand
addressing modes

Dn, An
(An)
(An)+, −(An)
d(An), d(An,Xi)
ABS.W, ABS.L
d(PC), d(PC,Xi)
imm

MOVE from CCR

Copy (i.e. move) data from CCR to destination

Operation:

```
[destination] ← [CCR]
```

Assembler syntax:

```
MOVE  CCR,<ea>
```

Attributes:

Size = word

Description:

Move the contents of the status register to the destination location. The source operand is a word, but only the low order byte contains the condition codes. The upper byte is all zeros. Note that although MOVE from CCR is a word operation, the instructions AND, OR, EOR to CCR are byte operations.

Application:

The MOVE from CCR instruction permits the programmer to read the bits of the CCR without using a conditional branch or a bit test instruction. For example, you might want to use the CCR in later testing.

```
MOVE.W    CCR,D7        Save CCR in D7
 .
 .                      Do operations that change CCR
 .
MOVE.W    D7,CCR        Restore CCR
BEQ       Test1         Now do a test on the old CCR
BMI       Test2
```

Condition codes:

```
X  N  Z  V  C
-- -- -- -- --
```

Destination operand
addressing modes

Dn
(An)
(An)+, −(An)
d(An), d(An,Xi)
ABS.W, ABS.L

MOVE to CCR

Copy (i.e. move) data to CCR from source

Operation:

```
[CCR] ← [source]
```

Assembler syntax:

```
MOVE  <ea>,CCR
```

Attributes:

Size = word

Description:	Move the contents of the source operand to the condition code register. The source operand is a word, but only the low order byte contains the condition codes. The upper byte is neglected.
Application:	The move to CCR instruction permits the programmer to preset the CCR. For example, MOVE #0,CCR will clear all the CCR's bits.
Condition codes:	X N Z V C * * * * *
Source operand addressing modes	Dn (An) (An)+, −(An) d(An), d(An,Xi) ABS.W, ABS.L d(PC), d(PC,Xi) imm

---

MOVE from SR

Copy (i.e. move) data from SR to destination

Operation:	[destination] ← [SR]
Assembler syntax:	MOVE SR,<ea>
Attributes:	Size = word
Description:	Move the contents of the status word to the destination location. The source operand is a word. Note that this instruction is not privileged in the 68000 but is privileged in the 68010, 68020, and 68030. Attempting to execute a MOVE SR,<ea> on these processors will result in a privilege violation trap.
Condition codes:	X N Z V C – – – – –
Destination operand addressing modes	Dn (An) (An)+, −(An) d(An), d(An,Xi) ABS.W, ABS.L

MOVE to SR

Copy (i.e. move) data to SR from source

Operation:	If [S]=1
	   THEN [SR] ← [source]
	   ELSE TRAP

Assembler syntax:	MOVE <ea>,SR
Attributes:	Size = word
Description:	Move the contents of the source operand to the status register. The source operand is a word and all bits of the status register are affected.
Application:	The MOVE to SR instruction permits the programmer to preset the contents of the status register. This instruction permits the trace mode, interrupt mask and status bits to be modified. For example,

MOVE #$2700,SR moves 00100111 00000000 to the status register which clears all bits of the CCR, sets the S-bit, clears from T-bit, and sets the interrupt mask level to 7.

Condition codes: X N Z V C
                 * * * * *

Source operand
addressing modes

Dn
(An)
(An)+, −(An)
d(An), d(An,Xi)
ABS.W, ABS.L
imm
d(PC), d(PC,Xi)

MOVEM

Move multiple registers

Operation:

```
REPEAT
   [Destination_register] ← [Source_register]
UNTIL all registers in list moved
```

Assembler syntax:
```
MOVEM   <register list>,<ea>
MOVEM   <ea>,<register list>
```

Example syntax: MOVEM.L D0-D7/A0-A6,$1234

Example syntax: MOVEM.L (A5),D0-D2/D5-D7/A0-A3/A6

Example syntax: MOVEM.L (A7)+,D0-D6/D7/A0-A6

Attributes: Size = word, longword

Description:

The group of registers specified by ⟨register list⟩ is copied to or from consecutive memory locations. The starting location is provided by the effective address. Any combination of the 68000's 16 address and data registers can be copied by a single MOVEM instruction. Note that either a word or a longword can be moved and that a word is sign extended to longword when it is moved (even if the destination is a data register). When a group of registers are transferred to memory, the registers are transferred starting at the specified address and up through higher addresses. The order of transfer of registers is data register 0 to 7, followed by address register 0 to 7. For example, MOVEM.L D0-D2/D4/A5/A6,$1234 would move registers D0,D1,D2,D4,A5,A6 to memory, starting at location $1234 (in which D0 is stored) and moving to locations $1238, $123C,... If the effective address is in the predecrement mode (i.e., −(An)), only a register to memory operation is permitted. The registers are stored starting at the specified address minus two and down through lower addresses. The order of storing is from address register A7 to address A0, then from data register D7 to data register D0. The decremented address register is updated to contain the address of the last word stored. If the effective address is in the postincrement mode (i.e., (An)+), only a memory to register transfer is permitted. The registers are loaded starting at the specified address and up through higher addresses. The order of loading is the inverse of that used by the predecrement mode and is D0 to D7 followed by A0 to A7. The incremented address register is updated to contain the address of the last word plus two.

Application:

This instruction is invariably used to save working registers on entry to a subroutine and to restore them at the end of a subroutine.

```
          BSR         Example
                      .
                      .
Example   MOVEM.L     D0-D5/A0-A3,-(SP)    Save registers
                      .
                      .

          Body of subroutine
                      .
                      .
          MOVEM.L     (SP)+,D0-D5/A0-A3    Restore registers
          RTS                              Return
```

Condition codes:

```
X N Z V C
- - - - -
```

Source operand
addressing modes
(memory to register)

(An)
(An)+
d(An), d(An,Xi)
ABS.W, ABS.L
d(PC), d(PC,Xi)

Destination operand
addressing modes
(register to memory)

(An)
−(An)
d(An), d(An,Xi)
ABS.W, ABS.L

MOVEP

Move peripheral data

Operation:

[destination] ← [source]

Assembler syntax:

```
MOVEP Dx,(d,Ay)
MOVEP (d,Ay),Dx
```

Attributes:

Size = word, longword

Description

The MOVEP operation moves data between a data register and a byte-oriented memory mapped peripheral. The data is moved between the specified data register and alternate bytes within the peripheral's address space, starting at the location specified and incrementing by two. This instruction is designed to be used in conjunction with 8-bit peripherals connected to a 16-bit data bus. The high order byte of the data register is transferred first and the low order byte transferred last. The memory address is specified by the address register indirect mode with a 16-bit constant. If the address is even, all transfers are to or from the high order half of the data bus. If the address is odd, all the transfers are made to the low order half of the data bus.

Application:

Consider a memory mapped peripheral at address $08 0001 which has four 8-bit internal registers mapped at addresses $08 0001, $08 0003, $08 0005 and $08 0007. The longword in D0 is to be transferred to this peripheral.

```
LEA       $080001,A0
MOVEP.L   0(A0),D0
```

This code results in the following actions:
```
[M(080001)] ← [D0(24:31)]
[M(080003)] ← [D0(16:23)]
[M(080005)] ← [D0(8:15)]
[M(080007)] ← [D0(0:7)]
```

Condition codes:
```
X N Z V C
- - - - -
```

MOVEQ

Move quick (copy a small literal to a destination)

Operation: `[destination] ← <literal>`

Assembler syntax: `MOVEQ #<data>,Dn`

Attributes: Size = longword

Description: Move the specified literal to a data register. The literal data is an eight-bit field within the MOVEQ op-code and specifies a signed value in the range −128 to +127. When the source operand is transferred, it is sign extended to 32 bits. Consequently, although only 8 bits are moved, the MOVEQ instruction is a longword operation.

Application: Used to load integers into a data register. Beware of its sign extension – the operations MOVE.B #12,D0 and MOVEQ #12,D0 are not equivalent. The former has the effect [D0(0:7)] ← 12, while the latter has the effect [D0(0:31)] ← 12 (with sign extension).

Condition codes:
```
X N Z V C
- * * 0 0
```

MULS,MULU

Signed multiply, unsigned multiply

Operation: `[destination] ← [destination] * [source]`

Assembler syntax:
```
MULS <ea>,Dn
MULU <ea>,Dn
```

Attributes: Size = word

Description: Multiply the destination operand by the source operand and store the result in the destination. Both the source and destination are 16-bit word values and the destination result is a 32-bit longword. The product is therefore a correct product and is not truncated. MULU performs multiplication with unsigned values and MULS performs multiplication with two's complement values.

Application: MULU D1,D2 multiplies the low-order words of D1 and D2 and puts the 32-bit result in D2. MULU #$1234,D3 multiplies the low-order word of D3 by the 16-bit literal $1234 and puts the 32-bit result in D3.

Condition codes:
```
X N Z V C
- * * 0 0
```

Source operand addressing modes

Dn
(An)
(An)+,−(An)
d(An), d(An,Xi)
ABS.W, ABS.L
d(PC), d(PC,Xi)
imm

NBCD

Negate decimal with sign extend

Operation:	[destination] ← 0 - [destination] - [X]
Assembler syntax:	NBCD <ea>
Attributes:	Size = byte

Description

The operand addressed as the destination and the extend bit are subtracted from zero. The subtraction is performed using decimal (BCD) arithmetic. The instruction calculates the ten's complement of the destination if the X bit is clear, and the nine's complement if X = 1. This is a byte only operation. Negating a BCD number has the effect of subtracting it from 100 (i.e., one hundred).

Condition codes:

```
X N Z V C
* U * U *
```

Destination operand
addressing modes

```
Dn
(An)
(An)+,-(An)
d(An), d(An,Xi)
ABS.W, ABS.L
```

NEG

Negate

Operation:	[destination] ← 0 - [destination]
Assembler syntax:	NEG <ea>
Attributes:	Size = byte, word, longword

Description:

Subtract the destination operand from 0 and store the result in the destination location. The difference between NOT and NEG is that NOT performs a bit by bit logical complementation while a NEG performs a two's complement arithmetic subtraction. All bits of the condition code register are modified by an NEG operation. For example, if D3.B = 11100111, NEG.B D3 results in D3 = 00011001 (XNZVC = 10001) and NOT.B D3 = 00011000 (XNZVC = -0000).

Condition codes:

```
X N Z V C
* * * * *
```

Destination operand
addressing modes

```
Dn
(An)
(An)+,-(An)
d(An), d(An,Xi)
ABS.W, ABS.L
```

NEGX

Negate with extend

Operation:	[destination] ← 0 - [destination] - [X]
Assembler syntax:	NEGX <ea>

Attributes:	Size = byte, word, longword
Description:	The operand addressed as the destination and the extend bit are subtracted from zero.
Condition codes:	X N Z V C * * * * *

| Destination operand addressing modes | Dn
(An)
(An)+, −(An)
d(An), d(An,Xi)
ABS.W, ABS.L |

NOP   No operation

Operation:	None
Assembler syntax:	NOP
Attributes:	Unsized
Description:	Performs no operation. The processor state, other than the PC is not modified. Execution continues with the instruction following the NOP.
Application:	NOPs can be used to introduce a delay in code without incurring side-effects. Some programmers use it to provide space for later 'patches'. Two or more NOPs can later be replaced by branch or jump instructions to fix a bug. This use is most seriously frowned upon as errors should be corrected by reassembling the code.
Condition codes:	X N Z V C – – – – –

NOT   Logical complement

Operation:	[destination] ← NOT[destination]
Assembler syntax:	NOT <ea>
Attributes:	Size = byte, word, longword
Description:	Calculate the logical complement of the destination and store the result in the destination location. The difference between NOT and NEG is that NOT performs a bit by bit logical complementation while a NEG performs a two's complement arithmetic subtraction.
Condition codes:	X N Z V C – * * 0 0

| Source operand addressing modes | Dn
(An)
(An)+, −(An)
d(An), d(An,Xi)
ABS.W, ABS.L |

OR

OR logical

Operation:	[destination] ← [source] + [destination]
Assembler syntax:	OR <ea>,Dn OR Dn,<ea>
Attributes:	Size = byte, word, longword
Description:	OR the source operand to the destination operand and store the result in the destination location.
Condition codes:	X N Z V C – * * 0 0

Source operand addressing modes	Dn (An) (An)+, –(An) d(An), d(An,Xi) ABS.W, ABS.L d(PC), d(PC,Xi) imm
Destination operand addressing modes	Dn (An) (An)+, –(An) d(An), d(An,Xi) ABS.W, ABS.L

ORI

OR immediate

Operation:	[destination] ← <literal> + [destination]
Assembler syntax:	ORI #<data>,<ea>
Attributes:	Size = byte, word, longword
Description:	OR the immediate data to the destination operand. Store the result in the destination operand.
Condition codes:	X N Z V C – * * 0 0

Destination operand addressing modes	Dn (An) (An)+, –(An) d(An), d(An,Xi) ABS.W, ABS.L

ORI to CCR

Inclusive OR immediate to CCR

Operation:	[CCR] ← <literal> + [CCR]
Assembler syntax:	ORI #<data>,CCR
Attributes:	Size = byte

| Description: | OR the immediate data to the condition code register (i.e., the lsb of the status register). For example, the Z flag of the CCR can be set by MOVE #$04,CCR |
| Condition codes: | X N Z V C
* * * * * |

X: = set if bit 4 of data one: unchanged otherwise
N: = set if bit 3 of data one: unchanged otherwise
Z: = set if bit 2 of data one: unchanged otherwise
V: = set if bit 1 of data one: unchanged otherwise
C: = set if bit 0 of data one: unchanged otherwise

ORI to SR

Inclusive OR immediate to status register

Operation:	IF [S]=1
	      THEN
	      [SR] ← <literal>+[SR]
	      ELSE TRAP

Assembler syntax:	ORI #<data>,SR
Attributes:	Size = word
Description:	OR the immediate data to the status register and store the result in the status register. All bits of the status register are affected.
Application:	Used to set bits in the SR (i.e., the S, T, and interrupt mask bits). For example, ORI #$8000,SR sets bit 15 of the SR (i.e., the trace bit).
Condition codes:	X N Z V C * * * * *

X: = set if bit 4 of data = 1: unchanged otherwise
N: = set if bit 3 of data = 1: unchanged otherwise
Z: = set if bit 2 of data = 1: unchanged otherwise
V: = set if bit 1 of data = 1: unchanged otherwise
C: = set if bit 0 of data = 1: unchanged otherwise

PEA

Push effective address

Operation:	[SP] ← [SP] −4; [M([SP])] ← <ea>
Assembler syntax:	PEA <ea>
Attributes:	Size = longword
Description:	The effective address is computed and pushed onto the stack. The difference between PEA and LEA is that LEA calculates an effective address and puts it in an address register, while PEA calculates an effective address in the same way but pushes it on the stack.
Application:	PEA is a very powerful instruction used to calculate an effective address that can be used later in address register indirect addressing. In particular, it facilitates the writing of position independent code. For example, PEA TABLE(PC) calculates the effective address of 'TABLE' with respect to the PC. This address can be read by a procedure and then used to access the data to which it points. Consider the example:

```
        PEA     Parameter  Push the parameter on the stack
        BSR     Subroutine Call the procedure
        LEA     4(SP),SP   Remove the space occupied by the parameter
        .
Subroutine LEA  -4(SP),A0  A0 points to the parameter (under the return address)
        MOVE.W  (A0),D2    Access the parameter
        .
        RTS
```

Condition codes:

```
        X N Z V C
        - - - - -
```

Source operand
addressing modes

(An)
d(An), d(An,Xi)
ABS.W, ABS.L
d(PC), d(PC,Xi)

RESET

Reset external devices

Operation:

```
IF [S] = 1 THEN
        Assert RESET line
        ELSE TRAP
```

Assembler syntax: RESET

Attributes: Unsized

Description: The reset line is asserted causing all external devices connected to the 68000's RESET output to be reset. The RESET instruction is privileged and has no effect on the 68000 itself.

Condition codes:

```
X N Z V C
- - - - -
```

ROL, ROR

Rotate left/right (without extend)

Operation: [destination] ← [destination] shifted by <count>

Assembler syntax:

```
ROL  Dx,Dy
ROR  Dx,Dy
ROL  #<data>,Dy
ROR  #<data>,Dy
ROL  <ea>
ROR  <ea>
```

Attributes: Size = byte, word, longword

Description: Rotate the bits of the operand in the direction indicated. The extend bit, X, is not included in the operation. A rotate operation is circular in the sense that the bit shifted out at one end is shifted into the other end. That is, no bit is lost or destroyed by a rotate operation. The bit shifted out is also copied into the C bit of the CCR, but not into the X bit. The shift count may be specified in one of three ways. The count may be a literal, the contents of a data register, or the value 1. An immediate count permits a shift of 1 to 8 places. If the count is in a register the value is from 1 to 64. If no count is specified, one shift is made (i.e., ROL <ea>).

Condition codes:	X N Z V C
	– * * 0 *

Destination operand addressing modes	(An)
	(An)+, –(An)
	d(An), d(An,Xi)
	ABS.W, ABS.L

ROXL, ROXR — Rotate left/right with extend

Operation:	[destination] ← [destination] shifted by <count>
Assembler syntax:	ROXL Dx,Dy
	ROXR Dx,Dy
	ROXL #<data>,Dy
	ROXR #<data>,Dy
	ROXL <ea>
	ROXR <ea>
Attributes:	Size = byte, word, longword
Description:	Rotate the bits of the operand in the direction indicated. The extend bit of the CCR is included in the rotation. A rotate operation is circular in the sense that the bit shifted out at one end is shifted into the other end. That is, no bit is lost or destroyed by a rotate operation. Since the X bit is included in the rotate, the rotation is performed over 9 bits. (.B), 17 bits (.W) or 33 bits (.L). The bit shifted out is also copied into the C bit of the CCR as well as the X bit. The shift count may be specified in one of three ways. The count may be a literal, the contents of a data register, or the value 1. An immediate count permits a shift of 1 to 8 places. If the count is in a register the value is from 1 to 64. If no count is specified, one shift is made (i.e., ROXL <ea>).
Condition codes:	X N Z V C
	* * * 0 *

Destination operand addressing modes	(An)
	(An)+, –(An)
	d(An), d(An,Xi)
	ABS.W, ABS.L

RTE — Return from exception

Operation:	IF [S] = 1 THEN
	$\quad$ [SR] ← [M([SP])]; [SP] ← [SP]+2
	$\quad$ [PC] ← [M([SP])]; [SP] ← [SP]+4
	ELSE TRAP
Assembler syntax:	RTE
Attributes:	Unsized
Description:	The status register and program counter are pulled from the stack. The previous values of the SR and PC are lost. Note that the behaviour of RTE depends on the nature of both the exception type and processor type.

The 68010 etc pushes more information on the stack following an exception than the 68000. In all cases, the processor determines how much to remove from the stack.

Condition codes:
```
X N Z V C
* * * * *
```

RTR

Return and restore condition codes

Operation:
```
[CCR] ← [M([SP])]; [SP] ← [SP]+2
[PC] ← [M([SP])]; [SP] ← [SP]+4
```

Assembler syntax: RTR

Attributes: Unsized

Description: The condition codes and program counter are pulled from the stack. The previous condition codes and program counter are lost. The supervisor portion of the status register is not affected by this operation.

Application: If you wish to preserve the CCR before entering a procedure, you can push it on the stack and then retrieve it with RTR.

```
MOVE.W    CCR,-(SP)    Save CCR on stack
BSR       Proc1        Call procedure
  .         .            .
  .         .            .
Proc1                    Body of procedure
  .         .            .
  .         .            .
RTR                      Return and restore CCR
```

Condition codes:
```
X N Z V C
* * * * *
```

RTS

Return from subroutine

Operation:
```
[PC] ← [M([SP])]; [SP] ← [SP]+4
```

Assembler syntax: RTS

Attributes: Unsized

Description: The program counter is pulled from the stack and the previous value of the PC is lost. An RTS is effectively equivalent to a JMP (SP)+ instruction.

Condition codes:
```
X N Z V C
- - - - -
```

SBCD

Subtract decimal with extend

Operation:
```
[destination] ← [destination] - [Source] - [X]
```

Assembler syntax:
```
SBCD  Dy,Dx
SBCD  -(Ay),-(Ax)
```

Attributes: Size = byte

Description: Subtract the source operand from the destination operand together with the extend bit, and store the result in the destination operand. Subtraction is performed using BCD arithmetic. The only legal addressing modes are data register direct and memory to memory with address register indirect using auto decrementing.

Condition codes:

X N Z V C
* U * U *

Z: Cleared if result is non-zero. Unchanged otherwise
(Z bit can be used to test for zero after a chain of multiple precision operations).

Scc

Set according to condition cc

Operation:

IF cc = 1 THEN [destination] ←1s
         ELSE [destination] ← 0s

Assembler syntax:

Scc <ea>

Attributes:

Size = byte

Description:

The specified condition code is tested. If the condition is true, the bits at the effective address are all set to one (i.e., $FF). Otherwise the bits at the effective address are set to zeros (i.e., $00).

SCC	set on carry clear	$\overline{C}$
SCS	set on carry set	C
SEQ	set on equal	Z
SGE	set on greater than or equal	$N.V + \overline{N}.\overline{V}$
SGT	set on greater than	$N.V.\overline{Z} + \overline{N}.\overline{V}.\overline{Z}$
SHI	set on higher than	$\overline{C}.\overline{Z}$
SLE	set on less than or equal	$Z + N.\overline{V} + \overline{N}.V$
SLS	set on lower than or same	C + Z
SLT	set on less than	$N.\overline{V} + \overline{N}.V$
SMI	set on minus (i.e., negative)	N
SNE	set on not equal	$\overline{Z}$
SPL	set on plus (i.e., positive)	$\overline{N}$
SVS	set on overflow clear	$\overline{V}$
SVS	set on overflow set	V
SF	set on false	0
ST	set on true	1

Condition codes:

X N Z V C
– – – – –

Destination operand
addressing modes

Dn
(An)
(An)+, −(An)
d(An), d(An,Xi)
ABS.W, ABS.L

STOP

Load status register and stop

Operation:

IF [S] = 1 THEN
              [SR] ← <data> ; STOP
         ELSE TRAP

Assembler syntax:	STOP #<data>
Attributes:	Unsized
Description:	The immediate operand is copied into the entire status register, and the program counter is advanced to point to the next instruction to be executed. The processor then stops all further processing and halts. Execution of instructions resumes when a trace, interrupt, or reset exception occurs. A trace exception will occur if the trace bit is set when the STOP is encountered. If an interrupt request arrives whose priority is higher than the current processor priority, an interrupt exception occurs, otherwise the interrupt request has no effect. If the bit of the immediate data corresponding to the S-bit is clear (i.e., user mode selected), execution of the stop instruction will cause a privilege violation. External reset will always initiate reset exception processing.
Condition codes:	X N Z V C * * * * * (set according to the literal)

SUB · Subtract binary

Operation:	[destination] ← [destination] − [source]
Assembler syntax:	SUB <ea>,Dn SUB Dn,<ea>
Attributes:	Size = byte, word, longword
Description:	Subtract the source operand from the destination operand and store the result in the destination location.
Condition codes:	X N Z V C * * * * *
Source operand addressing modes	Dn, An (An) (An)+, −(An) d(An), d(An,Xi) ABS.W, ABS.L d(PC), d(PC,Xi) imm
Destination operand addressing modes	Dn (An) (An)+, −(An) d(An), d(An,Xi) ABS.W, ABS.L

SUBA · Subtract address

Operation:	[destination] ← [destination] − [source]
Assembler syntax:	SUBA <ea>,An
Attributes:	Size = word, longword
Description:	Subtract the source operand from the destination address register and store the result in the destination address register.

Condition codes:

X N Z V C
- - - - -

Source operand
addressing modes

Dn, An
(An)
(An)+, −(An)
d(An), d(An,Xi)
ABS.W, ABS.L
d(PC), d(PC,Xi)
imm

SUBI

Subtract immediate

Operation: [destination] ← [destination] − <literal>

Assembler syntax: SUBI #<data>,<ea>

Attributes: Size = byte, word, longword

Description: Subtract the immediate data from the destination operand. Store the result in the destination operand.

Condition codes:

X N Z V C
* * * * *

Destination operand
addressing modes

Dn
(An)
(An)+, −(An)
d(An), d(An,Xi)
ABS.W, ABS.L

SUBQ

Subtract quick

Operation: [destination] ← [destination] − <literal>

Assembler syntax: SUBQ #<data>,<ea>

Attributes: Size = byte, word, longword

Description: Subtract the immediate data from the destination operand. The immediate data must be in the range 1 to 8. Word and longword operations on address registers do not affect condition codes register.

Condition codes:

X N Z V C
* * * * *

Destination operand
addressing modes

Dn, An
(An)
(An)+, −(An)
d(An), d(An,Xi)
ABS.W, ABS.L

SUBX

Subtract extended

Operation: [destination] ← [destination] − [source] − [X]

Assembler syntax:	SUBX Dy,Dx SUBX -(Ay),-(Ax)
Attributes:	Size = byte, word, longword
Description:	Subtract the source operand from the destination operand along with the extend bit, and store the result in the destination location. The only legal addressing modes are data register and memory to memory with address register indirect using auto decrementing.
Condition codes:	X N Z V C * * * * * Z: Cleared if result is non-zero. Unchanged otherwise (Z bit can be used to test for zero after a chain of multiple precision operations).

SWAP

Swap register halves

Operation:	[Register(16:31)] ← [Register(0:15)]; [Register(0:15)] ← [Register(16:31)]
Assembler syntax:	SWAP Dn
Attributes:	Size = word
Description:	Exchange the 16-bit words of a data register.
Application:	Enables the higher order word in a register to take part in word-operations by moving it into the lower order position. SWAP Dn is effectively equivalent to ROR.L #16,Dn (except that SWAP clears the C bit of the CCR while ROR sets it according to the last bit to be shifted into the carry bit).
Condition codes:	X N Z V C - * * 0 0 N: set if msb of 32-bit word set, cleared otherwise Z: set if 32-bit result is zero, cleared otherwise

TAS

Test and set an operand

Operation:	[CCR] ← tested([operand]); [destination(7)] ←1
Assembler syntax:	TAS <ea>
Attributes:	Size = byte
Description:	Test and set the byte operand addressed by the effective address field. Bits N and Z of the CCR are updated accordingly. The high order bit of the operand (i.e., bit 7) is set. This operation is indivisible and uses a read-modify write cycle. Its principle application is in multiprocessor systems.
Application:	The TAS instruction permits one processor in a multiprocessor system to test a resource and claim it if it is free. Because the operation is indivisible, no other processor can access the memory between the testing of the bit and its subsequent setting.
Condition codes:	X N Z V C - * * 0 0

Source operand addressing modes	Dn
	(An)
	(An)+, −(An)
	d(An), d(An,Xi)
	ABS.W, ABS.L

TRAP

Trap

Operation:
```
[SSP] ← [SSP] − 4; [M([SSP])] ← [PC];
[SSP] ← [SSP] − 2; [M([SSP])] ← [SR];
[PC] ←vector
```

Assembler syntax:
```
TRAP  # <vector>
```

Attributes: Unsized

Description: The processor initiates exception processing. The vector number used by the TRAP instruction and is in the range 0 to 15.

Condition Codes:
```
X N Z V C
− − − − −
```

TRAPV

Trap on overflow

Operation:
```
IF V true THEN:
[SSP] ← [SSP] ← 4; [M([SSP])] ← [PC];
[SSP] ← [SSP] ← 2; [M([SSP])] ← [SR];
[PC] ←[M(01C)]
ELSE no action
```

Assembler syntax:
```
TRAPV
```

Attributes: Unsized

Description: If the V bit in the CCR is set, then initiate exception processing. The exception vector is located at address 01C.

Condition codes:
```
X N Z V C
− − − − −
```

TST

Test an operand

Operation:
```
[CCR] ← tested([operand])
i.e., [operand] − 0; update CCR
```

Assembler syntax:
```
TST  <ea>
```

Attributes: Size = byte, word, longword

Description: The operand is compared with zero. No result is saved, but the contents of the CCR are set according to the result.

Condition codes:
```
X N Z V C
− * * 0 0
```

Source operand
addressing modes

Dn
(An)
(An)+, −(An)
d(An), d(An,Xi)
ABS.W, ABS.L

UNLK   ## Unlink

Operation: $[SP] \leftarrow [An]; [An] \leftarrow [M([SP])]; [SP] \leftarrow [SP]+4$

Assembler syntax: UNLK An

Attributes: Unsized

Description: The stack pointer is loaded from the specified address register. The address register is then loaded with the longword pulled off the stack.

Application: UNLK is used in conjuction with LINK. The LINK creates a stack frame at the start of a procedure and the UNLK collapses the stack frame prior to a return from procedure.

Condition codes:

X N Z V C
− − − − −

Index